The Two-Party South

Second Expanded Edition

ALEXANDER P. LAMIS

D0070818

OXFORD UNIVERSITY PRESS
New York   Oxford
1990

Oxford University Press

Oxford   New York   Toronto
Delhi   Bombay   Calcutta   Madras   Karachi
Petaling Jaya   Singapore   Hong Kong   Tokyo
Nairobi   Dar es Salaam   Cape Town
Melbourne   Auckland

and associated companies in
Berlin   Ibadan

Copyright © 1984, 1988, 1990 by Alexander P. Lamis

First published in 1984 by Oxford University Press, Inc.,
200 Madison Avenue, New York, N.Y. 10016.

First issued in paperback by Oxford University Press, 1986

Issued as a new edition in paperback by Oxford University Press, 1990

Oxford is a registered trademark of Oxford University Press

Library of Congress Cataloging-in-Publication Data
Lamis, Alexander P.
The two-party south / Alexander P. Lamis. — 2nd expanded ed.
p. cm.   Includes bibliographical references and index.
ISBN 0-19-506579-4
1. Southern States—Politics and government—1951–
2. Political parties—Southern States—History—20th century.   I. Title.
F216.2.L35   1990   324.275—dc20   90-45997

1 3 5 7 9 8 6 4 2

Printed in the United States of America
on acid-free paper

The Two-Party South

To the memory of my mother,
Olympia (Lynn) Lamis,
and
To my father,
Pano A. Lamis

Preface

Alexander Heard in 1952 entitled his study of electoral politics in the eleven states of the former Confederacy *A Two-Party South?* Over three decades later no one could deny that the question mark should be dropped. The two-party South exists, and this book explains why and how it developed.

The period under scrutiny generally follows the Second Reconstruction, which encompassed the civil rights struggles of the 1950s and much of the 1960s, and is a period I call, for lack of a better term, the post-civil rights era. The term *post-civil rights era* refers to the apparent national resolution by the late 1960s of the question of basic political and legal rights for blacks and does not imply that race has ceased to be a major political consideration in the South, or throughout the nation as well.

For the issues addressed in this book, I adopted a broad contextual approach, one that was eclectic in both data gathering and method of analysis. I was guided by the advice of V. O. Key, Jr., the master of American political analysis: "In work relating to the electoral behavior of geographical units . . . one needs to bring into the analysis every scrap of evidence to be had."*

My interest in the subject began in the late 1960s, when as a television news reporter in Charleston, South Carolina, I observed in action many of the leading political figures who were stirring the region, such as—to name a few who left vivid impressions—George Wallace, Martin

*A *Primer of Statistics for Political Scientists* (New York: Thomas Y. Crowell, 1954), 125.

Luther King, Jr., and Strom Thurmond. During the 1972 election season, as a newspaper reporter in Columbia, South Carolina, I watched the Palmetto State's Democratic leaders grapple with the growing inevitability of George McGovern's candidacy as their party's presidential standard-bearer and followed McGovern's inability to make a dent in the still heavily Democratic South. While covering this campaign, I became fascinated with the tensions present in the emerging party structure of the incipient post–civil rights era South. After entering graduate school in political science at Vanderbilt University, I encountered the analytical tools and instruction I needed to make sense of what I had been witnessing. That in a nutshell is the origin of this book, which is a thoroughly rewritten and expanded version of my doctoral dissertation at Vanderbilt.

As far back as my first semester in graduate school, Professor J. Leiper Freeman, my dissertation chairman, provided me with invaluable assistance, serving as something of a one-man introduction committee to the discipline of political science. I very much appreciate the countless hours he devoted to my education. I also want to thank the other members of my dissertation committee—Professors Robert H. Birkby, William C. Havard, John T. Dorsey, Jr., and Dewey W. Grantham, as well as Professor Emeritus Avery Leiserson, who served until his retirement.

Marshall Hix, then an undergraduate at Vanderbilt and now a lawyer in Nashville, provided important and timely aid by running the university computer for me while I was living in Baltimore; this involved his becoming on-the-scene programmer for the thousands of calculations that needed to be done on the county-level election data. Without his conscientious help, I could not have accomplished the initial phases of the project. (An explanation of how these calculations were used in the book is found in the Appendix.)

To the one hundred politicians and political observers who took the time to give me their assessments of electoral developments in their states, I must record my deep gratitude. These interviews, which ranged in length from twenty minutes to over three hours (the average running about forty-five minutes), were conducted in Washington in 1978, 1979, and 1982; half of them were tape-recorded. Each person interviewed is identified by his or her position at the time of the interview.

I also examined interviews conducted, mainly in 1974, by Jack Bass and Walter DeVries and deposited by them in the oral history section of the Southern Historical Collection in the Wilson Library of the University of North Carolina at Chapel Hill. Portions of twenty-five of these interviews are published here with the kind permission of the Collection's director. Bass and DeVries deserve commendation for making their excellent interviews available to other researchers.

I am profoundly thankful for her support and deeply indebted to her for
the many sacrifices she made so that I could write this book.

Oxford, Mississippi   A.P.L.
March 1984

Note on the Expanded Edition*

The expanded edition contains three new chapters. The first, Chapter
16, treats the 1984 presidential election in the South and various other
important elections in the eleven states that year. Chapter 17 examines
the 1986 elections plus the contests in Virginia in 1985 and Louisiana
and Mississippi in 1987. Chapter 18 offers an overview of several recent
developments and ends with a consideration of the much-discussed realignment question. The original fifteen chapters are unchanged except
that all the figures have been updated.

Much has happened in Southern in politics in four years. Yet, as the
new chapters indicate, the most striking feature of the recent period is
continuity with the patterns depicted in the original edition. The 1988
election season promises to be a banner political year for the South—
from Super Tuesday through the summer national conventions in Atlanta and New Orleans to the fall struggle for electoral votes.

I am very appreciative to have received kind assistance from many
people in writing this edition, including Sandra DiGiovanni, Hastings
Wyman, Jr., Paul D. Mitchell, Elizabeth Hutcherson, Alice V. Mc-
Gillivary, Alan I. Abramowitz, David E. Sturrock, Kathleen A. Hughes,
Rich Weiner, Patrick Plumlee, Helen J. Green, Julie Cissel, Ann L.
Murphy, and Sheldon Meyer and his able assistants at Oxford University
Press Rachel Toor and Stephanie Sakson-Ford. Also, my students helped
significantly by gathering hundreds, if not thousands, of articles from
Southern newspapers. My gratitude in this regard goes to those students
in my research courses at the University of Mississippi in the fall of 1984,
at the University of North Florida in the spring of 1986 and the fall of
1987, and in Troy State University's European program in Zaragoza,
Spain, in the spring of 1987.

Jacksonville, Florida   A.P.L.
March 1988

*This paperback edition, the Second Expanded Edition, contains a
postscript chapter, chapter 19, that analyzes the 1988 elections throughout the South and Virginia's historic 1989 gubernatorial election. It
projects possible future trends for the 1990s and beyond.

Cleveland, Ohio, June 1990

Two established writers in this field, Hugh D. Graham and Numan V. Bartley, generously offered me guidance and advice at key points along the way, which I greatly appreciate. Hugh Graham, who read the study both as a dissertation and in its present, revised form, especially spurred me on through a balanced mixture of encouragement and criticism, the latter tempered by a remarkable willingness in the early stages to give me the benefit of the doubt. I will never forget this exemplary treatment.

During the revision process I had the fortunate experience to work for James L. Sundquist of the Brookings Institution while he was preparing a new edition of his *Dynamics of the Party System*. In addition to learning by observing an excellent political analyst at work, I also profited from the use in my book of material I accumulated for Sundquist's book, particularly the important party-strength figures that appear throughout and the national survey data used extensively in Chapter 15.

Patrick R. Cotter, Stephen D. Shaffer, Richard Murray, and Arnold Vedlitz graciously shared with me hard-to-get data that they had gathered, a courtesy I appreciate very much.

Many others along the way offered assistance and suggestions, including Charles R. Wilson, Charles East, Marc A. Bernier, Charles W. Eagles, James C. Cobb, Larry S. Bush, Alice V. McGillivary, Eric V. Armen, Ray Albert (Al) Furr, Jr., Marc R. Baker, Darrell N. Blaylock, Jr., Phil Ashford, and the students in my Southern politics seminar at the University of Mississippi during the fall semesters of 1981, 1982, and 1983. I am very thankful to have had the benefit of their aid.

For the splendid manner in which he handled my manuscript, I owe a special debt of gratitude to Sheldon Meyer of Oxford University Press. I am convinced my guardian angel worked overtime to deliver me into such capable hands. His assistant, Melissa Spielman, deserves my praise and appreciation for her many valuable editorial suggestions as well as for the cheerful manner in which she facilitated the publication process. I am very thankful also for the careful work of Otto Sonntag, the book's copy editor, whose good judgment I learned to value during our long-distance contact. To Paul D. Mitchell, an Oxford, Mississippi, artist-illustrator, who drew the maps and figures, I am most grateful both for his skillful work and for the pleasant way in which he handled our many consultations.

The longer the list of appreciations—and mine, I am happy to note, is a long one—the greater the need to absolve all of the above from responsibility for any errors of fact or interpretation that appear here, because that burden, of course, rests solely with me.

Finally, and most important to Karen Lamis, my wife and best friend,

Contents

List of Figures

List of Maps

List of Tables

The Two-Party South

1

Region in Ferment

Outsiders more frequently than not find the South's approach to politics something of a mystery. Strange things go on down there, more than a few casual observers have concluded during the last several decades as news of the South's political turmoil filtered out of the region.

First and foremost, there was that odd creature the one-party system, and it refused to go away in a rational fashion when it was supposed to. Virtually all electoral activity continued to be carried on within the Democratic party in the states of the former Confederacy for nearly fifteen years after the first break in the Solid South occurred during the Dixiecrat revolt of 1948. Republican party strength did appear suddenly for sure in the 1952 presidential election and continued in the 1956 and 1960 balloting for President. However, despite this early GOP spurt and the accompanying premature heralding of the collapse of the Democratic South,[1] Republicans had very few electoral victories until the early 1960s.[2]

The one-party Democratic South thus lived on into the 1960s. Yet spectators from afar could not help but note that this same dominant Democratic party, especially its presidential wing, was the object of bitter denunciations by white Southerners—most of them Democrats— throughout the turbulent civil rights struggles of the early and middle 1960s. In fact, casual observation of Southern political life in the entire decade of the 1960s could produce only one sane conclusion: partisan chaos reigned from one end of the region to the other. And the 1970s and early 1980s, though less chaotic, contained their share of turmoil.

Understanding what the political figures who crossed the Southern

3

center stage were up to, and what they stood for, required more than a little effort. No wonder spectators away from the scene—and residents as well—were at times perplexed. Of course, the politicians offered scant assistance in any search for understanding. Although they engaged constantly in political communication, they infrequently contributed to political education, especially when the telling of what they were up to was not always pleasant.

But the complex story of the death of the solidly Democratic South and the accompanying emergence of the current top-heavy Southern two-party system ought to be understood by those in the region and outside who have a strong interest in public affairs. It is a story full of irony and even a touch of drama. It was rarely dull.

New Twist on an Old Issue

For generations Southern politics has been inextricably linked to the race issue. The Southern one-party system[3] had many effects, but its overriding purpose, the preservation of white supremacy, ought never to be underemphasized. The argument was simple. If whites divided their votes between two parties, blacks would hold the balance of power and could bargain for concessions to end their second-class status. Later, when outside action threatened the South's system of racial segregation, solidarity was thought necessary to thwart the outsiders, the Southern rhetoric calling for unity in the face of the Northern enemy.

The destruction of the underlying reason for the one-party South began in the late 1940s and proceeded in an uneven fashion until the critical events of the mid-1960s, the passage of the Civil Rights Act of 1964 and the Voting Rights Act of 1965, both sponsored by national Democratic leaders. The "betrayal" of the white South on civil rights— starting gradually with Harry Truman and ending momentously with Lyndon Johnson—precipitated the death of the one-party system. The events of the decade and a half leading to the climactic legislative actions of 1964 and 1965 are related in the next chapter. The main body of this book begins with the confused electoral picture that emerged after the national Democratic party's total embrace of the cause of blacks and traces the destruction of the one-party South at the state and presidential levels.[4]

The unraveling of the solidly Democratic South in the post–civil rights era proved to be a far more subtle and complex process than the wholesale punishment of Democratic presidential nominees at the height of the civil rights drama. Full comprehension of this Democratic transformation in major state contests, that is, in elections for governor and U.S. senator, is partly obscured by the need to chart eleven separate movements at the same time. The situation in each of the Southern states exhibited differing characteristics depending on the peculiarities of each state's political traditions, the ambitions of the various actors, and events unique to each state, among other reasons. Despite the diversity, however, a central theme involving a new twist on the old issue of race emerges to add some order to recent Southern politics.

Race in the South of the post–civil rights era occupied a far different place than it did in its original role as the rationale for the one-party South. By the early 1970s—the timing differed from state to state—one could discern a distinct lessening of racial tension in the region. The word that seems best to describe the situation is *abatement*, a diminishing of the intensity that had surrounded the race question.[5] Essentially, by the end of the 1960s the dreaded event—racial integration—had occurred, and the world did not come to an end. A general acquiescence among whites, if not uniform acceptance, of this nationally imposed reality settled in throughout the region.

How the altered racial environment contributed to the development of two-party electoral politics is explained in Chapter 3 and amplified in the state chapters. Briefly, a key element was the ability of Southern Democrats to capitalize on the new situation that followed both the civil rights upheavals and the rise of Republican challenges below the presidential level. The altered situation was this: the racial tension that had alienated traditionally Democratic white voters lessened, and at the same time large numbers of blacks carrying strong Democratic party leanings entered the electorate. The potential flowing from this new situation was not lost on a host of Democratic office seekers, who put together potent black-white coalitions in the early 1970s. It became a mere matter of arithmetic in some states for the Republicans to recognize that these black-white Democratic coalitions arrayed against them were powerful indeed. How the challengers sought to break this formidable alliance is described in all its variation in the state chapters. It is important to remember, however, that such coalitions could not have developed had the racial atmosphere remained at the intense levels reached in the mid-1960s. Furthermore, these black-white coalitions—on which a modest Democratic resurgence in the South in the middle 1970s was built—rested on a fragile, ideologically diverse foundation that offered future promise to the challenging Republicans.

Other ingredients were important as well. It was necessary to place the region's electoral development within the context of the last major political party upheaval in the nation, the New Deal realignment of the 1930s. In addition, the persistence—although in reduced form—of widespread Democratic party allegiance, a heritage of the Solid South era, had to be evaluated. Other more transient elements, such as the impact of the regional backgrounds, personalities, strategies, and party-building inclinations of the national leaders who occupied prominent positions during the period, were also considered.

Before launching into the politics of the post–civil rights era, one must lay a firm historical groundwork. This is the task of Chapter 2, which traces events leading up to the electoral turbulence that broke loose in the region in the early and middle 1960s. Then, taking a regionwide view, Chapter 3 analyzes the consequences of the civil rights revolution for the South's party system, examining key racial and non-racial elements that merged as a result of the collapse of the rationale for the one-party Democratic South. In a sense this overview chapter, which treats the significance to the South of the period's presidential elections, fleshes out in regional terms the central themes involved in the rise of Southern two-party politics and provides a preview for the book's abrupt shift to the heart of the political action, the state level, where eleven variations on the central themes are charted in consider-able detail in Chapters 4 through 14. While regional generalization has the distinct advantage of offering an understanding of the larger progres-sion of significant factors, the election-by-election state-level analyses offer a sober realization that the overall interpretation is but a collection of the colorful and often chaotic actions of individuals struggling for political ascendancy amid forces not always clearly understood by con-temporary observers. Following this journey through the varied state experiences, Chapter 15 analyzes the composition of the South's two parties in the early 1980s and concludes with speculation concerning future trends in Southern politics.

2

Democratic Rupture over Civil Rights

The bitter controversy over civil rights in the Democratic party, visible in the 1948 presidential election, had its origins in the early 1930s. One could go back to the Civil War, the time of John C. Calhoun, or the beginning of slavery in North America, but for the purposes of this book the New Deal era is sufficient. The economic appeal of the New Deal undermined the Republican loyalty of black voters outside of the South, and this shift of Northern blacks to the Democratic party occurred at the same time the black exodus from the South was in full swing.[1]

Perhaps a quotation from Sen. Ellison D. (Cotton Ed) Smith of South Carolina describing his abrupt departure from the 1936 Democratic National Convention in Philadelphia provides, in the words of George B. Tindall, "a symbolic prelude to the disruption of the Democratic party":

> . . . when I came out on the floor of that great hall, bless God, it looked like a checkerboard—a spot of white here, and a spot of black there. [Actually there were thirty black delegates or alternates.] But I kept going, down that long aisle, and finally I found the great standard of South Carolina—and, praise God, it was a spot of white!
>
> I had no sooner than taken my seat when a newspaperman came down the aisle and squatted by me and said, "Senator, do you know a nigger is going to come out up yonder in a minute and offer the invocation?" I told him, I said, "Now don't be joking me, I'm upset enough the way it is." But then, bless God, out on the platform walked a slew-footed, blue-gummed, kinky-headed Senegambian!
>
> And he started praying and I started walking. And as I pushed

through those great doors, and walked across that vast rotunda, it
seemed to me that old John Calhoun leaned down from his mansion
in the sky and whispered in my ear, "You did right, Ed. . . . "[2]

In addition to seating black delegates for the first time, the 1936 convention abolished the two-thirds rule for presidential nomination, elimina-
ting the South's ability to veto a nominee who would not accept its
policy of racial segregation.

A less colorful but even more germane illustration of what was to
befall the Democratic party occurred on the floor of the U.S. Senate in
1938 when an antilynching proposal sponsored by Northern Democrats
was under debate. Sen. James F. (Jimmy) Byrnes of South Carolina
reminded his listeners that a similar proposal had been sponsored in
1921 by Republican congressmen and at the time had been defeated
with the aid of Northern Democrats. The reversal on the issue among
Northern Democrats, he said, had come about because "90 percent of
the Negroes in the North . . . are voting for Democratic candidates."
Byrnes hinted that, although the South "had never voted for a Republican candidate," it might have to reappraise the situation. It is clear, he
said, that "the white people in the South in supporting the Democratic
Party [had been guided by] the belief that when problems affecting the
Negro and the very soul of the South arose, they could depend upon the
Democrats of the North to rally to their support."[3]

The Democratic party's dilemma over race festered for another decade while the nation's attention centered on World War II. The
commitment of Northern Democrats to blacks grew during the war,
and at the same time the war emergency strengthened the incipient
civil rights movement by opening new opportunities for blacks. Immediately after the war the urgency of the situation was enhanced by
several highly publicized incidents of violence in the South against
black servicemen who had returned home after release from the
military.[4]

Responding to the mounting political pressure for action,[5] President
Harry S Truman in early 1947 established a civil rights commission to
examine the plight of America's blacks. Its recommendations, published
that October under the title *To Secure These Rights*, were "a sweeping
denunciation of all governmental and of some private sanctions of race
discrimination or segregation." Truman called the report "an American
charter of human freedom" and implemented many of its suggestions
within his power, such as the integration of military units.[6] Sen. John J.
Sparkman of Alabama said at the time, "The people of the South are so
bitter that they will never accept Truman as a candidate."[7]

The Dixiecrat Revolt

A few days after the 1948 Democratic National Convention had adopted a strong civil rights platform and heard Mayor Hubert H. Humphrey of Minneapolis exclaim that it was time "for the Democratic Party to get out of the shadow of states' rights and to walk forthrightly into the bright sunshine of human rights,"[8] the most fervent segregationists convened in Birmingham, Alabama, and nominated Gov. Strom Thurmond of South Carolina and Gov. Fielding Wright of Mississippi as the States' Rights (or Dixiecrat) candidates for president and vice-president. Two historians described the scene: "The assembled company waved the Confederate flag, snake-danced under the portrait of Robert E. Lee, and condemned as 'infamous and iniquitous' the suggestion of equal rights for Negroes."[9]

The link between the Dixiecrat campaign and the civil rights position of both President Truman and the 1948 Democratic convention needs no elaboration. Thurmond quickly sized up the situation after Truman's civil rights initiatives. Even before the national convention, he told a gathering in Jackson, Mississippi, "The leadership of the Democratic party may as well realize that the South's electoral votes are no longer in the bag for the Democratic nominee."[10] Later, in accepting the States' Rights nomination, Thurmond declared, "There are not enough laws on the books of the nation, nor can there be enough laws, to break down segregation in the South."[11] And during a New York City campaign visit, he asserted:

> If you people in New York want no segregation, then abolish it and do away with your Harlem. Personally, I think it would be a mistake. . . . And by the same reasoning, no federal law should attempt to force the South to abandon segregation where we have it and know it as best for both races.[12]

In November, Thurmond swept the Deep South, carrying Mississippi with an overwhelming 87.2 percent of the votes cast, Alabama with 79.7 percent,[13] South Carolina with 72.0 percent, and Louisiana with 49.1 percent. But the movement failed to deny the election to Truman. In fact, the four states won by Thurmond were the only ones in which the Dixiecrats expropriated the regular Democratic ballot position. Elsewhere in the South, where they stood on their own, they lost to Truman.

The abrupt departure from Democratic domination that occurred in the 1948 election is pictured in Figure 2-1, which traces Democratic and Republican presidential voting strength from 1932 to 1980. The figure discloses that the diminished strength of the Democratic nomi-

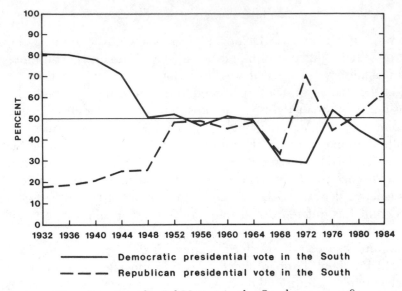

Figure 2-1. Trends in Presidential Voting in the South, 1932–1984

nees persisted around the 50 percent line in the four elections following
the Dixiecrat bolt. It also reveals that the Republican party, which was
not a major beneficiary of the 1948 revolt, gained a sizable number of
adherents for its presidential standard-bearer in the 1952, 1956, and
1960 elections. The figure does not, however, adequately represent the
critical nature of the 1964 election, which appears merely as an extension of the trend of the preceding three elections. The task of explaining
the significance of the 1964 election, an electoral landmark on the order
of 1948, is reserved for the last part of this chapter. For the uneasy and
uncertain period of the next three elections, however, Figure 2-1 offers
a preview.

   Another guide to these elections is presented in Figure 2-2, which
employs a venerable intraregional classification—the Deep South–Rim
South division. The major difference between the two subsections is the
relative concentration of blacks, who were proportionately more numerous in the Deep South.[14] For the Deep South whites of Mississippi,
South Carolina, Alabama, Georgia, and Louisiana, so the reasoning
went, blacks were a more serious threat, and as a result the race issue
held greater sway over political life there than in the Rim South states of
Texas, Florida, Tennessee, Virginia, North Carolina, and Arkansas.
Even in the halcyon days of the Solid South, from 1932 through 1944,
support for the Democratic presidential candidate was over ten percentage points greater in the Deep South, where the rationale for Democratic solidarity obviously had its most vehement adherents. When the

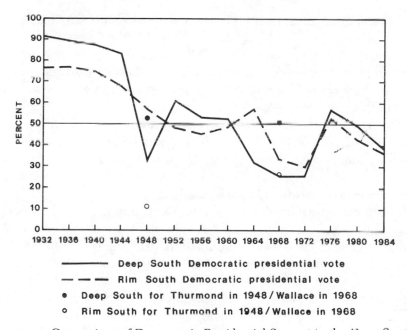

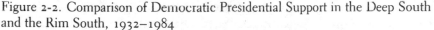

Figure 2-2. Comparison of Democratic Presidential Support in the Deep South and the Rim South, 1932–1984

break over race came, its force was also sharper in the Deep South. From the 85 percent mark in the Deep South in 1944, the Democratic nominee's share fell to 30 percent in 1948, a staggering drop. Perusal of the Deep South–Rim South differences in Figure 2-2 during the 1952, 1956, 1960, and 1964 elections substantiates the continued soundness of this intraregional division.[15]

No Clear Choice Appears

In the years immediately following the 1948 revolt, the speculation concerning what the election meant for the future ran along three lines:[16]

1. It was the beginning of a quadrennial effort to deadlock the electoral college and demand concessions to the Southern point of view.
2. It was only a temporary bolt, and the traditional adherents would soon be found back in the Democratic party.
3. It was the beginning of a two-party South.

As Tindall pointed out, "It proved, in fact, to be all of these things."[17]

The three contradictory tendencies stand out during the 1952 and 1956 elections. The Southern Democrats' shock at finding that their

traditional arrangement with the national Democratic party on segregation had been abrogated may have led to the blind rage of the Thurmond bolt, but the power realities of the situation appear always to have
been evident to the region's influential members of Congress. In particular, they knew how impotent the civil rights advocates were in the
Southern-dominated Senate.

The 1952 Democratic National Convention nominated Gov. Adlai
E. Stevenson of Illinois for president. Although Stevenson endorsed the
party's strong civil rights platform, there was no large-scale Southern
boycott. One concession to the South was Stevenson's choice of a
running mate, Alabama's Senator Sparkman.

The postnomination debate of one Deep South state's Democratic
party illuminates the predicament Southern Democrats faced.* In August 1952, after Stevenson's nomination, the South Carolina Democratic Convention reassembled in Columbia to decide what attitude to
adopt toward the national nominee.[18] Both of South Carolina's U.S.
senators urged the convention to back Stevenson. Sen. Burnet R. Maybank told the delegates that remaining with the national party would
keep Southern senators in a position where they could head off civil
rights legislation. Maybank reminded the assembly that only acts of
Congress, not party platforms, really counted. He added, "Our place is
within the party so we may maintain a voice in the party."[19] Sen. Olin
D. Johnston reached the same conclusion:

> I have read both the Republican and Democratic platforms in
> full. To me there is absolutely no difference between the aims and
> desires of the civil rights plank for both parties. Both have hidden
> teeth in them. Neither forms the South's viewpoint on this mat-
> ter. . . . I am sticking to the Democratic nominees of the Demo-
> cratic party.[20]

Other delegates, of lesser status in the South Carolina political hierarchy, felt differently. Francis Coleman, the mayor of Mount Pleasant, a
small coastal town near Charleston, said:

> How can we subscribe to the policies of the national convention?
> If we endorse the national party platform, it will be a mandate to the

---

*To follow all of the often contradictory Southern reactions to the national shifts on
race during the uneasy period from the late 1940s to the early 1960s would require
telling eleven separate stories, a strategy adopted in this book only for the post-1964
period. Yet, the complex state-level reactions to the cataclysmic changes that were
under way are too important for what comes later to ignore entirely. Thus, in the
remainder of this chapter I have interspersed discussion of the national developments
with a view of how the politicians of one state, South Carolina, were responding. The
choice of South Carolina places emphasis on the Deep South perspective.

U.S. Supreme Court to do away with segregation in the South. I beg you not to endorse the nominees of the Democratic national party and thus put a straitjacket on South Carolina.[21]

Thomas P. Stoney of Charleston rhetorically asked:

How can you repudiate a platform and then vote for the men on it? . . . [The delegation leadership] says the 1952 civil rights part is stiffer than in 1948, and you come with your mouths open and think with your bellies and not with your brains.[22]

Siding with Senators Maybank and Johnston, the state convention voted to support Stevenson.

A month later Jimmy Byrnes, who had been elected governor of South Carolina in 1950, proved he was true to his Senate warning of 1938. He endorsed Gen. Dwight D. Eisenhower for president. Byrnes's stated reasons for supporting the GOP nominee included Eisenhower's "stature as a world leader."[23] Also among his reasons was Eisenhower's opposition to federal legislation aimed at ending racial discrimination in employment practices. Byrnes contended, furthermore, that Stevenson planned to use his influence as president to urge the Senate to end Southern filibusters on civil rights measures.[24]

Shortly after Byrnes made his endorsement, Eisenhower visited Columbia. The press proclaimed the event as the first campaign visit ever of a presidential nominee of either party to South Carolina, one immediate result of party competition. During his speech from the State House steps, Eisenhower made no mention of civil rights. He did, however, rise to his feet promptly when the band played "Dixie." "I always stand when they play that song," the general told the cheering throng,[25] a gesture that was quite politic in the South.

Stevenson carried South Carolina—narrowly, 50.7 percent to 49.3 percent—and the other four Deep South states, plus North Carolina and Arkansas, while being swamped nationwide by the popular war hero Eisenhower. But the dilemma facing Southern Democrats remained and intensified over the next few years.

In 1954 the U.S. Supreme Court dramatically altered the situation by declaring segregated public schools unconstitutional in the famous *Brown* vs. *Board of Education* decision. There followed "massive" Southern resistance.[26] In March 1956 most of the region's members of Congress signed the Southern Congressional Manifesto, which condemned the Supreme Court for having "substituted naked power for the established law of the land"[27] and which called for resistance to integration. The school segregation decision, rendered by a Court led by Eisenhower's appointee as Chief Justice, Earl Warren, no longer made

Eisenhower's candidacy in 1956 the vehicle for protest it had been in some Southern circles in 1952, when the greatest danger to segregation appeared to come from Northern Democrats.

Whereas the 1952 election highlighted one of the three contradictory tendencies sketched above—that is, that a large portion of the Southern Democracy could remain loyal to the party, if by sharply reduced margins—the 1956 election offered evidence for the other two tendencies as well.

Prior to the 1956 Democratic National Convention, Strom Thurmond[28] declared:

> It is the desire of our state to work within the framework of the national party without going so far as to destroy the only weapon the South has that can bring effective results—fear on the part of the national party that the South will take independent action. . . . If the national party knows the South will not bolt . . . then it is apparent our fight to get concessions is lost.[29]

Thurmond's remarks were prompted by what he called the dangerous position Southern Democratic party chairmen had taken at a preconvention gathering in Atlanta. The party leaders had said, "We do not favor any bolts . . . or third parties."[30]

The 1956 debates of South Carolina Democrats after the national party had renominated Stevenson cast further light on the situation as viewed from the state level. The chief controversy at the Columbia gathering centered on a resolution by Shepard K. Nash, the Sumter County Democratic party chairman, stating that any South Carolina Democrat could vote for—and presumably campaign for—someone other than the Democratic presidential nominee in the fall without jeopardizing his party status.[31]

Several quotations from speakers opposed to the Nash resolution demonstrate that the debate dealt openly with fundamentals and that Democratic leaders (except Thurmond, of course) were quite convinced that their strategy of continued allegiance to the national party was the correct one. U.S. Sen. Thomas A. Wofford, a short-term appointee, speaking against the resolution, charged, "Eisenhower has done more damage in three and a half years in the South than Mrs. Roosevelt can do in twenty years. . . . We never have in the South gotten anything out of the Republican party." Gov. George Bell Timmerman, Jr., the successor to Governor Byrnes who had recently called for federal transportation of blacks to Northern states, where he said "race mixing" was favored, told the delegates, "The South made significant gains at Chicago, and these gains marked a turning point in political attitudes toward the South." Senator Johnston asserted at the convention, "We can best serve the people of South Carolina by remaining in the Democratic party."[32] In late October, during a visit to the State House to urge support for Stevenson, Johnston made the establishment's argument as explicit as it appears anywhere in the published record: "We can fight for segregation better through the Democratic party than in any other way. . . . Now if the Republicans get a majority in the Senate, and if Republicans head committees, we in the South are lost."[33]

Two other statements from the 1956 South Carolina Democratic convention, also from the party establishment's side although not from top officeholders, reveal the bitterness present at the gathering. Lonnie A. Causy of Horry County shouted at the "Eisenhowercrats" in the balcony to get out. "I came here because I love Adlai Stevenson," he exclaimed. Causy promised the delegates "to stump South Carolina against Jimmy Byrnes as I did in 1952 when the state was saved for Stevenson," and, according to a newspaper account, Causy "jeered at Senator Thurmond as a States' Righter." William T. Jones of Greenwood told the delegates, in the words of *The State*, that "if they couldn't support the nominees of the party they weren't Democrats. He suggested that if they wanted to vote for independents to get into the independent party, and if they wanted to vote for Eisenhower, to get into the Republican party."[34] The Nash resolution was defeated 168½ to 147½, and, as the results of the election were to show, many South Carolinians in November took Jones up on his offer.

Immediately after the state convention a hundred delegates met to start a ballot petition under the name South Carolinians for Independent Electors. The leadership of this movement came from officials of a state association of white citizens' councils, led by Farley Smith of Lee County, a son of Sen. Cotton Ed Smith. After securing a ballot position, this group— whose racist appeal needs no elaboration—pledged its electors to Sen. Harry F. Byrd of Virginia for the presidency and to U.S. Rep. John Bell Williams of Mississippi for the vice-presidency. The threat of party sanctions probably kept Thurmond from endorsing the Byrd slate. Former Governor Byrnes became the only prominent South Carolina politician to back the white citizens' council slate of electors. Byrnes's reasons for switching from the "world leader" Eisenhower to Byrd, given on a statewide radio hookup, are instructive:

> Though we regret it, we must admit that next to the peace of the world, the issue that commands most attention in the South is the attempt to force integration of the races in our schools, in violation of state laws. On this issue there is little to choose between Mr. Stevenson and President Eisenhower. . . . But he [Eisenhower] has

said and done enough about integrating the races in the District of
Columbia to cause us to realize that on this subject, we need not
expect assistance from either President Eisenhower or Mr.
Stevenson.[35]

The South Carolina results from this 1956 three-way election indicate
that each of the three contradictory courses of action advocated by
various political leaders—stay with the Democrats, join the Republican
party, or bolt—all securely tied to the impact of outside forces threaten-
ing segregation, had sizable support among the voters. Stevenson carried
the state with a plurality of 45.4 percent. The independents for Byrd
finished second with 29.5 percent, and the Republicans were third with
25.2 percent. That Stevenson nearly equaled his 1952 showing directs
attention to the massive defection from Eisenhower to the ticket backed
by the white citizens' councils. The most pronounced drop in Eisenhower's vote came in the state's Black Belt.[36] Among these counties,
with their heavy concentration of disfranchised blacks, Eisenhower's
vote went from 62 percent in 1952 to 17 percent in 1956, an indication
of the hold the most blatantly racist appeal had on a segment of the
Southern electorate. A postelection commentary in *The State* summed
up the election succinctly: "Segregation, in fact, has been the overriding
issue of the campaign in South Carolina."[37]

Stevenson again lost decisively in the nation, but he still carried a
majority of the Southern states—Mississippi, Alabama, Arkansas, North
Carolina, and Georgia along with South Carolina.

In 1957 Eisenhower sent troops to Little Rock, Arkansas, to enforce a
school desegregation order, and in both 1957 and 1960 he supported
mild civil rights bills in Congress. Although the Eisenhower actions
may have seemed quite timid to civil rights advocates, they were strong
enough in the eyes of some white Southerners to make the Democratic
party appear attractive again.

As the 1960 elections drew near, several things worked to discourage a
Southern exodus from the Democratic party. Because of the one-party
system at the state level and the rule of seniority in Congress, the
region's congressmen and senators held important leadership positions
in Washington that would be lost if they switched parties. In the states
themselves, the Democratic politicians had "a vested interest in the
office-holding industry."[38] Moreover, the Republican party, the party of
Lincoln and Reconstruction, did not offer a satisfactory alternative on
the race issue. Eisenhower's action in Little Rock and his support for
civil rights legislation provided no comfort to those Southerners ready to
flock to any candidate willing to give them hope of maintaining blacks
in an inferior position.

The 1960 presidential election stands out as one not dominated by the civil rights issue, mainly because Sen. John F. Kennedy of Massachusetts, the Democratic nominee, and Vice-President Richard M. Nixon, the Republican nominee, held almost identical civil rights positions. Quotations from accounts of the candidates' campaign visits to South Carolina show that segregationists received no outward comfort from either. Kennedy declared in Columbia, "Some of you may disagree with my views [on civil rights], but at least I have not changed my principles in an election year." He added that progress must be made on civil rights "if we are to be true to our ideals and responsibilities." Presidential leadership would be necessary for such progress, he said, and charged that Nixon was double-talking on the issue: "Up there he stresses how quickly he will act in this area. Down here he says he knows this is a difficult problem."[39] *The State* gave only the following report of Nixon's mention of the issue while in Columbia:

> The Vice President referred only incidentally to civil rights. He said he recognized that many in the audience would not agree with all his positions. But he said he believed he is respected by Southerners as a man "who talks the same way in the West and the South and the North and the East."[40]

The delicate posturing by Nixon and Kennedy on civil rights reflected campaign necessity. Although there were Southern states to win by appearing the least progressive on this issue, there were black voters in the large industrial swing states to attract by appearing the most progressive.

To understand how Southern Democratic leaders were able in 1960 to win six states—South Carolina, Georgia, Arkansas, North Carolina, Louisiana, and Texas—and thus to contribute to the narrow victory of the Kennedy-Johnson[41] ticket, it is important to remember that the electorate did not identify the civil rights developments of the 1950s with a Democratic president. While Truman was an aberration to many Southerners, there was reason to hope that the venerable party of Jefferson and Jackson would again be led by a man who would treat the South's racial institutions—as Franklin Roosevelt had done—as beyond the realm of the federal government's responsibility. This would prove to be wishful thinking, but it was a plausible rationalization considering how slowly the outside challenges to segregation were actually affecting the South's dual society. In 1960, Southern blacks were treated little better than in 1940. The power of the federal government had yet to be brought to bear—as it was in the middle and late 1960s—in sufficient strength to realize the changes portended by the resolutions of Northern

Democrats and the unenforced pronouncements of the Supreme Court. With the accession of the Kennedy administration, this was all to change.

National Democrats Champion Civil Rights

Concurrent with the maneuvers of elected politicians, black activists, led most prominently by Martin Luther King, Jr., applied pressure for national action by staging protests throughout the region in the late 1950s and early 1960s. During the first two years of the Kennedy administration, support from Washington for the civil rights movement gradually increased. By 1962 the course had been·set; in that year, amid strong white resistance, the young Democratic President ordered troops to enforce integration at the University of Mississippi. Other federal actions followed.[42]

If there was any ambiguity in the situation, Lyndon Johnson removed it shortly after succeeding to the presidency upon Kennedy's assassination in November 1963. Johnson seized the initiative on civil rights and was a powerful force pushing the 1964 Civil Rights Act through Congress.

All the worst fears of Southern segregationists soon came to fruition. With a Democrat in the White House leading the federal integration efforts, the message was clear: The national Democratic party had truly "walked into the bright sunshine of human rights" and would no longer protect racial segregation in the South. By the mid-1960s one could safely say that white Southerners knew where the party of their grandfathers stood on the issue Byrnes had called the "soul of the South."

Still, President Johnson's championing of the cause of civil rights for blacks would not have had the partisan impact in the South that it did without the highly publicized opposition to the Civil Rights Act by the Republican presidential candidate in 1964. Sen. Barry Goldwater of Arizona, the GOP nominee, voted against the imposition of cloture to break the Southern filibuster—which was the critical decision and which succeeded by only four votes—and against the bill itself. Despite Goldwater's protestations that he was "unalterably opposed to discrimination of any sort" and that he voted against the bill because parts of it "fly in the face of the Constitution,"[43] his vote was heralded in the South during the 1964 campaign by Republicans as well as by those bolters who were dissatisfied with the lack of choice on the race issue that the 1960 presidential candidates presented. For example, Farley Smith, of the South Carolina white citizens' councils, announced, "Independents should join under the banner of the Republican party. . . . The issues are clearly drawn."[44]

In November 1964 Johnson won a landslide Democratic victory nationwide, but the Republican Goldwater swept the Deep South states of Mississippi (with 87.1 percent of the vote!), Alabama (69.5 percent), South Carolina (58.9 percent), Louisiana (56 8 percent), and Georgia (54.1 percent).[45] Bernard Cosman, in *Five States for Goldwater*, corroborates the importance of the issue of race for Goldwater's Southern success: "In 1964, the Deep-South vote polarized around race. The Goldwater candidacy alienated Negroes, while simultaneously bringing together the white voters from all status levels who had been angered by the racial policies of Presidents Kennedy and Johnson."[46]

The significance of Goldwater's candidacy can scarcely be overestimated. Nor should one forget that Goldwater did little more than step forward to pick up what national Democratic leaders had cast aside: the votes of those Southern white Democrats who placed the preservation of racial segregation above all other issues. This discard marked the end of the road for a Southern Democracy based on white racial unity. In each state years of sorting out were still to come. But 1964 closed out an era and opened the way for the development of a Southern political order of a different sort. The next chapter considers all the forces, racial and nonracial, that merged in the post-1964 period to create this new order.

3

The Emergence of Southern
Two-Party Politics

Electoral chaos reigned in the South following President Johnson's complete embrace of the cause of equal rights for blacks in the middle 1960s. During the next several years Southern politicians and voters groped in various directions as they wrestled with their drastically altered partisan environment. The new situation exhibited three chief features.

First, the national Democratic party, the prime enforcer of the breakdown of segregation after 1964, suffered large defections in the South. These defections were manifest in the presidential elections of 1968 and 1972, in which the party's national ticket could muster only about 30 percent of the vote in the region. Although the complex story of how the defectors from the national party treated statewide Democratic candidates is depicted in all its variation in the state chapters, one generalization is possible here: When state Democratic nominees were convincingly branded as Kennedy-Johnson-Humphrey-McGovern integrationists, they suffered significantly at the polls through 1972. After 1972 the abatement of the race issue made defeat far less certain, and white Southern Democrats, in fact, discovered that alliance with blacks had become a crucial part of their majorities in the post–civil rights era.

Second, the total collapse of the rationale for the one-party Democratic South that occurred during the Kennedy and Johnson administrations unleashed a torrent of Republican activity in the region. The fuel for this spurt of Republicanism was substantial white antagonism toward all things remotely connected with the national Democratic integrationists. It was no accident that a significant increase in Republican victories for various offices in the South below the presidential level did not begin in earnest until the Goldwater candidacy of 1964. Figure 3-1, charting the GOP's uneven growth in the South, shows that the major Republican leap forward began in the mid-1960s.

Third, the collapse of the racial rationale for the one-party South allowed the economic and philosophical foundation of party politics that existed outside of the South to filter into the region's emerging partisan structure. This development is crucial for understanding how Republicans in the region were able to build a substantial and lasting base of support in the post–civil rights era. In the relative calm of the 1980s, Southern Republicans stress this aspect of their party's growth, while they understandably play down or even deny the role of the race issue.

The first two features—which are, of course, opposite sides of the same coin—need no further background elaboration. The third, however, requires familiarity with changes in the national party system since the New Deal era.

The New Deal Realignment and the South

When the Great Depression hit at the end of the 1920s, the Republican party had been the country's dominant political organization for seven decades. Students of America's political parties split the years from the Civil War to the Great Depression into two parts, the division coming during the Populist upheaval of the 1890s. For this inquiry it is unnecessary to characterize these two earlier party systems except to note that their primary organizing principle was not economic class. Rather, sectional, ethnic, religious, and urban-rural cleavages dominated,[1] and the major beneficiary of these cleavages was the Grand Old Party.

The situation changed abruptly in the 1930s. President Herbert Hoover, a man philosophically opposed to the use of the national government to direct the country's economic and social affairs, and the Republican party were discredited in the eyes of a substantial portion of the nation's citizens by their handling of the Depression. These voters, many of them entering the electorate for the first time, overwhelmingly supported the Democrat Franklin D. Roosevelt and his efforts to use the national government either to return prosperity or to ameliorate the effects of the hard times. From 15 million votes in 1928, Democratic presidential support reached 27.5 million for President Roosevelt's first re-election, in 1936.[2] The shift was of such a magnitude as eventually to make the Democratic party the country's majority party in the parti-

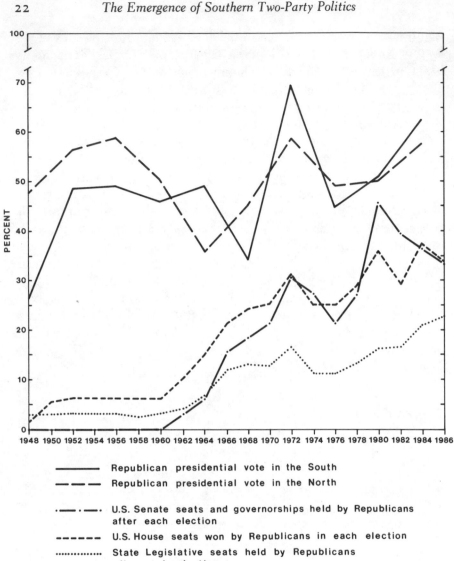

Figure 3-1. The Uneven Growth of the Republican Party in the South, 1948–1986

san configuration that resulted from the New Deal realignment. The organizing principle of the new system revolved roughly around economic-class issues and the related question of the proper role of the national government in promoting the interests of "those who have less."[3] As described by James L. Sundquist, the New Deal earthquake reoriented voters along economic-class lines: "Businessmen and professional men were preponderantly Republican; the working class predominantly Democratic."[4] For example, in 1940 the following responses by income group were given to the question "Which party would you like to see win the presidential election in 1940?":[5]

	Democratic (%)	Republican (%)
Upper Income	36	64
Middle Income	51	49
Lower Income	69	31

The New Deal realignment was first of all a realignment at the presidential level. Millions of voters flocked to Roosevelt's Democratic standard, not necessarily to whatever constituted the old opposition party in their locales. In the North, the realignment required three decades to work its way down to the state and local levels, a period that witnessed substantial divergence between the strength of the parties in presidential and state elections. More than a few Northern voters identified themselves as "Roosevelt Republicans" and supported FDR and the New Deal but retained their Republican voting patterns in state contests.[6] Sundquist elaborated:

> Various barriers prevented the electorate from conforming all at once, in every state and locality, to the new rationale of the party system . . . . As the barriers were removed, local realignments occurred. These appeared sometimes almost as independent changes in the party system, but since the essential result of each change was to bring a state or locality into conformity with the alignment established in the country as a whole in the 1930s, each must be considered an integral part—no less so merely because it was delayed—of that realignment episode.[7]

In the South the barriers to the penetration of the New Deal alignment were formidable indeed. Not the least of these was the obvious fact that the realignment—if successful—would have placed the Southern Republican party, then practically nonexistent, in a minority status in the national scheme. And Southern conservative Democratic politicians, who would have been expected to lead such a realignment, or any politicians for that matter, did not relish jumping from a majority-status party to one in the minority.

But by far the most serious barrier in the South was race. The Democratic party in the South, above all else, was the party of segregation. In his 1952 study of the prospects for two-party development in the region, Alexander Heard wrote:

> At the origin of the Southern one-party system stood the single figure of the Negro. The system . . . is now shored up by inertia and its own vested rights. But the origin was the Negro, and the Negro must be supplanted by other concerns before one-party supremacy will break down.[8]

The actions of three Democratic Presidents, starting with Truman's civil rights efforts, continuing with Kennedy's integration initiatives, and culminating in Johnson's complete embrace of the civil rights cause, resulted in the lifting of this formidable barrier to the penetration of the New Deal economic-class alignment into the South's politics.

The barrier did not fall all at once. It began to crumble first at the presidential level. In the 1952, 1956, and 1960 presidential elections, at least in the South's urban areas, a distinct class cleavage emerged consistent with the New Deal alignment established two decades earlier in the North.[9] (See Table 3-1, which presents classified precinct breakdowns by class and race for New Orleans and Atlanta.) For example, in Atlanta in 1952 Adlai Stevenson, the Democratic standard-bearer, received 76 percent of the votes of lower-income whites and 36 percent of those of upper-income whites; the Republican Dwight D. Eisenhower won only 24 percent of the votes of lower-income whites but 64 percent in upper-income white precincts. Precinct data from a score of other Southern cities confirm this trend.[10] This phenomenon has been referred to as presidential Republicanism or urban Republicanism.[11] It is the extension of the New Deal realignment at the presidential level to the least traditional areas of the South, its cities.[12]

Confluence of Race and Class

In the 1950s the impediment to class-based partisan voting in presidential elections (at least in the cities) was thus substantially weakened. But the barrier still held at the state level, where the GOP had yet to stir in any meaningful way. And the state level would remain unaffected until the cataclysmic political events of the early and middle 1960s discredited the rationale for Southern Democratic solidarity and gave the Republican party a powerful boost in the region.

When the transformation over race finally took place,[13] it marked the collapse of the Southern barrier to the penetration of class-based two-party politics below the presidential level.[14] But herein lies an important wrinkle: After the transformation over race knocked down the barrier to class politics, the race issue did not quietly go away. Quite the contrary, race became enmeshed in the emerging potentially class-based two-party structure that took hold in the South in the years after 1964. Thus, at

Table 3-1. Presidential Vote by Class and Race in New Orleans and Atlanta, 1952–1960

	Lower Income	Middle Income (Whites)	Upper Income	Blacks
		New Orleans		
		1952		
Stevenson	51%	37%	27%	87%
Eisenhower	49	63	73	13
		1956		
Stevenson	45%	31%	27%	44%
Eisenhower	52	65	69	54
States' Rights	4	4	3	2
		1960		
Kennedy	50%	44%	39%	75%
Nixon	17	28	39	24
Independent	32	29	22	1
		Atlanta		
		1952		
Stevenson	76%	65%	36%	74%
Eisenhower	24	35	64	26
		1956		
Stevenson	76%	74%	46%	15%
Eisenhower	24	26	54	85
		1960		
Kennedy	64%	60%	40%	42%
Nixon	36	40	60	58

SOURCE: Numan V. Bartley and Hugh D. Graham, *Southern Elections: County and Precinct Data, 1950–1972* (Baton Rouge: Louisiana State Univ. Press, 1978), 363, 368. The middle-income category was derived by averaging Bartley and Graham's two middle classifications.

this critical juncture in Southern political history, the twin forces of class and race merged, and in that merger is found a central feature of the partisan structure that arose in the region.

As the Republican party began to build at the state level, propelled by the white reaction to the end of segregation, the party made its most faithful converts among those attracted by its conservative position on New Deal–type economic-class issues. But it also picked up substantial support from white Democrats angered by their national party's "betrayal" on the race issue. Twisted into the situation was the logical compatibility of conservative economic-class Republicanism with the racial protest. The GOP, as the party philosophically opposed to an activist federal government in economic matters (a policy that favored the well-to-do North and South), gained adherents also from those who objected to federal intervention in the racial affairs of the states, and in more than a few cases they were the same people.

How could the two streams of protest be separated easily in the political arena? They could not, of course, and the Republican candidates, who recognized that they were beneficiaries of both prongs of reaction, rarely made the effort. Southern Republican candidates gladly took white racist support, careful especially in later years to acknowledge it as philosophical support for the abstract principle of limiting the federal government and nothing more. This attitude remains prevalent in Southern GOP circles today.*

As the Republicans began building their party and contesting elections, however, they discovered that Southern Democrats were not about to abandon the conservative field on either race or class. With the passage of the Voting Rights Act of 1965 and the rapid increase of black registered voters,[15] who faithfully carried Democratic party affiliation in gratitude to the party's national leadership for its efforts on their behalf, many Southern Democratic politicians abandoned their segregationist

---

*The GOP's pleasure at the subtle confluence of these issues in the 1980s was apparent during a 1981 interview with a Republican official in Ronald Reagan's White House who handles political matters. The topic was the place of race in Reagan's "new Southern strategy," to use the official's phrase. Part of the interview follows:

Official: As to the whole Southern strategy that Harry Dent and others put together in 1968, opposition to the Voting Rights Act would have been a central part of keeping the South. Now [the new Southern strategy] doesn't have to do that. All you have to do to keep the South is for Reagan to run in place on the issues he's campaigned on since 1964 . . . and that's fiscal conservatism, balancing the budget, cut taxes, you know, the whole cluster. . . .

Questioner: But the fact is, isn't it, that Reagan does get to the Wallace voter and to the racist side of the Wallace voter by doing away with Legal Services, by cutting down on food stamps . . . ?

[The official answered by pointing to what he said was the abstract nature of the race issue today.]

Official: You start out in 1954 by saying "Nigger, nigger, nigger." By 1968 you can't say "nigger"—that hurts you. Backfires. So you say stuff like forced busing, states' rights, and all that stuff. You're getting so abstract now [that] you're talking about cutting taxes, and all these things you're talking about are totally economic things and a by-product of them is [that] blacks get hurt worse than whites. And subconsciously maybe that is part of it. I'm not saying that. But I'm saying that if it is getting that abstract, and that coded, that we are doing away with the racial problem one way or the other. You follow me—because obviously sitting around saying, "We want to cut this," is much more abstract than even the busing thing *and* a hell of a lot more abstract than "Nigger, nigger."

The interview was conducted in Washington on July 8, 1981, by the author and a newspaper reporter. Needless to say, how much one is doing away with the race issue in this context is debatable.

posture and reached out—at first quietly, then more openly—to this new and powerful electoral force. Some Democrats came around faster than others; for example, Georgia's Jimmy Carter was a path breaker in this regard, but George Wallace felt no need to court blacks vigorously until he sought to recapture the Alabama governorship in that state's transformed partisan environment of 1982.

While the segregationist facet of the Southern Democratic party eroded rapidly in the early 1970s, the economically conservative portion of the party had greater staying power. Since the 1930s leaders of the Southern Democracy have split over basic governmental philosophy. The Byrds of Virginia and the Talmadges of Georgia were anti–New Deal conservatives; others, such as Lister Hill of Alabama and Olin D. Johnston of South Carolina, supported their national party's liberal positions on economic-class matters.[16] These philosophical divisions, however, had no institutional permanence in state political life because of the lack of separate, established party structures to carry on the battle in an orderly fashion over a long period of time.[17]

Even the fitful and undeveloped class politics that existed in the one-party South fell victim to the intensification of the race issue in the early 1950s when the legal onslaught against segregation grew serious. Numan V. Bartley and Hugh D. Graham documented the devastating impact the flaring of the race question had on Southern economic liberals in the 1950s.[18] For example, Sen. Claude Pepper, a Florida New Dealer, lost his Senate seat to a race-baiting opponent in the 1950 Democratic primary.[19] In North Carolina that same year Frank P. Graham, a pro-labor senator and former president of the University of North Carolina, went down after a vicious primary runoff campaign in which the promoters of his Democratic primary opponent, Willis Smith, urged "white people [to] wake up before it's too late"[20] and told North Carolina Democrats that a vote for Graham was a vote for "your children sitting in Negro schools."[21] In describing the Graham campaign, Samuel Lubell wrote, "Packaged in with the racial issue were opposition to 'communism,' to the CIO, to government spending, to health insurance, to the 'drift toward socialism.' "[22] This early confluence of race and class that Lubell noticed, however, occurred within the Democratic party and not between parties.

The twisting together of racial and economic-class issues continued after the start of vigorous two-party competition at the state level. Those Democrats occupying, often unwillingly, the liberal position on both issues frequently were defeated in the early years of party competition, roughly 1964 to 1972.[23]

After the abatement of the race issue in the 1970s, a favorable attitude by a Democratic candidate toward blacks and issues of concern to blacks lost much of its sting. Yet on economic-class issues separable from the race issue many white Democratic politicians continued to shy away from the left side of the political spectrum. This stance is better addressed after the various personalities and nuances of their positions have been laid out in the state chapters. Therefore, a portion of the concluding chapter treats this question, which encompasses a discussion of how far the class alignment begun in the 1930s has penetrated into the region's two-party system. At this point, a return to the presidential level elucidates further the context within which state politics developed.

Democrats' Nadir in the South: The 1968 and 1972 Elections

The 1968 and 1972 Democratic presidential nominees, Hubert Humphrey and George McGovern, shouldered the full brunt of the Southern reaction to the national party's abandonment of the white South. In the 1968 election the partisan situation was clouded by George Wallace's third-party candidacy. The Alabamian and the Republican nominee, Richard Nixon, divided the South; Humphrey won only President Johnson's home state of Texas. Wallace carried Alabama (with 65.8 percent of the votes cast), Mississippi (63.5 percent), Louisiana (48.3 percent), Georgia (42.8 percent), and Arkansas (38.9 percent). Strom Thurmond's vigorous campaign for Nixon in South Carolina denied Wallace a clean sweep of the Deep South states; Nixon won the Palmetto State's electoral votes with 38.1 percent, but the Alabama segregationist was second with 32.3 percent. Nixon carried five Rim South states; in two of them, Tennessee and North Carolina, Wallace placed second. The majority of Humphrey's Southern votes in 1968 probably came from blacks.

When the fury of the race issue hit, whites ceased to vote along class lines as they had done in the 1952, 1956, and 1960 presidential elections. In 1964 Goldwater, who had earlier announced he was going "hunting where the ducks are,"[24] did slightly better among lower-income whites in Atlanta (58 percent) than among upper-income whites (55 percent); in New Orleans the Democratic nominee still did a little better among lower-income whites than among the well-to-do, but Goldwater won a clear majority among all whites (see Table 3-2). This disintegration of class-based presidential voting was stronger in 1964 in the Deep South than in the Rim South.[25] However, in 1968 and again in 1972, class distinctions virtually disappeared among whites in nearly all Southern cities, and the Deep South–Rim South split was far less significant.[26]

Table 3-2. Presidential Vote by Class and Race in New Orleans and Atlanta,
1964–1972

	Lower Income	Middle Income (Whites)	Upper Income	Blacks
		New Orleans		
		1964		
Johnson	43%	35%	33%	97%
Goldwater	57	65	67	3
		1968		
Humphrey	21%	19%	17%	93%
Nixon	25	42	54	1
Wallace	53	39	29	6
		1972		
McGovern	19%	19%	17%	68%
Nixon	77	79	79	13
		Atlanta		
		1964		
Johnson	42%	37%	45%	99%
Goldwater	58	63	55	1
		1968		
Humphrey	19%	22%	32%	98%
Nixon	33	42	58	2
Wallace	48	36	10	0
		1972		
McGovern	17%	21%	19%	92%
Nixon	83	79	81	8

Source: Numan V. Bartley and Hugh D. Graham, *Southern Elections: County and Precinct Data, 1950–1972* (Baton Rouge: Louisiana State Univ. Press, 1978), 363, 368–69.

McGovern in 1972 was a weak finisher outside of the South, getting 39.7 percent of the vote in the rest of the nation, but he did especially poorly in the South, receiving only 28.9 percent. Although there were national reasons for his defeat unrelated to Southern politics, McGovern's pronounced weakness in the region suggests continuity with Humphrey's candidacy four years earlier. Data in the state chapters confirm that the two Democratic nominees performed similarly throughout the region.

The major difference in the South between the 1968 election and that of 1972 was the lack of the Wallace alternative in the latter contest. Most observers speculated that Nixon would be the chief beneficiary of

Wallace's absence from the Southern ballot in 1972, and survey data verify this expectation, showing that those Southerners who supported Wallace in 1968 voted for Nixon by a margin of three to one.[27] In his landslide victory Nixon carried all the Southern states and in fact the entire nation except Massachusetts and the District of Columbia.

Since the major beneficiary of the South's rejection of Humphrey and McGovern was Richard Nixon, an examination of Nixon's approach to the region is in order. In his 1960 campaign he cautiously advocated civil rights for blacks, but in his 1968 comeback attempt and in his 1972 re-election effort the Republican standard-bearer courted the white South. Contemporary observers labeled Nixon's attentiveness to the Southern scene his Southern strategy. Reg Murphy and Hal Gulliver, editors of the *Atlanta Constitution* who examined the topic in a 1971 book, wrote, "The Southern Strategy rested, finally, on a calculated appeal to white segregationist sentiment. It was anti-black, not with passion but with a cool, clear-eyed political cynicism."[28]

Nixon, whose keen insight into even the most subtle aspects of national political life cannot be denied, clearly comprehended what had occurred in the region since his 1960 campaign. Seeing his opportunity in 1968, he shrewdly allied himself with Sen. Strom Thurmond, the former Dixiecrat who had switched to the Republican party in 1964. Murphy and Gulliver asserted that Nixon

> sat in a motel room in Atlanta in the early spring of 1968 and made *his* political deal. Senator Strom Thurmond of South Carolina was there. There were others. The essential Nixon bargain was simply this: *If I'm president of the United States, I'll find a way to ease up on the federal pressures forcing school desegregation—or any other kind of desegregation.* Whatever the exact words or phrasing, this was how the Nixon commitment was understood by Thurmond and other Southern GOP strategists.[29]

For Nixon the alliance with Thurmond paid off in 1968 in more than Republican convention delegates; the former Dixiecrat stumped the South for the GOP nominee and contributed to Nixon's accumulation of Southern electoral votes.

Whether Nixon himself ever paid off, or whether in fact there ever was a deal,[30] remains unclear. Nixon did nominate two conservative Southerners to the Supreme Court in his first opportunity to fill a vacancy, but the Senate rejected both men. School integration under court direction, however, continued during the Nixon administration. Nixon certainly did not turn back the clock on civil rights; as President his interests were centered elsewhere.

Jimmy Carter and Democratic Resurgence in the Mid-1970s

The steady Republican growth[31] in the South ended temporarily in the middle 1970s when the GOP suffered a short-lived decline of varying magnitude, depending on which office is considered. Figure 3-1 charts this dip; Figure 3-2, however, provides a more revealing view of the trend by identifying the Republicans who won the major statewide offices, those of governor and U.S. senator. Both figures show that the drop in Republican victories bottomed out in 1976 and that by 1978 the party was once again on the upswing.

Why did the GOP decline in these years? The most common explanation attributes the drop to the detrimental effects of the Watergate scandal and the subsequent resignation of President Nixon. There can be no doubt that Watergate was a Republican disaster nationwide and that its effects were felt in several Southern elections; for example, the Democrat Ray Blanton in Tennessee's 1974 gubernatorial election used the issue effectively against the Republican Lamar Alexander, who had the misfortune of being closely identified with the pre-Watergate Nixon White House.

But to attribute the GOP downturn solely to Watergate, or to other national causes, such as the economic recession of 1974–75, is to overlook certain underlying dynamic elements at work in Southern politics. As was previously mentioned, a key regional element contributing to this Democratic upsurge was the abatement of the race issue in the early 1970s and the impetus this altered situation gave to the formation of potent black-white Democratic coalitions throughout the region.

Importance of the Abatement of the Race Issue

The electoral advantage that accrued to Southern Democrats in the post–civil rights era as a result of their support by the black-white coalition that formed after the hot battles over race had cooled in the 1970s cannot be emphasized enough. In the early and middle 1960s, however, such an outcome was far from apparent. Near the time of the Goldwater candidacy most Southern Republican candidates at the state level were unconcerned with losing what they were later to denounce as the "bloc vote." With exceptions (most notably Winthrop Rockefeller of Arkansas), the challenging Republicans sought to tie the Southern Democrats to the unpopular racial policies of Presidents Kennedy and Johnson and to reap anticipated electoral benefits.

The strategy almost worked for the Republican senatorial hopeful James D. Martin in Alabama in 1962; Sen. Lister Hill barely defeated him that year.[32] Sen. Ernest F. (Fritz) Hollings, Democrat of South

NOTE: Republicans held none of the thirty-three posts from 1925 to 1961

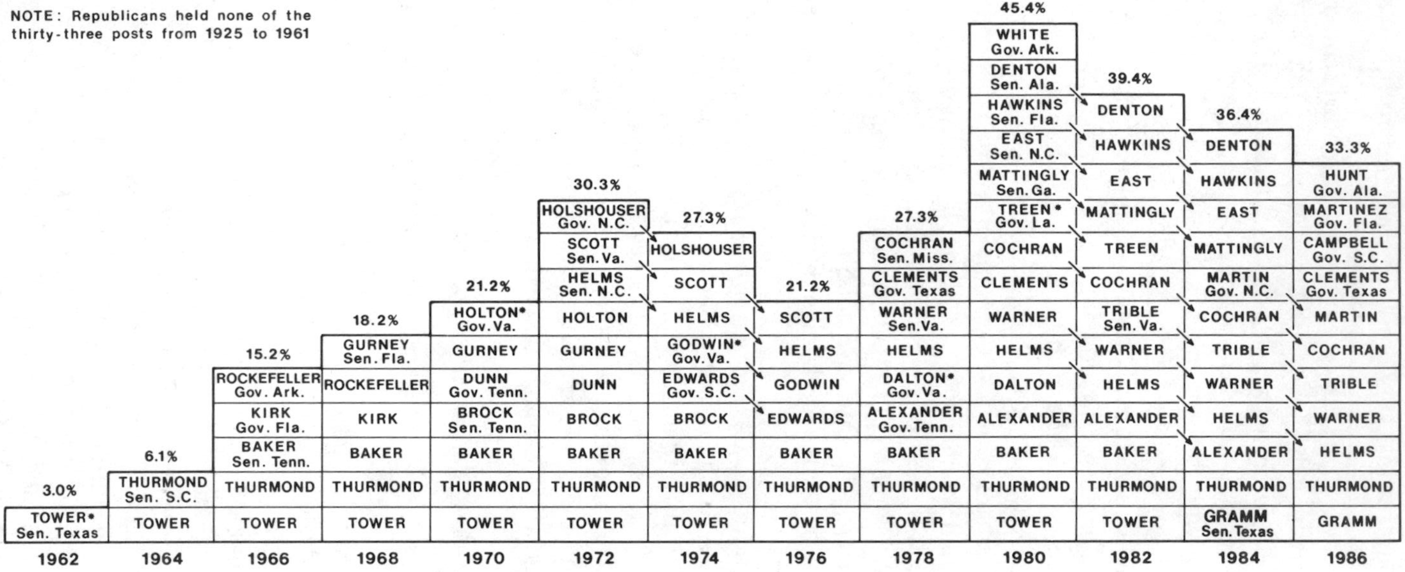

[* Elected in the preceding year]

Figure 3-2. Republican Successes in Senatorial and Gubernatorial Elections, 1961–1986

	1962 3.0%	1964 6.1%	1966 15.2%	1968 18.2%	1970 21.2%	1972 30.3%	1974 27.3%	1976 21.2%	1978 27.3%	1980 45.4%	1982 39.4%	1984 36.4%	1986 33.3%
										WHITE Gov. Ark.			HUNT Gov. Ala.
						HOLSHOUSER Gov. N.C.	HOLSHOUSER		COCHRAN Sen. Miss.	DENTON Sen. Ala.	DENTON	DENTON	MARTINEZ Gov. Fla.
			ROCKEFELLER Gov. Ark.	GURNEY Sen. Fla.	HOLTON* Gov. Va.	SCOTT Sen. Va.	SCOTT	SCOTT	CLEMENTS Gov. Texas	HAWKINS Sen. Fla.	HAWKINS	HAWKINS	CAMPBELL Gov. S.C.
			KIRK Gov. Fla.	ROCKEFELLER	GURNEY	HELMS Sen. N.C.	HELMS	HELMS	WARNER Sen. Va.	EAST Sen. N.C.	EAST	EAST	CLEMENTS Gov. Texas
		THURMOND Sen. S.C.	BAKER Sen. Tenn.	KIRK	DUNN Gov. Tenn.	HOLTON	GODWIN* Gov. Va.	GODWIN	HELMS	MATTINGLY Sen. Ga.	MATTINGLY	MATTINGLY	MARTIN
	TOWER* Sen. Texas	TOWER	THURMOND	BAKER	BROCK Sen. Tenn.	GURNEY	EDWARDS Gov. S.C.	EDWARDS	DALTON* Gov. Va.	TREEN* Gov. La.	TREEN	MARTIN Gov. N.C.	COCHRAN
			KIRK	THURMOND	BAKER	DUNN	BROCK	BAKER	ALEXANDER Gov. Tenn.	COCHRAN	COCHRAN	COCHRAN	TRIBLE
			THURMOND	TOWER	THURMOND	BROCK	BAKER	THURMOND	BAKER	CLEMENTS	TRIBLE Sen. Va.	TRIBLE	WARNER
			TOWER		TOWER	BAKER	THURMOND	TOWER	THURMOND	WARNER	WARNER	WARNER	HELMS
						THURMOND	TOWER		TOWER	HELMS	HELMS	HELMS	THURMOND
						TOWER				DALTON	ALEXANDER	ALEXANDER	GRAMM
										ALEXANDER	BAKER	THURMOND	
										BAKER	THURMOND	GRAMM Sen. Texas	
										THURMOND	TOWER		
										TOWER			

Carolina, whose narrow election to a two-year term in 1966 rested on the support of blacks, voted in 1967 against the confirmation of the first black appointed to the Supreme Court, an indication of how fearful he was of facing a Republican challenger in 1968 with such an endorsement of a Johnson civil rights gesture on his record. One Democrat from the Deep South who stayed with the national party noted that, if the Republicans had been "gut-cutters," they could have "painted the Democratic party as the party of black people and the Republicans as the party of the white people" and gone on to victory.[33]

But in Alabama in 1966 the Republicans were stopped dead in their tracks by a "poor man's segregationist,"[34] George Wallace, who successfully ran his wife for governor when he was barred by law from running himself. That same year the Republican Howard (Bo) Callaway did his best with the race issue in Georgia, but race could not work against Lester Maddox, himself a symbol of segregation. In some cases the effort to portray the Democratic candidate as a Kennedy-Johnson integrationist was ludicrous, as when the Republican Prentiss Walker tried to do it to Mississippi's Sen. James O. Eastland in 1966. A Republican gubernatorial candidate in Louisiana in 1964 made no headway against John J. McKeithen, the self-styled "100 percent segregationist" but not a "hater."[35] In South Carolina the race-baiting Republican Albert Watson was a narrow loser to the Democrat John West in 1970.

The strategy did work, however, against several nonsegregationist Democrats with moderate-to-liberal credentials on economic-class issues. The Republican Edward J. Gurney in Florida defeated LeRoy Collins for a Senate seat in 1968 on the basis of race. Bill Brock used the race issue to retire Sen. Albert Gore in Tennessee in 1970, and in 1972 race contributed to Jesse Helms's victory over Nick Galifianakis in North Carolina and aided the unseating of a Democratic moderate in Virginia, William B. Spong, Jr.

In the altered racial atmosphere of the early 1970s, however, the Republicans increasingly came to recognize the weak position the loss of black support left them in. It was, of course, ironic that the traditional party of segregation in the South should become the home of, and dependent on, black voters, many of whom were enfranchised by the national Democrats' passage of the Voting Rights Act. The irony was not lost on one Georgia Republican party chairman who ruefully bemoaned the diverse coalition that demolished GOP statewide challenges in his state, complaining that there was "no tie-in" between the twin pillars of the Georgia Democratic party during the post–civil rights era—rural, small-town whites of South Georgia and black voters. "They're as far apart as night and day," he noted. And yet, "They're voting hand in hand, and . . . they're squeezing the lives out of us."[36] And in North Carolina one defeated statewide Republican candidate articulated the difficulty of being a Southern Republican: "You start out with a certain number of Negro bloc votes against you and a certain number of people who vote straight Democratic no matter who the candidate is."[37]

Blacks in the Deep South constituted a larger percentage of the population than in the Rim South, as Table 3-3 shows, and this contributed to a contradictory result during the post–civil rights era. The larger percentage of blacks in the traditionally race-conscious Deep South made it easier for white Democratic candidates to win there than in the Rim South. At the same time, however, the black-white coalition in the Deep South was more volatile because of the long history of racial antagonism there. This Deep South volatility was exhibited in Mississippi in 1978 when blacks abandoned the Democratic senatorial nominee for the independent candidacy of a charismatic black leader, Charles Evers, resulting in the first statewide victory by Mississippi Republicans in a century.[38]

A second aspect of the abatement element is that it removed the major issue that in the 1960s had driven many whites from the Democratic party's presidential nominees and from those statewide candidates who could be tied to the national party's racial policies. With the race issue in relative quiescence, many of those white traditional Democratic voters in both the Deep South and the Rim South who had followed Goldwater, switched to Wallace, and favored Nixon over McGovern returned to the Democratic party in statewide elections and to vote in 1976 for Jimmy Carter, the epitome of the Southern Democracy of the mid-1970s.

The power of traditional Democratic party allegiance joined with the abatement of the race issue to bring back these once-disgruntled Democrats. This combination was especially noticeable in the small towns and rural areas, where the county-level voting returns most vividly depict the defectors' return to statewide Democratic candidates during the post–civil rights era. One Arkansas politician-observer expressed the point well: "Tradition is important to rural people. They are looking for ways to stay with the Democratic party; they have to be run off."[39] Three decades ago V. O. Key, Jr., articulated the powerful nature of this element: "Although the great issues of national politics are potent instruments for the formation of divisions among the voters, they meet their match in the inertia of traditional partisan attachments formed generations ago."[40] Jimmy Carter himself pointed to this strong force in a November 1973 interview, when he was governor of Georgia:

In general, I'd say that . . . all the trends have shown that you've got . . . a very detectable reservoir of Democratic party allegiance among the people who have weathered this aberration toward the Republican party based on the race issue and who have now come back to the Democratic party as their permanent home.[41]

Table 3-3. Percentage of Blacks in Each Southern State, 1970 and 1980

	1970	1980
Deep South		
Mississippi	36.8%	35.2%
South Carolina	30.5	30.4
Louisiana	29.8	29.4
Georgia	26.2	26.8
Alabama	26.2	25.6
Rim South		
North Carolina	22.2	22.4
Virginia	18.5	18.9
Arkansas	18.3	16.3
Tennessee	15.7	15.8
Florida	15.3	13.8
Texas	12.5	12.0

SOURCE: U.S. census, 1970 and 1980.

Precision in dealing with the notion of Democratic allegiance is not possible; its importance obviously differed from election to election. But responses to the standard party-identification question regularly asked in public opinion surveys[42] can give a rough measure of this notion. A comparison of responses to this question in 1960 and in 1976, made in Table 3-4, reveals that the political events of the 1960s had taken a heavy toll on Southern white Democratic party identifiers, who declined from 61 percent in 1960 to 46 percent in 1976. White Republican identifiers, at 21 percent, showed no increase during the sixteen-year period, while the proportion of whites claiming independence jumped from 18 percent to 33 percent. Despite the decline, Democratic allegiance among white Southerners remained relatively high in the mid-1970s, thirteen percentage points above the comparable figure for whites in the rest of the nation. It was this foundation of partisan allegiance that came to the rescue of Southern Democratic nominees in the mid-1970s.[43]

Thus, as the race issue was fading, skillful Democratic politicians, who were often successful products of their state's political institutions, lost no opportunity to appeal to the great "reservoir of Democratic party

Table 3-4. Party Identification of Southern and Northern Whites,
1960 and 1976

	South		North	
	1960	1976	1960	1976
Democratic	61%	46%	39%	33%
Republican	21	21	36	27
Independent	18	33	25	40
	100%	100%	100%	100%
	(N = 542)	(N = 755)	(N = 1158)	(N = 1782)

SOURCE: National Election Studies, 1960 and 1976. Center for Political Studies, University of Michigan. For both years the number of respondents is a weighted figure.

allegiance" that Carter had spoken of and that the survey data measured. Sen. Lawton Chiles of Florida touched on an aspect of this in reference to the Wallace voters of North Florida when he said, "They consider themselves Democrats, and, if you give them a Democrat they can accept, they'll vote for him."[44]

To be acceptable to many of these Democratic voters, whose allegiance to the Democratic party often developed from forces other than Roosevelt's New Deal, an approach to campaigning that did not create or exacerbate antagonisms in the electorate was crucial. This is exactly what these Democrats (such as Dale Bumpers of Arkansas, Sam Nunn of Georgia, Richard Riley of South Carolina, William Winter of Mississippi, Charles Robb of Virginia, and Robert Morgan of North Carolina, to name a few) offered. Chiles's 1,000-mile walk through Florida in 1970 exemplified this method of approaching the voters. Although these politicians took various stances on the issues, rarely did their positions form a coherent approach that allowed them to be easily labeled in recognizable partisan terms. And through this straddling process, they managed to remain acceptable to white traditional Democrats, who preferred to stay with their party if it was at all possible. These astute Democratic politicians with their innocuous campaigns made it possible.

Related to the Democratic-allegiance element were the advantages of incumbency and the overwhelmingly dominant position of Democrats at the local level. Incumbency was important to well-established Southern Democrats in frightening off challenges by serious Republican candidates; for example, incumbency aided Sens. Russell B. Long of Louisiana and John C. Stennis of Mississippi as well as governors constitutionally able to seek second, consecutive terms. Moreover, Republican candidates, especially in the Deep South, often offered little or no previous political experience; the Democrats were able to campaign on the experience issue alone. The Democratic candidates were therefore aided in regaining voters who had abandoned the party because of race by the many advantages that accrue to a party that has been "the only game in town" for decades, namely a storehouse of experienced and ambitious politicians who have credibility as candidates.

Carter's Singular Role and the Return of Class Voting

And then there was Jimmy Carter's singular regional and national role. His impressive personal achievement in securing the 1976 Democratic presidential nomination despite the great odds against him was a godsend to Southern Democratic leaders. They were now being led by one of their own, and their campaigns were upbeat, vigorous, and confident. For the first time since the 1960 elections, most Democratic politicians throughout the South united behind their party's national standard-bearer.

Carter embodied both segments of the newly formed Southern black-white Democratic coalition. His support among blacks was solid, dating from his positive treatment of blacks and their interests while he was governor of Georgia. And his personal background was firmly rooted in the culture of the white rural South. He spoke a language that Wallace voters could relate to; many of them trusted Carter and counted him as one of them. For Carter this coalition in 1976 was nothing new. It was the same one he had put together in the 1970 general election to win the Georgia governorship. The nature of Carter's broad Southern coalition was exemplified by the contrasting personalities who campaigned for him in 1976: George Wallace and Martin Luther King, Sr., the father of the slain civil rights leader.[45]

But as important as one intuitively knows Carter's "Southernness" to have been to his sweep of the region,[46] and as important as it was for Southern Democratic politicians, who only shortly before had had to carry the albatross of Humphrey and McGovern, it must not be allowed to obscure the changed nature of Democratic party support in the South after the disruptions of the civil rights era. In the 1976 presidential election, with the race issue in abatement, white voters throughout Southern urban areas again divided along class lines. Table 3-5, which gives precinct percentages for four Southern cities in the 1976 election, reveals that sharp economic-class divisions among whites again took hold at the presidential level and were even more pronounced than during the 1952–60 period, which a comparison of Table 3-5 with Table 3-1 confirms. Using survey data, Paul R. Abramson reported a similar class breakdown for the South as a whole.[47] Abramson also found that there was virtually no difference between the level of class voting among Southern whites and that among whites in the rest of the

Table 3-5. Presidential Vote in 1976 by Class and Race in New Orleans,
Atlanta, Memphis, and Houston

	Lower Income	Middle Income (Whites)	Upper Income	Blacks
		New Orleans		
		1976		
Carter	62%	44%	21%	97%
Ford	38	56	79	3
		Atlanta		
		1976		
Carter	63%	53%	36%	98%
Ford	37	47	64	2
		Memphis		
		1976		
Carter	54%	38%	21%	96%
Ford	46	62	79	4
		Houston		
		1976		
Carter	59%	36%	21%	98%
Ford	41	64	79	2

SOURCE: Richard Murray and Arnold Vedlitz provided these data, which are presented in summary form only in their "Racial Voting Patterns in the South: An Analysis of Major Elections from 1960 to 1977 in Five Cities," *Annals of the American Academy of Political and Social Science* 439 (Sept. 1978), 29–39.

nation. In the South 56 percent of the white working class voted for Carter; outside the South 57 percent voted for him. In the South 40 percent of the white middle class backed Carter; in the North 39 percent did so.[48]

Nevertheless, although Southern whites were dividing along class lines in 1976, a majority of them did not vote for Carter. The Republican standard-bearer, President Gerald R. Ford, a Midwestern Republican, received 53 percent of the Southern white vote to Carter's 46 percent.[49] Carter's victory margins in the South therefore rested partly on his solid support among Southern blacks.

Thus, Carter's sweep of his native region contained several elements. His "Southernness" was one, although the available instruments for measuring voter choice are too crude to isolate precisely how much of his support was based on regional pride alone. During the campaign

Carter lost no opportunity to play up his regional ties; he often told cheering Southern audiences, "Come January we are going to have a President in the White House who doesn't speak with an accent."[50] Second, the national Democratic party, even when led by a Deep South politician, could not muster a majority of the votes of white Southerners, the force that had been the party's mainstay in the Solid South era. Finally, in the reconstituted voting patterns of the post–civil rights era, the Southern Democratic party at the presidential level, and to an increasing extent at other levels as well, rested on a potent black-white coalition whose white segment had a tendency to break along economic-class lines consistent with the New Deal–style alignment.

The 1980 Reagan Victory and the 1982 Midterm Elections

The Republican Ronald Reagan swept to victory nationwide in 1980 over President Carter, 50.7 percent to 41.0 percent, with John Anderson, the independent, receiving 6.6 percent. While Reagan carried ten of the eleven Southern states, the regional picture was anything but a clean rout. Six of the ten states fell to Reagan by extremely narrow percentages: Tennessee (48.7 percent to 48.4 percent), Arkansas (48.1 to 47.5), Mississippi (49.4 to 48.1), South Carolina (49.4 to 48.1), Alabama (48.8 to 47.4), and North Carolina (49.3 to 47.2). Three states were Reagan's by large margins: Florida (55.5 percent to 38.5 percent); Texas (55.3 to 41.4); and Virginia (53.0 to 40.3). Louisiana occupied a middle position, going for Reagan 51.2 percent to 45.7 percent. Carter carried his home state of Georgia, 55.8 percent to 41.0 percent.

This election witnessed an upsurge in Southern Republican fortunes for offices other than the presidency; Figures 3-1 and 3-2 display this trend. After the 1980 balloting the Republican party held 45.4 percent of the South's combined twenty-two U.S. Senate seats and eleven governorships. The U.S. House seats won by the GOP in 1980 amounted to 36.1 percent of the total, while its state legislative seats increased three percentage points but, at 16.6 percent, still lagged behind the other offices.

The most visible gains came in the five Republican statewide successes in 1980. They were the Senate seat victories of John East in North Carolina, Jeremiah Denton in Alabama, Mack Mattingly in Georgia, and Paula Hawkins in Florida and the capture of the governorship in Arkansas by the Republican Frank White.[51] For a complete view of these GOP victories, it is necessary to describe the circumstances of each, which the respective state chapters do. At this point, however, an important item to keep in mind is the relationship of each of the five

GOP victories to Reagan's showing in these states—that is, to the *national* tide running against the Democratic party, then in power.[52] In several of these races Reagan's candidacy made the difference for the GOP candidate.

In 1980, as Figure 3-1 shows, the South reacted to a presidential campaign in about the same way as the rest of the country,[53] drawing attention to the increased importance of national factors for politics in the region. The national aspects of this election are well known: discontent with high inflation, with high interest rates, and with relatively high unemployment; frustration over the Iranian hostage situation; the perception that Carter lacked leadership ability; and the unfavorable reaction to Carter's vicious attempt to paint Reagan as an irresponsible warmonger, to mention a few of the most prominent ones. Carter received similar support from white voters in all regions: 35 percent in the South, 33 percent in the Northeast, 34 percent in the Midwest, and 31 percent in the West.[54]

There was some speculation when Ronald Reagan and his brand of conservatism captured the GOP nomination that the former California governor would generate the type of enthusiasm in the South that his ideological forerunner Barry Goldwater had occasioned sixteen years earlier. One Mississippi Delta Republican declared, "I consider that God is giving the country a second chance to elect Barry Goldwater."[55] But 1980 was a far cry from 1964. The transformation of the region's partisan structure had by 1980 created a political environment far more sophisticated and complex than that faced by the Arizona Republican in 1964. The partisan changes wrought by the civil rights revolution had taken hold throughout the South, and, despite the tide running against the Democrats, the black-white Democratic coalition still gave the Carter-Mondale[56] ticket a respectable Southern vote.

The 1982 midterm elections demonstrated both the continuing strength of the black-white Democratic coalition in the South and the increasing importance of national factors in the region's electoral behavior. Nationwide the trend in 1982 was toward the Democrats, partly as a reaction to the deep recession of 1981–82, with its double-digit unemployment rates, and partly as a response by "those who have less" to the perception that the policies of Reagan's administration excessively favored the interests of the nation's well-to-do. Democrats gained 26 seats in the U.S. House overall in 1982, a quarter of them coming from the South. Southern Republican representation in the House, which had reached 36.1 percent two years earlier, dropped to 29.3 percent in 1982. A comparison of seats won and lost between the two elections is slightly complicated because the South gained 8 new House seats after the 1980 census. In 1980, when the region was allocated 108 seats, 39 Southern Republicans were elected to the U.S. House. Of the South's 116 seats available in 1982, the GOP won only 34.

In the highly visible contests for governorships and U.S. Senate seats in 1982, the GOP suffered a net loss of 2 of the 33 positions, dropping from 45.4 percent in 1980 to 39.4 percent in 1982. Two first-term Republican governors lost: the conservative Democrat Mark White defeated Gov. Bill Clements in Texas, and Bill Clinton, the former Democratic governor, won back his office by outpolling Gov. Frank White in Arkansas. In Virginia the Republican Paul S. Trible, Jr., fought the tide, picking up the Senate seat held by the Independent Harry F. Byrd, Jr., who retired.[57] (See Figure 3-2.)

Besides these Democratic breakthroughs, the 1982 elections also featured a host of other statewide contests that, without resulting in partisan changes, cast considerable light on the nature of the partisan struggle in the region in the early 1980s. Heading the list was George Wallace's recapture of the Alabama governorship as a bona fide post–civil rights era Democrat ironically dependent on the same black voters he had once vowed to keep segregated forever. Furthermore, the potent black-white Democratic coalition was at work—if less visibly—in Georgia and South Carolina, assuring both states four more years of Democratic gubernatorial leadership.[58] And there were other important 1982 elections elsewhere in the region that illuminated the South's current partisan configuration. As with the 1980 GOP surge, a fuller understanding of the 1982 Democratic victories is gained from an exploration of the particulars of these contests, a task left to the state chapters.

Descent into the Political Whirlpool

The preceding overview of Southern politics provides an introduction to eleven separate versions of the end of the one-party system and the beginning of partisan competition in the region. How two-party politics developed in each state's political system is the topic of Chapters 4 through 14, where the elements introduced thus far are more fully considered within the context of each state's political traditions and peculiar circumstances.

One final regional illustration previews what comes next. Paul T. David constructed a useful index of political-party strength by combining the total vote for a party's candidates for governor, U.S. senator, and U.S. representative into a biennial percentage figure, giving each of the three types of offices equal weight.[59] When David's Democratic party-strength index, which is calculated separately for each state, is totaled

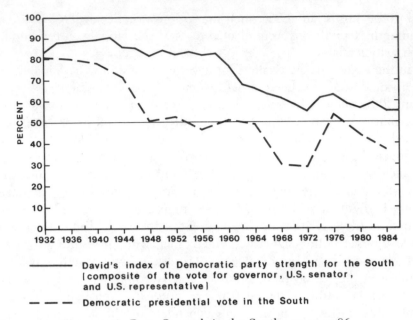

David's index of Democratic party strength for the South
(composite of the vote for governor, U.S. senator,
and U.S. representative)

— — — Democratic presidential vote in the South

Figure 3-3. Democratic Party Strength in the South, 1932–1986

for the region[60] and portrayed graphically, the result (given in Figure 3-3) is a simple picture of the death of the solidly Democratic South. Similarly, in each of the state chapters, this Democratic party-strength index is set forth, along with each state's Democratic presidential vote, providing eleven revealing comparative variations on the composite picture in Figure 3-3.

To the States

The order of the eleven state chapters is based on the venerable Deep South–Rim South division. Although some sections within the Rim South were indistinguishable from their Deep South neighbors, overall the six Rim South states exhibited far less preoccupation with race, the chief criterion for separating the two regional subsections. The five Deep South states are presented first, because in these most Southern of states the intense political concern with race[61] and the ironies that accompanied the transformations of the post–civil rights era appeared most vivid.

In the Deep South, Mississippi, with its marvelous ability to strip everything to stark essentials, makes an excellent first state. South Carolina follows chiefly because its political behavior in the post–civil rights era offered a sharp contrast to that of the Magnolia State, its twin sister from the days of the Dixiecrat adventure. The order of the other three has no strong justification, although the longevity and prominence of Alabama's leading politician probably won that state the third spot. Louisiana, which proved to be singularly weak in two-party terms, received last place as a result, automatically leaving fourth place to Georgia.

In some ways Arkansas occupies a middle ground between the subsections, causing its placement in the Rim South to be arbitrary. This decision becomes less noticeable, however, by making Arkansas the sixth state and thus a bridge between the subsections.

North Carolina, Virginia, and Tennessee share a common Mountain Republican tradition dating from the Civil War. Their experience with the other party during the pre–civil rights era provided enough similarity to justify lumping the three together in the arrangement of the state chapters, although the ordering among them is random. Both Florida and Texas have undergone enormous population and economic growth and change in recent years. These two rapid-growth states are the final ones to be considered. Texas, always the least Southern of the states of the former Confederacy, comes last, no doubt an uncommon position for the proud and boastful Lone Star State.

With the agenda set, the regional approach is temporarily abandoned, and attention shifts to the heart of the action.

4

Mississippi:
It's All Black and White

Mississippi's entry into the era of two-party competition exhibited in an extreme manner many of the political tendencies observed throughout the region.* The outstanding feature was the difficulty that black and white Democrats had in bringing about the biracial coalition that became so important for the Southern Democracy in the post–civil rights era. The situation can only be understood in the context of the state's heavy preoccupation with race.

The successes of Republican presidential candidates in Mississippi are easily linked to the national Democratic party's advocacy of civil rights for blacks. As early as 1960 an unpledged slate of presidential electors, supported by Gov. Ross Barnett and other Democratic segregationists,[1] carried the state with 39.0 percent of the vote to continue the protest that had begun in the 1948 Dixiecrat revolt, when Mississippi's Gov.

---

*The consistent ability of Mississippi to stand out from the pack inspired V. O. Key, Jr., in 1949 to open his chapter on the state's politics with this memorable paragraph: "Mississippi adds another variant to the politics of the South. Northerners, provincials that they are, regard the South as one large Mississippi. Southerners, with their eye for distinction, place Mississippi in a class by itself. North Carolinians, with their faith that the future holds hope, consider Mississippi to be the last vestige of a dead and despairing civilization. Virginia, with its comparatively dignified politics, would, if it deigned to notice, rank Mississippi as a backward culture, with a ruling class both unskilled and neglectful of its duties. And every other southern state finds some reason to fall back on the soul-satisfying exclamation, 'Thank God for Mississippi!' Yet Mississippi only manifests in accentuated form the darker political strains that run throughout the South." *Southern Politics*, 229.

Fielding Wright was Strom Thurmond's running mate.[2] In 1964, Mississippians gave Barry Goldwater 87.1 percent of their votes, chiefly on the basis of his stance against the Civil Rights Act.[3] Any illusions about the partisan meaning of the heavy Republican vote in 1964 were dispelled four years later when the Republican Richard Nixon mustered only 13.5 percent. George Wallace in 1968 carried the Magnolia State with 63.5 percent; Humphrey received 23.0 percent. Without Wallace on the ballot in 1972, President Nixon swept Mississippi, holding George McGovern to 19.6 percent, his lowest finish in the South.

These wild fluctuations in presidential voting are delineated in Figure 4-1. The voting returns suggest that few white people in Mississippi supported the national Democratic party in the late 1960s and early 1970s. Humphrey's backing in 1968 came primarily from the heavily black counties along or near the Mississippi River, from which one can infer that the blacks there voted overwhelmingly Democratic. This supposition is substantiated by a comparison of the fifteen counties having the largest percentage of black residents with Humphrey's fifteen strongest counties. (See Map 4-1.) McGovern's poor showing in the state four years later was nearly identical to Humphrey's.[4]

White resistance was so vehement in Mississippi throughout the 1960s that there occurred a complete organizational rupture between the state and local white Democratic officeholders, who led the fight for segregation, and a coalition of blacks and white liberals loyal to the national party. In fact, the regulars were denied seating at the 1968 Democratic National Convention in Chicago for their failure to remove racial discrimination from party affairs, as the national convention of 1964 had mandated. Instead the national party recognized the loyalist black-white coalition as the official Democratic party in Mississippi.[5] Charles Evers, the brother of Medgar Evers, the murdered black civil rights leader, became the state's Democratic national committeeman.

In this polarized racial atmosphere the nascent state Republicans sought to carve out a place for themselves. In 1963 the Republican Rubel L. Phillips challenged the winner of the Democratic gubernatorial primary runoff, Lt. Gov. Paul B. Johnson, Jr. Campaigning under the slogan "K.O. the Kennedys,"[6] Phillips tried—unsuccessfully, as it turned out—to capitalize on the race issue by emphasizing that as a Republican he was in no way connected with President Kennedy and the national Democratic party's civil rights effort. One of his campaign brochures stated:

> Rubel Phillips is a staunch segregationist. He condemns the use of federal power or threats of reprisals to force integration on Mississippians to curry favor with minority voters in the big Northern and

Eastern cities. As Governor, he will fight for genuine racial harmony
in keeping with Mississippi traditions. Having no obligations to the
Kennedys or their liberal henchmen, Rubel Phillips cannot be
forced into a political "deal" on the race question.[7]

Against Paul Johnson, a fellow segregationist, Phillips's effort to take
advantage of the racial turmoil went nowhere. The GOP nominee
received 38.1 percent of the votes cast to Johnson's 61.9 percent.

In the 1964 Goldwater landslide, Mississippians elected Prentiss
Walker their first Republican congressman in the twentieth century.
Two years later Walker tested the capacity of the state's newly found
Goldwater Republicanism by challenging Sen. James O. Eastland. Neal
R. Peirce described Walker's effort as follows:

A chicken farmer by profession, Walker had first won notice as
chairman of the 1960 unpledged elector slate in Mississippi. Walker
demonstrated his limited political acumen by trying to suggest that
Eastland had merely been pretending for 25 years that he was a real
conservative. (I have always been amused by the image conjured up
by Walker's charge that Eastland, unbeknown to the good people of
Mississippi, "hobnobs and prances" with the Kennedy political clan in
Washington.) The argument that Walker was the truer Mississippian
simply didn't wash; as state AFL-CIO chief Claude Ramsey pointed
out, Walker was trying to "outsegregate" Eastland and "this, of
course, was impossible. You just don't outsegregate Jim Eastland."[8]

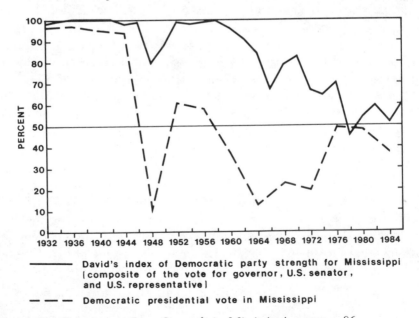

Figure 4-1. Democratic Party Strength in Mississippi, 1932–1986

In 1967 the Republican Phillips again ran for governor. The civil rights issue dominated the Democratic primary; the winner was the segregationist John Bell Williams, a white citizens' council stalwart and a congressman stripped of his House Democratic seniority for having openly backed Goldwater in 1964. Phillips did less well in 1967 than four years earlier, winning only 29.7 percent of the vote. But this time he failed after becoming the more racially moderate candidate. For example, Phillips contended in a television appearance during the campaign that "change offers the only avenue of hope for the underdeveloped states like Mississippi. If nothing changes, Mississippi will remain last forever—last in education, material wealth and national influence."[9] Regarding the Democrats, Phillips added:

> Are they discussing ways of finding a practical solution to the race issue? No. They are discussing ways of preventing change. . . . They [Mississippi's Democrats] believe the world is flat . . . and that the edge of the world is the Mississippi state line. Their world does end there, but yours and mine doesn't.[10]

On the eve of the November election, the executive committee of the Mississippi Freedom Democratic party, an organization of blacks, endorsed Phillips:

> We do not agree with all that Mr. Phillips projects but the most important factor is that some segment of white Mississippi has finally realized that when black people and poor white people in Mississippi are oppressed, discriminated and denied education, all of Mississippi suffers.[11]

Phillips responded to this endorsement by saying that he did not know "who was responsible for the endorsement or what the motive was, but I do know for certain that this endorsement was designed to hurt me. This was the 'kiss of death' type of endorsement with which we are all familiar."[12] In his losing statewide endeavor, Phillips received 71 percent of the vote in the black precincts of Jackson, the state's capital and largest city.[13]

The delineation of Democratic party strength in Figure 4-1 demonstrates the failure of the GOP to find a distinct place for itself in the chaotic political environment existing in Mississippi in the late 1960s. One result of the Republicans' difficulties, the figure reveals, was an upsurge of Democratic strength following the initial decline through 1966. This weakness and disarray among the Republicans was exemplified by the party's failure to run a candidate for governor in 1971.

Despite the lack of GOP representation in the 1971 gubernatorial campaign, this election is important for what it discloses about black-

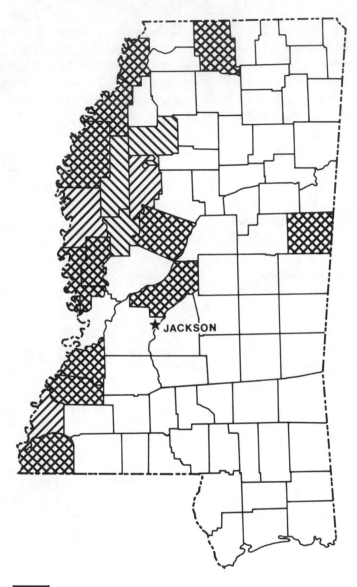

Map 4-1. Race and Democratic Presidential Voting in Mississippi in 1968

white Democratic relations. In most of the South by the end of the 1960s, there was considerable movement toward accommodation and cooperation among white and black Democratic leaders in statewide elections. But in Mississippi, where the resistance to nationally enforced efforts on behalf of blacks was extreme, the white Democratic establishment was unable to close the gap in any meaningful way until 1975, and what occurred in the 1978 election—which is described in detail below—suggests that the mid-1970s compromise contained a tendency to become unraveled.[14]

The separation of the loyalist Democrats—the coalition of blacks and white liberals recognized by the national party—from the state's Democratic establishment[15] contributed to the independent gubernatorial candidacy in 1971 of the black leader Charles Evers, who vigorously espoused the cause of the state's long-oppressed minority.[16] Evers received 22.1 percent of the votes cast, most of them from blacks.[17] William Waller, a former segregationist who won the Democratic primary running as a self-proclaimed populist,[18] was elected overwhelmingly.

The next statewide two-party contest after Phillips's 1967 race came in the 1972 re-election campaign of Senator Eastland. The Republican Gil Carmichael, an automobile dealer from Meridian, ran a credible race against Eastland. Carmichael gained some national notoriety when the Nixon administration went out of its way to praise Eastland for his service on its behalf in the Senate and to see that Carmichael was snubbed when Vice-President Spiro Agnew made a campaign visit to the state.[19]

Carmichael, who is considered a moderate (or even a "dangerous liberal") by many Mississippi Republican leaders in the early 1980s, explained why he relished the opportunity in 1972 to challenge Senator Eastland:

> Mississippi . . . is a [potentially] productive land. It's got all sorts of resources. And yet it was 50th . . . on the bottom. And so the only thing I could equate with that was that damn politics in Mississippi was the reason Mississippi was on the bottom. There were about four or five hundred elite families in this state who benefited beautifully by the politics of Mississippi. There was a ton—millions of people—who didn't benefit. I looked on Mississippi as almost a third-world country. . . . I didn't like that. So, this is where I was coming from. And, when I came home in 1961, I said I was going to help organize the Republican party. . . . I was very business oriented, free enterprise oriented. . . .
>
> I figured Mississippi was on the bottom because the old Democratic machine of this state had misused it, abused it and wasted it.

And I saw it as an enemy. I saw Jim Eastland as being the number
one head honcho of that old system. So, when I ran against him in
1972, some people—some of the Republican leadership—wanted
me to run just to get James Meredith out of the picture. [Meredith,
the first black to enroll at the University of Mississippi, sought the
GOP senatorial nomination, to the dismay of the state's Republican
establishment.]

And when the primary got through, everybody said, "Now, Gil,
lay down and play dead. You aren't going to run against Jim, are
you?" They had picked the wrong boy. . . . Because to me that old
cigar-chomping son-of-a-gun [Eastland] was the reason this state was
on the bottom. [20]

According to the Jackson *Clarion-Ledger*, "Waging an active campaign,
Senator Eastland argued that Mississippi and the South could not afford
to lose key congressional committee chairmanships now in the hands of
Southern Democrats."[21] Eastland won with 58.1 percent of the vote.

From 1972 to 1975 there was no statewide election in Mississippi.
During those years the accommodation and easing of the race issue that
had been apparent in most of the rest of the South since about 1970
took place in Mississippi. Although Governor Waller brought blacks
into state government for the first time,[22] it remained for the 1975
campaign and victory of the self-styled populist Cliff Finch, the winner
of the Democratic gubernatorial primary, to bring the warring white-
black factions of the Democratic party together organizationally. Finch,
a lawyer from Batesville, in northern Mississippi, was a former segregationist who supported Gov. Ross Barnett in Barnett's effort to resist
integration at the University of Mississippi in 1962.[23] Finch called himself the workingman's candidate and used a lunch pail with his name
printed over it as his campaign slogan.[24] A *New York Times* pre-election
report stated:

Mr. Finch has the support of almost all of the state's leading Democrats from Senator James O. Eastland, who is backing him heartily,
to Aaron Henry, the black chairman of the liberal loyalist faction,
who endorsed him with obvious reluctance. Mr. Finch was once
known as a segregationist. . . .

Observers attributed Mr. Finch's black support to his workingman
theme, which apparently elicited blue-collar sympathy across racial
lines.[25]

Carmichael was the Republican nominee for governor in 1975. He
presented himself, as his remarks quoted above suggest, as "a reform
Republican in the mold of the late Winthrop Rockefeller of Arkansas."[26]
The *New York Times* reported that

a Democrat-for-Carmichael organization has been formed to appeal to those who accuse Mr. Finch of being too close to the courthouse politicians and big-money interests that have long run the state. . . . He [Carmichael] detaches himself from the national Republican party and reminds voters that President Nixon turned his back on him when he ran against Senator Eastland in 1972.[27]

Carmichael's moderation considerably upset Mississippi Republican leaders, who would have preferred a more doctrinaire conservative. For example, Clarke Reed, the party's chairman, was described in one newspaper account as "somewhat perplexed by Mr Carmichael and his campaign. Mr. Reed said he thought 'about half of Gil's positions are crazy.' But he was inclined to let Mr. Carmichael do whatever he wanted, Mr. Reed added, 'because for some reason I don't understand, it seems to be working.' "[28] In a 1982 interview Carmichael elaborated on his differences with the dominant state GOP leadership. "Probably the role I play is moderate. That's one of the reasons I'm so aggravating—I'm so dogmatic in my moderate role. I keep talking about bringing the blacks into the Republican party and making it a viable, broad-based party." He said his conception of the party's future ran counter to that of Dixiecrat-turned-Republican leaders who prefer a "lily-white Republican party." Carmichael elaborated:

> Wirt [Yerger, a state GOP leader] had a dream of pulling out the white Dixiecrats [from the Democratic party] and . . . forming the new Republican party. . . . Then a fellow like Carmichael comes along, and he goes to Jackson State [a predominantly black university in the state's capital] and as a Republican starts talking to the black people, wanting them in the Republican party. "Come on, join the Republican party." . . .
>   I didn't want [there] to be a white Republican party and a black Democratic party. I didn't want that at all. To me that is just destruction. . . . We've gone nowhere if the Republican party in 1990 is the reverse of what [existed in the one-party era, all whites in one party and blacks isolated]. The reason we wanted to be the governor was to break the chain that has kept Mississippi on the bottom since the Civil War.[29]

Newspaper accounts of the 1975 general-election campaign stressed the absence of race as an issue.[30] Finch won with 52.2 percent, after having assembled the same black-white coalition that had been electing Democrats elsewhere in the South since the start of the post–civil rights era. Carmichael, who received 45.1 percent of the vote, said that despite his effort his Republican party label scared the "black and the poor vote."

He added, "What other reason would the redneck and the black person come together, if the [Republican] candidate didn't scare them?"[31]

The inauguration of Governor Finch, who in early 1976 was credited with performing "a minor political miracle"[32] by bringing together the black leadership and the white regulars, set the stage for an organizational unification of the Democratic party in Mississippi. Both white and black Democratic factions agreed to call simultaneous precinct meetings for the selection of delegates to the 1976 national convention, and this led to a unified delegation and the re-entry of the regulars into the national party. At the 1976 convention, cochairmen for the unified party were chosen: Aaron Henry, the loyalist black leader, became one cochairman; Tom Riddell, a white representative of the regulars, the other. The unified party leadership worked enthusiastically for the election of fellow Southerner Jimmy Carter. And in 1976 the Democratic party's presidential nominee carried Mississippi for the first time since 1956; Carter received 49.6 percent of the votes cast to Gerald Ford's 47.7 percent.

The fragile nature of the black-white Democratic unity forged in 1975 and 1976 was demonstrated at the voter level in the 1978 U.S. Senate election to fill the seat held by Eastland, who had decided to retire. Charles Evers ran as an independent and captured 22.9 percent of the votes, most of them coming from blacks.[33] Deprived of the black support that had carried the state for Finch in 1975 and Carter in 1976, the Democratic nominee, Maurice Dantin, received only 31.8 percent of the votes cast and was defeated by U.S. Rep. Thad Cochran, the Republican nominee, who received 45.0 percent.[34] A close examination of this three-way campaign offers insight into the precarious nature of the Democratic coalition in Mississippi during the post–civil rights era.

According to the *Washington Post*, Dantin ran as "a Democrat's Democrat, trying to capitalize on traditional party ties. His chief pitch to the voters is that a Democrat can do more for Mississippi in the Senate."[35] Toward the end of the campaign, both Senator Eastland and Sen. John C. Stennis stumped for Dantin. The *Clarion-Ledger* reported that Eastland told one gathering:

> He [Dantin] will not be a party hack. He is going to do what he thinks is right just as me and John have done. . . . He's going to be elected and he'll serve the state with distinction.
>
> If I didn't know where the interests of our people are, I wouldn't be telling you, for God's sake, to elect a Democrat. The Democratic Party is a big tent. Not to be in that big tent means you're going to be cold outside—you'll just get what's left and that's not very much.[36]

And Stennis, in his milder manner, followed by saying, "The seniority system has given us a very distinct, superior advantage. . . . It is in the Congress of the United States that Mississippi has its political power."[37]

Friends and foes of Evers agree on one thing: he is a charismatic and wily politician.[38] Evers asserted in the campaign that the two major parties "have been against anything that would benefit the mass of the people."[39] A *Clarion-Ledger* article at the end of the election reported this exchange, noting that "tempers were showing":

> The candidate himself [Evers] was angered by the remark made early in the week by Republican Thad Cochran that Democrat Maurice Dantin "takes Evers seriously. I just laugh at him."
>
> Evers, in a press conference Thursday [November 2, 1978], replied, "I want Mr. Cochran to know he's laughing at poor whites, at poor blacks, at the left-outs. If he can laugh at Charles Evers and all those folks, I bet he's going to be sorry on November 7."[40]

Evers staged a star-studded, eleventh-hour Delta tour to encourage interest in the election among black voters.[41]

Cochran acknowledged the obvious: the black-white Democratic split was the cause of his good fortune. A month before the election he told a *Washington Post* reporter, "It's a fluke, a most unusual set of circumstances that happen to benefit me. If I had to write a script, I couldn't have done a better job."[42]

The bitterness among white Democrats after the Cochran victory was captured in this *Clarion-Ledger* report:

> "The black people of this state have been had," said Jack Harper, Sunflower County chancery clerk, who headed the state party's campaign committee. "It's absolutely discouraging to those who have worked to bring blacks and whites together to see some fly-by-night, some unusual set of circumstances tear your party up.
>
> "Evers led them [blacks] right on down the road and out of the party and now he's got them on a limb.
>
> "We did everything we could to make the Democratic party appealing to blacks," Harper continued, "but Evers had that glorified conscientious objector [the boxer Muhammad Ali] come in and interfere with the emotions of the black citizenry who are in the process of adjusting to party politics. . . . We thought we could pick a good black vote off Evers in the Delta and that was our greatest disappointment."[43]

In an interview a senior Mississippi Democratic officeholder summed up the situation this way:

Blacks made the difference for Carter. So when the blacks stay
with the Democrats, we can just about win, but when they leave, we
can't. . . .

I think what happened to Dantin was [this]: Aaron Henry, the
black, did support him and also labor did support him, and that hurt
him. Then they didn't get out and vote for him. Labor didn't vote
and the blacks voted for Evers. Then the white people voted for
Cochran.[44]

As the 1978 Senate election indicated, the future of the two parties in
Mississippi is closely related to the position black voters and leaders take.

Conservative and moderate white Democrats were obviously upset
over the Evers-inspired defections. U.S. Rep. G. V. (Sonny) Montgomery, one of the most conservative of the Southern Democrats in
Congress,[45] took issue in an interview with an Evers campaign remark:
"[Evers's] statement that the Democrats have not done anything for the
blacks is totally wrong. Under the Democratic Congress, the blacks have
certainly gained, especially in Mississippi."[46] Montgomery did not point
out that he had opposed most of this legislation. And herein lies a
tension that has not been lost on Mississippi Republican leaders.

U.S. Rep. Trent Lott, the Gulf Coast Republican elected to the
House with Cochran in 1972, described the plight of Mississippi Democrats as he saw it (or perhaps as he hoped it would be):

They're in a bind with the national Democrat party. If they subscribe to the national Democrat party's principles, platform, they are
clearly going to alienate the overwhelming majority of the white
people in Mississippi. If they don't do it, they are going to offend the
black folk in Mississippi. . . .

So, if they go with the typical national Democrat base, they wind
up with blacks and labor and your more liberal, social-oriented
Democrats, white people. Put those groups together and they are a
minority in Mississippi. . . .

So, they [statewide Democratic candidates] have got to have some
of these old redneck George Wallace white voters. If they have these
other groups, they alienate that group.[47]

Throughout the South, statewide Democratic candidates generally
have been able to hold together the biracial coalition that Lott viewed as
being in danger of falling apart in Mississippi. It must be remembered,
too, that in Mississippi the coalition failed in 1978 only because of a
fluke resulting from the effort of a charismatic black leader. Many black
leaders have not given up on the Democratic party, nor have white
Democrats ranging from Montgomery's conservative side of the spec-

trum to the more liberal side. The *New York Times* reported in early 1979:

> [Aaron] Henry . . . has warned in recent letters to Mr. Evers, and to those who might be inclined to follow him [in future independent candidacies] that [such efforts] would "put a section of the black community outside the political world—outside the decision-making processes of the real political world."
>
> This, Mr. Henry said in an interview, "could have a devastating effect" on the black community.
>
> "The black political structure," he said, "is as much or more involved with the decision-making in this state's Democratic Party as they are in any place else in the country. And we tell everyone that when you lay down with Independents, you wake up with Republicans."[48]

Henry's warning may have had some effect, because in 1979 the Democratic white-black alliance held together long enough to elect a governor. William Winter, the 1979 Democratic gubernatorial primary winner,[49] assembled this formidable, if volatile, coalition to soundly defeat the Republican Gil Carmichael's third attempt at statewide office, by a margin of 60.9 percent to 39.1 percent.[50] Winter, a former lieutenant governor, had been identified as a moderate on civil rights in the 1960s, and this identity was blamed for his defeat in the 1967 Democratic gubernatorial runoff primary by John Bell Williams, the outspoken segregationist.

During the early 1980s the uneasy biracial Democratic statewide coalition remained in place.[51] Although President Carter narrowly lost the state to Reagan in 1980, the coalition experienced no serious disruptions unrelated to the national forces prevalent in that election.[52] Incidentally, in 1980 former Governor Williams endorsed Reagan, toasting the GOP nominee as an "advocate of a Jeffersonian philosophy," while saying that Carter had "put aside Jefferson and picked up Karl Marx."[53]

When Senator Stennis ran in 1982 for a sixth term, at the age of eighty-one, he drew a well-financed challenge from a thirty-five-year-old Republican, Haley Barbour. The two men shared the same conservative philosophy. The Barbour strategy thus became a one-note attempt to convince Mississippians that they needed, to quote the GOP nominee's slogan, a "Senator for the '80s," and by less-than-oblique implication not a "Senator in his 80s." Stennis won with 63.9 percent of the vote to Barbour's 36.1 percent. It was one of the relatively unnoticed ironies of the 1982 elections that Stennis, who in his thirty-year Senate career had vigorously opposed civil rights for blacks, received overwhelming black support in this election—support that partly accounted for his wide victory margin.[54]

While black voters were doing Senator Stennis an undeserved favor, white Democratic voters in the Mississippi Delta did not reciprocate for a black Democratic congressional nominee. State Rep. Robert G. Clark, the only black to serve in the Mississippi legislature during the first half of the 1970s, defeated several white candidates in the primary to win the Democratic nomination for the court-created Second Congressional District. The creation of the district, which had a 53.7 percent majority of black residents but a black minority among registered voters,[55] resulted from a prolonged legal battle to undo two decades of racial gerrymandering by the Mississippi legislature in the drawing of the state's congressional district lines.[56] After Clark's nomination, the state's major Democratic officeholders, led by Governor Winter, warmly endorsed him and aided his campaign. Clark, an amiable politician who had backed the Republican Carmichael in 1975, centered his campaign on economic issues, attacking Reaganomics. A *New York Times* reporter wrote that Clark spoke cheerfully about "mending fences and really doing something in Mississippi that has never been done before, trying to build a coalition that works two ways rather than just one."[57]

The Republican nominee was Webb Franklin, a former state judge and a Democrat who switched parties to make the 1982 race. Franklin campaigned as an economic conservative, calling Clark too liberal for Mississippi. While the surface campaign sounded like a standard Democratic versus Republican affair, the real issue was plain to everyone. A clever *New York Times* headline writer captured it: "Mississippi Race, Whatever They Say, Is About Race."[58] Subtle and not-so-subtle efforts by the Franklin organization to appeal to racial prejudice appeared throughout the campaign. The *New York Times* reported:

> [A Franklin] television commercial opens and closes with a view of [an] ornate Confederate monument [in Franklin's home town of Greenwood] while Mr. Franklin says:
> "You know, there's something about Mississippi that outsiders will never, ever understand. The way we feel about our family and God, and the traditions that we have. There is a new Mississippi, a Mississippi of new jobs and new opportunity for all our citizens. We welcome the new, but we must never, ever forget what has gone before. We cannot forget a heritage that has been sacred through our generations."
> Danny Cupit, the Democratic state chairman, attacked this ad as an effort "to inflame racial passion." He said that was the only way

the Republicans could hope to win here. He said this ad was part of an expected "subtle effort to inject race into the latter stages of the campaign."

Mr. Franklin scoffed at that interpretation. He said he took the film crew to the monument because he identified with the courthouse behind it, where he served for four years as a circuit judge, and for no racial purpose. "Certainly not," he said when asked if the purpose was racist.

The Republican is also using the rather unusual approach of putting his opponent's picture in fliers and newspaper supplements that point out their differences on issues . . . . One leading campaign adviser, speaking on the condition he not be quoted by name, said that the pictures were being used to remind voters that Mr. Clark was black.[59]

In an extremely close election, Franklin defeated Clark by a margin of 50.3 percent to 48.4 percent. What had happened was quite simple: few white Democrats voted for the black Democratic nominee. Clark's fellow Democrat Stennis, for example, carried the Second District with 61.3 percent of the votes cast. Robert Walker, the Mississippi NAACP field secretary, summed up the situation concisely, "I wouldn't be so foolish to say [Clark] didn't get white votes, because he did. He didn't get enough."[60]

The recent electoral history of another congressional district—the Fourth—highlights the tenuous nature of the black-white Democratic coalition as well as its strength when led by a skillful white politician with good relations among blacks. From 1972 to 1980, Democrats lost all elections for this seat, primarily as a result of the black-white split. The Fourth District, which includes Jackson and several rural, small-town counties stretching to the south and west from the capital, elected a Republican in 1972 when Thad Cochran received his first boost from a black independent candidacy. In that year Cochran defeated the Democrat Ellis B. Bodron, by 47.9 percent of the votes to 44.0 percent, while Eddie L. McBride, a black independent, won a critical 8.2 percent. When Cochran ran for the Senate in 1978, his assistant, the Republican Jon C. Hinson, captured the seat with a bare simple majority, 51.6 percent, against the Democratic nominee, John H. Stennis, Senator Stennis's son, who received 26.4 percent, and Evan Doss, a black independent candidate, who captured 19.0 percent. Two minor candidates took the remaining 3.0 percent.

Hinson's re-election in 1980 came as a result of the continuing division among the district's white and black Democrats. The white Democratic nominee that year, Britt R. Singletary, actually finished third with

29.4 percent of the vote. The black independent Leslie McLemore, a
political science professor at Jackson State University, was second with
31.6 percent. Hinson won with 39.0 percent.

The Republican's second term, however, was a short one. Hinson,
who in the 1980 campaign had denied being a homosexual, was ar-
rested early in 1981 in a Capitol Hill restroom and charged by District
of Columbia police with committing oral sodomy with a black male
employee of the Library of Congress.[61] He resigned in April.

The rules of the special election to fill Hinson's seat, which was held
in the summer of 1981, worked against an independent black candidacy. All candidates were required to run in the first election (a type of
open primary), the runoff being restricted to the top two candidates
regardless of partisan affiliation. The Republican Liles B. Williams, a
suburban Jackson businessman, placed first in the first election with 45
percent of the votes cast and faced Wayne Dowdy, the white Democratic mayor of McComb, who was second with 25 percent. The Voting
Rights Act, which was coming up for extension in Congress that fall,
became the decisive factor in the runoff. Williams said he would vote
against extension; Dowdy vowed to support the act in its current form,
rallying black groups to his banner. The district was 45 percent black.
The *New York Times* reported:

> In radio advertisements and in person Mr. Dowdy reminded
> blacks of the voting act and his stand. Black ministers, like Horace
> L. Buckley of Cade Missionary Baptist Church in Jackson, urged a
> big turnout. On Sunday Mr. Buckley told his parishioners that it was
> their duty as "Christian patriots" to vote and made it clear that they
> should support Mr. Dowdy because "segregationists and racists were
> planning to turn the clock back."[62]

Dowdy won narrowly, by a margin of 50.5 percent to 49.5 percent.

In the 1982 general election Williams unsuccessfully tried to unseat
Dowdy, receiving 45.4 percent of the vote to Dowdy's 52.8 percent.
The black independent who had started it all in 1972, Eddie McBride,
entered the 1982 race but was ignored by most black leaders and finished with only 1.8 percent. Several months before the election, William Wright, Dowdy's black administrative assistant, said in an interview that he did not fear a black independent candidacy. "With
Wayne's voting record and the things that he stood for, you are going to
see blacks stand with him in really significant numbers," Wright correctly predicted.[63]

Dowdy's success in holding black support despite the presence of a
black independent was repeated by the Democratic gubernatorial nomi-

née in 1983, Atty. Gen. Bill Allain of Natchez.[64] During the fall campaign Charles Evers made his third independent bid for statewide office, contending that blacks and other minorities "want our fair share"[65] and asserting that the "state is run by 11 percent of its people . . . mostly stuffy, redneck, old white men."[66] This time most of Mississippi's black leaders shunned Evers. Their 1983 decision to support Allain appeared to represent a triumph of practicality over emotion.[67] David Jordan, a black politician from Greenwood, explained, "We're not going to give Ronald Reagan a base in Mississippi in the governor's office. The trick . . . will not work on us this time. Our eyes are open. We went for that trick in '78 and a Republican senator came in the back door. The game is over and school is out."[68] In the November balloting Evers's support was minuscule compared with his two previous showings; he received only 3.9 percent of the vote and was an insignificant factor in the gubernatorial outcome.

Despite Evers's poor finish, the 1983 governor's race proved to be an explosive, if seamy, affair for reasons without parallel in recent statewide partisan conflict. Allain's main opponent was the Republican Leon Bramlett, a wealthy Clarksdale planter and champion of the most conservative elements in the state GOP hierarchy. Through early October, Bramlett, who had been state Democratic party chairman under the segregationist Gov. John Bell Williams in the late 1960s, conducted a lackluster campaign replete with generalities about the importance of improving education and the need to "bring the forces of government and business together to work harmoniously."[69] With the Democratic black-white coalition apparently holding firm, most political analysts concluded that Bramlett was a sure loser. In a syndicated column in early October, Bill Minor, the dean of Mississippi's political writers, found strong evidence that the "Mississippi Republican Party has abandoned hope for Leon Bramlett . . . and is concentrating on several lesser races the GOP thinks it can win."[70] Minor quoted one Republican leader: "The Wallace Democrats just aren't coming on board, there are no blacks at all, and the Evers campaign doesn't seem to be helping, so some of us can't see the Bramlett campaign going anywhere, even though he is probably the best candidate we have ever had."[71]

What had appeared through early October to be a humdrum affair, however, was transformed by the end of the month into one of the most spectacular and emotional gubernatorial campaigns in recent memory. The change started gradually. In mid-October, Republican orators, led by Ebbie Spivey, the party chairwoman, began to call attention to Allain's marital status—the Democratic nominee was divorced in 1970 after a seven-year marriage and had no children—by arguing that the voters should elect a "family man" as governor.[72] Joining the attack, Bramlett's wife, Virginia, told one campaign audience, "I'm running for first lady and I'm unopposed."[73] Bramlett added the theme to his standard speech, opening a campaign office in Forest, for example, by saying, "He [Allain] has no family, never has had one to any extent. I know more in a minute about educating a child than he'll ever know, because I've done it."[74] JoAnn Klein, Allain's campaign manager, responded by calling the Republicans' remarks "an insult to all people in the state of Mississippi who are not married."[75] Allain countered similarly; referring to his former wife's three sons by a prior marriage, he said, "I know the problems of raising a family. I helped to raise three boys."[76]

Then, with exactly two weeks left before Election Day, W. D. (Billy) Mounger and several other of Bramlett's major financial supporters charged, through their attorney, William Spell, Sr., that Allain "frequently has engaged in homosexual acts with male prostitutes."[77] The allegations, which were made on October 25 at news conferences in Jackson, Columbus, and Tupelo after the Republicans had failed privately to persuade state news organizations to report the charges on their own authority,[78] were accompanied by sworn statements from three black transvestites, two of whom claimed they had had sexual relations with Allain.[79] Spell also released statements of current and former police officers in Jackson who said they had observed Allain on numerous occasions "in a pattern of conduct consistent with solicitation of male prostitutes." And there was a statement from a part-time maintenance man at Allain's Jackson apartment house who said he had seen homosexual magazines and paraphernalia in one of Allain's closets.[80] In its coverage of the Spell allegations, the *Clarion-Ledger* reported that the three prostitutes had been tested independently by a Memphis polygraph expert employed by the newspaper and had passed the tests. Spell also said that he and the Bramlett supporters had given the prostitutes polygraph tests as part of their investigation and that the prostitutes had passed the tests.[81]

These bizarre allegations—especially their elaborate nature—stunned nearly everyone in Mississippi who was following the campaign.[82] Allain immediately called the charges "damnable, vicious, malicious lies"[83] and on the next day threatened to file a libel suit.

Bramlett at first attempted to distance himself from the allegations, saying his supporters had acted independently of him. But by the last few days of the campaign he embraced the charges to the point of offering to withdraw from the race if Allain submitted to and passed three independent lie detector tests refuting the allegations of homosexuality.[84] Partly responding to Bramlett's challenge and to pressure from more neutral sources, Allain privately took a polygraph test in New Orleans that was arranged by his lawyer and announced that he had passed.[85]

Besides the sparring over lie detector tests, the homosexual-allegations story—which overshadowed everything else in the campaign—took various twists and turns during the thirteen days left before Election Day. But when Mississippians went to the polls on November 8, the central question remained unanswered: the truth or falsity of the allegations had not been determined to the satisfaction of any neutral observer.*

Judging from the returns, the indeterminacy of the allegations probably had a neutralizing effect. Allain won with 55.2 percent of the votes cast to Bramlett's 38.9 percent. After it had become apparent that Evers had failed to materialize as a significant force in the election, and before the Mounger-Spell bombshell, it was safe to expect the black-white Democratic coalition to deliver Allain about a 55 to 60 percent victory. The allegations probably cost Allain several percentage points, causing him to finish in the low range of the coalition's strength.[86] Thus, despite the sensational events of this election, Allain won the governorship essentially because he was able to hold together Mississippi's potent biracial Democratic coalition. The governor-elect acknowledged as much two days after the voting during an appearance before representatives of half of that alliance. Addressing the Mississippi NAACP convention in Clarksdale, Allain told the delegates:

> I want to thank you for being with me during these last few weeks of trials and tribulations, when Mississippi politics got into the basement.
> I know I wouldn't be here as governor-elect tonight without your help. I'd be here as the outgoing attorney general. I know the people who elected me, and I won't forget you.[87]

---

* Two months after the election the three transvestites contacted the *Clarion-Ledger* to retract their stories. "It is time for the truth to come out," one said. "I wouldn't know Bill Allain if he walked in that door." Another of the trio added, "We are doing this now because we need to go on with our lives, and let Bill Allain go on with his. It never should have happened." Attorney Spell immediately discounted the retractions. "Since the election they have been constantly pursued by persons who wanted them to change their story to help Mr. Allain," Spell said. "The combination of threat and reward apparently caused them to deny their earlier sworn testimony which has been confirmed by three or more polygraph examinations." *Clarion-Ledger*, Jan. 15, 1984. (Allain never filed the libel suit he had threatened during the campaign.)

Mississippi—Conclusion

Mississippi is an excellent first state to examine because the lack of subtlety in the state's electoral politics makes the central elements easy to appreciate. In other states the politicians go to great lengths to obscure sensitive political conflicts; in Mississippi they are plainly on view for even the most casual observer to note.

The national Democratic party's advocacy of civil rights for blacks gave rise to statewide Republican challenges in the Magnolia State, starting with Phillips in 1963. But these early GOP challengers had little room to maneuver because white Mississippi Democratic nominees firmly staked out the segregationist side of the issue. In this regard the Mississippi pattern bears a close resemblance to what happened in Alabama, where the segregationist George Wallace and his allies stole whatever thunder the incipient GOP hoped to inherit from the racial turmoil.

As a result of the intensity of the civil rights struggle, the abatement of the race issue took hold later in Mississippi, which was also the only Southern state to experience a prolonged organizational rupture between white and black Democrats. But with Governor Finch's administration, the formidable black-white coalition that was so important to the Democratic party throughout the South formed also in Mississippi. The coalition's tenuous nature was dramatically illustrated in 1978 when Evers, the black independent, siphoned off substantial support among black voters to allow Mississippi Republicans to win their first statewide nonpresidential contest in the twentieth century. The election of a Democratic governor the following year, however, demonstrated that only unusual circumstances threaten this strong, if volatile, Democratic coalition. In the statewide elections of the early 1980s, including the bizarre Allain-Bramlett campaign, the uneasy alliance persisted despite continued strain.

This majority had only a weak connection to economic-class questions in the New Deal Democratic tradition. White candidates like Finch occasionally made gestures in the direction of a class appeal, but the record does not reveal any permanence to them. Rather, traditional Democratic party allegiance appeared to be largely responsible for the sustained support of statewide Mississippi Democratic candidates among whites. And when the state's blacks remained with these white Democrats, Republican candidates faced stiff obstacles in their effort to attain a statewide majority.

5

South Carolina:
No Place for "Wild Men"?

Of all the Deep South states—with the possible exception of Mississippi—South Carolina appeared the most promising for the Republicans in the early and middle 1960s. In the home state of Strom Thurmond, the Dixiecrat presidential candidate who formally embraced the GOP in 1964, the race issue seemed to give a powerful boost to two-party competition, first at the presidential level, then at the state level. But it was also in South Carolina that skillful white Democratic party leaders were quick to make a quiet accommodation with blacks, who after the events of 1964–65 rapidly became a pivotal force in the state's politics. This black-white Democratic coalition, although not easy to maintain, generally held through the 1982 elections, providing most Democratic candidates with comfortable statewide majorities. The story of the formation and maintenance of this diverse coalition, which requires delving into the personalities and issues that agitated the state, also illuminates serious tensions in the coalition that are a potential threat to its continued well-being.

As the South Carolina experience unfolds, it is instructive to remember what took place in Mississippi during the same period. The radically different approaches of the leaders in these sister states of the Solid South[1] emphasize the importance that the actions of elites have in altering patterns of behavior that are too often viewed as dependent on all-powerful sociological forces. Here political leadership made the difference, and two states with similar backgrounds diverged significantly.

Goldwater carried South Carolina in 1964 with 58.9 percent of the vote, chiefly on the basis of his opposition to the Civil Rights Act. Despite having fought Lyndon Johnson on civil rights, South Carolina Democratic leaders such as Sen. Olin D. Johnston campaigned for the President.[2] One result of this backing was to hold in line strong Democratic support in the state's Piedmont counties, those lying roughly in the plateau north of the fall line, which contained South Carolina's largest percentage of persons employed in manufacturing (see Map 5-1). The large white working class there remained with the Democratic standard-bearer in 1964.

National Democratic strength dropped again in all of South Carolina in the 1968 election, in which Hubert Humphrey finished third. The decline was led by the wholesale abandonment of the Democratic ticket by white working-class Democrats of the Piedmont, which was partly responsible for an abrupt shift in the Palmetto State's presidential-voting patterns in 1968.[3] The Piedmont became the weakest area of the state for the national Democratic standard-bearer, after having been Johnson's strongest region in 1964; George Wallace won a substantial plurality of these counties in 1968. The turnaround in the Piedmont is linked to resentment among the white working class toward Johnson's civil rights policies.[4]

Another group of South Carolina counties also flip-flopped in presidential voting between 1964 and 1968—the Black Belt counties, which are defined as those having a population over 50 percent black in the 1960 census (see Map 5-1). In 1964 President Johnson received his weakest support in these counties, where few blacks voted prior to the implementation of the Voting Rights Act of 1965. But large black voter registration made the Black Belt the strongest part of South Carolina for the Democratic nominee in 1968.

An understanding of how the changes at the presidential level affected statewide elections requires familiarity with the maneuvers of the prominent politicians who dominated the South Carolina electoral landscape during the last two decades. An overview of what was to befall Palmetto State Democrats can be gotten from Figure 5-1. This illustration shows that Democratic party strength remained high through the early 1960s[5] as South Carolinians, along with other Southerners, awaited the final push from Washington on integration. When it finally came, Democratic strength took a nose dive.

The Republican party mounted only one major assault against the Democrats before the state was completely "abandoned" on civil rights by the national Democrats. That exception was the campaign in 1962 against the Democratic Sen. Olin Johnston by the Republican William

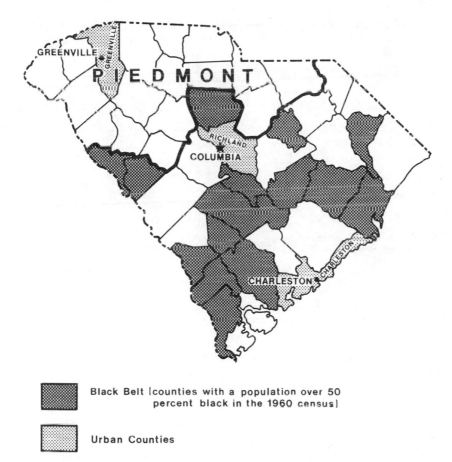

Black Belt (counties with a population over 50 percent black in the 1960 census)

Urban Counties

Map 5-1. South Carolina's Black Belt and Three Largest Urban Counties

D. Workman, Jr., a writer for the Charleston *News and Courier* who had recently published a book defending racial segregation.[6] Johnston, a staunch segregationist, was not directly vulnerable on the race issue. Rather, Workman, in the words of Numan V. Bartley and Hugh D. Graham, "attacked him as a handmaiden of the Kennedys and intimated that a vote for Johnston was a vote for the invasion of Mississippi by federal troops."[7] Johnston held on, but Workman's 42.8 percent of the total vote was an early sign of the potency of the white backlash that was to sweep the state in the next few years.

Apart from the Goldwater candidacy, the most important partisan event in South Carolina during the middle 1960s was the decision of Senator Thurmond in 1964 to switch to the Republican party. Thurmond understood, as one South Carolina political observer pointed out, that the Democratic primary would become a major obstacle for him

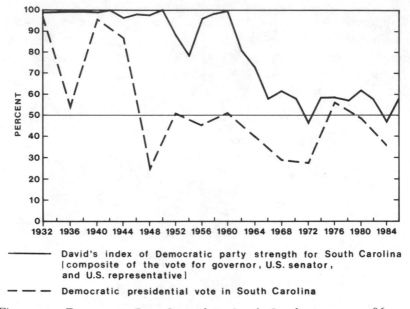

——————— David's index of Democratic party strength for South Carolina
(composite of the vote for governor, U.S. senator,
and U.S. representative)

— — — Democratic presidential vote in South Carolina

Figure 5-1. Democratic Party Strength in South Carolina, 1932–1986

now that blacks were starting to vote in large numbers.[8] Thurmond's decision contributed mightily to legitimizing the Republican party in the state in one quick move and to making it an immediate threat to the state's Democrats, a situation that encouraged white Democratic leaders to reach out to blacks for help in defeating the GOP challengers.

Buoyed by its presidential-level growth, the state Republican party in 1966 ran a gubernatorial candidate for the first time in the twentieth century. The GOP nominee, State Rep. Joseph O. Rogers, Jr., received 41.8 percent of the vote while losing to Robert E. McNair, the Democratic lieutenant governor who had succeeded to the governorship on the resignation and subsequent appointment to the Senate of Gov. Donald S. Russell. The unexpired two-year term of the late Senator Johnston was filled in the 1966 election, and a Republican challenger, Marshall Parker, came very close to winning. He received 48.7 percent of the vote in losing to Ernest F. (Fritz) Hollings, the former governor, who had defeated Russell in the Democratic primary mainly on the issue of Russell's "self-appointment" to the Johnston seat.

One Republican did win statewide in 1966, however. Senator Thurmond was re-elected with 62.2 percent of the votes cast. That the state's two most prominent Democrats, Russell and Hollings, chose to battle among themselves for Johnston's seat rather than challenge Thurmond indicates that these politicians had no illusions that Thurmond's new party affiliation would adversely affect his popularity at the polls.[9]

Senator Hollings presents a classic example of a Southern Democrat pressured by the sudden and successful exploitation of the race issue by a Republican party brought to life by the national Democratic party's vigorous espousal of civil rights.[10] As black voter registration was growing along with the white backlash over integration, Hollings had to stand up and be counted for nearly two years in the Senate before running for a full, six-year term in 1968. In the words of one observer, Hollings told blacks to "forget the rhetoric and look at what we do . . . I'm with you on the pocketbook issues, but in order to survive politically I must vote against [the U.S. Supreme Court nomination of Thurgood] Marshall,"[11] which he did in 1967. In the 1968 general election the Republican Parker, who again challenged Hollings, did everything he could to hang the national Democratic party around Hollings's neck,` and the former governor from Charleston skillfully kept his distance from the national party. Hollings said he was voting for Humphrey but was too busy with his own race to actively support the national nominee. Hollings won re-election with 61.9 percent of the vote.

The 1970 gubernatorial election marked an important watershed for the Republican party in South Carolina. Albert Watson, a former Democratic congressman who had supported Goldwater and then switched to the Republican party in 1965 when he was stripped of his seniority by House Democrats, ran a blatantly racist campaign.[12] The Democratic nominee, Lt. Gov. John C. West, a moderate, benefited from both overwhelming support among black voters[13] and strong backing among white establishment leaders who were upset over the virulent racial atmosphere the Watson campaign was encouraging and exploiting. West won with 51.7 percent of the votes cast. In Columbia and Charleston the Republican did better in lower-income white precincts than in upper-income white areas and received nearly no votes in black precincts.[14]

Following this election, Thurmond began his much-publicized courting of South Carolina blacks. Neal Peirce wrote:

> It is known that after the 1970 defeat, Harry Dent—a man of cooler temper than his erstwhile boss—took Thurmond aside and told him he would have to back away from a strong segregationist appeal. It was on Dent's urging that Thurmond put a black man on his staff. The strategy, Dent told an interviewer, was to get Thurmond "in a position where he can't be attacked like Watson by liberals as being a racist." When Thurmond appealed openly to

blacks, the white moderates who had been afraid of Watson were reassured.[15]

Thurmond won re-election in 1972. His Democratic opponent, State Sen. Nick Zeigler,* denounced Thurmond for his opposition to nearly all federal economic welfare legislation, from Medicare to aid to education. Focusing on bread-and-butter New Deal–type economic issues, Zeigler hoped to bring together blacks and the George Wallace Democrats who had abandoned Humphrey, especially in the heavily blue-collar manufacturing counties of the Piedmont. Zeigler failed in 1972, getting only 36.7 percent of the vote. In the polarized atmosphere of 1972, Zeigler drew votes in a pattern quite similar to that of McGovern's poor showing in the state.[16]

When the race issue began to wane in the early 1970s, the state's Democratic senator, Hollings, began positioning himself to avoid a primary challenge from the left. Amid considerable national publicity in 1969, he "discovered" hunger in his home state[17] and sought more open ties with black leaders. In his 1974 re-election effort Hollings faced weak opposition in both the Democratic primary and the general election, where his opponent was Gwenyfred Bush, a little-known Republican, who received only 28.6 percent of the vote.

Despite his posturing on the left, Hollings never veered far enough to alarm his corporate backers. One newspaper reporter who has observed Hollings closely remarked that he has had a "lot of success with this 'I'm a fiscal conservative and a moderate on social issues,' which means they talk a lot and don't come up with the money."[18] Hollings's challenges to economic interests never threaten the business establishment in South Carolina. On one issue, for example, that did pose something of a threat, the labor law reform bill of 1977–78, Hollings led Democrats opposed to the bill. While attempting to explain why the Democratic party has done so well in South Carolina, Hollings, in an interview with Neal Peirce, also provided some insight into his own political positioning:

---

*John Bolt Culbertson, a Greenville lawyer and state party maverick, challenged Zeigler, the party leadership's candidate, for the Democratic nomination. Culbertson, who was sixty-three at the time of the primary, called himself an economic liberal; he was quoted in the campaign as saying, "When I go to Washington, Hubert Humphrey, Abraham Ribicoff, Jacob Javits and the rest will be following me. I'll be more liberal than all of them." *Columbia* (S.C.) *Record,* Aug. 21, 1972. Culbertson lambasted the hypocrisy of the Democratic establishment in the state: "The regulars are more Republican than they are Democrat. Except for [Olin D.] Johnston and [Benjamin R. (Pitchfork Ben)] Tillman, this state has always had aristocratic rule, rule by privilege. That's what I've been fighting all my life." Ibid. Culbertson was defeated 58 percent to 42 percent.

The Democrats keep their iron grip, he [Hollings] said, because Democratic state legislators "have been habitually good public servants. A textile leader knows he's got good support and following among them. It's given him a good business climate, and he doesn't want to upset that good applecart." Anyway, Hollings said, the Democratic party in South Carolina "is more conservative than it is liberal," so that Republicans attacking from the right lack ideological ground in which to maneuver.[19]

In 1974 South Carolina elected a Republican governor in an election that can only be understood by describing the misfortune that befell the Democratic gubernatorial primary winner. Charles D. (Pug) Ravenel, a youthful reformer who ran the state's first professional media campaign blitz, defeated the ten-term Congressman William Jennings Bryan Dorn in the Democratic runoff. Less than two months before the general election, the South Carolina Supreme Court declared Ravenel ineligible because he had failed to meet a five-year residency requirement. After the state party substituted Dorn as the Democratic nominee, Ravenel refused to back Dorn in any meaningful way. It is not difficult to conclude that James B. Edwards, a Charleston oral surgeon who is a conservative in the Ronald Reagan mold, benefited from the Democratic party's nightmare.[20] The Republican nominee edged his way to victory with 50.9 percent of the vote.

South Carolina Democratic party leaders found in Jimmy Carter the first national nominee of their party in over a decade for whom they could comfortably and actively campaign, and in the election Carter carried the state with 56.2 percent of the vote. In 1976, with the race issue in quiescence, many white traditional Democrats in the Piedmont flocked to the banner of their fellow Southerner, making that part of the state once again a stronghold for the Democratic presidential standard-bearer. However, the Piedmont had to share top honors with the Black Belt as the most Democratic section of the state in 1976. The strongest national Republican parts of the state that year were its three largest urban areas, Charleston, Greenville, and Columbia (Richland County), and the counties surrounding them.

The Democratic presidential success, however, did not carry over to the party's vigorous attempt two years later to unseat Thurmond. In his second try for statewide office, the Democrat Ravenel concentrated, as had Zeigler six years before, on the Republican senator's opposition to traditional Democratic domestic economic programs. Thurmond, who is legendary for his attention to South Carolina affairs, began his campaign early and ran steadily, repeating that South Carolinians knew his record and supported it.[21] Thurmond won with 55.6 percent of the vote, the closest election of his Senate career. Ravenel's losing vote pattern closely resembled McGovern's and Zeigler's.[22] Although it could be argued that Thurmond is a political institution in the state because of his longevity and attention to his constituents and has a base of support that is independent of party or ideological considerations, these voting-pattern similarities suggest something more fundamental. By openly affiliating with the Republican party, Thurmond brought the national party cleavage to the forefront in statewide elections, at least in his races for the U.S. Senate. Thurmond hinted at this view himself in an interview. Asked about the future of the GOP in the South, he said in July 1978, "The party's growth in the South will come naturally. A two-party system is important from the standpoint of national elections—to give people clearly defined choices."[23] In an earlier interview, conducted by Peirce,

> Thurmond explained that when South Carolinians vote Republican for President, "They feel that's way out yonder and if they vote Republican there won't be any stigma. But in state elections, especially among the less enlightened people, there's still that stigma against Republicans that goes back to the military rule of 1866 to 1876." By the very fact that the Democrats control the machinery at the local and state level, Thurmond said, up-and-coming politicians see their best chance to be elected as Democrats, not Republicans.[24]

Two factors were prominent in South Carolina's 1978 gubernatorial election. The first was the importance of black voters to the Democrats and the concomitant difficulty Republicans had in overcoming that edge. The other was the importance of the Democratic candidate's ability to project a moderate to moderate-conservative stance.

The 1978 Democratic gubernatorial primary winner, State Sen. Richard W. (Dick) Riley of Greenville, fit the winning mold perfectly. As Lee Bandy, Washington correspondent for *The State*, South Carolina's largest and most influential newspaper, observed, "The business establishment in South Carolina supports and underwrites the Democratic party; these people backed Dick Riley."[25] Another observer, Joan McKinney, Washington correspondent of the Charleston *News and Courier*, described Riley's coalition this way: "He works hard in the black community; he gets upstate support and is acceptable to business. He is bankrolled by Greenville textile people and bankers. He doesn't frighten them; he is not a rabblerouser."[26]

There was a "rabblerouser" in the 1978 Democratic gubernatorial primary campaign, and he caused something of a stir for South Carolina. Tom Turnipseed, a former associate of George Wallace who announced he had seen the light and now was with "our black brothers," attempted to put together a coalition of blacks and poor whites in the Democratic primary. A *New York Times* reporter wrote:

> [Turnipseed] is mingling an undiluted populist attack on "vested interests" with calls for reconciliation between whites and those whom he insists on referring to as "our black brothers, mine and yours."
>
> "As long as you're wasting your energy hating the black man and not economic exploitation," Mr. Turnipseed admonishes voters, "you're doomed." . . . He relentlessly assails the utility companies, "big corporations," special interests, the state's patrician power structure, the State Assembly, corrupt politicians and all others who he contends have conspired to "preserve a cheap labor market, limit education and employment opportunities and otherwise rip off the people of South Carolina." . . .
>
> His fellow legislators [Turnipseed is a state senator] call him a "wild man," or a "dangerous demagogue," and some suggest that he has a "screw loose."[27]

Prior to the first primary, Turnipseed withdrew from the race, complaining of irregular heartbeats and saying that he was acting on the advice of his cardiologist. A leading editorial writer for *The State* summed up the impact of Turnipseed's withdrawal: "To the great relief of South Carolina's business and governmental establishment, State Senator Tom Turnipseed, the populist demagogue from Lexington, has withdrawn from the Governor's race, citing reasons of health."[28]

In the 1978 general election, Riley, the Democratic nominee, defeated his Republican opponent, Edward L. (Ed) Young, a former one-term U.S. representative, by a margin of 61.4 percent to 37.8 percent, a partisan division that roughly reflected the strength of the black-white Democratic coalition in post–civil rights era South Carolina.

Early in 1979 Carroll Campbell, a young, articulate businessman who had been elected to Congress as a Republican in 1978 from the Greenville-centered district, offered an analysis of this gubernatorial election that suggests the importance for the Democrats of holding the moderate to moderate-conservative position. Campbell, whose assessment was obviously tinged with partisan hope, said:

> The Democratic party, which has been a conservative party in the South, as we all know, has moved sharply to the left in the past few years in the South, particularly in South Carolina. The candidates they have been running have been far more liberal. The conservative Democrat is having a very difficult time getting through the Democratic primary.[29]

Campbell cited Ravenel as an example of these nonconservative nominees. About Governor Riley, Campbell said, "Riley is a moderate, not a conservative, but not a wild man." On a scale of one to ten, one being ultraliberal, he said he would put Riley at three or four. He added, "Dick was able to pick up some of your moderate conservative voters, pick up his black [supporters], and pick up virtually all of the liberal votes. You know that was a good coalition; it's good politics."[30] However, he cautioned that in the future the Democratic primary could produce winners to the left of Riley.

As to the 1978 Republican gubernatorial nominee's inability to break Riley's support among blacks, Campbell had some incisive comments. Before the fall campaign, Ed Young, the GOP nominee, had asserted, "All we need is 20 percent of the black vote and we've got it."[31] After his July prediction that there would be a break in the "black vote" in November, Young made a vigorous appeal to blacks during the fall campaign, but failed. Campbell offered the following observation concerning Young's appeal to blacks:

> It backlashed on him. He [Young] overdid it in my estimation. There is no question that the Republican party has got to recognize the need to attract black voters. And anybody who doesn't has got his head in the sand. However, the manner that you try to do this is all important. Young ran radio ads: "The Democratic party gave you George Wallace, the white primary and this, that and the other. Vote Republican."
>
> What do you do with all that? It turned off all the conservative George Wallace supporters in the state. And he failed to pick up blacks either. So, what I am saying is . . . you don't go out and move to an extreme position to try to do it.[32]

In the 1980 and 1982 elections, South Carolina Republicans continued to experience the detrimental effects of their inability to attract any significant portion of the state's blacks, who made up 27.8 percent of the registered voters in 1982.[33] And the Democrats managed successfully to hold together their winning post–civil rights era coalition.

Despite the myriad difficulties that faced President Carter in 1980, the incumbent only narrowly lost South Carolina to Ronald Reagan, by a margin of 48.1 percent to 49.4 percent. The county-level returns reveal that no significant shifts occurred in the presidential voting pattern established in 1976. A comparison of Carter's two races in the state shows that among the counties where Carter was strong or weak in 1976 he generally remained strong or weak in 1980. There occurred, however, an even falloff in nearly all counties as his 1976 statewide percentage of 56.2 dropped. The strongest Democratic counties remained those of the Black Belt and the Piedmont.

Senator Hollings easily won re-election in 1980, with 70.4 percent of the vote, over the Republican Marshall Mays. But in the same election the Republicans gained two congressional seats. In the district dominated by Charleston, a Republican state senator, Thomas F. Hartnett, narrowly beat Ravenel in the latter's third straight failure to attain public office. And U.S. Rep. John W. Jenrette, Jr., the Democrat who had been convicted in the Abscam scandal of illegally taking bribes, was unseated in the Sixth District by a thirty-three-year-old Republican attorney, John L. Napier, a former member of Thurmond's Washington staff. These gains gave the GOP a four-to-two edge in the state's six-member U.S. House delegation; four incumbents, two from each party, were returned in 1980.

Governor Riley was overwhelmingly re-elected to a second term in 1982, winning 69.9 percent of the vote.[34] Potentially strong GOP candidates, such as former Governor Edwards or Congressman Campbell, declined to challenge the popular Democratic incumbent. So the Republican nomination went to the man who had started it all in 1962, William Workman, by then a sixty-eight-year-old retired editor of *The State*. Workman's second try for statewide office, this time without the impetus of the civil rights issue, was a lackluster affair; he received only 30.1 percent of the vote, and the Republicans lost all contested elections for state constitutional offices. Surveying his party's weak 1982 showing, the state Republican party chairman, George Graham, observed, "We got a heavy turnout of people who vote blind, one-party politics. Regardless of anything, recessions, catastrophes or whatever, they vote Democratic. And that's about 40 percent of the vote."[35] Graham noted that blacks made up a substantial number of these voters.[36]

The most interesting election in South Carolina in 1982 also pointed to the importance of solid black support for Democratic victories. This race was Congressman Napier's vigorous attempt to hold his seat in the Sixth District, which had a black population of slightly over 40 percent. While losing the state narrowly in 1980, Carter had carried Napier's district with 54 percent of the vote, and Napier's 1980 victory would not have been possible without the Abscam difficulties of his Democratic opponent. By using the powers of incumbency to the hilt, Napier hoped to overcome the inherent weakness of being a Republican in that district, which stretched over ten rural, small-town counties north of Charleston, including Georgetown and Florence. The Democratic nominee, State Rep. Robert M. Tallon, Jr., hammered away at Napier's support for President Reagan's economic program, stressing that unemployment in the district had climbed to 13 percent.[37] In a pre-election interview, Napier described Tallon's strategy:

> He's trying to say that [the Reagan] administration is not for poor people, not for black people. . . . I think in the long-term people look and see that we had to make some of the decisions that were made. We simply cannot continue to get money out of an empty coffer. We don't have money up here. We have got to bring discipline to the federal structure. Thinking people understand that. I think our blacks . . . are a thinking group. And they cannot be just taken for granted that they are going to vote one way because they are "told to."[38]

As both sides figured, black voters were the key to the election, and they provided the foundation for Tallon's victory, with 52.3 percent of the vote to Napier's 47.7 percent.[39]

Despite the problems Republicans have in breaking the strong Democratic allegiance of black voters and in broadening their base generally, the Democrats have their troubles too. Top among them are the tensions inherent in the ideologically diverse Democratic coalition. Examination of the recent South Carolina electoral scene suggested that major statewide Democratic nominees invariably have been satisfactory to the state's conservative economic interests. Thus, these nominees do not advocate policies that on the national level would put them in their party's left-of-center mainstream and perhaps alienate their powerful state patrons and conservative Democratic voters generally. Governor Riley, for example, was no "wild man," as Huey Long–style Democrats often are termed; his business-establishment credentials were impeccable.

Therefore, when the Democrats can prevent the Republicans from cutting into the overwhelming Democratic support among blacks and when the Democratic nominee is not a "wild man," statewide Democratic ascendancy in South Carolina is safe. But if more left-of-center Democrats began to win Democratic primaries, tensions within the Democratic coalition would certainly increase. This would occur because activist Democrats, on the order of Henry Howell of Virginia or Reubin Askew of Florida, would probably advocate spending and taxing policies to benefit their natural constituencies—"those who have less" whether white or black—at the expense of the more affluent segments of the Democratic establishment. Whether such nominees lead to Democratic party defeats depends, of course, on how the particulars (the personalities and the issues) are handled. In the event the above scenario develops, the Howell example—as the Virginia chapter corroborates—offers promise for Republicans; the Askew experience in Florida, however, suggests that the Republican hope for a "wild man" Democratic nominee might not turn out as well as the South Carolina GOP, poised to capitalize on such a turn of events, would expect.

South Carolina—Conclusion

South Carolina's two-party development differed markedly from Mississippi's. First, South Carolina Democratic leaders, facing a formidable GOP threat after Thurmond switched to the Republican party in 1964, reached out early to black voters and used their support to fuse a winning biracial coalition that offered benefits both to the white leaders and to blacks (the latter benefiting, at least, from an end to white-supremacy rhetoric by statewide Democratic nominees and from a measure of influence in state affairs).

Second, the state's most prominent segregationist Democratic politician clarified the partisan situation early by joining the Republican party. Thus, when other Deep South states in 1970 were still witnessing strong candidacies by segregationist Democrats (such as Orval Faubus's abortive 1970 comeback attempt in Arkansas or the campaign of George Wallace, the winner of the Democratic gubernatorial primary in Alabama that year) or independent black candidacies (as in the case of Charles Evers in Mississippi in 1971), South Carolina fought out the race issue *between* the two parties and not within the Democratic party. In the critical 1970 gubernatorial election Watson, the GOP nominee, sought vigorously to use white resentment over integration to win the governorship. However, West, a moderate Democrat, beat him with substantial support from blacks. And since then, this diverse biracial coalition has held together.

The coalition could not, however, stop the well-established Thurmond from winning re-election three times as a Republican. (A Republican also won the governorship in 1974, but the peculiar circumstances of that election mark it as a singular event not to be confused with the broader trends; the weak GOP showing in the gubernatorial races of 1978 and 1982 further substantiated the deviant nature of Edwards's election.) A result of Thurmond's forthright embrace of the Republican party was to permit economic-class issues to be fought out in partisan terms in his general election campaigns, and this certainly was the case with Thurmond's races in the 1970s, against Zeigler in 1972 and against Ravenel in 1978. Class issues, which were closely akin to those from the New Deal era, were rarely found, however, to predominate in other statewide Deep South general elections the way they did in these two South Carolina elections for U.S. senator.

6

Alabama: Mesmerized by
a "Poor Man's Segregationist"

Alabama's electoral development for over two decades has been dominated by the charismatic segregationist George C. Wallace. The simple fact that he was an Alabama Democrat who led a major regional—and to some extent nationwide—revolt against the national Democratic party over race goes a long way toward explaining why the Republican party had such a difficult time in the state. On the initial crest of the wave of racial protest in the early 1960s, the Republican party in Alabama was able to make substantial early gains, but these were nearly obliterated by Wallace's domination of the state until his 1978 "retirement." In the first post-Wallace elections, in 1978, the challenging Republicans ran a credible but losing statewide race and then captured a U.S. Senate seat two years later while Ronald Reagan was winning Alabama's electoral votes, all of which strongly suggested that two-party competition had gotten a second start in the incipient post-Wallace era.

Then, to the consternation of those who had cheerfully watched Wallace retire from the governorship in January 1979, the still feisty though infirm Wallace, who had by then joined the new era by apologizing to blacks for his racist past and by seeking their votes, declared himself a candidate for governor in 1982 and fought his way back to office through two tough primaries and the general election. But the Wallace who emerged triumphant in November 1982 no longer represented a lingering aberration in Southern politics. Quite the contrary, his general election victory in 1982 over an aggressive Republican candidate was fashioned in the standard manner that had been used by scores of statewide Southern Democratic victors in the 1970s—that is, by forming a potent, ideologically diverse black-white Democratic coalition. It was a new trick for Wallace. But it was old hat for other white Southern Democrats who lacked the mesmerizing powers of the younger, pre-assassination-attack Wallace and had been unable single-handedly to retard GOP growth in their states by using the politics of race, as Wallace had done in Alabama. Thus, when Wallace returned triumphant in 1982, after four years on the sidelines, he did so as a reputable post–civil rights era Democrat, breaking sharply with his earlier electoral appeal. Before the new Wallace of the 1980s can be placed in proper perspective, his earlier political career and its impact on Alabama politics must be explored.

Serious two-party competition in Alabama began in 1962 with the near upset of Sen. Lister Hill. The Republican James D. Martin, a businessman, attempted to capitalize on the unpopularity of the Kennedy administration's civil rights initiatives in campaigning against Senator Hill. Numan V. Bartley and Hugh D. Graham described the election as follows:

> . . . Martin set the tone of attack, calling for "a return of the spirit of '61—1861, when our fathers formed a new nation" to support their principles. "God willing," Martin concluded, "we will not again be forced to take up rifle and bayonet to preserve these principles. . . . Make no mistake, my friends, this will be a fight. The bugle call is loud and clear! The South has risen!" Hill countered as best he could with appeals to fading memories of the "Republican depression" and Herbert Hoover and by emphasizing the New Deal's contribution toward alleviating the misery of depression and underdevelopment in Alabama, his own consistent support of TVA, and the advantages of his seniority.[1]

Hill's narrow victory, with 50.9 percent of the vote, was a precursor of President Johnson's losing campaign in Alabama two years later.[2]

Goldwater swept the state in 1964, with 69.5 percent of the vote, shattering previous Alabama presidential election patterns[3] and carrying into office five Republican congressmen, including Martin. The Republican standard-bearer's civil rights stance was especially appealing throughout the southern two-thirds of the state, starting slightly below Birmingham (Jefferson County), an area where race was a potent issue[4] and where blacks were effectively disfranchised. However, the Black Belt of South Alabama—counties that contained rich, black soil and were heavily populated by blacks, as shown in Map 6-1—abandoned the surrounding southern counties soon after the Goldwater-Johnson elec-

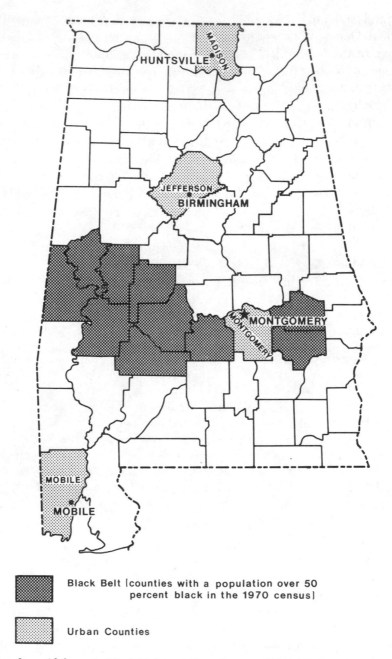

Map 6-1. Alabama's Black Belt and Four Largest Urban Counties

tion and suddenly became the strongest part of the state supporting national Democratic nominees. This occurred because after the 1965 passage of the Voting Rights Act blacks in these counties began to vote in large numbers for the first time and to cast their ballots consistently for their national champions, but not for Alabama Democrats—at least not initially.

Governor Wallace, who was first elected in 1962, occupied himself while in office with, among other things, vain attempts to fulfill his famous inaugural cry of "segregation today, segregation tomorrow, segregation forever."[5] He was constitutionally prevented from succeeding himself in 1966, and his effort to change the state constitution on this point failed.

With the prospect of Wallace off the ballot in 1966, the Republicans—riding high after the Goldwater "landslide"—prepared for a major push, hoping to pick up segregationist voters. Martin gave up his U.S. House seat to run for governor, and the state Republican party chairman, John Grenier, challenged Alabama's other veteran U.S. senator, John Sparkman. It was the misfortune of the state GOP that Wallace decided to run his wife, Lurleen, for governor, and the Wallaces prevailed in the Democratic primary without a runoff. Against a Wallace, the Republican Martin's 1962 electoral strategy had no chance.[6] As Donald S. Strong put it, "No one doubted that Congressman Martin was an Alabama segregationist, but it is hard for a rich man's segregationist to beat a poor man's segregationist."[7]

Sparkman, a New Deal liberal like Hill, had remained "right" on civil rights, and the veteran senator experienced little trouble turning back the GOP threat in 1966, gaining re-election with 60.1 percent of the vote. The voting pattern in his race bore little resemblance to any other candidate's, national or state, pointing to the ability of this entrenched incumbent to remain apart from the issues that were stirring the Alabama electorate.[8]

In 1968 James B. Allen, Wallace's lieutenant governor and a close political ally, was the Democratic nominee to replace Senator Hill, who decided to retire. No clearer case of Alabama Republicans' total helplessness against George Wallace exists. The *Montgomery Advertiser* reported that Allen based most of his campaign on his affiliation with Wallace.[9] The Republican nominee, Perry Hooper, did what he could. He avoided supporting Nixon's candidacy, saying he would cooperate with Wallace should the Alabamian win the presidency. Hooper's campaign speeches were strongly against "crime and disorders" and federal intervention in local government.[10] Allen's 1968 victory, with 70.0 per-

cent of the vote, followed a county-level pattern quite similar to that of
Wallace's winning presidential vote in the state that year.[11]

In 1970 the major Alabama electoral activity occurred in the Democratic primary for governor. Wallace's chief opponent was Albert
Brewer, who as lieutenant governor had succeeded to the governorship
in 1968 upon the death of Wallace's wife. Brewer made it to the runoff
on the basis of strong support from blacks, which prompted Wallace to
fall back on his old race-baiting tactics. For example, one Wallace
campaign advertisement had this message:[12]

IF YOU WANT TO SAVE
ALABAMA AS WE KNOW ALABAMA
REMEMBER!
THE BLOC VOTE (NEGROES AND THEIR
WHITE FRIENDS) NEARLY NOMINATED
GOV. BREWER ON MAY 5TH. THIS
BLACK AND WHITE
SOCIAL-POLITICAL ALLIANCE
MUST NOT DOMINATE
THE PEOPLE OF ALABAMA!
THIS SPOTTED ALLIANCE MUST BE DEFEATED!
THIS MAY BE YOUR LAST CHANCE.
VOTE RIGHT—
VOTE WALLACE

Wallace narrowly defeated Brewer for the Democratic nomination, winning 51.6 percent of the votes cast.

The Republicans did not run a candidate for governor in 1970. However, Dr. John L. Cashin, a black dentist from Huntsville, entered the
general election as a candidate of the National Democratic Party of
Alabama (NDPA), a black third-party effort in Alabama that was not as
successful as a similar effort in Mississippi.[13] In campaigning against
Cashin, Wallace once more warned against the "black bloc vote" and
encouraged a large turnout of whites.[14] Cashin received 14.7 percent of
the vote.[15] Wallace was returned to the governorship in his own right
with 74.5 percent. A. C. Shelton, a white independent, finished third
with 8.9 percent.

Running for the Senate against Sparkman two years later, the
NDPA's candidate, John LeFlore, received less than 3 percent of the
vote in a three-way contest. As a result of this poor showing, the NDPA
was virtually moribund as a statewide force.[16]

Robert Vance, the chairman of the state Democratic party from the
mid-1960s through the mid-1970s and one who identified with the

national party, is given part of the credit for avoiding a Mississippi-style breach within the state party. As Neal Peirce wrote, Vance "easily outmaneuvered the NDPA by proving to the national party that he was making a serious [and successful] effort to include black people in the regular party."[17] Because of his central role in party affairs, Vance's views on this period of electoral flux are especially interesting. When asked in 1974 what would happen if Wallace left the scene, he said:

> I think that everything will probably come out very nicely from my point of view. Had he left . . . in the mid-1960s and had the Republicans been interested in taking a cold, pragmatic view of political development in Alabama, they could have torn this state apart. We could have flopped over into the Republican column very quickly. But I am inclined to believe that that opportunity is past. I don't think they can do it now under any circumstances and I doubt that the opportunity will again be comparable to that. I think that we were very nearly in a position in the middle 1960s where the Republicans, if they had been real "gut-cutters," could have painted the Democratic party as the party of the black people and the Republican party as the party of the white people, at least south of Birmingham. . . . And with him [Wallace] on the scene it got a little shaky around '68, exactly where we were going. But I just don't think that exists anymore.[18]

In 1972 the Republican Winton M. (Red) Blount, postmaster general in the Nixon administration, attempted to unseat Sparkman. According to the *Montgomery Advertiser*:

> Blount made an all-out effort to link Senator Sparkman and the Democratic presidential candidate, Senator George McGovern. His speeches and advertising tried to convince voters that Sparkman and McGovern were a "team" and that they were alike, ideologically.[19]

Regarding this tactic of Blount's, Ray Jenkins, a veteran editor of the *Alabama Journal*, observed:

> The big issue as far as Blount was concerned was trying to tie John Sparkman to McGovern. The McGovern crowd . . . he was part and party of the same system, and . . . that is just a little bit too much bull . . . for the most unsophisticated Alabama voters. It was an insult to them in a way.[20]

For his part, Sparkman campaigned in his usual fashion, stressing the importance to the state of his Senate seniority and reminding voters about the federal money he had brought to Alabama. The Republican Blount received only 33.1 percent of the vote for his well-financed effort, compared with Sparkman's 62.3 percent.[21]

The Republican party did not officially nominate a candidate for governor in 1974 to oppose Wallace's re-election. To the chagrin of GOP leaders, a Republican, Elvin McCary, ran anyway, receiving only 14.8 percent of the vote.[22]

A thorough treatment of Alabama politics must contain an in-depth consideration of the Wallace phenomenon and its impact on the state's Republican party. Untangling Wallace's racial appeal from his populist appeal is an especially difficult, if not impossible, task. Jenkins, the newspaper editor, approached the problem in this manner:

> [A] thread that runs back through Alabama's history [is] the conserva-
> tive South Alabama voting Dixiecrat and the somewhat liberal North
> Alabama voting Loyalist.
>
> When he came along, in any case, Wallace had the effect of
> obliterating the old Dixiecrat-Loyalist split. He just didn't fit into
> either one at all, and he just completely obliterated it. His support
> cut completely across the board. . . .[23]

Although Wallace, a native of the South Alabama county of Barbour, is well known for his racial position, his populism needs some elaboration. The comments of Jenkins, who has observed Wallace throughout the successful politician's career, are instructive:

> Wallace, if you are using the old definitions of populism, could
> be called justifiably a pseudo-populist. He wasn't like Gene Tal-
> madge, one of those fake populists who gets up and mouths all of
> these things about what he is going to do for the people, and then
> makes his covert deals with the economic powers of the state. Gene
> was the most vivid example of the faker, the man who spoke for the
> people, but represented everything against their interest. . . .
>
> Well, Wallace wasn't this at all. He came out of the Folsom[24]
> tradition and his rhetoric was extremely populist, no doubt about it
> whatever. To a large extent he tried to carry it out. A good example
> of it is that junior college and trade school program which he
> built. . . . But like so much of Wallace's stuff in concept it didn't
> take the practical consideration of how you are going to pay for this
> sort of thing, where you are going to get faculties. . . . What it
> amounted to was that they raided the high schools for their faculties
> and just added two years to the high schools, which wasn't too
> bad . . . but nonetheless the idea was still there and it was a good
> idea and it represents Wallace's populism. . . .
>
> But then when you get over to the other side of the populist issue,
> this is where you have a . . . departure from Jim Folsom. Folsom's
> idea was to hitch up the Big Mules. That was his term: "We're going
> to hitch up the Big Mules." [The idea was] to put it on the damn
> corporations for a while, like Huey Long did in Louisiana. But

Wallace didn't do this. His taxing programs went straight to the consumers. . . . Almost none [of his taxes] were put on the corporations and industries. . . .

So then, you see, he is a pseudo-populist. He has done all of these things, but he has gotten it out of the people, not out of the corporations like the old populists wanted to do.[25]

For Alabama Republicans, Wallace's combined appeal, both pseudo-populist and racial, was devastating, and Wallace, as Jenkins aptly phrased it, "managed to totally arrest the development of the Republican party."[26]

When asked in 1974 what was retarding the growth of the GOP in Alabama, Wallace answered that the people of Alabama had been satisfied with the Democratic party. He continued:

People with all shades of opinion can participate in the Democratic primaries. Everybody can participate in the Democratic primary. Even if you're a Republican, you vote in the Democratic primary. . . . you've had conservatives, you've had liberals, you've had middle-of-the-roaders [run for office]. And it's not a matter of not getting a choice. You just get a choice in the Democratic primary.[27]

Prominent Alabama Republicans describe the situation in about the same way, although their emphasis is different. Bill Harris, the state GOP chairman, pointed to the broad nature of the Alabama Democratic party in the late 1970s and called it "the only game in town,"[28] adding:

Wallace certainly made it much more difficult for us. But Jim Allen also made it tough for us. So here I was saying, "Be a Republican, join the responsible, conservative party . . . ." Well, the Democrat says, "I am a Jim Allen supporter and he stands for all those things."[29]

In 1979 U.S. Rep. Jack Edwards, a Republican who was first elected in the Goldwater sweep of 1964 and has retained his seat from the Mobile-dominated district since then, emphasized the dispiriting consequence of facing such an entrenched and broadly based opposition:

One of our major problems is the perception that we cannot win statewide. And it is hard for me to argue with young people that . . . we can win and we need to pioneer and we need good people to run if we are ever going to win. Of course, all that is true, but for a guy who really wants to be attorney general or governor, you have to look at the cold, hard facts, that we have not been winning statewide races.[30]

A number of observers of the Alabama GOP have pointed to the party's preoccupation with ideological questions as a major drawback. For example, Jenkins said in 1974 that the Republicans

> just don't understand politics for one thing. [They] are given to these profoundly boring ideological disputes, and petty disputes at that. Republican politics is characterized by petty personal hatreds of one another. These even override ideological differences, and there are few ideological differences. It is basically Goldwater Republican philosophy. It is sort of a "Let them eat cake" philosophy . . . .[31]

The GOP chairman Harris, in an interview four years after Jenkins's assessment, said:

> There is no doubt the Republican party has been plagued . . . with ideological purity. . . . It is a death syndrome, and we have just got to get over it before we can win.
> We are viewed as cold, calculating people who don't give a damn about anybody. . . . Let them starve in the streets. Balance that budget. And that is not true.[32]

Congressman Edwards also lamented this GOP preoccupation with conservative ideological purity:

> Too often Republicans make it uncomfortable for the moderate-to-liberal Republicans, and they don't feel comfortable and they quit running or they change parties. So, while we tend to keep a greater purity, if you will, than the Democrats do, we also tend to remain the minority because we can't seem to assimilate people of different views as well as the Democrats do.[33]

The retarding influence of Wallace on Republican growth is starkly illustrated in Figure 6-1. Similar party-strength figures for most of the other Southern states reveal that Democratic decline continued into the early and middle 1970s, at which time a mild resurgence occurred for reasons discussed elsewhere. But in Alabama the precipitous drop in Democratic party strength in the early 1960s halted abruptly in 1966, at a point above the 60 percent line, and the party's strength generally rose from then to a peak in 1974 with Wallace's triumphant re-election without official opposition from the "dispirited" Republican party.

The retirement of Sparkman, the death of Allen, and Wallace's decision to "retire" at the end of his term in January 1979, rather than to run for the U.S. Senate, all made 1978 a banner election year in Alabama.[34] With one exception the important action occurred in the Democratic primaries, calling further attention to the weakness of the GOP.[35] But the Republicans could take some comfort in the fact that the winner of the Democratic primary for governor, Forrest (Fob)

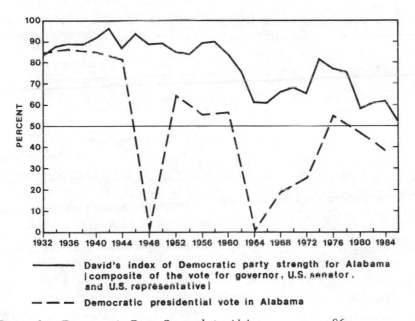

Figure 6-1. Democratic Party Strength in Alabama, 1932–1986

James, had been a member of the state Republican executive committee in the early 1970s and a major GOP fund-raiser.[36]

In the early Democratic gubernatorial speculation James was ignored. The race was supposed to be between Bill Baxley, the attorney general; Jere Beasley, the lieutenant governor; and Albert Brewer, the former governor.[37] Baxley was considered the most liberal; one newsman called him "the hope of the liberals outside of the state."[38] James, a millionaire industrialist, "ran a media-oriented campaign, promising to bring 'a new beginning to Alabama.' "[39] He finished four percentage points ahead of Baxley, to lead the first primary. In the runoff James's past GOP affiliation became a major issue. The *Washington Post* reported:

> Attorney General Bill Baxley, a fiery populist with strong black support, doesn't let voters forget James's Republican ties.
>
> He delights in telling audiences about his "millionaire Republican opponent" who raised money for Richard M. Nixon in 1972 and the Republican candidate for Alabama Lieutenant Governor in 1974.
>
> "His [James's] advertising company has sold him to a lot of decent Alabamians as a fresh face who has never been in politics," Baxley said last week in a swing through Arab and a half dozen other northern Alabama cities. "But he's been in politics longer than Bill Baxley. He's been in politics up to his ears. It's been Republican politics."[40]

James ignored most of Baxley's daily attacks. On the question of his party loyalty he would say:

> I was born a Democrat. I was raised a Democrat. During the early 1970s, I strayed away from the Democratic party. In recent years, I've seen the error of my ways. I've come home, and I've come home to stay.[41]

James won the runoff with 55.2 percent of the total vote.

James was not the only former Republican to run as a Democrat in 1978. Charlie Graddick, who had been elected district attorney of Mobile in 1974 as a Republican, won the Democratic nomination for attorney general[42] and was unopposed in the general election. The James and Graddick victories led Congressman Edwards to remark in early 1979 that "we really won two of the top three offices last year."[43]

Guy Hunt, a former probate judge in Cullman County in North Alabama, was the formal Republican nominee in the 1978 gubernatorial race. Hunt was little known in the state and was not considered a formidable opponent even before a former Republican won the Democratic nomination.[44] Hunt received only 25.9 percent of the vote in his loss to James.

Senator Allen's widow, Maryon, who was appointed to her husband's seat after his death, in June 1978, sought but was denied the Democratic nomination for the remaining two years of Allen's term in an upset by State Sen. Donald Stewart. Stewart, an Anniston attorney, originally entered the crowded race for Sparkman's seat but shifted after Allen's death. According to the *Washington Post*, Stewart had a moderate to liberal reputation in the legislature and was

> outspoken on a number of issues, including utility company regulation and education. Blasting "the fat cats" and Alabama Power Co., the state's most popular whipping boy, Stewart courted labor and black support . . . .[45]

For the Senate race the Republicans, in the words of Congressman Edwards, "pulled out our old war-horse—Jim Martin."[46] Like Stewart, Martin had also entered the race for Sparkman's seat, but when the Democratic primary was won by Howell Heflin, a former chief justice of the Alabama Supreme Court, Martin in early October decided that Stewart would be a less formidable opponent than the well-known and respected Heflin, and the GOP nominee switched races.[47] An election-eve summary of the Stewart-Martin general election stated, "A well-financed, business-backed campaign depicted Stewart, a longtime foe of the utility companies, as a labor-oriented liberal—a tactic Stewart has tried to counter by emphasizing his strong defense and conservative fiscal views."[48] Stewart won with 55.1 percent of the vote. Martin's 43.3 percent was the best GOP result in a nonpresidential race since Martin's near upset of Hill sixteen years earlier. After his defeat Martin announced that the 1978 senatorial campaign would be his last race for public office. As reported by the *Birmingham News*, the three-time GOP loser said "his failure to draw more black and labor support cost him the race. . . . Martin said some voters were just 'prejudiced' against him because he is a Republican."[49]

The most significant aspect of Stewart's 1978 victory was that it successfully brought together the same black-white, ideologically diverse Democratic coalition that had been forming throughout the South for over a decade. This coalition was weak in Alabama because Wallace and his allies had shown consistently that they could control Democratic nominations without the support of blacks and could then devastate Republican opposition—if there was any—without blacks. But in 1978 Stewart needed the support of blacks to stop the Republican Martin. And the same was equally true for the Democratic nominee in 1980, when the full, six-year term of the late Senator Allen came up.

The 1980 U.S. Senate election in Alabama became intertwined with the Reagan-Carter presidential race, an examination of the voting returns discloses. Reagan carried Alabama with 48.8 percent of the vote to President Carter's 47.4 percent, and in the process the Republicans won the Senate seat with their nominee, Jeremiah Denton, a retired navy admiral and former prisoner of war in North Vietnam. Reagan and Denton ran similarly in all parts of the state,[50] which strongly suggests that national influences were the critical ones in the Senate election.

The clear-cut nature of the GOP win was clouded by the outcome of the Democratic primary. James Folsom, Jr., who relied both on the popular image of his famous father—Big Jim Folsom—and on a conservative approach to the issues, narrowly defeated the newly elected Senator Stewart for the Democratic nomination. In the primary Folsom, who was thirty-one years old, contended that Stewart was too liberal for the state, saying that "he, Folsom, would better represent the state's conservative political mainstream."[51] (Stewart's less-than-charming personality also contributed to his defeat.)[52]

Denton's approach to the campaign was encapsulated by a *New York Times* reporter: "He is mixing his reputation as a patriotic war hero with a call for pay-as-you-go, free-enterprise economics and the recitation of a series of moral and family values that he says America is forsaking."[53]

Alabama voters were thus faced in November 1980 with a choice of two conservatives. One newspaper article concluded:

> Both [candidates] want less government interference in personal lives
> and business. Both want more attention given to military strength
> and national prestige. Both want to curtail government spending and
> waste and encourage work incentives for welfare recipients.[54]

In this battle of conservatives Denton emerged victorious with 50.2
percent of the vote to Folsom's 47.1 percent. Despite the similarity of
the candidates' ideological appeal, the election represented a clear two-
party division in sources of support among the electorate. The conservative Democrat Folsom did best in the heavily black counties of the
Black Belt. Denton was strongest in the state's largest cities and their
surrounding counties. If classified precinct data were available, they
would no doubt reveal class and racial cleavages along standard partisan
lines: lower-income whites and blacks for the Democrat Folsom; the
more well-to-do generally for the Republican Denton.[55] For Alabama's
victory-starved Republicans, Denton's success was a welcome shot in
the arm. On election night Bill Harris, the GOP chairman, said:

> After you've campaigned in this state for years as a Republican
> and this finally happens—it's super, I just don't know quite what to
> say.
>   This signals the start of something new in Alabama, a real, work-
> ing two-party system.[56]

When George Wallace announced, in May 1982, that he would seek
a fourth term as governor, he faced his first serious electoral opposition
in the state since his narrow victory in the Democratic primary runoff in
1970. In the interval, and especially since 1978, the nature of Alabama
elective politics had been transformed, presenting Wallace with two
major obstacles. One was a revitalized Republican party that had two
years earlier captured a U.S. Senate seat and that was fielding a seasoned, tough-talking politician, Mayor Emory Folmar of Montgomery,
as its candidate for governor in the 1982 general election. Second, black
Alabamians, whom Wallace had worked to keep segregated from whites,
were now a key element in Democratic primaries and in general elections when the Republicans offered strong candidates, as they did in
1978 and 1980.

In 1970 Wallace had confronted only the second of these obstacles,
and his strategy in that close runoff against Governor Brewer, who had
solid backing from blacks, was to warn against Brewer's "spotted alliance" with the "black bloc vote."[57] But whereas in 1970 Wallace had
faced no Republican opponent in the general election, the sixty-three-
year-old former governor now needed blacks if he was going to defeat
the Republican Folmar in November. Thus, in 1982, to the amused

surprise of many observers,[58] Wallace openly sought black support, starting with the Democratic primary campaign.

Wallace's major Democratic opponents were Lt. Gov. George McMillan, a moderate with strong support among black leaders, and House Speaker Joe McCorquodale, a conservative.[59] In the first primary Wallace led the field with 42.5 percent of the vote to McMillan's 29.6 percent; McCorquodale, who ended up endorsing Folmar in the general election,[60] was eliminated from the Democratic runoff with 25.0 percent.

Wallace concentrated his campaign on the issue of Alabama's high unemployment—second highest in the nation during the fall of 1982 at 14.5 percent—and contended that his experience as governor and his national and international recognition made him eminently qualified to lure new industries, and thus new jobs, to the state.[61] McMillan ran a polished, if bland, campaign stressing the state's need to "move forward."[62] The thirty-nine-year-old lieutenant governor's rhetoric turned harsher in the last week of the bitter runoff campaign. The *New York Times* reported that he

> told members of the Birmingham Chamber of Commerce . . . that in the almost 16 years Mr. Wallace controlled the state government "there was a void of leadership" and "mismanagement" that deprived Alabama of the economic growth experienced by other Southern states.
>
> He criticized what he called Mr. Wallace's "shallow, superficial political rhetoric" and said the state needed leaders "with a desire to solve problems, not politically exploit problems."
>
> He also accused Mr. Wallace of coming down on both sides of the issues and said, "If the people of this state are dumb enough to buy that kind of hypocrisy, then they deserve what they get."[63]

McMillan was counting heavily on overwhelming black support. In late August the Alabama Democratic Conference (ADC), the state's largest black political group, endorsed him. At the time of the endorsement, Joe L. Reed, ADC's long-time chairman, said that he thought the group's backing "will translate into 85–90 percent" of the votes among blacks.[64] But in the first primary Wallace surprised many observers by winning up to 40 percent of the votes of blacks in the rural Black Belt counties.[65] Delores Pickett, a black actress and public-relations woman who was, to use her official title, Wallace's state coordinator for black support, explained the Wallace campaign's approach in an interview shortly after the first primary: "All we've done is ask black people to weigh the negative things with the positive things and make a personal decision. And the positive things George Wallace did outweigh the negative."[66] She said many blacks had forgiven Wallace for his segregationist stance:

> It's in our Christian upbringing, and it's something that Martin Luther King taught us, too. George Wallace has been saying that he made mistakes and has changed and I think people have started to believe him . . . .
>
> [S]egregation was of the South. He was just doing what the majority of the voters at that time wanted him to do. . . .
>
> Even when he was making those speeches—and I was one of the blacks out there demonstrating in those days—I could see some things were happening that were good for black people. There were schools being built, junior colleges, jobs available.[67]

Black leaders, alarmed at the success of Pickett's work on Wallace's behalf, counterattacked in the runoff. Reed's ADC, according to the *Birmingham News*, "bought ads on black-owned radio stations, playing excerpts from Wallace's 'Segregation Forever' speech . . . . The ads conclude by asking citizens to vote for McMillan."[68] In the last days before the runoff vote, Coretta Scott King, the widow of the civil rights leader, and the Reverend Jesse Jackson, the Chicago-based black organizer, visited Alabama to speak for McMillan. Mrs. King told a black Selma audience:

> Mr. Wallace may have changed and I think he probably has, but the fact that he has changed does not mean you have to put him in the same position he held before. What he symbolizes is a spirit and an attitude that America has rejected.[69]

Not enough blacks agreed with Mrs. King, however. Wallace narrowly defeated McMillan, 50.9 percent to 49.1 percent, receiving a critical 33 percent of the votes among blacks.[70]

With the Democratic nomination secure, Wallace turned quickly to his GOP opponent, Montgomery's Mayor Folmar. The night of his runoff victory Wallace asserted, "The philosophical line will be drawn [in November]. We'll talk about people who are unemployed and hungry and about Republicans who only have to worry about who will mow their beachfront lawns."[71] The GOP nominee, according to the *New York Times*, did not see the election that way:

> Mayor Folmar, a former marine with a stern visage, military bearing and country club connections, who made millions as a shopping center developer, says the option for voters is "not the traditional Democrat-Republican partisanship but the choice of progressive, strong, active leadership or moving the clock back . . . ."[72]

If Republicans had hoped to make inroads among blacks as a result of Wallace's candidacy, they chose the wrong candidate. Folmar's reputation among blacks was poor, at best. Joe Reed, the ADC chairman who was also a Montgomery city councilman, said of Folmar, "I think deep down he's a racial bigot. I think he dislikes blacks, period, and poor whites . . . ."[73] Asked why blacks opposed Folmar, Peggy Roberson, Washington correspondent of the *Montgomery Advertiser*, said, "He has tweaked their noses and insulted them at every opportunity in Montgomery. . . . Folmar comes out of that old Montgomery high society crowd. He hasn't done anything to court the black people."[74]

Approximately 90 percent of Alabama's black voters supported Wallace in November,[75] helping him to attain a winning 59.6 percent of the vote to Folmar's 40.4 percent.[76] The black-white, ideologically diverse Democratic coalition that won for Wallace in the general election was, of course, nothing new in the South. It was the same coalition that had been successfully electing moderate Southern Democrats throughout the 1970s. Nor was this the first time that the coalition had carried a former Democratic segregationist back to office. Its uniqueness in Alabama in 1982—prompting widespread national attention—came because the beneficiary was the most prominent of all those who had fought for racial segregation during the civil rights era. His victory was the supreme irony in a regional transformation littered with ironical outcomes.

Alabama—Conclusion

The Republican party in Alabama received a major boost in the early 1960s as a result of the national Democratic party's integrationist policies. But the early gains were obliterated when the state Democratic leadership remained firmly in the hands of Wallace and his allies. This Alabama pattern sharply contrasts with the South Carolina experience. The key difference between these two Deep South states—as is true when one compares Mississippi and South Carolina—is the manner in which the white Democratic leadership approached black voters. In South Carolina, Democratic leaders made an early and successful effort to accommodate blacks. In Alabama, Vance moved successfully to prevent a Mississippi-style rupture, but other, more important Democrats, led by the widely popular Wallace and Allen, did not participate, and a South Carolina–style accommodation failed to materialize.

Wallace's potent appeal mixed racial and economic-class politics, but the latter was never of the sort that showed results in both sides of the governmental equation—the expenditure *and* the taxation sides—as Jenkins suggested. In addition, economic-class issues rarely appeared in two-party contests. Hill's narrow victory over Martin in 1962, in which the veteran incumbent barely survived the Republican Martin's racist assault by relying on memories of New Deal accomplishments in the state, was the last general election until the late 1970s that stressed economic-class questions. Stewart's victory in 1978 and Wallace's in 1982 hinged to some extent on these issues; Wallace, for example, lost no opportunity to remind the voters of the wealthy people backing his GOP opponent.

By the late 1970s the Alabama Democratic party had so successfully dominated statewide politics that serious Republican candidates chose to seek office through the Democratic primary. Congressman Edwards stressed the difficulty his party had in persuading candidates to run statewide when the record of such GOP challenges was one of total defeat until the late 1970s. But there was hope even at this low point. At the time of Wallace's departure and Allen's death, the major barrier encountered by Alabama Republicans in the middle 1960s—fervent and popular Alabama segregationist Democrats—was no longer the mighty roadblock to Republicanism it had once been. And, in 1980, by staying close to Ronald Reagan and riding the national anti-Carter tide, Denton gave Alabama Republicans their first statewide victory, taking a U.S. Senate seat. In essence, with both Martin's credible 1978 showing and Denton's victory two years later, two-party politics at the state level received a second start.

Initially the abatement of racial tension contributed less to Democratic dominance in Alabama than it did in other Deep South states, because Wallace and his allies had shown consistently that they could control Democratic nominations without the support of blacks and could then also demolish Republican opposition without blacks. But in 1978 Stewart needed the support of blacks to stop Martin. The same was true of Folsom in his losing 1980 race with Denton. And, remarkable as it was, even George Wallace, back from the sidelines in 1982, found the support of blacks critical to his success in recapturing the governorship.

Wallace's reappearance on the political scene in 1982 seemed at first glance to cloud the partisan situation once more. It is important, however, to remember that Wallace won election this last time in a manner that did not run counter to the emerging two-party structure in Alabama and the rest of the South. Rather, he won the 1982 general election at the head of the standard, post–civil rights era Southern Democratic coalition. While his force of personality was still strong enough to carry him back to office, the forces he led in the 1960s, when he almost single-handedly retarded the growth of the Alabama GOP, have dissipated. There is thus no reason to believe that the "new" Wallace will deliver Republicans another decade-long knockout blow.

7

Georgia: Triumph of
a "Night-and-Day" Alliance

As in other Deep South states, in Georgia the Republican party became
an instant threat to statewide Democratic dominance with the Goldwater sweep in 1964. Like its neighbors Alabama and South Carolina,
Georgia elected a governor in 1966, offering an important first opportunity to the hopeful Republicans. But in Georgia this initial GOP challenge was turned back only narrowly by a segregationist Democratic
candidate, Lester Maddox. By contrast, in Alabama a segregationist
Democrat won overwhelmingly in 1966, and in South Carolina the
Democratic nominee for governor that year won without making an
overtly racist appeal; in fact, it was a time in which the South Carolina
Democratic party was quietly seeking black support. Because the Georgia Republican party was not overwhelmed early by a Wallace and
because the Georgia Democrats were slow to accommodate the growing
numbers of black voters, the late 1960s and early 1970s were years that
offered the Republicans prospects of real growth in this Deep South
state.

What happened is illustrated in Figure 7-1, which depicts the rapid
decline of Democratic party strength in Georgia from 1962 to 1966.
The party went from the 93 percent line to slightly above the 70 percent
mark in only four years. Thereafter, the going became much rougher
for the GOP, and, in fact, in the 1970s Georgia Democrats maintained
one of the highest party-strength averages in the South. An examination
of the political events and maneuvers during this period offers insight

93

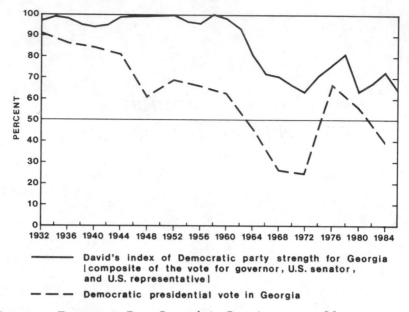

Figure 7-1. Democratic Party Strength in Georgia, 1932–1986

into why the Republicans failed to become a statewide force in a promising state or, to put it the other way, how the Democrats managed to regain virtually unchallenged supremacy statewide.

The presidential elections in Georgia followed the standard Deep South scenario. Goldwater's victory with 54.1 percent obliterated prior consistent presidential-voting patterns.[1] The strongest rejection of Johnson, Humphrey, and McGovern came in the rural, small-town, predominantly white area of South Georgia. After blacks registered in significant numbers following the passage of the Voting Rights Act, the Black Belt counties (shown in Map 7-1) became the strongest in the state for Humphrey and McGovern. But the Black Belt had to share top Democratic honors by the mid-1970s with its neighboring South Georgia counties, where blacks were less numerous. The rural white Democratic voters of South Georgia, who had been lured away first by Goldwater, then by Wallace in 1968, and finally by Nixon in 1972, returned overwhelmingly in 1976 to the national party when it was led by one of their own, the South Georgia native Jimmy Carter. The importance of the behavior both of these South Georgia white voters and of Georgia's blacks to Democratic party dominance from 1966 through 1982 cannot be stressed enough. The GOP victory in a U.S. Senate race in 1980 contained features that set it apart from the dominant Georgia trend.

Throughout the post–World War II era and into the early 1970s, the

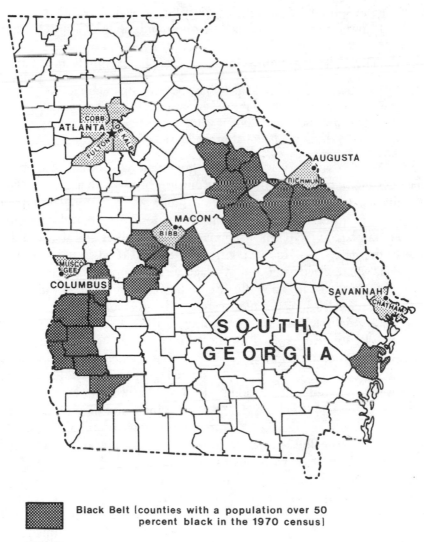

Black Belt (counties with a population over 50 percent black in the 1970 census)

Urban Counties

Map 7-1. Georgia's Black Belt and Seven Largest Urban Counties

Democratic primary witnessed recurring struggles between "rural, lowland, lower-status whites," on the one hand, and the North Georgia uplands, metropolitan Atlanta, blacks, and higher-status whites, on the other.[2] The Talmadge family forces in Georgia exemplify this pattern:

> [They] prospered in rural areas, ran best in rural counties in the southern half of the state, thrived in lower-status white precincts in the cities, lost the more affluent white precincts, and might as well have not been on the ballot at urban black polling places.[3]

Lester Maddox's victory in the 1966 gubernatorial primary was in the classic pattern of the Talmadges. Running third in that primary and missing the runoff was Jimmy Carter, then a state senator. His support in 1966 was quite different from Maddox's. Joseph L. Bernd wrote that Carter "ran best in 'dynamic Georgia' areas, the cities and the northern part of the state. . . . He ran poorly in the small rural counties of static Georgia, where Goldwater and Wallace were strongest."[4]

Against Maddox in 1966 the Republicans nominated Howard (Bo) Callaway, a U.S. representative elected on Goldwater's coattails. Callaway sought to win by combining race-conscious South Georgia and the Republican voters in the cities. While both Maddox and Callaway pursued the Goldwater voter, white liberals and blacks organized a write-in for Ellis Arnall, a former governor. The Republican Callaway barely outpolled Maddox, by a margin of 46.5 percent to 46.2 percent, with Arnall getting 7.3 percent. Under the Georgia constitution, if no candidate receives a simple majority of the votes, the legislature must choose the winner from the top two. The overwhelmingly Democratic legislature voted for Maddox.

In 1968 Sen. Herman E. Talmadge, seeking a third term, was opposed by a little-known Republican, E. Earl Patton, who received only 22.5 percent of the vote. According to the *Atlanta Constitution*, Patton's strategy was to concentrate on the large urban areas.[5] Talmadge, as always, ran well in South Georgia.

Wallace carried Georgia easily in the 1968 presidential election, winning 42.8 percent of the votes cast to Nixon's 30.4 percent and Humphrey's 26.7 percent. Roy V. Harris, a veteran Georgia political operator who ran Wallace's state campaign,[6] summed up the 1968 campaign this way: "When you get down to it, there's . . . only one issue, and you spell it n-i-g-g-e-r."[7]

In October 1968, amid much publicity, five Democratic state constitutional officers switched to the Republican party; they were the state comptroller general, the commissioner of agriculture, two members of the Public Service Commission, and the state treasurer.[8] The comptroller general, Jimmy L. Bentley, Jr., an associate of Senator Talmadge, made the switch with the intention of running for governor in 1970 as the Republican nominee.[9] Perhaps in Bentley the GOP could have found a candidate able to put together a coalition of Republican urban well-to-do voters and South Georgia rural whites, the coalition that won the state for Goldwater. With the exception of Callaway, however, the switch by Bentley and the other four was not greeted with enthusiasm by the state's Republican party leadership. Bentley, who characterized his reception as sickening, assessed his new party during an interview several years after the switch:

> The Republicans in this state . . . keep themselves restricted to small groups and small pockets. They're far more interested in internal Republican politics than in external Republican politics. I didn't give a damn who the state chairman of the Republican party was . . . . I wanted to see a hundred Republicans in the state legislature. . . . I wanted to see a [Republican] governor and a lieutenant governor and some Republican State House offices. . . .
>
> The Republicans just couldn't see that. They never could grasp that vision. . . . I told them they'd either take over the state government in 1970 or they'd lose it for twenty years . . . .[10]

In 1970 the Georgia Republicans held their first statewide primary, which drew few nonurban voters. And Bentley was soundly defeated for the gubernatorial nomination by Hal Suit, an Atlanta television newsman little known outside of the Atlanta area.[11]

On the Democratic side in 1970 a shrewd electoral manipulator rose to prominence, and in his maneuvers lies another part of the answer to the Democrats' ability to defeat the GOP challenge in Georgia. Jimmy Carter, a Sumter County farmer and businessman, faced former Gov. Carl Sanders in the Democratic runoff for the gubernatorial nomination in 1970. Sanders was closely identified with the Atlanta-centered, upper-income white and black faction of the Georgia Democratic party—that is, the anti-Talmadge, anti-Maddox forces, the same groups Carter had sought to rally in 1966. In this election Carter positioned himself quite differently. A newspaper account contended that Carter "ran a populist-type campaign [in which he] said he wanted the votes of the supporters of George Wallace as well as those of poor blacks."[12] It was a novel approach for Georgia and received its share of cynical rebukes. On the race issue Numan V. Bartley and Hugh D. Graham wrote, "Although eschewing outright race-baiting, Carter struck hard at busing, identified himself with the Maddox administration . . . and promised to invite George Wallace to visit Georgia."[13]

After Carter defeated Sanders in the runoff 59.4 percent to 40.6

percent, Carter's press spokesman was quoted in the *Atlanta Constitution* as hailing "the victor's high vote as a sign that 'we have brought the Wallace people back into the fold and made them feel they can now be a part of the state Democratic Party.' "[14] Wallace's 1968 presidential pattern in Georgia and Carter's 1970 runoff pattern showed a significant similarity.[15] Charles Kirbo, a close friend of Carter's, commented on this strategy during a 1974 interview, when Kirbo was the Georgia Democratic party chairman:

> Jimmy can and does appeal to the Wallace voter, but not on the racial thing. Wallace has got a lot of support from people . . . [who] are just down on the government. And he's got a lot of populist support. Jimmy is a populist.[16]

During the runoff campaign

> Carter labeled Sanders "Cufflinks Carl" and portrayed himself as the common-man candidate. One of Carter's more effective television commercials pictured the door to a country club and contained a message that began: "This is the door to an exclusive country club, where the big-money boys play cards, drink cocktails and raise money for their candidate: Carl Sanders. People like *us* aren't invited. We're busy working for a living. That's why our votes are going for Jimmy Carter. . . ."[17]

Sanders's view of Carter and the campaign, given at length in a 1974 interview, depicts the major transformation Carter made from candidate to governor and adds further insight into this important 1970 runoff:

> Jimmy Carter very deliberately and very insidiously, I might add, over a period of three or four years, went around the state and totally misrepresented himself and his political philosophy, as a conservative, George Wallace–type conservative. Of course, conservatism in 1970 in this state was growing rampant. He bottled up what I would call, for lack of better description, an attractive bottle of political snake oil. And he sold that snake oil far and wide. He also, as part of his what you might call deceitful type of campaign, he sold also the theory that there I was, the big corporate lawyer, and here he was, the little peanut farmer. And since I had left office and I had been very successful, and that the reason I had been successful was because while I was governor of Georgia . . . I had done a lot of favors for a lot of people. Now they were my friends, my clients. All that kind of horse manure. And he went around and gave that song and dance far and wide, north, south, east, west.
>
> Of course, the reason he's had such a disastrous time [as governor], just four years, is that the day he made his inaugural speech, he completely changed the color that he had been flying under in

the campaign. And I'd say . . . that he probably had four years of the most personally discredited type of administration that's ever been in Georgia, for simply the reason that nobody in the state—with the exception of a small, marked corps of loyal people who you always have around the governor's office—nobody in this state, I think, would tell you that he really carried out what he campaigned for. He did just the opposite. He's totally distrusted. Maybe some very liberal people have been pleasantly surprised, because based on his campaign, they would have been inclined to think totally otherwise. But the moderates and the conservatives of the state don't believe him.[18]

After acquiring the Democratic nomination, the coalition builder Carter added substantial urban black support to his solid support in rural regions and small towns and among the urban working classes[19] to defeat the Republican Suit in the November 1970 general election, by a margin of 59.3 percent to 40.6 percent. As governor, Carter made a serious effort to bring blacks into state government and, in general, to fulfill his inaugural assertion that "the time of racial discrimination is over."[20]

Carter may be criticized, as Sanders and others have done, for not turning out to be another Maddox, but in looking at the ascendancy of the Democratic party in Georgia in the 1970s and early 1980s, one cannot ignore the importance of black voters for Democratic success. It was Carter who first brought Wallace voters together with blacks, and he did it early. There is no question that the Democrats would have lost the 1972 general election to fill the seat of the late Sen. Richard B. Russell had blacks not voted overwhelmingly for the Democratic nominee, although they had little reason to do so. Furthermore, from 1972 through 1978 no statewide Republican candidate received more than 30 percent of the vote against this formidable coalition. Although others after Carter deserve the credit for holding the coalition together, he first forged it in 1970. Somewhat ruefully, the Republican state chairman, Robert Shaw, acknowledged the difficulty this coalition created for his party:

> So what catches us is that you find the conservative rural vote going in voting the straight party ticket, and by the same token you find the urban blacks voting the straight party ticket. And they'd be considered a liberal element, with the South Georgia farmer voting conservative. And yet they're voting hand in hand, and when they do, they're squeezing the lives out of us. And yet there's no tie-in between the two at all. Ideologically, they're as far apart as night and day.[21]

In 1972 Sam Nunn, a thirty-four-year-old lawyer, rallied the traditional Talmadge-Maddox rural forces to win the Democratic Senate nomination. His general-election opponent, Congressman Fletcher M. Thompson,

> seized the busing issue, addressing rallies . . . to ban the use of buses to achieve integration. During the senatorial campaign, Thompson sometimes seemed to be running less against his Democratic opponent . . . than against school buses, McGovern, and actress Jane Fonda and former Attorney General Ramsey Clark, both of whom had visited North Vietnam and who, according to Thompson, should be charged with treason. Visits by President Nixon, Vice-President Agnew, Senator Goldwater, and others evidenced the concern of national Republican leaders for Thompson's campaign.[22]

Faced with this formidable GOP opposition, Nunn sought support from a neighbor to the west. David S. Broder described the Democratic nominee's course of action:

> [Nunn] flew to Alabama in mid-campaign to receive Wallace's endorsement, and publicly condemned Carter for refusing to nominate Wallace for President at the Democratic convention. "George Wallace represents the real views of Georgians," Nunn said. He echoed Wallace's rhetoric in his attacks on "judicial tyranny," his denunciation of school-busing orders and his calls for referendum elections on federal judges every six years. The crypto-Wallace campaign was enough to counter Thompson's effort to alarm whites with charges that Nunn would receive the black "bloc vote."[23]

Nunn won with 54.0 percent. Despite his alliance with Wallace, Nunn received overwhelming support from blacks, who opted for the candidate carrying the Democratic label as the lesser of two evils.[24] Precinct data reveal that Nunn received about 90 percent of the votes of blacks in Atlanta and Macon.[25]

Lester Maddox, who had been elected lieutenant governor in 1970, when he was ineligible to succeed himself as governor, placed first in the initial Democratic gubernatorial primary in 1974. George Busbee, a Georgia House veteran of eighteen years, defeated Bert Lance, a North Georgia banker and a Carter ally, to gain the runoff spot against Maddox. Howell Raines, political editor of the *Atlanta Constitution*, wrote, "Busbee, taking a gamble, managed to appeal to the black voter directly while holding on to white votes in conservative central and south Georgia."[26] Winning overwhelmingly in the urban counties and splitting the others, Busbee defeated Maddox by 59.9 percent to 40.1 percent in the runoff. Dave Nordan, former political editor of the *Atlanta Journal*, noted that, in appealing to blacks, "Busbee knew he would pick up more black votes than he would lose in white votes."[27] In the general election Ronnie Thompson, the mayor of Macon, received only 30.9 percent of the vote against Busbee. Talmadge also won easy re-election in 1974, with 71.7 percent over the Republican Jerry Johnson's 28.2 percent.[28]

The pattern for Democratic success was established by the second half of the 1970s,[29] and the 1978 elections brought no surprises. Because of a change in the state constitution, Busbee was eligible to seek a second term in 1978. Rodney M. Cook, the Republican party state chairman, received only 19.3 percent of the vote[30] against the incumbent governor. Senator Nunn was re-elected over the Republican John W. Stokes, who received 16.9 percent. What chance the race issue had given the Republicans in the crucial years after the Goldwater sweep had vanished. By 1978 the major electoral contests in Georgia were again being fought out in the Democratic primary.

If the above sketch of Georgia two-party politics is correct, how then does one account for the 1980 victory of the Republican Mack Mattingly over Senator Talmadge? The answer lies in the peculiar circumstances of this multifaceted campaign.

Senator Talmadge's personal problems—which one writer concisely described as "a public bout with alcoholism, a sensational divorce, and a damaging Senate probe of his personal and official finances"[31]— brought out a large field of challengers in the August Democratic primary. Despite his personal liabilities, Talmadge managed to lead the field but failed to win the nomination outright. In the runoff three weeks later, he faced Lt. Gov. Zell Miller, a seasoned politician who had a moderate-to-liberal image and who actively sought the support of blacks, the one-time targets of legendary Talmadge race baiting. The *Atlanta Constitution* aptly described Miller's effort to ally himself as closely as he could to Governor Busbee's winning position on the political spectrum:

> The night of the first primary vote, when reporters began asking anew whether the lieutenant governor wasn't risking a white backlash with all of his high profile black support, Miller noted that Julian Bond [a prominent black politician and state legislator who supported Miller] had campaigned for George Busbee in 1974 and he [Bond] was more controversial then than he is now.
>
> And when he was asked whether his plain-spoken advocacy of increased welfare benefits might not ruffle feathers in rural Georgia and the conservative suburbs, Miller said the welfare package he backed was written into the state budget by none other than George Busbee.

If wrapping himself in the reasonableness of Busbeeism wasn't enough, Miller fielded Talmadge's "big labor" charge by pointing out that Talmadge has some "big labor" boys in his corner too.[32]

Talmadge's strategy was to portray Miller as a free-spending liberal who favored big-government solutions to all problems. The *Atlanta Journal* concluded after television debates between the two men that the veteran senator had some success in depicting Miller as, among other things, a proponent of comprehensive national health insurance, increased federal aid to education, and nationalization of the welfare system.[33]

Black leaders, such as Mayor Maynard Jackson of Atlanta, played an active role on Miller's behalf. During the runoff Jackson told blacks that a vote for Talmadge, a former segregationist, was the moral equivalent of "spitting on the grave of Martin Luther King, Jr."[34] Miller's highly visible black support coupled with Talmadge's attempt to brand Miller as, in the words of the *Washington Post*, "a Kennedyesque liberal with deficit spending dreams,"[35] added a strong racial overtone to the runoff.[36]

Talmadge defeated Miller by 58.6 percent of the vote to 41.4 percent, with huge margins in the rural, small-town counties of South Georgia. Miller, who carried only a dozen counties, won in the populous Atlanta area, carrying Fulton and De Kalb counties. The failure of Miller's "highly touted coalition of blacks, teachers, and union members,"[37] moved the loser to assert, "[H]istory will prove us right. . . . Some have the job of planting seeds, while others reap that harvest."[38]

With the Democratic nomination secure, Talmadge's attention shifted to the Republican nominee, Mattingly, a former state GOP chairman and a businessman who had moved to Georgia from Indiana in 1951. A *Congressional Quarterly* pre-election report rated Mattingly's chances as slim, adding that he had the image of "a quintessential 'country club' Republican."[39] The Mattingly strategy was linked to the troubles of the Democrats, as an *Atlanta Journal* article revealed six months before the November balloting:

> They [Mattingly's backers] are banking on the Democrats' divisiveness costing them the election and they are hoping Talmadge will survive a runoff, probably with Lt. Gov. Zell Miller. If that happens, a key Mattingly strategist says, the anti-Talmadge vote would likely go to Mattingly.[40]

With the polls showing the general election tight, the incumbent, in the finest Talmadge tradition, branded his GOP challenger a carpetbagger:

> My opponent came down here from Indiana a number of years

ago. Now we're glad he came down here to settle. But he wasn't content with that. He got a hired gun from Washington, D.C., to serve as his campaign manager. Then he got an advertising man all the way down from Detroit.

The whole thing has been an invasion similar to Sherman's march to the sea. A long time ago, they were called carpetbaggers.[41]

Apparently by 1980 either the carpetbaggers had become a majority or Georgia's voters had decided that outside origins and contacts were no longer disqualifying features in state politics. At any rate, Mattingly's slim victory, by 50.9 percent of the vote to Talmadge's 49.1 percent, was one of the major upsets of the 1980 elections. Since President Carter carried his home state with 55.8 percent (a decline from his 1976 figure of 66.7 percent), there were no obvious Reagan coattails in Georgia.[42] Rather, Mattingly's victory was based on a strong showing in the state's cities, especially in the populous Atlanta area. Mattingly ran ahead of Reagan in the state's largest urban counties. For example, in the Atlanta metropolitan counties of De Kalb and Cobb, Mattingly led Reagan 69 percent to 45 percent and 71 percent to 54 percent, respectively.[43] In one sense urban, or "streetcar,"[44] Georgia finally got its revenge on the once powerful, rural-based Talmadge forces.

But the urban-rural aspect of this election ought not obscure what happened in 1980 to Georgia's winning post–civil rights era Democratic coalition. Mattingly was able to do what no Georgia Republican in the 1970s had managed to accomplish: he cut substantially into solid Democratic support among blacks, receiving over a third of the votes of Georgia's blacks.[45] After the general election, Mayor Jackson declared, "Talmadge's defeat demonstrates that Afro-American voters cannot any longer be taken for granted in Georgia—you cannot spit in our eye and tell us it's raining."[46]

This is no new phenomenon for the growth of Southern Republicanism. John Tower in Texas won his U.S. Senate seat in 1961 because of the disgust of liberal Democrats with the very conservative nominee of their party, and in Virginia in 1969 many black and white supporters of the liberal Democrat Henry Howell— who had been defeated in the primary—bolted to the Republican Linwood Holton to give the GOP its first statewide victory there. In 1978 Mississippi blacks abandoned the Democratic nominee for the Senate in favor of an independent, resulting in the first GOP statewide win in the Magnolia State.

The Mattingly victory, however, cannot be seen as heralding the arrival of strong statewide two-party competition in Georgia. The coalition that held the state for politicians like Busbee and Nunn was put to a severe test in 1980 with a peculiar campaign colored by the legacy of a deep rural-urban schism, the participation of a member of the state's most controversial political family, and a divisive primary that strained the ideologically diverse, black-white coalition that is the mainstay of the Georgia Democracy. The results of the 1982 gubernatorial election confirmed this interpretation of the Republican "breakthrough" of 1980.

Joe Frank Harris, an eighteen-year veteran of the Georgia House from Cartersville, in North Georgia, defeated U.S. Rep. Bo Ginn, the front-runner who represented the Savannah area in Congress, in the September 2 runoff, to win the 1982 Democratic gubernatorial nomination. Harris, a conservative, gained considerable publicity with his campaign pledge not to raise taxes, which was credited with earning him a runoff slot against the well-financed Ginn.[47] In the last weeks of the campaign, sensing Harris's surge, Ginn attacked Harris's close ties with Tom Murphy, the Georgia House speaker, contending Harris would be Murphy's pawn.[48]

The Republican gubernatorial nominee, State Sen. Bob Bell, a conservative from the Atlanta suburb Tucker, expanded on Ginn's criticism of Speaker Murphy:

> This is a campaign that puts the good, honest, decent people of Georgia against a corrupt, abusive, entrenched gang of politicians who are more interested in staying in power than they are in cleaning up our state.[49]

When pressed for specifics, Bell added:

> I never said Joe Frank Harris was corrupt, abusive or entrenched. I said there is a group of politicians that allow the corruption to exist. . . . You don't have to be a corrupt politician to be a part of a system that allows corrupt politicians to exist.[50]

A reporter asked Bell at the outset of the general-election campaign how he would differentiate himself from the other conservative—Harris—in the campaign. Bell responded by saying that Georgia's "paralyzed political system" cannot be changed by a Democratic insider. If Harris is elected, Bell contended, "it will mandate the status quo. . . . If I'm elected, it will be a mandate for the reform that I'm talking about. There's the basic difference."[51]

Harris stuck to his theme of a "common-sense government" with no tax increase.[52] Toward the end of the campaign, the most prominent "issue" was Harris's refusal to release a personal financial statement. Bell, who had issued such a statement, contended that his opponent had something to hide.[53] According to the *Atlanta Constitution*, the result of Bell's constant attacks on the state's Democratic power structure caused Democratic officials to close ranks behind Harris:

The Democratic Party poured thousands of dollars into a "get out the vote" campaign, while Harris joined hands with Democratic Lt. Gov. Zell Miller [who successfully sought re-election in 1982, after his 1980 primary loss to Talmadge] to run as a team.[54]

And a united Georgia Democracy was still hard for a suburban Atlanta Republican to beat. Harris won with 62.7 percent of the vote to Bell's 37.3 percent. A review of the returns showed:

Bell managed only a trickle of votes in the [South Georgia] Farm Belt, did poorly in the [Atlanta] metro fringe counties, and was losing in the smaller cities—Columbus, Savannah, Macon, and Augusta. He was left with only the [Atlanta] suburbs, and the suburbs were not nearly enough.[55]

Bo Ginn summed up the general election for the *Constitution:*

Georgia is still basically a conservative-to-moderate Democratic state. While Sen. Bell certainly put forward as good a campaign for the governorship as a Republican has, other than Bo Callaway, it's just simply a reality that Georgia is still . . . very much a Democratic state.[56]

Republicans could take some comfort, however, in Bell's losing performance. It was eighteen percentage points higher than the GOP gubernatorial showing four years earlier, which inspired the following assessment in an *Atlanta Constitution* editorial

Even in defeat, however, Republican Bob Bell may have made Georgia history. . . . [He] got the Democrats off their duffs and out working. . . .

[The Democrats] were running scared in the final hours of the contest, and that is good for Georgia. For it may mean that the Democratic Party can no longer take the Georgia voter for granted. The old saw, "winning the Democratic primary is tantamount to election," is at least weakened—forever, let's hope.[57]

Georgia—Conclusion

The Georgia experience with two-party development highlights both the early efforts of the challenging Republicans to exploit the race issue in the aftermath of the Goldwater candidacy and the skillful manner in which white Georgia Democrats, starting with Carter in 1970, fashioned a strong biracial coalition that regularly won healthy majorities— with one exception—in statewide races through 1982. The lessening of racial tensions after the national resolution of the issue of basic legal and political rights for blacks contributed significantly to this Democratic success.

Irony abounded in the Georgia situation. The efforts of national Democrats on behalf of civil rights solidified black support for the white Georgia Democratic nominees who faced general-election challenges from Republicans hoping to ride the white backlash into office. But with the reduction of racial tensions many of those white voters—a number of them residing in South Georgia—who had been lured away from the Democrats because of the race issue returned to their traditional Democratic allegiance. Shrewd Democratic candidates, such as Carter and Busbee, brought them back with campaigns that often straddled racial issues long enough for the votes to be counted. (Little evidence of the exploitation of economic-class issues by Georgia Democrats was found.) No wonder the state Republican chairman observed that this seemingly awkward biracial Democratic coalition in Georgia, which he called ideologically "as far apart as night and day," had sapped the once-bright potential of the GOP in Georgia.

8

Louisiana:
Sui Generis like Huey

When Louisiana's most famous politician, Huey P. Long, was pressed once to explain his singular political style, he responded, "Oh, hell, say that I'm *sui generis* and let it go at that."[1] No more appropriate characterization can be found for his state's recent experience with two-party politics. While the same regional trends observed elsewhere were also at work in this Deep South state, the result in partisan terms often deviated so far from the norm as to approach the unique. And as if to seal itself off for good, Louisiana in the mid-1970s adopted an electoral law that abolished separate party primaries, adding substantially to the state's partisan air of difference. Yet despite the peculiarities, common ground with the rest of the region could be spotted from time to time.

The legacy of a centuries-old migration contributed more than a little to the state's distinctive status. When French Catholics were forced to leave Acadia (Nova Scotia, Canada) in the 1750s, they settled in the southern part of Louisiana, known today as Acadiana. The impact their descendants, the Cajuns, had on political life was described by the newspaperman Tom Sancton, as related by the critic A. J. Liebling:

> [Louisiana is] the most complex state in the South. In just about every one of the others you have the same battle between the poor-to-middling farmers on the poor lands—generally in the hills—that didn't justify an investment in slaves before the war, and the descendants of the rich planters on the rich lands, who held slaves by the dozen to the gross. . . . We had that same conflict, but in addition,

we have a lot that are all our own. In other states it was just between
the poor Anglo-Saxon Protestant whites and the rich Anglo-Saxon
Protestant whites. But here we got poor French Catholic whites and
poor Anglo-Saxon whites and rich French Catholic whites. Sometimes the Catholic French got together against the Anglo-Saxon
Protestants and sometimes the rich of both faiths got together against
the poor, or the poor against the rich.[2]

Huey Long, the "flamboyant advocate of the subversive doctrine of
'Every Man A King,' "[3] left a legacy as well: a strong bifactional one-
party system in which the Longs and the anti-Longs did battle for nearly
three decades after Huey's assassination in 1935. V. O. Key, Jr., wrote,
"Louisiana factionalism more nearly approaches the organizational realities of a two-party system than that of any other southern state."[4] By
the early 1960s, however, this Democratic bifactionalism had dissolved
into a bevy of multifactional and personality splits.[5] Even the Longs
were found in competing camps.[6]

It was at this point that the Republican challengers first made a
serious entry into the "festival in a labyrinth," as Louisiana politics has
been appropriately dubbed.[7] An examination of Louisiana presidential-
voting patterns offers initial guidance to the state's path of two-party
development. Kennedy's Catholicism aided the 1960 Democratic standard-bearer in carrying Louisiana with 50.4 percent of the vote; his
strongest support came from South Louisiana's heavily Catholic parishes. Also in the 1960 balloting Nixon received 28.6 percent, and a
States' Rights slate finished third, with 21.0 percent.[8]

In 1964 Goldwater won the state with 58.6 percent of the vote to
Johnson's 43.2 percent. However, there was no abrupt break in the
parish-level pattern.[9] When Goldwater's opposition to the Civil Rights
Act of that year drew to him hard-core segregationists throughout the
Deep South, the Catholic parishes, with their heritage of racial
moderation,[10] remained with the Democratic nominee, President Johnson. In predominantly Protestant North Louisiana the Democratic
nominees were weak in 1960 and 1964.[11]

By 1968 even the Louisiana areas of staunchest Democratic strength
had succumbed to the racial turmoil. The state gave its electoral votes to
Wallace, who received 48.3 percent; Humphrey was a distant second
with 28.2 percent, followed by Nixon at 23.5 percent.[12] While Humphrey did slightly better in South than in North Louisiana, the Democratic nominee's strongest parishes were those that contained the highest
percentage of blacks. This racial polarization of the Louisiana electorate
persisted in 1972.[13] Thirteen of the sixteen parishes with the highest percentage of blacks were among McGovern's top sixteen parishes.

Except for the extra strength that Kennedy found among Louisiana's Catholics, the presidential results were not unlike those in the other Deep South states. The Democratic presidential trend line in Figure 8-1 substantiates this observation when compared with presidential trends in the other states. However, the Democratic-party-strength trend line in Figure 8-1 behaves strangely compared with party-strength trend lines pictured in the other state chapters.[14] Likewise, an overview of Republican statewide challenges reveals no logical, steady pattern of growth. Rather, one finds a weak minority party battling against great odds and being content to benefit from whatever sources came along.

In the March 1964 gubernatorial general election, the Republican party ran a wealthy sixty-nine-year-old oil company owner, Charlton H. Lyons, hoping to take advantage of the divisive first and second Democratic primaries of the preceding December and January.[15] Lyons, an admirer of Barry Goldwater, conducted a vigorous campaign, inviting the neighboring Republican segregationists Rubel Phillips of Mississippi and James Martin of Alabama to campaign for him. Perry H. Howard wrote that Lyons also

> brought in the Hollywood charmer Ronald Reagan for a three day political road show for Louisiana audiences. Like the fabled "Hadacol" medicine salesman of days past, Reagan was involved in entertaining and selling. His "medicine" was prescribed for the cure of a disease he called "Fabian socialism" or sometimes in layman's language "liberal welfare philosophy."[16]

The unprecedented GOP effort did not appear to unnecessarily concern the Democratic gubernatorial nominee, John J. McKeithen, who had survived two difficult primary battles and earned "a reputation as a 'street fighter' with deadly aim for the political jugular of opponents."[17] McKeithen treated Lyons gingerly, referring to the GOP nominee as "my honorable elderly opponent."[18] But McKeithen saw to it that the segregationist Lyons could not get to his right on the race issue; he proclaimed himself, for example, a "one-hundred percent segregationist" but not a "hater."[19]

McKeithen's victory, with 60.7 percent of the vote, exhibited virtually no parish-level relationship with the patterns of his party's presidential nominees in 1960 and 1964.[20] Lyons's 38.5 percent, while not dismal, was not of a magnitude to encourage a host of imitators. Eight years passed before the Louisiana GOP mounted another statewide challenge. Figure 8-1 reveals that Democratic party strength, after having dipped nearly twenty percentage points, to 73 percent, during the six years from 1958 to 1964, shot up to 93 percent in 1968, the highest level in the South that year.

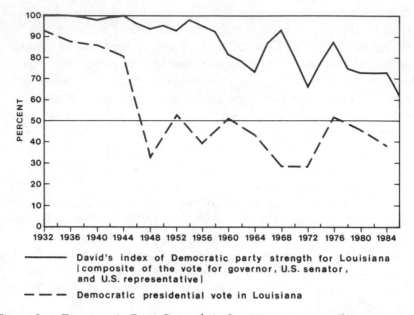

David's index of Democratic party strength for Louisiana
(composite of the vote for governor, U.S. senator,
and U.S. representative)

— — — Democratic presidential vote in Louisiana

Figure 8-1. Democratic Party Strength in Louisiana, 1932–1986

The 1971–72 gubernatorial election witnessed the emergence of two politicians of opposite parties who were to figure prominently in every gubernatorial race from that one through the 1983 elections: Edwin W. Edwards, a French-speaking Democratic congressman from Crowley, in South Louisiana, and David C. Treen, a suburban New Orleans conservative Republican who had been active in the 1960 States' Rights presidential electoral slate effort. To win the Democratic nomination in the December 1971 Democratic runoff, Edwards narrowly defeated State Sen. J. Bennett Johnston of Shreveport, in North Louisiana. Treen, the GOP nominee who had earlier run unsuccessfully for Congress, based his 1972 gubernatorial campaign on his outspoken conservative beliefs, "assaulting the federal Medicare program, attacking organized labor, and generally upholding an uncompromising social, economic, and philosophical conservatism."[21] Edwards, a witty and charismatic campaigner, built on his South Louisiana base by appealing to black voters.[22] Newspaper accounts of the campaign reported that Edwards projected a moderate-to-liberal image.

Edwards won, with 57.2 percent of the vote to Treen's 42.8 percent. An examination of the results, at both the parish and the precinct levels, reveals the strength of Cajun and black power, to use the phrasing of Charles E. Grenier and Perry H. Howard.[23] In a 1973 interview Edwards emphasized that he was the first governor of Cajun descent elected in the

The 27 parishes giving Edwards
his strongest support in 1972

[The 27 parishes below the solid line contained the highest
proportion of Louisiana's Catholics in the 1970 census]

Map 8-1. Edwards's Strength in Louisiana's Catholic Parishes in the 1972 Gubernatorial General Election

twentieth century, adding, "I was elected by a coalition of blacks, farmers, people from South Louisiana of French Cajun descent."[24] Map 8-1 demonstrates that Edwards's strongest parishes were indeed in Acadiana; the three parishes outside of the predominantly Catholic region were those with heavy black populations. Precinct data presented in Table 8-1 indicate that there was a mild class cleavage in the cities of New Orleans, Baton Rouge, and Shreveport, where lower-status whites were more likely to vote for Edwards than for Treen. Blacks in all three cities were overwhelmingly for the Democrat. Concerning his solid black support, Edwards said, "I was making overtures and had a record as a city councilman, state senator, and member of Congress [as one] who showed a

Table 8-1. Louisiana Gubernatorial Vote in 1972 by Class and Race in New
Orleans, Baton Rouge, and Shreveport

	Lower Income	Middle Income (Whites)	Upper Income	Blacks
New Orleans				
Edwards	51%	40%	35%	91%
Treen	49	60	65	9
Baton Rouge				
Edwards	45%	36%	23%	97%
Treen	55	64	77	3
Shreveport				
Edwards	30%	22%	18%	96%
Treen	70	78	82	4

SOURCE: Numan V. Bartley and Hugh D. Graham, *Southern Elections: County and Precinct Data, 1950–1972* (Baton Rouge: Louisiana State Univ. Press, 1978), 368–71.

willingness to accommodate black needs, which in most instances were the same as the needs of the poor whites."[25]

There were three significant side items flowing directly from the 1971–72 gubernatorial election. First, six months after his gubernatorial loss, Treen won a seat in Congress in the November 1972 general elections, becoming Louisiana's first Republican member of the U.S. House in modern times. He was re-elected to Congress three times and in 1979 became the Republican party's "representative" in the gubernatorial election of that year. Second, after his defeat in the Democratic gubernatorial runoff, Bennett Johnston filed in the Democratic primary against Sen. Allen Ellender and won the nomination by default when Ellender died shortly before the primary. Former Governor McKeithen[26] unsuccessfully challenged Johnston in the general election as an independent, receiving only 23.1 percent of the vote. Ben C. Toledano, a Republican, finished third, with slightly less than 20 percent.

The third, and most important, of the side items from the 1971–72 gubernatorial election was the impetus given to a major change in Louisiana's election laws: the establishment of an open-primary system that has done away with separate party primaries.* Edwards began push-

*Under the new law *all* candidates are listed on a single ballot along with party labels (or, if a candidate chooses, as an independent). If no candidate gets a simple majority, the top two candidates regardless of party affiliation compete in the general election, which for federal elections is held in November. For example, in the 1978 re-election effort of Sen. Bennett Johnston, no Republican filed for the open primary but Johnston had a Democratic challenger, State Rep. Louis (Woody) Jenkins. Because Johnston received a simple majority (59 percent) in the open primary, there was no "runoff" general election for U.S. senator in November.

ing for the new system as a gubernatorial candidate. He said the open primary

> would save this state about $2 million a year, and most of all we would get away from stirring up this bitterness and hatred which Republicans have been able to do after our primaries, sitting back as scavengers and waiting to move into the ranks of the losers and stirring up continued hatred among the disillusioned and the unhappy and disappointed people whose candidates didn't win in the Democratic primary.[27]

Or as Jack Bass and Walter DeVries wrote, "The new law, promoted by Edwards, was advocated on the basis of 'fairness': it wasn't fair for Democrats to fight through two politically bloody primaries and then face a fresh Republican opponent."[28]

Four years elapsed after the Edwards gubernatorial victory before Louisiana was provided with its next two-party contest—the 1976 presidential election. Carter narrowly carried the state, winning 51.7 percent of the vote. Election returns at the parish level indicate that the Catholic parishes remained strong for the Democratic nominee, as they had been for Edwards in 1972. Precinct data from New Orleans show that this election produced the strongest class cleavage of the presidential elections since 1960. Carter received 62 percent of the vote in lower-income white precincts, 44 percent in middle-income areas, and 21 percent in upper-income areas; among black voters he won 97 percent. The type of class cleavage that had begun in the nation with the New Deal realignment was thus plainly evident in New Orleans in 1976. A less pronounced form of class division had existed among whites in the presidential voting in New Orleans in 1960 and to a lesser extent in 1964; but for the Democratic nominees, under the pressure of racial considerations here, and elsewhere in the South, this cleavage disappeared in 1968 and 1972, as Table 3-2 revealed.

In Louisiana the obstacles to long-term GOP growth below the presidential level were, as in other Deep South states, the overwhelming support for Democrats among blacks, the long-time attachment of whites to the party at the state level, and the fact that many state Democratic candidates were at least as conservative as their Republican challengers. On this latter point, Victor Bussie, the veteran Louisiana labor leader, elaborated:

> Basically, Louisiana has been a Democratic party state for many years. Now we have, what I call, a Republican philosophy within the Democratic party. . . . We have an ultra-conservative group within the party. We have an ultra-liberal group, and then we have

people who travel fairly down the middle of the road. So, while we have one party, we have the whole philosophy involved in that party. It has been hard to get people to separate themselves from that. They still call themselves Democrats, but they will vote for people [who] would normally represent the Republican philosophy, or they would vote for candidates [who] normally represent the Democratic philosophy. The name Republican in the state has not caught on like it has in many states . . . .[29]

The chief Republican successes in Louisiana, until the unusual 1979 gubernatorial election, did not come at the state level or at the parish or legislative-district level; rather, they occurred in congressional races. Two years after Treen's election to the House, the Republican W. Henson Moore won the Baton Rouge–centered congressional seat. His 1974 victory followed a bitter Democratic primary struggle.[30] And in 1977 the Republican Robert L. Livingston, Jr., won a seat representing a district east of New Orleans. Livingston's special-election victory came after the Democrat elected in 1976 resigned, following his indictment for election fraud.[31]

From this middle level the Republican party hoped to expand in both directions. Congressman Livingston contended that most people in the state were fundamentally conservative. He added, "And they see three Republican congressmen doing a good job and saying things they believe in. The national trend of the Democratic party is liberal, increase government services. They don't like that."[32] Slowly the voters are going to come around to the GOP, Livingston said. "I don't say we'll dominate, but we'll continue to grow until we are on parity—30 percent registration in five or more years."[33]

Indeed, GOP registration[34] more than doubled from 1978 to 1983 (see Table 8-2). Until the open-primary system was adopted in 1975, Republicans had argued that minuscule GOP registration reflected the desire of potential Republican registrants to retain the right to participate in selecting local officials, who were nearly always determined by the outcome of the Democratic primary. For example, David Treen in 1974 said, "There was just no percentage in getting registered Republican because you don't vote in . . . what everybody considers to be the election [the Democratic primary]—I mean for your school board or for your sheriff or all your local officials. . . . So we didn't have any registered Republicans."[35] The adoption of the open-primary system invalidated that argument. Still at 9.1 percent registration in 1983, the Louisiana GOP has a long way to go.

Republicans candidly admit that their party is years away from being a strong competitive force in state politics. "If all things are equal, they'll

Table 8-2. Republican Party Registration in Louisiana, 1960–1983

	Total Registered	Republicans Registered	GOP Percentage
1960	1,151,449	10,871	.9%
1970	1,434,427	29,447	2.0
1972	1,784,828	46,787	2.8
1974	1,713,183	47,497	2.8
1976	1,863,487	70,380	3.8
1978	1,821,494	80,869	4.4
1980	1,997,214	149,605	7.5
1982	1,958,676	165,031	8.4
1983	2,135,771	195,136	9.1

SOURCE: Parish Report of Registered Voters, Louisiana Commissioner of Elections, Baton Rouge. The figures are for the quarter ending Dec. 31, except for the 1983 figures, which are for the quarter ending Sept. 21.

vote for the Democrat . . . it's ingrained to be a Democrat in Louisiana," said Jay Stone, a former executive director of the Louisiana Republican party.[36] Stone added that the main problem Louisiana Democrats have is their national party. "We try to hang the national Democratic label around their necks, when we can," he said.[37] Congressman Livingston pointed out that the broad spectrum of views represented in the Louisiana Democratic party left his forces with a difficult situation to break up. "Anyone who can hold that spectrum is not vulnerable to the so-called Republican threat," Livingston said.[38]

In the annals of recent Southern elections, there is none stranger than Louisiana's 1979 gubernatorial election. On its face it was a GOP breakthrough. Congressman Treen, the sole Republican[39] in a field with five Democrats, led the open primary—if barely, with 21.6 percent—and then narrowly defeated the Democrat who won the other runoff spot, Louis Lambert, the chairman of the state's Public Service Commission.

There were, however, some bizarre features in this first Republican statewide victory since Reconstruction that clouded its meaning in two-party terms. The four Democrats who failed to reach the runoff—Lt. Gov. James E. (Jimmy) Fitzmorris; E. L. (Bubba) Henry, Speaker of the Louisiana House; State Sen. Edgar (Sonny) Mouton; and Paul Hardy, Louisiana's secretary of state—all endorsed and campaigned for the Republican Treen, amid cries of traitor from state Democratic party officials.[40] The last of the four Democrats to come out for the GOP candidate, Fitzmorris, actually led Lambert in the preliminary open-primary count but lost second place by 1,989 votes in the official total, which put Lambert at 20.8 percent of the votes cast to Fitzmorris's 20.6 percent.[41] The Louisiana Supreme Court refused to order a new election as a result of Fitzmorris's allegations of voting irregularities. When Fitzmorris backed Treen, he made clear his belief that a spot on the general election ballot "was stolen from me, from my supporters and from the people of the state."[42] After the election all four Democrats accepted positions with Governor Treen's administration.[43]

Superimposed on this remarkable display of Democratic disunity was a rhetorical battle between Treen and Lambert that had all the markings of a classic American two-party ideological struggle, with echoes of the Treen-Edwards contest of 1972. Lambert, who as PSC chairman regularly fought utility-rate increases, accused Treen, in the words of one writer, of "being a heartless conservative, voting in Congress against the interests of the sick, elderly and working people."[44] The New Orleans *Times-Picayune* said, "Treen emphasized fiscal responsibility . . . [and] election integrity."[45] The newspaper added:

> Treen ran with the backing of the state's business establishment and the major newspapers. Lambert had the backing of organized labor and black organizations. . . .
> Lambert stumped the state in the final weeks of the election attempting to paint Treen as an "ivory tower" Republican and himself as a populist concerned with the poor and working people.[46]

Governor Edwards endorsed Lambert, telling one audience that "if you like what you've had, this [Lambert's candidacy] is your best bet for it to continue."[47]

Treen vigorously rebutted Lambert's attempt to portray him as an uncaring conservative ideologue. The Baton Rouge *Morning Advocate* reported:

> Treen claimed Lambert's forces are spreading rumors that he's not for supplemental pay for firemen and policemen. "I say certainly I'm going to protect supplemental pay," Treen said, adding he is sending out letters to firemen and policemen emphasizing his stand.
> He also said Lambert is claiming that he is against homestead exemptions, while that is untrue. "I'm for increases in supplementary pay and teacher pay—to catch up with inflation."[48]

Treen called Lambert's statements distortions; two of his newly found Democratic allies were less circumspect. Secretary of State Hardy labeled Treen's Democratic opponent "lying Louie," and House Speaker Henry declared at an Alexandria rally, "If you like Spiro Agnew, you'll love Louis Lambert."[49]

Given the unusual nature of this campaign,[50] Treen's narrow victory with 50.3 percent of the vote to Lambert's 49.7 percent was open to different interpretations. George Despot, the state GOP chairman, said after the December 1979 balloting, "The growth of the Republican Party is a natural evolution that has been accelerated by Republican leadership. What we have in Louisiana is a directional flow to a two-party government. You can't hold the tide down."[51] Jesse Bankston, the Louisiana Democratic party chairman, observed, "We were beaten not by Republicans. We were beaten by disgruntled Democrats."[52] A perusal of the voting returns suggests as well a role for friends-and-neighbors voting:[53] Treen carried his populous New Orleans area home parish of Jefferson with 83,099 votes to Lambert's 46,047, a difference that was nearly four times larger than Treen's statewide victory margin of 9,557 votes. At any rate, Treen's victory, whatever the reasons for it, was certainly a major boost for the Louisiana Republican party.

Ronald Reagan carried Louisiana with 51.2 percent of the vote in 1980 to President Carter's 45.7 percent, but that election year also again pointed to the GOP's lack of depth in the state. No Republican challenged Sen. Russell B. Long, the veteran Democrat and son of Huey Long, who won re-election over a determined Democratic gadfly, State Rep. Louis (Woody) Jenkins.[54] Nor was a Republican on the ballot in 1978 when Senator Johnston won re-election in the open primary over the Democrat Jenkins's first attempt to go to the U.S. Senate. And when Treen resigned his seat in Congress prior to his gubernatorial inauguration, he was replaced by a Democrat, W. J. (Billy) Tauzin, in a special election, leaving Livingston and Moore the only Republicans in Louisiana's eight-member U.S. House delegation.

In 1983 Governor Treen was soundly defeated for re-election by former Governor Edwards, who captured 61.9 percent of the votes to the Republican incumbent's 36.8 percent.[55] Popular and well financed, Edwards had been preparing for the race almost from the day he left office. Since both candidates had extensive public records, they conducted a vigorous series of public debates, which focused on a variety of public-policy issues.[56] The policy questions frequently became tied, however, to personal issues, as is illustrated in this report by the *Morning Advocate*'s John LaPlante of a televised Treen-Edwards debate:

> Lively discussion of the issues—particularly crime, the environment, spending and taxes, education and integrity—was sprinkled with increasingly pointed personal attacks.
> Gov. Treen continued to stress integrity, repeatedly calling former Gov. Edwin Edwards a liar and accusing him of promoting "a government that uses taxpayers' money to try to help out friends."
> "Dave Treen will never do anything to make you ashamed of the governor of Louisiana," he said in his closing statement. . . .
> Edwards again stressed what he called Treen's ineptitude, compar-

ing it to his own reputation for getting things done. At one point he
described Treen as "having a lack of anything between your ears."
"We need to go back to the era of excellence which we had in the
1970s," Edwards said.[57]

During the campaign Treen made a strong attempt to attract black
voters, arguing, for example, that he had appointed more blacks to state
boards and commissions in his single term than Edwards did in two
terms.[58] His efforts won him the backing of several black groups and
their leaders.[59] Edwards countered by distributing literature reminding
blacks that Treen was "a member of the States' Rights Party which was
associated with racial segregation in the late 1950s and early 1960s."[60]
On Election Day, Treen's efforts to break into the solidly Democratic
voting patterns of blacks went nowhere. After the balloting, George
Despot, the GOP chairman, conceded that Treen's black support was
practically nonexistent,[61] adding, "When almost all the black vote goes
to one candidate, it is necessary to get around 67 percent of the white
vote to win."[62]

Assessments of the significance of Treen's defeat for the future of
Louisiana partisan politics were immediately forthcoming from political leaders. Jesse Bankston, the Democratic party chairman, said, "I
think we will always have a Republican Party of strength . . . even
though they got a tremendous defeat in terms of a complete repudiation of their kind of administration. . . . I hope there's always some
place for the reactionaries." "I don't think anybody expected Treen to
win," commented Congressman Moore. "I think David started out as an
underdog from the beginning [because he faced] the most accomplished
politician this state has seen since Huey Long," Moore added. Despot
said the Republican party's base "is very well-established. . . . We're
optimistic about our prospects for growth over the next 10 or 12 years."[63]
Congressman Livingston also looked to the future:

> We loved and worked for Dave Treen . . . [but] he is just one
> man out of thousands.
> He brought us to the forefront of being a two-party state and we
> will always be a two-party state. It is up to the rest of us to pick up
> the pieces.[64]

Louisiana—Conclusion

Of all the Southern states Louisiana had the fewest seriously contested
two-party elections during the period under scrutiny. After contesting

the initial elections of both Governor McKeithen in 1964 and Governor Edwards in 1972, the GOP failed to oppose the re-election efforts of these Democrats. Rarely were the U.S. Senate seats challenged by Republicans.

The 1972 Edwards-Treen election suggests that the biracial coalition assembled by Democrats elsewhere in the South provided the edge that year in Louisiana as well, and this interpretation was confirmed in the 1983 Edwards-Treen rematch. However, cleavages unique to the state, especially the Catholic-Protestant split, contributed to the electoral configuration that emerged in Louisiana in the post–civil rights era. A mild form of economic-class voting was also detectable in several elections.

The only statewide victory for the GOP came with Treen's election to the governorship in 1979, but the peculiar nature of that campaign obscured its partisan significance. And Treen's weak showing in 1983 highlighted the singular nature of that first Republican breakthrough. A more complete assessment of two-party development in Louisiana must await a period of more vigorous and sustained GOP challenges.

9

Arkansas: Roller-Coaster Style Partisan Change

Arkansas's experience with two-party politics over the last two decades divides distinctly into three phases. First, there was the atypical Southern Republican coalition put together by Winthrop Rockefeller in the middle to late 1960s, which included strong black support and which had vanished by the early 1970s. Next, starting with Rockefeller's defeat in 1970, attractive, skillful moderate Democratic leaders capitalized on strong white-voter allegiance to the Democratic party coupled with black support, which became solidly Democratic in the post-Rockefeller era, to reduce statewide Republican challenges from 1972 through 1978 to no more than nominal contests.

In the 1980 elections, gaining impetus from the national GOP tide as well as from a peculiar local situation, Arkansas Republicans captured the governorship. Two years later, when both national and local circumstances were less favorable to the GOP, the Democrats regained the governorship. This third period of partisan competition, however, contained features that could lead to a longer period of serious two-party competition than was witnessed in the two earlier phases.. The Democratic-party-strength trend line in Figure 9-1—which after the early 1960s resembles the path of a roller coaster—illustrates these three phases of partisan development.

Orval Faubus's domination of Arkansas Democratic politics, enhanced by the Little Rock school desegregation confrontation of 1957, continued until Faubus's first retirement in 1966. That year the Demo-

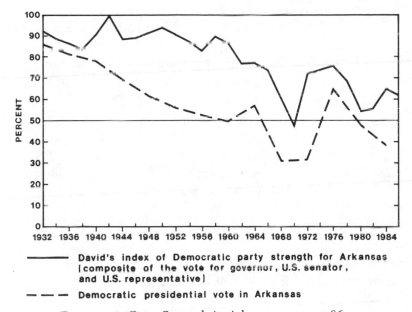

PERCENT

1932 1936 1940 1944 1948 1952 1956 1960 1964 1968 1972 1976 1980 1984

———— David's index of Democratic party strength for Arkansas (composite of the vote for governor, U.S. senator, and U.S. representative)

— — — Democratic presidential vote in Arkansas

Figure 9-1. Democratic Party Strength in Arkansas, 1932–1986

cratic primary produced another segregationist gubernatorial nominee, James D. Johnson, a former president of the Arkansas citizens' councils. Two years later[1] the party's nominee was also a man in the Faubus mold—Marion Crank, a former speaker of the Arkansas House of Representatives.

Both Johnson and Crank lost to Winthrop Rockefeller, the Republican nominee, who had first run for governor in 1964, when he lost to Faubus.[2] Rockefeller, an heir to the John D. Rockefeller fortune, had come to the state in the 1950s and invested a considerable amount of his money in promoting both his candidacy and the state's Republican party.[3] Rockefeller, however, differed from most of his fellow Southern Republicans. He was an integrationist who openly appealed to black voters and received their support.[4] In 1966 he defeated Johnson for the governorship with 54.4 percent of the votes cast; in 1968 he was re-elected over Crank with 52.4 percent.[5]

In the 1968 presidential election[6] Faubus and Johnson worked for Wallace,[7] who carried the state. According to the *Arkansas Gazette*, Crank, the Democratic gubernatorial nominee, "judiciously has avoided aligning himself with Humphrey at all. He will vote for him because of the Democratic label, Crank says without enthusiasm."[8]

While Crank attacked Rockefeller's "fiscal irresponsibility and promised to cut the fat in state government,"[9] Rockefeller told campaign audiences that a vote for Crank would return the state to Faubus-style machine rule.[10] The Republican's victory pattern in 1968 was similar to his 1966 support.[11]

Charles Bernard, the GOP nominee who faced Sen. J. William Fulbright in 1968, could not repeat Rockefeller's winning pattern. The *Arkansas Gazette* said Bernard's campaign speeches offered

> mostly traditional Republican fare calling for fiscal responsibility and a tougher foreign policy. Somewhat surprisingly for an East Arkansas planter, Bernard also says that America can't afford second-class citizenship and that he would have voted for civil rights bills that Fulbright voted against.
>
> Fulbright is not especially popular with Negroes and Bernard might pick up some votes there, considering that Governor Rockefeller . . . is highly popular with Negroes.[12]

Fulbright won with 59.2 percent of the vote.[13] Jim Ranchino, an Arkansas electoral analyst, found that, while 90 percent of the blacks voted for Rockefeller, only 30 percent supported Bernard.[14]

Rockefeller's strongest support came from both the traditionally Republican northwest hill country[15] and the heavily black eastern delta counties along the Mississippi River. Map 9-1 locates the counties with high proportions of blacks and also shows the persistence of GOP voting in the northwestern hill counties. In Little Rock, the capital and the largest city in the state, Rockefeller received 81 percent of the votes of blacks in 1966 and 88 percent in 1968.[16]

If Faubus had won the Democratic gubernatorial nomination in 1970 in his first comeback effort, there is little doubt Rockefeller would have continued to dominate the black precincts of Little Rock. Starting in 1970, however, the Democratic primary winners, with the exception of Sen. John McClellan, broke with the segregationist inclination of the Arkansas party's previous nominees. This break with the past enabled a new breed of Arkansas Democratic politician to establish strong support among blacks while appealing successfully to the bulk of Arkansas's white voters.

In the crowded 1970 Democratic primary field, Dale Bumpers, an articulate moderate who ran a skillful media campaign, narrowly made the runoff against Faubus. Faubus turned to the busing issue with a vengeance, but the racial approach failed him this time.[17] Calling the runoff campaign vicious, the *Arkansas Gazette* reported:

> As for busing, he [Faubus] told the crowd that Bumpers had said it was not an issue in the campaign and added that, if Bumpers were elected, the message would go out to the nation from the *Arkansas*

Gazette that a Governor had been selected who didn't think busing was a problem.

"Every bureaucrat in Washington and every federal judge is going to say, 'Why this busing is all right that we're pushing on the people because down there they have elected a man that says busing isn't an issue,' " Faubus said. "For that reason alone, he [Bumpers] should be rejected."[18]

Bumpers's victory over Faubus in the runoff, with 58 percent of the vote, caught Rockefeller unprepared. A newspaper reporter explained:

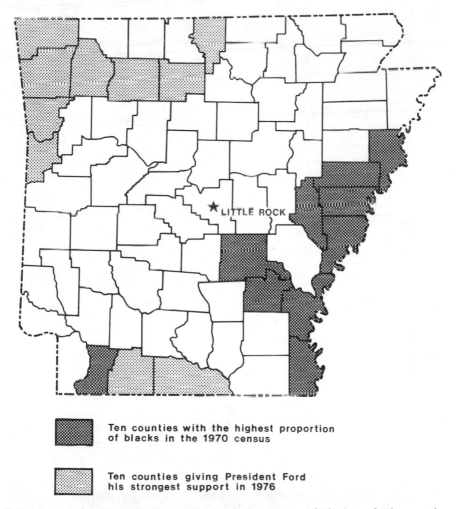

Ten counties with the highest proportion of blacks in the 1970 census

Ten counties giving President Ford his strongest support in 1976

Map 9-1. Arkansas Counties with a High Proportion of Blacks and Those with a Strong Republican Voting Preference

He [Rockefeller] has been a candidate loaded with ammunition for a
target that doesn't exist. The entire Rockefeller organization—and it
is a formidable one—had been geared to run against, and in all
probability, defeat, Orval E. Faubus. . . .

In Jim Johnson four years ago, and in Marion H. Crank two years
ago, there was enough segregationist extremism or outright political
ties with the Faubus machine to provide Rockefeller with his target.[19]

Bumpers defeated Governor Rockefeller soundly, 61.7 percent to 32.4
percent. A third candidate, Walter L. Carruth of the American party,
who called both major candidates ultraliberals,[20] received 5.9 percent.
The county-level returns and the available precinct data from Little
Rock indicate part of the reason for Bumpers's victory. Although the
heavily black counties along the Mississippi River gave Rockefeller his
strongest support, the percentages were lower than in 1966 and 1968. In
Little Rock's black precincts, Bumpers edged out Rockefeller, 54 percent to 46 percent.[21] Using survey data, Ranchino concluded:

The story of 1970 was the white moderate's return to the Democratic
Party. This group which had split in the presidential race of 1968,
gave a majority to Rockefeller in 1966 and 1968, had now changed
the face of the electorate in Arkansas. . . . [The] great middle class
of voters had moved from a rather conservative, intolerant posture in
1960, toward a greater degree of tolerance and moderation in
1970. . . .[22]

Bumpers's 1970 pattern was atypical for victorious statewide Democrats; when Bumpers won re-election in 1972 with 75.4 percent of the
vote, there was virtually no relationship between that race and his 1970
victory.[23] A scatter diagram of these two Bumpers races suggests the
reason for his disparity: the heavily black counties in 1972 shifted completely away from the Republican nominee, who that year was Len E.
Blaylock, the welfare commissioner under Rockefeller, and became the
Democrat's strongest counties.

Thus, the Republicans who came after Rockefeller, who died in
1973, were unable to capitalize on his inroads among black voters.[24]
Shortly after the 1970 election, the defeated GOP candidate for lieutenant governor, Sterling R. Cockrill, asserted, "[The Republican party]
will not die with the defeat of the Governor, myself or any other candidate, because the Republican Party has brought competition to government and a choice to the people."[25] Despite Cockrill's claim, in the
seven general elections for governor and senator from 1972 through
1978, no Republican received as much as 40 percent of the vote. When
asked about this rapid decline, U.S. Rep. Ed Bethune, the Republican
whose own election in 1978 signaled the end of the downhill slide, said:

Well, it was natural that [the decline] would occur because the party was all built around one individual. And none of us who were privy to the Rockefeller effort and were supporters of the Rockefeller effort were well-known enough or well-heeled enough to sustain the force. And . . . another thing that happened is that the Rockefeller effort—the moderate Republican approach—was co-opted by the Democrats. . . . Dale Bumpers picked up the Rockefeller programs almost verbatim and carried them forward.[26]

Whatever the reason, the focus of electoral politics in Arkansas in the 1970s was once again to be found in the Democratic primary.

In the 1972 Democratic senatorial primary, Senator McClellan narrowly won renomination over U.S. Rep. David Pryor, who had a moderate-to-liberal voting record.[27] McClellan made the runoff campaign a single-issue show by hammering away at Pryor's support from labor unions.[28] Pryor, on the defensive, responded by saying that his labor support was not from "outside labor bosses" but from Arkansas working people. He added that he was proud of such support.[29] After disposing of Pryor, McClellan won the general election, with 60.8 percent of the vote, over the Republican Wayne H. Babbitt, a veterinarian whom Rockefeller in the late 1960s had appointed director of the state's Livestock and Poultry Commission. There was speculation that Babbitt's vote total was inflated by dissatisfied Pryor supporters.[30]

In 1974 Pryor received the Democratic gubernatorial nomination by soundly defeating Faubus, who was making a second attempt at a comeback. Pryor received 65.6 percent of the vote in the general election against the Republican Ken Coon, a former executive secretary of the state GOP.[31]

The Republicans continued to limp along in other elections of the mid-1970s. In 1974, after serving four years as governor, Bumpers defeated Senator Fulbright in the Democratic primary and faced only a nominal GOP challenge in November from John Harris Jones, who won a mere 15.1 percent of the vote. The GOP challenge to Governor Pryor's 1976 re-election effort was also minimal. The Republican candidate, Leon Griffith, a plumber and building contractor from Pine Bluff, was "unknown even in his own party until the day he filed."[32] Griffith

received little help from Republicans around the state, spent less than $10,000 and relied almost completely on the small staff that the Republican state headquarters furnished him. . . .

He attacked Governor Pryor regularly, but, if the Governor ever responded or even acknowledged Griffith's presence in the race, it escaped the attention of the press. The Governor did buy a few political advertisements Sunday [prior to the election].[33]

In reporting on Pryor's 83.2 percent landslide, the *Arkansas Gazette* noted, "It was the most lopsided defeat for a Republican candidate for Governor since 1952, a decade before the Republican resurgence led by the late Winthrop Rockefeller."[34]

Lack of serious two-party competition at the state level persisted in the 1978 elections. After a tough primary contest in 1978,[35] Governor Pryor won, with 76.6 percent of the vote, the Senate seat left open by McClellan's death.[36] Tom Kelley, the Republican, received 16.3 percent and an independent got the rest. Shortly after the July 1978 primary, a Bumpers assistant noted that Pryor was house hunting in Washington, adding, "The Republicans are just not a problem . . . ."[37] Bill Clinton, the then thirty-one-year-old attorney general, was the 1978 Democratic gubernatorial nominee. He won, with 63.3 percent of the vote, over A. Lynn Lowe, the state GOP chairman.[38]

How have the Democrats in Arkansas managed to dominate so successfully at the statewide level? Is there a possibility that the party's broad spectrum is in danger of coming apart? Pat Moran, Senator Bumpers's administrative assistant and a former Arkansas Public Service Commission chairman, did not foresee that possibility in a 1978 interview:

> Some of the ultra-conservatives are ripe to be picked off by a Republican party with a strong personality, but until they are able to recruit a few of those persons, they can't hope to pick them. . . . We'll keep those [conservative, rural voters]; the Republicans aren't going to beat us there. [This is because] tradition is important to rural people. They are looking for ways to stay with the Democratic party; they have to be run off.[39]

U.S. Rep. Bill Alexander observed:

> We Democrats have done such a good job. We are a progressive party that has moderated. There is room in the Democratic party for liberals and conservatives. We have a good balance that permits the Democratic party to survive.[40]

Alexander said that the liberal label is a threat to the continued prosperity of the Arkansas Democratic party. He defined liberal as meaning "in a national sense social consciousness over fiscal responsibility," adding that he was not a liberal by that definition.[41] Bumpers described the GOP's dilemma as follows: "They have got to offer candidates a chance of winning in order to get attractive ones, and they have to have attractive candidates to win."[42] Bumpers said in 1978 that he did not foresee much prospect for either, but noted that that could change.[43]

In 1978 a second wave of GOP activity began when Ed Bethune won an open congressional seat from the Little Rock–centered district.[44]

After Bethune's victory with 51.7 percent of the vote, the personable and attractive campaigner[45] said, "There seemed to be more conservatism in the air this year and I think I reflected that conservatism."[46]

While Bethune's victory was a shot in the arm, the 1980 elections completely revived the GOP as a statewide threat. Aiding the Republican assault was Reagan's victory in the state with 48.1 percent of the vote to Carter's 47.5 percent, an impressive turnaround since Carter had received 65.0 percent in Arkansas four years earlier. Part of Carter's drop was attributable to a local issue: the unpopular housing of Cuban refugees at Fort Chaffee, in the northwestern part of the state. Sebastian County, where Fort Chaffee is located, presents an example of the power of the Cuban issue for that part of Arkansas. Carter, who received 47.0 percent of the vote in Sebastian County in 1976, received only 27.5 percent there in 1980.

The major partisan development of 1980 came in the Republican recapture of the governorship. Although the pro-Reagan national sentiment affected the gubernatorial outcome, this GOP breakthrough had chiefly local causes—namely, the style, personality, and mistakes of the youthful Democratic incumbent, Bill Clinton.[47]

Frank D. White, a Little Rock financial executive who switched to the Republican party in early 1980, ran a well-financed campaign that sought to take advantage of Clinton's unpopular increase of automobile-license fees and the hostility over the Cuban refugees.[48] In fact, "car tags and Cubans" became the convenient label for White's victory with 51.9 percent of the vote to Clinton's 48.1 percent.

That Clinton was vulnerable was signaled in the May primary when a seventy-seven-year-old retired turkey farmer won 31 percent of the vote against him.[49] Two *Arkansas Gazette* reporters, John Brummett and Steele Hays, wrote that Clinton's "liberal, Eastern establishment reputation" and his personal style contributed to his defeat. They said:

> [V]oters saw Clinton as arrogant, aloof, inaccessible or egotistical. The national attention he received [he was portrayed in the press as someone with a bright future in national politics] instead of helping may have hurt him, causing voters to view him as overly ambitious and being more interested in his political future than in them.[50]

Clinton gave credence to this interpretation of his defeat when he announced his candidacy for the governorship in early 1982. He said in a television commercial, "Many of you have told me you were proud of things I did, but that I often seemed out of touch; that I worked hard at doing what I wanted to do, but didn't always seem to care about doing what you wanted me to do." As an example, he said that he increased automobile-tag fees to get more money needed for state roads. "But it was a mistake because so many of you were hurt by it, and I'm really sorry for that."[51]

Even Senator Bumpers was affected by the local and national dissatisfaction with Democrats in 1980. The veteran politician faced what seemed like a nominal challenge from the Republican Bill Clark, a conservative Little Rock businessman. Summarizing the campaign, the *Arkansas Gazette* wrote, "Clark called Bumpers a liberal and says he doesn't care how his Arkansas constituents feel on issues, as illustrated by his votes for the Panama Canal treaties and against legislation for voluntary prayer in schools."[52] Bumpers had been preparing himself for an assault from the right in the years leading up to the election. For example, he abandoned his usual organized-labor allies in 1978 to help defeat the labor law reform bill.[53] On the stump, he "criticizes Senate liberals such as Edward M. Kennedy . . . for resorting to their traditional 'throw another government program' at a problem when he says 'creative thinking' is what's needed."[54] On Election Day, Clark surprised the political community[55] by receiving 40.9 percent of the votes to Bumpers's winning 59.1 percent.

At first glance, the 1982 elections seemed to suggest that the Republican roller coaster, after a brief upward surge in 1980, was on its way to another descent. But, in fact, that election year contained signs that a more stable era of two-party competition may be settling into place in Arkansas.

In 1982 Clinton fought his way back to the governorship through two tough primaries[56] and the general election to defeat Governor White with 54.9 percent of the vote to 45.1 percent for the incumbent Republican. The impact of local and national factors on this election was the reverse of what had occurred two years earlier. Dissatisfaction with President Reagan's economic policies, especially with high unemployment, contributed to Clinton's success. And the local issues were going Clinton's way this time. In place of "car tags and Cubans," the twin issues became utility rates and jobs. Regarding the former, White was on the defensive. The *New York Times* reported:

> In Mr. White's term, electric utility rates increased by more than $130 million, after approval by his appointees to the State's Public Utilities Commission, and utility earnings rose by 47 percent.
>
> It seemed less than coincidence to some voters that Mr. White was a stockholder in one utility holding company and a board member of a utility before becoming Governor. And the Governor sent at least one of his two nominees to the commission to a power company official for an "interview" before making the appointment.[57]

Clinton's repeated apologies for having raised the automobile-license fees and his vigorous person-to-person campaigning throughout the state muted the arrogance issue of 1980.[58] Clinton's Craighead County campaign manager, Dan Pierce of Jonesboro, in northeast Arkansas, said:

> The people in this county decided that Bill Clinton had learned a lesson. They had spanked him and sent him to his room. They always knew he had the ability and they had decided he had matured to the point where they were willing to give him a second chance.[59]

Beneath the local policy and personality issues, this 1982 gubernatorial election contained partisan elements found throughout the South's emerging two-party system. Governor White's postelection comments were instructive. First, he pointed to the national features present in his defeat: "Any candidate in office is wedded to his party. Perhaps that rubbed off. I couldn't do anything about it, but I was blamed for unemployment. The trend in this country was against me. You can't overcome the national trends."[60] Next, he turned to the racial aspect of partisan politics in his state:

> The black vote was devastating. The perception was that I was insensitive[61] and I just couldn't overcome it. Bill got almost 100 percent of the black vote. We could have spent a million dollars more and it wouldn't have changed the outcome. The black vote went where they feel comfortable, in the Democratic Party. There was nothing I could have done to change that.[62]

Finally, in the words of a newspaper article:

> A reporter suggested that the state Republican Party now is in a shambles, but White said, "Quite the contrary." He said the GOP's gain of 3 seats in the legislature—to 10 of the 135 seats—shows the party is doing well. "I think there's a tremendous following, a lot of new, young blood," White said. "It makes me think the Republican Party is here to stay."[63]

Arkansas—Conclusion

Under Rockefeller's leadership Arkansas Republicans did not attempt—as did so many of their Southern partisan associates—to exploit white racial fears for electoral gain. Rather, until the 1970 Democratic gubernatorial primary victory of Bumpers, the Democrats were the race-baiting champions. This atypical GOP pattern in Arkansas was not solidified by the Republicans who followed Rockefeller in the 1970s, and white Democratic moderates enticed blacks back to the party of Lyndon Johnson.

The element that Arkansas exhibited in perhaps a slightly larger measure than did other Southern states was traditional Democratic loyalty
among whites. As Moran said, "Tradition is important to rural people.
They are looking for ways to stay with the Democratic party; they have
to be run off." Arkansas Democratic candidates did all they could to
make themselves acceptable to these people. And the effect was devastating for Republican statewide candidates through 1978.

The abatement of the race issue was less important to Democratic
domination in Arkansas in the 1970s than it was in neighboring Deep
South states. The huge Democratic majorities in two-party contests
through 1978 suggest that the support of blacks was not essential for victory. Neither did economic-class issues predominate. But by 1982 the situation was different. The same black-white Democratic coalition found
elsewhere in the South propelled Clinton back to the governorship.

Furthermore, following White's 1980 GOP gubernatorial victory,
nearly total Democratic dominance in the first post-Rockefeller decade
gave way to a competitive environment in which the Republicans appeared to be more firmly established than in the 1970s. With leaders
like Bethune, the GOP is building for the future, ready to take advantage, when possible, of local and national issues in its favor. Given this
relative maturity in the Arkansas party system, future partisan ups and
downs are likely to be less steep than the roller-coaster style swings
witnessed in the last two decades.

10

North Carolina:
Clash of Polar Forces—Hunt vs. Helms

Two-party competition in North Carolina did not suddenly emerge amid chaotic electoral fluctuations caused by the race issue. Rather, in this first of three Mountain Republican states[1] to be considered, a remarkable partisan stability persisted, although the disruptions that did occur were significant, if not as intense as those found in the Deep South states. And with the exception of the potent Jesse Helms phenomenon, moderate North Carolina Democrats—led most recently by Gov. James B. Hunt, Jr.—successfully contained through the 1970s the forces that shattered the Democracy in neighboring Virginia. By the early 1980s, however, the opposing partisan forces that developed in North Carolina in the post–civil rights era—the Helms Republicans and the Hunt Democrats—split a pair of elections, with Helms's group triumphant in 1980 and Hunt's allies victorious in 1982. No matter who wins the 1984 elections, when the battle lines between these two opposing philosophies are to be manned by their respective leaders, their clashes have sharply delineated the state's emerging partisan structure. A review of the last two decades of party competition highlights the current two-party struggle in North Carolina.

Map 10-1, which divides the state into four analytically useful regions, offers an introduction to North Carolina's political geography.[2] The mountain counties are those where Republicanism can be traced to the Civil War, as was true of the Appalachian highlands of neighboring Virginia and Tennessee.[3] The eastern coastal plains counties are pre-

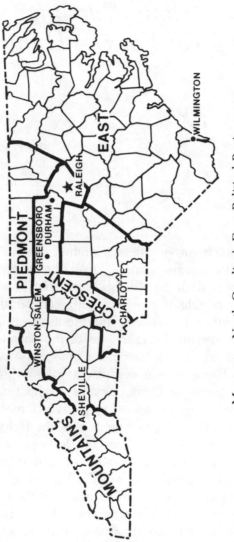

Map 10-1. North Carolina's Four Political Regions

dominantly agricultural and contain the heaviest concentration of the state's blacks, who made up 37.4 percent of the population of this region in the 1970 census. Within the Piedmont, eleven counties form a crescent that contains the major cities of the state: Raleigh (Wake County), Durham, Greensboro (Guilford), Winston-Salem (Forsyth), and Charlotte (Mecklenburg).[4] The winning Democratic pattern generally consisted of mild support in the mountain counties, overwhelming support in the East, and strong but not overwhelming support in the Piedmont and Piedmont Crescent, which were the battlegrounds in normal statewide elections.

In the 1964 presidential election, Goldwater's racial appeal did not conquer North Carolina or any other Rim South state.[5] Especially noteworthy was the failure of North Carolina's eastern counties to flock to the Goldwater standard along with the counties of the South Carolina coastal plains, South Georgia, South Alabama, among others.[6] Goldwater was put on the defensive in the eastern part of the state by his lack of enthusiasm for federal agricultural programs, which had strong support among farmers in this rural section of North Carolina. When Goldwater came to Raleigh during the campaign, he said he would not end farm price supports immediately, but added, "My position [is] to confer with farmers . . . to get the broad burden of government eventually off the backs of farmers."[7] A month later Johnson visited Raleigh and warned of a farm depression if Goldwater became president, referring to Goldwater's support for "prompt and final termination of the farm subsidy program."[8] The Raleigh *News and Observer* wrote, "[Johnson's] words were well received by Tar Heel Democratic strategists, who are making extensive use of the farm issue to take some sting out of the issue of civil rights."[9] Johnson's winning pattern did not lead to the abrupt break in voting patterns found elsewhere in the region in 1964.[10]

In 1968 Humphrey ran third in the state, with 29.2 percent of the vote to Wallace's 31.3 percent; Nixon carried North Carolina with a plurality of 39.5 percent. Four years later McGovern received slightly fewer votes than Humphrey, getting 28.9 percent in the 1972 Nixon landslide. The Democratic presidential-vote decline in both elections in North Carolina was especially noteworthy in the eastern counties.[11] The presidential results, while interesting in themselves, also provide background for what happened to statewide Democratic candidates during these years.

The 1968 gubernatorial election witnessed a determined effort on the part of the Republican nominee, James C. Gardner, a young, attractive businessman elected to Congress in 1966, to capitalize on the national woes of the Democrats. Robert W. Scott, the Democratic gubernatorial nominee, did not actively support Humphrey, although he announced that he would vote for all Democratic nominees. "Confident that liberal Democrats would not support his Republican adversary," Preston W. Edsall and J. Oliver Williams wrote, "Scott and his managers worked hard to hold the east, where George Wallace was strong and where Gardner was conducting a vigorous drive."[12] The Republican Gardner, who was taking no chances in his presidential choices, endorsed both Nixon and Wallace.[13] He announced early that the East would be a battleground:

> Take 1964, Bob Gavin [the GOP nominee for governor that year] led Dan Moore [the Democratic nominee] until he got to Greensboro and from there eastward he got almost nothing.
>
> The East has kept the Democrats in power for many years. Our question, and our theme is: What has it gotten them? The answer is 67 years of promises and mediocrity.[14]

Sen. Sam J. Ervin, Jr., running for re-election in 1968, faced a weaker Republican opponent than did Scott; Ervin was therefore less reluctant to stand with Humphrey. In Fayetteville, Ervin endorsed the Democratic presidential standard-bearer, describing Humphrey as "the greatest friend the farmers of this nation have ever had."[15]

Both Scott and Ervin won, the former with 52.7 percent of the vote and the incumbent senator with 60.6 percent. Despite Gardner's vigorous effort in the East, he failed to carry the region; he did better there, however, than any previous GOP nominee, winning 43 percent of the vote to Scott's 57 percent.[16] Scott's winning pattern generally resembled Gov. Dan Moore's in 1964.[17] In addition, Scott received overwhelming black support in the cities. Precinct data from Greensboro, Charlotte, and Raleigh show that the Democratic nominee won 98 percent of the vote in black precincts.[18] The point was not lost on Gardner, who had this to say in a postelection interview:

> Certainly the size of the Negro vote was much larger than we had anticipated and it went totally against us . . . .
>
> It's hard to explain to me the Negro in North Carolina. He's been terribly dissatisfied. The Democrats have been in charge, yet they [blacks] go out every year in a bloc vote for any Democrat running.
>
> It's not the easiest thing to run as a Republican in North Carolina. You start out with a certain number of Negro bloc votes against you and a certain number of people who vote straight Democratic no matter who the candidate is.[19]

The year 1972 was one of triumph for the Republican party in North Carolina, the party capturing both the governorship and a U.S. Senate seal. However, the reasons behind the twin victories differed markedly, as is indicated by the electoral patterns and an examination of contemporary accounts of the elections. James E. Holshouser, a Republican from the mountain area, defeated Gardner for the GOP gubernatorial nomination. The Republican nominee for the Senate seat, the arch-conservative Jesse Helms, had an entirely different background from Holshouser. Helms was a former Democrat and a native of Raleigh who was widely known in eastern North Carolina because of his television commentaries carried throughout that region by a Raleigh station.[20] In an editorial supporting Helms's Democratic opponent, the Raleigh *News and Observer* wrote:

> Helms once denounced Social Security as a system of "doles and handouts," the Medicare program as "socialized medicine" and rural electric co-ops as "socialized electricity." During this campaign, in quest of votes, he has retreated from these bold stands with general assertions of concern for the aged, the sick and rural residents.[21]

It is questionable whether Holshouser was any less conservative than Helms, but there was a difference in image and style. As a former Republican state senator, Phil Kirk, who served as Governor Holshouser's administrative assistant, put it, "Holshouser is probably as conservative as Helms but not as vociferous."[22]

Hargrove (Skipper) Bowles, a well-to-do Greensboro businessman who defeated Lt. Gov. Pat Taylor for the 1972 Democratic gubernatorial nomination, presented a moderate candidacy not unlike that of the outgoing governor, Scott. But the Democratic nominee for senator, Nick Galifianakis, was different; for one thing, he received the nomination by defeating the incumbent, Sen. B. Everett Jordan, in the Democratic primary, a victory accomplished with strong support from blacks.[23] Galifianakis, a former Duke University law professor, was described by the *News and Observer* as having earned the reputation of a liberal in his three terms in the state legislature and three terms in Congress for supporting such issues as tax reform, national medical insurance, and U.S. withdrawal from Vietnam.[24]

During the Senate campaign Helms attempted to tie Galifianakis to McGovern, calling his opponent "soft on drug abuse and a profligate spender" and saying Galifianakis favored amnesty for Vietnam draft evaders. "No one has ever called Jesse Helms a namby-pamby on forced busing or extravagant federal spending,"[25] Helms asserted.

By contrast the Holshouser-Bowles contest was more of a standard North Carolina Republican-Democratic campaign, which was reflected in the voting patterns. Bowles's defeat, with 48.5 percent of the vote, did not result from any major shift in the state's partisan voting patterns. In securing his narrow win, Holshouser obviously benefited from Nixon's huge victory margin in the state—69.5 percent.

Galifianakis was more closely associated with McGovern than was Bowles, county-level returns reveal.[26] The key breakthrough for Helms was clearly in the East, where he ran ahead of his Democratic opponent in many counties.[27] Statewide, Helms won with 54.0 percent of the vote. How much of Helms's success in these Democratic bastion counties can be attributed to the perception of Galifianakis as a racially liberal McGovern ally and how much can be credited to Helms's many years of association with the region through his television commentaries is difficult to ascertain.[28]

Two years after the 1972 defeats, Democratic resurgence began in a strong way in North Carolina. Figure 10-1, which charts Democratic party strength in the state, illustrates the abrupt Democratic turn in 1974 away from steady decline. State Atty. Gen. Robert B. Morgan handily defeated Galifianakis for the 1974 Democratic nomination for the Senate seat being vacated by Ervin, who retired at the end of his term. Morgan, "a native of the East, a participant in politics for a quarter of a century and a champion of Eastern causes,"[29] brought a political record to the campaign that Neal Peirce described as follows:

> Back in 1960, Morgan had managed segregationist I. Beverly Lake's campaign for governor against Terry Sanford; later he defended North Carolina's repressive law banning Communists and fellow-travelers from speaking at state universities. Twice elected attorney general, however, he built a reputation as a consumer advocate, fighting higher utility and milk prices. He also hired blacks for his staff and won the endorsement of some major black organizations in the state's larger cities. On the other hand, Morgan had defended the Nixon administration's Vietnam policy, and it was impossible for the Republicans to pin on him the "liberal" tag that had sunk Galifianakis.[30]

During the 1974 general election campaign, Morgan worked closely with county Democratic leaders while trying, in the words of the *News and Observer*, "to capitalize on the national economic woes of increasing inflation and spending stagnation to entice voters back to the Democratic Party."[31] He attacked President Ford's proposal for an income tax surcharge, arguing that a first priority should be to close tax loopholes favorable to the wealthy. He warned farmers in the eastern part of the state that the Republicans planned to dismantle federal farm programs. As one North Carolina political writer expressed it, "Morgan's obvious attempts were to bind together a Democratic coalition, including both

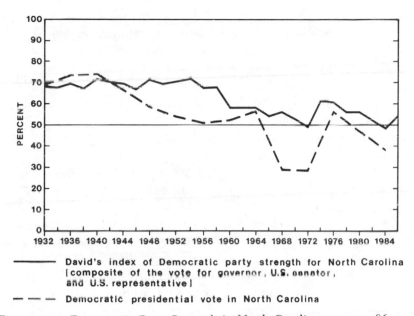

Figure 10-1. Democratic Party Strength in North Carolina, 1932–1986

blacks and liberals and Eastern conservatives. He has done so . . . by stressing the economic issues and by having his campaign take on something of a populist tone."[32]

Against this experienced Democratic political tactician, the Republicans offered a furniture company executive, William F. Stevens, Jr., who had no experience in government. Several North Carolina observers pointed to the weakness the GOP has in fielding candidates with the credentials to give them credibility with voters, one noting that the Republican party "simply has no stable of talent" to draw on.[33] According to press reports, Stevens tied his campaign closely to the GOP organization in the state.[34] Morgan won with 62.1 percent of the vote.

Morgan skillfully courted blacks while keeping his strong support among Wallace voters in eastern North Carolina, where his political origins lay. He held this coalition together with a campaign appeal that was populist, or working-class directed. Such a strategy succeeded because race was not a significant issue in 1974. Black voters drawn to Morgan because of his Democratic affiliation provided critical support, and, at the same time, with the race issue in eclipse, economic-class appeal was a factor in retaining support among white Democrats, some of whom had defected to Helms in 1972. But Morgan's class appeal was by no means sharp, showing nowhere near the level or consistency of Henry Howell's in Virginia, for example.

Although it is therefore true that the abatement of the race issue allowed white and black Democrats to find a common ground in backing statewide Democrats like Morgan, something other than economic class was also drawing many of these white Democrats back to their party after they had abandoned both McGovern and a North Carolina Democrat identified with McGovern (Galifianakiş). That draw appears to have been Democratic party allegiance. Thus, while Morgan's class appeal was part of his success, some white Democrats probably supported him at least equally because of the pull of party loyalty.[35]

Lt. Gov. James B. Hunt, Jr., the 1976 Democratic gubernatorial nominee, won a smashing victory over his Republican opponent, creating a vote pattern almost identical to Morgan's two years earlier.[36] After his 1972 election to the lieutenant governorship, Hunt had spent considerable time campaigning around the state, both for himself and in an effort to revitalize the Democratic party.[37] Regarding Hunt's 1976 campaign, one reporter wrote, "Hunt placed himself in the moderate-to-progressive tradition of former Governors Kerr Scott, Luther Hodges and Terry Sanford and attracted a broad-based Democratic coalition."[38] Against this unified Democratic coalition, the Republican David T. Flaherty, who served as human-resources secretary under Governor Holshouser, received only 34.9 percent of the vote.

Political observers from North Carolina consider Hunt a shrewd politician whose moderate positions do not threaten either the conservative or the liberal elements of the state party. Even the Republican Phil Kirk, the former Holshouser assistant, noted that the Democratic coalition is "not fragile as long as Hunt is governor." Hunt's position is not unlike Riley's in South Carolina. He is a moderate who does not threaten the more conservative Democratic business-industrial establishment of North Carolina. At the same time, he is far more appealing to blacks and white liberals than any Republican alternative. Rob Christensen, Washington correspondent of the Raleigh *News and Observer*, explained how Hunt holds together this disparate coalition:

> He's a very skillful politician, a very skillful coalition builder. He's a middle-of-the-road (for North Carolina) politician. He's a tremendous hard worker. . . . He is by common consensus, with perhaps Terry Sanford, the best postwar governor North Carolina has had. You might throw in Luther Hodges. . . .
>
> He manages a balancing act essentially. He's tough on law and order, which appeals to conservatives. He did not free the Wilmington ten [black defendants in a celebrated trial], although he reduced their sentences. But on the other hand, he appoints a lot of blacks to high, prominent positions—to judgeships. He's very

pro-education, pro–public schools, which is kind of viewed as a liberal position. . . .

He talks a good game. When he speaks before black groups, he talks of a new day in North Carolina. He speaks the language of hope, of racial harmony, of working together, of change in racial attitudes. Talk's cheap I suppose, but he is generally perceived by blacks as a friendly politician. When you compare him with the other major political figure in the state, who is Jesse Helms, who certainly raises racial code words all the time in busing and cutting food stamps and in general in a very subtle way the race issue, by comparison Hunt looks good to blacks.[39]

North Carolina Democratic moderates, who were in clear control in 1976, had no trouble accepting the national party's nominee in 1976. Ferrel Guillory of the *News and Observer* summarized the campaign:

> Through the use of strong anti-Carter advertising and with Governor James E. Holshouser, Jr., and U.S. Senator Jesse A. Helms both campaigning, Republicans adopted a strategy of attacking Carter and the national Democratic platform as too liberal and pro-union . . . .
>
> With growing Ford momentum becoming apparent, and angered by what they regarded as distortions in the GOP campaign advertising, leading Democrats launched an aggressive pro-Carter counter effort last week.
>
> U.S. Senator Robert Morgan denounced the Republicans for "Watergate-type tactics." James B. Hunt, Jr., the Democratic candidate for governor, vouched for Carter's moral character and fiscal conservatism. Radio and television advertisements to bolster the Carter candidacy and to encourage a Democratic turnout were put into use, featuring such diverse personalities as former U.S. Senator Sam J. Ervin, Jr., Alabama Governor George C. Wallace and the Reverend Martin Luther King, Sr.[40]

Carter's victory pattern in North Carolina, with 55.2 percent of the vote, corresponded closely to Hunt's.[41] The *News and Observer* reported on the optimism prevalent in state Democratic circles after the 1976 elections: "After substantial defections to Republicans and third-party candidates in 1968 and 1972, Democrats see the 1976 results as an indication their party could reassemble a winning statewide coalition for philosophically moderate candidates."[42]

The Democratic nominee who opposed Senator Helms in 1978, the self-styled populist John Ingram, the state's insurance commissioner, was not in the Hunt-Morgan mold. Spending less than $50,000, he upset Luther H. Hodges, Jr., a Charlotte banker and son of the former governor, to win the senatorial nomination. Hodges, who spent over

$700,000 in the primary,[43] was squarely identified with the more moderate leadership of the North Carolina Democracy. The *New York Times* reported that Hodges's positions "were generally moderate to conservative—he opposed pending labor law changes that would benefit labor, but said government programs to employ the jobless were needed."[44] In the primary Ingram relied "almost exclusively on his record of opposing insurance rate increases and his portrayal of himself as the friend of the working people."[45] The *New York Times* article added, "On the issues, he generally took a more liberal position than Mr. Hodges, indicating that he felt the labor revision act, for example, could be of some benefit to working people."[46]

During the fall campaign Ingram lacked the enthusiastic and well-financed backing that Governor Hunt receives. Against Helms's celebrated war chest of $7 million, Ingram raised only $300,000. The *Washington Post* wrote:

> Many traditional [Democratic party] loyalists have been slow to flock to the Ingram banner because of his populist rhetoric.
>
> The *Charlotte Observer*, for example, reported that more than 50 of the 165 influential Democrats Governor Jim Hunt keeps on a secret list refused to buy or help sell tickets for an Asheville reception for President Carter last month because the proceeds were to go to Ingram. Four former Democratic state chairmen have endorsed Helms.[47]

On the stump Ingram charged, "If he [Helms] had a record of fighting for people like I do, he wouldn't need $6 million . . . . But he has a record of being against our young people, our senior citizens, our farmers, our veterans and our working people."[48]

Helms's well-financed effort focused on both projecting the image of "a Christian gentleman" and explaining that Helms is "working for you in Washington."[49] A *Congressional Quarterly* report noted:

> Helms has held onto his personal popularity as he continues to promote his image as a conservative statesman with a national following. He has strong support in the business community and will be able to keep most Republicans behind him.[50]

The incumbent senator, who refused to debate or to appear with his opponent, lost no opportunity to label Ingram too liberal for North Carolina.[51]

Helms won with 54.5 percent of the votes cast. A county-level analysis reveals that Ingram's vote broke sharply with the Hunt-Morgan pattern. The eastern counties were quite weak for Ingram relative to the other two Democrats. The populous Piedmont Crescent was also less strong for Ingram; he was simply unable to hold enough of the Hunt-Morgan Democratic coalition to win statewide.[52]

With his 1978 re-election behind him, Helms consolidated the control he had increasingly exercised over the North Carolina GOP since 1976, when he installed his choice for state party chairman.[53] The vehicle for Helms's activities was his political-action committee, the Congressional Club, which effectively uses mass-mailing techniques to raise large sums of money nationwide for right-wing causes. The club is directed by Thomas F. Ellis, Helms's friend and political associate of over three decades.[54] W. Lee Johnston wrote that after the 1978 elections Helms and Ellis

> made the Congressional Club the core of the state's Republican Party. Helms' people occupied the key leadership positions in the party from Executive Director through staffing positions. These people were ideologically and personally tied to Helms and his brand of conservatism.[55]

For the 1980 elections Helms and the Congressional Club selected the major GOP candidates: John P. East, a virtually unknown political science professor at East Carolina University and an ideological conservative, for the U.S. Senate, and, for the governorship, I. Beverly Lake, Jr., a state senator from Raleigh whose father had been a segregationist Democratic gubernatorial candidate in 1960 and 1964. The major effort went into East's race to unseat Senator Morgan and not into Lake's challenge to Governor Hunt, which generated little enthusiasm. Ellis observed after the election, "Hunt had nothing negative we could campaign against. He had a personal and party organization; he had plenty of money, and we just couldn't raise the money we thought we could for the Lake campaign."[56] On Election Day, when there was little good news for Democrats nationwide, Governor Hunt coasted to re-election with 61.9 percent of the vote to Lake's 37.4 percent.

The Senate race went differently. East's campaign stressed saturation television commercials that portrayed Morgan as a "big spender on social welfare programs but tight-fisted when it came to defense."[57] His attacks on Morgan centered on three themes: the "giveaway" of the Panama Canal, U.S. aid to "Marxist" Nicaragua, and Morgan's "opposition" to the B-1 bomber.[58] East's television spots, financed by a nationwide direct-mail appeal to conservatives that raised $1.1 million,[59] sought repeatedly to tie his candidacy to Ronald Reagan's; one claimed, for example, "Ronald Reagan needs John East in the Senate."[60] Asked about this six weeks before the election, East said, "If you want to put it in practical terms, Governor Reagan has a tremendous number of ad-

mirers and supporters in this state. And if those people who support
Governor Reagan also support me . . . that's an awful lot of votes."[61]
An advertisement put it another way: "If you want some improvements,
you're not only going to have to change the White House, but you're
going to have to change the Congress."[62]

Morgan, on the other hand, relied on the strength of the state's
Democratic coalition, conducting a traditional campaign. As one newspaper reported, Morgan "blended television and radio exposure with
numerous appearances at county political rallies, pigpickings and on the
civic club circuit. He stressed his proven record and his experience."[63]
In summarizing the election, the *News and Observer* wrote:

> The campaign sometimes slipped to the personal level with East
> characterizing Morgan as an inept follower of President Carter and a
> liberal who was close to the philosophy of Sen. Edward M. Ken-
> nedy, D-Mass.
> Morgan portrayed East as a far-right conservative of the ilk of the
> John Birch Society.[64]

East won the extremely close election with 50.0 percent of the vote to
Morgan's 49.4 percent. Precise explanations for such a close outcome
are impossible. One reporter attributed it to East's success in convincing
enough voters through his heavy television advertising that Morgan was
too liberal for North Carolina: "The Republicans in 1980 were able to
distort the voting record of a moderately conservative Democrat and
make him look like a liberal and make it stick."[65] If this view is correct,
then it supports the conclusion that moderate Democrats in the Hunt-
Morgan mold generally command majority support; Morgan's defeat
becomes an exception only because the incumbent senator was portrayed effectively as something he was not. Another source of East's
victory was certainly Reagan's candidacy.[66] At every turn East tied himself to Reagan, and when Reagan carried the state—in a victory based
on national issues—East was swept along with him.

During the campaign the 1980 elections were frequently described as
a test of the power of Jesse Helms and his Congressional Club.[67] If they
were such a test, the East victory gave Senator Helms a substantial
boost. Still, there remained in North Carolina a potent Democratic
coalition led by a popular and undefeated politician, Governor Hunt,
and in 1984 Hunt is challenging Helms's second senatorial re-election
effort. In fact, the political talk in the state since at least 1980 has
centered on the impending Helms-Hunt clash, which received a dress
rehearsal in the 1982 congressional elections.

Encouraged by the East victory and the gain of two U.S. House seats in 1980, the Congressional Club recruited and heavily backed a slate of challengers against the seven incumbent Democratic congressmen.[68] Unlike in 1980, when he had been preoccupied with his own race, Hunt this time organized a statewide group, "Unity Campaign '82," to push his party's candidates. The Republicans' effort to unseat U.S. Rep. Ike Andrews, a Democrat with a political background like Morgan's, illustrates the 1982 campaign's similarity to East's challenge as well as the difference Hunt's involvement made. The *New York Times* reported that

> television advertisements crafted by the Congressional Club's advertising subsidiary hammer at "Ike Andrews and his liberal buddies in Congress" and mass mailings remind voters that [the Republican candidate] is a "Christian" while Mr. Andrews has "wine bars" at his receptions.
>
> This assault from the Helms camp initially paralyzed Mr. Andrews, according to Democratic officials. Then Mr. Hunt stepped in, gave Mr. Andrews a sharp-tongued pep talk and installed some Hunt supporters in his campaign. . . .
>
> National Democratic officials credit [Hunt] with inspiring Mr. Andrews and some other Democrats to fight the Helms organization instead of surrendering in the face of its superior technology and spirited attacks depicting Democrats as soft on social issues such as school prayer and abortion.[69]

The 1982 congressional balloting produced a smashing Democratic success. All seven Democratic incumbents won (Andrews made it with 51.9 percent), and both freshmen Republican congressmen elected in 1980 were defeated, leaving only two Republicans in the state's eleven-member House delegation, the lowest GOP representation in twenty years. The Democratic successes in North Carolina as well as elsewhere in 1982 were aided by the poor performance of the economy during President Reagan's first twenty-two months in office. But in North Carolina considerable credit accrued to Governor Hunt.[70] Even Holshouser, the former Republican governor, said, "From a North Carolina standpoint only, the big winner yesterday was Jim Hunt. Where he campaigned hard, the Democrats came out ahead."[71]

Observers were cautious when it came to predicting what this election meant for the much-heralded Helms-Hunt contest of 1984. Former Senator Morgan said that Helms and the Congressional Club had been damaged but that it would be wishful thinking to believe that the damage would be permanent. "Jesse and Tom Ellis . . . are mean, but dumb they are not," Morgan said.[72] Ellis himself acknowledged that "there's going to be a problem" defeating Hunt, but added, "I don't think this has made him invincible. There's still a lot of knots on that old tree and we'll just see."[73]

North Carolina—Conclusion

North Carolina's experience supports the importance of the abatement of the race issue for Democratic strength in statewide elections. Republicans in the state built upon their base in the mountain counties to win the governorship in the 1972 Nixon landslide. In that same year, however, Helms exploited racial tensions to give the GOP a victory based on another approach—one that substantially differed in voter support from Holshouser's.

With the rise of moderates like Hunt and Morgan (in place of a candidate like Galifianakis, who was easily identified with McGovern), a potent biracial Democratic coalition formed to provide winning majorities for Morgan in 1974 and for Hunt in 1976 and 1980. Economic-class issues in the New Deal style played a role in these campaigns. At least of equal importance for this Democratic coalition, however, was the pull of Democratic party allegiance at a time when the divisive issue of race was in eclipse.

Some of the tensions present in the broad North Carolina Democratic coalition were visible in the 1978 Senate race, in which Helms won a second term. The challenger, Ingram, lacked the moderate image of Morgan and Hunt, a deficiency that cost him both campaign money and support among the right-of-center white segments of the coalition. Candidacies such as Ingram's (others included Turnipseed's in South Carolina and Howell's in Virginia) invariably put considerable strain on the ideologically diverse Democratic coalition. While Ingram's performance pointed to tensions in the North Carolina Democracy, Hunt's skillful maneuvers emphasized the continued vitality of this potent force in North Carolina politics.

Its most serious challenge came from Senator Helms and his conservative allies. In the 1980 and 1982 elections these two forces could each claim a victory. In November 1984, when Helms and Hunt square off against each other, the strength of the potent North Carolina Democratic coalition will receive its most important test in the post–civil rights era.

11

Virginia:
Transformed by a "Loser"

In Virginia the demise of the Byrd organization during the mid-1960s resulted in a period of prolonged, bitter Democratic factional squabbling that was motivated as much by policy considerations as by personality differences. During the early 1970s, as a result of a variety of circumstances, the middle ground in the Democratic party underwent a rapid decline and the two antagonistic poles ruptured the party beyond easy repair. In the process a substantial number of conservative Democrats switched to the Republican party, which had expanded from its mountain base[1] to encompass a wide spectrum of right-of-center to moderate forces from throughout the commonwealth. All through the 1970s the GOP demonstrated it could win consistently, if narrowly, in statewide elections. An overall look at Virginia electoral politics in the post–civil rights era yields a clear conclusion: party realignment struck with a vengeance.

From a few years before the start of Franklin Roosevelt's presidency until 1965, Harry F. Byrd dominated Virginia politics through an organization whose "effectiveness . . . rivaled the success of the urban political machines of its day."[2] How the Byrd organization used the poll tax and the resulting small electorate to control state government is a fascinating story that is treated in depth elsewhere.[3]

Senator Byrd's philosophy of frugal, limited government, characterized by his pay-as-you-go principle, survived several noteworthy electoral challenges during the first decade after World War II.[4] But any

145

moderating trends operating on the organization came to an abrupt halt
with the famous 1954 school desegregation decision. Ralph Eisenberg
wrote:

> The decision thrust a new, albeit very old, issue to the forefront of
> politics. Great effort was expended by Senator Byrd and the orga-
> nization to sell "massive resistance" to Virginians. In doing so, the
> organization revived racial issues and fears that had plagued state
> politics for so long in the past. Against the specter of integration
> ("race-mixing"), antiorganization and moderate organization leaders
> could do little to rouse a popular following to their progressive
> causes.[5]

In 1961 the organization's successful candidate for governor, Albertis S.
Harrison, Jr., was not closely identified with the school closers of the
massive-resistance effort and was considered something of a moderate.
Therefore, to "assuage the organization's more conservative group, State
Senator Mills E. Godwin, Jr., who had been a principal organization
spokesman for massive resistance, was the candidate for lieutenant governor on the same ticket."[6] Godwin, who was to play an important role
in future elections, won easily in 1961.

An early sign that the Byrd organization was slipping came at the
1964 state Democratic convention. The delegates repudiated Senator
Byrd's "golden silence" position on presidential elections and voted to
endorse President Johnson,[7] who carried the state with 53.5 percent of
the vote to Goldwater's 46.2 percent.[8] Goldwater in 1964 swept Southside Virginia, the rural, small-town area that is not unlike sections of
eastern North Carolina. This racially conservative area had been a
mainstay of the Byrd organization, and Johnson's statewide victory
without this Democratic bastion signaled that major changes were in
progress.

In 1965 Lieutenant Governor Godwin, despite his origins in the more
conservative section of the Byrd organization, was able to unite all
Democratic factions and secure the gubernatorial nomination without a
primary fight. Godwin's coalition was all-encompassing, including,
among others, Byrd Democrats from rural, small-town areas, labor
union members, and blacks. The Republican candidate, Linwood Holton of Roanoke, "a young and attractive candidate who campaigned
with a moderate platform,"[9] struck out verbally at this diverse assort-
ment of allies united in opposing him. Holton attacked the

> incredible logic under which he [Godwin] was able on September
> 14, 1965, to send Armistead Boothe to Arlington to proclaim him a
> liberal in the finest tradition of the Great Society while he was also

able on October 6, 1965, to send Bill Tuck to Danville to attest he was a true conservative in the tradition of Harry Byrd.[10]

A reaction to Godwin's apparent move away from the right led to the formation of the Virginia Conservative party, which ran a John Birch Society member for governor in 1965.[11]

In November 1965 Godwin was elected with 47.9 percent of the vote to Holton's 37.7 percent; the Conservative party candidate, William J. Story, Jr., received 13.4 percent, with strong support in Southside Virginia, as Map 11-1 shows. This map also illustrates the importance of the mountain counties to the Republican nominee. A precinct analysis reveals that Godwin swept black areas in Richmond and Norfolk.[12] As governor, Godwin pushed through a state sales tax and advanced major new programs for expenditures on education and mental health, areas that had been neglected under the now discarded pay-as-you-go doctrine.[13] J. Harvie Wilkinson III wrote that Godwin "swept to victory behind a coalition of Byrd and anti-Byrd elements and fused a dynamic consensus of these elements when in office."[14] At this juncture it appeared that the disparate elements of the Democratic coalition could be held together, and, as one newspaper said of Godwin, the "professional at politics," it may be that "Mr. Godwin is just the man to bring off the balancing act."[15]

Senator Byrd resigned in 1965 and died the following year. His son, Harry F. Byrd, Jr., a state senator, was appointed to his father's seat and sought election in his own right in 1966 to the remaining four years of the Senate term. Sen. A. Willis Robertson, a seventy-nine-year-old conservative Democrat and Byrd ally, ran for re-election that same year. Wilkinson described the divisive 1966 Democratic primaries for these two U.S. Senate seats as follows:

> Whereas the organization finally settled on the most conservative of all possible combinations [Byrd, Jr., and Robertson], the opposing camp put forward two men with whom they hoped to gain middle-of-the-road support. The most liberal of the potential candidates, state Senator [Henry] Howell of Norfolk and Congressman [W. Pat] Jennings of the Ninth District, withdrew in favor of the more moderate Armistead Boothe of Alexandria and state Senator William B. Spong of Portsmouth. Boothe would oppose Byrd, Jr., while Spong was to run for Robertson's seat.[16]

Both Boothe and Spong, starting in the mid-1950s, had been associated with Democratic urban interests that had sought to end the lethargy of state government under the organization's control.[17]

The 1966 primary results were extremely close: Byrd defeated Boothe,

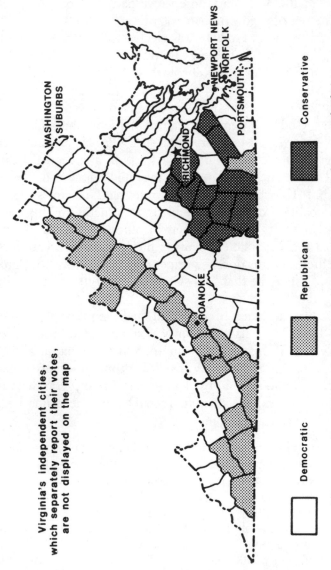

Virginia's independent cities,
which separately report their votes,
are not displayed on the map

WASHINGTON
SUBURBS

RICHMOND

NEWPORT NEWS

NORFOLK

PORTSMOUTH

ROANOKE

Democratic   Republican   Conservative

Map 11-1. Party Strength by County in Virginia's 1965 Gubernatorial Election

148

50.9 percent to 49.1 percent, and Spong retired Senator Robertson by a 614-vote margin, or 50.1 percent to 49.9 percent. In addition, Congressman Howard W. Smith, the conservative chairman of the House Rules Committee and another Byrd ally, was defeated in the Democratic primary by State Delegate George C. Rawlings, Jr., of Fredericksburg, a liberal Democrat.[18] Black voters played an important role in Robertson's defeat, giving Spong over 92 percent of their primary votes in Richmond and Norfolk. Blacks in these two cities cast only 2 percent of their votes for Byrd in the primary. In the general election black voters remained with Spong but overwhelmingly supported Byrd's Republican opponent, giving him 87 percent of their votes in Norfolk and 96 percent in Richmond.[19] Both Spong and Byrd defeated their Republican and Conservative opponents in the November balloting, Spong with 58.6 percent of the vote and Byrd trailing him by over five percentage points, at 53.3 percent.[20]

Thus, the Byrd organization, which had been weakened by Godwin's moves to broaden his base of support, suffered two major defeats in 1966 that presaged the organization's complete electoral collapse in the 1969 gubernatorial primary. It was becoming clear that black voters were exercising a critical role in the Democratic primary and were consistently voting for the Byrd opponent whether in the primary or in the general election, a situation that was to lead Byrd, Jr., to bypass the Democratic primary in his re-election effort in 1970.

The Spong victory, according to Eisenberg, "gave birth to a moderate wing of the Democratic Party which had evolved about his candidacy."[21] These moderates included "younger men, some from the organization, others who had worked with the organization on certain issues, and still others who were antiorganization but unwilling to align themselves with the party's liberal wing."[22] Opposing this group was the liberal faction led by State Sen. Henry E. Howell, Jr., of Norfolk. Howell, a lawyer, had gained considerable attention through his court battles to require legislative reapportionment. In the Tidewater region and increasingly in other parts of the state, Howell developed strong ties with blacks and organized labor.[23] A third faction consisted of what was left of the Byrd organization. Godwin was its nominal leader, but his abandonment of the organization's principles as governor left this once-dominant element of the Virginia Democracy in an uncertain position as the 1969 gubernatorial election approached.

There was no statewide election in 1968. In the presidential contest Nixon carried Virginia with 43.4 percent of the vote; Humphrey was second with 32.5 percent; and Wallace trailed badly at 23.6 percent. Wallace's strength was centered in the Southside counties.

The Byrd organization's candidate in the 1969 Democratic gubernatorial primary was Lt. Gov. Fred G. Pollard, an unabashed conservative. The standard-bearer of the moderate forces was Spong's campaign
manager, William C. Battle, who had managed John Kennedy's 1960
campaign in Virginia and served as ambassador to Australia but who
had never held elective office.[24] The liberals were led by their persistent
champion, State Senator Howell. Eisenberg described Howell's campaign this way:

> He ran a "people's campaign" with a slogan pledging to "keep the
> big boys honest." His antiestablishment campaign made effective use
> of billboards and television, which portrayed him as defender of the
> "little man." The Howell campaign admittedly was a populist one
> that sought to win the nomination on a base of blacks, labor, white
> small farmers, and blue-collar workers.[25]

Battle took the middle road, stressing the need for new leadership and
modernization in state government.[26] Pollard was unable to overcome his
identification with the disintegrating conservative Byrd organization and
finished a distant third in the July 1969 first primary, with 23.3 percent of
the vote. Battle led with 38.9 percent to Howell's 37.8 percent.

Accounts of the runoff, which was held a month later, stressed the
importance of Governor Godwin's "unprecedented" intervention in the
primary to support Battle, an act that infuriated the Howell camp.[27]
Battle defeated Howell 52.1 percent to 47.9 percent, but emerged from
the primaries with the "enduring wrath of the Howell forces."[28]

The major beneficiary of this intraparty dissension was Holton, the
skillful Mountain Republican politician who carried the GOP's gubernatorial banner again in 1969. Charles McDowell, a veteran Richmond
journalist, perceptively explained, in a 1973 interview, the splits in the
Democratic party that took place in 1969:

> At best, Henry [Howell] sulked in his tent. At worst, he invited his
> supporters to go over to Holton. In any event, a mass of black voters
> in Virginia went to Holton, and Holton put together [an] incredible
> coalition that he could have never put together if Henry Howell had
> really been there for Battle and if Battle had been . . . receptive of
> Henry's help. . . .
>
> They don't trust each other to this day. . . . Bill Battle regarded
> Howell as a radical troublemaker, never appreciated his good quali-
> ties. Howell regarded Battle as just another lion in the Byrd orga-
> nization. Battle was trapped in that whole situation, by the Byrd
> organization regarding him as an anti-Byrd candidate, and the left
> wing of the Democratic party regarding him as the Byrd candidate.
> Well, he pleased neither group in the Democratic party.[29]

Classified precinct results from Richmond and Roanoke in Table 11-1 indicate that the divisions between Battle and Howell were roughly reflected in the Democratic primary electorate. McDowell offered this excellent assessment of the differences between the squeezed forces of the middle and the Howell faction of the party:

> There aren't any intermediaries between the middle faction of the Democratic party and the Howell left, as it is called. The middle of the Democratic party really grew out of the Byrd wing. The middle of the Democratic party, the Byrd-Spong wing . . . really is those younger people, those sons of old Byrd people who've moved left, but their base is still in the establishment. Bill Spong . . . was general counsel for the biggest bank in his home town, the son of an established family, former president of the Virginia bar. That is where the Battle wing lives . . . . I mean it is the same people that are the Byrd wing except they are more enlightened, progressive people. They really mistrust Howell. In six years as a senator, Spong and Howell never had a productive discussion.[30]

Holton defeated Battle with 52.5 percent of the vote to 45.4 percent. As was indicated above, the dissension in the Democratic party clearly permitted this important gain for the Republican party.[31] One analyst of this election, Larry Sabato, concluded:

> Holton's victory, then, was due in good part to division in Democratic Party ranks. Howell's primary vote—an urban base of blacks, liberals, Wallaceites, and labor—proved decisive, and urban defection to Holton provided his victory margin.[32]

The wrath of the Howell forces in 1969 did not extend to the other two statewide Democratic nominees: J. Sargeant Reynolds, a member of the wealthy Reynolds Metals Company family, who was the nominee for lieutenant governor; and the candidate for attorney general, Andrew P. Miller, son of the Byrd organization's vociferous foe of the 1950s, Francis Pickens Miller. Labor and black groups that backed Republican Holton also supported the Democrats Reynolds and Miller,[33] who were both elected. After the election the moderates looked to Reynolds as the leading gubernatorial candidate for 1973 and as one who could bridge the split between the moderate and liberal wings of the party and return the governorship to the Democratic party. However, in 1971 Reynolds, thirty-four years old, died of a brain tumor.[34]

Rawlings, the liberal Democrat who had defeated Smith in the 1966 Eighth Congressional District Democratic primary, only to lose to the Republican William L. Scott in the general election, announced early that he would seek the 1970 Democratic nomination for the seat held

Table 11-1. Virginia Gubernatorial Vote in 1969 by Class and Race in
Richmond and Roanoke

	Lower Income	Middle Income (Whites)	Upper Income	Blacks
		Democratic Primary Runoff		
		Richmond		
Howell	60%	18%	12%	93%
Battle	40	82	88	7
		Roanoke		
Howell	60%	40%	13%	91%
Battle	40	60	87	9
		General Election		
		Richmond		
Battle	38%	40%	36%	37%
Holton	62	60	64	63
		Roanoke		
Battle	48%	41%	36%	61%
Holton	52	59	64	39

SOURCE: Numan V. Bartley and Hugh D. Graham, *Southern Elections: County and Precinct Data, 1950–1972* (Baton Rouge: Louisiana State Univ. Press, 1978), 406–7.

by Byrd; Rawlings was supported by Howell in this campaign.[35] Facing a determined liberal challenger in the Democratic primary, Senator Byrd announced he would seek re-election as an independent. A Virginia newspaperman noted that Byrd "didn't mention what . . . unofficial reports had hinted earlier: that a poll commissioned by Byrd had shown he would face considerably more trouble in a Democratic primary than he would running as an independent in the general election."[36]

The Republicans staged a bitter dispute at their July 1970 convention over whether to run a candidate against Byrd. The conservative Republican forces, led by U.S. Rep. Joel T. Broyhill of Northern Virginia's Tenth District, favored an endorsement of Byrd or, better still, neutrality between Byrd and his Democratic opponent, and no Republican candidate. But Governor Holton insisted and eventually prevailed in having the party nominate State Delegate Ray L. Garland of Roanoke.[37]

Senator Byrd won re-election with 53.5 percent of the vote to 31.2 percent for the Democratic nominee, Rawlings, and a weak 15.3 percent for Republican Garland. Byrd ran a strong race in all parts of the state.[38] Black voters, as would be expected given Byrd's showing among this group in 1966, overwhelmingly supported Rawlings.[39] But, as Sabato reported, "Rawlings, despite the strong support of Henry Howell, was not able to tap Howell's strength among Wallace voters. A survey of sample Wallace precincts . . . indicates that Harry Byrd secured the vast majority of Wallace voters."[40]

Beginning with the 1969 gubernatorial election and the three-way Senate race of 1970, the early 1970s were full of intraparty and interparty regrouping, the label independent often serving as a convenient resting point in the midst of the electoral turmoil. Byrd's decision to abandon the Democratic label was an important signal for conservative supporters of the Byrd family. Former Governor Godwin was a pivotal figure during this period of transition. Godwin backed Byrd in 1970 and also supported President Nixon's re-election in Virginia in 1972.[41] His complete conversion to the Republican party in 1973, as the GOP's gubernatorial candidate, offered conservative Democrats an unmistakable message to abandon their party, and substantial numbers of them did so. However, before considering the crucial 1973 gubernatorial election, one must mention important developments in 1971 and 1972.

While the Godwins and Byrds were moving slowly toward the Republican party, the moderate forces in the Democratic party were by no means conceding the party to Howell and his liberal allies. The death of Reynolds required an election in 1971 to fill the remaining two years of the lieutenant governor's term. Howell became a candidate and made no secret of his motive: "I'm running for Lieutenant Governor in order to be able to run for Governor [in 1973]."[42] Over the objections of the liberal forces, the Democratic State Central Committee in mid-June 1971 voted to nominate the party's candidate by convention rather than by primary.[43] Convinced that the convention nominating process was not in his interest, Howell sought the office as an independent.[44]

As the Democratic convention drew near, party leaders, Sabato wrote, "began talking earnestly again of a moderate-conservative coalition which . . . would return the Democratic Party to political dominance in Virginia."[45] After considerable maneuvering among the candidates,[46] the convention nominated State Delegate George J. Kostel of Clifton Forge, a moderate who aggressively sought conservative backing. Godwin (not yet in the full embrace of the GOP) became Kostel's campaign manager, and Senator Byrd endorsed him.[47] The Republicans, after a divisive convention, nominated a supporter of Holton, George P. Shafran. In the three-way race in November, Howell won with 40.0 percent of the vote to Kostel's 36.9 percent, the GOP nominee being a distant third at 23.1 percent.

In 1972, aided by the McGovern campaign, the liberals controlled the state Democratic convention, electing a Howell ally as party chairman. McDowell, the newspaperman, observed:

> They swept everything before them . . . . [However] Howell was never enthusiastic about McGovern. Howell spotted McGovern as a sure loser in Virginia from the first day that McGovern ever emerged as a candidate. But Howell reached out, and his group used, not in any bad sense, the McGovern movement to take over the party. Howell came to that convention not as a delegate but as an observer. He sat in the balcony and watched it and gave interviews about how he felt sure that when he ran for governor after a convention of this kind, he'd probably have to run as an independent; that this party down on that floor is just not strong enough to support a gubernatorial candidate . . . it is not broadly enough based.[48]

In the November balloting Nixon received 67.8 percent of the vote to McGovern's 30.1 percent in Virginia, and the Republican presidential sweep contributed to the election of Virginia's first outright Republican U.S. senator in the twentieth century.

Senator Spong was opposed for re-election in 1972 by U.S. Rep. William L. Scott, the conservative Republican who had won Smith's seat in 1966. Until the last few weeks of the campaign, Spong appeared to have a safe lead. Then an influx of national GOP aid—both in finances and personnel—revived Scott's lagging chances. The campaign launched "a television-radio blitz that linked Spong to gun control, busing, and George McGovern and pictured Scott firmly on the side of patriotism and Richard Nixon."[49] Scott won with 51.4 percent to Spong's 46.1 percent. McDowell concluded that the race issue, which he said in Virginia "now hides under the busing cover," was an important element in Spong's defeat.[50] Spong's own explanation of his defeat, given in a 1974 interview, stressed the predicament he saw himself in:

> You would have had to be awful dumb not to perceive this split that was coming along. Ideologically it had to be translated as liberal or conservative and just left anybody of moderate persuasion in bad shape. Traditionally Democrats have been able to prevail in presidential years because there was a Democratic governor for insulation purposes. I had none of that. Reynolds and Battle were my closest allies, and Battle was defeated and Reynolds died, and there was no insulation, nobody to take the heat off at all as it came. For the first time you could not separate a state race from a national race.[51]

By 1973 the moderate Democrats were in total disarray.

The Democratic party did not run a candidate for governor in 1973, but Howell's independent candidacy carried the Democratic identification in all but name. Godwin, now formally a Republican, received the GOP nomination. The newspaper reports before the gubernatorial voting in 1973 were full of references to realignment. For example, a *Washington Post* reporter wrote, "A victory for Godwin, who has called himself a 'Byrd Democrat-Republican' was seen as possibly leading to a realignment of conservatives under the GOP banner . . . ."[52] Another *Post* article captured the flavor of the campaign:

> Godwin, a conservative Democrat turned Republican, attacked Howell as a candidate of "labor bosses" and radical Democrats and characterized himself as a protector of Virginia's tradition of "stability, continuity, and predictability" in government.
>
> Howell . . . sought to portray Godwin as a proponent of special business interests and [aimed] for a populist-style coalition of liberals, blacks and blue-collar whites.
>
> Another key issue was the state's 4 percent sales tax on food and nonprescription drugs, which Howell proposed to repeal and replace with a package of new taxes aimed at more affluent Virginians . . . . Godwin denounced the plan as fiscally irresponsible.[53]

Godwin attempted to make school busing an issue, contending that, before running for governor in 1973, Howell had favored busing to achieve racial integration. But Howell said he opposed busing.[54] The election result was extremely close, Godwin winning with 50.7 percent of the vote to Howell's 49.3 percent.

An examination of the voting patterns from Virginia's counties and independent cities in the 1973 election illuminates the Democratic electoral pattern that emerged in the 1970s. Virginia's major population centers are located in what is called the urban corridor,[55] running from the heavily populated Washington suburbs in Northern Virginia (population of 920,000 in the 1970 census) through Richmond (518,000) and Petersburg–Colonial Heights (129,000) to the populous Tidewater cities in the Hampton Roads area, Newport News–Hampton (290,000) and Norfolk-Portsmouth (680,000). The other two large urban areas of the state are Roanoke (181,000) and Lynchburg (123,000), located in the Valley of Virginia. Howell carried the Tidewater cities; in Norfolk his majority was 65.6 percent, and in Portsmouth it was 67.7 percent. In Richmond, however, Howell's majority was only 51.8 percent, not nearly enough to offset Godwin's strength in the populous and conservative suburban counties of Henrico and Chesterfield, where Godwin's majorities were 72.5 percent and 71.2 percent, respectively. The two candidates ran nearly even in Northern Virginia.

Godwin swept Southside Virginia, the former bastion of the Byrd organization and the area that heavily backed Goldwater in 1964 and

Wallace in 1968. Many, but not all, of the traditional Republican counties throughout the Valley of Virginia and the Shenandoah Valley supported the Democrat-turned-Republican Godwin. Extensive classified precinct data were not available for this election, but Sabato reported that blacks gave Howell about 95 percent of their votes.[56]

A comparison of this important 1973 election with Carter's narrow loss to Ford in 1976, 48.0 percent to 49.3 percent, reveals a strong similarity in electoral patterns. Howell and Carter also ran similarly among blacks and among whites who had backed Wallace in 1968.[57] Thus, the kind of coalition that Carter put together throughout the South in 1976 was already in place three years earlier in Virginia. When Howell ran for governor again in 1977, his general election campaign once more conformed to this pattern.[58]

In 1976 the Republicans, unsuccessful in their efforts to get Senator Byrd to join their ranks, did not run an opponent against him in his campaign for re-election that year. Democratic candidates were not scrambling for the opportunity to oppose Byrd either; the party's nomination went by default to retired Adm. Elmo Zumwalt, a former chief of naval operations. Byrd was easily victorious with 57.2 percent of the vote to Zumwalt's 38.3 percent. A Republican moderate, Martin Perper, who had sought to oppose Byrd as his party's nominee but was barred by the party's decision not to oppose Byrd this time, ran as an independent and received 4.5 percent of the vote.[59]

Lt. Gov. John N. Dalton of Radford, a Republican elected in 1973, was the GOP candidate for governor in 1977. Andrew Miller, the state's attorney general, elected first in 1969 and re-elected in 1973, was expected to win the Democratic gubernatorial nomination. But Miller, who represented moderate forces in the Democratic party, was upset, 51.4 percent to 48.6 percent, by the champion of the liberals, Howell, in a Democratic primary marked by an extremely low turnout.[60]

Accounts of the 1977 gubernatorial general election indicated that the chief issue was Henry Howell, by then Virginia's most controversial political leader. A sampling of the campaign rhetoric follows:

> The depth of feeling was capsuled in a biting, anti-Howell phrase by Governor Godwin, putting the liberal challenger outside the pale of acceptability: In a campaign swing last week, the Governor called the Democratic candidate "not a Virginia gentleman."
> Mr. Howell fired back that "the Tories of Virginia—King George and King Godwin—can't stop us . . . .
> "Lucifer is loose in Virginia," Mr. Howell said [on the eve of the election]. "We in Virginia are turkeys for the utilities, and I don't know about you, but I am tired of being plucked. We have more

soldiers than the other fellow has. Let's identify those who are liberals and those who believe in life after birth."[61]

Dalton's victory with 55.9 percent of the vote to Howell's 43.3 percent
was of landslide proportions considering the closeness of the elections
throughout this period. One analyst concluded:

> While Dalton had no high positive rating, he also had a minuscule
> negative rating; and so Howell's attacks, whatever their merits, did
> not seem credible. In essence, Dalton made a poor target because he
> was an electoral tabula rasa, the antithesis of a sharply defined candi-
> date such as Howell.[62]

The next statewide election of the period was the 1978 race to fill the
Senate seat vacated by the Republican Scott, who decided not to seek a
second term. The Republicans, at a huge convention attended by over
7,500 delegates, nominated Richard Obenshain, a Blacksburg native
and former party chairman, on the sixth ballot.[63] Obenshain was considered the most conservative of the three leading candidates; the other
two were former Navy Secretary John W. Warner, who finished a close
second in the balloting; and former Governor Holton, who was third.[64]
In early August, Obenshain died in a plane crash, and the GOP state
committee gave the nomination to Warner.[65]

Former Attorney General Miller, the moderate who had good relations with the conservative sectors of the Democratic party, received his
party's nomination at its June 10, 1978, convention after three ballots.[66]
One newspaper account of the campaign stressed Miller's conservative
ties:

> Mr. Miller was putting on his own display of conservative backing
> at a solidarity breakfast . . . in Richmond. The head table included
> many of the most famous figures from the days when the common-
> wealth was resisting desegregation under the leadership of the late
> Harry Flood Byrd, Sr.
> Former Representative Watkins Abbitt, calling himself a "super-
> conservative," . . . testified that Andy Miller was now a satisfactory
> distance right of center . . . .[67]

Miller also had the backing of the leading state labor organizations and
other Howell supporters,[68] although there was a noticeable decline in
enthusiasm among some of these elements after Miller decided not to
ask Howell to take part in the campaign.[69]

Warner won the extremely close election with 50.1 percent of the
vote to Miller's 49.7 percent. The electoral patterns were similar to
those of the last two gubernatorial elections and Carter's presidential

race, indicating a persistence of the basic two-party pattern established in the crucial Howell-Godwin contest of 1973.

In 1980 Virginia was one of the three Southern states that Ronald Reagan won by a substantial majority. The California Republican, who received the endorsement of Senator Byrd,[70] won 53.0 percent of the vote to Carter's 40.3 percent.[71] In addition, the Virginia GOP made a nearly clean sweep of the state's U.S. House delegation, winning nine of the ten seats.[72] (The lone Democratic victor, incidentally, carried a solidly Republican voting record.)

Figure 11-1 depicts the disintegration of Virginia's once-powerful Democratic party. None of the comparable party-strength figures presented in the other ten state chapters shows a Democratic decline as deep and prolonged as the one in Virginia.

In the 1981 gubernatorial election, however, a chastened and transformed Virginia Democracy made a comeback. Lt. Gov. Charles S. (Chuck) Robb, the Democratic nominee, won the governorship by abandoning the sharp liberal appeal of the Howell campaigns. Robb, a son-in-law of former President Johnson who was invariably described in newspaper accounts as a conservative, skillfully walked the line between the disparate and mistrustful elements of the Virginia Democratic party and assembled the same biracial, ideologically diverse coalition that had provided winning statewide margins for Democrats in the other Southern states throughout the 1970s. Robb's approach to the electorate is illustrated by the themes he struck in his kickoff campaign address in March 1981. In it Robb sought to claim the Byrd mantle of governmental restraint by reminding his audience that "Democrats in Virginia— not Republicans—chiseled the commandments of fiscal conservatism into the laws and traditions of our commonwealth." At the same time he urged the repeal of Virginia's sales tax on food, asserting that the tax "impacts so disproportionately" on the poor and the elderly.[73] This delicate balancing act drew an approving comment from Virginia's NAACP director, Jack Gravely: "His speech had a little something in it for everybody."[74]

The outspoken liberals were skeptical of Robb. In late May 1981, during the Virginia Beach convention that unanimously nominated Robb, Henry Howell—who was not invited by the new party leadership to address the gathering—summed up the situation this way, as reported in the *Washington Post*:

> "Hell," scoffed Howell, "Democrats—real Democrats—haven't won an election [for governor] in Virginia for 100 years."
> If that's the case, Howell was asked, why shouldn't Robb portray

himself as conservative as possible in an effort to defeat his [Republican] opponent . . . ?

"Because you ought to stand for something more than just wanting to win," Howell replied.

"This used to be a one-party state," he explained. For more than half a century, he said, followers of the late Sen. Harry Flood Byrd Sr. controlled the party. "They were Republicans in philosophy. The state Democratic Party never believed in the principles of the national Democratic Party.

"But now that the Byrd Democrats are where they belong, in the Republican Party, we should be trying to build a coalition that represents most of the people—labor, blacks, farmers.

"Instead, Chuck has gone out of his way to bring back Bill Tuck [an anti-union, segregationist former governor] and Watt Abbitt [an ultraconservative former congressman]."[75]

Howell did say, however, that he would vote for Robb [76]

Robb's strategy was aided by a simple desire among Democrats to recapture the governorship after twelve years on the outside. One veteran political reporter, Melville Carico, articulated this spirit after listening to a Robb speech in Roanoke: "There was nothing in it anyone could argue with. But it doesn't matter a damn what he says. The Democrats want to win this one for a change."[77] And in the end the liberals, with no place to go, followed Howell's lead and voted for Robb,

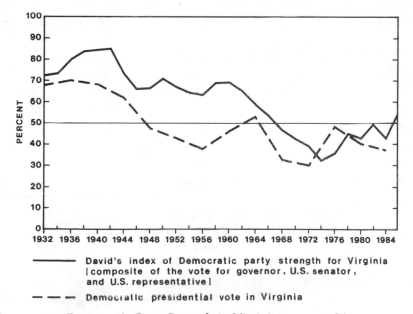

Figure 11-1. Democratic Party Strength in Virginia, 1932–1986

who received 53.7 percent of the vote[78] to 46.3 percent for the Republican nominee, Atty. Gen. J. Marshall Coleman.

Coleman had his own troubles. Godwin and his associates were less than enthusiastic about Coleman, viewing him as overly brash, self-confident, and even a bit too liberal. According to a newspaper report, Coleman angered "old-line conservatives when he defeated Democrat Edward Lane in 1977 [for attorney general] by resurrecting Lane's segregationist past, a past many of the old guard shared."[79] Ironically, racially charged remarks by Godwin at a Richmond rally for Coleman, which was attended by President Reagan, became a last-minute campaign issue that was credited with contributing to a high turnout among blacks, few of whom supported Coleman. The remarks that caused the furor were reported as follows in the *Washington Post*:

> Godwin, whose personal distaste for Coleman has been a poorly concealed secret throughout this campaign, had little to say about his party's nominee tonight. He lashed out instead at Robb's support of the Voting Rights Act, contending that extension of the key federal civil rights legislation of the 1960's "would keep this state in bondage to the Department of Justice."[80]

Coleman denied the resulting charge that his campaign was using racist tactics: "I resent being branded a racist," he said a few days later during the final debate between the two candidates.[81]

Robb's victory breathed new life into the Virginia Democratic party. Although the party failed to capture the U.S. Senate seat vacated in 1982 by Senator Byrd's retirement, it picked up three U.S. House seats that year[82] and sizably increased the party's strength as measured in Figure 11-1. Lt. Gov. Richard J. Davis, a sixty-one-year-old former mayor of Portsmouth who had been elected with Robb in 1981, lost the 1982 Senate race to the Republican Paul S. Trible, Jr., an aggressive, thirty-five-year-old former county prosecutor and three-term congressman from the Tidewater area; Trible received 51.2 percent of the vote to Davis's 48.8 percent. In a year in which Republicans suffered setbacks throughout the South and the nation, Trible's accomplishment was a significant personal achievement. Davis's fellow Democrats tended to attribute their nominee's narrow loss to Davis's lack of consuming desire to win and to Trible's personal attractiveness.[83]

Although the return of figures more moderate than Henry Howell to leadership in Virginia's Democratic party contributed to lifting the party from its low point at the end of the 1970s, it cannot be forgotten that the political events of recent decades have transformed Virginia's partisan landscape. This is abundantly illustrated by a poll conducted at the

College of William and Mary in early 1982. The differences in demographic characteristics among those Virginians who identified with the two parties reflect the changes. For example, blacks made up 31 percent of those in the poll who identified with the Democratic party. Among the more well-to-do, Republican identifiers were more numerous; for example, Virginia Republicans made up 43 percent of those earning over $30,000 a year while Democrats constituted only 23 percent of that category.[84] On various issues and in overall ideology, the Democratic identifiers were far more liberal than the Republicans.[85] On the basis of the findings of their survey, Alan I. Abramowitz, John McGlennon, and Ronald Rapoport concluded:

> Along with the emergence of the Republican Party, the past three decades have also witnessed a transformation of the Virginia Democratic Party due to the expansion of the black electorate, migration from the North, and defection of large numbers of conservative former Democrats to the GOP. Even with the election of a team of moderate-to-conservative Democrats to the top three state government offices in 1981, the Virginia Democratic Party cannot return to the Byrd era. Charles Robb, Richard Davis, and Jerry Baliles [who was elected attorney general in 1981] would not have been elected without the solid support of liberal and black Democrats. They cannot afford to ignore the views of their liberal and black supporters any more than they can afford to ignore the views of the moderate-to-conservative whites whose return to the Democratic Party also made the 1981 victories possible. Holding this diverse coalition together will be a difficult test for these new Democratic leaders.[86]

Virginia—Conclusion

In Virginia, as in Tennessee, it is inappropriate to talk of Democratic statewide dominance. The record of two-party competition over the last two decades demonstrates that the Virginia Democratic party underwent enormous changes amid bitter feuding between rival party elements, some of whom ended up in the Republican party.

One central theme in Virginia was the movement of Byrd Democrats, who represented economic conservatism along with white supremacy, into the Republican party. Godwin was a pivotal figure in this process. The other theme, which is related, was the demise in the 1970s of the moderate Democrats, who were squeezed between the Godwin-style Democrats turned Republicans and the followers of the persistent liberal champion, Howell. Throughout the South the Democratic moderates—West and Riley in South Carolina, Carter and Busbee in Georgia, and Hunt in North Carolina, to name a few—were able, in general, to hold the center against the more conservative and the more liberal Democrats. Virginia's moderates, the Spongs and the Battles, were defeated by the early 1970s, and the state party was captured by the Howell forces.

These bitter factional disputes resulted in the first Republican statewide success, Holton's election in 1969. Similarly, the inability of the wings of the Democratic party to reach accommodation led Godwin to embrace the GOP completely in 1973. And Godwin's narrow victory over Howell in 1973 cemented the movement of a number of conservative Democrats into the Republican party. This GOP coalition has shown its ability to win statewide majorities on several occasions since 1973.

The abatement of the race issue by the early 1970s and overwhelming black support were important to Howell's ability to put together a black-white coalition roughly along economic-class lines. Howell, unlike the Democratic senatorial nominee Rawlings in 1970 or McGovern in 1972, was able to attach to his coalition a large number of low-income whites, many of whom had supported Wallace in 1968. However, Howell's manner of polarizing campaigns with his clear left-of-center economic appeal permitted little ambiguity in the choice, and Godwin was able to pick up enough support from more traditional white Democrats to win. If Howell had been elected governor, perhaps he would have been able to add to his coalition and push it into the range of a safe majority. The fact remains, though, that the Howell wing of the Democratic party was a loser in Virginia throughout the 1970s.

But in the 1981 gubernatorial election, Virginia Democrats under a leader far less liberal than Howell were able to regain the governorship. In his campaign Robb demonstrated the coalition-building skills that have served Democrats so well elsewhere in the South during the post–civil rights era. That Democratic coalition is likely to remain under heavy strain, given the state party's legacy from the bitter years of factional squabbling when Henry Howell led a fundamental transformation of Virginia party politics.

12

Tennessee:
Composite of All the South

Tennessee offers one of the more intricate Southern scenarios for state-wide two-party development. Of the three Mountain Republican states, Tennessee had the strongest Republican party dating its origins from the Civil War conflict and the Unionist sentiment of the people in the highlands.[1] As a result, in East Tennessee, one of the state's three grand divisions, Republicans have traditionally won state legislative elections and both congressional seats. The link between the Republican party's strength there and the antisecessionist movement of the 1860s prompted V. O. Key, Jr., to write in 1949:

> Persistence of partisan loyalties in Tennessee should give pause to those who predict drastic party realignments in the short run. Social mechanisms for the transmission and perpetuation of partisan faiths have an effectiveness far more potent than the political issue of the day. And the consequences of the projection of the past into the present for Tennessee politics are great.[2]

Because of its geographical and historical diversity, the state contains a complex mixture of nearly all of the important elements found throughout the South. In West Tennessee, an area virtually indistinguishable from nearby parts of the Deep South, the race issue was a major factor in voting-pattern shifts during the civil rights and post–civil rights eras. In Middle Tennessee, where the New Deal earthquake had a significant impact, a relatively strong class-based voting division took hold early and withstood longer than elsewhere the lure of the racial issue. And, of course, the traditional Republicanism of East Tennessee provided the challenging party with a substantial base on which to build. East Tennessee is also noteworthy because it exhibited signs that the barriers to a New Deal–style party alignment were breaking down from the other direction as well: Democratic economic policies began to weaken the Civil War–era cleavage that favored the Republicans in the area.

Within this diverse state mix, skillful politicians of both parties battled throughout the 1970s and early 1980s, taking advantage of national influences, such as Watergate, the 1974 recession, and a Southern farmer's becoming the national Democratic standard-bearer, and of peculiar state events, such as the tainting of a Democratic administration with corruption. And they developed a highly competitive two-party system at the state level, perhaps by 1982 the most competitive in the South.

Eisenhower defeated Stevenson by roughly one percentage point in both 1952 and 1956, and Nixon in 1960 carried the state with 52.9 percent of the vote to Kennedy's 45.8 percent.[3] In at least one city for which classified precinct data were available, Nashville, whites divided sharply along class lines, Stevenson winning 76 percent of the votes of lower-income whites but only 38 percent of those of upper-income whites.[4]

In the 1964 presidential election in Tennessee, Goldwater lost decisively to Johnson, 44.5 percent to 55.5 percent. Cited most often to account for the Republican presidential decline that year after three straight GOP successes was Goldwater's lack of support for the Tennessee Valley Authority and other federal initiatives. "[R]acial fears," Bartley and Graham wrote, "were not strong enough to overcome old New Deal loyalties among lower-income whites and strong reservations about Goldwater's hostility to TVA, social security, and other economic mainstays of the New Deal tradition."[5] In the GOP defeat of that year, what could not be overlooked was that in Memphis, the state's largest city, Goldwater's racial appeal obliterated class distinctions among whites. As Table 12-1 reveals, 66 percent of the lower-income whites in Memphis chose the Republican Goldwater over Johnson. Apparently these voters made no distinction between national and statewide candidates, because the two Republican senatorial candidates in 1964 did about as well as Goldwater among this previously untapped (by Republicans) and lucrative source of voters.[6]

Prior to 1964 the Republican party, at that time still centered in East Tennessee, rarely contested statewide elections, preferring instead to support conservative Democrats in the Democratic primary.[7] The death

Table 12-1. Presidential, Senatorial, and Gubernatorial Vote by Class and
Race in Memphis, 1960–1972

	Lower Income	Middle Income (Whites)	Upper Income	Blacks
		1960		
Kennedy	50%	42%	30%	66%
Nixon	50	58	70	34
		1964		
Johnson	34%	32%	30%	99%
Goldwater	66	68	70	1
		1966		
Clement	32%	30%	25%	96%
Baker	68	70	75	4
		1968		
Humphrey	9%	11%	16%	98%
Nixon	24	35	62	2
Wallace	67	54	22	0
		1970		
Gore	27%	30%	21%	98%
Brock	73	70	79	2
Hooker	29%	25%	14%	98%
Dunn	67	72	85	2
		1972		
McGovern	24%	10%	10%	88%
Nixon	74	87	88	12
Blanton	32%	27%	18%	60%
Baker	68	73	82	40

SOURCE: Numan V. Bartley and Hugh D. Graham, *Southern Elections: County and Precinct Data, 1950–1972* (Baton Rouge: Louisiana State Univ. Press, 1978), 392.

of the fervent New Dealer Sen. Estes Kefauver in 1963 offered Republicans a chance at two Senate seats in 1964; Sen. Albert Gore, a left-of-center Democrat like Kefauver, also came up for re-election that year. The traditional section of the Tennessee Republican party put forward one of the two candidates for the U.S. Senate seats, Howard H. Baker, Jr., the son of an East Tennessee congressman; Baker sought the remaining two years of Kefauver's term. Dan H. Kuykendall of Memphis challenged Gore for the full six-year term. Kuykendall was a representative of a "new guard" of Goldwater Republicans who sought to expand the party into a statewide force. Norman L. Parks described this element:

Politically inexperienced, but deeply ideological and impatient with
the supineness of the Old Guard, the New Guard proposed to bring
to politics the hard sell, the grass roots drive, and the systematic
organization which generated success in the business world. Their
goal was the merging of the Democratic Party traditionalists, the
West Tennessee planter belt, the white supremacists, the representatives of banking, finance, industry, and insurance, and ideological
conservatives in general under the Republican banner.[8]

In addition to Kuykendall, an executive with Proctor & Gamble in
Memphis, another leader of the "new guard" was William E. (Bill)
Brock III, heir to the Brock candy-manufacturing fortune, who had
captured the Chattanooga-centered U.S. House seat in 1962.

Despite the different political backgrounds of Baker and Kuykendall,
their vote patterns in 1964 were nearly identical.[9] Both GOP candidates
lost in 1964, but they ran better than Goldwater. Senator Gore defeated
Kuykendall, 53.6 percent to 46.4 percent, and Congressman Ross Bass,
a Kefauver liberal, defeated Baker, 52.1 to 47.4 percent.

In 1966 Senator Bass lost the Democratic nomination to Gov. Frank
Clement[10] in a bitterly divisive primary, which is one factor cited to
explain Clement's defeat by Baker in the general election.[11] Baker's
victory, with 55.7 percent of the vote to Clement's 44.3 percent, was
also caused in part by the racially spurred Democratic defections in
West Tennessee. In Memphis, Baker captured 68 percent of the vote in
lower-income white precincts; he managed only 4 percent in black
districts there.[12] Other, more localized reasons have been offered for
Baker's victory.[13] Whatever the reasons, with Baker's statewide victory in
1966 "the dam had truly broken, and the Republicans were on their
way with a statewide appeal."[14]

The 1968 Wallace candidacy in Tennessee obliterated prior consistent patterns of Democratic presidential support[15] and left the national
party nominee in third place with 28.1 percent. Nixon carried the state
with a 37.9 percent plurality to Wallace's 34.0 percent. The precinct
returns from Memphis (Table 12-1) and from the state's second-largest
city, Nashville (Table 12-2), show that lower-income whites flocked to
Wallace.[16] In Nashville this was especially noteworthy because this
same class of whites had held firm with Johnson only four years earlier.
A county-level analysis shows that Wallace did especially well in West
Tennessee. Race was, of course, the chief cause of this 1968 outcome.[17]

The statewide elections of 1970 in Tennessee proved to be the most
successful for the Republican party in the South up to that point. They
deserve careful scrutiny.

In 1970 Senator Gore narrowly survived a Democratic primary chal-

Table 12-2. Presidential, Senatorial, and Gubernatorial Vote by Class and
Race in Nashville, 1960–1972

	Lower Income	Middle Income (Whites)	Upper Income	Blacks
		1960		
Kennedy	60%	52%	34%	68%
Nixon	40	48	66	32
		1964		
Johnson	67%	60%	36%	98%
Goldwater	33	40	64	2
		1966		
Clement	58%	56%	38%	87%
Baker	42	44	62	13
		1968		
Humphrey	22%	22%	21%	94%
Nixon	22	30	62	4
Wallace	56	48	17	2
		1970		
Gore	60%	53%	31%	97%
Brock	40	47	69	3
Hooker	53%	47%	21%	97%
Dunn	44	50	78	3
		1972		
McGovern	32%	24%	20%	92%
Nixon	64	73	79	7
Blanton	54%	41%	18%	64%
Baker	46	59	82	36

SOURCE: Numan V. Bartley and Hugh D. Graham, *Southern Elections: County and Precinct Data, 1950–1972* (Baton Rouge: Louisiana State Univ. Press, 1978), 391.

lenge and faced a November campaign against Congressman Brock, the Chattanooga Republican. At the heart of this election, which attracted considerable national attention, was the race issue, although with a more subtle presentation for the newly arrived post–civil rights era. David Halberstam captured the Brock approach:

> It is made all the more shabby by the fact that he [Brock] injects this stuff into the atmosphere at one level and then acts the nice young man. His newspaper ads and television ads are hitting away daily at the most emotional issues they can touch. His media firm came down here a year and a half ago and found that the five most emotional issues were race, gun control, the war, busing, and prayer, and they are making this the campaign. Keep Gore answer-

ing false charges. It is not the old, sweaty, gallus-snapping racism that was once used against Claude Pepper; rather it is cool and modern. And while I have covered shabby racist campaigns in the past, there is something about this one which is distinctive. This is the first time that a campaign like this has been tied to the President, the Vice President, and the Attorney General of the United States. [18]

To the charge that he had lost touch with his home state, Gore responded by conducting a vigorous campaign,

> barnstorming the hustings, appearing in shirt-sleeves at supermarkets and factory gates, while Brock played to the receptive junior chambers of commerce. Gore proclaimed that he had grown up "with Tennessee dirt on my hands, not Chattanooga chocolate," that he and a majority of Tennessee's congressional delegation had voted for fifty bills that involved federal aid to Tennessee while Brock had voted against all fifty. [19]

In the fight to capture the sizable Wallace Democrats, the election boiled down to New Deal–style economics versus race. In 1970 in West Tennessee the latter won out. Brock swamped Gore in the lower-income white precincts of Memphis and carried a majority in most West Tennessee counties [20] to go along with traditional GOP majorities in East Tennessee. Gore's appeal to Democratic pocketbook issues did bring back many of the lower-income white Wallace voter in Nashville, where Gore's margin in these precincts was 60 percent to Brock's 40 percent (see Table 12-2). [21] Statewide Brock's winning margin was 51.3 percent to 47.4 percent for Gore.

In contrast to what had occurred in 1966, when the Republicans had not offered a gubernatorial nominee, in 1970 they fielded a challenger; Winfield Dunn, an attractive Memphis dentist who had been active in party affairs throughout the 1960s, received the GOP nomination for governor. The Democratic nominee, John J. Hooker, Jr., a vigorous, liberal-leaning lawyer, was handicapped in the race by publicity about his financial difficulties involving a fried-chicken enterprise. [22] During the campaign Hooker bore down on the economic issue, telling one group:

> The Republican economists in Washington believe that you can control inflation through unemployment and high interest rates . . . .
> The Democratic party believes in productivity and in people working.
> We are involved in a contest with the farmers and working people of the Democratic party on one side, and the silk stockings, the do-nothings . . . on the other. [23]

There is no doubt that the Gore-Brock race and the Hooker-Dunn race influenced each other.[24] Dunn's victory margin was slightly larger than Brock's; Dunn received 52.0 percent of the vote to Hooker's 46.0 percent. (The Memphis and Nashville precinct returns were similar for both contests.)

In 1972 Nixon won Tennessee's electoral votes overwhelmingly by combining his 1968 support with Wallace's.[25] Senator Baker easily won re-election that year over U.S. Rep. Ray Blanton, a conservative West Tennessee Democrat, 61.6 percent to 37.9 percent. Tables 12-1 and 12-2 demonstrate that Baker received considerable support among urban blacks in 1972; Blanton had once supported Wallace.[26]

Capitalizing on his name recognition from his losing 1972 Senate race, Blanton won the 1974 Democratic gubernatorial nomination over a large field with only 22.7 percent of the vote.[27] The Republicans nominated Lamar Alexander, a youthful lawyer who had served on the pre-Watergate Nixon White House staff. With the 1974 recession and the Watergate scandal prominent in the minds of the voters, Blanton was able to unify the Democratic party with a skillful campaign. Jack Bass and Walter DeVries described the race this way:

> Blanton ran a methodical campaign sticking closely to bread-and-butter issues, playing heavily on the Democratic tide. He spoke out against higher interest rates and against Tennessee's fair trade laws that limited retail discount sales, and he made a populist pitch against banks and insurance companies. His polls showed that Lamar Alexander, a smoothly articulate lawyer who had managed campaigns for Dunn and Baker, was being hurt by the fact that he had worked for a while in the Nixon White House. Blanton took Democratic congressional candidates to Washington to meet with labor officials and later declared, "At least when I go to Washington I can see my friends; he [Alexander] has to go to the Lewistown prison" (where several former White House aides were serving Watergate-related sentences).[28]

Blanton's victory was the first indication in Tennessee that the Wallace voters were coming back to the Democratic party. A comparison of Blanton's winning pattern with Gore's 1970 effort[29] reveals that the heavily pro-Wallace West Tennessee counties were the main deviants; these counties gave Blanton roughly fifteen percentage points more than Gore.[30] In the lower-income white precincts of Memphis, Blanton improved considerably on the showing of all Democratic candidates since Kennedy in 1960, although Alexander outdrew him, 55 percent to 45 percent.

Two years later similar patterns resulted in two more Democratic

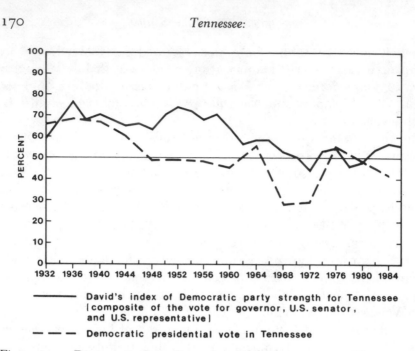

Figure 12-1. Democratic Party Strength in Tennessee, 1932–1986

victories: in the races for Brock's Senate seat and for Tennessee's 1976 presidential electoral votes.[31] An examination of these elections illuminates certain key ingredients at work in the state that, in the main, accounted for a mild resurgence of Democratic party strength during the middle 1970s. This Democratic resurgence appears clearly in Figure 12-1.

In 1976 James R. (Jim) Sasser, a Nashville lawyer and former chairman of the state Democratic party, defeated Senator Brock with 52.5 percent of the vote to 47.0 percent. During the campaign Sasser described his main theme to a reporter:

> Brock is a special-interest senator who represents exclusively money interests—banks and insurance companies. He votes right down the line with the oil companies. AMA [American Medical Association] has him in their hip pocket. He votes against the tax cut bill, against strengthening the anti-trust laws and against Medicare in 1965.[32]

The same reporter asked Brock to define the difference between himself and Sasser, and received this reply:

> My philosophy is less government, his philosophy is more. My philosophy is less taxes, his is more. My philosophy is less spending, his is more. My philosophy is more freedom and I think his would lead to less.[33]

As these quotations from the candidates suggest, this election stressed fundamental economic issues that have divided the two national parties since the 1930s; accounts of the election make no mention of the race issue.

The Democratic senatorial candidate in 1976 did not have to carry the liability of an unpopular national party nominee. In all the pre-election polls Jimmy Carter ran ahead of Sasser,[34] and in the election he defeated Ford for the state's ten electoral votes, 55.9 percent to 42.9 percent, or over three percentage points higher than Sasser's total. This election provides a strong example of the importance to state Democrats of the removal of the race issue from center stage and the ascendancy as national standard-bearer of a moderate Southerner not identified with the divisive civil rights efforts that the Northern wing of the party had led in the 1960s. In the West Tennessee counties that had abandoned Gore in 1970, Sasser won majorities, as is shown in Map 12-1.[35] (Precinct data in Memphis reveal that Carter polled over a majority in the city's lower-income white precincts.)[36]

A comparison of the county-level support for Johnson in 1964 with that for Carter in 1976 illustrates the persisting regional nature of Tennessee two-party competition.[37] Middle Tennessee counties provided the highest percentages for both Democratic standard-bearers. The weakest counties for the Democrats were located mainly in East Tennessee, although there were exceptions. The West Tennessee counties were chiefly in the middle ranges.

The voters of Middle Tennessee have been plainly less receptive to the Republican appeal, which is exemplified by Brock's 1976 statement of his philosophical differences with Sasser. U.S. Rep. Albert Gore, Jr., the son of former Senator Gore, whose largely rural, small-town district covered much of Middle Tennessee east of Nashville, provided a reason why the Republican appeal has been weakest in his area of the state:[38]

> You can't underestimate the historical trends. Look at the impact of TVA and the New Deal on this district. In many ways the New Deal was a great shaft of light that filled the lives of many people with hope that had not been there. They saw the tremendous benefit that can come to a people, to a region as well as to an entire nation, from dynamic, progressive leadership not afraid to change traditional patterns. People who lived without electricity and got it as the result of rural electrification are not classic conservatives when it comes to every new government program. People who saw industry come into the region not as the result of the invisible hand of Adam Smith but rather as the result of dynamic programs stimulated by a vision of the future that first came from government leaders do not trust the free enterprise system to solve each and every problem.

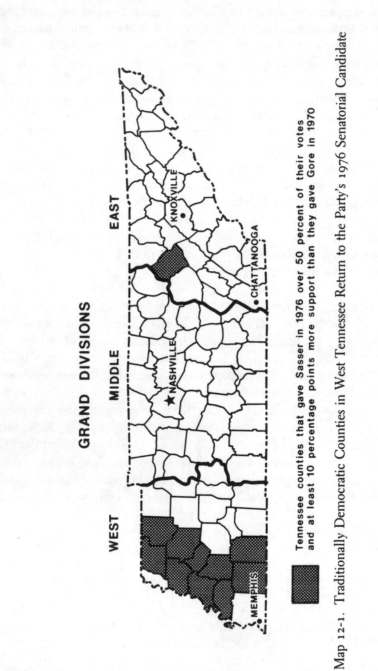

Map 12-1. Traditionally Democratic Counties in West Tennessee Return to the Party's 1976 Senatorial Candidate

So, to accept a label of rural conservative as applicable to Middle Tennessee, I think misses the mark. There is a populist heritage there. There is a respect for the value of progressive programs.[39]

Another interesting phenomenon in Tennessee was the growth of Democratic strength in East Tennessee, especially in the far eastern counties.[40] This confirms the spread of the New Deal–style alignment from a direction directly opposite to the Southern norm. In East Tennessee traditional Mountain Republican voting has declined as poorer whites have supported the economic policies of the Democratic party.[41] Shirley Chapman, in a study entitled *Democrats Challenge Traditional Republicanism in Upper East Tennessee*, stated what Democratic observers there believed would be necessary for the Democratic party to grow in that region of the state:

> Democrats all agree that the area is moving toward two-party activity and seem to be universally optimistic about Democratic gains in elections in the near future. Several noted that if candidates would run as "Democrats" and not as individuals waging campaigns personally, the party would gain recognition and acceptance in the area faster.[42]

Chapman added:

> If the Democrats are to produce a constant challenge, as they now do in Sullivan County alone, they must produce strong candidates who are from among the district's influential citizens. They cannot switch their Democratic votes at the local legislative district level to vote for the established Republican leaders.[43]

Of course, statements similar to these were also uttered by hundreds of Republican party activists throughout the South as they grappled with the difficulty of party building below the presidential level.

In 1978 Senator Baker won re-election with 55.5 percent of the vote to 40.3 percent for Jane Eskind, the Democratic nominee, and 4.0 percent for an independent, Thomas J. Anderson. One reporter described the campaign as follows: "But while the central theme of Eskind's campaign is that Baker is not representing the state but using [his Senate seat] to further his own national ambitions, there is little evidence that the incumbent's popularity is on the wane."[44] In 1978 the Senate election, however, was overshadowed by the gubernatorial election.[45]

The GOP recaptured the governorship in 1978 in an election that was not dominated by national issues. Rather, local matters involving the styles and personalities of the candidates and the controversies surrounding the unpopular outgoing governor, Blanton, who was indicted and convicted of extortion, conspiracy, and mail fraud after leaving office, were most prominent in this election.[46] Jake Butcher, a wealthy Knoxville banker, won the Democratic nomination in a bitter primary in which he spent $2.1 million. In the general election Butcher again spent his own money freely, especially on television commercials, and this spending itself became an issue. Even the Memphis campaign consultant who handled Butcher's advertising campaign, DeLoss Walker, supported this view: "You can spend too much money and reach the urp-ing point in exposure. I think Jake reached it."[47] Another observer added, "Butcher didn't present an aura of trust. People are suspicious of someone who makes a lot of money fast. He never established integrity, and his lavish campaign spending called attention to that."[48]

The beneficiary of the Democrat's woes was the politician whom the now discredited Blanton had defeated four years earlier, the Republican Lamar Alexander. Concerned about the image he believed he had in 1974 as a stuffy country club Republican, Alexander took a chapter from the 1970 campaign book of Lawton Chiles of Florida and made a 1,000-mile walk across Tennessee.[49] As a result his 1978 image became one of a "folksy, down-to-earth person walking . . . to meet with and listen to the people."[50] A Memphis *Commercial Appeal* reporter wrote:

> Alexander, in a red and black checked shirt, managed to sell himself as a man of the people—a working man. He also managed to sell Butcher as the rich guy who lives up on the hill and looks down at the little people.
> It eventually boiled down to Alexander's walk and Butcher's money, and . . . the walk won.[51]

In regard to this election J. Leiper Freeman concluded:

> The Democrats failed to achieve unity in the fall campaign. Not only did Butcher's money campaign cause troubles, but he had great difficulty in coping with the Republicans' criticism of Blanton without offending the Governor. Furthermore, several Democratic officials announced their defection after the primary . . . .[52]

Alexander was elected governor with 55.6 percent of the vote to Butcher's 44.0.

The 1982 elections brought another full round of heated two-party contests.[53] In the end the two incumbents holding statewide office, Sasser, the Democratic senator, and Alexander, the Republican governor, won re-election, but a review of what occurred highlights the nature of two-party politics in the state in the early 1980s.

Sasser started early. Twenty-two months before the election a *New*

York Times article reported on his intense schedule of appearances around the state. Asked about this fast pace with the election so far off, Sasser responded, "I've known since I knocked off Bill Brock, one of the big boys, that they'd be after me in '82. . . . I'm the new bull in the pasture. . . . I've got to prove that the first election was for real."[54]

The conservative Republican Robin L. Beard, a five-term congressman who represented a district that stretched from the outskirts of Nashville to the Memphis suburbs, conducted a hard-hitting campaign, attacking Sasser's voting record on issues such as school busing, prayer in public schools, abortion, and foreign aid.[55] Beard's tactics were partly responsible for prompting the *Nashville Banner* to withdraw its endorsement of Beard, saying, "Rep. Beard has shunned the mood of the people of this state and has instead decided to continue his Senate election drive by campaigning on outdated conservative demagoguery."[56]

Sasser labeled Beard's attacks vicious distortions and responded with a recitation of his own conservative positions on many of these social issues.[57] The *New York Times* wrote that, when a school prayer measure was considered in the Senate during the fall campaign, Sasser voted with Sen. Jesse Helms, the arch-conservative North Carolina Republican, "at every opportunity."[58] The *Times* also reported that Sasser expressed concern over Beard's emphasis on social issues: "Obviously these attacks are calculated to go after the blue collar working-class people and fundamentalists who are Democratic voters in the South. They are trying to portray me as unpatriotic and un-American and ungodly."[59]

Apparently Sasser was not saved because of the backfiring of the Beard charges. Eddie Mahe, Beard's political consultant, contended that the onslaught, especially on abortion, cut Sasser's lead from thirty percentage points to fifteen. Rather, President Reagan's handling of the faltering economy had moved social issues to the back burner for many voters. Mahe acknowledged the difficulty: "The damned economy is not working the way we hoped or thought it would."[60] Sasser defeated Beard with 61.8 percent of the vote to 38.2 percent.

In the 1982 gubernatorial race Governor Alexander's Democratic challenger, Mayor Randy Tyree of Knoxville, did all he could to make the contest against Alexander a referendum on President Reagan's economic policies, especially the high unemployment rate. Tyree said in a September debate with Alexander:

> I'm not satisfied with leadership that fails to take aggressive action when . . . we're in a recession. I don't think we can afford anything less in the next four years than the decisive leadership this state needs. The stakes are simply too high.

[Tyree then pointed to the importance of the political party in providing such leadership.]

I'm proud, very proud to be representing the Democratic party. The party of Franklin Roosevelt, Harry Truman, and John F. Kennedy—the party that's led the way on Social Security, Medicare and aid to education.

My opponent, a Republican, represents and supports the party under Ronald Reagan which has cut aid to education, has reduced Social Security benefits and has brought on the worst recession we've had in this country in recent history.[61]

Alexander countered by claiming that he was not responsible for the nationwide economic decline. The *Congressional Quarterly* described one effort of Alexander's to avoid blame for the performance of the economy:

[Alexander's] most skillful attempt to blunt the economic issue came at the expense of Kentucky Gov. John Y. Brown, a Democrat, who came south to campaign for Tyree. Alexander aides pressed reporters to ask Brown if he thought governors were responsible for unemployment in their states. Brown, who faces a joblessness problem in Kentucky comparable to Tennessee's, admitted that he did not think a governor should be blamed.[62]

At every opportunity Alexander sought to separate national affairs from state matters. In the debate with Tyree, he said:

I believe the state government is doing exactly what it ought to be doing.

We don't need a governor who can announce that we have problems in Washington. We have newscasters who can do that. We need a governor who can take specific action that will pay off in results, and I submit we've been doing that.[63]

According to the *Nashville Tennessean's* report of the September debate,

Alexander went on to list his accomplishments: attracting industries to the state such as Nissan; developing the Technology Corridor near Oak Ridge; formulating the basic skills program for the schools and repairing roads throughout the state.

"My opponent needs to address the one question that challenges him in this campaign and that is 'What would you do and how would you do it differently or better?' " Alexander said.

"I respectfully say he hasn't given a single answer to that question."[64]

Alexander bucked the national Democratic trend to win re-election with 59.6 percent of the vote to Tyree's 40.4 percent. In a television program shortly after the election, Alexander was asked to explain how he had won. His response was both a commentary on what he had just accomplished and a lecture to his fellow Southern Republicans:

> *Questioner:* Do you have a code on how a Republican gets to be re-elected in the South . . . ?
>
> *Alexander:* Get a lot of Democrats to be for you. That's about the only way you can do it. And this year especially was a Democratic trending year in the Southern states. I think there's another thing Southern Republican candidates for state and local offices can do that they usually don't. They usually are converted to Republicanism . . . by national issues, so they run for tax assessor, arguing about the gold standard, and for the [state] legislature, talking about the unbalanced federal budget, when most people care more about sewers, jobs, better schools, health care of the children down the block; and they run on the wrong issues.[65]

Tennessee—Conclusion

Tennessee's experience with two-party politics contained an interesting mixture of the major political elements found throughout the region. In fact, so many aspects of the region's politics were visible in this long state, stretching from the western tip of Virginia to the Mississippi River, that it seemed a composite of all the South.

The state's electoral history offers evidence of the role of the abatement of the race issue. Primarily in race-conscious West Tennessee in the middle to late 1960s, the challenging Republicans were the beneficiaries of the reaction to the national Democratic effort to end segregation. Republican candidates were thus able to add to their traditional base in East Tennessee with support among protesting Democratic voters in the west. This is illustrated by the Memphis results in low-income white precincts. Brock's victory over Gore in 1970 hinged on this support, which had its roots in the white reaction to the national Democratic party's civil rights policies. By 1976 many of these Democratic defectors (both in Memphis and in many West Tennessee counties) had returned to their traditional Democratic voting patterns, and in the process they helped elect Blanton to the governorship in 1974 and Sasser to the U.S. Senate in 1976. The major change between 1970 and 1976 was the easing of racial tension.

A mild form of economic-class appeal was also detectable in the state's emerging party structure. This was visible in Blanton's 1974 campaign, in which he stressed Republican responsibility for the recession of that year. Sasser, who was in the Kefauver mold, campaigned in

1976 against Brock's opposition to Democratic economic initiatives such as Medicare; Sasser's appeal to the voters was not unlike Ravenel's in South Carolina in 1978. And Tyree in 1982 sought to identify himself with popular national Democratic domestic initiatives. But there were also indications that some Democratic defectors who returned to their party's nominees at a time when the race issue was no longer salient did so as much because of the pull of traditional Democratic party allegiance as for economic-class reasons.

The overall result in Tennessee was to make the GOP highly competitive at the state level. During the last decade the Republican party, permanently expanded from its East Tennessee base, reached a position from which it is able to win statewide by taking advantage of local errors committed by the Democrats (as Alexander did in 1978) or of national trends in its favor—or even to sidestep such trends, as the popular incumbent Alexander did in 1982.

13

Florida:
Recast by Rapid Growth

Florida has undergone staggering demographic changes since World War II. Rapid population growth—37.1 percent in the 1960s and 30.2 percent in the 1970s—and extensive urbanization completely transformed South and Central Florida and had an impact on the predominantly rural, more traditionally Southern region of North Florida. A comparison with another Southern state illustrates the stunning proportions of this human expansion. In the 1940 census South Carolina and Florida had the same number of people within their borders—1.9 million each. Four decades later Florida's population reached 9.7 million. South Carolina in the 1980 census had only 3.1 million.[1] Given this kind of change, it is amazing that Florida maintained any link at all with its past traditions. But an examination of the state's political history finds electoral patterns similar to those in other Southern states through the early 1970s. After that, the regional link faded fast.

The influx of Northerners—many carrying Republican affiliation—provided the basis for the start of two-party competition. Republican challenges during the 1950s and the first half of the 1960s did not, however, pose a serious threat to statewide Democratic nominees. Then, when the race issue became enmeshed in two-party politics, the GOP received a spurt that was strong enough during the last half of the 1960s to produce two major victories—in races for governor and for U.S. senator. But in the crucial 1970 elections the Democratic party won back the governorship and retained an open Senate seat.

Florida Democrats remained dominant statewide through the early 1980s, losing only a Senate seat in the Reagan sweep of 1980. Despite the continued Democratic strength, however, in the last ten years Florida's politics gradually split away from Southern patterns and began to have more in common with other fast-growing states outside of the South. In a sense it was as if the state's rapid demographic change had suddenly caught up with its political life and the "faintly tropical rebel yell"[2] of the 1940s that V. O. Key, Jr., detected became inaudible.

Early Republican presidential strength in Florida was centered in an "urban horseshoe" that runs from Sarasota and the Gulf Coast counties south of St. Petersburg, up through Orange County (Orlando) in Central Florida, to the Atlantic and down the East Coast to Broward County, directly north of Miami.[3] These were the counties in which the largest immigration occurred. Map 13-1, which displays the highest quartile of counties for the 1960 Republican presidential standard-bearer, Richard Nixon, illustrates the importance for the GOP of this horseshoe.[4] The state's urban areas are not all included, nor are all the counties in the horseshoe consistently Republican; for example, Hillsborough County (Tampa) is an urban Democratic bastion.

The 1964 presidential election brought a sharp break in the state's presidential voting patterns.[5] Florida came very close to being the sixth Southern state to go for Goldwater, who received 48.9 percent of the vote. An analysis of the near-random relationship between Kennedy's vote pattern and Johnson's provides insight into the voter disruption that began in the presidential election of 1964 and later was carried over to statewide contests. Two elements were at work in Florida in 1964, one quite compatible with what was occurring in the Deep South, the other somewhat analogous to the Rim South's general problem with Goldwater but with a twist peculiar to Florida.

North Florida contains the state's highest percentage of blacks, and many white Democrats of this region were more preoccupied with maintaining segregation than were those in the boom sections of the state to the south.[6] Thus, Johnson's support for civil rights and the Goldwater candidacy's appeal for Southern racists were enough to cause the North Florida counties to flip-flop in presidential voting between 1960 and 1964. These Panhandle counties had been the strongest for Kennedy but became the weakest for Johnson four years later.[7]

Goldwater's suggestion that the Social Security system could be made voluntary did not play well in the Republican urban horseshoe, an area with a heavy concentration of retirees. These counties had been the strongest for Eisenhower and Nixon in the three preceding presidential elections in Florida; they were Kennedy's weakest counties. But in 1964

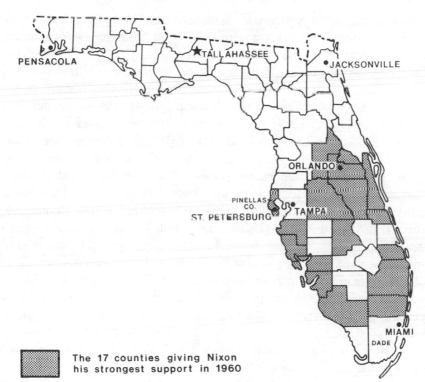

The 17 counties giving Nixon his strongest support in 1960

Map 13-1. Florida's Republican "Urban Horseshoe"

Johnson significantly improved on Kennedy's showing in these Republican bastions. Charles Stafford, Washington correspondent of the *St. Petersburg Times,* noted, "Goldwater came to St. Petersburg and made a speech on crime in the streets. With all the concern over his statements on Social Security, all he had to do there was to say he supported the current system and he would have carried the county by a wide margin."[8] In the 1964 election Pinellas County (St. Petersburg) jumped from 35 percent for Kennedy in 1960 to 55 percent for Johnson, a sharp repudiation of Goldwater by Republicans there.

The defection of GOP voters ended in 1968 when the less dogmatic Nixon avoided Goldwater's anti–Social Security position; in fact, Nixon in carrying Florida in that three-way election ran a vote pattern similar to Eisenhower's 1956 pattern.[9] For the Democrats, the disruption persisted at the presidential level; Humphrey showed a negative relationship to Kennedy's county-level pattern of support,[10] and the presidential-voting pattern for the Democrats remained unchanged in 1972. Humphrey and McGovern, in their weak races in the state, drew support from the same areas.[11]

At the state level a staunch segregationist, Farris Bryant, won the Democratic nomination for governor in 1960 by defeating a candidate backed by the outgoing governor, LeRoy Collins; Collins was considered a racial moderate by Southern standards at the time.[12] In the closest general election up to that date, Bryant won with 59.9 percent of the vote. Four years later Haydon Burns, the mayor of Jacksonville, defeated Robert King High, the mayor of Miami, in a bitter 1964 Democratic primary, in which Burns charged that High was "the candidate of the NAACP."[13] Burns won the general election with 56.1 percent.

The 1966 Democratic runoff primary was a replay of 1964 with a different outcome. After two undistinguished years in office, Governor Burns could muster only a third of the votes in the first Democratic primary and faced Mayor High in the runoff. Burns "became increasingly vituperative, attacking his archrival's 'ultraliberal philosophy' and indebtedness to the 'Negro bloc vote' and calling upon Floridians to 'follow the lead of the people of Alabama,' presumably offering himself as Florida's George Wallace."[14] High won the nomination with 58.3 percent, but the divisiveness of the primary spilled over into the general election.

The Republican gubernatorial nominee, Claude R. Kirk, Jr., according to David R. Colburn and Richard K. Scher,

> benefited from the continued public dissatisfaction with Lyndon Johnson and his Great Society. . . . High had alienated many conservative Democrats in the state with his progressive racial views and his political ties with the Kennedys of Massachusetts. . . . Indeed, Governor Burns refused to support High's candidacy because of these views . . . .
>
> Realizing the discord within the Democratic party, Kirk played up the differences in political views between himself and High. In particular he criticized High's racial attitudes. . . . Kirk also exploited public dissatisfaction with race riots in the cities, Vietnam, and inflation. In fact, he spent most of the campaign addressing these issues and attacking Johnson's domestic and foreign policies. It was difficult to tell at times whether Kirk was running against Johnson or High . . . . One seventy-year-old Florida woman commented, "The name [Republican] offends my sensibilities but actually in some ways it is more like the old Democratic party I once believed in."[15]

Kirk defeated High, 55.1 percent to 44.9 percent, doing well in the counties where Burns had been strongest, especially in North Florida.

The 1968 Senate election in Florida previewed what was to befall other Southern Democrats running along with McGovern four years later, such as Nick Galifianakis in North Carolina and Nick Zeigler in

South Carolina. Former Governor Collins, who in the 1960s assisted Presidents Kennedy and Johnson in their civil rights efforts, won a bitter Democratic primary fight for the Senate seat nomination. The Republican nominee, Edward J. Gurney, labeled his opponent Liberal LeRoy, and in the rural areas of North Florida the Gurney campaign circulated a photograph showing Collins walking with Martin Luther King, Jr.[16] After Gurney's victory with 55.9 percent of the vote, the *Tallahassee Democrat* concluded in an editorial:

> It was the civil rights issue that was the undoing of LeRoy Collins—specifically, to begin with, the U.S. Supreme Court school desegregation decision.
>   He saw it as an opportunity to lead Florida, and the South, into the mainstream of national affairs. The nation was willing, but Florida and the South weren't.[17]

Collin's vote pattern closely corresponded to Humphrey's poor showing.[18] Collins went down in defeat carrying the brand of a national Democrat at a time when association with the Kennedy-Johnson-Humphrey integrationists was a liability in the South.

The significance of the 1970 elections for Florida's Democratic party cannot be emphasized enough. The party entered these elections in statewide disarray. Figure 13-1 documents the Democratic decline, marking 1968 as the nadir. In 1966 and 1968 the Democrats had lost the governorship and one Senate seat, and in 1970 the Democratic incumbent, Sen. Spessard Holland, was retiring, providing the GOP challengers with the target of an open seat. The race issue, which had defeated Collins, showed no sign of easing. At this critical juncture, with the Republicans seemingly in the ascendancy, two articulate, moderate state senators emerged victorious from the Democratic primaries for governor and U.S. senator—two men who were able to put together a winning Democratic coalition that remained strong in Florida into the early 1980s.

In the 1970 gubernatorial election Reuben Askew, the Democratic nominee from Pensacola in the North Florida Panhandle, generally benefited from the antagonism caused by Governor Kirk's more flamboyant activities.[19] Newspaper accounts indicated that Askew based his primary campaign on one issue: taxes. He said Florida businesses were not paying their fair share:

> It is easy for any candidate to declare himself against pollution and crime, for better schools and for economy in government.
>   It is not so easy to say that a certain segment of society should pay more taxes.[20]

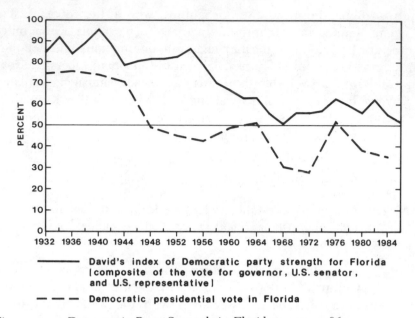

Figure 13-1. Democratic Party Strength in Florida, 1932–1986

Askew sought a corporate income tax for the state. On this issue Kirk went after Askew in the general election:

> "The working man is realizing, finally, that this [Askew's corporate income tax] is not a tax on corporations; it is a tax on him. If 'Taxyou' is elected," Kirk said, waving at the table in front of him, "all of these eggs and grits and gravy and biscuits will carry a tax."[21]

Kirk also stressed school busing. In a speech in Fort Lauderdale, the Republican governor charged, "Florida's school children are being bused around like pawns in an insane numbers game played by a handful of irrational federal judges."[22]

Askew stuck to his main issue. On the stump near the end of the campaign, he asserted, "It takes real courage to face the tax freeloaders—the phosphate companies and other privileged interests—and tell them in no uncertain terms that they have avoided paying their fair share of taxes long enough."[23] For his part, Kirk lost no chance to remind voters of Askew's national Democratic party connection, declaring that Askew would "support Humphrey or McGovern or some other permissive liberal" for the presidency in 1972 while he, Kirk, would back Nixon's re-election.[24]

In the 1970 Senate race Lawton Chiles, the Democratic nominee, who was from Lakeland (Polk County), in Central Florida, received a boost from a publicity man's stroke of genius: a 1,000-mile walk across the state. Chiles has been described as a representative of "the aw-shucks school of politics,"[25] and, considering the way the issues were running for Democrats, it was not a bad time for a Florida Democrat to have style triumph over substance. A newspaper report summarized his approach:

> Chiles, who didn't create any big waves during his 12 years in the State Legislature, campaigned in the style of generations of Southern Democrats. The 40-year-old Lakeland attorney shucked his coat, put on khaki pants, and tried to identify with the working man. He nimbly side-stepped the racial issue.[26]

Retiring Senator Holland joined Chiles on the campaign trail, asserting at one point:

> In the primary, he [Chiles] got more votes than I got in Polk County. . . . I see his opponent calling Lawton a liberal. But we in Polk County don't elect anybody but conservatives. I'm a moderate conservative and Lawton Chiles is a moderate conservative.[27]

In this 1970 election the Republicans carried the burden of a divisive primary for their senatorial nomination. William C. Cramer, Mr. Republican of Florida politics up to that time,[28] was challenged by G. Harrold Carswell, Nixon's appointee to the U.S. Supreme Court who had been rejected by the Senate. Governor Kirk, who backed Carswell's unsuccessful primary effort, was himself forced into a runoff by Jack Eckerd, a millionaire owner of a drugstore chain who was to make two major statewide GOP races in 1974 and 1978. Kirk won the nomination.

The Republicans thus confronted two fresh faces who also offered geographical diversity: Askew from the Panhandle and Chiles from the heart of Central Florida. Both could count on populous Dade County (Miami) in South Florida, with a large Jewish and minority concentration, to provide strong Democratic support.

Askew and Chiles won with 56.8 percent and 53.9 percent of the vote, respectively. North Florida provided the highest percentages for both Democrats. The pull of party tradition in 1970 was a major factor in bringing these North Florida Democrats back to their party's attractive ticket after the defections of 1966 and 1968. Later Chiles observed, "While Democrats in Florida have voted 'for the man' for years, still, when you get into North Florida areas, they consider themselves Democrats and, if you give them a Democrat they can accept, they'll vote for him."[29] Askew assessed these twin victories in an interview four years later:

Both of us represented in a different sort of way a new attitude in politics and a new confidence in the people. You know, if a politician was willing to be honest with them and to try to properly motivate them, they would respond. And I think Lawton did this by his walk. And I think that we did it essentially by the type of program we had, on a willingness to take on a lot of the 'sacred cows' frontally . . . and to set really a new tone.[30]

There were no statewide races in 1972. In the contest for an open Senate seat[31] in 1974, Richard Stone, the Democratic nominee, put together a winning combination that resembled the Chiles-Askew pattern, although the forceful campaign of a third-party candidate, John Grady, who ran under the American party label and received 15.7 percent of the vote, cut into Stone's margins in North Florida. Stone, who is Jewish and had resided in Miami before being elected Florida's secretary of state in 1970, made a determined effort to appeal to white Democrats in North Florida. When he took office, he changed his official residence to Tallahassee.[32] As a Republican congressman put it,

Republicans can carry those counties of North Florida when the Democrats have a candidate from South Florida who is perceived as a liberal. But Stone was perceived as a conservative. . . . He spent all of his time [as secretary of state] in the rural areas playing the harmonica. He wasn't perceived as a Jewish candidate from Miami.[33]

A newspaperman said it even more bluntly: "Stone ran as a redneck in North Florida and in South Florida as a Jew."[34] And the strategy worked.[35] Stone's Republican opponent, Jack Eckerd, could not break the combination even by bringing Strom Thurmond to North Florida for a two-day campaign swing.[36] Stone received 43.4 percent of the vote to Eckerd's 40.9 percent.

Governor Askew won re-election in 1974, getting 61.2 percent to 38.8 percent for the Republican Jerry Thomas, a former Democratic lieutenant governor. A review of the election returns reveals a remarkable divergence of Askew's 1974 pattern from the reinvigorated Democratic vote pattern of 1970.[37] An examination of this 1974 campaign and Askew's first term suggests the reasons for this divergence. Martin Dyckman, writing in the Tallahassee bureau of the *St. Petersburg Times,* summed up part of Askew's four-year record in a post-election article, saying that Askew:

Cajoled the Legislature into fulfilling his campaign promise to levy a corporate profits tax . . . .

Outraged landed interests by supporting environmental legislation that gives the state control over local developments with potentially devastating impact on nature.

Tempted fate by saying it was worse to segregate schoolchildren than to bus them, and opposed amending the U.S. Constitution to forbid busing or authorize school prayers.

Sponsored a model consumer protection act that gives the state a hand swift enough to deal with frauds almost as fast as they are invented.[38]

On the other hand, Thomas, Askew's GOP opponent, again to quote from the Dyckman article,

has filled the autumn air with the thunder of biting rhetoric and broad charges but has been unable to crack—much less, crumble—Askew's firmly based tower of public trust.

Throughout the campaign, Thomas has hammered away at his favorite campaign themes, charging that Askew is an advocate of forced busing,[39] has been soft on crime and is a spendthrift administrator who squanders tax dollars to build up a "red-tape bureaucracy" in Tallahassee.

Picturing himself as a strict constitutional conservative, Thomas has proclaimed his opposition to busing, stressing his reputation as a strong law-and-order advocate and has pledged to impose a moratorium on the growth of government.[40]

Most North Florida counties gave Askew significantly less support in 1974 than he and Chiles had received there in 1970. Many of the populous urban counties that generally favored Republicans, such as Sarasota, Lee, Orange, and Palm Beach, gave Askew higher percentages than they were to give Carter two years later. The busing issue, or race, is the most plausible explanation for the North Florida defection from Askew. Askew's increased strength elsewhere in the state represented a new element in Florida Democratic politics.

The main outlines of the Carter win in Florida were already suggested in the account of the 1974 Stone victory. The North Florida counties swung back in 1976 for Carter as the national nominee. Moreover, six of the top fifteen urban counties gave Carter from 53 to 62 percent of their votes.[41] Classified precinct data were not available for Florida cities in the 1976 election, but judging from the class results found in other Southern urban areas in this election, it is plausible to assume that lower-income white groups in these six cities, along with black voters,[42] were largely responsible for this victory.[43]

Chiles was re-elected in 1976 with little difficulty (63.0 percent to 37.0 percent) against John Grady, who had been the American party candidate against Stone in 1974 but who ran as a Republican in 1976. In the campaign Grady attacked Chiles "as a liberal who is soft on defense and spendthrift on social programs,"[44] but the attacks from the right did not work, because, as one partial observer noted, "nothing about Lawton's performance smacked of ultraliberalism; he was not vulnerable in a philosophical sense."[45] Also, Chiles stayed close to Florida during his first term, returning for a week every month as he had promised in 1970. And Chiles matched his walk gimmick of 1970 with another successful one in 1976: he limited all campaign contributions to $10, something of a record for an incumbent U.S. senator facing serious opposition.[46]

The Democrats in 1978 continued their successful hold on statewide elections in Florida by retaining the governorship. Robert Graham, a former state senator and a millionaire developer and lawyer from Miami, won an upset in the Democratic primary runoff over Atty. Gen. Robert Shevin. Declaring, "I was not born with a silver spoon in my mouth," Shevin, a merchant's son, claimed the voters faced a choice between "a moderate administration of Bob Shevin or a liberal one under Bob Graham . . . who has supported more spending bills than anyone in the Legislature."[47] Graham countered with a professionally orchestrated campaign that had at its core a gimmick as successful as Chiles's 1970 walk. He worked at a hundred different jobs in a hundred days, from bartender to garbage collector. A *Miami Herald* reporter wrote:

> Yes, Graham has "done" more than 100 different jobs in an effort to identify with the "hopes, dreams and aspirations" of the working man and to obscure his own background as a wealthy Dade developer who championed urban causes. It has worked masterfully. Graham's "work-days" campaign, his well-financed TV blitz and his stay-loose, easy-going campaign style lured a flood of blue-collar votes in the Democratic primaries, particularly in the staunchly conservative Panhandle . . . .[48]

Graham also benefited in the Panhandle by his choice of Wayne Mixson, a veteran legislator who "cherishes his image as a good ol' boy from North Florida,"[49] as his running mate.

Graham's Republican opponent was Jack Eckerd, the drugstore-chain owner who spent $2.3 million from his $57 million fortune in making his third unsuccessful bid for statewide office. Eckerd ran a strong media campaign along conservative lines with the theme "send a businessman to Tallahassee."[50] But Graham, straight from his dazzling primary performance with its appeal to all segments of the Democratic party,[51] was a hard target to hit. Eckerd probably lost some support because of the exposure during the campaign of scandals in the U.S. General Services Administration, which he had headed at the time of some of the wrongdoing.

The 1978 gubernatorial general election generally fit the pattern of other recent statewide races.[52] When the Democrats field a candidate who can hold together the traditional North Florida Democratic vote with a coalition of blacks and blue-collar whites in the large urban centers, plus the heavily Democratic areas of South Florida, they are usually able to win with a modest statewide majority, as they demonstrated throughout the 1970s. Graham followed the pattern perfectly, winning with 55.6 percent of the vote in 1978.

In 1980 Florida was Ronald Reagan's strongest state in the South; he carried it with 55.5 percent of the vote to Carter's 38.5 percent. National factors were chiefly responsible for this result, although Reagan campaigned effectively and extensively in the state, paying attention to matters of local interest. Unlike Goldwater, Reagan lost no opportunity to assert, as he did in St. Petersburg near the end of the campaign, "I will maintain the integrity of the Social Security system."[53] In South Florida, where Cuban refugees were the source of local concern, Reagan called the refugee influx "a national problem deserving federal attention," adding, "The President of the United States is ducking this issue and is, to a large extent, trying to shift the burden onto the backs of Florida residents."[54] Also, Carter's Mideast policies apparently antagonized a number of longtime Democratic Jewish voters in South Florida. The combination of national and local matters spelled disaster for the Democratic national ticket in the state.

Reagan's Florida landslide unquestionably influenced the narrow Republican victory in 1980 for a U.S. Senate seat. But the Democrats helped, too. Senator Stone lost his first try for renomination to Bill Gunter, the state's insurance commissioner, who had unexpectedly lost to Stone in the 1974 Democratic senatorial runoff. Gunter, considered a more conservative politician than Stone, criticized the incumbent for "flip-flopping" on the Panama Canal treaties (which Stone supported at the last minute) and on prayer in the public schools, among other questions.[55] Stone refused even to speak to Gunter after the runoff, much less to personally endorse the Democratic nominee.[56]

The Republican nominee was Paula Hawkins, a former two-term member of the Florida Public Service Commission.[57] A Maitland housewife, as she describes herself, Hawkins is a feisty consumer advocate who told voters she would not be one of the club in the Senate. Her positions on the issues are quite similar to those of Reagan's brand of conservatism.[58] On the stump she argued that "government was meant to be our protector, not our provider" and said she would vote to cut off benefits to all but those she described as the worthy poor. Even that group, which she never defined, would be required to work for benefits, she said.[59]

In addition to the divisiveness of the primary and the coattails factor, one newspaper article suggested that Gunter was hurt by his failure to emphasize clear differences with Hawkins. A *Miami Herald* reporter said, "Fearful of alienating his conservative Democratic constituency, Gunter offered bland pronouncements on issues . . . and wound up sounding like the incumbent."[60] Hawkins received 51.7 percent of the vote to Gunter's 48.3 percent. In explaining why Hawkins won, Patrick McMahon, Washington correspondent of the *St. Petersburg Times*, emphasized her statewide exposure as a twice-elected GOP official, her sex, and her proconsumer positions: "I think all of those things helped her have a wider base than most Republican white males, who tend to be probusiness, prodevelopment like Eckerd."[61]

Governor Graham and Senator Chiles were both re-elected in 1982. Graham won 64.8 percent of the votes cast to easily defeat the Republican nominee, U.S. Rep. L. A. (Skip) Bafalis, whose campaign was plagued with a series of setbacks that left the outcome in no doubt by Election Day.[62] The *St. Petersburg Times* wrote:

> Against an opponent [Bafalis] who never seemed to score by calling for a draconian crackdown on crime, Graham offered a well-rounded program that emphasized increased spending for education, law enforcement, roads and the environment and relentless recruitment of out-of-state industries.
>
> But the foundation was the same formula that Graham rode from obscurity into the Governor's Mansion four years ago, his "workdays." In fact, [his] commercials featured 4-year-old film of Graham hoisting sponges in Tarpon Springs, hauling garbage in Tampa and performing other blue-collar tasks.[63]

Chiles was considered vulnerable initially,[64] but the effort of his Republican opponent, State Sen. Van B. Poole, to "portray the low-key, moderate Chiles as a big-spending Washington liberal"[65] never took hold. Chiles increased his limit on campaign contributions this time to $100 but would accept money only from Floridians. Poole's commercials attacked Chiles's votes on school prayer, the Panama Canal treaties, and abortion, and asked the voters to give "Lawton Chiles his walking papers."[66] Newspaper reports suggested that Poole was hurt by weak public-speaking skills and by a drawn-out Republican primary season that did not end until four weeks before the election. "Hardly [getting] his walking shoes dusty," as one reporter put it, Chiles received 61.8 percent of the vote to Poole's 38.2 percent.[67]

Despite the easy Democratic victories in 1982, the accumulated changes of recent decades had left Florida with a sharply altered partisan environment. Party-registration figures were one indication of the new

Table 13-1. Republican Party Registration in Florida, 1940–1982

	Total Registered	Republicans Registered	GOP Percentage
1940	725,470	43,402	6.0%
1950	1,006,560	60,595	6.0
1952	1,339,538	116,794	8.7
1954	1,359,780	136,376	10.0
1956	1,606,750	210,797	13.1
1958	1,607,214	233,743	14.5
1960	2,016,586	338,340	16.8
1962	2,052,134	360,274	17.6
1964	2,501,546	458,156	18.3
1966	2,463,832	465,605	18.9
1968	2,765,316	619,062	22.4
1970	2,797,000	711,090	25.4
1972	3,487,458	974,999	28.0
1974	3,621,256	1,035,510	28.6
1976	4,094,308	1,138,751	27.8
1978	4,217,187	1,178,671	27.9
1980	4,809,721	1,429,645	29.7
1982	4,865,636	1,500,031	30.8

SOURCE: Division of Elections, Florida Department of State, Tallahassee. The figures are for Oct. of the year reported.

situation. In 1950 only 6.0 percent of Florida's registered voters affiliated with the Republican party. By 1982 the figure for Republican registration had risen to 30.8 percent. (See Table 13-1.) Although the GOP was far from parity with the Democrats in registration, these figures verified Florida's steady movement away from one-party status. Survey data on party identification gathered by Paul Allen Beck at Florida State University likewise show an upward trend for the Republican party.[68] Thus, Florida Democrats must be mindful that a potentially strong counterforce exists that is capable, when short-term factors run its way, of winning majorities statewide.

Florida—Conclusion

Florida's two-party development fitted into broader regional themes through the first part of the 1970s. In the late 1970s and early 1980s, common Southern elements persisted to some extent, but the dramatic demographic changes that swept over the state in recent decades left a political mix containing many new elements without readily apparent parallel elsewhere in the region.

The issue of race played an important role in early Republican successes in Florida, namely Kirk's in 1966 and Gurney's in 1968. In 1970, however, two attractive Democrats without any strong attachment to the racial troubles of the 1960s emerged triumphant from the primaries and won crucial statewide races. Askew and Chiles differed in the extent to which they made economic-class appeals in the style of the New Deal; Askew was more willing to take left-of-center positions, while Chiles straddled the center. Both candidates benefited from overwhelming black support, although the percentage of blacks was not large enough in Florida to make this the critical element it was in neighboring Deep South states.

As a result of a variety of circumstances, the Republican party developed a firm base in Florida despite its failure in all but one of the major statewide elections from 1970 through 1982. The recent path of the GOP's development in Florida, however, does not neatly conform to regional themes. In Mississippi, by way of example, the breakup of the tenuous black-white Democratic alliance stands out as paramount for future Republican gains in the Magnolia State. By contrast, the Sunshine State offers no easily grasped Southern key to its partisan future. The key may very well be simply that Florida is no longer a part of the dynamic elements of Southern politics as they were operating by the early 1980s.

14

Texas:
A World unto Itself

To an even greater extent than Florida, the gigantic, oil-rich, rapidly growing state of Texas split off from the political South during the period covered by this book. The dynamic elements found in the politics of Alabama, South Carolina, or Tennessee, to name only a sample of Southern states, had only a passing relationship to Texas politics in the 1960s and 1970s. To be sure, Texas was a member of the one-party South, with its origins in the Civil War and racial segregation, and an important legacy of that past remained in strong Democratic party allegiance among the electorate. But the coalitions that formed in this highly complex state more closely related to matters that either were peculiar to Texas or could be found just as easily in other parts of the nation as in the Southern states to the east.

This view of Texas's Dixie status is by no means novel. A glance at the state's demography reveals a strikingly non-Southern fact: Texas has a relatively small percentage of blacks—12.0 percent in the 1980 census and 12.5 percent in the 1970 census. Indeed, a much larger ethnic minority in Texas consists of Mexican-Americans.[1] When V. O. Key, Jr., a West Texas native, began his Texas chapter, he noted that "the presence of large numbers of Negroes [in the other ten states] has been influential in determining [their] lines of political division and often in diverting the attention of the electorate from nonracial issues."[2] But Texas, he wrote, did not conform to this pattern:

Yet, like other southern states, it is a one-party state because in 1860 a substantial part of its population consisted of Negro slaves. Most of its people then lived in East Texas, and the land to the west was largely undeveloped. The changes of nine decades have weakened the heritage of southern traditionalism, revolutionized the economy, and made Texas more western than southern. Democratic supremacy persists, although its original basis has shrunk to minor significance. In 1940 only one Texan in seven was a Negro. White Texans, unlike white Mississippians, have little cause to be obsessed about the Negro. The Lone Star State is concerned about money and how to make it, about oil and sulfur and gas, about cattle and dust storms and irrigation, about cotton and banking and Mexicans.[3]

Three decades ago Texas was still, however, a one-party state although its politics had even then a different cast, and the story of its departure from one-party status completes the regional picture. Figure 14-1 illustrates Texas's path away from solid Democratic dominance, a move that came earlier here than in any of the other ten save the Mountain Republican states.

The key to understanding the rise of two-party competition in Texas at the state level is to be found in the fate of the remarkably successful and durable conservative Democratic faction. As long as the conservative Democrats remained dominant, they served as a check on the potential growth of the Republican party.[4] An examination of the state's major electoral struggles reveals how the conservatives kept the upper hand most of the time and also suggests the current potential for major partisan changes in the 1980s.

Key concluded in 1949 that Texas had "developed the most bitter intra-Democratic fight along New Deal and anti–New Deal lines in the South."[5] These factional contests continued in the 1950s, a decade that witnessed several heated fights between the conservative Democrats led by Allan Shivers, the master of the right-of-center forces who was elected governor for three two-year terms starting in 1950,[6] and the liberal New Deal Democrats led by Ralph Yarborough, who lost several close gubernatorial races but won a special election to the U.S. Senate in 1957. Yarborough remained the mainstay of the liberal wing until his primary defeat in 1970 and comeback failure in 1972. A sampling of Yarborough's view of Texas politics, given in 1974, captures the flavor of the struggle:

> The Republican party and the people who control the Democratic party are identical in ideology. It's money [that] controls Texas. This is the happy hunting ground. Senator [Lee] Metcalf has written a book, a study of utility regulation in the United States. And he

points out that people in Texas are gouged worse by utilities than any other state in the Union. . . . Texas is the happy hunting ground of predatory wealth in the Union, out of the fifty states.[7]

In 1960 a seemingly quixotic challenge to Sen. Lyndon B. Johnson's "insurance" re-election effort marked the beginning of serious Republican challenges at the statewide level. An obscure Wichita Falls government professor, John G. Tower, received an astonishingly high (for a Republican in Texas) 41.1 percent of the vote, as that statewide election became tied in the voters' minds with the presidential choice,[8] since Johnson was also on the ballot as John F. Kennedy's vice-presidential running mate.

To fill Johnson's seat temporarily and to designate the anointed heir, Gov. Price Daniel, a conservative Democrat and a Shivers ally, appointed William A. Blakely, described by one observer as a dull, plodding, oil-rich conservative who was at least as far to the right as the Republican Tower.[9] Liberal Democrats, without the spoken approval of Yarborough, decided that a Tower victory was in their best interest, the argument being that a viable Republican party would soon draw to it conservative Democrats.[10] In the 1961 special election, Tower won with 50.6 percent of the vote, becoming the first Republican senator from the South in the twentieth century.

In 1962 the backlash over the Kennedy administration's civil rights

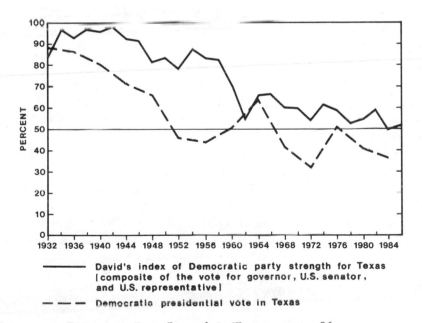

Figure 14-1. Democratic Party Strength in Texas, 1932–1986

initiatives helped the GOP win two congressional seats and gain a respectable 45.6 percent of the vote for Jack Cox in the gubernatorial election against the Democratic nominee and Johnson protégé, John B. Connally. This 1962 Republican activity plus Tower's two races in 1960 and 1961 are reflected in Figure 14-1; they resulted in the sharp dip of Democratic party strength from 82 percent in 1958 to 55 percent only four years later.

The elevation of Johnson to the presidency in November 1963, after President Kennedy's assassination, had a significant effect on electoral developments in Texas. The master manipulator Johnson worked skillfully to contain factional Democratic squabbling so that, among other results, the party would present a unified front during his 1964 election campaign. For example, he "muscled" several conservative Democrats out of a primary challenge to Yarborough in 1964.[11]

Senator Yarborough defeated a spirited effort in the 1964 general election by the Republican George Bush, 56.2 percent to 43.6 percent.[12] Governor Connally, benefiting from his "brush with death" in Dallas, swept past weak Republican opposition in 1964 with 73.8 percent of the vote.[13] This Democratic unity among presidential, senatorial, and gubernatorial candidates is in sharp contrast to the situation in many other Southern states in 1964 and demonstrates the inability of the Goldwater civil rights stance to disrupt the Texas Democracy, at least under the shrewd maneuvers of Texas's most famous Democrat, President Johnson. Figure 14-1 shows that 1964 was a year of Democratic resurgence in Texas, an atypical Southern performance.

In 1966 Senator Tower defeated his second conservative Democratic opponent, Waggoner Carr, an associate of Connally's. Tower ran a highly professional campaign financed by Texas and national conservative sources. Texas liberals were again given reason to be offended at the conservatism of their party's nominee and, along with a sizable number of Mexican-Americans, deserted Carr.

The Tower victories were important exceptions. In other races, however, the conservative Democrats were able to maintain their dominant position from the mid-1960s through most of the 1970s. In contests for either governor[14] or senator, conservative Democrats won every nomination except that for governor in 1978 and went on to win every general election against Republican nominees except in the gubernatorial race in 1978 and against the incumbent Tower. When the nomination stayed with the conservative wing, the challenging Republicans had little room for maneuver and could not put together a statewide majority.[15] The Democratic conservative wing was consistently able to dominate the nominations and win the general elections using an interesting strategy, which was perceptively depicted by Numan V. Bartley and Hugh D. Graham:

> The pattern in Texas illustrates the shrewd ability of conservative Democratic governors to rally to their standards in the hard-fought primaries sufficient upper-income voters to edge the liberal coalition of blacks and lower-income whites. Then in the general elections the Democratic voters remained in the fold, and the G.O.P. suffered biannual humiliation. Little wonder that the morale of both liberal Democrats and loyal Republicans remained chronically low in Texas.[16]

This clever conservative Democratic pattern, which might be termed a reverse-scale strategy, worked beautifully in the 1968 gubernatorial election for Preston Smith, the conservative Democrat who ran second in the first primary to the liberal Don Yarborough (no relation to Sen. Ralph Yarborough). Smith defeated Yarborough in the runoff with 55.3 percent of the votes, winning overwhelming support in the white upper-income precincts of Houston (83 percent) but trailing Yarborough in lower-income areas (42 percent to 58 percent) and receiving few votes from blacks (2 percent). After disposing of his liberal Democratic challenger, Smith reversed his voter-support pattern in the general election to defeat Paul Eggers, the Republican nominee and a Tower associate, 57.0 percent to 43.0 percent. This time Smith won considerably more support among Houston's lower-income whites, going from 42 percent to 58 percent. Among blacks his support rose dramatically, from 2 percent to 71 percent. But in the upper-income white precincts that he had carried with 83 percent in the runoff, Smith polled only 32 percent against the Republican Eggers in November. (See Table 14-1.)

In the general-election campaign Eggers attempted to tie Smith to the Democratic presidential standard-bearer, Hubert Humphrey. But Smith kept his distance from the national nominee, even though a major Johnson-encouraged effort was made in Texas for Humphrey during the closing weeks of the campaign.[17] Remaining aloof, Smith declined to appear at an election-eve rally for Humphrey in Houston, saying, "I am going to vote for Humphrey but the fact that I'll do this doesn't mean I'm for all the programs that come out of Washington, D.C."[18]

As it turned out, the liberal Minnesota Democrat did not need Smith's help. Humphrey carried Texas, defeating Nixon by a margin of 41.1 percent to 39.9 percent. Wallace finished third with 19.0 percent. This was the only Southern state that the Democrats' national candidate won in 1968; Texas was Wallace's weakest state in the region.

The 1970 election witnessed the high point of conservative Democratic success in Texas. Not only did Governor Smith coast to renomi-

Table 14-1. Gubernatorial and Senatorial Vote by Class and Race in Houston, 1968 and 1970

	Lower Income	Middle Income (Whites)	Upper Income	Blacks
1968 Democratic Gubernatorial Runoff				
Yarborough	58%	47%	17%	98%
Smith	42	53	83	2
1968 Gubernatorial General Election				
Smith	58%	49%	32%	71%
Eggers	42	51	68	29
1970 Democratic Senatorial Primary				
Yarborough	55%	44%	23%	97%
Bentsen	45	56	77	3
1970 Senatorial General Election				
Bentsen	53%	38%	22%	83%
Bush	47	62	78	17

SOURCE: Numan V. Bartley and Hugh D. Graham, *Southern Elections: County and Precinct Data, 1950–1972* (Baton Rouge: Louisiana State Univ. Press, 1978), 398–99.

nation and defeat Eggers in a rematch but the nemesis of the right-of-center forces for two decades, Senator Yarborough, was defeated in a bitter primary by the conservative Democrat Lloyd M. Bentsen, Jr., a Houston millionaire who was one of those Johnson had forced out of the Senate primary race in 1964. Bartley and Graham described the contest as follows:

> Bentsen was a conservative Democrat of the Connally persuasion who attacked Yarborough for his dovishness on Vietnam and his unsouthern votes against the confirmation of Haynesworth and Carswell. [Clement F. Haynesworth, Jr., and G. Harrold Carswell were the Southerners whom Nixon appointed to the Supreme Court but who were rejected by the Senate.] . . . Yarborough responded, as he always had, in vibrant, even dogmatic defense of liberalism's challenge to the vested interests, which certainly included Houston millionaires. . . . Yarborough held together his New Dealish coalition of blacks and lower-status whites, although his margins in working-class white districts were less impressive than they had been in previous elections. But the countryside belonged to Bentsen, who won hefty majorities not only in west Texas but in the east Texas towns and counties that had once been Yarborough country as well. Yarborough carried only the heavily Chicano south Texas region, to lose statewide with 46.9 percent of the vote.[19]

Bentsen's general-election campaign against the Republican George Bush, who had been elected twice to Congress from a Houston district since his 1964 statewide senatorial defeat, is a classic example of a conservative Southern Democrat using New Deal–style economics to rally the lower-income voters to defeat a Republican after he had beaten a proven and consistent champion of these same voters in the primary. (Table 14-1 also portrays this second illustration of the reverse-scale strategy.) A *Houston Chronicle* article presented the following summary of the 1970 campaign:

> While Bush poured money into a TV campaign developing an image as a concerned, sincere candidate with the nebulous claim that "he can do more," Bentsen bore down on an appeal to the voters' pocketbook.
>
> Bentsen blamed the Nixon administration for failure to curb inflation, increasing unemployment, recession, high interest rates and a depressed stock market. . . .
>
> Bentsen seized on a visit by [Vice-President Spiro] Agnew to West Texas and Dallas as the leverage needed to persuade labor, blacks and Mexican-Americans that they should not send a second Republican senator to Washington.
>
> They [Bentsen's campaign people] told them, in effect: "Look, you people simply can't let Texas elect a Republican to support Nixon's economic policies and Agnew's rhetoric."[20]

Bentsen won with 53.5 percent of the vote to Bush's 46.4 percent. The election, primary and general, in the words of Bo Byers, chief of the *Houston Chronicle*'s Austin bureau, "put another damper on the push of Republicans and liberal Democrats for a stronger two-party system in Texas."[21]

In 1972 the Democratic gubernatorial nominee was Dolph Briscoe, a wealthy, conservative West Texas rancher. Briscoe, who has been described as a "gentleman whose overwhelming blandness rivaled Preston Smith's,"[22] projected "a staunchly conservative image."[23] His opponent in the primary was State Sen. Frances (Sissy) Farenthold of Corpus Christi. In the words of a *Houston Chronicle* reporter, Farenthold

> stirred the enthusiasm that liberals showed for Yarborough in the 1950's [but] she had too many political liabilities . . . . She was a crusading liberal, a woman, a Roman Catholic—underfinanced and lacking organization. Environmentally conscious, she wouldn't use billboards.[24]

Briscoe won the nomination with slightly over 55 percent of the vote.

Despite Briscoe's conservatism, the GOP nominee, State Rep. Henry C. Grover, a former Houston schoolteacher, asserted shortly after the

primaries that "whatever Briscoe's label now, their November battle will
be on the issue of conservative versus liberal," Grover being the
conservative.[25] The election turned out to be extremely close because
many Mexican-Americans supported a third-party candidate, Ramsey
Muñiz of La Raza Unida, who received 6.3 percent of the vote. Briscoe
defeated Grover by a margin of 47.9 percent to 45.0 percent. Grover did
well in the large metropolitan counties, but strong Briscoe support in
the rural areas helped offset this, and Briscoe once more demonstrated
the reverse-scale strategy by doing well in the same black and lower-status white precincts that he had lost to Farenthold in the primary.[26]

Briscoe had little trouble keeping his distance from McGovern; for
one thing, he voted for George Wallace at the 1972 Democratic National Convention.[27] Such was not the case for Barefoot Sanders, the
1972 Democratic nominee in the race against Senator Tower. Before
taking on Tower, Sanders defeated former Senator Yarborough's comeback effort in the primary. Among other things, Sanders charged that
Yarborough was "an ultraliberal advocate of school busing."[28] In the
general election, the Democratic senatorial nominee, who was a former
legislative counsel to President Johnson,[29] sought to benefit from popular Democratic programs, telling his audience at one rally that Texans
"know Tower supported the private interests when he voted against
Medicare."[30] Tower's campaign strategy was illustrated in this comment
in a *Houston Post* article about Tower's activities on a pre-election trip
to Beaumont: "As usual, most of his really harsh criticism was reserved
for Democratic presidential candidate George S. McGovern, who—as
he carefully pointed out—has been endorsed by Sanders."[31] The effort
by Sanders to walk the Democratic tightrope failed; he received 44.3
percent of the vote to Senator Tower's 53.4 percent.

A comparison of the Sanders loss with the Bentsen victory two years
earlier is suggestive of the voting-pattern shifts under way in the state
early in the 1970s. Democratic dominance of the small towns and rural
areas had unquestionably been the party's mainstay; when Republican
competition began, GOP strength was centered in the urban areas.[32]
But the issues raised in the 1972 senatorial campaign, especially Tower's
hammering away at Sanders as a local equivalent of McGovern, whose
positions on race and other social issues were decidedly unpopular
among some white small-town and rural dwellers, apparently were per-
suasive. Nearly fifty staunchly Democratic rural and small-town
counties that had been strongly for Bentsen in 1970 (giving him over 70
percent of their votes) gave Sanders at least twenty percentage points less
support, signaling a significant weakening of Democratic strength in the
countryside.[33]

Governor Briscoe had little trouble winning re-election in 1974. In the year of Watergate, Texas Republicans lost two U.S. House seats, and their gubernatorial nominee, Jim Granberry, a former mayor of Lubbock, ran the weakest statewide GOP race in eight years, getting only 31.1 percent of the vote. Muñiz, of La Raza Unida, received 5.6 percent, but he was not an important factor this year, because the election was not close; Governor Briscoe won with 61.4 percent. All of the often contentious segments of the Democratic party fell in behind Briscoe. The *Houston Chronicle* wrote, "Organized labor has cozied up to Briscoe, confident that he is much more responsive to their legislative program than Granberry would be."[34] Likewise, the rural areas of both East and West Texas remained predominantly Democratic. For Texas Republicans, as for Republicans around the nation, 1974 was a setback. Byers, of the *Houston Chronicle*, wrote:

> Republicans long have agreed that if they are to crack the Democratic stranglehold on state government they must win the governorship . . . . But their dream of continued steady progress toward a gubernatorial victory and a real two-party state was shattered Tuesday.[35]

Because Texas Republicans lost both statewide contests in 1976—for presidential electors and for Senator Bentsen's seat—it was generally overlooked that the 1976 election was not in fact a disaster for the GOP.[36] (Figure 14 1 indicates that Democratic party strength actually dropped a few percentage points in 1976.) When a Southern small-town farmer receives only 51.1 percent of the vote as the Democratic nominee to a Midwestern Republican's 48.0 percent, Texas is anything but a one-party state. The key point is that many conservative Democratic voters (those, for example, who had helped provide Johnson with his 63.3 percent Texas victory in 1964) were not returning in 1976 to an attractive regional product.

A look at the 1976 presidential returns reveals that GOP strength in Texas, as in the other rapid-growth state, Florida, was concentrated in the urban areas. Map 14-1 isolates all counties that gave Ford at least 52 percent of the vote, that is, four or more percentage points over his statewide average. In the eastern part of the state, the huge urban centers of Houston and Dallas and their surrounding counties were Ford strongholds.[37] In the rest of the state, GOP strength in 1976 was found in the medium-size cities of San Angelo, Odessa, Lubbock, and Amarillo as well as in the counties adjacent to San Antonio. Other important cities, as was true in Florida, remained Democratic-majority areas; the most notable of these were Fort Worth, Corpus Christi,

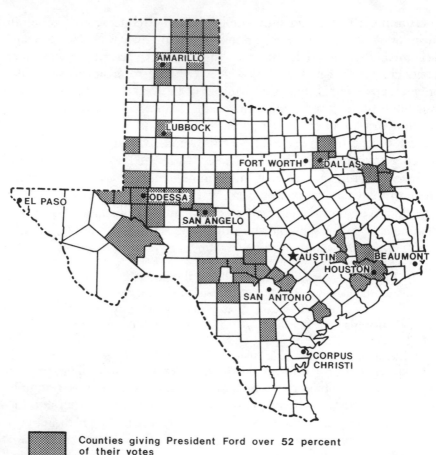

Counties giving President Ford over 52 percent
of their votes

Map 14-1. Strongest Republican Counties in Texas in 1976

Austin, San Antonio, Beaumont, and El Paso. Within the cities the
economic-class breakdown in 1976 was decidedly in the mold of the
New Deal alignment. For example, upper-income whites in Houston
preferred Ford to Carter by a margin of 79 percent to 21 percent;
lower-income whites backed Carter with 59 percent of their support to
Ford's 41 percent.[38]

Senator Bentsen was re-elected in 1976. After his 1970 victory
Bentsen moderated his policy positions to appeal to less conservative
Texas Democrats.[39] Probably as a result of this moderation, he drew no
Democratic primary challenge from the left in 1976. Rather, he re-
ceived weak opposition from a right-wing economics professor, Phil
Gramm, who charged that Bentsen had been unfaithful to his conserva-
tive campaign commitments of 1970. (Gramm later won a seat in Con-

gress as a Democrat, became a prominent ally of President Reagan, and switched to the Republican party in 1983.)[40] According to newspaper accounts, Bentsen's Republican opponent, U.S. Rep. Alan Steelman, sought to project the image of a liberal Republican—at least on environmental issues—and called Bentsen the "darling of special interests."[41] Steelman received 42.2 percent of the vote in the November balloting to Bentsen's 56.8 percent.

The elections of 1978 brought the long-awaited breakthrough for Texas Republicans: capture of the governorship. The Republican Bill Clements defeated State Atty. Gen. John Hill, the Democratic nominee, 50.0 percent to 49.2 percent. The most prevalent explanation for the victory of Clements, a multimillionaire oil-drilling contractor who had served as deputy secretary of defense in the Nixon administration, was money. Clements gave or lent over $4 million of his own fortune to his $7 million campaign.[42] Several observers of Texas politics pointed to the heavy personal spending by Clements, especially on a large-scale phone-bank operation.[43]

Two *Dallas Morning News* reporters, Stewart Davis and Sam Kinch, Jr., wrote after the election:

> Clements was "sold" like soap: forceful, conservative, a corporate manager, a rich man who doesn't need politics for a living, a man who came up from the ground without family resources, a man who knows how to meet a payroll and get the job done. Increasingly, based on an accurately perceived anti-politician sentiment among the electorate, that Clements image was contrasted, often starkly, against a picture of Hill as a seedy-looking, greedy, over-anxious politician who had been seeking public office too long.[44]

Another theme of the Clements campaign, the reporters said, was that "Hill is a liberal who, when nominated, let the liberals take over the Democratic party as well. That scare tactic was one of the more effective Clements lines, particularly when combined with the opprobrious 'career politician.' "[45]

Clements's vociferous onslaught—unprecedented for a Texas GOP gubernatorial candidate—benefited substantially from the division in Democratic ranks caused by Hill's primary nomination. Hill, a moderate, had narrowly defeated Governor Briscoe, the leader of Texas's conservative Democrats, and Briscoe supporters found it hard to forgive Hill in November. The two Dallas newspapermen summed up the attitude of these conservatives: "[W]hy help the guy who beat our man? Clements actively sought and got many of those folks. And many of Hill's local organizers took the mistaken attitude that they simply didn't need the Briscoe people."[46]

While Hill did all he could in the campaign to avoid the liberal label,[47] he unquestionably stood to the left of the conservative Briscoe.[48] Arthur E. Wiese, chief of the *Houston Post*'s Washington bureau, noted, "In going to leaders like Hill, the party has made a substantial shift from Shivers conservatives to moderates."[49] After Hill's narrow defeat in the general election, the Briscoe conservatives were quick, according to Wiese, to point an accusing finger: If you veer to the left with a Hill, then there is disaster in November.[50] A county-level comparison of where Hill's support declined relative to Briscoe's winning pattern in 1972 indicates that Hill experienced critical losses in the countryside, primarily in the small-town, rural areas of West Texas—Briscoe country.[51]

Most observers agreed that the Clements effort probably made the difference for Senator Tower,[52] who won re-election in 1978 by an even narrower margin than Clements, receiving 49.8 percent to 49.3 percent for U.S. Rep. Robert Krueger, Tower's Democratic opponent. An English professor and a dean at Duke University before returning to his home of New Braunfels to run for and win a congressional seat in 1974, Krueger championed the interests of the Texas oil industry and was associated with the more conservative elements of the Democratic party. He defeated former State Sen. Joe Christie, an opponent of "big oil," in the Democratic primary.[53]

In the general election, despite Krueger's right-of-center credentials, Senator Tower denounced his opponent, in the words of a *Baltimore Sun* account, "as a tool of organized labor who plans to start 'cozying up to Northeast liberals' so he can run for President."[54] In Krueger, a vigorous and articulate campaigner, Tower faced the toughest opposition of his political career, and plainly he was aided by the strong Clements campaign. U.S. Rep. Charles Wilson, an East Texas Democrat who had considered opposing Tower in 1978, was one who credited Tower's victory to the pull of the lavish Clements effort:

> Tower would have never made it without Clements. He's a very lucky man. He got elected on a fluke to start with. Then the next time he had a Democrat more conservative than he was, and all the liberals voted for him. Then the next time he got to run when his opponent was strapped with McGovern. He's just lucky.[55]

What these Democratic defeats—especially the loss of the governorship—meant for Texas's partisan future was the object of much speculation by all interested groups.[56] In liberal Democratic circles the notion that the election of the first Republican governor in the twentieth century would drive "closet Republicans" from the Democratic party was not altogether unpleasing.[57] Party moderates, especially those with state-wide ambitions, vehemently objected to such a course. Bill Hobby, the Democratic lieutenant governor, told a party gathering a month after the defeats that, to quote from an article in the Austin *American-Statesman*, "there should be no efforts to 'purify' the party by driving out conservatives."[58] Hobby added, "We have a job to do, not only of organization, but of ideology. We can't be purifiers. When we [are], we lose elections."[59]

If there was to be large-scale party switching, presumably those rural, small-town Democrats who deserted Hill would lead the way. An examination of the views of the congressmen who represent some of these Democrats is instructive. A number of the 1978 bolting Democrats resided in the huge, sprawling West Texas Twenty-first Congressional District.[60] In 1978 the Twenty-first elected a Republican, Tom Loeffler, with 57.0 percent of the votes cast. Neither Representative Loeffler nor his chief campaign assistant, Howard Adkins, expressed confidence that significant numbers of conservative Democrats had given up on their party. Adkins said:

> These people are not voting party labels; they are voting for individuals. . . . It is a conservative area, but they are finally beginning to realize, and I think for the first time in Texas that, just because their granddaddy voted Democrat, they are having to take another look and find out if that Democrat is a conservative or liberal, and they are starting to differentiate on that basis.[61]

North of Loeffler's district, in the Nineteenth Congressional District,[62] which contained the Republican strongholds of Lubbock, Midland, and Odessa, a conservative Democratic state senator, Kent Hance, defeated a vigorous Republican challenge in 1978 by George Bush, Jr., the son of Reagan's Vice-President. Representative Hance understandably did not foresee massive conservative Democratic defections on the horizon. He said bitterness over Hill's primary defeat of Briscoe, a West Texas native, caused some conservative rural Democrats in that part of the state to vote for Clements, but he viewed this as a passing thing.[63] Hance, who became a prominent Democratic "boll weevil" in the U.S. House, said he tries to avoid the ideological squabbling found in Texas Democratic party affairs:

> I go around [at state conventions] and shake hands. Then when they pull out their guns and start shooting at each other . . . I leave. Democratic conventions are always going to have a big fight. You got too many from [supporters of] George Wallace to George McGovern and everything in between . . . .[64]

Representative Wilson, who served for twelve years in the Texas legislature before being elected to the U.S. House in 1972 from the rural,
small-town Second Congressional District, in East Texas, was not coy
when asked for his assessment of the 1978 election for Texas politics.
He said this election made the Texas Republican party "totally
viable,"[65] and offered this analysis:

> My district is pretty much Deep South and the rural areas tradi-
> tionally have been heavily Democratic. The cities have been where
> the Republican votes are. Now, the rural areas are beginning to vote
> much more Republican. The rural areas are growing, changing.
> Instead of being all poor farmers, factory workers and all that, you
> get tons of white-collar insurance salesmen, real-estate people, all
> that kind of stuff. And they're voting Republican. . . . Where my
> district would come in 70 percent for the Democratic candidate for
> governor, it is now coming in 58 percent. Also, there is a big drop-
> off in the black vote in the rural areas, in quantity. All of them who
> vote, still vote Democratic, but [fewer] are voting.[66]

Wilson concluded that those who do not think the conservative Democrats are going Republican "are just fooling themselves."[67]

Wilson's remarks were indicative of the ferment in the Texas Democracy following the narrow GOP victories in 1978. For example, late in
1979 several Democratic state legislators from the Dallas area switched
to the Republican party. When State Rep. Anita Hill changed parties,
she announced, "I don't consider I am leaving the Democratic Party but
that it has left me." The more liberal Democrats in Dallas welcomed
the defections. "I'm glad they admitted what they are," said State Rep.
John Bryant. "It weakens the Democratic Party for them to use our
label. I'm tired of seeing Democrats for Nixon, Democrats for Ford,
and Democrats for Clements." Others in the Democratic party sought a
middle way. One said it was necessary to do "everything to make the
Democratic Party welcome to conservatives as well as liberals." Another
added, "We have a strong party because of its diversity."[68]

After Reagan's clean rout of President Carter in Texas in 1980, by a
margin of 55.3 percent to 41.4 percent, the partisan ferment intensified,
especially as Democratic candidates of various ideological persuasions
began lining up for the 1982 elections. The *Texas Observer*, the faithful
voice of Texas's minority of outspoken liberals, wrote in the spring of
1981:

> We are fed up hearing the lying-down Democrats . . . say the
> reason the Republicans have taken over is, the Democrats are too
> liberal. This flies against common sense.
> Jimmy Carter was too left? Jimmy Carter, the Democrats' re-

sponse to the McGovern cataclysm, proves that Reagan won because the Democrats are too liberal?

In Texas the Republicans are ascendant with Tower, Clements, Bush, gains in Congress and the legislature. Yet Speaker [Bill] Clayton and Lt. Gov. Hobby tell us, with straight faces, that after 29 years of Governors Allan Shivers, Price Daniel, John Connally, Preston Smith, and Dolph Briscoe—"Democrats" all—the reason for Clements' victory is the Democrats are too liberal!

Come on, now. The truth is as plain as the Reagan strategy, soak the poor to further enrich the rich.[69]

But when the dust settled after the 1982 Democratic primaries, all factions of the party—from the conservatives to the liberals—had something to cheer about, and the result was Democratic unity to a degree not seen in Texas in recent years. Atty. Gen. Mark White, a forty-two-year-old conservative, won the gubernatorial nomination with a centrist campaign that alienated few people. But the liberals had their own nominees in several lesser positions on the Democratic ticket, including a former editor of the liberal *Texas Observer*, Jim Hightower, the Democratic primary winner for the post of agriculture commissioner.[70] (The *Observer* called Hightower "a populist as tough as any of the Texas populists of the Nineteenth Century.")[71] This liberal representation made 1982 different for left-of-center Texas Democrats, rendering it easier to accept a conservative at the top of the ticket.

The unity theme pervaded the Democratic state convention in Dallas in September. Former Governor Briscoe told the conclave, "Texas is a Democratic state, and with your help, we'll prove it once again this November with a victorious ticket all the way from the top to the bottom."[72] Former Atty. Gen. Hill declared, "Republicans can't win statewide races, if we'll just stick together, so this time—this time—this time, let's stick together!"[73] Hightower set the partisan tone for the impending fall campaign, saying at the convention, "It's going to be more fun running against these little right-wing Republicans than choking chickens."[74]

During the general-election campaign, White spoke out forcefully against rising unemployment and soaring utility rates. On the latter point he criticized Governor Clements for his appointments to the Public Utilities Commission, the body that approved the unpopular rate increases.[75]

Governor Clements, who spent a record $12 million on his re-election effort, ran an aggressive campaign in his characteristic style, which the *New York Times* described as "folksy, contentious, often abrasive."[76] The Republican governor frequently referred to White as incompetent and a bumbler, declaring at one point that White "doesn't know any

more about management than a hog knows about Sunday. He's never
even run a hot dog stand."[77] Clements stressed his tough anticrime
program and his support for reducing governmental bureaucracy and
improving education; he reminded Texans of the strong fiscal position
of the state (Texas had a $1.3 billion budget surplus in 1982).[78] Sub-
stantive issues aside, the personality of the highly visible governor became an ever-present issue. Carl P. Leubsdorf, Washington bureau
chief of the *Dallas Morning News,* said that Clement's accomplishments—including his attention to building the Republican party while
in office—were "offset by the fact that he rubs so many people the
wrong way. He's very controversial. He's always shooting his mouth off.
So he has had high negatives all the way."[79] Late in the campaign
Clements was put on the defensive by the utility-rate issue.[80] He tried to
ignore White's constant attacks over high utility costs, but his occasional
blunt responses when questioners pressed him on the issue usually back-
fired. Once he said, "People are just going to have to conserve more.
When I grew up, there was no air conditioning, and I got along fine."[81]

White won with 53.8 percent of the vote to Clements's 46.2 percent,
and the entire statewide Democratic ticket was swept into office. Senator
Bentsen defeated his Republican challenger, U.S. Rep. James Collins,
59.1 percent to 40.9 percent. Collins ran a single-note campaign, attacking Bentsen as a "man who talks like Herbert Hoover but votes like
George McGovern,"[82] a notion that apparently went nowhere with the
Texas electorate. Democrats also won twenty-two U.S. House seats to
the Republicans' five.

Precinct data from Houston reveal that sharp class divisions were present among urban white voters in the gubernatorial election. Lower-income whites backed Mark White with 71.0 percent of their votes; upper-
income whites gave the Democratic nominee only 16.3 percent. Blacks
were nearly unanimous in their choice of White.[83] Eighty-six percent of
the state's Mexican-Americans who voted were reported to have supported White, a critical increase of ten percentage points over the Democratic nominee's showing among Texas Hispanics four years earlier.[84]
Also, county-level analysis indicated that many rural, small-town counties that had abandoned Hill in 1978 returned to the Democratic fold.

The unity of all segments of the Texas Democratic party and the
unfavorable reaction to the state of the economy under the Republican
administration in Washington clearly were the leading reasons for the
1982 outcome. Taking a longer view of Texas elections, however, one is
struck by how far the state has moved away from one-party dominance.
While the Democrats were riding high after their 1982 triumphs, they
had to be mindful that a potentially strong opposition now existed ready
to offer Texans an alternative, should circumstances run against the

Democrats. In fact, Republicans were predicting that the disparate elements of the Texas Democracy would come apart as the responsibility for governing returned. "They will find themselves a slightly less united party, if not a greatly less united party," forecast Chet Upham, the Republican state chairman.[85] Travis McBride, a West Texas State University professor, appropriately summed up the partisan situation soon after the balloting in an interview with an *Amarillo Daily News* reporter:

> There is a solid base of more than one million Republican voters in this state, and it tells the Democrats you'd better do things properly, or you're in trouble. The Republicans are going to be winning some offices in the future, and I think it's great the two-party system is alive here.[86]

Texas—Conclusion

Texas stands out as one Southern state where the race issue did not dominate electoral politics. Even during the one-party era economic issues were found to be more important than racial concerns. And, not surprisingly, Texas's development of a two-party system reflected this primacy of the economic.

Both Republicans and members of the liberal wing of the Texas Democratic party suffered numerous defeats at the hands of the dominant conservative Democrats throughout most of the period under study. In the 1978 elections, however, there was a reversal as the conservative Democratic governor, Briscoe, lost renomination and the primary victor, Hill, was defeated by the well-financed Republican Clements. But in 1982 a unified Democratic party regained the governorship with the conservative White at the head of a ticket that included a few left-of-center Democrats.

In an overall look at the Texas experience in the Southern context, the outstanding feature remains the weakness of the race issue. In the turbulent 1968 presidential election, Texas was the only state in the South to stay with the national Democratic party nominee. Furthermore, when other Southern states were developing potent black-white majorities in the early 1970s to fend off Republican challenges, Texas partisan developments were revolving around other questions, some Texas oriented, others more national in scope. In fact, this huge state had grown so diverse and complex that comparison with other Southern states became a risky task. Several decades ago, when the established norm throughout the South was the one-party system with its tie to racial segregation, it was far more appropriate to seek peculiarly Southern qualities in Texas politics. Today the common regional thread is hard to find in the Lone Star State.

15

Southern Politics in the 1980s

The complex and diverse story of how and why the one-party Democratic South expired is of more than antiquarian interest. Out of the dynamic elements involved in this great regional transformation of the past several decades comes the foundation for whatever course Southern politics will take in the middle to late 1980s and beyond. And perhaps with a little luck what has gone before will yield clues as to what is coming up. The effort to peer cautiously forward is prompted less by a desire to mimic the soothsayer than by the spirit of adventure engendered by the long, multifarious journey already traveled so far through Southern political life. Why stop now simply because the calendar has come up short of more elections to pore over?

An excursion into the findings of survey research in the early 1980s offers guidance in the attempt to glimpse the region's likely political direction. The polling information reported in the next two sections illuminates the makeup of the two major blocs of voters examined in eclectic fashion in the state chapters—namely, the potent black-white Democratic coalition and the configuration of support for the challenging Republicans.

Composition of the Parties in the Early 1980s

Public opinion surveys provide the most precise information possible on electoral behavior. Unfortunately, they are not always available to answer all the questions a researcher has. For the type of analysis done in this book, separate statewide surveys for all eleven states conducted in each

election year since 1960, asking scores of politically relevant questions
(and keeping the same questions from year to year), would be the equivalent of a political science heaven. This heaven, however, does not exist.
Faced with reality, one does as I have done in the state chapters: search
for hints about voter behavior wherever they can be ferreted out.

There are bright spots in the spare reality of survey-research availability. More and more academic state polls have been established in the
last few years,[1] and their findings may some day fill in, for a future era,
all the analyst would like to know. Several early returns from this
potential data bonanza were made available to me by the directors of
two Southern university polls: Patrick R. Cotter, of the Alabama Capstone Poll at the University of Alabama in Tuscaloosa, and Stephen D.
Shaffer, of the Mississippi Poll at Mississippi State University in Stark-
ville. State poll findings reported in several political science conference
papers also proved helpful.

At the national level the analyst's heaven is realized in the National
Election Studies conducted every two years since the 1950s by the
University of Michigan's Center for Political Studies (CPS). Allowing
for problems in defining the South,[2] the CPS polls can be used to chart
broad regional patterns. But because the CPS surveys' samples are nationally and regionally based, one cannot use them to understand the
sharp political differences that exist between, for example, Mississippi
and Virginia, or Louisiana and Tennessee, or North Carolina and Georgia. That there are significant state differences is apparent to all involved
and has been documented in this book's state chapters. Still, the CPS
surveys are helpful in outlining general trends, especially when coupled
with the few available state polls.

In seeking to identify Southern partisan coalitions in the early 1980s,
one faces two competing approaches to their measurement. First, actual
voter choice in an important election could be used to define voter
blocs; the logical candidate here is the 1980 presidential election. Second, voter responses to the standard survey question about party identification could be used. Both have strengths and weaknesses.[3] Using voter
choice in 1980 enmeshes the resulting partisan insights with the short-
term peculiarities of the Carter-Reagan contest. The use of partisan
identification is weakened by uncertainty over whether a respondent's
partisan choice expressed during the poll-taking process means anything
for long-term voting behavior. Compounding this problem is the growing propensity of many respondents to claim they are independents,
which further obscures the electoral link. There is no completely satisfactory resolution to the problem of choosing a measure. In fact, both
measures—voting behavior and partisan self-identification—are used

here, and the reader is cautioned to consider the inherent limitations imposed by each.

The partisan-identification figures in Table 15-1 verify the dominance of the Democratic party in the South as well as in the North (the North is included throughout for comparison). All the panels of the table demonstrate black antipathy for the Republican party. Among the four Southern states for which state polling data were available, Alabama had the largest percentage of whites identified as Democrats, which makes sense given the broad nature of the Wallace-led party there. Virginia had the weakest Democracy; among whites in the Old Dominion the Democratic-Republican gap was quite narrow. This finding should come as no surprise after one has followed the political developments depicted in Chapter 11, where the demise of Virginia's Howell-led Democrats was traced.

Racial Split

The results from the 1980 presidential election in Table 15-2 starkly demonstrate the deep racial cleavages present in the actual voting behavior of Southerners. The contours of the black-white Democratic coalition in Alabama, where Carter was a narrow loser in 1980, can be glimpsed in the table's first panel.[4] Virtually all blacks supported Carter, but only 38 percent of the whites favored the Democratic President. The CPS survey presents the same basic picture for the South as a whole, although the strength of the Democratic coalition for the region is weaker than that shown for the single Deep South state of Alabama, which should be expected since the CPS sample includes many respondents from Southern states that Reagan won overwhelmingly—specifically, Texas, Florida, and Virginia.

Table 15-2, however, is of little help in the attempt to figure out what constituted Reagan's Southern victory coalition except to confirm that it was made up almost exclusively of whites. Table 15-3 adds a little more by showing the party affiliations of the 1980 presidential electorate. Among whites in Alabama and the South generally, nearly all the Republicans voted for Reagan, but only two-thirds of the white Democrats backed Carter. Three-quarters of the white self-identified independents went with Reagan. Regardless of party affiliation, blacks voted for Carter; of course, most blacks were Democrats,[5] as the panels of this table further illustrate.

Economic-Class Divisions

While party affiliation played a role in sorting out the 1980 Southern voters, many aspects of the partisan coalitions remain unexplained. Two

Table 15-1. Race and Party Identification in the Early 1980s

	Alabama (1982)			Mississippi (1982)		
	All	Whites	Blacks	All	Whites	Blacks
Democrat	54%	46%	80%	53%	42%	77%
Republican	19	22	8	16	20	6
Independent	28	32	12	31	37	17
	101%	100%	100%	100%	99%	100%
N	1779	1410	369	859	593	256

	Virginia (1982)			Tennessee (1981)		
	All	Whites	Blacks	All	Whites	Blacks
Democrat	34%	28%	69%	42%	39%	65%
Republican	20	22	2	25	28	9
Independent	47	50	29	33	33	26
	101%	100%	100%	100%	100%	100%
N	610	514	96	419	373	46

	South (1980)			North (1980)		
	All	Whites	Blacks	All	Whites	Blacks
Democrat	49%	43%	77%	38%	35%	73%
Republican	21	25	4	24	26	6
Independent	30	33	19	38	39	21
	100%	100%	100%	100%	100%	100%
N	539	449	90	1018	928	90

	Nation (1980)		
	All	Whites	Blacks
Democrat	42%	37%	75%
Republican	23	26	5
Independent	35	37	20
	100%	100%	100%
N	1577	1377	180

SOURCE: The documentation for Tables 15-1 through 15-7 is contained in this source note.

The figures for the South and North are from the 1980 American National Election Study, Traditional Time Series, conducted by the Center for Political Studies of the University of Michigan. Pre-election interviews were conducted in Sept. and Oct. 1980, and postelection interviews with the same sample were done in Nov. and Dec. 1980.

The Alabama party-identification figures in Table 15-1 and Table 15-7 are from the Capstone Poll conducted June 22 to Aug. 25, 1982, by Patrick R. Cotter, director of survey research and service, University of Alabama, Tuscaloosa. The Alabama figures in Table 15-2 through Table 15-6 are from Capstone Poll No. 3, conducted Oct. 26 to Nov. 2, 1980. Special cross-tabulations for both polls were done for this book by Professor Cotter, for which the author is very grateful.

The Mississippi data are from the Mississippi Poll, conducted Sept. 7–18, 1982, by Stephen D. Shaffer of Mississippi State University. Professor Shaffer performed the Mississippi cross-tabulations especially for this book; the author is very appreciative of his aid.

The Virginia and Tennessee figures, which appear only in Table 15-1, were reported in separate conference papers. The William and Mary Virginia Poll was conducted Feb. 16–Mar. 18, 1982, by Alan I. Abramowitz, John McGlennon, and Ronald Rapoport and reported in their "The Transformation of the Virginia Electorate" (Paper delivered at the Annual Meeting of the Southern Political Science Association, Atlanta, Oct. 28–30, 1982). The Tennessee figures are from a Mar. 1981 poll conducted by Robert H. Swansbrough and reported in his "Changing Partisanship in a Border State—Tennessee" (Paper delivered at the 1982 Citadel Symposium on Southern Politics, Charleston, S.C., Mar. 15–17, 1982).

Table 15-2. Race and Voter Preference in the 1980 Presidential Election

| | Alabama | | South | | North | |
	Whites	Blacks	Whites	Blacks	Whites	Blacks
Carter	38%	96%	35%	93%	33%	92%
Reagan	58	4	61	7	56	6
Anderson	5	1	4	0	12	2
	101%	101%	100%	100%	101%	100%
N	568	137	269	57	572	49

SOURCE: See documentation in Table 15-1.

Table 15-3. Race, Party Identification, and Voter Preference in the 1980 Presidential Election

Alabama

| | Whites | | | Blacks | | |
	Dem.	Rep.	Ind.	Dem.	Rep.	Ind.
Carter	67%	6%	20%	98%	78%	93%
Reagan	28	93	74	1	22	7
Anderson	5	1	6	1	0	0
	100%	100%	100%	100%	100%	100%
N	242	111	159	107	9	14

South

| | Whites | | | Blacks | | |
	Dem.	Rep.	Ind.	Dem.	Rep.	Ind.
Carter	69%	4%	22%	96%	100%	67%
Reagan	28	95	70	4	0	33
Anderson	3	1	9	0	0	0
	100%	100%	101%	100%	100%	100%
N	109	81	79	49	1	6

North

| | Whites | | | Blacks | | |
	Dem.	Rep.	Ind.	Dem.	Rep.	Ind.
Carter	66%	4%	26%	93%	0%	100%
Reagan	26	87	56	5	100	0
Anderson	8	9	18	2	0	0
	100%	100%	100%	100%	100%	100%
N	193	180	199	42	1	5

SOURCE: See documentation in Table 15-1.

more variables—economic-class and generational differences—cast further light on the composition of the Southern electorate. The first panel of Table 15-4 reveals that economic class in 1980, as in 1976, consistently differentiated white Southern voters. The Democratic standard-bearer received 58 percent of the votes of those with family incomes less than $15,000 but only 23 percent of the votes of those whites with incomes over $35,000. The 1980 Alabama survey did not ask respondents their income, but the notion of economic class can be approached by the use of another variable that the survey did record, the education level of respondents, since those with less education frequently occupy a lower status in society and usually earn less. Among Alabama whites with at least some college education, the third panel of Table 15-4 shows, 66 percent supported Reagan while only 27 percent favored Carter. Among whites with a high school education or less, Carter did considerably better with 46 percent, but he still trailed Reagan's 51 percent.

These findings confirming the existence of New Deal–style cleavages at the presidential level in 1980 appear also when party identification is substituted for candidate choice as the chief partisan measure, which is done in Table 15-5. Southern white Democrats are far more numerous among "those who have less," according to the first panel. The Alabama and Mississippi state polls display the same general pattern, but intriguing differences appear between these two neighbors. Substantially fewer white Mississippians earning over $20,000 identify with the Democratic party than do whites in Alabama. Perhaps some of this difference can be attributed to the prominent retarding influence on Alabama GOP growth of George Wallace, the charismatic "poor man's segregationist."[6]

Generational Differences

One fascinating finding of survey research in recent years has been the sharp differences in partisan behavior among generations.[7] For the South, divisions among age groups are quite distinct and contain important suggestions concerning future trends. Table 15-6 discloses that for white Southerners Carter's support was proportionally highest among those over sixty years of age; Carter defeated Reagan in that age category by 49 percent of the vote to 47 percent. In Alabama the older white generation favored Carter by an even larger margin, 56 percent to 43 percent. But among younger voters Reagan was the big winner. White Alabamians eighteen to forty years old favored the Republican nominee by 63 percent of the vote to Carter's 31 percent, and for the entire South younger voters chose Reagan by 66 percent to Carter's 29 percent.

Table 15-4. Class and Voter Preference in the 1980 Presidential Election

	Southern Whites			Northern Whites		
	Under $15,000	$15,000 to $35,000	Over $35,000	Under $15,000	$15,000 to $35,000	Over $35,000
Carter	58%	36%	23%	43%	34%	31%
Reagan	38	61	75	49	56	50
Anderson	5	3	2	8	10	20
	101%	100%	100%	100%	100%	101%
N	151	101	47	246	242	95

	Alabama Whites	
	High School Education or Less	Some College and Higher
Carter	46%	27%
Reagan	51	66
Anderson	3	7
	100%	100%
N	314	250

SOURCE: See documentation in Table 15-1.

Table 15-5. Class and Party Identification in the Early 1980s

	White Southerners (1980)			White Northerners (1980)		
	Under $15,000	$15,000 to $35,000	Over $35,000	Under $15,000	$15,000 to $35,000	Over $35,000
Democrats	53%	38%	21%	40%	32%	31%
Republicans	22	23	44	22	26	33
Independents	25	39	35	38	41	36
	100%	100%	100%	100%	99%	100%
N	195	147	57	386	346	120

	White Alabamians (1980)			White Mississippians (1982)		
	Under $10,000	$10,000 to $20,000	Over $20,000	Under $10,000	$10,000 to $20,000	Over $20,000
Democrats	61%	50%	45%	54%	42%	33%
Republicans	16	19	23	11	23	42
Independents	23	32	32	35	34	25
	100%	101%	100%	100%	99%	100%
N	250	348	168	112	188	211

SOURCE: See documentation in Table 15-1.

Table 15-6. Age and Voter Preference in the 1980 Presidential Election

	White Southerners			White Northerners		
	18–39	40–59	60 & Over	18–39	40–59	60 & Over
Carter	29%	29%	49%	29%	33%	39%
Reagan	66	68	47	53	58	58
Anderson	5	3	4	18	9	3
	100%	100%	100%	100%	100%	100%
N	114	75	81	244	182	145

	White Alabamians		
	18–40	41–60	61 & Over
Carter	31%	37%	56%
Reagan	63	57	43
Anderson	6	5	1
	100%	99%	100%
N	305	150	113

SOURCE: See documentation in Table 15-1.

The same pattern appears when one examines party identification and age among white Southerners, which Table 15-7 does. The gap between Democratic and Republican partisans narrows considerably for the generation that came of voting age in the past twenty years. Those younger citizens who entered the electorate during and after the great partisan watershed of the middle 1960s were considerably less likely to identify with the Democratic party than were members of the older generation, whose partisan leanings were influenced by the Solid South mentality that persisted until the civil rights question had been resolved. Among white Mississippians eighteen to thirty-six years old, for example, only 30 percent in 1982 identified with the Democratic party, compared with 57 percent among white Mississippians sixty-one years of age or older. Figures similar to these led Raymond Wolfinger and Robert B. Arseneau to conclude, "The actuarial odds are all on [the Republicans'] side. Older Southerners are more likely to be Democrats, younger ones to be Republicans. If the only influence on southern population composition were the normal pattern of death and maturation, every passing year would help the Republicans."[8]

Although these generational findings offer hope for the GOP, it would be an error to view the trend of Republican growth among the young as predetermined. Such an interpretation would deny to political forces their true, pivotal role. All the major changes covered in this book have had political causes at their core. The Solid South was not destroyed by the inevitable movement of all-powerful socioeconomic

Table 15-7. Age and Party Identification in the Early 1980s

	White Southerners (1980)			White Northerners (1980)		
	18–39	40–59	60 & Over	18–39	40–59	60 & Over
Democrats	38%	39%	56%	31%	35%	42%
Republicans	26	21	25	21	29	32
Independents	36	40	19	48	36	26
	100%	100%	100%	100%	100%	100%
N	202	122	124	434	271	222

	White Alabamians (1982)		White Mississippians (1982)		
	18–36	37 & Over	18–36	37–60	61 & Over
Democrats	40%	51%	30%	46%	57%
Republicans	25	19	31	15	14
Independents	35	30	39	39	30
	100%	100%	100%	100%	101%
N	577	827	213	251	121

SOURCE: See documentation in Table 15-1.

forces—such as the rise to middle-class prosperity of many white Southerners after World War II. Socioeconomic factors play a role in shaping the political environment, but the primacy of the political ought never to be forgotten. The history of the death of the one-party Democratic South—which at its center was a political story—should demonstrate that conclusively to any doubters. Rather, the ultimate partisan division of the current younger generation of Southerners, and the next one, will be decided in large measure by the future actions of political elites, although these actions will be tempered by the socioeconomic circumstances they confront. Therefore, if these observations are correct, Republican strategists cannot rest on the inevitable passing of the torch from one generation to another. They can, however, remain thankful that with the destruction of the Solid South mind-set, they are now getting a fairer shot at making lasting partisan gains among the South's youth. How well they do will rest far more on their political skill than on the inexorable passage of time.

Diverse Issue Cleavages in the Southern Electorate

While the survey information examined so far adds a measure of insight into the partisan divisions existing in the South in the early 1980s, much more can be learned by focusing on what public opinion polls disclose about various issue positions prevalent among the electorate.

Voter responses in the 1980 CPS survey to eight political questions, ranging from broad inquiries about the proper role of the national government to specific ones concerning abortion, busing, and prayer in public schools, are revealing mileposts in the effort to chart the contours of Southern partisan divisions.

The answers to each question are broken down into five categories: four of the categories are made up of whites for Reagan or for Carter in the South or in the North; the fifth is for Southern blacks voting for Carter.[9] These five categories allow multiple comparisons on each question. First, the attitudes of the two major partisan voting blocs of Southern whites in 1980 can be compared—that is, Southern Reagan white voters versus Southern Carter white voters. Next, the two regional wings of each major party's white supporters can be compared with each other: Reagan's white voters in the North versus his white Southern supporters; and white Carter supporters in the North versus those in the South. Finally, the two parts of the potent black-white Democratic coalition in the South can be contrasted by an examination of Carter's Southern black supporters and his Southern white backers.

The 1980 CPS survey asked a marvelous question for tapping the central issue that has divided the nation's parties since the New Deal: "Some people feel the government in Washington should see to it that every person has a job and a good standard of living. Others think the government should just let each person get ahead on his own. Where would you place yourself [on a seven-point scale]?"[10] The first position on the scale represents the view that government should see that everyone has a job and a good standard of living; the seventh, that government should let each person get ahead on his own. For ease of handling, the seven-point scale has been collapsed into three categories. Position four, the middle slot, is labeled neutral. Those picking points one through three are taken together as supporting some type of governmental role; respondents choosing positions five through seven are viewed as favoring more emphasis on the responsibility of the individual.

Table 15-8 displays the responses by the five regional and racial categories. The sharpest differences are between Carter's black and white Southern allies. Sixty-seven percent of the Southern blacks favored a government role, but only 28 percent of Carter's Southern white backers were so inclined. This result quantitatively confirms part of the basis for the tensions described throughout the state chapters as existing in the ideologically diverse, black-white Southern Democratic coalition. Table 15-8 also shows that Southern whites for Carter were more inclined to favor a role for government than were Southern whites for Reagan, by a margin of 28 percent to 21 percent. Carter's Northern

Table 15-8. Attitudes on Whether the National Government Should See That Every Person Has a Job and a Good Standard of Living

| | Southern Whites | | So. Blacks | Northern Whites | |
	Reagan	Carter	Carter	Reagan	Carter
Favors role for government	21%	28%	67%	13%	40%
Neutral	22	22	16	16	30
Favors stress on individual	57	50	18	71	30
	100%	100%	101%	100%	100%
N	148	78	45	273	164

Question: "Some people feel the government in Washington should see to it that every person has a job and a good standard of living. Others think the government should just let each person get ahead on his own. Where would you place yourself [on a seven-point scale]?" Point 1 was labeled "government see to a job and good standard of living," and point 7 was labeled "government let each person get ahead on his own." Points 2 and 3 were combined with point 1; points 5 and 6 went with point 7. Point 4 is labeled neutral since it came in the middle. Center for Political Studies (CPS), University of Michigan, 1980 National Election Study.

For this table and for Tables 15-9 through 15-13, the major-party vote for the presidency is used; that is, John Anderson's 1980 vote is ignored so that the attitudes of those supporting the nominees of the two established parties may be examined.

white supporters stood farther to the liberal side on the question than did their Southern counterparts, 40 percent to 28 percent.

Another question in the CPS survey also strikes at the public's basic attitude toward the proper role of the national government. "Some people are afraid the government in Washington is getting too powerful for the good of the country and the individual person. Others feel that the government in Washington is not getting too strong. What is your feeling, do you think the government is getting too powerful or do you think the government is not getting too strong?" Table 15-9 displays the results. This question, which admittedly is far less precise and as a consequence less useful than the first one, elicited partisan unity among the five categories. The three groups of Carter supporters had similar scores, and Reagan's white backers North and South were in virtual unanimity in their fear of powerful government—however they defined it—on the banks of the Potomac.

Racial attitudes were solicited in the following well-phrased query: "Some people feel that the government in Washington should make every effort to improve the social and economic position of blacks and other minority groups, even if it means giving them preferential treatment. Suppose these people are at one end of the scale at point number 1. Others feel that the government should not make any special effort to help minorities because they should help themselves. Suppose these

Table 15-9. Attitudes on Whether the National Government
Is Growing Too Strong

| | Southern Whites | | So. Blacks | Northern Whites | |
	Reagan	Carter	Carter	Reagan	Carter
Government too powerful	88%	59%	58%	87%	64%
Not getting too strong	12	41	42	13	36
	100%	100%	100%	100%	100%
N	130	58	24	237	113

Question: "Some people are afraid the government in Washington is getting too powerful for the good of the country and the individual person. Others feel that the government in Washington is not getting too strong. What is your feeling, do you think the government is getting too powerful or do you think the government is not getting too strong?" CPS, 1980 National Election Study.

people are at the other end at point 7. And, of course, some other people have opinions somewhere in between . . . . Where would you place yourself on [a seven-point] scale?" Table 15-10 reports the tabulations after the scale has been collapsed for ease of interpretation in the manner adopted for the first question. Differences between white and black Southern supporters of Carter stand out: 44 percent of the blacks see a role for the national government but only 16 percent of the whites take that position. This discrepancy in the dominant Southern alliance again quantitatively corroborates the existence of potential tensions and conflict over racial issues in Dixie's powerful "night-and-day" coalition. Furthermore, Northern whites for Carter were twice as favorable to the liberal position as were their Southern counterparts. Republicans of both regions overwhelmingly favored leaving minorities to their own devices. A question on busing produced similar results (see Table 15-11).

Sharp differences appear between Southern whites for Carter and their Northern allies over the issue of prayer in the public schools. Ninety-one percent of the former were in favor of allowing prayer; only 58 percent of the Northerners would allow it (see Table 15-12). On this issue Carter's Southern blacks and whites were identical in their stances. On another highly charged social issue—abortion—Carter's Southern whites were the most conservative among the five voter categories. While 46 percent of Carter's Northern white supporters favored the view that a woman should always be able to get an abortion, only 26 percent of his Southern white supporters selected the prochoice position. The GOP responses across the two sections of the country were again similar, pointing to the homogeneous nature of national Republican politics (see Table 15-13).

Table 15-10. Attitudes on the Proper Role of Government in Aiding Blacks

| | Southern Whites | | So. Blacks | Northern Whites | |
	Reagan	Carter	Carter	Reagan	Carter
Favors gov't help for minorities	7%	16%	44%	12%	32%
Neutral	27	35	21	24	34
Minorities should help themselves	<u>66</u>	<u>48</u>	<u>35</u>	<u>64</u>	<u>34</u>
	100%	99%	100%	100%	100%
N	151	74	48	283	176

Question: "Some people feel that the government in Washington should make every effort to improve the social and economic position of blacks and other minority groups, even if it means giving them preferential treatment. Suppose these people are at one end of the scale at point number 1. Others feel that the government should not make any special effort to help minorities because they should help themselves. Suppose these people are at the other end at point 7. And, of course, some other people have opinions somewhere in between at points 2, 3, 4, 5, or 6. Where would you place yourself . . .?" Points 2 and 3 were combined with point 1; points 5 and 6 went with point 7. Point 4 is labeled neutral. CPS, 1980 National Election Study.

Table 15-11. Attitudes on Busing to Achieve Racial Integration of the Public Schools

| | Southern Whites | | So. Blacks | Northern Whites | |
	Reagan	Carter	Carter	Reagan	Carter
Bus if needed to achieve integration	1%	7%	31%	2%	13%
Neutral	5	10	13	1	9
Keep children in neighborhood schools	<u>94</u>	<u>84</u>	<u>56</u>	<u>96</u>	<u>78</u>
	100%	101%	100%	99%	100%
N	159	91	48	303	176

Question: "There is much discussion about the best way to deal with racial problems. Some people think achieving racial integration of schools is so important that it justifies busing children to schools out of their own neighborhoods. Others think letting children go to their neighborhood schools is so important that they oppose busing. Where would you place yourself on [a seven-point scale]?" Points 2 and 3 of the scale were combined with point 1; points 5 and 6 went with point 7. Point 4 is labeled neutral. CPS, 1980 National Election Study.

Table 15-12. Attitudes on Prayer in the Public Schools

| | Southern Whites | | So. Blacks | Northern Whites | |
	Reagan	Carter	Carter	Reagan	Carter
Allow prayer in schools	86%	91%	91%	76%	58%
Religion does not belong in schools	14	9	9	24	42
	——	——	——	——	——
	100%	100%	100%	100%	100%
N	136	80	45	254	165

Question: "Some people think it is all right for the public schools to start each day with a prayer. Others feel that religion does not belong in the public schools but should be taken care of by the family and the church. Which do you think—schools should be allowed to start each day with a prayer or religion does not belong in the schools?" CPS, 1980 National Election Study.

Table 15-13. Attitudes on Abortion

| | Southern Whites | | So. Blacks | Northern Whites | |
	Reagan	Carter	Carter	Reagan	Carter
Never permit abortion	13%	10%	28%	10%	8%
Allow only in case of rape, etc	31	49	26	35	34
Allow when need is clearly established	22	16	16	23	13
Always allow woman choice of abortion	34	26	30	32	46
	——	——	——	——	——
	100%	101%	100%	100%	101%
N	156	94	50	306	179

Question: "There has been some discussion about abortion during recent years. Which one of the opinions on this page best agrees with your view?
   1. By law, abortion should never be permitted.
   2. The law should permit abortion only in case of rape, incest or when the woman's life is in danger.
   3. The law should permit abortion for reasons other than rape, incest, or danger to the woman's life, but only after the need for the abortion has been clearly established.
   4. By law, a woman should always be able to obtain an abortion as a matter of personal choice."
CPS, 1980 National Election Study.

On the equal rights amendment (ERA), 66 percent of the white Southern Reagan backers disapproved of it but only 33 percent of Carter's Southern whites did so. Between Carter's Northern and Southern wings of white support, the ERA gap was not wide; two-thirds of the Southerners favored the women's rights amendment, while three-fourths of the Northerners did so. Eighty-eight percent of Carter's Southern blacks favored the ERA. (Similar divisions came in response to a question on environmental protection.) In an inquiry concerning support for increasing defense spending, Reagan's white voters North and South were in agreement, 82 percent of them favoring more money for the Pentagon. Carter's Southern white voters were far more willing to increase spending on arms (75 percent) than were the Democrat's Northern supporters (56 percent), his Southern blacks falling in between (65 percent).[11]

This excursion into survey research, especially the results in Tables 15-8 through 15-13, documents the existence of significant partisan cleavages in the electorate of the early 1980s. White Southern and Northern Reagan voters more frequently than not had very similar positions on the propositions examined. The Democrats, as one would expect, given the diverse character of their party, exhibited far greater differences. The white Southern and Northern wings of the party—as measured by presidential candidate support—showed sizable attitudinal differences, especially on racial and social matters.

On the one question that best captured support for the national government's involvement in economic matters (displayed in Table 15-8), important differences appeared among the major groupings of Carter supporters. Two-thirds of the Southern blacks strongly favored a central role for the national government in seeing that everyone has a job and a good standard of living, while only about a quarter of Carter's Southern whites took that view; Northern whites for Carter fell somewhere in between. The cleavages on this basic economic question relate directly to two broad themes running throughout this book: the extent of the Southern penetration of New Deal–style partisan politics below the presidential level and the existence of tensions in the ideologically diverse, black-white Southern Democratic coalition. The next section returns attention to these themes.

Southern Penetration of the New Deal Alignment

Electoral politics in the South prior to the 1960s was characterized by isolation from the great debates of national politics; the nonracial issues that agitated the country faced impenetrable Southern barriers. These obstacles were breached in presidential elections after the rationale for the Solid South evaporated with the beginning of Northern Democratic civil rights initiatives. At first the result of the fury of the race issue in the 1960s was to punish the Democratic party's national nominees, but by 1976, after the hottest battles were over and the race issue was in relative abeyance, the party's standard-bearer (albeit a Southerner) was able to carry the region with an electoral pattern that divided along class lines consistent with the New Deal alignment as it had evolved in the nation. And these same Southern class differences were also visible in the 1980 election,[12] as Table 15-4 shows.

At the state level the altered situation circa 1964 created considerable confusion for the once-unchallenged Democratic candidates who were accustomed, as a general rule, to functioning in isolation from nonracial national questions. As barriers were lifted, permitting the penetration below the presidential level of national issues in an organized partisan fashion, the electoral scene in each state simultaneously became entangled with the emotional issue of race, which had played such an important part in keeping the South a region apart. It was with this highly confused situation in existence during the middle years of the 1960s that the main part of this book began. Now that the course of Southern electoral politics has been charted into the early 1980s, it is appropriate to ask how far the convergence with the national New Deal–style partisan alignment has progressed in the South below the presidential level.[13]

Even in Northern states, where there was no major barrier to the penetration of the national partisan configuration to the state level, the realignment process was one of an uneven filtering, or, as Professor Key put it, "These [national] debates seep down into the battles between their [national parties'] subsidiaries, and perhaps become blurred in the process . . . ."[14] How blurred the process is depends to a considerable extent on the actions of the various personalities working within each state's political traditions. As the two-party structure emerged, some Southern politicians pushed the penetration of the national alignment further along than others. Thurmond's forthright embrace of the Republican party aided in clarifying the two-party situation in South Carolina; Stennis in Mississippi and Talmadge in Georgia blurred it. Certainly the Howell campaigns in Virginia stand out as having brought these questions to the fore. There were others who sought to play a role similar to Howell's but were unable to win in the Democratic primary.

In general, through the 1970s economic-class cleavages were more prevalent in the elections of the Rim South than in those of the Deep South, but there were signs that the distinction between the two subsections was growing far less sharp.

Few elections in the Deep South during the first decade of the post–civil rights era—Thurmond's re-election campaigns in South Carolina are exceptions—revolved around class issues. In Georgia in 1972 Nunn did not wrap himself in the New Deal legacy; his narrow victory over the Republican Thompson came, rather, as a result of a union of the Talmadge-Maddox white Democrats with blacks in an appeal that was nonideological. Only in the 1978 Senate election of the Democrat Stewart over the Republican Martin did the Alabama general elections deal with these issues; in 1982, however, Wallace made gestures in the direction of a class appeal when he was confronted with a credible Republican opponent. The on-again, off-again black-white Democratic alliance in Mississippi dominated elections there to the near exclusion of economic-class issues, although Finch made use of workingman symbols to cement the state's biracial Democratic coalition. In Louisiana the infrequent number of GOP challenges made the question difficult to consider there.

The Rim South presents a different picture. A number of elections during the 1970s in Texas, Virginia, North Carolina, Tennessee, and Florida revolved around at least mild economic-class division.[15] Most prominent were the losing campaigns of Howell in Virginia in 1973 and 1977; the Tennessean Sasser's defeat of Brock in 1976 and of Beard in 1982; Morgan's victory for a U.S. Senate seat from North Carolina in 1974 and his defeat by East six years later; Senator Bentsen's Texas victories in 1970, 1976, and 1982; and Askew's successful campaigns for the Florida governorship in 1970 and 1974. In other elections in these states, the use of New Deal–style economic issues by the Democratic nominees was less noticeable but still stronger than in the Deep South. These included Briscoe's winning campaigns for the governorship of Texas in 1972 and 1974; Miller's narrow senatorial loss to the Republican Warner in Virginia in 1978; and Blanton's gubernatorial victory in Tennessee in 1974.

Regardless of how the Southern elections are classified in terms of the extent of economic-class appeal by the Democratic nominees, there is no question that two-party contests in the Rim South were more concerned with these questions than were those in the Deep South. By the early 1980s, though, this convenient intraregional distinction was becoming less important.

The Persisting Political South

Above all else and for generations, race made Southern politics distinct from politics in other parts of the nation.[16] When the race issue was transformed, there surfaced in much of the South a residual cohesiveness that provided the basis for a continued regional link; and this cohesiveness cut across the old Deep South–Rim South split now that the race issue—the foundation for the intraregional division—had undergone a metamorphosis.

The common feature visible in state after state became the centrality of the ideologically diverse, black-white coalition to the well-being of the Southern Democracy or, from the other side, to the future prospects of the challenging Republicans. Where this coalition and its attendant dynamics were not found to be dominant, the existence of a bond to distinctively Southern political trends was called into question. Such was the case with Florida and Texas,[17] and by the late 1970s and early 1980s both of these fast-changing states appeared to have less in common with the other nine in partisan terms than with states elsewhere in the nation that were also experiencing the same type of rapid growth.

But for the nine states of the persisting political South, insight into the partisan situation in one offered aid in understanding what was happening in the others. Recollection of the nature of two-party competition as sketched in the state chapters should support this observation. When the Republican Trent Lott in Mississippi warned about the precarious nature of the Democratic coalition in his state, about the critical importance of Wallace voters and blacks for Democratic majorities, and about the difficulties he hoped his opponents would have in holding these disparate elements together, he could just as easily have been talking about the situation in South Carolina, Alabama, Georgia, Louisiana, Arkansas, North Carolina, Virginia, and Tennessee. In many of the state chapters observations appear—either from newspaper sources or interviews—that are quite similar to Lott's. Essentially, in an amorphous manner these politicians and political observers were touching on the key elements of race, class, and traditional Democratic affiliation as they came together to form the dominant regional coalition in the post–civil rights era.

The tensions visible in present-day Southern politics are pivotal for, among other things, the prospects of continued penetration of New Deal–style cleavages in the region. For example, in South Carolina Tom Turnipseed, a "rabblerouser" and a "wild man," made a vigorous—if short-lived—effort to win the governorship in 1978 with a sharp appeal to low-income whites and blacks. If he had succeeded, the penetration of the economic-class alignment would have progressed further in this Deep South state; conservative and moderate Democrats in South Carolina, whose ties to their state's Democratic party were often based on noneconomic considerations that have weathered the racial revolution, would have been put under intense pressure to abandon a Democratic party led by such a nominee. This is what happened to the Howell-led Democracy in Virginia in the 1970s. The future implications of the tensions illustrated by the Turnipseed and Howell cases are explored in the last part of this chapter.

Furthermore, it appears just as likely that the future chance arrival to prominence of a Howell-like figure will occur in a Rim South state as in the Deep South. And the result will be the same in whichever state or states such a development occurs—to push along the already existing tendency of the state parties in the South to mirror more closely the dominant national partisan cleavage.[18]

Newer National Influences

The future course of the economic-class alignment in all the Southern states will be affected, of course, by political developments outside of the region. A look at the New Deal alignment in the nation in recent decades leaves no doubt but that the cleavages formed in the era of the Great Depression have undergone substantial changes in the rest of the country. Sundquist concluded that in the North the realignment begun in the 1930s had widely penetrated below the presidential level by the early 1960s.[19] But even by that time the nature of the coalition had changed drastically, as Samuel Lubell has pointed out in a series of incisive books,[20] and since then a panoply of issues and conflicts affecting the national party system has arisen.

To what extent the national party system has been altered is a matter of considerable debate.[21] It is my opinion that no fundamental realignment has occurred since the 1930s in the nation, but that the race issue brought about a reshuffling of forces nationwide since 1964 within the basic broad ideological and economic-class cleavage that persists. One element contributing to this reshuffling within the continuing New Deal alignment has been the racial antagonism that is evident between Northern working-class whites, who are a key element of the Democratic party's support there, and Northern blacks, who virtually cut their state-level ties with the Republican party after 1964.

The key issue for this book, however, is not what the changes in the national party system are—for that would require an investigation of considerable detail—but rather that there have been important changes and, in fact, the national party system was in considerable flux by the early 1980s.[22] Thus, as an older national realignment finally pierced formidable Southern barriers, newer and different national forces were also at work that could overtake the earlier forces in the South before they are fully played out.

Future of the Southern Black-White Democratic Coalition

Although it cannot be denied that Southern politics in the early 1980s was subject to greater national influences than at any time since the Civil War, the region's political future will be determined by more than merely what happens in the country at large, as important and unpredictable as changes in the bigger arena are. Instead, a healthy portion of the South's political future is wrapped up in the fortunes of the dominant black-white Democratic coalition. What of this alliance? Its potency has been demonstrated time and again. Its tensions, present and potential, have surfaced frequently. Where is it going and what difference does it make?

Thus far, this broad Democratic coalition has held together partly as a result of the canny maneuvers of white Democratic leaders, who are its chief beneficiaries. They often walk a political tightrope that requires Olympian balancing. It is a straddling performance that ought to evoke periodic standing ovations from the gods of equivocation, if such exist. Since the future of the Southern Democracy is intertwined with the success of this tightrope act, a candid description of it by one of its more skillful practitioners is illuminating.

Such a description came from U.S. Rep. David R. Bowen, a Mississippi Democrat elected to the House in 1972. Bowen represented the state's 45 percent black Second District until January 1983; he chose not to run for a sixth term in 1982 after a federal court, responding to two decades of racial gerrymandering, had dismembered his district to create a Delta district with a black majority.[23] One popular guide to Congress, noting that Bowen had not attracted much attention in the House, described him as "a moderate by Mississippi standards, although in fact his voting record is not far out of line with traditional Mississippi conservatism."[24]

In a 1982 interview I asked Bowen whether the tightrope analogy fit the way he viewed his political situation. He responded:

> Yes, it was a little bit [like walking a tightrope]. Of course, I had a lot of very conservative white people supporting me, a lot of conservative farmers and businessmen, people like that. And at the same time a large bloc of the black community. I think if you don't have a hard-core doctrinaire position on something in which you lock yourself in by saying, "I am a liberal and I believe in a liberal program, which is the following," and therefore you sort of announce that "I am going after labor votes and black votes and that's that and if I can pick up any more on friendship or personal charm or on whatever, well, I'll get a few more someplace else." That's one way.
>
> Or you can go to the other side and say, "I am a conservative and

I am going to get business votes and wealthy farmer votes and I am going to pick up any others wherever I can." Obviously, I was not either of those two extremes. . . . And I had no particular reason to be. . . .

[At this point Bowen helped the interview along by asking himself the next logical question.]

It's easy enough when you are in [the first] campaign to make everybody happy because you never had to vote on anything . . . but how'd you stay in office for ten years? I think I just didn't do anything to alienate either of those two blocs that I had put together. Obviously, there were a lot of white votes I didn't get. Because if my high-water mark was 70 percent of the votes and I was getting maybe 90 percent of the black votes, there were a lot of white votes I was not getting. But my voting record was often on the conservative side, but it varied across the middle of the board. It was not far right or far left. In all these national organizations that rate you, I might range from 35 to 85 . . . . My ADA and liberal-type votes were usually in the low numbers. The conservative organizations were more often in the high numbers, but usually in the middle ranges somewhere.

So it was not a very doctrinaire sort of pattern. You could look at it and you could say, "I don't know whether it falls under liberal or conservative." That's pretty much the way it was. No one could really stamp me as a liberal or a conservative. I never did anything to alienate the black support that I had. I never did anything to alienate the business support that I had. There were never very many issues that came along which were kind of no-win issues where you would totally outrage half the people whatever you did. . . .

Take things like food stamps. . . . Theoretically, a lot of the people who do not receive food stamps are against them. Of course, almost all the black community is for them as well as a lot of the whites. I'm on the Ag[riculture] Committee and I have to write food stamp legislation. Of course, blacks stayed with me because I voted for food stamps. And [to] the whites, I was able to explain that I was tightening up the legislation, improving it. And it would have been a lot more costly and a lot less efficient if I were not in there trying to put amendments in there to improve it—conditions that require recipients to register for work and accept work if it is offered and to make sure that people don't draw food stamps who are able-bodied and unwilling to work. So, generally those conservatives who would cuss and holler about food stamps all the time would say, "Well, David's doing a good job trying to improve the program. They are going to pass the thing . . . anyhow. He's in there trying to improve it, trying to tighten it up, trying to cut out the fraud, the waste." But I would certainly vote for the program after I got through tightening it up.

> So, . . . what makes good politicians, I guess, is someone who can
> take whatever his vote is and do a good job of explaining it . . . . If
> you can explain it to those who are against it and make them like it,
> even though you voted for it, and then, of course, let the ones who are
> for it know that you voted for it . . . then you are in good shape. And I
> think that is probably what I did. . . . It's just kind of a matter of
> personal skill and packaging what you do and explaining it.[25]

Trends are at work in the South that could make the delicate positioning of nonideological Democratic straddlers like Bowen more and
more difficult to maintain. Thus far it has been stressed that the black-
white Democratic coalition is ideologically diverse. Although that is
true in the main and was the coalition's most striking feature, especially
in the first years of the post–civil rights era, by the early 1980s there was
a growing tendency for rank-and-file Democrats of both races to recognize their common stake in policies that favor their interests. Tables
15-4 and 15-5 show that low-income whites are far more likely to be
members of the Southern Democratic coalition than are upper-income
whites. Furthermore, a deeper perusal of the issue responses in Tables
15-8 through 15-13 uncovers a substantial percentage of whites in agreement with the views of the black wing of the alliance. And the tendency
is in the direction of greater ideological, or issue, agreement. In national terms, the same phenomenon has been charted in this book
under the heading of the penetration of the New Deal–style alignment
into Southern politics.

The pace at which this tendency proceeds will depend, as suggested
above, on the rise to prominence of left-leaning Southern Democratic
leaders who will advocate policies favorable to "those who have less" of
both races. Exactly when and where these leaders will surface cannot be
predicted, but the result can be: to push more conservative Democrats
over to the Republican party. How strong the Republican party will
grow in the South in the next decade or so involves too many impon-
derables—national as well as Southern—for even a guess. But grow it
will, for its foundations are secure in the new partisan configuration that
emerged in the South following the great political transformation the
region has experienced since the early 1960s.

Consequence for "Those Who Have Less"[26]

One of the sternest criticisms leveled at the South's one-party system
was its detrimental effect on the political interests of the region's
poorer citizens. Professor Key explained why these people lose out in
the disorganized political environment that results from the lack of
party competition:

Politics generally comes down, over the long run, to a conflict between those who have and those who have less. . . .

It follows that the grand objective of the haves is obstruc-
tion . . . . Organization is not always necessary to obstruct; it is
essential, however, for the promotion of a sustained program in
behalf of the have-nots . . . . It follows, if these propositions are
correct, that *over the long run the have-nots lose in a disorganized
politics. They have no mechanism through which to act* and their
wishes find expression in fitful rebellions led by transient dema-
gogues who gain their confidence but often have neither the technical competence nor the necessary stable base of political power to
effectuate a program.[27]

Party competition has now firmly settled into the region, and the
prognosis favors its growth. Has this two-party system provided "those
who have less" with the permanent organizational structure in political
life necessary for the sustained promotion of their interests? The assessment of the extent of economic-class politics prevalent in the region,
presented at the end of the state chapters and summarized in this chapter,
makes the answer unmistakable: Not yet, but it could be coming.

Given the historical and current roles of America's two national
parties, the vehicle for the lower-bracket groups in the South must be the
Democratic party. Therefore, the future of the Southern Democracy is of
more than passing interest to those who want government to serve the
interests of the region's less prosperous citizens of both races. Since elites
are the dynamo behind political change, it follows that, in order for
"those who have less" to get more, faithful champions of their cause must
arise to supplant the clever Democratic straddlers who have dominated
the first decade and a half of the post–civil rights era Democracy. Only
then will the South's well-to-do meet their match in the political arena.

The potential in the South for such a partisan configuration to take
hold is greater today than at any time since the Populist dream of an
alliance of the dispossessed across racial lines collapsed nine decades ago
before the reality of racial prejudice. The task of fulfilling that dream in
the mature years of the post–civil rights era rests on the shoulders of
those future Southern leaders dedicated to the admirable goal of the
Populists—a more equitable distribution of the fruits of this potentially
bountiful region, a region that has yet to yield a just political harvest for
the majority of its citizens, white and black. If that harvest ever comes,
it will have been made possible because of the groundwork laid by those
who led the nation and the South through the last several decades of
political change to the point where a brighter political future could be
in the offing.

16

The 1984 Elections

The 1984 elections represented no sharp break with the partisan developments that fueled the rise of the two-party South. These elections did, however, dramatically highlight the key elements at work in Southern politics in the 1980s.

President Reagan's electoral triumph with 58.8 percent of the popular vote to Walter Mondale's 40.6 percent was first and foremost a nationwide phenomenon. It was based on various national factors that have received extensive treatment[1] since the November 1984 balloting—such as, the apparent strength of the economy with a low inflation rate, the President's personal popularity, and the generally negative reception given to Mondale's proposal to increase taxes. These national elements, among others, operated in the South roughly as they did elsewhere, which in itself shows how far the South had come from the Solid South era when regional considerations dominated presidential elections there. For example, a cross-tabulation of voter choice with responses to a question on whether one was better off financially in 1984 compared with a year earlier demonstrates both the importance of the state of the economy for voting in 1984 as well as the similarity in behavior of Southern and Northern whites. See Table 16-1.

Still, there were important regional differences in the presidential voting. Contained within the national Republican victory was a noticeably stronger Southern finish. In the eleven states of the former Confederacy, Reagan won 62.4 percent compared with 57.6 percent for the other thirty-nine states. This divergence represents a return, although in reduced fashion, to the pattern present in the 1964 and 1972 elections,

Table 16-1. Attitudes on Financial Well-Being and Vote
for President in 1984

	Better Off	Southern Whites Same	Worse Off
Reagan	83%	65%	37%
Mondale	17%	35%	63%
	100%	100%	100%
N	144	92	81

	Better Off	Northern Whites Same	Worse Off
Reagan	76%	57%	39%
Mondale	24%	43%	61%
	100%	100%	100%
N	423	269	194

Question: Would you say that you (and your family living here) are better off or worse off
financially than you were a year ago?

SOURCE: National Election Study, 1984, Center for Political Studies, University of Michigan. All
the 1984 survey calculations in this chapter were performed by the author using the University of
North Florida computer facilities.

when the Southern GOP vote far outstripped its non-Southern counterpart. See Figure 3-1 in Chapter 3. Before attempting to unravel the
1984 presidential result and before looking at the other major elections
in the South that year, a brief consideration of how the campaign went
in the region is in order.

Neither presidential ticket can be faulted for ignoring the South, as a
quick review of the candidates' forays below the Mason-Dixon line illustrates. In early October, President Reagan brought his "Morning in
America" theme to a large crowd in Gulfport, Mississippi. He praised
the South for nourishing the "traditions and values that shape our land"
and added: "We've come here for one reason and one reason only—to
win—and we ain't just whistling Dixie."[2] Lambasting the Democrats as
preachers of "gloom and doom," the President said:

> America is stronger, more prosperous and bursting with patrio-
> tism. This isn't a Reagan recovery, this is an American recovery.
> This great nation is moving forward again, and we're not going back
> to that unhappy past.
>
> Well now, despite the strength of this expansion, there's one sure
> way to ruin it. You'd have to be something of an expert to do that,
> but when it comes to bringing economic growth to a grinding halt,
> our opponents are experts.
>
> After decades of a rising tax burden, they want to give the Ameri-
> can people a massive tax increase. They call it bitter medicine, but

that's just because they think they can get us to swallow anything. I think the word shrimp means something different to our opponents than it does to Gulfport. To you, it's a livelihood. To them, it's your paycheck after they get their hands on it.[3]

Speaking in Greenville, South Carolina, later in October, Reagan told a gathering at a technical college:

Today there is a phenomenon that many of the pollsters can't understand. I have seen it everywhere I go. Young people from every background have rejected the politics of pessimism and are four-square behind a strong, vibrant and growing America.

I don't think it is selfish for you to want a good job, to own a home, and to have a decent standard of living. America's young people deserve that kind of future and we aren't going to let our opponents tax it away.[4]

Walter Mondale and his running mate Geraldine Ferraro were attentive to the South as well, especially in the early months. For example, they began their post-convention campaign with a visit to Jackson, Mississippi, and a nearby farm. Although the issues of the campaign were discussed, the trip is remembered for the "great blueberry muffin test" that Ferraro, the first woman vice-presidential nominee and a New Yorker, underwent at the playful hands of Jim Buck Ross, Mississippi's veteran commissioner of agriculture and a self-proclaimed defender of Southern manhood. The widely reported exchange took place while Ross was explaining Mississippi's catfish industry to the candidates. The *New York Times* account captured the scene well:

"Now I'm for research and education," said Mr. Ross, who wore a cowboy hat and black-and-gray cowhide boots. "Here in Mississippi we have four new crops. One is catfish." He turned to Mrs. Ferraro. "Have you eaten any catfish?"

"Not yet," she replied.

"You haven't lived, young lady," the 70-year-old Mr. Ross said to the 48 year-old candidate.

As Mrs. Ferraro smiled wanly, Mr. Ross said that the state was developing catfish, crayfish, grapes and blueberries.

"Those I grow," said Mrs. Ferraro.

"You grow 'em?" remarked Mr. Ross with a grin at Mrs. Ferraro, who has the endorsement of numerous feminist groups. "Can you bake a blueberry muffin?"

The audience, including Mr. Mondale and Mrs. Ferraro, broke into laughter.

"I sure can," Mrs. Ferraro finally responded. "Can you?" The comment drew longer laughter.

Grinning, Mr. Ross said, "Down here in Mississippi the men don't cook."[5]

At the very bottom of the same *Times* article, Mondale's message was reported:

In 1984 it is realism to tell the truth about these deficits. This debt will kill our economy unless we cut it down.

The question is, who will pay and how much? I take my stand today. I don't want the average American and low-income Americans to pay more so that millionaires and big corporations pay less or nothing at all.[6]

In mid-September, Mondale held a question-and-answer session in Tupelo, Mississippi. He attacked President Reagan for failing to offer a deficit-reduction plan and said that during the 1980 campaign he had predicted that Reagan, if elected, would seek to cut Medicaid and Social Security. "Right after the election, what did he do? He . . . took a hatchet out and went after Social Security and Medicaid. There he goes again." The Democratic nominee warned that, if Reagan is re-elected, he will advocate sharp cuts in Medicare. "Mr. Reagan's plan on Medicare," Mondale said, "is nothing short of official cruelty. My plan is simple decency."[7]

During the appearance Mondale received several hostile questions dealing with religion and abortion. The Memphis *Commercial Appeal* wrote:

Speaking to an overflow crowd of 2,300 sweltering in the Tupelo High School gymnasium, Mondale disputed one questioner's description of the Democratic platform as "anti-religious" and said he did not like to see religion being raised in the presidential race.

"I have my faith and it's my whole being," said Mondale, the son of a Methodist minister. "Our faith is between ourselves, our consciences and our God."

"We don't have to clear our faith by passing muster with some politician who happens to be running against us."[8]

Later, in response to another question, Mondale argued that it would be wrong for government to interfere in the "very difficult personal decision" of abortion.[9]

Mondale visited Tupelo at the invitation of the city's mayor, Jimmie Caldwell, one of the Minnesotan's strongest Southern supporters. Caldwell attracted national attention at a meeting of mayors in St. Paul when he defended the Democratic ticket's appeal in the South. "Walter Mondale's and Geraldine Ferraro's cares, concerns, philosophies and family

Table 16-2. Vote for President in 1984 in Each Southern State

	Reagan	Mondale	Percentage Black 1980
Deep South			
Mississippi	61.9%	37.4%	35.2%
South Carolina	63.6	35.6	30.4
Louisiana	60.8	38.6	29.4
Georgia	60.2	39.8	26.8
Alabama	60.5	38.3	25.6
Rim South			
North Carolina	61.9	37.9	22.4
Virginia	62.3	37.1	18.9
Arkansas	60.5	38.3	16.3
Tennessee	57.8	41.6	15.8
Florida	65.3	34.7	13.8
Texas	63.6	36.1	12.0

values are just as Southern as catfish, corn bread and cotton," Mayor Caldwell asserted at a news conference, and the colorful sentence was televised throughout the country.[10] But the November returns did not back up his comment.

Table 16-2 displays the Reagan–Mondale vote in each of the Southern states. The focus in the following analysis is on the behavior of white voters since black Americans continued in 1984 to give the Democratic presidential nominee roughly 90 percent of their votes as they have since 1964. Among Southern whites, Mondale's support was weaker than it was among whites in the North. The precise regional percentages are difficult to attain because the survey information is not available in the exact division one might want. A fair estimate, however, is that the overall regional difference was about eight to ten percentage points, putting Mondale's support among Southern whites at a regional average of 28 percent.[11]

Among the Southern states, however, the percentage of whites for Mondale varied significantly. A glance at the Table 16-2 state-by-state percentages for Mondale compared with the percentage of blacks in each state, which is displayed in the table's right-hand column, indicates the scope of the variations, when one considers the Democratic solidarity of black voters. Take Mississippi and Florida, for example. Leaving aside the turnout question, since Mississippi was 35.2 percent black in 1980 and since Mondale received only 37.4 percent in Mississippi, the percentage of whites in the Magnolia State for Mondale must have been considerably lower than it was in Florida, where Mondale received

Table 16-3. Exit Poll Estimates of Vote by Race
in the 1984 Presidential Election

| | Whites | | Blacks | |
	Reagan	Mondale	Reagan	Mondale
Mississippi	85	14	9	89
Alabama	82	17	6	93
Texas	77	22	12	86
North Carolina	76	24	12	85
Virginia	74	25	10	90
Florida	71	29	13	84
Tennessee	69	31	5	95
South (includes Kentucky and Oklahoma)	72	28	9	89
Nation	64	35	7	89

SOURCE: Various Election Day exit polls as reported by the Joint Center for Political Studies and compiled by Harold W. Stanley in Table 13-2 of his "The 1984 Presidential Election in the South: Race and Realignment" in Robert P. Steed, Laurence W. Moreland, and Tod. A. Baker, eds., *The 1984 Presidential Election in the South: Patterns of Southern Party Politics* (New York: Praeger, 1986), p. 315.

34.7 percent in a state with a black population of only 13.8 percent. The above line of reasoning is confirmed by the findings of several television network exit polls, shown in Table 16-3.

Regardless of what the exact numbers were, the important question remains: Why was Mondale unable to assemble very much of the white wing of the South's often potent black-white Democratic coalition? Further, why was he more successful in gaining white votes in some Southern states than in others? Or to phrase the inquiry another way: Why was Reagan so popular among Southern whites (and Northern whites, for that matter), and why was he more popular among whites in the Deep South than in the Rim South?

When Southern white voters[12] (Northerners are included here for comparison but deserve a separate inquiry themselves) are examined using the variables of partisan identification, age, and income, the resulting cross-tabulations reproduce tendencies visible in past presidential elections that are now well-known patterns: lower-income voters more favorable to the Democratic nominee, although by substantially reduced margins from those of 1976 and 1980; the over-60 generation more partial to the Democrats; and the self-identified Democrats less faithful to their party's national nominee than the Republican identifiers. There was also a notable gender gap in 1984, with males more partial to

Reagan than females. See Table 16-4. Yet the divisions among Southern whites on these variables are not strong enough to deflect attention from the overriding question raised above concerning Southern white voter behavior.

One explanation put forward to account for Reagan's strength among whites centered on racial prejudice. Bill Moyers, the CBS commentator, expressed this point of view forcefully on election night. The following is Moyers's view:

> You know, the overwhelming reason, I think, is race. It's not white drift so much as it is white flight. . . . when they say in the South that the national Democratic party is too liberal what they really mean is that Jesse Jackson is too powerful in the Democratic Party. [Moyers next mentioned several racially charged positions taken by the Reagan administration.] They've retreated from affirmative action. They have supported tax exemptions for schools that practice racial [discrimination]. They're opposed to busing. The President went down to Charlotte and made a speech . . . saying busing had failed when in fact busing had succeeded in Charlotte. The newspaper the next day had to call his hand on that but by then the message had gone out on local television that the President was against busing. George Bush was in Mobile, Alabama . . . and made to an all-white group a speech saying the party of Mondale and Ferraro and Tip O'Neill is not the Democratic Party that the people of Alabama remember. Well, the party that the people of Alabama remember is the party of the old George Wallace and Bull Connor and the days when the white segregationists were in control of the South. [1]

Moyers's analytical outburst was also influenced by learning of the near unanimous support for Mondale among blacks. But the black support for the Democrats should have been no surprise since it has been present in every presidential election since 1964 and is rooted in the manner in which the parties lined up on the great issues that dissolved the Southern one-party system. Furthermore, the overwhelming white support for a Republican presidential nominee was present in the Deep South in 1964 and throughout the region in 1972 (and in 1968, if you combine the votes of Richard Nixon and George Wallace), and, even the Democrat Jimmy Carter, a Deep South native, did not win a majority of Southern whites in 1976, much less in 1980.

For anyone keeping the 1984 election in historical perspective, it would be unwise not to look at the lingering race issue as a partial explanation of these voting results. But race in the 1980s in the South, and in the nation as well, was a far more subtle element than it was in

Table 16-4. The 1984 Presidential Vote by Party Identification,
Income, Age, and Sex

	Democrats	Southern Whites Republicans	Independents
Reagan	31%	97%	83%
Mondale	69	3	17
	100%	100%	100%
N	124	87	108

	Democrats	Northern Whites Republicans	Independents
Reagan	22%	96%	65%
Mondale	78	4	35
	100%	100%	100%
N	289	334	274

	Under $15,000	Southern Whites $15,000 to $35,000	Over $35,000
Reagan	56%	67%	77%
Mondale	44	33	23
	100%	100%	100%
N	91	115	83

	Under $15,000	Northern Whites $15,000 to $35,000	Over $35,000
Reagan	53%	62%	69%
Mondale	48	38	31
	101%	100%	100%
N	200	365	256

	18–39	Southern Whites 40–59	Over 60
Reagan	69%	69%	56%
Mondale	31	31	44
	100%	100%	100%
N	150	97	75

	Northern Whites		
	18–39	40–59	Over 60
Reagan	62%	62%	64%
Mondale	38	38	36
	100%	100%	100%
N	397	271	220

	Southern Whites	
	Males	Females
Reagan	71%	62%
Mondale	29	38
	100%	100%
N	147	175

	Northern Whites	
	Males	Females
Reagan	65%	61%
Mondale	35	39
	100%	100%
N	394	504

SOURCE: National Election Study, 1984. Center for Political Studies, University of Michigan

the pre-1964 period, when there was substantial support in the North for dismantling legal segregation in the South. That task having been accomplished in the 1960s, there were very few people who wanted the country to go back to the era of segregation. But in the aftermath of these major nationally imposed racial changes, the race issue did not disappear, as was demonstrated in Chapter 3. Rather, it became enmeshed in the emerging two-party structure of the region.*

During Reagan's first term, the President's positions on race-sensitive issues did not go unnoticed, as previewed by Moyers. One could put forward logical, nonracial arguments in defense of Reagan's policies on affirmative action, tax exemption for schools that discriminate, voting rights issues, and the like. A good review of all these civil rights-related questions can be found in the debate over the confirmation of William

*The reader is urged at this point to review the interpretation made on pages 24–27 in Chapter 3 concerning the manner in which racial and nonracial streams of protest merged in the politics of the post-civil rights era. Special attention should be paid to the candid remarks of a "new Southern strategist" in the Reagan White House, which are quoted in the note at the bottom of page 26 and which powerfully convey the nature of racial politics in the 1980s.

Bradford Reynolds as associate attorney general.[14] Reynolds, whom Reagan defended as "a tireless fighter against discrimination,"[15] was the administration's point man on these issues as the assistant attorney general in charge of the civil rights division; the Senate did not confirm him in the new position.

After surveying the Reagan record, one would be naive not to recognize that the President's policies sent coded signals to those whites who do not like blacks. Reagan's stance on a North Carolina voting-rights case, for example, so offended Republicans in Congress that they filed a brief in the case opposing the administration. Senator Robert Dole of Kansas, then the majority leader, remarked as follows on the display of Republican disunity in this case: "I think too often we're sort of on the periphery. We're never really in there when black Americans need our help."[16]

Looking alone at the variation in 1984 voting among the Southern states, it is not hard to see that the message—subtle or not-so-subtle—was picked up in at least some quarters. As noted above, Mississippi, the Southern state most preoccupied with race, produced the lowest white support for Mondale. In the Rim South the white figure was still low, but it was at least double the Mississippi result. South Carolina, the state with the second highest percentage of blacks and Mississippi's partner from the Dixiecrat revolt of 1948, probably was a close second, with Alabama not far behind.[17] When particular Southern states where race remains an ever-present major issue are acting similarly, these state-by-state variations are not the result of chance.

However, to make the point that race was a factor in the Southern white support for Reagan (or, for that matter, among traditionally Democratic white blue-collar workers in the Northern big cities) is not the same thing as saying it was *the* factor. How much of a factor it was in every locality and to every voter cannot be determined given both the subtlety and complexity of race in American society as well as the crude nature of the tools at the analyst's disposal.[18] Nor is it sufficient to say that Southern whites are conservative and thus voted for the more conservative of the two candidates. This popular explanation is entirely, and obviously, too simplistic. It is so commonly used, however, that a brief examination of Southern and Northern white voter attitudes may further illuminate both some of the reasons for the 1984 decision as well as the political sophistication of the electorate.

What is often missing in the discussion of Southern conservatism (or liberalism, progressivism, populism, or whatever term is applied to left-of-center positions) is the recognition that the use of such shorthand labels masks several distinct dimensions into which such concepts logically divide. Three such dimensions are 1) economic-class and role-of-government questions; 2) foreign policy and defense questions; and 3) a cluster of social questions that include public morality issues, race relations, and women's rights.[19] Table 16-5 examines the responses of Southern and Northern white voters in 1984 on a variety of issue questions grouped under these three dimensions.

Overall, the various panels of Table 16-5 confirm once more V. O. Key's observations in *The Responsible Electorate*[20] concerning voter rationality. "[V]oters are not fools," Key reminds us, because against all odds—or so it sometimes seems—they show a remarkable inclination to line up their votes with their policy preferences.[21] As Professor Key phrased it:

> From our analyses the voter emerges as a person who appraises the actions of government, who has policy preferences, and who relates his vote to those appraisals and preferences. One may have misgivings about the data and one can certainly concede that the data also indicate that some voters are governed by blind party loyalty and that some others respond automatically to the winds of the environment of the moment. Yet the obtrusive feature of the data is the large number of persons whose vote is instrumental to their policy preferences.[22]

Given the positions of President Reagan and Walter Mondale on the issues of the day, the voters—South and North—demonstrated a pronounced tendency to cast their presidential ballots for the candidate who came closer to sharing their issue preferences. For example, those who favored cuts in government services were much more likely to vote for Reagan, whose reputation as one who preferred reducing the role of government certainly stood higher than Mondale's. Those who favored a role for the federal government in providing jobs and a good standard of living were much more likely to back Mondale, whose fondness for positive governmental action in these areas was undisputed and far outstripped the President's. Perusal of the other issues in the table generally produces similar findings. While it is comforting to affirm again that voters are not fools, the panels of Table 16-5 reveal more than merely this.

The percentages at the very bottom of each cross-tabulation in Table 16-5 allow for comparison of voter opinions in the South and the North on all these issues. When the responses of Southern whites are compared with those of Northern whites, there were noticeable sectional differences among the issues grouped under two of the three conservatism-liberalism dimensions: foreign-defense policy issues and social issues. On the economic-class and role-of-government dimension, however, the South-North differences were quite small indeed. Thirty-three

Table 16-5. Attitudes on Various Public Policy Issues
and the Vote for President in 1984

1. Economic Class and Role-of Government Questions
Cut Services to Save Money

	Southern Whites			Northern Whites		
	Cut	Neutral	More Services	Cut	Neutral	More Services
Reagan	90%	59%	47%	85%	60%	38%
Mondale	10	41	53	15	40	62
	100%	100%	100%	100%	100%	100%
N	113	91	77	297	262	249
	(40%)	(32%)	(27%)	(37%)	(32%)	(31%)

Question: Some people think the government should provide fewer services, even in areas such as health and education, in order to reduce spending. Suppose these people are at one end of the scale at point number 1. Other people feel it is important for government to provide many more services even if it means an increase in spending. Suppose these people are at the other end, at point 7. And, of course, some other people have opinions somewhere in between. . . . Where would you place yourself on this scale . . . ? [Points 2 and 3 were combined with point 1 for ease in handling; points 5 and 6 went with point 7. Point 4, the middle slot, was labled neutral. All seven-point scales in the table were handled in this manner.]

Health Insurance

	Southern Whites			Northern Whites		
	Gov't	Neutral	Private	Gov't	Neutral	Private
Reagan	63%	66%	78%	49%	67%	76%
Mondale	37	35	22	51	33	24
	100%	101%	100%	100%	100%	100%
N	46	29	63	136	78	169
	(33%)	(21%)	(46%)	(36%)	(20%)	(44%)

Question: There is much concern about the rapid rise in medical and hospital costs. Some people feel there should be a government insurance plan which would cover all medical and hospital expenses for everyone. Others feel that all medical expenses should be paid by individuals, and through private insurance plans like Blue Cross or other company-paid plans. Where would you place yourself [on a seven-point scale]?

Role of Government on Jobs and Standard of Living

	Southern Whites			Northern Whites		
	Gov't Do It	Neutral	Self Help	Gov't Do It	Neutral	Self Help
Reagan	40%	64%	83%	42%	53%	76%
Mondale	60	36	17	58	47	24
	100%	100%	100%	100%	100%	100%
N	62	66	156	199	203	502
	(22%)	(23%)	(55%)	(25%)	(25%)	(50%)

Question: Some people feel the government in Washington should see to it that every person has a job and a good standard of living. Others think the government should just let each person get ahead on his own. Where would you place yourself [on a seven-point scale]?

2. Foreign Policy and Defense Issues
Level of Defense Spending

| | Southern Whites | | | Northern Whites | | |
	Decrease	Neutral	Increase	Decrease	Neutral	Increase
Reagan	40%	70%	79%	37%	70%	83%
Mondale	60	30	21	63	30	17
	100%	100%	100%	100%	100%	100%
N	63	92	135	280	282	272
	(22%)	(32%)	(47%)	(34%)	(34%)	(33%)

Question: Some people believe that we should spend much less money for defense. Others feel that defense spending should be greatly increased. Where would you place yourself [on a seven-point scale]?

Involvement in Central America

| | Southern Whites | | | Northern Whites | | |
	More	Neutral	Less	More	Neutral	Less
Reagan	84%	72%	52%	77%	75%	47%
Mondale	16	28	48	23	25	54
	100%	100%	100%	100%	100%	101%
N	85	53	100	175	176	412
	(36%)	(22%)	(42%)	(23%)	(23%)	(54%)

Question: Some people think that the United States should become much more involved in the internal affairs of Central American countries. Others believe that the U.S. should become less involved in this area. Where would you place yourself [on a seven-point scale]?

Proper Approach to the Russians

| | Southern Whites | | | Northern Whites | | |
	Cooperate More	Neutral	Get Tougher	Cooperate More	Neutral	Get Tougher
Reagan	47%	68%	80%	39%	72%	77%
Mondale	53	32	20	61	28	23
	100%	100%	100%	100%	100%	100%
N	83	63	133	311	185	331
	(30%)	(23%)	(48%)	(38%)	(22%)	(40%)

Question: Some people feel it is important for us to try to cooperate more with Russia, while others believe we should be much tougher in our dealings with Russia. Where would you place yourself [on a seven-point scale]?

Table 16-5. (Continued)

3. Cluster of Social Questions
A. Race Relations Questions
Pace of Civil Rights Effort

	Southern Whites			Northern Whites		
	Too Fast	About Right	Too Slowly	Too Fast	About Right	Too Slowly
Reagan	67%	70%	54%	81%	56%	36%
Mondale	33	30	46	19	44	64
	100%	100%	100%	100%	100%	100%
N	64	74	13	141	257	36
	(42%)	(49%)	(7%)	(33%)	(59%)	(8%)

Question: Some say that the civil rights people have been trying to push too fast. Others feel they haven't pushed fast enough . . . . Do you think that civil rights leaders are trying to push too fast, are going too slowly, or are they moving at about the right speed?

Government Help for Minorities

	Southern Whites			Northern Whites		
	Gov't Should Help	Neutral	Should Help Selves	Gov't Should Help	Neutral	Should Help Selves
Reagan	52%	64%	78%	43%	63%	75%
Mondale	48	37	22	57	37	25
	100%	101%	100%	100%	100%	100%
N	67	85	134	239	286	293
	(23%)	(30%)	(47%)	(29%)	(35%)	(36%)

Question: Some people feel that the government in Washington should make every effort to improve the social and economic position of blacks and other minority groups. Others feel that the government should not make any special effort to help minorities because they should help themselves. . . . Where would you place yourself [on a seven-point scale]?

B. Public Morality Questions
Prayer in Schools

	Southern Whites		Northern Whites	
	Allow Prayer	Keep Prayer Out	Allow Prayer	Keep Prayer Out
Reagan	67%	50%	74%	46%
Mondale	33	50	26	54
	100%	100%	100%	100%
N	202	44	422	247
	(82%)	(18%)	(63%)	(37%)

Question: Which do you think—schools should be allowed to start each day with a prayer or religion does not belong in the schools?

Abortion

	Southern Whites				Northern Whites			
	Never	Only Rape, etc.	Clear Need	Always	Never	Only Rape, etc.	Clear Need	Always
Reagan	67%	64%	66%	68%	75%	71%	66%	51%
Mondale	33	36	34	32	25	29	34	49
	100%	100%	100%	100%	100%	100%	100%	100%
N	43	104	65	101	85	237	200	355
	(14%)	(33%)	(21%)	(32%)	(10%)	(27%)	(23%)	(41%)

Question: There has been some discussion about abortion during recent years. Which one of the options on this page best agrees with your view?

1. By law, abortion should never be permitted.
2. The law should permit abortion *only* in case of rape, incest or when the woman's life is in danger.
3. The law should permit abortion for reasons *other than* rape, incest or danger to the woman's life, but only after the need for the abortion has been clearly established.
4. By law, a woman should always be able to obtain an abortion as a matter of personal choice.

C. Women's Rights Questions
Place of Women in Society

	Southern Whites			Northern Whites		
	Equal Role	Neutral	Place in Home	Equal Role	Neutral	Place in Home
Reagan	64%	66%	70%	56%	75%	77%
Mondale	36	34	30	44	25	23
	100%	100%	100%	100%	100%	100%
N	157	67	63	548	171	174
	(55%)	(23%)	(22%)	(65%)	(20%)	(15%)

Question: Recently there has been a lot of talk about women's rights. Some people feel that women should have an equal role with men in running business, industry, and government . . . . Others feel that women's place is in the home . . . . Where would you place yourself [on a seven-point scale]?

Government Help for Women

	Southern Whites			Northern Whites		
	Gov't Should Help	Neutral	Should Help Selves	Gov't Should Help	Neutral	Should Help Selves
Reagan	53%	69%	78%	41%	67%	78%
Mondale	47	31	22	59	33	22
	100%	100%	100%	100%	100%	100%
N	88	88	104	279	262	260
	(31%)	(31%)	(37%)	(35%)	(33%)	(32%)

Question: Some people feel that the government in Washington should make every effort to improve the social and economic position of women. Others feel that the government should not make any special effort to help women because they should help themselves. Where would you place yourself [on a seven-point scale]?

SOURCE: National Election Study, 1984. Center for Political Studies, University of Michigan.

percent of the Southerners and 36 percent of the Northerners preferred some sort of governmental medical insurance system as opposed to leaving the matter to the private sector. On the question of cutting services in fields such as health and education to reduce government spending, there was again virtually no difference between the regions. And the third question used to tap this dimension—involving the role of government in providing jobs and a good standard of living—revealed similar agreement across regions. Thus, on this one important dimension there emerges a picture of a white South sharply divided and far from monolithically conservative, and scarcely more conservative than the white North.

On the other two dimensions, the South-North differences were more sizable. In the national security arena, white Southerners were far more willing to favor increased defense spending, more United States involvement in Central America, and a tougher stance toward the Russians. On the six questions that fall under the social-issue cluster, the differences between the North and South were closer to those in the national security area, but there were exceptions. Forty-two percent of the white Southerners found civil rights leaders pushing too fast compared with 33 percent of the white Northerners; a similar difference was found on the question concerning government help for minorities. On whether women should play an equal role with men in society, there was a ten-percentage-point gap, with weaker support for an equal role found in the South. Interestingly, on abortion the responses were somewhat the same in the two parts of the country except that the pro-choice position had support from 41 percent of the white Northerners compared with 32 percent of the white Southerners. Whether prayer should be allowed in the public schools produced the sharpest North-South divergence. Eighty-two percent in the South favored allowing prayer as compared with 63 percent in the North.

It is not my purpose here to explain precisely the entire 1984 national decision, a major topic in itself best left to those concentrating on national electoral change. Rather, the above excursion into survey research was meant to demonstrate—in addition to arguing for the value of more dimensional reasoning in electoral analysis—the weakness in viewing Southern whites as merely a bastion of conservatism and using such a conclusion to explain the South's vote in 1984. The Southern reality as reflected in responses to these survey questions is far more complex.[23] In fact, as Table 16-5 illustrates, the attitudinal basis exists in the region for a two-party competition not unlike that found in the rest of the nation, although the South's historical legacy will continue for a time to give it certain singular characteristics.

The 1984 Elections in the States

As it became readily apparent in the last weeks of the fall campaign that Reagan would sweep the South, attention increasingly shifted to the numerous two-party struggles throughout the region. And, although the presidential results gave Southern Republicans much to cheer about, they came away from these other contests with mixed results.

While making the strongest GOP presidential showing since 1972, the party in the South fought the Democrats to a standstill over the major statewide offices—U.S. senator and governor. The governorship of North Carolina, previously held by a Democrat, went to a Republican, and a Democrat took an open Republican Senate seat in Tennessee, leaving the GOP with twelve of these thirty-three top positions, or 36.4 percent. See Figures 3-1 and 3-2. (Both figures show a slight decline in 1984 for the Republicans because the Democratic recapture of the Louisiana governorship in 1983, described in Chapter 8, is reflected in the 1984 totals.)

The best news for the Republicans came in the battle for the South's 116 U.S. House seats, where the GOP made major breakthroughs in North Carolina and Texas, picking up three and four seats, respectively. The GOP gain of a Georgia seat in 1984 was offset by the loss of one in Arkansas. Added to this seven-seat gain were two seats earned initially through party switches—one in Florida in 1984 and one in Texas in 1983. In the Florida case the incumbent won in 1984 under the GOP label; the Texas seat was retained by another Republican in 1984. The net result was to increase the GOP total to 37.1 percent (43 seats) compared with 29.3 percent (34 seats) in 1982, a notable gain. Republican state legislative seats, although continuing to lag behind, showed the sharpest increase since the early 1970s, rising to 21.0 percent in 1984 compared with 16.7 percent two years earlier; this trend is also displayed in Figure 3-1.

These regional aggregates mask a substantial amount of variation from state to state. In order to understand the nuances present in the politics of the eleven Southern states, one must look individually at what happened in each. Thus, it is to this diverse and complex picture that attention now turns. A comparative analysis follows this venture into the political personalities and issues that aggitated the Southern states below the presidential level in 1984.

North Carolina

North Carolina was the South's premier partisan battleground of 1984. Not only did it contain the region's most highly publicized and expensive Senate race—the titanic $26 million struggle between Jesse Helms and Jim Hunt—and a spirited race for governor, but six of its eleven U.S. House districts had contests that were decided by fewer than two percentage points. And, when it was over, the Republican party laid claim to an impressive cumulative victory, even though its winning margins were narrow.

If everything that was written about the Hunt-Helms election could be gathered in one place, the material would probably fill a small library. One book on the race has already appeared,[24] and others may follow. Although the saturation point in coverage was no doubt reached, the substance of the struggle certainly deserved the extensive treatment it received.

Governor Hunt epitomized the moderate white Democratic leaders who arose in the 1970s to lead the post-civil rights era biracial Democratic coalition. He was highly successful in maintaining good relations with blacks, white traditional Democrats, and the state's business establishment. When faced with situations that had the potential to disrupt the coalition, Hunt skillfully mediated them, often giving just enough to each group to preserve his diverse alliance. In the heated partisan atmosphere of 1984, Hunt needed all the skill he possessed to continue successfully his tightrope performance.

Helms, too, represented an important stream in the growth of the Republican party in the South. His political roots were tied to segregationist Democratic politics, and his first Senate victory, in 1972, contained strong anti-black overtones. He was also a forceful advocate of economic conservatism and a vociferous champion of the conservative side of various social issues of the day.

All the elements in the political backgrounds of these men were fully played out in 1984. A *Washington Post* reporter concluded that "race has been a strong undercurrent in the Helms campaign" and that "Helms is believed to have stirred a backlash among conservative white voters. . . . "[25] The article said that the Helms organization "put out a campaign newspaper picturing Hunt with Jesse L. Jackson and telling of a mounting registration by blacks and a 'Hunt-Jackson plan' to register more. . . . "[26] Earlier in the year Helms led a losing battle in the Senate against a national holiday honoring Martin Luther King, Jr.

Helms repeatedly called Hunt a "Mondale liberal," saying: "I'm a Reagan conservative and proud of it, and Mr. Hunt is a Mondale liberal and ashamed of it."[27] Hunt countered in two ways. First, he attacked Helms as a leader of a "radical right" that is out-of-step with mainstream opinion in the Tar Heel State. Second, Hunt sought to identify with Southern Democratic moderates and conservatives, likening himself to

Chuck Robb of Virginia, Dick Riley of South Carolina, and Sam Nunn of Georgia. He said they believe in "a balanced budget, economic growth for jobs, and racial justice and people working together. Those are the things I subscribe to, regardless of who's president."[28] In addition to emphasizing his links to President Reagan, his seniority in the Senate, and his work for the state's agricultural interests, Helms countered the right-wing extremist charge by attacking Hunt's "wrong-wing extremists"[29] and argued for a closer connection between religion and government to counter the drift toward a "secular humanist society."[30]

Helms won with 51.7 percent to Hunt's 47.8 percent. The victor asserted that his election "sent a signal throughout the world that North Carolina is a God-fearing, conservative state . . . a state where people believe a bloated, all-powerful central government is a threat to the liberties of the American people. . . . "[31] Hunt attributed his loss to the President's big win in North Carolina. "The truth is," Hunt said, "the avalanche of Ronald Reagan overswept us in the election."[32] The Helms-Hunt election is considered further in the comparative overview at the end of the chapter.

James G. (Jim) Martin, a veteran Republican congressman from Charlotte, won the governorship for the GOP with 54.3 percent to the Democrat Rufus Edmisten's 45.4 percent. Martin, who was associated with the more moderate elements of the state's Republican party, conducted a very different campaign from Helms's, one that centered on state issues—especially economic growth and tax reduction—and lacked the ideological stridency of the Helms appeal. Edmisten, the state's attorney general, stood on his record of defending consumer interests and fighting utility rate increases. One drawback his candidacy carried resulted from his hard-fought and divisive runoff primary victory over Eddie Knox, a former Democratic mayor of Charlotte. After his narrow loss, Knox joined the Reagan campaign and later received a position in the Martin administration; he eventually switched his voter registration to the Republican party.

Three incumbent Democratic congressmen in North Carolina lost their seats in 1984, and two others—Stephen L. Neal and W. G. (Bill) Hefner—came very close to the same fate. The Democrat Ike Andrews, the veteran incumbent from Raleigh who had such a tough time in 1982, lost a rematch with the Republican William W. (Bill) Cobey, a former University of North Carolina athletic director, 50.6 percent to 49.4 percent. Former Congressman William M. (Bill) Hendon, a Republican who lost the state's western-most district in 1982 after one term in office, won it back from the Democrat James McClure Clarke, 51.0 percent to 49.0 percent. And the first-term Democrat Robin Britt was defeated by Howard Coble, a Republican state representative, in the district that includes Greensboro; the vote there was 50.6 percent to 49.3 percent. In the Charlotte district the Republican J. Alex McMillan 3d defeated the Democrat D. G. Martin by 319 votes out of nearly 220,000 cast to hold the seat vacated by Governor Martin. Along with the usual candidate and district factors, these contests mirrored themes in other states and in the Hunt-Helms battle. For example, Cobey repeatedly called the choice: "Reagan-Cobey as opposed to Mondale-Andrews."[33] After the November voting, the GOP share of the state's eleven-member U.S. House delegation increased to five.

Alabama

Senator Howell Heflin, the folksy, first-term Democratic incumbent, had little trouble withstanding a GOP effort to brand him a "Mondale liberal." He was re-elected with 62.8 percent of the vote to 36.3 percent for his Republican challenger, Albert Lee Smith, a former one-term congressman from Birmingham. At every turn Smith stressed his support for President Reagan and attempted to tie Heflin to Mondale and the Democratic standardbearer's plan to increase taxes. "If they [Alabamians] vote for Ronald Reagan and vote for Howell Heflin, they're cancelling their votes,"[34] the Republican told one campaign audience. He attacked Heflin, in the words of a *Birmingham News* reporter, "for what he called an inconsistent stand on school busing, opposition to the CIA-backed mining of Nicaraguan harbors, and failure to take the lead on prayer in classrooms."[35]

For his part, Heflin endorsed the national ticket and even introduced Mondale at a rally near Huntsville early in the election year. But the incumbent, who is often pictured as an affable grandfather figure, was quick to point out: "That doesn't mean I'm a party puppet or a party robot."[36] Heflin said his voting record shows that he supported Reagan more than he did President Carter, 60 percent of the time for the Republican President compared with 55 percent when the Georgia Democrat was in the White House. The senator also said he was against portions of the Democratic platform, including the part on homosexual rights; he made it clear that he did not favor Mondale's tax plan.[37]

As a newspaper profile of "down-home Heflin" put it: "Armed with a jowly countenance and a reputation as one of the best storytellers in Washington, Heflin is telling voters that he stands for 'traditional Alabama values.' Stressing his support for a balanced federal budget, better science education, and prayer in schools, Heflin so far has been able to brush aside charges . . . that he has joined the liberal 'Washington crowd.' "[38] Perhaps sensing the difficulty of ousting such a well-liked and respected incumbent who had positioned himself so carefully on the issues, national and state Republican officials were less than enthusiastic Smith backers during the fall campaign and gave more attention to two hotly contested House races.[39]

H. L. (Sonny) Callahan, a former Democratic state senator who switched to the GOP to run for Congress, narrowly won the Mobile-dominated district that had been held by the Republican Jack Edwards since the Goldwater sweep of 1964; Edwards decided to retire in 1984 after ten terms. Callahan received 51.0 percent to the Democrat Frank McRight's 49.0 percent. According to *The Political Report*, McRight, a little-known attorney who represented Mobile-based corporations in labor cases, ran "an effective and expensive media campaign . . . that promoted him as the candidate for people who were 'tired of politicians putting their interests ahead of ours.' "[40] In the Birmingham-centered district, the first-term Democrat Ben Erdreich easily turned back a spirited challenge from Jabo Waggoner, another Democrat-turned-Republican state legislator, 59.6 percent to 39.8 percent. Waggoner charged that a vote for Erdreich was a vote for Speaker Thomas P. (Tip) O'Neill and for Mondale.[41] Erdreich responded by distancing himself from Mondale on particular issues, although he gave the national ticket nominal support. On O'Neill, the Democrat told a Birmingham public radio audience: "He doesn't represent my views . . . . The good news I can convey is, the speaker is retiring. The bad news is, it won't happen for two more years."[42]

Mississippi

Senator Thad Cochran, the Republican first elected in 1978 when blacks abandoned a white Democratic nominee to support a black independent, won re-election easily over the Democrat William Winter, 60.9 percent to 39.1 percent. After months of vacillation, Winter, the former Democratic governor, entered the race in February 1984 and conducted a vigorous campaign. He argued that Mississippi, one of the country's poorest states, had been unfairly hurt by the Republican administration's budget cuts. A Jackson *Clarion-Ledger* article described the appeal:

> Winter said Mississippi's efforts to better itself economically had been "stymied" by a "false economy" at the federal level, resulting in "disproportionate" cuts in federal aid.
>
> "I'm not content to see the people of Mississippi enjoy less than parity," Winter said, adding that the South needs a "more articulate spokesman."[43]

To Cochran's charge that he is a liberal, Winter responded late in the campaign: "If being a liberal means that one is concerned about seeing that everybody has an equal opportunity, then I confess being a liberal. They said that back in the 1960s when I said I thought the Constitution ought to apply to everybody in this country."[44]

Cochran emphasized his Washington experience and his Senate seniority, frequently pointing out that he chairs the Agriculture Appropriations subcommittee and is a member of the Defense Appropriations subcommittee. He said these posts enable him to "assure Mississippi gets its fair share."[45] The incumbent charged that "it's not Mississippians who are supporting" Winter, but rather liberal Democrats in Washington who "dreamed up this campaign."[46] "I don't think we want somebody in Washington just representing the interests of the national Democratic party."[47]

When in a joint appearance Winter criticized Cochran's support for the 1981 Reagan tax cut, saying, "You cannot cut taxes to the extent that they were cut and increase appropriations as much as they have been increased, for defense for example, and expect us to have a solvent country," Cochran responded, as reported in the *Clarion-Ledger*:

> "If William Winter had been in the Senate and voted on the other side of that issue, he would have been in a very small minority. And I would say exercising a judgment that wasn't widely shared anywhere in the country."
>
> Cochran said Winter wanted to continue the "economic mess" created by the Carter administration. . . .
>
> "I would say trying to provide workers and consumers in America with more of a share of what they were working to earn was eminently fair and correct. I know that adding one more person to the Democratic side of the aisle in the Senate is not going to help the spending problem there," Cochran said.[48]

As these excerpts from the rhetorical battle indicate, both men embraced the basic positions of their national candidates, although naturally both at various points sought to sidestep national positions or images they viewed as unhelpful to their campaigns.

In the end Mississippi voters apparently linked the presidential and senatorial contests closely, and the racial polarization that occurred in the presidential balloting spilled over to the Senate race. A precinct analysis of Jackson indicated that Winter did only about a percentage point better than Mondale's very poor showing among whites in the capital.[49] Also, Winter's strongest counties were those with the highest proportion of blacks, as was the case with Mondale.[50]

One of the most publicized House races in the nation was the rematch between the white Republican Webb Franklin and the black Democrat Robert Clark in the Second District, which Franklin again won narrowly—50.6 percent to 48.9 percent. While Franklin had the incumbency edge, Clark was the beneficiary of a January 1984 court-ordered redistricting that increased the district's black population to 58.3 percent and the black voting-age majority to 52.8 percent.[51]

The *Clarion-Ledger* recorded the following comments when the two men appeared together at an NAACP meeting in Raymond:

> "When Webb Franklin runs my picture and his and says 'I'm one of you,' I believe he's saying, 'I'm one of those who sold my [Clark's] great-grandmother' " in slavery, Clark said.
>
> Franklin prefaced his remarks . . . by saying that he was "sick and tired" of Clark "whining that I have not been responsive to black issues and interests."[52]

A full month before Election Day, the main concern in the Second District had become turnout.[53]

In Mississippi's Fourth District, David Armstrong, a 32-year-old GOP challenger, tied his campaign to President Reagan and charged that Congressman Wayne Dowdy was in league with the "free-spending liberals" in Washington. Vice President George Bush, visiting Natchez to boost Armstrong's candidacy, declared: "A vote for David Armstrong is a vote for President Reagan's programs. . . . Don't tie one hand behind the President's back. Give us David Armstrong."[54] Dowdy, a personable politician in his early forties, stressed his constituency service. A newspaper reporter wrote:

> Some observers remain baffled by Wayne Dowdy's aw-shucks political success, but not folks in this tiny southwest Mississippi community [of Progress].
>
> "He meets with his people," says J. D. Jones. "You can talk with him. A lot of people who get elected to Congress are above all that. But Wayne will come and talk, shoot a game of pool."[55]

As for the charge of being a liberal, Dowdy responded: "Some people in Washington would snicker if they heard someone with my voting record called a liberal. I'm a progressive Southerner."[56] When the returns were in, of the four Democrats (Mondale, Winter, Clark, and Dowdy) running in Mississippi in 1984, Dowdy was the only one who held together the state's black-white Democratic coalition, winning with 55.3 percent of the vote.

South Carolina

Senator Strom Thurmond, the Dixiecrat-turned-Republican, easily won his sixth full term at the age of eighty-one with 66.8 percent of the vote to 31.8 percent for his little-known Democratic opponent, Melvin Purvis, Jr., a Florence minister. Thurmond's virtual invincibility at the polls was signaled in 1983 when several prominent Democrats declined to make the race and several others endorsed Thurmond.[57] Purvis, whose fall campaign was nearly invisible, won the Democratic nomination by only a few hundred votes out of 290,000 cast over Cecil J. Williams, a black Orangeburg newspaper publisher who claimed he was robbed of the primary victory and launched an ineffective write-in campaign.[58]

In South Carolina's six U.S. House districts, evenly divided between the parties, five incumbents received spirited opposition. All five—the Republicans Thomas F. Hartnett, Floyd Spence, and Carroll Campbell, and the Democrats Butler Derrick and Robin Tallon—were reelected with vote percentages close to the 60 percent line.

Arkansas

Arkansas was treated to a partisan battle royal in 1984 as the Republicans launched an all-out effort to take the Senate seat from David Pryor, the Democratic incumbent. U.S. Representative Ed Bethune, the GOP nominee, did all he could to make the race a referendum on President Reagan's policies, asserting at every opportunity that Pryor frequently voted against the President. As an *Arkansas Gazette* reporter noted, Bethune argued that "there was a 'new wave' in politics founded on a coalition of Southern and Western conservatives who were optimistic about the future and that Pryor was part of the old liberal Democratic coalition that always spent too much and collected too much in taxes."[59]

Senator Pryor, a former congressman and governor who won the seat in 1978, countered with a year-long campaign, featuring extensive person-to-person tours throughout the state and emphasizing his attention to Arkansas interests. His slogan was "Arkansas Comes First." At Hot Springs, among other places, Pryor responded to Bethune's main line of attack: "The major charge [in the campaign] is that I have voted against this president too often. I've served under five presidents. My record has been independent of all those presidents I have served under. I do not represent presidents. I represent the people of Arkansas."[60]

Pryor's hard work paid off in a 57.3 percent victory over Bethune's 42.7 percent. Diane K. Blair, a University of Arkansas political scientist, contends that Reagan's coattails were

> anxiously anticipated and cleverly minimized . . . . Pryor had taken careful note of Senator Dale Bumpers's "embarrassing" loss (through

a lackadaisical low-budget campaign) of 41 percent of the vote in 1980 to an unimpressive Republican challenger. Pryor, therefore, raised and spent nearly $1.5 million, repeatedly praised the "ferociously independent" Arkansas voter, hired superb professional consultants, and campaigned tirelessly for a year as though he were an underdog. The coattails might well have been there in 1984, but coattails anticipated are far less damaging than coattails unforeseen.[61]

The Democrat Bill Clinton won a third two-year term as governor with 62.6 percent of the vote to 37.4 percent for the Republican Woody Freeman. Freeman, a Jonesboro contractor who had never run for public office, labeled Clinton a "professional politician" with an unimpressive record, asserting: "It's time to put the government back in the hands of the people once again and allow government to be run by the will of the people instead of the will of the backroom politicians."[62] With his surprise upset defeat for a second term in 1980 still fresh in his mind, Clinton campaigned with vigor, stressing his educational reform program and other accomplishments in office. For example, on a swing into the Republican stronghold in Ozark, in the words of a newspaper reporter, Clinton "was quick to point out that he had the business acumen to eliminate four state agencies, the most by any administration in the last forty years by his own account,"[63] and he promised to do more of the same if given another term.

Bethune's Little Rock-centered congressional seat was won by a controversial law-and-order Democrat, Sheriff Tommy Robinson of Pulaski County (Little Rock), in an interesting three-way race. Robinson received 47.1 percent to the Republican Judy Petty's 41.5 percent. The independent Jim Taylor won 11.4 percent running a shoestring campaign in which he argued in favor of quick American action to end the nuclear arms race, supported the Supreme Court's decisions allowing abortion and barring school prayer, and suggested that a tax increase might be needed to reduce the federal deficit.[64]

Although Taylor added a novel air to the campaign, the contest was between Robinson and Petty. Petty, who had run a strong losing race in 1974 against Congressman Wilbur Mills, stuck close to the main Republican themes of 1984. One reporter wrote: "Petty says she is proud that she will be part of the Republican team that will keep taxes down, build a strong defense, continue the economic recovery and reduce federal interference in local affairs."[65] Robinson assailed a federal judge's decision consolidating three public school districts in Pulaski County to further racial integration and promised to introduce legislation to limit the power of federal judges in such cases.[66] In the fall campaign (the court issue had first arisen in the primaries), Robinson made an appeal to traditional Democrats by opposing reduction in certain federal programs; the sheriff also spent considerable time campaigning in the district's rural counties, which proved critical to his victory.

Georgia

Senator Sam Nunn, the conservative Democrat who maintained good relations with Georgia's Republican establishment, had only token opposition in 1984, winning with 79.9 percent.

Wyche Fowler, the white Democrat who had represented the central Atlanta district since 1976, won renomination in 1984 with 63.6 percent of the vote over Hosea L. Williams, a black state legislator and veteran civil rights activist. Under court pressure, Fowler's district had been redrawn to increase its percentage of blacks to 65. Williams unsuccessfully argued to the voters that such a district should be represented by a black.[67]

The only 1984 partisan surprise in Georgia came in an Atlanta-area district represented for five terms by the Democrat Elliott H. Levitas. Pat Swindall, a 33-year-old Republican lawyer, unseated Levitas with 53.1 percent of the vote. Swindall mounted an aggressive advertising campaign aimed at portraying Levitas as too liberal for the district. One advertisement compared the incumbent's voting record to Geraldine Ferraro's, asserting that the two Democrats had voted together 73 percent of the time. Levitas, the ad concluded, is "the best congressman Queens, New York, ever had."[68] Post-election analyses emphasized the loss to Levitas of a portion of his black supporters, who were put in Fowler's district when the lines were redrawn.[69] Until Swindall's election, Newt Gingrich, of another suburban Atlanta district, was the only Republican in the Peach State's ten-member U.S. House delegation.

Louisiana

The pronounced weakness of the Republican party in the Pelican State persisted in 1984. Senator J. Bennett Johnston, a two-term Democrat, faced no serious opposition—Republican or Democratic—in the state's unique open primary, coasting to victory without a runoff. He received 85.6 percent of the vote.

All eight of Louisiana's members of the U.S. House—six Democrats and two Republicans—were also re-elected without runoffs. The only incumbent who faced a tough race was the Democrat Lindy Boggs of New Orleans, and her opposition came from another Democrat, Israel M. Augustine, Jr., a black former state judge. Under pressure from a federal court, the state legislature redrew Boggs's district, making it the state's only black majority district, with 55.8 percent of the registered voters black.[70] Boggs won with 60.1 percent to Augustine's 38.6 percent.[71]

Tennessee

In 1984 U.S. Representative Albert Gore, Jr., the fast-moving, articulate young congressman from Middle Tennessee, claimed the Senate seat vacated by Senator Howard Baker, Jr., the Republican majority leader. Gore won 60.7 percent against the Republican Victor Ashe's 33.8 percent. Ed McAteer, a religious fundamentalist, received 5.3 percent running as an independent.

Gore, whose father served three terms in the U.S. Senate, nimbly avoided Ashe's repeated attempts to link him to left-of-center Democratic politicians. Calling Gore "two-faced," Ashe asked rhetorically: "Just who is the real Albert Gore? Well, the real one is the one who votes in Washington and has earned the financial help and close friendship of Ted Kennedy, Jerry Brown, Tip O'Neill, Walter Mondale and a host of other political figures who are equally out of step with Tennessee."[72] To attacks like this, Gore would respond: "The old labels—liberal and conservative—have far less relevance to today's problems than the efforts to find solutions to those problems. There's no need to rely on an outdated ideology as a crutch."[73] The issues he stressed in his eight years in the House—hazardous waste, organ transplants, infant formula, genetics, shifts in the nature of employment in a high technology society—led the *Nashville Tennessean* to describe him as "in the first wave of a branch of politics variously labeled Yuppie, neo-liberal or technocratic. It is more geared to the pragmatic solution of problems than reliance on the old credos of Democratic liberalism."[74] Further, Gore had developed a reputation for careful attention to his constituents through frequent visits to all parts of his district, and he promised to expand these open meetings to all the state's counties.

Against this skillful approach, Ashe, an acerbic state legislator from Knoxville who was viewed as something of a GOP maverick, conducted a strong campaign tied closely to support for President Reagan. But his efforts failed to tarnish the solid image Gore projected. For example, in their second debate, Ashe repeatedly accused Gore of speaking in "Washington gobbledygook" and pressed the Democrat to explain why he supports Mondale for president. Gore countered effectively as follows: "I'm loyal to my party. I support the nominee of my party. This is a race for the U.S. Senate. It's a race to see who's going to represent Tennesseans. . . . and I'll tell you one thing—I've never been a rubber stamp or a coattailer, and I never will be."[75]

The ratio of six Democrats to three Republicans in the Tennessee

U.S. House delegation remained unchanged in 1984, as the Democrat Bart Gordon held Gore's seat. In the Chattanooga-dominated district, the Democrat Marilyn Lloyd received an unexpected close call when the Republican John Davis held her to 52.4 percent of the vote.

Virginia

Senator John W. Warner, a first-term Republican, swept to an easy re-election over the Democrat Edythe C. Harrison, a little-known former state legislator from Norfolk. Warner received 70.0 percent of the vote.

Harrison, who was drawn into politics by the influence of Henry Howell, the left-of-center Virginia Democratic champion, had weak financial support (less than half a million dollars) and only lukewarm backing from the state's Democratic establishment. On the other hand, Warner, who was personally popular, had few weaknesses to go with his $2.4 million war chest.[76] As Larry Sabato concluded: "The Senate race was as lopsided as an election probably can become in the era of two-party competition."[77]

Warner made an attempt to improve upon the weak support among blacks he had received six years earlier. A Warner assistant characterized the effort this way: "I know no reason why black Virginians would single out John Warner for a vengeance vote . . . . He has done nothing to polarize the black voters."[78] Campaigning in the Tidewater in late October, Warner termed Harrison's attempt to tie him to Jesse Helms[79] "tragically erroneous," adding: "To the extent that minorities support me, it is an indication that they are following closely the votes of their U.S. senator."[80] A precinct analysis put Warner's black support at about 21 percent, nearly triple his 1978 showing[81] and quite high for a Southern Republican.

Virginia's U.S. House delegation retained its partisan division of six Republicans to four Democrats. Nine incumbents were returned, although five of them had strong challengers who received respectable vote totals. In the Seventh District, a retiring Republican was replaced by another Republican, D. French Slaughter, Jr., who received 56.5 percent of the vote to the Democrat Lewis M. Costello's 40.2 percent; an independent won the rest.

Texas

Along with North Carolina, Texas was the other Southern state to experience a major GOP surge in 1984. U.S. Representative Phil Gramm, a conservative Democrat who joined the Republican party the previous year, defeated state Senator Lloyd Doggett, a Democrat who narrowly won his party's nomination in a bitter runoff against an opponent who attacked him as a liberal. Gramm received 58.5 percent of the vote to Doggett's 41.4 percent. In addition, the Texas Republicans gained four U.S. House seats and made a respectable showing in other lesser races.

The Gramm-Doggett contest degenerated into an acrid, no-holds-barred affair replete with more than the usual campaign exaggerations on both sides. For example, the New York Times reported on the "name-calling" in a late September televised debate:

> Mr. Gramm . . . referred to his opponent as a free-spending "millionaire lawyer" and accused him of accepting a campaign contribution raised at a strip show sponsored by a San Antonio homosexual group.[82]
>
> Mr. Doggett . . . in turn assailed Mr. Gramm for running what he termed a "buy-and-lie campaign."[83]

A difficulty Doggett carried into the general election involved the manner in which he won the Democratic nomination. He defeated U.S. Representative Kent Hance, a conservative West Texas Democrat, by several hundred votes out of nearly a million cast in the hard fought runoff. Hance, who joined the GOP in 1985, focused on Doggett's reputation as a liberal, contending that the label would help the Republicans win the general election. He also criticized Doggett for accepting $5,000 from Senator Edward M. Kennedy's political action committee. "I understand why Ted Kennedy would give money to Lloyd Doggett. They're birds of a feather; they should flock together."[84] For his part, Doggett

> stuck close to his habit of raking over the voting records of his opponents. He accused Hance of having voted to slash Social Security benefits and federal funding for education, and reminded voters that Hance had cosponsored President Reagan's tax cut bill in 1981. One Doggett television commercial depicted a servant, sporting white gloves, delivering a fancy volume entitled "Kent Hance Tax Cuts for the Rich, 1981" to a wealthy master. "Kent Hance isn't a congressman," said the voice-over, "he's a butler."[85]

In the fall Hance made no effort, perhaps understandably given the bitter nature of the runoff, to assist Doggett among the rural, small-town voters who were Hance's chief supporters.

In the meantime, Gramm made a vigorous effort to win over these same traditionally Democratic voters, assisted by his drawling,[86] unkempt demeanor. The *Dallas Morning News* noted that Gramm sought "to appeal to the farm and ranch folks as a 'redneck' rather than 'country club' Republican."[87] And like all Republicans running in 1984, Gramm linked his campaign to President Reagan's at every opportunity.[88]

Reagan's coattails also aided GOP challengers in defeating three Democratic House incumbents. In the Dallas area the Republican Dick Armey defeated first-term Representative Tom Vandergriff, 51.3 percent to 48.7 percent. Beau Boulter, a Republican attorney from Amarillo, retired a five-term incumbent, Jack Hightower, in the Pandhandle district by a vote of 53.0 percent to 47.0 percent. And in a central Gulf Coast district, Mac Sweeney, a 28-year-old Republican who had worked in the Reagan White House, conducted an energetic door-to-door campaign to defeat Representative William Patman, who was seeking a third term; Sweeney won 51.3 percent of the vote to Patman's 48.7 percent. The fourth GOP gain came in Hance's West Texas district where two former congressional assistants faced each other. The Republican Larry Combest defeated the Democrat Don R. Richards, 58.1 percent to 41.9 percent. A Republican, Joe L. Barton, held Gramm's congressional seat. Thus, when the Ninety-ninth Congress convened in January 1985, there were ten Republicans and seventeen Democrats in the House delegation from Texas, a 100 percent increase for the GOP over 1982.

Florida

Florida was the only Southern state without even a nominal statewide contest in 1984, a situation that was corrected in 1986 with an abundance of major two-party battles, as the next chapter reveals.

All nineteen of Florida's congressmen were re-elected in 1984, but because of a party switch the partisan balance shifted by one seat. U.S. Representative Andy Ireland, a conservative who had represented a central Florida district since 1976, left the Democratic party for the GOP in March 1984, arguing that the Democrats were too far to the left. Patricia Glass, a Manatee County commissioner with a strong record as an environmentalist, won a Democratic runoff to gain the nomination to oppose Ireland, but she received only 38.1 percent in the general election to Ireland's 61.9 percent.

Two South Florida Democratic congressmen, Dan Mica and Larry Smith, had strong Republican opponents, but both won with 55.4 percent and 56.4 percent, respectively. The other challenged incumbents were re-elected with at least close to 60 percent of the votes; eight were unopposed. After the election, Florida's U.S. House delegation consisted of twelve Democrats and seven Republicans.

Comparative Assessment of the State Results

These individual treatments of the candidates, their personal styles, and the issues present in their campaigns may be viewed, perhaps, as the correct approach to understanding the state results—that is, by reference to the untidy details of the individual struggles. In fact, the campaign profiles may be seen as too brief and superficial, and they are. Yet, despite the recognition of the value of more details, a few general observations are appropriate.

Obviously, all the Republican candidates in 1984 chose to link their efforts to President Reagan, hoping to benefit from his popularity. Equally understandably the Democratic candidates sought to distance themselves from their national nominee. For the Republicans, the winners were those whose voting patterns corresponded most closely to Reagan's.[89]

Why were certain Democrats—Heflin, Gore, Pryor, for example—able to withstand the Reagan landslide, and why were others—Hunt and Doggett—unable to do so? Beyond the personal characteristics of individual candidates, which is no small factor, the power of incumbency clearly jumps out as an important element in many contests. Nunn and Johnston, on the Democratic side, and Thurmond and Warner, on the Republican side, scared off potentially strong opponents and really faced only nominal opponents. Incumbency gave Cochran and Helms the edge and assisted Heflin and Pryor. Yet incumbency was not everything, and, of course, the contests in Texas and Tennessee were for open seats.

Heflin, Gore, and Pryor presented the voters with appealing images of independent, effective legislators who would place their state's interests before party, president, or anything else. On the issues their positions differed: Heflin more to the right, Pryor slightly to the left, and Gore often staking his ground on non-ideological "new" issues. The result in each case was to win substantial numbers of white voters to add to overwhelming black support. For example, in Alabama Heflin probably received around 50 percent of the white vote and 90 percent of the black vote.[90] Given Reagan's huge majority among whites, the ticket-splitting in Alabama in 1984 had to have been at phenomenal levels. A closer look at Alabama's split-ticket white voters—provided by the University of Alabama's Capstone Poll—indicates that they were more likely to identify as independents, to have higher incomes, and to be members of the younger generation.[91] Fewer white Tennesseans probably split their ballots for president and senator in 1984—based on a comparison with the Tennessee Poll, conducted at the University of Tennessee at Chattanooga—but their profile is similar to their counterparts in Ala bama.[92] (One would like to compare these voters on attitudinal questions, such as those examined in the presidential election section based on the 1984 National Election Study, but such comparable state information is not available.)

Governor Hunt in North Carolina was able to attract substantially more white support than Mondale, but he fell considerably short of the Heflin, Gore, Pryor achievement. In essence, Hunt had the correct formula for Southern Democratic success, but he faced an aggressive incumbent in a polarized environment that did not permit the type of ambiguity that Southern Democrats find necessary to hold together their diverse biracial coalition. In Mississippi, Winter also sought that ambiguity, but, for a variety of reasons (many peculiar to the Magnolia State and to that particular contest), he failed. And Doggett in Texas, suffering from a divisive runoff primary victory, lost the more conservative white Democrats to the Republican Gramm, himself a former conservative Democratic champion.

The results of 1984 were such that both sides in the South could find some comfort. With the presidential landslide uppermost in their minds, Republican leaders talked of a fast-approaching realignment in Southern politics. Survey information detecting movement toward the GOP in partisan identification became the evidentiary centerpiece for those who envisioned a bright immediate future for the Republican party in Dixie. Democrats, pointing to their 1984 victories below the presidential level, were unwilling to concede that the future belonged to the new opposition party. They counseled patience until the 1986 elections could be held, content in knowing they would not have Ronald Reagan on the ballot again. In such a state of partisan anticipation and uncertainty, the mid-term elections of 1986—the topic of the next chapter—were conducted.

17

The 1986 Elections

Mid-term elections, by their very nature, usually defy easy characterization. They break into scattered individual struggles that vary from state to state and district to district, and for complete understanding careful attention must be given to the peculiarities of each. Yet, on election night it is the composite result that draws attention, and the South found itself in the national spotlight on November 4, 1986.

The premier event of the 1986 elections was the Democratic recapture of the U.S. Senate. Half of the party's impressive eight-seat gain came in the South.[1] Republican seats in Alabama, Georgia, North Carolina, and Florida, all picked up in the Reagan sweep of 1980, went to Democratic challengers, and a Democrat took an open Democratic seat in Louisiana against a strong Republican opponent. In the U.S. House of Representatives the Democrats gained only five seats nationwide, fewer than generally expected in the mid-term election of a president's second term,[2] but four of them came in the South.[3] Overall, the Southern Democracy put on an impressive display of its depth, complexity, tensions, and future potential.

All was not bleak, however, for the GOP in Dixie. The party in 1986 won four governorships previously occupied by Democrats—in Alabama, South Carolina, Florida, and Texas.[4] And the Republicans quietly continued their steady, if glacial, gains in the region's state legislatures, moving from 21.1 percent in 1984 to 22.7 percent of total legislative seats controlled after the 1986 elections.[5] The results for all categories are reflected in Figures 3-1 and 3-2 in Chapter 3.

Before considering a comparative assessment of these elections, the circumstances of the many interesting and varied Southern electoral contests of 1986 ought to be fresh at hand. Thus, as has been the pattern throughout this book, attention turns to the candidates, campaigns, and issues—the live stuff of politics.

Alabama

With four experienced and well-known politicians after his job and with voters expressing increasing concern about his health,[6] George Wallace announced in April 1986 that he would not seek another term as governor. "After much prayerful consideration, I feel that I must say I have climbed my last political mountain," the veteran of four decades of Alabama political life told an emotional gathering in Montgomery.[7]

His departure set the stage for one of the most amazing gubernatorial elections in state history. Unraveling the diverse twists and turns of this controversial contest, which was fought as much inside courts of law as on the campaign trail, sheds considerable light on the current nature of partisan life in Alabama. In the end Guy Hunt, a Republican, given practically no chance at the beginning, became Wallace's successor. And, in a second important 1986 election in the state, one that was tame by comparison, Senator Jeremiah Denton, a first-term Republican, narrowly lost to a conservative Democrat, U.S. Representative Richard Shelby.

The clear front-runner to succeed Wallace was Lt. Gov. Bill Baxley, the former attorney general who lost his first try for governor in 1978 and opted for the second spot in 1982 rather than face Wallace. Baxley had the support of the state's two major black organizations, the Alabama Democratic Conference and its newly formed competitor, the Alabama New South Coalition, the latter led by Mayor Richard Arrington, Birmingham's first black mayor.[8] Organized labor, represented by the Alabama Labor Council, and the state's teachers, through the Alabama Education Association, also backed him.[9]

On the stump Baxley sought to identify himself with Alabama's populist tradition, as depicted in the following *Birmingham News* profile article:

> A tobacco-chewer and hot-pepper eater with a thick Wiregrass accent, Baxley stops just as often to shake hands with long-haired, tatooed men, farmers in dirty breeches and women in tank tops and jeans as he does with dark-suited lawyers and business leaders.
>
> Likening himself to George Wallace and Big Jim Folsom, Baxley tells crowds that, "Besides my experience, there's one thing that sets me apart from other candidates, and that's the sincere compassion I have for the average person."[10]

Of the other three candidates in the Democratic primary, George McMillan, the former lieutenant governor who nearly defeated Wallace in the 1982 Democratic runoff, consistently held fourth place in the polls during the several months prior to the June 3 first primary. "It's Time for Excellence" was his theme. "I'm not out to pit the rich against the poor, the blacks against the whites . . . . We've had that stuff too long."[11] McMillan finished last with 12 percent. Forrest (Fob) James, the former governor, carried into the race a high negative rating tied to his four years in office; he also could count on a strong core of loyal supporters. He ran third with 21 percent.[12]

The man with the best chance of stopping Baxley in the last few months before the Democratic primary was thought to be Charles Graddick, the two-term law-and-order attorney general who had won his first public office in 1974 as a Republican. Graddick, known as "Charcoal Charlie" for his vehemence on capital punishment, claimed to be the "new face" in the race since the other three had been either governor or lieutenant governor and had all run previously for governor, which he had not done. A *Birmingham News* reporter wrote that Graddick often told rallies: "We have been Baxleyed, we have been McMillaned and we have been Fobbed. And what do we have to show for it?"[13] Saying he planned to make Alabama the "comeback state," Graddick offered a program that emphasized increased industrial recruitment and improvements in education.[14]

Baxley led the first primary with 37 percent to Graddick's 29 percent. The runoff campaign proved to be so hard-hitting that a *New York Times* article proclaimed that the long-anticipated birth of a new era (that is, the post-Wallace era) had become "mired in a campaign so fraught with name-calling and accusations of racial politics that it is more evocative of the Alabama politics of the past than the future."[15] The racial element entered when Graddick ran television commercials attacking Baxley as a pawn of special interest groups, particularly mentioning several prominent black Alabamians. One of the black leaders, Joe Reed, responded: "In the old days, they used to cry 'nigger, nigger.' Now they just say 'black politician,' but everyone knows that's a code word that means the same thing."[16]

The name-calling picked up after a televised debate on June 15 resurrected an episode from the spring campaign. In March the *Birmingham News* reported that state troopers assigned to protect Baxley drove a woman reporter for the Associated Press to Baxley's Montgomery apartment on various occasions. The reporter resigned her job; Baxley, whose wife resided in their Birmingham home, initially denied the story. Later he admitted using state cars to transport private citizens, claimed no impropriety in the use of the vehicles, and offered to repay the state. He refused further comment on the matter, saying he would answer to no one but his wife concerning the woman's visits.[17] When the issue was raised during the debate, Graddick said nothing as Baxley repeated his previous positions on the matter, but the next day Graddick charged Baxley had lied about it.

Concurrent with the campaign charges and counter-charges, there took place a series of maneuvers concerning the 33,000 people who had voted in the June 3 Republican primary. Alabama does not have registration by party, but in 1979 the state Democratic party adopted a rule prohibiting anyone from voting in a Democratic runoff primary who had voted in the first primary of another party, a rule that had never been enforced. After the first primary, John Baker, chairman of the state Democratic party, wrote county party and election officials urging them to enforce the anti-crossover rule by asking each potential runoff voter if he or she had voted in the GOP primary and then barring those who said they had. Alabama's Republicans countered by claiming that crossover voting was legal and urging Republicans to vote. Graddick did likewise, but he went even further in his capacity as attorney general. He had Susan McKinney, the assistant attorney general in charge of the voter fraud division, write county election officials shortly before the June 24 balloting to tell them that the anti-crossover rule was unconstitutional and that officials could "subject themselves to civil liabilities under state and federal law" if they invoked the rule to prevent any registered voter from casting a ballot.[18]

When the ballots were counted, Graddick had won a narrow victory with 460,051 votes to Baxley's 451,295. Baxley refused to concede defeat, contending that the 8,756 margin of victory was made up of illegal Republican crossover votes. There followed a dispute of such gigantic proportions that it overshadowed all else in the election. To tell the complete story of the next few months of legal and partisan wrangling would require many more pages than can be devoted here. In brief, on August 1, a panel of three federal judges in Montgomery invalidated Graddick's runoff victory, ruling that the attorney general had violated the Voting Rights Act by having his assistant warn voting officials not to enforce the anti-crossover rule. The plaintiffs in the suit, a black couple from Pike County, argued successfully that this action in effect was a change in voting procedures and under Section 5 of the Voting Rights Act all such changes must receive preclearance in Washington, which obviously had not been done for this election-eve action.[19] The court ordered party leaders to hold a new runoff "unless the Democratic party determines pursuant to its procedures and the stringent rules under

Alabama law for an election contest that Mr. Baxley received the majority of the legally cast votes."[20]

A few days later Graddick announced he would not appeal and called for a new runoff. "My style is not to win elections in courthouses or committees," he said.[21] The public overwhelmingly favored this option; a Capstone Poll found 70 percent of its respondents in favor of a new election and only 18 percent for the party naming Baxley the nominee.[22]

Despite the availability of this seemingly sensible solution to the dispute, the party's five-member subcommittee mandated to examine the problem decided on August 15, after four days of raucous hearings, that Baxley had received a majority of the legal votes and declared him the nominee. Relying on a Baxley-supplied list of 10,406 alleged Republican crossover voters and on testimony from pollsters who estimated that crossovers favored Graddick at a rate between 83 percent and 88 percent,[23] the panel concluded: "We believe such evidence is convincing to a reasonable person and we are satisfied that the illegal actions of the attorney general and his staff [in encouraging crossover votes] resulted in thousands of illegal votes in favor of Graddick and that Baxley received the majority of the legal votes cast."[24]

Graddick fought back with a two-track strategy: he began a write-in candidacy for the November election and at the same time continued the legal battle. The latter brought forth a favorable ruling in mid-September from a federal judge in Birmingham, who ordered a new runoff if Graddick dropped his write-in campaign. This judicial decision, however, was overturned on October 1 by an appeals court in Atlanta,[25] and Graddick's efforts over the next two weeks to get the U.S. Supreme Court to grant an emergency petition failed. Finally, five days before the November 4 election Graddick dropped his write-in candidacy, saying he had determined that he could not win and was aware that he might help Baxley win. He added: "I will not permit the hand-picked candidate to have any chance to win when he has the support of only the minority of our people."[26]

The major beneficiary of this unprecedented turmoil was, of course, Guy Hunt, the GOP nominee, who was virtually ignored earlier in the year. Typical of Hunt's early treatment was this mention in a *New York Times* article on the eve of the second primary: "The runoff winner Tuesday is all but assured victory in November over Guy Hunt . . . . The state's Republican Party is concentrating on the Senate contest."[27] Not so by October. "The best way to describe what has happened," an Alabama political scientist told a reporter on the eve of the election, "is to say that Guy Hunt has been standing in the middle of an Alabama political road, and it looks like he's just been run over by the governorship."[28] Hunt, a former county probate judge, a farmer, and a part-time operator of a sales distributorship who had no formal education beyond high school, projected a clean-cut, down-home image. Although he had not held statewide elective office, he did run Ronald Reagan's 1980 and 1984 campaigns in the state and was appointed by the President as state director of the U.S. Agricultural Stabilization and Conservation Service, serving from 1981 to 1985.

Sensing the surge to Hunt, Baxley turned his attention on the Republican candidate with a barrage of negative television commercials that attacked Hunt's educational and professional qualifications, even poking fun at him as "a vacuum cleaner salesman."[29] Hunt answered the charges this way:

> They've said I was a vacuum cleaner salesman, and as far as I can remember I've never sold a vacuum cleaner in my life. But right now people have a whole lot more respect for vacuum cleaner salesmen than they do lawyers and politicians. . . .
>
> No, I don't have much experience with Montgomery politics. I thank God I don't. I'm glad I don't.
>
> People want a fresh face. And the fight in Alabama isn't between Democrats and Republicans. It's between right and wrong.[30]

On November 4, Alabama's voters finally had their chance to respond to the chaos that had surrounded the governor's race since late June, and they gave Hunt a substantial victory with 56.4 percent of the votes cast to Baxley's 43.5 percent. One pre-election survey indicated that 87 percent of the Graddick runoff voters favored Hunt.[31] Hunt's supporters were overwhelmingly white; two exit polls estimated that between 69 percent to 73 percent of the whites backed Hunt. Blacks remained solidly for Baxley at 96 percent or 97 percent. See Table 17-1 at the end of this chapter.

In general the Alabama governor's race had all the markings of a first-class partisan shakedown cruise. The state's GOP, as discussed in Chapter 6, remained artificially weak as a result of the powerful retarding influence of George Wallace, a situation that led ambitious Republicans to seek the highest statewide office through the Democratic primaries. James did it in 1978 and Graddick tried in 1986; for example, Graddick's Democratic runoff vote clearly resembled President Reagan's pattern in Alabama.[32] The ploy was so open that four Republican state senators appeared in a television commercial for Graddick before the runoff describing him as "a known Republican choosing to run as a Democrat for politically pragmatic reasons."[33] Obviously in an environment without a twentieth-century tradition of party competition and without registration by party, the Southern norm on both counts, and where, furthermore, there was a slow and atypical post-1964 Republican start, the potential existed for such a fluid partisan situation to blow up. And that is what the protracted Graddick-Baxley controversy, with its production of a Republican governor, represented—a quick, explosive jolt toward partisan maturity.

Despite the confusion in the governor's race, Congressman Shelby, a hard-hitting, "boll-weevil" Democrat, narrowly defeated Senator Denton, 50.3 percent to 49.7 percent. Shelby rose steadily in the polls from a distant position at the outset of the campaign, apparently reaping the benefit of television commercials that claimed Denton had favored Social Security cuts and that struck at Denton's less-than-total devotion to regularly making the circuit "back home." The latter point was supported in a Shelby commercial with a film clip featuring Denton complaining: "I can't be down here [in Alabama] patting babies on the butt" and still get things done in Washington.[34] Shelby's Social Security charges, which Denton denied, drew the attention of a *Washington Post* reporter doing a story on the nationwide use of negative campaign tactics in 1986. The reporter described the attacks in part as follows:

> The first spot . . . noted that Denton had "voted against Social Security four times. . . . Go to your local library to check the Congressional Record."
>
> Denton responded with an ad featuring his mother testifying that the charge was untrue—"because he's my son."
>
> Shelby swiftly answered with another spot: "We've seen the proof that Senator Denton voted to cut Social Security. . . . " Denton's picture suddenly appears on a copy of the Congressional Record. Now, the narrator said, there was something "even more shocking": Denton had voted to give Social Security to "illegal aliens. . . . Again, check the Congressional Record." Then, in white lettering against a black background: "Denton votes to cut your Social Security. . . . and give it to illegal aliens."[35]

President Reagan visited Alabama several times to campaign for Denton. At a Montgomery rally on September 18 the Chief Executive repeatedly praised Denton for fully supporting him during the first six years of his presidency. Reagan then took the occasion to direct a plea to Alabama Democrats to support the Republican senator: "I used to be a Democrat myself, and I must tell you from my heart that Jerry Denton represents your views far better than the liberals who run the Democratic Party in Washington and right here in Alabama."[36] At another point, Reagan said.

> I just have to believe that, with Jeremiah Denton chairing the
> Senate subcommittee on Security and Terrorism, every nickel-and-
> dime fanatic and dictator knows that if he chooses to tangle with the
> United States of America, he'll have to pay a price.[37]

Asked about this display of high-level backing for his opponent, Shelby
quipped: "It is kind of funny in that if the President visits any more
often, he will know his way around this state more than Senator Denton
does."[38]

On the daily give-and-take of campaign politics, Shelby and his associates must be credited for their effectiveness, and this rhetorical battle
clearly allowed Shelby to have a shot at the incumbent. In other words,
it allowed him to pull in enough white support to join with his solid
backing among blacks, who viewed Shelby as the better of two less-than-
satisfactory choices. (See Table 17-1 at the end of this chapter for estimates of the vote by race.) In addition to his conservative voting record
in Congress, Shelby had voted against the extension of the Voting
Rights Act and opposed the establishment of the Martin Luther King,
Jr., national holiday.[39] Perhaps the realization that his political success
rested on black support led Shelby in the fall of 1987 to become one of
the first of the conservative Southern Democratic senators to announce
his opposition to the nomination of Judge Robert Bork to the Supreme
Court, an appointment vigorously opposed by civil rights groups.

It should also be noted that the 1986 elections in Alabama witnessed
the advance of scions of two famous Alabama political families. George
Wallace, Jr., won election as state treasurer and Jim Folsom, Jr., became lieutenant governor; both are Democrats.[40] Shelby's Seventh Congressional District seat went to the Democrat Claude Harris, Jr., a
former circuit judge from Tuscaloosa. Harris defeated the Republican
Bill McFarland, a Tuscaloosa businessman who had recently switched
to the GOP, by a vote of 59.8 percent to 40.2 percent. There were no
other seriously contested congressional races, leaving the U.S. House
delegation from Alabama with two Republicans and five Democrats.

Georgia

The defeat of Senator Mack Mattingly, the first-term conservative Republican, by U.S. Representative Wyche Fowler, the left-of-center At-
lantan, raised more than a few eyebrows among those who viewed
Southern politics through popular stereotypes. How could a big city
liberal, blasted throughout the campaign in television advertisements as
one of those "tax-and-spend" national Democrats, win a majority in
Georgia? In an election as close as this one, 50.9 percent to 49.1

percent, any number of factors could be credited with having carried the day for the Democrat.

In proclaiming "Anti-Talmadge Vote Was Gone—And So Was Mack Mattingly," one newspaper headline pointed to an obvious element.[41] In 1980 more than one-third of the state's black voters cast Republican ballots and thus denied to a member of a once virulently racist political family the full benefit of the post-civil rights era black-white Democratic coalition. Furthermore, the Talmadge legacy was anti-city, and urban dwellers got their revenge in the close election of 1980, all to the benefit of Mattingly, a novice who had not held public office previously.

In 1986 Mattingly had to stand on his own, and, given the weakness of the GOP in statewide Georgia politics, plus the lack of a presidential election that year, the opportunity his vulnerability offered the right challenger was obvious.[42] Few people, however, viewed Fowler as the right Democrat for the task.

A lawyer who represented a heavily black Atlanta district in Congress for ten years, Fowler was little known in the rural, small-town expanses of South Georgia, the heart of Talmadge country. Further, his voting record, although in the middle ranks for all his U.S. House Democratic colleagues, was considerably less conservative than the other Georgia Democrats in Congress. For example, from 1981 to 1985 Fowler's conservative score as rated by the *National Journal* was 33 percent. For the other Georgia Democrats the figure was 62 percent; the House Democratic average was 31 percent.[43]

Aware of his weaknesses, Fowler early on gave extensive attention to areas far from Atlanta. Exhibiting, as a reporter put it, "a remarkable ability to put on a down-home show"[44] when outside of the capital, the soft-spoken, conservatively dressed Fowler lost no opportunity to identify with his audiences. Following one of his southern forays a full year before the election, the *Atlanta Journal* reported:

> In Columbus last week, U.S. Representative Wyche Fowler let the crowd know he had put in his time as a soldier at Fort Benning.
>
> In Valdosta, he mentioned that his grandfather was a farmer, and in Albany, he let slip that his mother had been born just outside of town.
>
> But he saved the fish farm for Americus.
>
> "You know the fish hatchery down the road in Dawson? the Atlanta Congressman asked proudly. "The Steve Cox Fish Hatchery? That's named after my uncle."[45]

Despite the attention he gave to these areas, Fowler found the initial going tough, encountering more than a few skeptics. Wilbur Gamble, chairman of the Terrell County Commission and the Georgia Peanut Commodity Commission, expressed the doubts this way:

> He's got an image—I'm not saying it's an earned image—of a liberal. And I'm sure the Republicans will jump on that . . . .
> And I'll be honest with you, being from a black district will hurt him with the whites, not like it would have 10 years ago, but it will hurt him. Folks worry that he'd vote for every fool spending bill, especially the ones that have to do with minorities.[46]

What made believers of the skeptics came nearly nine months after the visit described above: Fowler's mid-August nomination victory without a runoff over several candidates, including Hamilton Jordan, Jimmy Carter's former assistant, who ran as a conservative. "Wyche really surprised me," commented one Democratic state representative, Cas Robinson, after the primary. "When I saw the numbers he was coming up with in some pretty conservative counties, I knew we had a man who could win."[47] Adding to Fowler's acceptability was an early fall endorsement by Senator Sam Nunn, the Peach State's popular, conservative senior senator.[48]

Mattingly conducted an expensive television campaign that lambasted Fowler for being too liberal for Georgia (a "roaring liberal," he called the Democrat)[49] and for having the worst attendance record in Congress on roll-call votes in 1986.[50] The Republican also aired commercials that emphasized his support for the President and pictured Reagan several times complimenting Mattingly; other spots discussed particular things the incumbent had done for Georgians.[51] In early October, President Reagan campaigned in the state for Mattingly. Likening Fowler to Senator Edward M. Kennedy, the president exclaimed: "You wouldn't want a senator who's as liberal as Teddy Kennedy, would you?"[52]

Mattingly's low-key style, his "refreshing humility," came into sharp contrast with that of his more assertive opponent. Apparently Mattingly, in the words of a sympathetic bank lobbyist, "just looks at himself as an average guy who is really surprised that he's up there [in the Senate] . . . . Some of them [senators] act like God around you."[53] While such self-effacing qualities might be endearing in a friend or associate, they can hurt in a tough political campaign, as the candidates' only televised debate, on October 20 showed. In the words of Hal Straus of the *Atlanta Journal*, Fowler "vigorously attacked . . . Mattingly on the issues of deficit spending, foreign policy and personal honesty . . . while the GOP incumbent tried to paint his opponent as a tax-and-spend liberal."[54] They probably came off about even in charges and counter-charges. Their styles, however, differed sharply. To again quote from Straus's post-debate article:

> [Mattingly] seemed generally passive during the encounter compared to the constantly attacking Atlanta congressman.
>
> When Fowler accused Mattingly, for example, of voting to kill the federal peanut program and to "destroy" farm export markets, the incumbent didn't respond.
>
> When Fowler came close to calling Mattingly a liar, the senator again had no response. "Mack, I don't know whether you won't tell the truth, or whether your aides won't tell you right," Fowler said. [55]

In the days immediately after the debate, Fowler showed a noticeable increase in various state polls. [56] No doubt sensing the edge the contrast of styles provided him, the Democratic challenger used the advantage effectively on the stump. For example, in an address to ninety businessmen in Albany, Fowler cautioned the group: "If you tolerate people in public office, like you saw Mack Mattingly in the debate, who would not answer questions—if you tolerate and accept that, you will never get aggressive, effective leadership." [57]

Fowler carried the entire Black Belt and over half of the South Georgia counties. The metropolitan Atlanta counties gave the Democrat a 10,000 vote margin, which differed sharply from Mattingly's 160,000 vote-margin there six years earlier. [58] Survey data indicated that the bulk of the state's blacks were joined by around 40 percent of the whites to bring in another victory for the state's "night-and-day" alliance. See Table 17-1.

Governor Joe Frank Harris won re-election easily with 70.5 percent to 29.5 percent for Guy Davis, Jr., a Republican lawyer who surprised state party leaders by declaring his gubernatorial candidacy right before the filing deadline. The GOP had decided not to challenge Harris and never gave full support to Davis's doomed candidacy. [59] The governor, who kept his 1982 pledge not to raise taxes, was widely popular. [60]

Nineteen eighty-six marked the election of the second black to Congress from Georgia since Reconstruction; Mayor Andrew Young of Atlanta was the first. John Lewis, a veteran civil rights leader, defeated Julian Bond, a former colleague from the protest days of the 1960s, to win the Democratic nomination for the Atlanta seat vacated by Fowler. Lewis's upset victory in the runoff—he had trailed Bond by twelve percentage points in the first primary—was widely described as a blow to the city's black establishment, which favored Bond. [61] Lewis easily defeated Portia A. Scott, a black Republican, in November.

The state's two Republican congressmen were re-elected along with seven Democratic incumbents. U.S. Representative Pat Swindall, the youthful Republican elected in 1984, managed 53.2 percent against the Democrat Ben Jones's 46.8 percent. Jones drew national publicity because he had played Cooter, the redneck mechanic, in the television show "Dukes of Hazzard."[62] U.S. Representative Newt Gingrich, who had distinguished himself as a leader of young conservative Republicans in the House, defeated the Democrat Crandle Bray, administrator of Clayton County, with 59.5 percent to 40.5 percent. State Democratic leaders, irritated by Gingrich's confrontational partisan style, went out of their way to find and support a candidate to oppose the four-term incumbent.[63]

Louisiana

Senator Russell Long's announcement in early 1985 that he would not seek re-election provided the Pelican State with an unexpected contest for an open seat. The Republican party quickly coalesced behind U.S. Representative W. Henson Moore, of Baton Rouge, who had been contemplating a statewide race at least since 1979.[64] Thirteen Democrats entered the open primary, but U.S. Representative John B. Breaux, of Crowley, a protégé of Governor Edwin W. Edwards, eventually emerged as the Democrat with the best chance to catch Moore.

Because the September 27 open primary came more than a month before the November 1986 mid-term elections and because Moore was running far ahead in the polls, Republican national leaders were hoping Moore would win the seat outright by getting a simple majority and thus give the party a boost in its fight to retain control of the Senate.[65] Moore did lead the field with 44.2 percent, but he was forced to face Breaux, who received an unexpectedly high 37.4 percent, in the "runoff" general election on November 4.

The Republican tried to turn the two-man race into a referendum on Governor Edwards, whose popularity had declined considerably since his smashing re-election three years earlier. On the other hand, Breaux sought to concentrate attention on the faltering of Louisiana's oil-sensitive economy, which he blamed on President Reagan's policies. The following sample from their rhetorical combat conveys the campaign's tone.

Moore repeatedly linked Breaux to Edwards, a fellow Cajun who gave Breaux his start in politics and whose congressional seat Breaux won in 1972 when Edwards became governor. A Moore television advertisement told viewers:

The Edwin Edwards connection goes back a long way. Breaux was Edwards' top aide in Congress and hand-picked successor. And now Breaux is the Edwards candidate for senator. Edwards' friends, backers, money and political machinery are on the line for Breaux . . . one contribution after another to Breaux from the Edwards money machine. A Breaux-Edwards connection. Isn't it time we changed all that?[66]

Breaux is part of "the politics of the past [that] has been holding us back," Moore asserted. "You have never heard John Breaux criticize the political system in Louisiana."[67]

For his part, Breaux, who had a generally conservative voting record in the House, bore down on pocketbook issues. Careful to acknowledge Reagan's personal popularity, the Democrat argued that the President's policies were not working. On the stump, he said:

> If you're satisfied with what you've got, send Moore to Washington and confirm that you're happy and satisfied. If you don't like the fact that you're out of work, if you don't like the price of cotton and soybeans, if you don't like what's happening in the energy business, if you don't like the closing of plants in Louisiana, then don't send Moore to Washington. Then, there's no more Moore."[68]

Breaux could count on drawing laughs when he told this story, which was often:

> I ran across two guys . . . talking about the election. One was saying to the other, "You know, they told me six years ago that, if I voted for the Republicans and the Republican party, things would start picking up. You know something, they were right. I voted for the Republicans. Last month, they picked up my car, my truck, my house and my boat."[69]

If the election boiled down to the state's depressed economy versus the tarnished image of Louisiana's racy governor, the former won in 1986. Breaux went to the Senate with 52.8 percent of the votes cast to Moore's 47.2 percent. Exit polls showed 39 percent of the state's whites joined with about 90 percent of its blacks to form Breaux's victory coalition. See Table 17-1.

Breaux received an unexpected boost from the national GOP that helped to spark enthusiasm for the Democrat's candidacy among black voters. The episode involved the Republican party's "ballot integrity" program, which was aimed at areas that voted overwhelmingly for Walter Mondale in 1984. Essentially the program involved sending mail to all registered voters in the targeted precincts, nearly all of which in Louisiana were predominantly black, then following up with challenges in those cases where the mail was returned as undeliverable. William Greener, political director of the Republican National Committee, vigorously defended the program. "I'm tired of having Democrats say Republicans are intimidating black voters. We are participating in efforts to discourage voter fraud. . . . We are against dead and nonexistent people voting."[70]

The Democrats filed suit in several locations to halt the program. In Louisiana a federal judge in September ordered a preliminary injunction stopping the Republican party from forcing state registration officials to check the names of 30,000 Louisiana voters identified through the mailings.[71] The judge said that blacks had been "singled out . . . in violation of their state and federal constitutional rights."[72] The issue was rekindled just ten days before the election when a federal judge in New Jersey, who was handling the main suit in the dispute, released a statement quoting a national GOP official as saying that the "ballot integrity" program "could keep the black vote down considerably" in Louisiana.[73]

The infusion of support the voter-purge controversy gave Breaux among blacks was expressed well in this *Washington Post* article which bore the headline, "GOP Plan To Cut Black Vote Backfires in Louisiana":

> Wherever Breaux traveled this week, he was embraced by large and enthusiastic crowds of blacks. His campaign took on the fervor of the civil rights movement.
>
> "The Republicans are saying they don't want black people to vote," Breaux told a gathering of community leaders and dock workers at the longshoreman's hall [in Lake Charles].
>
> "There's a reason to be angry about this election. The dream of equality, of voting rights, shines, but there are people in Louisiana who would like to turn those lights off."[74]

It is difficult to say for certain what the impact of the controversy was on the outcome. A fair guess would be that it improved black turnout. At any rate, Moore said he wished the episode had not happened. He called the voter-purge plan "a big mistake" when asked about it during a televised debate October 19. "It was something that shouldn't have been done," he said, adding that he had no advance knowledge of it and that it was stopped at his request.[75]

A Republican replaced Moore in Congress. State Representative Richard H. Baker, who switched parties in 1985, won the Baton Rouge-centered seat in the open primary with 51.0 percent to 45.0 percent for state Senator Thomas H. Hudson, a Democrat. After the open primary it was certain that Breaux's southwest Louisiana seat would go to a Democrat because under the state's unique voting system two Democrats earned berths in the "runoff" general election; the only Republican in the race finished a distant fourth on September 27. The victor was Jimmy Hayes, a developer, who received 57.0 percent to state Representative Margaret Lowenthal's 43.0 percent.

Although all other congressional incumbents were returned, a third open seat, formerly held by a Democrat, the late Gillis Long, was won by a Republican. An initial five-candidate field was reduced to the required two after the open primary: Faye Williams, a black Democratic lawyer, the leader with 25.6 percent, and Clyde Holloway, a white Republican businessman, the runner-up with 23.1 percent. The sprawling Eighth District in central Louisiana, which stretched from Lake Pontchartrain in the east to Alexandria, was 36 percent black; Mondale won 49.0 percent of the district's votes in 1984. Holloway had run unsuccessfully twice before for the seat. Williams, an Alexandria native and Grambling State University graduate, lived outside of the district for over twenty years until shortly before the election, although she contended she had maintained her official residence there all along.

The substantial issue differences between the two candidates had to compete with an October revelation of an event in Williams's personal life fifteen years earlier when she was a graduate student in Los Angeles. A *New York Times* article headlined "Politics Gets Personal in Louisiana's 8th Congressional District" recapitulated the event and Holloway's comments concerning it:

> [Williams's] estranged husband, . . . a black television broadcaster from whom she had filed for divorce, had broken into her house, beaten her and shot to death the man she had been seeing . . . a white college professor and prominent political activist.
>
> "The part that worries me about her past is not the love affair," Mr. Holloway said. "The part that concerns me is that the guy who was killed was a known Communist in the Los Angeles area. The old saying out in the street is that if you sleep with a dog, you get fleas."[76]

Williams said the incident was irrelevant to her candidacy, pointing out that, after all, she was not the perpetrator of the crime but the victim of it. Instead of concentrating on this matter, she said voters should be concerned with the fact that "we have the highest unemployment rate, the highest illiteracy rate, the highest dropout rate, the highest welfare rate and the second highest teen-age pregnancy rate in the nation."[77]

How the much-talked-about incident figured into the decision was unclear as was the impact of her race. With 48.6 percent of the vote she virtually matched Mondale's performance in the Eighth District, although she ran behind Breaux. Holloway's victory with 51.4 percent left the state's U.S. House delegation after the 1986 elections containing five Democrats and three Republicans, a net gain of one for the GOP.

In 1987, Governor Edwards's electoral winning streak came to an end. As befits a state that offers the best in political theater, the glib, fast-talking Democratic governor put on a good show before abruptly bringing down the curtain. Many doubted he would run for a fourth term considering what had befallen him since resuming power after the 1983 election. He had endured two lengthy federal trials on racketeering and fraud charges, and, although the first ended in a hung jury and he won acquittal in the second, his public standing had plummeted, partly as a result of the state's poor economic condition.

Four serious candidates entered the race to replace him. The lone Republican was U.S. Representative Robert L. (Bob) Livingston, Jr. He was originally thought to have the best chance to make the runoff against Edwards in view of his apparent entitlement to the state's hard core GOP voting bloc. There were three other Democrats: Secretary of State Jim Brown; U.S. Representative W. J. (Billy) Tauzin; and U.S. Representative Buddy Roemer. All the candidates liberally attacked Edwards except Brown, who argued: "Voters are sick of personal attacks. They know what Edwin's faults are."[78] Everyone appeared to be convinced that the trick was to get into the runoff with Edwards, the theory being that the voters were ready for "anybody but Edwards." Edwards wanted that person to be Livingston, believing he could deflect from his unpopularity with a free-wheeling runoff campaign of Republican-bashing, at which he excelled.

A month before the October 24 open primary, a Mason-Dixon poll conducted for several Louisiana television stations September 25–30 revealed the following: Edwards, 22 percent; Tauzin, 19 percent; Livingston, 18 percent; Brown, 15 percent; Roemer, 12 percent; undecided or don't know, 13 percent.[79] Into this fluid situation, the state's newspapers weighed in forcefully. On September 27 in a front-page editorial the New Orleans *Times-Picayune* endorsed Roemer, the North Louisiana conservative who promised to "scrub the budget," and within a few weeks seven other daily newspapers followed suit. Calling what came next "the Roemer surge," Jack Wardlaw, a veteran newspaperman, observed: "The talk on the street, in the Capitol and down the byways of Louisiana is that the Roemer candidacy has caught fire . . . ."[80]

In the open primary Roemer, who had a reputation as a spellbinding speaker to go with his "boll weevil" Democratic voting record in Congress,[81] polled 32.7 percent to Edwards's 28.3 percent; Livingston finished a distant third with 18.6 percent.[82] In a dramatic moment on election night, Edwards surprised nearly everyone by announcing that he would not challenge Roemer in a runoff,[83] abruptly ending his long tenure at the top of Louisiana politics.[84]

In two-party terms the weak showing of the Republican Livingston highlighted once again the failure of the GOP to carve out a permanent role for itself in Louisiana's "festival in a labyrinth." Several analysts pointed to "the ghost of Henson Moore's failed bid" for the Senate in 1986, citing especially Moore's post-election comment that, in the words of a newspaper paraphrase, "a good Republican could never beat an acceptable Democrat in a statewide race."[85] Livingston himself said: "I'm laboring under the misperception created by Henson Moore that a Republican can't win, and I violently disagreed with him when he said it, and I violently disagree with him now."[86]

South Carolina

In 1986 the South Carolina Republican party won the governorship for the second time since Reconstruction, and this time the GOP did it without the assistance of chaos on the Democratic side, as occurred in 1974 during its first breakthrough. The victory in and of itself marked a milestone for the party on the road to maturity. Another mark of its growth could be seen in the fact that the party had a choice of two aggressive, ambitious, and articulate conservative congressmen who wanted to run for governor, Carroll Campbell of Greenville and Thomas F. Hartnett of Charleston. In the end Hartnett decided against a primary challenge to Campbell, opting instead to run for lieutenant governor.[87]

On the Democratic side, Lieutenant Governor Mike Daniel won the gubernatorial nomination after the runner-up in the first primary, Phil Lader, a former president of Winthrop College, decided not to seek a runoff.[88] Daniel's personality contrasted sharply with the combative Campbell, who received his first major boost in political life when he led white Greenville citizens in protests against a large-scale, court-mandated school busing plan in 1970, even organizing a march on Columbia.[89] A newspaper profile article of Daniel during the fall campaign, for example, contained these descriptive phrases: "never been considered an exciting and inspirational public figure," "safe but bland," "never been noted for drive or ambition."[90] Profiles of Campbell were full of references to his ambition for high office. One newspaperman, Henry Eichel, of the *Charlotte Observer*'s Columbia bureau, wrote: "From Governor Dick Riley down, Democrats portray Campbell as an

opportunist who makes threats and plays a mean brand of politics."
Eichel added that "Campbell says the Democrats fear him because they
know they can't push him around" and he quoted Campbell on the
point: "I don't back off. I'm not threatened very easily . . . . The ones
that don't like me probably feel intimidated by me."[91]

The campaign proper, which featured, among other things, a squab-
ble between the two nominees over submitting to drug testing, moved a
visiting journalist to observe: "It's a mean gubernatorial campaign unfold-
ing in South Carolina, almost a caricature of modern politics, chock-
full of warmed-over emotional issues that have little to do with lifting a
poor state out of its economic and educational doldrums."[92] One of the
reporter's examples:

> Another loaded issue emerging from the campaign is the Confeder-
> ate battle flag on the Capitol. Blacks complain that it's a symbol of
> the state's one-time dedication to slavery, but Campbell said in their
> debate that he would keep the flag flying. "It's part of our heritage,"
> he said.
>   Daniel danced around the same question with a long response
> that never actually answered it. The real issue here was racial politics
> and Daniel looked as if he was trying to salvage as many white votes
> as he could.[93]

Campbell won with 51.0 percent to Daniel's 47.9 percent. For Daniel, the black-white Democratic coalition came up woefully short on
white votes. He received only 35 percent of the white vote compared
with 96 percent of the black vote, exit polls revealed. See Table 17-1.
One analyst, Glen T. Broach of Winthrop College, noted that "suburban Republicans came to the polls in droves," but turnout among blacks
was lackluster.[94]

Senator Ernest F. (Fritz) Hollings, the veteran Democrat, had no
trouble attracting white voters—57 percent—to add to near unanimous
black support to win easy re-election to a fourth term over the Republican Henry D. McMaster, a former U.S. attorney. Hollings received
63.1 percent to McMaster's 35.6 percent.

The Democrats picked up Campbell's U.S. House seat when state
Senator Elizabeth J. Patterson, the daughter of Senator Olin D. Johnston, defeated Mayor William D. Workman of Greenville with 51.4
percent to 47.3 percent for the Republican.[95] State Senator Arthur Ravenel, Jr., a Charleston Republican, held Hartnett's seat for the GOP by
defeating the Democrat Jimmy Stuckey with 52.0 percent to Stuckey's
48.0 percent. The other congressional incumbents were re-elected, leav-

ing the Palmetto State's U.S. House delegation with four Democrats and two Republicans.

Mississippi

On third try, Mississippi's majority-black Second Congressional District voted to send a black Democrat to Washington. In 1986 Mike Espy, a 32-year-old former assistant state attorney general, defeated U.S. Representative Webb Franklin, the two-term Republican incumbent, with 51.7 percent of the votes to 48.3 percent for Franklin.

No one was quite sure why Espy managed to accomplish what Robert Clark, the black candidate who ran in 1982 and 1984, failed narrowly to do. Bill Minor, the state's leading political analyst, pointed to Espy's "highly organized campaign that got out the black vote in impressive numbers" and to the weak state of the farm economy in this rural, small-town Mississippi Delta district, considerable blame for which fell on the Reagan administration's policies.[96] As Minor put it:

> Several thousand white farmers who formerly supported Franklin are believed to have "voted with their rumps" by staying home on election day. However, many other white farmers deliberately went to the polls and did something they never dreamed of doing before— they voted for a black to represent them . . . .[97]

Supporting Minor's interpretation, a Jackson *Clarion-Ledger* reporter wrote: "The farm crisis in the district was a major issue in the campaign, with Espy hammering away at Franklin's agricultural voting record and endorsing a moratorium on farm foreclosures, a one-year moratorium on farm debt interest and a mediation program between growers and lenders."[98]

Mississippi's four other congressmen were easily re-elected in 1986, which left the five-member delegation with only one Republican, Trent Lott, the number two Republican in the House minority leadership. The 1988 elections, however, will bring major changes to the delegation. Lott and U.S. Representative Wayne Dowdy, the Democrat from the Fourth District, are giving up their seats to run for the seat of Senator John Stennis, who at eighty-six announced in October 1987 that after four decades in the Senate he would retire.

The impending replacement of Stennis comes in the wake of the election in 1987 of the youngest man to be governor of Mississippi in over half a century: Ray Mabus, a 39-year-old Democrat who attained a reputation as a fighter of local corruption while occupying the post of state auditor. Mabus ran first in a crowded Democratic primary and then decisively defeated Mike Sturdivant, a Delta businessman, in the runoff. After that performance, he was expected to line up the state's dominant black-white Democratic coalition for an easy victory in November. He did win, with 53.4 percent of the votes, but the better-than-expected showing of his Republican opponent, Jack Reed, with 46.6 percent, led the GOP to claim a moral victory of sorts. [99]

The policy differences between Reed, a 63-year-old Tupelo businessman with a long record of civic and pro-education activities, and Mabus were viewed as minimal, both touted as "progressive reformers." The choice moved Minor to observe that the candidates "represent the most progressive, intelligent elements of our state, a far cry from the past when cheap demagoguery, offers of pie in the sky and shallow intellect ruled our politics." [100] Echoing this theme the day after his victory, Governor-elect Mabus called the election

> a 100 percent vote for change. Jack Reed and I may have had differences but the heart of our messages was the same—the need to change Mississippi for the better, the need to get better jobs for all our people and the need to make government accountable to the people who pay for it. [101]

Arkansas

Arkansas was no hotbed of two-party competition in 1986. Two veteran Democratic incumbents, Senator Dale Bumpers and Governor Bill Clinton, were easily re-elected.

Clinton first disposed of former Governor Orval Faubus, who at seventy-six made his first comeback try since two failed attempts in the early part of the 1970s. Considering that Clinton had twenty times more money than Faubus's $31,000 in contributions, [102] Faubus's nearly one-third of the vote should have been a comfort to the older man. Apparently he took his defeat hard, calling himself a "has-been" and labeling Clinton a representative of the "super-rich," according to a *New York Times* post-election article headlined "Faubus Angry After Arkansas Loss." [103]

In the general election the youthful veteran governor, who turned forty during the campaign and who was often mentioned as a potential presidential candidate, faced former Governor Frank White in their third contest. Because of a constitutional change, the prize this time was for the state's first four-year gubernatorial term. White never found a convincing issue and finished in November only a little better than Faubus with 36.1 percent to Clinton's 63.9 percent. [104]

Senator Bumpers faced a credible Republican opponent. Asa Hutchin-

son, a former U.S. attorney, who attempted to convince the voters that
the two-term incumbent did not represent the interests of the state in
Washington. "It's Time for Arkansas Again" was Hutchinson's slogan.[105]
Among other things, Bumpers stressed the specific federal projects he
helped bring to the state over the years as well as the 100 days he spends
at home each year. When called "too liberal," he responded by saying
that the "problems facing this country transcend labels like liberal, conservative, moderate or anything else."[106] Nor was he defensive about his
opposition to President Reagan's 1981 tax cuts. Bumpers said he feared
the cuts would "create deficits that would choke a mule" and argued that
he had been proven correct.[107] He won with 62.3 percent to Hutchinson's 37.7 percent.

The most lively race in Arkansas in 1986 came in the First Congressional District during the Democratic primary. U.S. Representative Bill
Alexander, a member of the House Democratic leadership, had a close
call when state Senator Jim Wood, Jr., held him to 52 percent of the
vote in the May primary. Alexander had received a barrage of negative
publicity when it was revealed that he used a military plane at a cost of
$56,000 to fly to Brazil for an alcohol fuels study even though he was
the only member of Congress on the trip, which included his daughter
and several assistants and guests. Wood used the "solo junket" episode as
an example, in the challenger's words, of Alexander's "flagrant disregard
for our tax money." Wood also called the nine-term veteran "arrogant,
too big for his britches."[108] Recognizing the damage, Alexander campaigned vigorously to save his seat. A few months after the primary he
held a press conference, characterized by a newspaper reporter as "the
most humble public statement of his career,"[109] in which he said he had
received the voters' message and would pay more attention to his district. He then withdrew as a candidate for an upcoming election for
House majority whip.[110] In November the Republicans fielded a 27-
year-old radio station owner, Rick (Ramblin' Rick) Albin, who had
moved to Arkansas from Missouri only three years earlier; Alexander was
re-elected with 64.2 percent to Albin's 35.8 percent. Arkansas's other
three congressmen—two Democrats and a Republican—were all comfortably returned to Washington.

North Carolina

North Carolina again distinguished itself as one of the most fiercely
partisan battlefields in the South. Many hard-fought House races were
conducted in 1986 alongside of a major two-party statewide race. And
after the votes were tabulated, the Democratic party had recovered sig-

nificantly from the setbacks it suffered in the wake of Senator Helms's triumph two years earlier.

Terry Sanford, a former Democratic governor, defeated Senator James T. Broyhill, a Republican who was appointed to the seat shortly after the June 1986 suicide death of Senator John East; East had announced in 1985 that he would not seek a second term. Sanford, a longtime president of Duke University, received 51.8 percent of the vote to 48.2 percent for Broyhill, a twelve-term congressman from Lenoir and a member of a well-known furniture manufacturing family.

Sanford won his party's nomination easily in the first primary against nine other candidates. Broyhill's route to the nomination, however, came only after a bruising battle with David Funderburk, a very conservative candidate who had the enthusiastic backing of the Congressional Club, the political action committe closely associated with Senator Jesse Helms.

The primary highlighted strains present in the North Carolina Republican party dating back at least to the clashes between Governor James Holshouser and Senator Helms in the early 1970s. The traditional wing of the party, which included Broyhill and Governor James Martin, tended to stress standard conservative economic and foreign policy issues, while the Helms forces focused on the emotional social issues, such as, prayer in the schools, abortion, affirmative action.[111] Television commercials by Funderburk, a former ambassador to Rumania and college professor, attacked Broyhill for his votes on various social issues, including one in favor of the Martin Luther King, Jr., national holiday.[112] Funderburk argued further that victory in November could only come with the nomination of a "strong conservative." "With Senator Helms and Senator East," he said, "we were able to attract a large number of conservative Democrats to switch over. But would we be able to do that if we had a candidate who represents the other wing or the other perspective?"[113] Funderburk drove home the point with reference to his mentor: "Jesse Helms says the only things you find in the middle of the road are a yellow stripe and a dead skunk. I don't think you'll find me in the middle of the road."[114]

Confident of victory, Broyhill, well-known and respected among state Republican activists, labeled himself the "conservative choice" and complained that Funderburk had distorted his voting record.[115] His television advertisements emphasized his extensive congressional record. The depth and longevity of Broyhill's political experience in state party circles paid off in the May primary. He defeated Funderburk by a two-to-one margin. A key unanswered question became how much support would the defeated wing of the party produce for Broyhill in November.

In the general election campaign, Sanford vigorously went after the Reagan administration's economic policies. In Asheville to mark the end of his pre Labor Day tour of all one hundred of North Carolina's counties, Sanford declared:

> There is a mess in Washington. The budget is out of hand, the national debt is out of hand, and we have been victimized, as have our children and grandchildren, by an absolutely dangerous MasterCharge economy. . . . It has been a sorry record of borrow and spend, borrow and waste, borrow and spend.[116]

When Broyhill tagged him an "old-time liberal," the 69-year-old Democrat homed in again on the budget-deficit issues: "We have just been the victims of the greatest example of fiscal irresponsibility in the history of America. Is that conservative or liberal? Is it conservative or liberal to abandon the North Carolina farmer? Is it conservative or liberal to betray the North Carolina apparel and textile worker?"[117]

Broyhill stuck close to Reagan. "I'm supporting the conservative majority, the majority that's friendly to the programs and policies of President Reagan," he said during an October debate.[118] At a late-October airport rally in Charlotte, the president praised the Republican as "part of the 1980 clean-up crew for the worst economic mess since the Great Depression."[119]

National issues were not the only ones raised. Broyhill reminded Tar Heel voters that, as governor in 1961, Sanford successfully extended the state's sales tax to include food, calling him "Food Tax Terry." Sanford responded aggressively, arguing that "the tax went for the most ambitious school program in the history of North Carolina" and said he showed leadership and political courage in taking an unpopular position that held promise for long-term benefits to the state and that, in fact, gave "us the finest business climate of anywhere in the country."[120] Noting that the tax cost the average citizen $18 a year, the Democrat asserted further: "[It's] the best buy North Carolina has ever gotten."[121]

In accumulating his victory margin, Sanford did well in the eastern part of the state—in the 60 percent range—and made a strong showing in the heavily populated Piedmont Crescent.[122] Several months after the election, Senator Helms attributed the loss primarily to Broyhill's inability to attract conservative Democrats in eastern North Carolina.[123] Others credited Sanford's vigorous, unapologetic approach to the role of positive government. Democratic observers noted that, as a result of Reagan's success with the theme "government isn't the answer to the problem, government is the problem," Democrats have been on the defensive on the question of government as innovator. Al Adams, a former law partner of Sanford's, put it this way, as reported by Ken Eudy and Tim Funk in the *Charlotte Observer:*

> "Democrats have been sort of apologizing instead of saying, 'Darn right, we did it and we're proud of it.' " Adams said. "Sanford stood up . . . and said he was proud of [the sales-tax extension]."
> "It was a brilliant exercise in political judo," said Gary Pearce, co-director of former Governor Jim Hunt's 1984 Senate campaign . . . . "The race was determined by Sanford's own instincts. The way he turned around the food tax issue was brilliant."[124]

The Democrats regained two House seats lost in 1984. In the Raleigh-dominated district, David E. Price, a Duke political science professor and former state party chairman, decisively defeated a first-term Republican, U.S. Representative Bill Cobey, 55.7 percent to 44.3 percent. In the western district, James McClure Clarke, a former one-term Democratic congressman, won back his seat from U.S. Representative Bill Hendon, the Republican who had defeated Clarke in 1984 and who had himself been defeated by Clarke in 1982. Clarke had 50.7 percent of the votes to Hendon's 49.3 percent. In an election not decided until weeks after the November 4 balloting, U.S. Representative Howard Coble, a Republican, held his seat by a margin of only 79 votes against the Democrat he had defeated in 1984. A Republican, Cass Ballenger, replaced Broyhill in the House, and the Democrat Martin Lancaster easily won election in a rural, small-town district in the southeastern part of the state. With the two GOP losses, the U.S. House delegation contained eight Democrats and three Republicans.[125]

Virginia

Virginia won a spot in the post-Reconstruction record books by becoming the first Southern state to elect a black to a nonjudicial statewide office. State Senator L. Douglas Wilder's 1985 victory for lieutenant governor with 51.8 percent of the vote to his GOP opponent's 48.2 percent overshadowed two other noteworthy occurrences in the Old Dominion during that election: the second consecutive gubernatorial victory by the Democratic party after twelve years in the political wilderness and the election of the first woman to statewide office (attorney general) in the commonwealth's history.

Few people could be found in the early months who thought Wilder, a Richmond liberal Democrat long active in politics, could win the general election. Although Wilder received the Democratic nomination without opposition at his party's state convention, the Republicans had a knock-down, drag-out battle for their lieutenant governor's nomination.

J. Marshall Coleman, the party's unsuccessful gubernatorial nominee in 1981, narrowly led in the first state convention ballot.[126] His opponent, state Senator John Chichester, of Fredericksburg, passed him on the second ballot and won a majority on the fourth roll call.[127] Considerable nomination assistance came to Chichester from senior conservatives in the party, such as Mills E. Godwin, Jr., the former governor, who never warmed to Coleman.[128]

In an excellent study of this election, Larry Sabato of the University of Virginia explains Wilder's victory primarily in terms of the effectiveness of his campaign strategy along with the mistakes of his opponent. "Wilder campaigned," Sabato wrote, "not as Jesse Jackson, concentrating his time and attention on the black community, but rather as a Tom Bradley (the Los Angeles mayor)—a mainstream black candidate widely acceptable to whites."[129] An Election Day survey indicated the success of the strategy: 44 percent of the white voters supported Wilder.[130]

Sabato elaborated on Wilder's successful approach:

> First, he put the GOP on the defensive and made Republicans reluctant to attack him by charging that their use of the term "liberal" to describe him had racial implications. Second, he took a nearly 4,000-mile station wagon trek through rural and small-town Virginia, in an attempt to meet the white voters supposedly most resistant to a black candidacy. An enormous quantity of free, favorable publicity in local and statewide media was generated along the way. Third, Wilder adopted a relaxed, sedate campaign style that belied his earlier reputation as a firebrand.[131] His smooth, direct delivery made him perhaps the best television personality of the six statewide candidates in 1985. In that, he had a decisive edge over John Chichester, whose television performances were often stiff, uneasy, and inarticulate. Fourth, Wilder cleverly shaved the liberal edges off of his public record, instead focusing on his legislative achievements, his Korean War valor, and the patriotic virtues and moderate-conservative Virginia values he claimed to possess.[132]

Also Wilder had strong backing among the state's newspapers and effectively used his television commercials. "The ad most frequently aired for Wilder," Sabato reported, "featured a rural white sheriff's deputy with a Southside drawl endorsing the Democrat—a memorable spot that helped to neutralize GOP charges that Wilder had not been tough enough on 'law-and-order' issues."[133] Sabato's detailed critique of Chichester's campaign ends with this summary sentence: "Overconfidence followed by incompetence contributed mightily to Chichester's defeat."[134]

Gerald Baliles, the Democratic attorney general, won the governorship in 1985 with 55.2 percent to his GOP opponent's 44.8 percent.

Baliles identified himself closely with the administration of Governor Charles S. (Chuck) Robb, who was constitutionally barred from seeking a second consecutive term. The popularity of Robb's brand of conservative-to-moderate Democratic politics apparently contributed significantly to Baliles's relatively easy victory over the Republican Wyatt B. Durrette, the man Baliles had beaten in 1981 for attorney general.[135]

State Delegate Mary Sue Terry amassed the largest Democratic margin in 1985 on the way to her pathbreaking victory with 61.4 percent to the Republican W. R. (Buster) O'Brien's 38.6 percent. Well financed and with a solid record in public life to rely on, Terry turned her sex into an advantage, drawing considerable news media attention.[136]

In the 1986 elections Virginia Democrats picked up an open congressional seat to bring the partisan division of the U.S. House delegation to an even five to five. Nine incumbents were re-elected and the Democrat Owen B. Pickett replaced a retiring Republican in the Norfolk-Virginia Beach area.[137] The results of the recent Democratic successes are reflected in the update of Figure 11-1 in the Virginia chapter, where the illustration charts the Virginia Democracy's rise from the depths it reached in the 1970s. Adding to the party's upbeat tone are its hopes to retake in 1988 the Senate seat being vacated surprisingly by Paul S. Trible, Jr., the first-term Republican incumbent. Robb is already running hard for the seat and is the odds-on favorite.[138]

Tennessee

In an era of television-dominated campaigning with its emphasis on the attractive and the flashy, few observers in Tennessee thought a rotund behind-the-scenes wheeler-dealer would hold much appeal for a statewide electorate. Discounting the experts, Ned McWherter, the House speaker and an eighteen-year legislative veteran, ploughed ahead and defeated two well-known Democrats in the primary and regained the governorship in the general election for the Democratic party.[139]

Since the Volunteer State has no provision for a runoff, McWherter's 43 percent of the vote was enough for the nomination in the August primary. Jane Eskind, head of the Public Service Commission, spent freely from her personal fortune, promoting an image of a fighter "for the people against the lobbyists and deal-makers,"[140] and finished with 30 percent of the votes. Mayor Richard Fulton of Nashville, despite what the Knoxville *News Sentinel* termed his "gubernatorial appearance," ran third, as he did in his 1978 campaign for the Democratic gubernatorial nomination, with 26 percent.

With Governor Lamar Alexander, the popular two-term Republican, constitutionally barred from a third term, the GOP turned to Winfield Dunn, its successful 1970 gubernatorial candidate. His campaign suffered a setback when it was disclosed that, by using tax shelters, he had paid no federal income tax in 1982 and 1983 on a total income in excess of a quarter of a million dollars. His response to inquiries on the matter: "It is my challenge and opportunity as a wage earner in this country to pay no more taxes than I have to . . . . I want to pay my fair share, but that's all I want to pay."[141] In East Tennessee several unpopular positions taken by Dunn as governor and particularly affecting that region were revived and used against him.

No sharp partisan differences between the two candidates appeared in the fall campaign. Dunn and McWherter sparred over taxes, the Democrat giving an unqualified pledge of no new taxes with the Republican unwilling to rule them out under all circumstances.[142] They also traded conflict-of-interest charges.[143] In securing his solid victory with 54.3 percent to Dunn's 45.7 percent, McWherter carried a slight majority among whites to go with his overwhelming support from blacks. See Table 17-1.

Tennessee's U.S. House delegation remained at six Democrats and three Republicans; all incumbents were re-elected in 1986. U.S. Representative Marilyn Lloyd survived a second consecutive close election, defeating the Republican Jim Golden with 53.9 percent to the challenger's 46.1 percent.[144]

Texas

In 1986 Bill Clements, the 69-year-old former Republican governor, defeated Governor Mark White, the Democrat who had beaten Clements four years earlier. The bitter rematch, fueled by the personal antagonism of the candidates, focused on several key public policy concerns: taxes, the poor state of the Texas economy, and education.

Clements won the GOP nomination without a runoff against U.S. Representative Tom Loeffler and former U.S. Representative Kent Hance, the "boll weevil" Democrat who joined the Republican party in 1985. Governor White also was renominated without a runoff, but his 54 percent of the vote against a field of generally unknown candidates did not augur well for the upcoming election.

The tenor of the fall campaign was illuminated in the following exchanges at an early October debate over the wisdom of a large tax increase that was adopted with White's support. The *Dallas Times Herald* reported:

> White said a dramatic drop in the price of oil precipitated the financial crisis and that a tax increase was needed to maintain minimal levels of state services.
> "We could have let our schools continue to deteriorate and our roads to decay," White said. "Everybody knows it but you, Bill. If

you don't think there is anything wrong with that, then you go tell them [the voters] that."

Clements, however, said the current fiscal crisis resulted from White's lack of budgetary experience and allowing "spending to go out of control."

"This is a classic example of no leadership," said Clements. . . . "Truth is that state revenues have increased $11.2 billion since White took office. We don't have a revenue shortfall. We have a spending problem."[145]

At another point, Clements charged: "We cannot stand any more of this tax, tax, spend, spend Mondale-mentality of the White administration."[146]

Post-election analyses of Clements's victory with 52.7 percent to White's 46.1 percent (a virtual reversal of their percentages four years earlier) also mentioned the backlash White experienced among Texas schoolteachers angry over educational reforms that required them to take reading and writing tests.[147] A Texas Poll taken after the election revealed strong anti-White sentiment among the voters. Thirty-eight percent said they chose Clements because they were against White.[148]

Texas Republicans in 1986 consolidated the gains they made in the state's congressional delegation two years earlier. All of their incumbents were returned as were all Democratic incumbents. In the only open seat, the contest in the Twenty-first District to replace Loeffler, the Republican Lamar Smith won easily, leaving the partisan split in the Texas U.S. House delegation unchanged at 17 Democrats and 10 Republicans.

Florida

In its two major statewide elections in 1986, Florida sent out conflicting signals. By virtually identical percentages, Bob Graham, the popular outgoing Democratic governor, defeated Senator Paula Hawkins, the Republican first-termer (54.7 percent to 45.3 percent), and Bob Martinez, a Republican, won the governorship over the Democrat Steve Pajcic (54.6 percent to 45.4 percent). The mixed outcome recalls V. O. Key's characterization of the state as "every man for himself,"[149] which, if expanded to be made gender neutral, holds some appeal for explaining this divergent partisan result.

That is the way Graham viewed his victory. On election night he asserted:

Floridians were doing what Floridians have traditionally done. They voted for who they thought would do the best job. It wasn't a referendum on Ronald Reagan. It wasn't a vote on partisan realignment. It was on who they wanted to employ as their senator the next six years.[150]

Despite his consistent lead in the polls, Graham conducted a fall campaign of attack on Hawkins's Senate record, which he found lacking in initiative. "Her definition of the job," Graham said in their only debate, "is that it's important for her to be there to vote, but not try to set the agenda."[151]

Hawkins emphasized her support for President Reagan, chiding Graham for once calling Reagan a "simpleton."[152] In their debate the senator reminded the governor that he had seconded the nomination of Jimmy Carter at the 1980 Democratic National Convention, adding sarcastically: "I know it was a great honor to second Jimmy Carter, but I personally would have declined it."[153] She stressed her record in battling drug abuse, championing the cause of abused children, and supporting Social Security cost-of-living increases. Recognizing her underdog status, she likened herself to Joan of Arc: "I like to slay dragons and put out fires."[154]

Her fellow Republican, Martinez, a former mayor of Tampa and a convert from the Democratic party in 1983, had better luck in November. His good fortune came partly from what happened to the Democrats. Pajcic, a former state representative from Jacksonville, narrowly defeated Attorney General Jim Smith in the September 30 Democratic primary runoff, 50.6 percent to 49.4 percent. Spending freely of his own money,[155] Smith, a "law-and-order" conservative who later joined the Republican party, vigorously attacked Pajcic's legislative record as representative of a 1960s liberalism that Smith said is totally out of step with Florida's mainstream.[156] For his part, Pajcic likened his record to Graham's "progressive policies," denounced Smith's negative campaign tactics, and argued that Smith was trying to deflect the race from a discussion of the problems Florida faces as a result of its rapid growth. Following his narrow loss, Smith made a perfunctory endorsement of Pajcic and then abruptly left the state for a widely publicized hunting trip in Colorado.

Republicans gleefully watched the bitter Democratic runoff fight. John Stipanovich, Martinez's campaign manager, expressed the mood in colorful language: "Jim Smith spent a few million dollars burying the harpoon of liberalism deep in Pajcic's chest, and we're not going to pull it out."[157] Martinez's Hispanic background—his grandparents came to Tampa from Spain at the turn of the century—generated considerable enthusiasm among Hispanics in populous Dade County.[158] Elsewhere, especially in North Florida, his Southern drawl served to counter any negative impact his ethnic origin might have had.[159] In the Panhandle, normally a Democratic bastion, Martinez's message was straight-forward: "Let me tell you, Smith supporters are joining us all over the state because they don't believe in this type of liberalism that he [Pajcic] will represent while he is in state government."[160]

An examination of the voting returns indicates that Martinez's victory was a convincing one statewide, but in North Florida he ran far better than Republicans usually do there, winning 25 of 36 counties above the frost line.[161] And, in Dade County, Martinez led with 205,171 votes to Pajcic's 199,379, also an atypical GOP performance.

Mark Stern of the University of Central Florida in Orlando correctly cautions that the importance of short-term factors in this second GOP gubernatorial victory of the century ought not to deflect attention from the Republican party's rapidly improving position in Florida.[162] Recent voter registration figures, for example, reflect strong GOP gains. Table 13-1 in the Florida chapter showed Republican voter registration had reached 30.8 percent in 1982. When the registration books closed in February 1988 prior to Super Tuesday, the figure had jumped to 37.8 percent.[163] Furthermore, Suzanne Parker of Florida State University has reported a sharp rise in the 1980s in the number of Floridians who identify with the Republican party when asked their party preference in surveys.[164] With Senator Lawton Chiles's announcement in late 1987 that he will not seek re-election in 1988, the impending partisan struggle to succeed the three-term Democrat will provide an unexpected early test of how far the GOP's progress in the fast-changing Sunshine State has come by November 1988.[165]

Comparative Overview of the State Results

No summary statement can convey completely the political diversity witnessed in the South during the 1986 elections and in the several odd-year contests conducted before and after the main event. Yet, a few comparative generalizations seem appropriate.

When surrounded by a sea of detail, resort to a statistical measure can provide a comforting analytical anchor despite the recognized limitations such mathematical constructs carry. Thus, exercising appropriate caution, a glance at the Paul David index of Democratic party strength proves helpful. See Figure 3-3 in Chapter 3 for the extension of David's index for the South through the 1986 elections. In 1982 Democratic strength stood at 59.5 percent, up several points from the 56.1 percent registered during the Reagan victory of 1980. In the year of Reagan's sweeping re-election, the Republican party in the South improved its position as indicated in the index's composite calculation of the vote for governor, U.S. senator, and U.S. representative. This GOP increase is shown in the figure as a Democratic decline in 1984 of slightly over four percentage points to 55.2, the Democratic party's lowest all-time level save for 55.0 in 1972. And what did 1986 do to the regional partisan indicator? Nothing. It remained the same at 55.2 percent, a standoff with something for both sides to cheer about.

For the Democrats, the Senate victories stood out. The quality of the candidates has been advanced more than a few times as an important explanatory element in these Democratic victories.[166] Up to a point the insight is a good one. Certainly in Florida, Bob Graham put on a masterful political display that overwhelmed the incumbent. In Georgia and Alabama, Mattingly and Denton seemed somehow to have been grafted onto the normal flow of political life in their states; neither had held elective office before getting caught up in lucky breaks in 1980, and neither really used the five years before the 1986 election to mesh into the political culture of their states. By contrast, Fowler and Shelby were unquestionably homestate products who knew the political ways of their respective states inside and out. In Louisiana and North Carolina, the candidates—Breaux and Moore, Sanford and Broyhill—were more evenly matched on this nebulous candidate-appeal standard, pointing to the need for consideration of other elements.

Beyond candidate personality, there were the normal factors peculiar to each contest. One cannot help but have a little sympathy for Moore when learning of the strategic assists his national party operators gave to Breaux, as related above. In North Carolina, GOP ideological squabbling flowing from a bitter primary prevented the formation of an enthusiastic united front in November. One ironic scenario from Alabama has it that Shelby, for whom blacks had no great love based on his record on issues of special concern to them, was pulled into office because blacks turned out in greater than expected numbers to support Baxley, the hapless Democratic gubernatorial candidate who was under criticism for being too close to blacks.[167] And there were other similar items brought out in the campaign sections above.

A look at the Table 17-1 percentages by race for the senatorial candidates calls attention once more to the biracial nature of the Democratic coalition in the South. Only the incumbents Bumpers and Hollings, along with Graham (who was widely looked upon as the incumbent in Florida because of his high visibility as governor and because he led in the polls from the beginning), had majorities among whites. Blacks overwhelmingly supported all the Democratic nominees. These patterns, of course, are well-established ones that have been much in evidence over the last decade and a half of the post-civil rights era and need no further amplification.

There was the Reagan factor. All five of the first-time Democratic senatorial victors—along with Bumpers and Hollings—had to contend with opponents who attached themselves closely to Reagan and the

Table 17-1. Exit Poll Estimates of the Vote by Race for Senator
and Governor in the South in 1986

| | Senator (ABC News) | | | |
| | Whites | | Blacks | |
	Democrat	Republican	Democrat	Republican
Alabama	37%	63%	94%	6%
Arkansas	58	42	95	5
Florida	54	46	82	18
Georgia	46	54	87	13
Louisiana	39	61	92	8
North Carolina	44	56	94	6
South Carolina	57	43	98	2
	(CBS News)			
Alabama	38%	62%	93%	7%
Florida	53	47	83	17
Georgia	40	60	81	19
Louisiana	39	61	88	12
North Carolina	43	57	92	8

| | Governor (ABC News) | | | |
| | Whites | | Blacks | |
	Democrat	Republican	Democrat	Republican
Alabama	27%	73%	97%	3%
Arkansas	61	39	96	4
Florida	46	54	79	21
Georgia	66	34	90	10
South Carolina	35	65	96	4
Tennessee	52	58	93	7
Texas	45	55	93	7
	(CBS News)			
Alabama	31%	69%	96%	4%
Florida	44	56	89	11
Georgia	71	29	90	10
Texas	40	60	78	22

SOURCE: Surveys conducted by ABC News and CBS News at polling places on November 4, 1986, and reported in *Public Opinion* (January–February 1987), p. 31.

revolution they told voters he had brought to the nation's political life. The President himself campaigned for them all and helped them raise money.[168] Given the arithmetic of biracial Democratic politics, the Democratic share of the white vote had to be kept near 35 percent in most of the states for the Republicans to win. With economic uncertainty rising in 1986 and with the normal lag experienced as a second-term presidency enters its twilight years, it was not surprising that some Reagan voters ignored the President's advice and instead supported qualified Democratic candidates who aggressively touted their independence of all interests except their state's or who frankly proclaimed the fiscal suicide they detected in the Reagan big-deficit policies.

In gubernatorial politics the GOP made important breakthroughs in 1986. The party's path to its four 1986 victories was varied, evincing no general pattern. In Alabama the governorship came as a result of an almost unbelievable sequence of events that favored the party's official nominee. In the Palmetto State the Governor's Mansion in Columbia fell to the GOP through hard, determined political struggle. Divisiveness among the Democrats aided the Florida Republican triumph, and an ailing Texas economy probably carried the day in the Lone Star State. No matter how these victories occurred, the mere fact of having four Republican governors—along with Governor Martin of North Carolina—should aid the party's growth in these states. Balancing off these Republican gains, the Democrats in 1986 won the governorship of Tennessee and retained the post in Arkansas and Georgia. Furthermore, in the odd-year elections Democrats won the gubernatorial contests in Virginia in 1985 and in Louisiana and Mississippi in 1987. Thus, at the end of 1987 the South's governorships were divided between five Republicans and six Democrats.

Black Democratic candidates won several high visibility contests that deserve note. The election of a black congressman from the Mississippi Delta was an event of no minor significance for the maturity of biracial politics in the region as was the statewide victory of a black to the office of lieutenant governor in Virginia. Also, Atlanta in 1986 joined Memphis and Houston in being represented in Washington by a black congressman, and it is only a matter of time before New Orleans follows suit.

In summary, this recent round of elections leaves the South littered with memories of many hard-fought two-party campaigns and gliding forward on a level partisan plane. As reported above, the Southern party strength index held steady in 1986 with the Democrats at 55.2 percent. No one knows where the next series of elections will take things; perhaps another season at even keel or a significant turn one way or the other, or something in between. The future, of course, has the annoying habit of refusing to reveal itself distinctly. And while the future ultimately must be left to take care of itself, there remain several questions pertaining to the past and the future worth pursuing in the final chapter.

18

Toward the Future

Beyond the holding of the 1984 and 1986 elections, what is new in Southern two-party politics? The personalities have changed for sure—a few politicians are gone for good, others have temporarily left the stage, and, of course, there are more than a handful of new actors in prominent positions. The underlying dynamics of partisan politics in the region, however, do not appear to have deviated significantly from their portrayal in the first fifteen chapters. Still, several items require refinement to account for more recent events. They occupy the first part of this chapter. The last part treats the perennial bugaboo of electoral analysis, the question of realignment.

Recent Developments: An Overview

Starting with the 1984 campaign, the Southern Democracy's delicately balanced black-white coalition had to contend with the forceful personality of Jesse Jackson, the civil rights leader who became the first serious black candidate for president. Jackson's presidential campaign generated considerable fervor among blacks throughout the South and in the Northern big cities as well. The chants of "Run, Jesse, run," the electricity of his rallies, and the impressive, high visibility parades of his supporters to voter registration centers were all memorable images from Jackson's 1984 campaign.[1] One newspaper reporter, attempting early to assess the impact, wrote, "Jesse Jackson is leading a revival of black political interests the likes of which black activists say they have not witnessed for many years."[2] "It feels a lot like the '6os," said Mary

Young, a black Georgia state representative from Albany. "And I don't think it's going to die."[3]

Jackson spoke of building a broad coalition. "Blacks, Hispanics, women, children, and workers need each other. That's the coalition. That's the rainbow coalition."[4] After pointing out that 24 million of the nation's 35 million poor people are white, the candidate asserted: "Now it is not the blackness or whiteness of the matter, because Reagan is so aristocratic and pro-rich that it doesn't matter what color the poor are. We must fight to open the door of opportunity . . . ."[5]

Despite the rhetorical appeal to whites, Jackson received most of his support in 1984 from blacks and focused the public spotlight on issues of particular concern to blacks. To white Democratic leaders in the South trying to hold together their uneasy biracial coalition, activity that called attention to racial divisions was not welcome. For example, Jackson argued that runoff primaries discriminate against blacks and urged their abolition, a course that drew heavy opposition from white leaders fearful of what would happen to their winning coalitions if more blacks became Democratic nominees.[6]

After the Mondale defeat, there was more than a little discussion within the Democratic party over whether blacks should have a lower profile in the party.[7] The debate, in fact, prompted state Senator Julian Bond of Georgia to remark: "If blacks lay any lower in the Democratic Party we will be in China. All of this talk is coming from those who, unlike blacks, couldn't deliver their constituencies for the ticket."[8] The debate lingered on unresolved into 1988 as Jackson began his second presidential campaign. In May 1987, Senator Ernest F. Hollings of South Carolina, no admirer of Jackson,[9] pointed the finger of blame at the black leader for what he saw as recent GOP gains in the South among conservative white Democrats: "When Jesse stood up and said, 'My time has come' and 'We want it all,' they went in droves and as a result we got a Republican governor in South Carolina."[10] Tyrone Brooks, a black state representative from Georgia who supported Jackson in 1984, expressed concern in late 1987 over Jackson's future effect: "I believe Jackson's candidacy may in fact contribute to the further alienation of conservative whites and Democrats, who will go and vote Republican in the general election."[11]

Various black and white Democratic leaders, some more partial to Jackson than those quoted above, held other and different views of Jackson's ultimate impact. A final assessment of his role must await the playing out of events yet to come. What is important to note here, however, is that the tensions highlighted by Jackson's vigorous presence on the political scene were merely a continuation of those evident in the

Southern Democracy throughout the post-civil rights era, tensions which remain central to the region's partisan future, as was emphasized in Chapter 15.

An updated snapshot of public partisan leanings reveals only small shifts since 1980 and thus corroborates other evidence pointing to the lack of any drastic change in the Southern partisan environment over the last few years. Table 18-1 shows a three percentage point decline in Democratic party identification among Southern whites, down to 40 percent in 1986 from the 43 percent in 1980 registered in Table 15-1. There was a two-point drop among white Northern Democrats. Republican party identification hardly increased at all among whites in the South but was five percentage points higher among Northern whites in 1986.[12]

In addition to the persistence of intra-Democratic tensions and the general stability of partisan identification, Southern states continued to experience further nationalization of their politics. Texas and Florida have been leaders in this process. Perusal of the party strength figures for the eleven states as extended to cover the 1984 and 1986 elections suggests that, as in other regions of the country, diversity within Dixie could become as important as regional similarity. The eleven figures, displayed in Chapters 4 through 14, reveal that from 1984 to 1986 six states witnessed a drop in Democratic party strength while the other five experienced a rise in Democratic strength. Earlier differences among the states over the arrival of two-party competition—also shown in the eleven figures—have been documented at length. The most recent divergences contain the hint that at some future point it may well be as hard to find common patterns concerning the partisan paths of, say, Alabama, Georgia, and South Carolina, as it is to do so for Illinois, Indiana, and Ohio. Certainly these three Midwestern states share common features in their electoral politics. Yet it is well recognized that they are distinctive political entities with different political traditions generated by various demographic, social, economic, and historical differences. Therefore, although a persisting Southern politics could still be discerned, its diminishing dimensions were manifest in the waning days of the 1980s.

Occasionally an indicator of the ongoing nationalization of Southern politics surfaces and causes the rest of the country to stand up and take note of a "new South." Such occurred in the fall of 1987 when every Southern Democratic senator save one voted against confirmation of the Supreme Court nomination of Judge Robert Bork, the conservative constitutional law scholar. President Reagan's choice was vigorously opposed by civil rights groups, and opposition in the Senate was led by

Table 18-1. Race, Region, and Party Identification in 1986

	All	South Whites	Blacks	All	North Whites	Blacks
Democrat	48%	40%	71%	37%	33%	78%
Republican	21	26	6	28	31	2
Independent	32	35	24	34	36	20
	101%	101%	101%	99%	100%	100%
	741	560	181	1333	1197	136

	All	Nation Whites	Blacks
Democrat	41%	35%	74%
Republican	26	29	4
Independent	33	36	22
	100%	100%	100%
N	2074	1757	317

SOURCE: National Election Study, 1986. Center for Political Studies, University of Michigan. These cross-tabulations were kindly provided by Professor Alan I. Abramowitz of Emory University, to whom the author is very appreciative for this help.

several of the party's prominent Northern liberals. While the Bork fight was a dramatic, high visibility episode, recent studies of congressional voting records have revealed growing cohesion among Democrats, North and South. Before the Bork vote, for example, the *Congressional Quarterly* published a cover story on what it called the "fading alliance" of Southern Democrats and Republicans, the famed Conservative Coalition. "What is clear right now," CQ wrote in August 1987, "is that Southern Democrats simply are not casting many votes with Republicans anymore."[13] In general, the interesting and important effect that the ongoing nationalization of Southern politics is having on America's major political institutions is only beginning to unfold and deserves to be followed closely in the future.

Realignment and Southern Politics

As politicians and political spectators pondered the results of the 1984 elections, there was much talk of realignment in the air. Scores of newspaper articles appeared asking, almost breathlessly, "Have we had a realignment?" "Is it just around the corner?" As polls in the first months following that election showed an increase in Republican party identification in the South and in the rest of the country, the question of realignment was raised again and again. When a few Southern politicians held news conferences to announce they were switching from the Democratic party to the GOP, the same term, realignment, was trotted out to explain what was happening. No doubt, in the 1988 election season more of the same will be heard.

The realignment literature is vast.[14] It began with V. O. Key's influential 1955 article "A Theory of Critical Elections."[15] In this article Key called attention to certain important elections that stood out from the rest and seemed to mark major changes. In discussing these critical elections, Professor Key defined the realignment concept in a back-handed fashion:

> Even the most fleeting inspection of American elections suggests the existence of a category of elections in which voters are, at least from impressionistic evidence, unusually deeply concerned, in which the extent of electoral involvement is relatively quite high, and in which the decisive results of the voting reveal a sharp alteration of the pre-existing cleavage within the electorate. Moreover, and perhaps this is the truly differentiating characteristic of this sort of election, the realignment made manifest in the voting in such elections seems to persist for several succeeding elections.[16]

As was characteristic of Key's modesty and sense of proportion, he did not get carried away with the patterns he depicted. "Obviously any sort of system for the gross characterization of elections," he wrote in conclusion, "presents difficulties in application." Key continued: "The actual election rarely presents in a pure form a case fitting completely any particular concept. Especially in a large and diverse electorate a single polling may encompass radically varying types of behavior among different categories of voters;[17] yet a dominant characteristic often makes itself apparent."[18]

A fuller understanding of Key's approach to realignment is to be found not in this article or in a second well-known one,[19] but in the approach he uses to explain electoral changes in his textbook *Politics, Parties, and Pressure Groups*.[20] There Key places strong emphasis on American political history. At every turn he stresses the complexity and constantly changing nature of the party system in our large and diverse country, asserting midway through the text, "The party system exists in a continual state of flux."[21] Employing careful generalizations firmly rooted in the historical context, Key in this book offers considerable analytical insight into the flux evident in his time. In my view, the most valuable and enduring lesson that Key teaches about electoral change is one of orientation to the study of the subject matter.

If Key offered guidance and a sense of the importance of political history, James L. Sundquist demonstrated the value of the systematic mining of the historical record in search of theoretical insight into the party system's "continual state of flux." Following the lead of Key and E. E. Schattschneider,[22] Sundquist defines realignment as "those redistributions of party support, of whatever scale or pace, that reflect a change in the structure of the party conflict and hence the establishment of a new line of partisan cleavage on a different axis within the electorate."[23] In the process of reaching this definition, Sundquist wrote an invaluable eleven-page conceptual guide to the often contradictory realignment literature, entitled "The Muddied Concept of Party Realignment."[24] He discusses various dimensions of the realignment concept—such as magnitude, durability, geographic scope, and pace of change—as well as the conflict-displacement dimension that he finds central to his definition of realignment. The bulk of Sundquist's book consists of a lucid examination of the candidates, issues, and events that agitated the nation from the 1830s into the early 1980s. Drawing from this vast record, he offers various propositions that flesh out his valuable concept of realignment, which amount to a series of sophisticated generalizations that comprehensively explain the major electoral changes in U.S. history up to the current era.

Both Key and Sundquist remind us that even during drastic changes in the party system, such as occurred during the Civil War era, there remains a not insignificant residue from what went before. Sundquist likens the process to the drawing of "new patterns on transparent overlays."[25] Key makes this same point by showing how the electoral map of Tennessee in the 1940s still reflected in pronounced fashion the cleavages formed in that state in the 1860s.[26]

This is not the place to review the realignment field further except to mention the widespread application of the realignment notion to recent Southern politics. It seems that nearly every writing on partisan developments in the region, no matter how brief or how thin the data base, must make some contribution to the realignment debate.[27] If realignment is not found, then something else—dealignment being the most handy current idea—is offered to account for the big changes that have taken place in the South.[28] This propensity to put insubstantial labels on complex historical processes is not carrying the task of understanding very far. The closer the acquaintance with the complex, contradictory reality of electoral politics, the greater should be the reluctance to engage in any premature quest to bring abstract order where it does not belong.

What then is the answer to the perennial question: Has there been an electoral realignment in Southern politics? A moment's reflection over the insights of Key and Sundquist coupled with a quick review of the considerable Southern electoral flux of the last several decades ought to put the realignment question in the proper perspective it needs and make the answer obvious.

What happened in the South? The story begins with the destruction of the rationale for the one-party system and traces in detail the rise of two-party competition both at the regional level and in each of the eleven states. The various party-strength figures throughout this book chart the tortuous course the historical process has taken. What explains the twists and turns visible in the rise of partisan competition in the various Southern states and in the region as a whole? Obviously, one must get close to the partisan scene in each state to have a chance of answering that question. And the answer will not come merely in the sentence: There was a partisan realignment (or dealignment or whatever) in the South.

In such superficial use of realignment, the concept becomes a mere synonym for change. And, of change there is and always will be plenty in human affairs. The point is not to see something change and to shout at it: There is change! Rather, one must try to understand the nature of the change, explain why it is happening, and analyze its antecedents and its likely direction.

These are all tasks in regard to Southern politics that this book has tackled, making it then, if one prefers the term, a lengthy treatment of the realignment (that is, of the considerable change) that has occurred in Southern electoral politics in recent decades. Thus, when the old re-alignment issue is resurrected after yet another sequence of elections in Dixie, one should recognize it for the shorthand that it has become and get on with the more exciting and meaningful labor of figuring out exactly what happened and what it means.

19
Postscript:
The 1988 Elections
and Beyond

No Southerner of whatever partisan inclination could complain about a lack of attention from the national parties during the 1988 presidential election season. Both national conventions were held in the South—the Democrats' in Atlanta and the Republicans' in New Orleans. Both national presidential standard-bearers had Southern strategies: Vice President George Bush's being endemic to his political roots and Governor Michael Dukakis's demonstrated by his selection of Senator Lloyd Bentsen of Texas as his running mate. (In the end Dukakis's seemed misplaced, but the hindsight of November is of no value in July.) And, of course there was that unprecedented event of March 8, 1988—Super Tuesday—when virtually the entire South (South Carolina being the lone exception) and the border states, along with a handful of Western and New England states, chose their convention delegates.

After sewing up the nomination prior to the Atlanta convention, Dukakis made a three-day campaign swing in June through seven Southern states, meeting with various Democratic politicians, including Alabama's George Wallace. The Massachusetts governor declared in Montgomery: "I'm serious . . . about campaigning hard in the South, working hard in the South and winning the South."[1] In introducing the candidate at an outdoor rally, Lt. Governor Jim Folsom, Jr., of Alabama, exclaimed: "Mike Dukakis believes in the same things Alabamians believe in. He believes in a strong defense, a strong family, a strong economy that provides jobs for all its citizens."[2] Throughout his Southern tour, Dukakis emphasized his record as a battler against crime and drugs. As Robin Toner of the New York Times reported: "He attended a flag-raising ceremony with police cadets in Miami. He preached the dangers of drug abuse to youngsters in Florence, S.C. He met with 60 criminal justice officials from around the country, accepted their endorsement and kicked off their efforts as 'crime fighters for Dukakis.' "[3]

Foreshadowing what was to come, Republican orators preceded Dukakis at each stop, branding him a "Teddy Kennedy liberal" who is soft on crime. Dukakis brushed off the GOP surrogates. To quote from Toner's account:

> "They sent some guy from Arizona [Senator John McCain] into Florida who doesn't know beans from brown bread," he said in Biloxi. "I don't think that's a particularly helpful or frankly winning campaign. I say that because I think the American people are tired of this stuff."
>
> Mr. Dukakis, who was also assailed by Vice President Bush last week as a Harvard liberal, indicated that he was not yet ready to fight back. "If I'm attacked there may come a time when I have to respond," he said. "I hope not."[4]

Of course, Dukakis's slowness to respond to Republican attacks against him on a variety of emotional issues became a central controversy in the fall campaign. These issues—his management of a Massachusetts prison furlough program that released Willie Horton, a black convicted murderer who went on to commit further crimes; his veto of a Massachusetts bill imposing penalties for public school teachers who refused to lead their students in the Pledge of Allegiance; his opposition to the death penalty, among others—dogged his campaign in the region and in the nation. The headline on a *New York Times* article about a Dukakis campaign rally in Hawkinsville, Ga., in late October conveyed the state of affairs: "Dukakis Fights Negative Image in South."[5] In a television appeal broadcast at the time of this rural Georgia rally, Dukakis lashed out at the GOP "campaign of distortion and distraction, of fear and smear."[6] The Georgia trip, incidentally, was one of the Democrat's rare Southern forays in the last part of the campaign, when the hope of a successful Democratic Southern strategy had evaporated. The Southern front was abandoned to the nominee's running mate, Senator Bentsen.[7]

While Willie Horton and the Pledge of Allegiance were smears to the Democrats, for Republicans they were simply symptomatic of what the public gets from "traditional liberals," as Bush labeled his opponent during a visit to Memphis. "If we are successful in getting the truth out there, they [Democrats] will be unsuccessful in drawing the traditional

Southern Democrats and Southwest Democrats back into the fold," the Vice President said at a rally held on a picturesque site near the Mississippi River.[8]

In a visit to Raleigh, N.C., President Reagan boosted his former running mate with a powerful dose of Democrat-bashing, at which he remained the recognized master: "The opposition can say that ideology and values don't matter. The opposition can try to hide what they believe. Wasn't George Bush right when he said the opposition is over there in left field . . . and their policies can only be described by the dreaded L-word—liberal, liberal, liberal."[9] The President asserted that the Republican party is now the party of Franklin D. Roosevelt and Harry Truman: "It is often said that the once-proud Democratic Party of FDR and Harry Truman is dead and gone. The party of FDR and Harry Truman couldn't be killed. . . . The secret is that when the left took over the Democratic Party leadership, we took over the Republican Party."[10]

Throughout the campaign, the Republican orators repeatedly stressed the economic growth and prosperity with low inflation that occurred during President Reagan's two terms, the strengthening of America's military forces, and the improvement of relations with the Soviet Union. They warned of dire consequences to economic and defense policies if the "Democratic wrecking crew" of the late 1970s—the Carter years—returned to power.

When the votes were counted, it was a decisive Republican victory nationwide, 53.4 percent to 45.6 percent. Bush handily carried all eleven Southern states (see Table 19-1) and twenty-nine others. Dukakis won ten states, running through the northern tier of the country from Massachusetts to Oregon and Washington, along with the District of Columbia.

Bush's Southern margin of victory far exceeded his vote in the rest of the nation. In the eleven states of the South, which accounted for a quarter of the popular votes, Bush had 58.3 percent to 40.9 for Dukakis; in the other thirty-nine states and the District of Columbia, the total was 51.7 percent to 47.1 percent. As is demonstrated in Table 19-2, the demographics of the various partisan categories of Southern voters did not differ greatly from those in the Reagan elections. (For a comparison in these categories with 1984, refer to Table 16-4 on pages 240–41.)

Dukakis improved on Mondale's support among Southern whites, going from a regional average of 28 percent in 1984 to 32 percent in 1988.[11] There were, of course, variations in white support among the Southern states; these are suggested in Table 19-1, which also lists the percentage of the population that is black in each state next to the

Table 19-1 Vote for President in 1988 in the South and in the Ten Highest
Democratic States Outside of the South

	Bush	Dukakis	Percentage Black 1980
Deep South			
Mississippi	59.9%	39.1%	35.2%
South Carolina	61.5	37.6	30.4
Louisiana	54.3	44.1	29.4
Georgia	59.8	39.5	26.8
Alabama	59.2	39.9	25.6
Rim South			
North Carolina	58.0	41.7	22.4
Virginia	59.7	39.2	18.9
Arkansas	56.4	42.2	16.3
Tennessee	57.9	41.5	15.8
Florida	60.7	38.5	13.8
Texas	56.0	43.3	12.0
Dukakis's States			
Rhode Island	43.9%	55.7%	2.7
Iowa	44.5	54.7	1.4
Hawaii	44.8	54.3	1.8
Massachusetts	45.4	53.2	3.8
Minnesota	45.9	52.9	1.3
West Virginia	47.5	52.2	3.3
New York	47.5	51.6	13.7
Wisconsin	47.8	51.4	3.9
Oregon	46.6	51.3	1.4
Washington	48.5	50.0	2.6

Democratic vote. Since blacks voted around 90 percent for Dukakis, Dukakis obviously received a higher proportion of white votes in states like Texas and Tennessee than he did in Mississippi and South Carolina. The exit polls in Table 19-3 confirm these patterns. (By way of contrast, the second panel of Table 19-1 shows Dukakis's vote in the ten states he won coupled with a display of the relatively low percentages of blacks in those states. These North-South comparisons are full of future national implications for both parties, but, unfortunately, that topic would carry us too far afield.)

The result of seeing the sharp racial polarization in the black-white Southern voting trends spurred yet another round of hand-wringing over "white flight" from the Democratic party by national commentators whose quadrennial focus on the Southern situation seems always to be accompanied by outbursts of amazement at patterns well established for

Table 19-2. The 1988 Presidential Vote by Party Identification, Income, Age, and Sex

| | | Southern Whites | |
	Democrats	Republicans	Independents
Bush	29%	97%	62%
Dukakis	71	3	38
	100%	100%	100%
N	103	87	82

| | | Northern Whites | |
	Democrats	Republicans	Independents
Bush	15%	91%	57%
Dukakis	85	9	43
	100%	100%	100%
N	220	308	238

| | | Southern Whites | |
	Under $15,000	$15,000 to $35,000	Over $35,000
Bush	51%	59%	71%
Dukakis	49	41	30
	100%	100%	101%
N	57	106	95

| | | Northern Whites | |
	Under $15,000	$15,000 to $35,000	Over $35,000
Bush	54%	56%	65%
Dukakis	46	44	35
	100%	100%	100%
N	142	252	304

| | | Southern Whites | |
	18–39	40–59	Over 60
Bush	63%	56%	65%
Dukakis	37	44	35
	100%	100%	100%
N	110	98	65

| | | Northern Whites | |
	18–39	40–59	Over 60
Bush	60%	58%	57%
Dukakis	40	42	43
	100%	100%	100%
N	282	257	229

Table 19.2. (Continued)

| | Southern Whites | |
	Males	Females
Bush	67%	55%
Dukakis	33	45
	100%	100%
N	133	140

| | Northern Whites | |
	Males	Females
Bush	59%	57%
Dukakis	41	43
	100%	100%
N	345	423

SOURCE: National Election Study, 1988. Center for Political Studies, University of Michigan.

over two decades. For example, Tom Wicker, the veteran *New York Times* writer, began a widely circulated post-election column as follows:

A fundamental reason why Democratic nominees have lost five of the last six Presidential elections . . . is that in these national contests Republican victories have been very nearly lily-white. . . .

Why has this happened? Unquestionably because the Democratic Party has become associated in the public mind with blacks—partly because blacks have been voting heavily Democratic . . . partly because the Democrats in their eight years of Presidential power since 1964 sponsored most of the programs that many whites think benefit blacks disproportionately . . . and partly because of recurrent campaign phenomena like Jesse Jackson's high visibility in the Democratic Party and Willie Horton's in this year's Republican television appeals.

Michael Dukakis would have lost the 1988 election in any case, because peace, prosperity and patriotism—all embodied in Ronald Reagan—were working for Bush. But white flight into the Republican Party, in all regions of the county but most spectacularly in the South, will be a palpable, continuing, virtually fatal problem for the Democrats as far ahead as a poll-taker can see.

This is not racism in a sheet and a hood; it is a race consciousness in a white as well as a blue collar. It is the dominant, underlying fact of modern national elections, year after year. Republicans who deny that they exploit it are disingenuous; Democrats who pretend that they can win anyway are whistling past the graveyard.[12]

No one could deny that Republicans have made subtle racial appeals in the Reagan era. Roger Ailes and Lee Atwater's effective use of Willie

Table 19-3. Exit Poll Estimates of the Vote for President
by Race in the South in 1988

| | Whites | | Blacks | |
	Bush	Dukakis	Bush	Dukakis
Alabama	72%	27%	9%	90%
Arkansas	65	34	9	91
Florida	63	36	23	77
Georgia	73	27	8	91
Louisiana	69	30	3	96
Mississippi	78	21	7	92
North Carolina	65	35	11	87
South Carolina	76	24	8	92
Tennessee	66	34	8	91
Texas*	65	34	6	93
Virginia	69	30	9	88
South**	67	32	7	92

*Texas Hispanics supported Dukakis by 75 percent to Bush's 24 percent.
**Includes Kentucky, Oklahoma, and West Virginia.

SOURCE: Surveys conducted by ABC News at polling places on November 8, 1988, and contained in the 874-page data book published by the television network as Carolyn Smith, ed., *The '88 Vote* (New York: Capital Cities/ABC, Inc., 1989).

Horton[13] had its counterparts in earlier campaigns, such as, Reagan's "welfare queen" of 1980. The racial element in the GOP's "new Southern strategy" has been recounted at several places above.[14]

Still, as with the Reagan results, to argue that race was a factor in Bush's Southern victory is not to contend it was *the* factor. I am convinced that the North-South disparity in white Democratic support would have lessened significantly had the public's attention in the campaign been focused on economic issues and not on highly charged social issues. Table 16-5 (pages 244–47) demonstrated that Southern and Northern whites hold similar views on economic and domestic role-of-government matters, but Southern whites are more conservative than Northern whites on racial and public morality issues (the famed Social Issue, as this cluster has been effectively dubbed) and on foreign and defense matters. The 1988 survey data conform to this general pattern; see Table 19-4. It is the hope of national Democrats that they can turn a presidential campaign on the questions that unite their white supporters across regions while continuing to attract nearly solid support among America's blacks.

Moving below the presidential level in the 1988 election season, one finds a partisan environment that is evolving along lines quite familiar to

Table 19-4. Attitudes on Various Public Policy Issues and the Vote for President in 1988

1. Economic Class and Role-of Government Questions
Cut Services to Save Money

	Southern Whites			Northern Whites		
	Cut	Neutral	More Services	Cut	Neutral	More Services
Bush	74%	62%	37%	78%	59%	37%
Dukakis	26	38	63	22	41	63
	100%	100%	100%	100%	100%	100%
N	90	74	70	252	199	214
	(39%)	(32%)	(30%)	(38%)	(30%)	(32%)

Question: Some people think the government should provide fewer services, even in areas such as health and education, in order to reduce spending. Suppose these people are at one end of the scale at point number 1. Other people feel it is important for government to provide many more services even if it means an increase in spending. Suppose these people are at the other end, at point 7. And, of course, some other people have opinions somewhere in between. . . . Where would you place yourself on this scale . . .? [Points 2 and 3 were combined with point 1 for ease in handling; points 5 and 6 went with point 7. Point 4, the middle slot, was labled neutral. All seven-point scales in the table were handled in this manner.]

Role of Government on Jobs and Standard of Living

	Southern Whites			Northern Whites		
	Gov't Do It	Neutral	Self Help	Gov't Do It	Neutral	Self Help
Bush	34%	52%	72%	38%	48%	73%
Dukakis	66	48	28	62	52	27
	100%	100%	100%	100%	100%	100%
N	47	42	154	133	162	379
	(19%)	(17%)	(63%)	(20%)	(24%)	(56%)

Questions: Some people feel the government in Washington should see to it that every person has a job and a good standard of living. Others think the government should just let each person get ahead on his own. Where would you place yourself [on a seven-point scale]?

2. Foreign Policy and Defense Issues
Level of Defense Spending

	Southern Whites			Northern Whites		
	Decrease	Neutral	Increase	Decrease	Neutral	Increase
Bush	30%	60%	81%	37%	64%	77%
Dukakis	70	40	19	63	36	23
	100%	100%	100%	100%	100%	100%
N	64	79	104	228	273	218
	(26%)	(32%)	(42%)	(32%)	(38%)	(30%)

Question: Some people believe that we should spend much less money for defense. Others feel that defense spending should be greatly increased. Where would you place yourself [on a seven-point scale]?

Proper Approach to the Russians

	Southern Whites			Northern Whites		
	Cooperate More	Neutral	Get Tougher	Cooperate More	Neutral	Get Tougher
Bush	52%	70%	72%	49%	64%	69%
Dukakis	48	30	28	51	36	31
	100%	100%	100%	100%	100%	100%
N	87	50	105	331	182	194
	(36%)	(21%)	(43%)	(47%)	(26%)	(27%)

Question: Some people feel it is important for us to try to cooperate more with Russia, while others believe we should be much tougher in our dealings with Russia. Where would you place yourself [on a seven-point scale]?

3. Cluster of Social Questions
Place of Civil Rights Effort

	Southern Whites			Northern Whites		
	Too Fast	About Right	Too Slowly	Too Fast	About Right	Too Slowly
Bush	71%	58%	33%	70%	60%	26%
Dukakis	29	42	67	30	40	74
	100%	100%	100%	100%	100%	100%
N	100	143	21	179	472	88
	(38%)	(54%)	(8%)	(24%)	(64%)	(12%)

Question: Some say that the civil rights people have been trying to push too fast. Others feel they haven't pushed fast enough. . . . Do you think that civil rights leaders are trying to push too fast, are going too slowly, or are they moving at about the right speed?

Abortion

	Southern Whites				Northern Whites			
	Never	Only Rape, etc.	Clear Need	Always	Never	Only Rape, etc.	Clear Need	Always
Bush	71%	66%	68%	48%	59%	68%	57%	51%
Dukakis	29	34	32	52	41	32	43	49
	100%	100%	100%	100%	100%	100%	100%	100%
N	34	96	53	89	73	244	159	282
	(13%)	(35%)	(20%)	(33%)	(10%)	(32%)	(21%)	(37%)

Question: There has been some discussion about abortion during recent years. Which one of the options on this page best agrees with your view?
1. By law, abortion should never be permitted.
2. The law should permit abortion only in case of rape, incest or when the woman's life is in danger.
3. The law should permit abortion for reasons *other than* rape, incest or danger to the woman's life, but only after the need for the abortion has been clearly established.
4. By law, a woman should always be able to obtain an abortion as a matter of personal choice.

SOURCE: National Election Study, 1988. Center for Political Studies, University of Michigan.

students of recent Southern politics. At the least visible level—state legislative races—Republicans continued their glacial upward movement, occupying 25.4 percent of the region's legislative seats after the 1988 elections compared with 22.7 percent following the 1986 balloting. Many of the gains came in North Carolina[15] and Georgia[16], where the GOP surge was impressive, but other states contributed here and there. The partisan balance in U.S. House seats remained the same, 39 of the 116 seats (or 33.6 percent) won by Republicans in 1988. The GOP picked up two seats in Florida while losing two in Texas, and a Democratic success in Georgia was offset by a Republican gain in Louisiana.[17] (In February 1989 a U.S. representative in Florida switched to the Republican party, and an Arkansas congressman made a similar move in July 1989. Thus, going into the 1990 elections, the GOP total increased to 41 seats.[18])

High-visibility statewide races were scarce in 1988. Only five U.S. Senate seats were up for election in the region, and there was a lone gubernatorial contest, in North Carolina, the only Southern state that still elects its major state officers in a presidential election year.

James G. (Jim) Martin, the Tar Heel State's popular moderate Republican governor, easily won re-election, defeating Lt. Governor Robert B. Jordan 3d, the Democratic nominee, 56.1 percent to 43.9 percent. According to the Raleigh *News and Observer*, Martin "carved out a record as a moderate conservative who emphasized tax cuts for business, a merit-pay program for teachers, and initiatives for building schools and more highways."[19] He deflected Democratic assertions that he was an inefficient, if congenial, governor, displaying in the words of a GOP partisan a "Teflon coating."[20] Jordan, a "moderate, business-oriented Democrat [with a] wooden speaking style," in the characterization of the *News and Observer*, committed a major gaffe early in the campaign during an address before black newspaper executives. He told the executives "he could not publicly support all the issues on which they agreed because he did not want to offend the 'redneck vote' in Eastern North Carolina."[21] The remark received wide publicity and did not help Jordan's effort to unify North Carolina's Democratic black-white coalition.

The only two incumbent U.S. senators running for re-election in 1988, both Democrats, were easily returned: Senator James R. (Jim) Sasser of Tennessee[22] and Senator Bentsen,[23] who followed Lyndon Johnson's 1960 example and wisely chose an "insurance" campaign in case of national defeat. Charles S. (Chuck) Robb, Virginia's former Democratic governor, effortlessly claimed a seat left open by the failure of a first-term Republican incumbent to seek re-election.[24]

The remaining two Senate elections were the only really interesting

Southern statewide battles of 1988—open seats being vacated by a pair of Democrats, Senator Lawton Chiles of Florida and Senator John Stennis of Mississippi. Hard-fought Republican victories in each gave the GOP a boost in the category of major statewide offices and made up for its Virginia Senate seat loss. After the 1988 elections, the party held twelve of the region's thirty-three governorships and U.S. Senate seats, or 36.4 percent, compared to eleven (33.3 percent) after the 1986 voting.

In Florida, U.S. Representative Connie Mack, a conservative Republican, edged out U.S. Representative Buddy MacKay, the Democratic nominee, 50.4 percent to 49.6 percent. Mack hammered at MacKay as too liberal for Florida, ending his many television spots with the refrain, "Hey Buddy, you're liberal!"[25] MacKay countered by calling Mack "an extremist" and placing himself in the mainstream. "Anyone who wants to call me liberal is having to defy the facts in order to do that," MacKay said.[26]

In Mississippi, U.S. Representative Trent Lott, the polished, aggressive, conservative House Republican whip, defeated U.S. Representative Wayne Dowdy, a folksy moderate Democrat who related well to rural and small-town whites and who cultivated strong ties with blacks. Lott received 53.9 percent to Dowdy's 46.1 percent. Lott's well-financed campaign quickly took the offensive to blunt any possible attacks on Lott's conservative record. According to a *Congressional Quarterly Weekly Report* summary, Lott "was on the air early with ads touting himself as a leader in strengthening the Social Security system, pledging his allegiance to student loans, and showing his concern for bringing in federal money to improve Mississippi's roads."[27] Lott sought support among rural and low-income whites by pointing out that "his father farmed cotton and drove a school bus [while calling] Dowdy, whose family owns a number of radio stations, a millionaire, country-club type."[28] Exit polls reveal Dowdy's weak support among whites in 1988. See Table 19-5, which displays the racial breakdowns for each of the 1988 senatorial elections.

The Republican party also scored several notable victories for lesser statewide offices, positions from which they had been virtually shut out until the 1988 elections. In North Carolina, James C. (Jim) Gardner, a former congressman and the GOP's 1968 gubernatorial nominee, narrowly won election as lieutenant governor, defeating state Senator Tony Rand, a Democrat from Fayetteville, 50.7 percent to 49.3 percent. In Florida, Jim Smith, a former Democratic state attorney general and unsuccessful Democratic gubernatorial runoff candidate in 1986, was elected secretary of state with 63.1 percent of the vote. Smith had switched to the

Table 19-5. Exit Poll Estimates of the Vote for Senator by Race
in the South in 1988

| | Whites | | Blacks | |
	Democrat	Republican	Democrat	Republican
Florida	45%	55%	80%	20%
Mississippi	27	73 '	91	9
Tennessee	57	42	94	5
Texas*	53	46	93	7
Virginia	67	33	83	17

*Texas Hispanics supported the Democrat (Bentsen) by 84 to his Republican opponent's 15 percent.

SOURCE: See documentation in Table 19-3.

GOP and been appointed to the post by Florida's Republican governor.[29] In Texas another Democrat-turned-Republican, Kent Hance, won a state-wide race with 55.0 percent of the vote for a seat on the Railroad Commission, a powerful state regulatory body. Hance had been appointed to a vacancy on the commission by the state's Republican governor.[30]

As usual when examining a multiplicity of partisan elections below the presidential contest, it is not always easy to find a dominant pattern. A useful statistic, relied on throughout this book, is Paul David's index of Democratic party strength, a composite of the vote for governor, U.S. senator, and U.S. representative. After the 1988 elections the regional figure for the Democrats went up to 58.3 percent from 55.2 percent in 1986. This consistently strong Democratic party-strength figure ought to give pause to anyone taking the view that the 1988 elections in the South contained something strikingly new. Careful pondering of the political events of that year should place the recent balloting within the context of an on-going regional transformation that is at least two and a half decades old. Such an exercise in taking the long view focuses attention squarely on Dixie's still dominant—if harried—black-white Democratic coalition.

A year later in Virginia the black-white alliance passed a dramatic test that drew national and even international attention to Southern politics. On November 7, 1989, Lt. Governor L. Douglas Wilder, a Democrat, became the first African-American elected governor of a state in the nation's history. In the closest gubernatorial election ever conducted in Virginia, Wilder defeated J. Marshall Coleman, the Republican nominee and a former state attorney general,[31] with 50.1 percent to Coleman's 49.8 percent, a margin of victory of only 6,854 votes out of nearly 1.8 million cast.

The abortion issue dominated the campaign. When the U.S. Supreme Court in July 1989 indicated in *Webster* that states may be allowed greater latitude in regulating abortions than permitted under the famous 1973 case of *Roe v. Wade*, abortion-rights activists were galvanized nationwide, and their energetic efforts showed results in several 1989 elections besides Virginia's. A mid-October *New York Times* article captured the issue's impact on the Wilder-Coleman race:

> The dominance of the abortion issue was starkly evident in a debate on Monday night . . . . Mr. Wilder, who favors few restrictions, repeatedly brought up the subject, each time reminding the statewide television audience that Mr. Coleman was on record as opposing all abortions except when the life of the pregnant woman is in danger [but making no exception in case of rape or incest] Mr. Coleman, seemingly frustrated by the Wilder tactic, finally snapped at his opponent, "It's the only issue you have."[32]

Race never became an overt issue in the campaign,[33] but it hovered in the background and suffused the contest in a subtle manner that was doubtless unavoidable given the historic potential of a Wilder victory. Larry Sabato, the youthful dean of Virginia's political analysts, skillfully evaluated the role of race in an invaluable 88-page analysis of the election. He wrote:

> No issue has been as powerful as or poisonous in Virginia history as race, so it was inevitable that Wilder's blackness would color the campaign from start to finish. Yet the impact of this simple fact was variegated and somewhat contradictory: race cut both ways, and simultaneously helped and hurt Wilder. . . .
>
> Wilder's color probably cost him tens of thousands of votes on election day. Exactly how many will never be known, but many conservative Democrats and independents otherwise inclined to vote Democratic simply could not pull Wilder's lever. That Coleman influenced them by introducing serious doubts about Wilder's character played a role, but race was likely part of the mix as well.
>
> The other side of the equation is at least as weighty, however: Wilder was assisted by his race in tangible ways. He was unopposed for the nomination for governor (and lieutenant governor in 1985) in part because of Democratic fear of losing the loyalty of black voters. Much of the money raised for his generously financed campaign came from national Democratic sources and an enthusiastic black middle class attracted by Wilder's unique status. Wilder's race (combined with party) virtually guaranteed the support of blacks and white liberals, giving Wilder the flexibility to move to the center (such as his reversal on the death penalty) without causing alienation among party activists. And in

upscale neighborhoods (especially in Northern Virginia) Wilder's race was an alluring element for high income, well educated suburbanites who seek to be cosmopolitan and sophisticated. . . . For white liberals, urbane suburbanites, and non-natives alike, a vote for Wilder became a badge of honor, objective proof that they were not racist, symbolic separation from Old Virginia and all that the painful past of segregation and massive resistance represented. . . .[34]

Exit polls show that Wilder received 41 percent of the white vote and 96 percent of the votes of blacks.[35] Black turnout (72.6 percent of those registered) was nearly eight percentage points higher than turnout for whites (65.0 percent), a figure that, Sabato reported, "startled even the Wilder camp."[36] The Democrat's strength lay in the state's two large population centers: Northern Virginia and the Hampton Roads cities of Newport News, Norfolk, and Portsmouth.[37]

Wilder's victory also represents a remarkable personal success story, which is conveyed well in a profile article written many months before the election by B. Drummond Ayres, Jr., of the *New York Times:*

[I]s Virginia . . . ready to make electoral history, ready to make a leap in racial faith?

"Absolutely," replied Mr. Wilder. "This is a far, far different state than it was when I got into politics 20 years ago. After all, I'm the Lieutenant Governor. A lot of people have moved into the state. There's been a lot of economic and social change, particularly up around Washington and down around Norfolk."

Mr. Wilder too has changed since those distant days when his black neighbors in Richmond's East End, newly enfranchised by changes in voting rights laws and legislative district lines, sent him to the Virginia Senate, the first black to serve there since Reconstruction.

Back then he wore his hair in a bushy Afro, voiced anger when white legislators did not invite him to their parties and pushed relentlessly for a liberal agenda from toughening anti-bias laws in housing to striking the words "massa" and "darkey" from the state song, "Carry Me Back to Old Virginia."

Today, the Afro is gone. Where once Mr. Wilder was quick to vent anger, he now is quick to head for the smoke-filled room and compromise. And one indication of how his agenda has changed is that he has begun voicing support for the death penalty.

In short, he has become a moderate in a state that is increasingly moderate.

"I'm as Virginian as any Virginian," he likes to say. "This race will not be decided on race. Virginia has moved away from that. Leadership and experience—that's what this race is all about, and that's what I've got."[38]

In Georgia in 1990 a well-known black politician and civil rights leader sought unsuccessfully to follow in Wilder's footsteps. Andrew Young, a former congressman, U.S. ambassador to the United Nations, and mayor of Atlanta, ran a low-key, centrist campaign for governor. Unlike Wilder, who was nominated by convention without opposition, Young faced two tough elections to win the Democratic nomination. Lt. Governor Zell Miller, a sixteen-year occupant of the Peach State's second spot and a wily white politician who gave Senator Herman Talmadge a spirited challenge in the Democratic primaries of 1980, easily led the field in the first primary, receiving 41 percent of the vote to Young's 29 percent with the rest going to three other white candidates. Miller handily won the August 7 runoff, garnering 62 percent of the vote to Young's 38 percent.[39]

In the earlier 1990 primaries two black candidates won major state-wide Democratic nominations, although both face heavily favored Republican incumbents in November. In South Carolina, Theo Mitchell, a veteran black state senator from Greenville, won the Democratic gubernatorial nomination with 59 percent of the vote against a white state senator from Charleston, Ernest Passailaigue, who was a relative newcomer to political life. The apparent strength of Governor Carroll Campbell, the Republican incumbent who is seeking re-election, dissuaded several prominent Palmetto State Democratic politicians from entering the race.[40] In North Carolina, Harvey Gantt, a former mayor of Charlotte and the first African-American to attend Clemson University, won a Democratic runoff primary for his party's nomination to oppose Senator Jesse Helms, the three-term Republican incumbent. Gantt received 57 percent of the vote in defeating Mike Easley, a county district attorney.[41]

There are several other interesting 1990 governor's races under way in the South as this expanded paperback edition goes to press. In Florida, Lawton Chiles, the former three-term U.S. senator who stepped down in 1988 complaining of "burnout," is seeking the Democratic gubernatorial nomination. His running mate is Buddy MacKay, fresh from his narrow 1988 Senate loss for Chiles's old seat. U.S. Representative Bill Nelson, a twelve-year Democratic incumbent from east-central Florida, was the nomination favorite prior to Chiles's late entry.[42] Governor Bob Martinez, the Republican incumbent who is running for re-election, had a low popularity rating going into the election, partly as a result of several political plunders he committed in office, starting with a fiasco over a proposed tax on services early in his term.

Ann Richards, the fiesty Texas state treasurer who came to national attention with her acerbic Bush-bashing keynote address at the 1988

Democratic National Convention, is the Democratic nominee for governor of Texas in 1990. She handily defeated Jim Mattox, the state's
attorney general, in an early April runoff that carried the "art" of negative campaigning via TV spots to new lows.[43] Clayton Williams, a folksy
multi-millionaire businessman who financed his campaign with at least
$5 million of his own money, won the Republican gubernatorial nomi-
nation without a runoff[44] and in the process established himself as a
straight-talking, homespun "cowboy" who, in the words of a newspaper
reporter, is "harkening voters back to a rugged and heroic past that is still
a large part of the Texan identity."[45]

Of the remaining three Southern governor's races in 1990,[46] one incumbent is expected to win handily: Governor Ned McWherter of Tennessee, a
Democrat, is unlikely to face a strong Republican opponent. In Alabama
there was no shortage of experienced Democratic political talent out to
defeat the first-term GOP governor, Guy Hunt, who won office as a result
of the bizarre Democratic gubernatorial events of 1986. The June 5 primary narrowed the field to two: Paul G. Hubbert, executive director of the
Alabama Education Association, who led the first primary with 32 percent
of the vote; and Don Siegelman, the state attorney general, who came in
second with 25 percent. Hubbert won the June 26 runoff and is expected to
be a strong fall opponent for Governor Hunt, who has performed his duties
credibly. Finally, in Arkansas, Governor Bill Clinton, the Democrat who
has served ten non-consecutive years in office and who harbors presidential
ambitions, is favored to win re-election, but his margin of victory will be far
narrower than in 1986. Sheffield Nelson, a wealthy Little Rock businessman and lawyer, won the Republican gubernatorial nomination in a spirited primary. Nelson defeated U.S. Representative Tommy Robinson, a
former Democrat who switched to the GOP in 1989.[47]

Ten of the South's twenty-two Senate seats come up for election in
the 1990 slot of the six-year cycle,[48] and all ten incumbents are running
for re-election. They are all favored to win in the early guessing, although out of ten it is not improbable to have a surprise upset. Seven
have only token opposition—three Democrats, Sam Nunn of Georgia,
Al Gore of Tennessee, and David Pryor of Arkansas, and, four Republicans, John Warner of Virginia, Phil Gramm of Texas, Thad Cochran of
Mississippi, and Strom Thurmond of South Carolina. The other three
senators—the Republican Helms of North Carolina, whose 1990 race
was discussed above, and two Democrats, Bennett Johnston of Louisiana and Howell Heflin of Alabama—should face more formidable opponents, but, five months before the voting, none was viewed as a loser.[49]

An update in one final area—party identification as reported by re-

Table 19-6. Race and Party Identification in 1988

	All	South Whites	Blacks	All	North Whites	Blacks
Democrat	41%	35%	61%	32%	29%	68%
Republican	22	26	9	32	34	3
Independent	37	39	30	36	37	29
	100%	100%	100%	100%	100%	100%
N	669	513	156	1259	1155	104

			Nation			
		All	Whites	Blacks		
Democrat		35%	31%	64%		
Republican		28	32	7		
Independent		36	38	30		
		99%	101%	101%		
N		1928	1668	260		

SOURCE: National Election Study, 1988. Center for Political Studies, University of Michigan.

spondents in surveys—is worth considering. Results from the latest National Election Study, the premier academic poll used throughout this book, are displayed in Table 19-6. The survey, which was gathered by in-person interviews, was conducted during the fall of 1988. Comparison with the 1980 results, which are found in the lower panels of Table 15-1 (page 213), reveals continued white defection from the Democratic party. Democratic identification among Southern whites dropped eight percentage points during the eight years. (The changes in the North, once again, are fascinating but are beyond the scope of the topic here.) The Republican column, however, was not the beneficiary using this measure, rising a mere percentage point.[50] Rather, Southern white respondents claiming independent status increased markedly and account for the bulk of the Democratic loss. As the decade of the 1990s unfolds, future updates of the cells of Table 19-6 will offer a first glimpse of new partisan directions.

Toward the Twenty-first Century

Shifting attention from the immediate past to the future, I wish to discuss four political trends that I foresee evolving in the years leading from the present into the next century.[51]

1. The black-white Democratic coalition will persist, but it will grow weaker as the deep tensions in that party drive portions of the white wing into the waiting arms of the Republicans. The broad-based nature of the

Table 19-7. Partisanship and Ideology of State Legislative Candidates
by Region in 1980

| | Democrats | | | Republicans | | |
	Deep South (n=43)	Rim South (n=77)	North (n=69)	Deep South (n=61)	Rim South (n=111)	North (n=74)
Strong National Identification	21%	50%	61%	70%	74%	74%
Strong State Identification	44	68	63	62	72	74
Supported Presidential Candidate	30	61	61	82	81	86
Ideological Liberalism	29	42	62	5	6	14
Issue Liberalism	36	46	66	15	19	25

SOURCE: Alan I. Abramowitz, "Party Leadership, Realignment, and the Nationalization of Southern Politics." Paper Delivered at the Annual Meeting of the Southern Political Science Association, Memphis, November 5-7, 1981, composite of Tables 1, 2, and 4.

resurgent Southern Democratic party of the 1970s resulted from a historical anomaly, the origins of which are described in detail above. As the Solid South era recedes into the distant past, the coalition faces very formidable odds, as is illustrated by some interesting data gathered nearly a decade ago.

Alan I. Abramowitz, then of the College of William and Mary and now of Emory University, mailed questionnaires in early 1981 to state legislative candidates in the South and the North (the Northern sample was smaller and served primarily as a reference point for the Southern data).[52] The candidates were asked about the strength of their party identification, both to the national party and to their state party, about their support for their party's presidential candidate in 1980, their ideological self-identification, and their positions on fifteen issues, which were used to construct a liberalism-conservativism issue scale. The Southern results were broken down by the venerable Deep South and Rim South divisions and are displayed in Table 19-7. Then, the Southern figures were further subdivided into rural, urban, and mixed districts; see Table 19-8.

The results bring a degree of precision to what one senses to be true through examination of more impressionistic data. First, and of less importance, the Republican party exhibits remarkable unity across the nation, although there are a few minor but interesting differences. For example, Southern Republicans are a little more conservative than their counterparts in the North. By comparison, however, the divisions among the Democrats are gigantic.

Table 19-8. Partisanship and Ideology by Degree of Urbanization and Subregion for Southern Democratic State Legislative Candidates in 1980

i	Deep South			Rim South		
	Urban Areas (n=15)	Mixed Areas (n=11)	Rural Areas (n=16)	Urban Areas (n=27)	Mixed Areas (n=26)	Rural Areas (n=24)
Strong National Identification	33%	18%	12%	59%	46%	44%
Strong State Identification	47	64	31	85	69	48
Supported Presidential Candidate	47	27	12	70	65	46
Ideological Liberalism	48	27	12	56	46	23
Issue Liberalism	40	39	30	62	46	32

SOURCE: Abramowitz, "Party Leadership, Realignment, and the Nationalization of Southern Politics," Table 6.

Democratic legislative candidates in the Deep South and particularly those in the Deep South's rural areas have very distinct differences with their counterparts in the North. For example, only 12 percent of the rural Deep South Democratic candidates had a strong national party identification or were ideological liberals, and only a similarly small percentage of them supported Carter in 1980. This contrasts sharply with the overall Northern figures, which are in the 60 percent range. Even within the Deep South, city and country showed significant differences on these questions. Is there any wonder that Michael Dukakis found the going tough in the Southern rural and small-town expanses?[3]

Although intra-Democratic cleavages are real and portentious, it does not follow that these divisions will translate into automatic GOP gains. The next three points treat other factors likely to be involved in the future process.

2. One prediction about the future is certain. The scene of competition will continue to penetrate below the high-visibility statewide level, where two-party competition is firmly rooted, to lower levels on the statewide ballot and to the state legislative and county and municipality levels.

The state legislative level is a good one to examine; to consider even less obscure offices—those at the local level—is extremely difficult because of the lack of comprehensive data. The GOP state legislative movement has been in a slow-but-steady upward direction since Watergate. See the trend line in Figure 3-1 (page 22). There are interesting variations among the states. Arkansas has an atypically weak GOP Rim South presence at this level, and South Carolina is particularly strong for the Deep South category. Detail examination of the elements peculiar to each state should suggest reasons for the state differences, but the overall future trends are of central interest here. David Sturrock, a young scholar who has investigated the Southern "down-ticket" process more thoroughly than anyone else, is at work testing a series of hypotheses concerning the process. Since his work represents the latest research in the field, his propositions are worth considering. They are:

A. Republican legislative strength will be greatest in:
   1. Counties that are urban, suburban, or are dominated by small small cities (population of 20,000 or more).
   2. Counties that regularly voted Republican before 1950, primarily mountain counties that opposed secession in the 1860s.
   3. "Interstate" counties—Those counties containing small but rapidly growing population centers, often situated on or near the periphery of major metropolitan areas, and usually traversed by an interstate highway.
B. Republican legislative strength will be least in:
   4. Historically Democratic, rural, non-interstate counties.
   5. Predominantly black areas, both rural and urban.
C. General characteristics of Republican legislative strength:
   6. Significant numbers of legislative candidacies (25 percent or more of the total number of seats in a state) and victories (10 percent of that total) will not be attained until after Republican victories have occurred in high-visibility races (both presidential *and* either gubernatorial or U.S. Senate) in a given state.
   7. Legislative strength will grow slowly and incrementally;
   8. Will be only modestly affected by strong Republican showings in high-visibility elections;
   9. Can be affected by significant state-specific political events or trends.[54]

In a preliminary report based on partial case studies in five states, Sturrock concluded that these propositions held up fairly well.

My own best guess is that by the turn of the century there will have occurred a spread of competition to these lower ballot levels that will have no counterpart in post-Reconstruction Southern political history. Areas that have known only intra-Democratic competition for local office will become hotbeds of two-party politics. Perhaps South Carolina will come to be viewed as a Deep South pacesetter in this process as Florida has been for the Rim South. Local politics rarely contains the ideological divisions that are present at the national level, and the variations found in local politics are absolutely dizzying. Without better data, it is difficult to say much more about the "down-ticket" arena even as it is today, much less as it will be in the future. Yet, it is hard to imagine how the Southern political system at this level could be worse off by having another organized vehicle for the contesting of public office—the general election. In that sense alone, one can take comfort that the cause of democracy in the South will likely be well served in the emerging new era.

3. The destruction of the one-party Democratic South and the rise of two-party competition have made Southern politics more closely resemble politics outside of the region. This nationalization of Southern politics is a powerful phenomenon, and it will continue. The causes of the transformation are fundamental and irreversible; over a century and a quarter after the Civil War the South is fast on the way to rejoining completely the national political mainstream.[55]

To predict a continuing nationalization of politics in Dixie is not to say that regional political features tied to the peculiar Southern experience will disappear. For some years to come, the viability of the black-white Democratic coalition will form the key to partisan developments in the region (as discussed in Point 1 above). We know that such will not be the case in Minnesota, Wisconsin, Iowa, Oregon, or Connecticut, to name a few Northern states. These states share political similarities with Southern states; after all, we are part of the same country. But the dynamics of politics outside the South frequently revolve around different considerations. In Northern industrial states with sizable black urban concentrations, Southern analogies are present and will persist. (In fact, as the race issue moved north in the late 1960s, it was partially correct to point to a "Southernization of America," as the author John Egerton did in his book with that subtitle.[56])

4. By the next century the Southern Democratic party will have made major strides toward becoming an organization that faithfully champions the interests of "those who have less" of both races. This development, if it materializes, will have important implications for the future course of left-of-center domestic politics and policy at the national level as well as within the region. The short-run effect of this trend may very well be a sharp decline in Southern Democratic strength, but the purified and unified party that emerges could, in league with a compatible Democratic party in the rest of the country, lead to a return of the Democrats to a position of dominance in presidential elections, a position they have not held in over two decades.

This last prediction is tinged with philosophical hope, but the hard data appear, at least tangentially, to support the prospect. The other three trends identified above are supportive of the outcome suggested under Point 4. A weakened Southern black-white Democratic coalition, slowly drained of its more conservative elements, faced with increasing opposition at the lower ballot levels, and subjected to strong nationalizing tendencies will be forced to abandon its current centrist, straddling posture and become a party with serious policy content and a meaningful program for its adherents. Such a posture will not be right of center; the Republicans have that ground staked out clearly in the region as they have had generally in the rest of the country since the New Deal.

If what I am predicting occurs, in essence, "those who have less" of both races will finally have attained the vehicle that Professor Key predicted in 1949 would flow from a dissolution of the one-party South. The consequences of such an outcome for Southerners who have less is simply that they will begin to win on the great questions of taxation and expenditure and those concerning in whose interest the government should function.

From time to time critics have pointed to Professor Key's prophesy and declared that he was wrong. I think the situation by the twenty-first century will show that Key was on target. He simply miscalculated the length of time needed for the complete dismantling of the one-party system. Also, he discounted the extent to which the race issue would linger on as a barrier to the coming together of blacks and whites to form a meaningful political force for the promotion of the interests of "those who have less" of both races. I am reminded of a famous quotation from an article written in 1892 by Tom Watson, the Georgia Populist, and entitled "The Negro Question in the South." Watson predicted that the Populist party would settle the race question by offering whites and blacks "a rallying point which is free from the odium of former discords and strifes. . . . by presenting a platform immensely beneficial to both races and injurious to neither. . . . by making it to the interest of both races to act together." Watson continued: "Now the People's Party say to these two men [one black and one white], 'You are kept apart that you may be separately fleeced of your earnings. You are made to hate each other because upon that hatred is rested the keystone of the arch . . . which enslaves you both.' "[57]

Today in the South and in the nation the race question is rarely an overt element in political discourse, but it lingers on and remains a barrier to the fulfillment of the trend outlined in Point 4. The barrier will be overcome only when leaders[58] openly confront the problem and convince their adherents of both races that they are, as Watson so powerfully asserted, kept apart so that they can be separately fleeced of their earnings.[59]

Appendix:
An Explanation of the
Correlation Technique

A complete understanding of recent Southern partisan change requires studying the results of hundreds of elections in greater detail than that provided by statewide percentages. Descending to the next level—the county level—means, however, confronting literally hundreds of thousands of individual county returns since the South has over 1,100 counties. To avoid being buried under an avalanche of numbers, I turned for help to the statistician and the computer.

In the main I was interested in one simple relationship for all these figures: how the candidates of the Democratic party for the major offices (president, senator, and governor) compared with each other in terms of their county-level voter support. Discovering precisely this relationship for various contests offered the promise of guiding the effort to chart the South's emerging partisan structure. The required precision was supplied by the use of Pearson's product-moment correlation coefficients.

For the contribution of the correlation solution to be fully appreciated, one needs to visualize the problem a researcher faces. Consider, for example, studying the electoral performance of two candidates in Alabama: James Allen, the victorious Democratic nominee for the Senate in 1968, and George McGovern, the national party's losing standard-bearer in 1972. One encounters two long columns of figures representing the percentages of support in Alabama's sixty-seven counties for both Democrats. Allowing the imagination to extend the columns completely, one finds that the numbers line up as follows:

County	Allen in 1968	McGovern in 1972
Autauga	60.8%	22.3%
Baldwin	80.6	15.9
Barbour	75.2	26.3
Bibb	80.1	19.7
Blount	72.8	19.4
Bullock	47.5	50.6
Butler	60.9	22.9
. . .	. . .	. . .
Wilcox	58.7	54.7
Winston	57.9	13.5
Total	70.0%	25.5%

For people lacking an intimate connection with Alabama political life, little can be gleaned quickly from perusal of these rows of figures beyond the obvious fact that Allen was considerably more popular than McGovern. Applying the correlation technique,. however, produces a coefficient of − .70, which instantly conveys valuable information—that is, as soon as one understands what such a coefficient represents.

Using the correlation technique* on columns of figures, such as those from Alabama, yields a coefficient that ranges from 1.0 to − 1.0. A coefficient approaching 1.0 means there is a nearly perfect relationship between the patterns of support of both candidates in the two elections being compared. In other words, the two Democrats received support in nearly the same proportion from the same counties. In South Carolina in 1978, for example, Charles D. (Pug) Ravenel's percentages in the Palmetto State's forty-six counties correlate with George McGovern's 1972 county percentages in the state at .81, indicating a fairly high degree of consistency in voter support for both candidates (something Ravenel would no doubt have chosen to avoid, since McGovern finished poorly in the state). This coefficient further demonstrated the relative stability of the developing partisan cleavage in post–civil rights era South Carolina.

A coefficient near − 1.0, on the other hand, suggests something quite

*The technique's mathematical basis is explained with considerable wit by V. O. Key, Jr., in A Primer of Statistics for Political Scientists (New York: Thomas Crowell, 1954), 58–129. See also Hubert M. Blalock, Jr., Social Statistics, 2d ed. (New York: McGraw-Hill, 1972), 361–428.

different: an inverse relationship between the strengths of the candidates. The Allen-McGovern Alabama coefficient of −.70, for example, indicates that in counties where the national Democrat McGovern was strong, Allen, the epitome of a George Wallace Democrat, was weak, and where Allen was strong, McGovern was weak.

When the correlation coefficient approaches zero, no relationship at all exists between the votes for the two candidates. For example, in Arkansas in 1964 the races of Winthrop Rockefeller, the GOP gubernatorial candidate, and Barry Goldwater, the party's national nominee—both, incidentally, losers in Arkansas that year—produce a correlation coefficient of .05, an early sign that Rockefeller's brand of Republicanism was attracting different adherents than Goldwater's.

Using correlations solely to produce a measure of association between candidates of the same party in different elections avoids a difficult causal question that may arise in working with aggregate data.* At several points in the book, however, correlation analysis is employed in a way that requires an assumption not necessary in the candidate-by-candidate comparisons. These instances involved the correlation of a candidate's county-level vote with one important demographic variable, the proportion of blacks at the county level. Where a high positive correlation exists between this variable and a candidate's vote, one can with moderate confidence assume that the candidate was drawing strong support from black voters (but an assumption is nevertheless being made). Charles Evers's vote in the three-way Senate race of 1978 in Mississippi illustrates this use of the technique. Evers's vote by county correlates with the county-level percentage of blacks in the state at .86, a strong indication that blacks heavily supported the veteran civil rights leader.

Every correlation coefficient can be graphically portrayed by a scatter diagram, and good practice requires an examination of these diagrams; this was done for all the coefficients reported in this book. Such a diagram for the type of data used here results from plotting each county's position on a graph using as coordinates the percentages both candidates attained in each county. This portrayal of the coefficient tells more than the coefficient alone and makes possible the valuable isolation of those counties that deviate from the dominant pattern—the "far-outliers." W. Phillips Shively observed:

---

*On the various general problems associated with aggregate data analysis, such as the ecological-fallacy issue, see Austin Ranney, "The Utility and Limitations of Aggregate Data in the Study of Electoral Behavior," in his edited volume *Essays on the Behavioral Study of Politics* (Urbana: Univ. of Illinois Press, 1962), 91–102.

> Users of [this type of] analysis in political science far too rarely go on to the creative and exploratory labor of examining the residuals [the far-outliers] . . . . Usually the spread of dots . . . is treated as an act of God, or as a measure of the basic uncertainty of human affairs. On the contrary, it is a trove in which new variables lie waiting to be discovered.*

In the Tennessee chapter, for example, a scatter diagram of the Gore-Sasser correlation coefficient of .89 identified a cluster of West Tennessee counties as far-outliers, which led to their presentation in Map 12-1 with an accompanying explanation for the pattern.

Another use of a scatter diagram came in the consideration of the sharp shift in Democratic presidential voting in South Carolina between 1964 and 1968. The correlation between Johnson's 1964 pattern and Humphrey's in 1968 is −.27. Examination of the scatter diagram showed that the Piedmont counties were the chief ones to abandon Humphrey, after having strongly supported Johnson only four years earlier. Of course, neither the coefficient nor the scatter diagram provides much help in explaining why the voters in these counties behaved as they did. Analysis can only begin with these research tools. As Professor Key wrote thirty years ago:

> Sole reliance on the numerical data fed into the product-moment formula is perilous. . . . In fact, experience develops a two-way working pattern. Correlation of statistical data points to inquiries to be made by interview and by examination of printed sources. In turn, such information gives substance to the correlation-centered analysis.†

*The Craft of Political Research, 2d ed. (Englewood Cliffs, N.J.: Prentice-Hall, 1980), 120.
†Primer of Statistics for Political Scientists, 125.

Bibliographical Note

Study of post–World War II political life in the South must begin with one of the finest books ever written on a political subject: *Southern Politics in State and Nation*, by V. O. Key, Jr., with the assistance of Alexander Heard (New York: Alfred A. Knopf, 1949). Key sagely analyzed the one-party system from its origins through the latter half of the 1940s, assessing its impact with a penetrating simplicity that cut away the plethora of myths too long attached to the subject.

Drawing on his research for Professor Key's project, Alexander Heard a few years later published his treatment of Southern Republicanism and its future prospects in *A Two-Party South?* (Chapel Hill: Univ. of North Carolina Press, 1952). Heard's prescient book offers a benchmark against which to measure the developments of the intervening three decades.

For my purposes, the politics of the uneasy period of transition from the late 1940s through the early 1960s is only a prelude to the big changes that swept through the region when the national deadlock on civil rights was broken in 1964 and 1965. But for those interested in this less-than-inspiring period of Southern political history, Numan V. Bartley tells the story extremely well in his *The Rise of Massive Resistance: Race and Politics in the South during the 1950s* (Baton Rouge: Louisiana State Univ. Press, 1969). Bartley's 33-page bibliographical essay provides an invaluable guide for further research.

Because events in the 1960s were fast-moving, books on Southern politics* in this decade faced a severe handicap, not unlike trying to

---

*Only books with a regional focus are considered in this bibliographical note. The existence of useful analytical works on the politics of individual states varies widely. For example, Virginia, through the efforts of Ralph Eisenberg and Larry Sabato, among others, possesses a good supply of quality studies. There are other such well-endowed states. The reader is referred to the state chapters for citations to books and articles dealing with individual states.

examine a hurricane's damage while still caught up in the midst of the storm; no doubt some writers finding themselves in the hurricane's eye prematurely concluded that the storm had ended. Along with Donald R. Matthews and James W. Prothro's well-crafted *Negroes and the New Southern Politics* (New York: Harcourt, Brace, and World, 1966), three useful collections of essays and research papers labored under this disadvantage: Allan P. Sindler, ed., *Change in the Contemporary South* (Durham, N.C.: Duke Univ. Press, 1963); Robert B. Highsaw, ed., *The Deep South in Transformation* (University: Univ. of Alabama Press, 1964); and Avery Leiserson, ed., *The American South in the 1960's* (New York: Praeger, 1964). The best book on Southern politics in the 1960s, Bernard Cosman's *Five States for Goldwater: Continuity and Change in Southern Presidential Voting Patterns* (University: Univ. of Alabama Press, 1966), remains the definitive study of the divergence of the Deep South from the Rim South in the watershed election of 1964.

Taken together, three important books appearing in the early and middle 1970s comprehensively analyzed Southern politics from World War II through the Second Reconstruction (the latter period is alternatively known as the civil rights era). The first, *The Changing Politics of the South* (Baton Rouge: Louisiana State Univ. Press, 1972), ably organized and edited by William C. Havard, is a 740-page compendium of information and analysis, containing overview chapters by Havard and eleven individual state chapters written by academic authorities on their respective states. My debt to Havard and his associates is reflected in the citations I make to their work in the note section of this book. The state chapter titles and their authors in order of appearance in Havard's book are Ralph Eisenberg, "Virginia: The Emergence of Two-Party Politics"; Manning J. Dauer, "Florida: The Different State"; Lee S. Greene and Jack E. Holmes, "Tennessee: A Politics of Peaceful Change"; O. Douglas Weeks, "Texas: Land of Conservative Expansiveness"; Richard E. Yates, "Arkansas: Independent and Unpredictable"; Joseph L. Bernd, "Georgia: Static and Dynamic"; Preston W. Edsall and J. Oliver Williams, "North Carolina: Bipartisan Paradox"; Donald S. Strong, "Alabama: Transition and Alienation"; Charles N. Fortenberry and F. Glenn Abney, "Mississippi: Unreconstructed and Unredeemed"; Perry H. Howard, "Louisiana: Resistance and Change"; and Chester W. Bain, "South Carolina: Partisan Prelude."

Within a year of each other in the mid-1970s, two quite different yet remarkably complementary books appeared by two pairs of authors: Numan V. Bartley and Hugh D. Graham, *Southern Politics and the Second Reconstruction* (Baltimore: Johns Hopkins Univ. Press, 1975), and Jack Bass and Walter DeVries, *The Transformation of Southern Politics:*

Social Change and Political Consequence since 1945 (New York: Basic Books, 1976).

Bartley and Graham employ the historical narrative, which they correctly assert is "the organizational structure best designed to reveal the evolution of political patterns over time" if "it is analytical as well as descriptive" (p. 21), to weave together a vast amount of information into tightly written thematic chapters. The authors first treat the Southern populist legacy in the decade of pure one-party politics that followed World War II and then trace the legacy's demise when the race issue after 1954 grew to dominate the persisting one-party system. An extensive treatment of the politics of turmoil during the 1960s and the rise of Republicanism comes next. A chapter dealing with what the authors call the "ambiguous resurgence of the New South" and one on the 1972 elections lead to the book's conclusion.

Bartley and Graham painstakingly collected and classified precinct data from twenty-seven Southern cities for major elections from 1950 to 1972, a massive and laborious undertaking for which all who work in this field are in their debt. These data provided their book with an original and revealing foundation upon which to base their interpretation of the primaries and elections they were studying. The authors later published a data book containing their classified precinct information (along with hard-to-find county-level Democratic primary results) in *Southern Elections: County and Precinct Data, 1950–1972* (Baton Rouge: Louisiana State Univ. Press, 1978). From the information in their data book, I constructed several tables important for my interpretation in this book. Bartley and Graham also thoroughly explored and used published sources, which is reflected in the scope of their exhaustive and highly valuable bibliographical essay.

Bass and DeVries's book ranges over much more than electoral and party politics, and that is both its weakness and its strength. As a result of the effort to cover Southern public life in all its manifestations, the book lacks the precision and well-integrated nature of Bartley and Graham's work. Bass and DeVries, for example, isolate their interesting voting statistics and illustrations in the appendixes rather than integrate them into the textual analysis. On the other hand, their all-encompassing approach conveys a vivid sense of the nature of the many social and political developments under way in the post-1945 South, a goal facilitated by the work's lively writing style.

The bulk of the Bass and DeVries book consists of eleven state chapters built around themes prominent in the traditions of each state and loosely linked to broader considerations. By far the greatest strength of the work derives from the impressive number of interviews the au-

thors conducted throughout the South with "more than 360 . . . active
and retired politicians—including governors, members of Congress, legislators, and other state and local officeholders—political party officials,
journalists, labor leaders, academic observers, and others in all 11
states" (p. x).

Like Bartley and Graham, Bass and DeVries are to be congratulated
for sharing their information with other researchers. After the publication of their book, Bass and DeVries deposited the audio tape recordings
from their interviews—as well as the typescripts for the almost 200
interviews that were transcribed—in the Southern Historical Collection
at the University of North Carolina at Chapel Hill. As a result, I was
able to use previously unpublished portions from twenty-five of these
interviews to supplement my own interviewing, which was directed
toward the narrower topic of the development of Southern two-party
politics.

Two other more specialized books published in the mid-1970s deserve
mention: Louis M. Seagull, *Southern Republicanism* (Cambridge,
Mass.: Schenkman, 1975), and Earl Black, *Southern Governors and
Civil Rights: Racial Segregation as a Campaign Issue in the Second
Reconstruction* (Cambridge, Mass.: Harvard Univ. Press, 1976). Approaching Southern electoral change with a focus on the Republicans,
Seagull combines documentary sources and his own extensive aggregate
data analysis—the weaknesses of which he carefully acknowledges—to
produce a concise interpretation of the major trends through the 1972
elections. He also presents a wealth of correlation coefficients among
GOP candidates. Black exhaustively and competently chronicles and
analyzes the changing position on racial segregation of white Southern
politicians running for governor in the period 1950–73. The differences
between Deep South and Rim South candidates emerge starkly; the
weakness of the race issue in Texas stands out in several imaginatively
constructed illustrations.

In his impressive series of books covering public affairs in all regions
of the United States, Neal R. Peirce devoted two volumes to the South
with individual chapters on each of the eleven states: *The Deep South
States of America: People, Politics, and Power in the Seven Deep South
States* (New York: W. W. Norton, 1974) and *The Border South States:
People, Politics, and Power in the Five Border South States* (New York:
W. W. Norton, 1975). Peirce's books offer excellent introductions to
the major issues, personalities, and traditions of each state. His treatment of political parties and elections invariably strikes at the central
issues, providing considerable insight.

Wayne Greenhaw's *Elephants in the Cottonfields: Ronald Reagan und the New Republican South* (New York: Macmillan, 1982) is not, as its title implies, an analysis of Southern Republicanism. Rather, the book consists of loosely connected profiles of various prominent Southern Republican politicians. The strength of the work is that Greenhaw accurately presents these Republicans exactly as they appear in their public guises. Having interviewed many of the same people he treats in individual chapters, I was struck by the accuracy of his extensive reproduction of what they have to say as well as by the consistency of what these public figures tell interviewers. What is amazing about Greenhaw is that he reports uncritically everything the politicians tell him. Still, the book is useful in the sense that all original data have value.

Starting in 1978, students of Southern politics have gathered at springtime every other year in Charleston, S.C., for what has become an invaluable institution—The Citadel Symposium on Southern Politics, which I have had the pleasure of participating in four times running. The conference organizers, Robert P. Steed, Laurence W. Moreland, and Tod A. Baker, all of The Citadel's political science department, have published three volumes of research papers from their symposia and are preparing a fourth, on the 1984 presidential election in the South. The three books to appear so far under their editorship are *Party Politics in the South* (New York: Praeger, 1980), *Contemporary Southern Political Attitudes and Behavior: Studies and Essays* (New York: Praeger, 1982), and *Religion and Politics in the South: Mass and Elite Perspectives* (New York: Praeger, 1984).

The foremost source for accurate general-election returns is the remarkable fifteen-volume *America Votes* series, compiled and edited by Richard M. Scammon and Alice V. McGillivary. These data books, which contain county-level voting statistics for major elections in all fifty states, have appeared after every general election for nearly thirty years and are currently published in Washington by Congressional Quarterly for Scammon's Elections Research Center. The statewide candidate percentages cited in this book for 1952 to 1982 were taken from these authoritative volumes, and for national elections from 1932 to 1948 the figures are from another book compiled by Scammon, *America at the Polls: A Handbook of American Presidential Election Statistics, 1920–1964* (Pittsburgh: Univ. of Pittsburgh Press, 1965).

Finally, in addition to state newspapers and academic journals, such as the Southern Political Science Association's *Journal of Politics*, two bimonthly publications are valuable for keeping up with political developments in the region—*Southern Exposure* and *Southern Changes*. The listing in the review section of *Southern Exposure*, a periodical issued by the Institute for Southern Studies in Durham, N.C., is the single best source for information on new books on Southern politics. *Southern Changes*, the journal of the Atlanta-based Southern Regional Council, stays at the cutting edge of Southern political life. For example, in the Oct.–Nov. 1983 issue, Bill Minor published a fascinating article, entitled "White Politics in a Black Land," that explored how powerful, conservative white Mississippi politicians with lengthy records of fighting for segregation are regularly able to win contested elections in majority-black counties, a topic that deserves more study and attention.*

*For mention of works published since 1984, consult the notes to Chapters 16, 17, 18, and 19.

Notes

Chapter 1: Region in Ferment

1. For an informative overview of the Southern Democracy through the early 1960s, see Dewey W. Grantham, *The Democratic South* (New York: W. W. Norton, 1965).
2. Figure 3-1 in Chapter 3 supports this observation by comparing the Republican presidential vote with GOP successes in Southern elections for governor, U.S. senator, and other offices.
3. V. O. Key, Jr., with the assistance of Alexander Heard, analyzed this system in the celebrated classic *Southern Politics in State and Nation* (New York: Alfred A. Knopf, 1949). Professor Key's work appeared at a point when the great changes that would sweep away the one-party system he had so brilliantly described were just beginning.
4. In a series of lectures at Mercer University in 1970, George B. Tindall perceptively sketched the main forces at work in this transformation. See his *Disruption of the Solid South* (New York: W. W. Norton, 1972).
5. The existence of this abatement of racial tension is based on a qualitative "feel for the times" that emerged from surveying contemporary newspapers and interviewing politicians and political observers. For example, when asked in 1974 to name the major change in Southern politics during his lifetime, Sen. John J. Sparkman of Alabama was quick to respond: "[T]he elimination of the civil rights question as a political issue." Interview with Sparkman, conducted by Jack Bass and Walter DeVries, Jan. 31, 1974.

A precise cause for the abatement is difficult to locate. An important element probably involved the U.S. Supreme Court decisions in the late 1960s that led to the desegregation of many Southern school districts, especially those in rural areas. With racial integration a fact of life in the one place—the public schools—where it had been fought the longest, it was certainly clear to all concerned that the South had run out of courts. An excellent narrative treatment of the civil rights issue during the late 1960s and early 1970s is presented in A. James Reichley, *Conservatives in an Age of Change: The Nixon and Ford Administrations* (Washington: Brookings Institution, 1981), 174–204.

Chapter 2: Democratic Rupture over Civil Rights

1. I. A. Newby, *The South: A History* (New York: Holt, Rinehart & Winston, 1978), 396–97.
2. George B. Tindall, *The Disruption of the Solid South* (New York: W. W. Norton, 1972), 31–32.
3. George E. Mowry, *Another Look at the Twentieth-Century South* (Baton Rouge: Louisiana State Univ. Press, 1973), 69–70. President Roosevelt, wily politician that he was, straddled the race issue during his years in the White House. See Frank Freidel, *F.D.R. and the South* (Baton Rouge: Louisiana State Univ. Press, 1965), esp. chap. 3, and James T. Patterson, "The Failure of Party Realignment in the South, 1937–1939," *Journal of Politics* 27 (Aug. 1965), 602–17. Patterson, for example, wrote that "the Roosevelt administration left touchy southern problems alone. . . . Roosevelt, anxious to retain southern congressional support, not only failed to introduce civil rights legislation for Negroes before 1940, but even tried to keep the anti-lynching bill from discussion in the Senate" (611–12).
4. William C. Berman, *The Politics of Civil Rights in the Truman Administration* (Columbus: Ohio State Univ. Press, 1970), 42–53. Berman wrote, "An extreme example of what was happening to Negroes in the South took place in Batesburgh, South Carolina. There, on February 13, 1946, Issac Woodward, a newly discharged black veteran, still in military uniform, was removed from a bus after a verbal tiff with the driver and was assaulted and blinded by the chief of police of that town. News of this crime received wide publicity, which in turn eventually produced demands for a federal investigation. The Justice Department brought an indictment against the alleged perpetrator of this deed, but he was acquitted in federal court in Columbia, South Carolina, on grounds of self-defense" (44–45).
5. For a perceptive discussion of these pressures, see Berman's monograph cited above, esp. pp. 3–78.
6. Both quotations are from Charles P. Roland, *The Improbable Era: The South since World War II*, rev. ed. (Lexington: Univ. Press of Kentucky, 1976), 32.
7. Francis B. Simkins and Charles P. Roland, *A History of the South*, 4th ed. (New York: Alfred A. Knopf, 1972), 590.
8. Robert A. Garson, *The Democratic Party and the Politics of Sectionalism, 1941–1948* (Baton Rouge: Louisiana State Univ. Press, 1974), 278.
9. Simkins and Roland, *History of the South*, 590.
10. *The State* (Columbia, S.C.), May 11, 1948.
11. Ibid., July 18, 1948.
12. Irwin Ross, *The Loneliest Campaign: The Truman Victory of 1948* (New York: New American Library, 1968), 232.
13. On the Alabama ballot there was no slate of electors pledged to Truman.
14. The percentage of blacks in the Southern states in 1950 and 1960, as reported by the U.S. census, was as follows:

	1950 (%)	1960 (%)
Deep South		
Mississippi	45.3	42.0
South Carolina	38.8	34.8
Louisiana	32.9	31.9
Alabama	32.0	30.0
Georgia	30.0	28.5
Rim South		
North Carolina	25.8	24.5
Arkansas	22.3	21.8
Virginia	22.1	20.6
Florida	21.8	17.8
Tennessee	16.1	16.5
Texas	12.7	12.4

15. By the 1970s, however, the gap between the two subsections had narrowed considerably.
16. The description of the three trends is adopted from Tindall, *Disruption of the Solid South*, 38.
17. Ibid.
18. The South Carolina material draws on my M.A. thesis, "The Disruption of a Solidly Democratic State: Civil Rights and South Carolina Electoral Change, 1948–1974" (Vanderbilt University, 1975), part of which was published in the *Journal of Political Science* 5 (Fall 1977), 55–72.
19. *The State*, Aug. 7, 1952.
20. Ibid.
21. Ibid.
22. Ibid.
23. Ibid., Sept. 19, 1952.
24. Ibid.
25. Ibid., Oct. 1, 1952.
26. For a fine treatment of the politics of this era, see Numan V. Bartley, *The Rise of Massive Resistance: Race and Politics in the South during the 1950s* (Baton Rouge: Louisiana State Univ. Press, 1969).
27. Simkins and Roland, *History of the South*, 596.
28. Governor Thurmond had been defeated by Sen. Olin D. Johnston in the 1950 South Carolina Democratic primary when Thurmond had attempted to unseat the then first-term senator. (In fact, Key wrote in 1949 that when Thurmond began his active role defending the South against Truman's civil rights initiatives, "Sage South Carolina politicians nodded and concluded that Strom was running for the Senate." *Southern Politics*, 18.) In 1954 Thurmond made it to the Senate, although in an unusual fashion. When Senator Maybank died after his unopposed renomination in the June 1954 Democratic primary, the state Democratic executive committee picked State Sen. Edgar Brown of Barnwell County to replace Maybank. Thurmond cried foul and beat Brown in the general election as a

write-in candidate, the only way Thurmond could get on the ballot when the party committee refused to call another primary. During the 1954 campaign Thurmond promised to resign in 1956 in order to run for the seat in the proper manner, that is, in the Democratic primary. Thus, in 1956 Thurmond was a candidate for the remaining four years of his own term, which he won unopposed. Alberta Lachicotte, *Rebel Senator: Strom Thurmond of South Carolina* (New York: Devin-Adair, 1966), 62–117.

29. *The State*, July 22, 1956.
30. Ibid.
31. This was, of course, a measure designed by politicians to protect themselves since a citizen could vote in secret for whomever he or she chose no matter what the convention did.
32. The Wofford, Timmerman, and Johnston quotations are from *The State*'s Aug. 28, 1956, account of the convention.
33. *The State*, Oct. 25, 1956.
34. The Causy and Jones quotations are from ibid., Aug. 28, 1956.
35. Ibid., Oct. 11, 1956.
36. For the location of the Black Belt counties, see Map 5-1, in the South Carolina chapter.
37. *The State*, Nov. 7, 1956.
38. Tindall, *Disruption of the Solid South*, 40.
39. *The State*, Oct. 11, 1960.
40. Ibid., Nov. 4, 1960.
41. Kennedy's selection of Sen. Lyndon B. Johnson of Texas as his running mate was a concession to Southern Democrats, an ironic concession as it turned out. At the Democratic National Convention in Los Angeles, Gov. Ernest F. (Fritz) Hollings of South Carolina urged Kennedy to select Johnson. "Let's face facts, Jack," Hollings is reported to have told the nominee. "As things stand this morning, you would lose South Carolina. When tempers calm down, we can take a more realistic look at the situation, and I do not know what our state will do, but Lyndon Johnson is your best bet for the support of the South." *The State*, July 15, 1960.
42. For an account of Kennedy's approach to the civil rights issue, see Carl M. Brauer, *John F. Kennedy and the Second Reconstruction* (New York: Columbia Univ. Press, 1977).
43. *The State*, June 19, 1964.
44. Ibid. In competition with Goldwater and other early Republican "Southern strategists," the first years of the 1960s witnessed the rise of a Southern Democratic segregationist hero who was to become a force in nearly every presidential race starting in 1964, Gov. George C. Wallace of Alabama. By July 1964 over 25,000 petition signatures had been secured—more than enough—to put Wallace on the ballot in South Carolina as an independent presidential candidate. Immediately after the Republican party nominated Goldwater, Wallace withdrew his candidacy. A South Carolina group promoting Wallace issued the following statement after Wallace's withdrawal: "And be it resolved that . . . knowing that the Democrats sponsored the Civil Rights Bill and in view of the fact that Sen. Barry Goldwater voted against the Civil Rights Bill . . . we, a group of South Carolina Independent Democrats, wholeheartedly endorse Sen. Goldwater for President . . . ." *The State*, Aug. 30, 1964.

45. The GOP nominee carried only one other state, his home state of Arizona.
46. Bernard Cosman, *Five States for Goldwater: Continuity and Change in Southern Presidential Voting Patterns* (University: Univ. of Alabama Press, 1966), 90.

Chapter 3: The Emergence of Southern Two-Party Politics

1. For a first-rate analysis of the cleavages in the American party systems from the 1850s through the 1920s, see James L. Sundquist, *Dynamics of the Party System: Alignment and Realignment of Political Parties in the United States* (Washington: Brookings Institution, 1973), 39–182. A revised edition of this book appeared in 1983.
2. V. O. Key, Jr., "The Future of the Democratic Party," *Virginia Quarterly Review* 28 (Spring 1952), 165–66. Key noted, "The chances are that Roosevelt and the New Deal converted to the Democrats comparatively few old-line Republicans. Rather, the Democrats gained the allegiance of persons who had not been enough concerned with public affairs to vote and of persons coming to voting age."
3. This phrase, which I use at several points below, is from V. O. Key, Jr., *Southern Politics in State and Nation* (New York: Alfred A. Knopf, 1949), 307. The Democrats favored an activist national government; the Republicans preferred to leave the regulation of economic and social matters to state and local governments. That there would be different winners and losers depending on which level of government handled these matters was clear to those involved, if not always articulated.
4. Sundquist, *Dynamics of the Party System*, 202.
5. Ibid.
6. Ibid., 213.
7. Ibid., 218. The barriers in the North were not inconsequential. Sundquist wrote that the Democratic party leadership in some Northern states "was too old or too conservative to appeal to Roosevelt supporters, or more deeply committed to the party's patronage than to its program" (239). Nevertheless, Sundquist concluded that the process was virtually complete in the North by the mid-1960s. Ibid., 244. See generally his chap. 11 ("Aftershocks of the New Deal Earthquake—in the North").
8. Alexander Heard, *A Two-Party South?* (Chapel Hill: Univ. of North Carolina Press, 1952), 9.
9. Some GOP presidential growth in the 1950s came from segregationist whites in search of an alternative on race, as the South Carolina example in Chapter 2 illustrates, and had nothing to do with economic class. This racial component of GOP support in the 1950s, however, should not obscure the movement toward class voting outlined in this chapter. The two trends operated simultaneously. Sorting them out precisely—given the crude tools at the analyst's disposal—was often impossible.
10. Numan V. Bartley and Hugh D. Graham, *Southern Elections: County and Precinct Data, 1950–1972* (Baton Rouge: Louisiana State Univ. Press, 1978), 345–407.
11. Donald S. Strong, *Urban Republicanism in the South* (University: Univ. of Alabama Bureau of Public Administration, 1960). Donald S. Strong, *The 1952 Presidential Election in the South* (University: Univ. of Alabama Bureau of Public

Administration, 1956). Bernard Cosman, "Presidential Republicanism in the South, 1960," *Journal of Politics* 24 (May 1962), 303–22. Donald S. Strong, "Durable Republicanism in the South," in Allan P. Sindler, ed., *Change in the Contemporary South* (Durham, N.C.: Duke Univ. Press, 1963), 174–94.

12. It is true that Republican activity in the South is found most consistently in the urban areas; this occurred first at the presidential level and later at other levels. County election maps regularly show this urban Republican strength. The urban aspect of this support, however, ought not to mask what is going on below the surface inside the urban counties: the development of distinct class divisions in partisan preference.

An example from the 1982 Texas gubernatorial election illustrates the point. The losing Republican candidate, Gov. Bill Clements, did better in Houston (Harris County) than statewide. He lost Houston to the Democrat Mark White, 49.0 percent (230,810 votes) to 51.0 percent (239,920 votes); Clements was defeated by White in the state 46.2 percent to 53.8 percent. Since 3.1 million votes were cast in this election, clearly the Republican candidate relied heavily on this populous urban county's support, and in general Houston has been a stronghold for Texas Republicans.

A closer scrutiny of Houston's Republican support reveals that there existed sharp class divisions among the city's whites in the election. The *Houston Post* on Nov. 4, 1982, reported the following classified precinct results:

	Clements	White
Affluent whites	82.9%	16.3%
Middle-income whites	63.0	36.2
Working-class whites	28.5	71.0

Thus, while this large urban county was providing strong Republican support, whites were voting on the basis of economic-class divisions consistent with the New Deal realignment of the 1930s. Therefore, it makes sense to characterize this phenomenon as a manifestation of changes in the national party system that were begun decades ago but that were delayed in their penetration of the South. (Houston's blacks, incidentally, cast their ballots nearly unanimously for the Democratic nominee in 1982.)

13. To be precise, this is what occurred when President Johnson embraced the civil rights movement in 1964.

14. Other writers object to an interpretation that views the New Deal configuration as surviving the breakup of the Democratic South. See, for example, Everett Carll Ladd, Jr., with Charles D. Hadley, *Transformation of the American Party System*, 2d ed. (New York: W. W. Norton, 1978), 129–77. The argument, greatly simplified, goes like this: The Solid South was a key feature of Roosevelt's coalition; now with the South no longer voting overwhelmingly Democratic in presidential elections, the Roosevelt coalition is shattered beyond repair. The central point that this view misses is that the class-based realignment begun by FDR's New Deal required decades to work its way into the nation's decentralized party system in both the North and the South. In the South, where the barrier was immense, the process lagged far behind.

In a sense this difference of interpretation revolves around definitions. Certainly the Roosevelt or New Deal *coalition* of big-city ethnics (many of them Catholics), farmers, Westerners, and virtually *all* Southerners is at an end. The New Deal *system* persists. The powerful tendency begun in the Depression era toward reshuffling the nation's party system roughly along economic-class lines with accompanying ideological doctrines—often focusing on the proper role of the federal government—took root in the 1930s and grew. The specific issues on the agenda at any one point have changed; in general, though, the Democrats continue to represent the interests of "those who have less," and the Republicans are still the party closely identified with the nation's well to do. There may be many exceptions, but in large measure these observations remain as true in the early 1980s as they were in the 1930s, when the party system first shifted in this direction on the initiative of FDR's New Deal.

15. In 1964 only 35.5 percent of the voting-age Southern black population was registered; by 1969 the figure had risen to 64.8 percent. The percentage of whites registered also increased. In 1964, 73.4 percent of the Southern voting-age white population was registered; in 1969 the percentage had reached 83.5. Steven F. Lawson, *Black Ballots: Voting Rights in the South, 1944–1969* (New York: Columbia Univ. Press, 1976), 331 (table 3).

16. Key discussed the "Southern political spectrum" in *Southern Politics*, 359–68. See also George B. Tindall, *The Emergence of the New South, 1913–1945* (Baton Rouge: Louisiana State Univ. Press, 1967), chap. 18. An undeveloped but rapidly growing area of Southern historiography is the New Deal era, a period about which many fascinating political questions remain unexplored. Frank Freidel, Numan V. Bartley, and six other historians mapped the terrain in a series of lectures delivered Oct. 12–14, 1983, at the University of Mississippi Chancellor's Symposium on Southern History. A volume of the proceedings of this "New Deal and the South" symposium is forthcoming from the Univ. Press of Mississippi.

17. The effect of these early spasmodic and transient expressions of class politics within the South's one-party factional structure is explained by Key in the renowned chap. 14 ("Nature and Consequences of One-Party Factionalism") of his *Southern Politics*. In short, Key concluded that the losers in such a disorganized political system were "those who have less." The last few pages of this book consider whether "those who have less" have improved their position as a result of the arrival of two-party competition during the post–civil rights era.

18. Bartley and Graham, *Southern Politics and the Second Reconstruction* (Baltimore: Johns Hopkins Univ. Press, 1975), 24–80.

19. Ibid., 25.

20. Samuel Lubell, *The Future of American Politics*, 3d ed., rev. (New York: Harper & Row, 1965), 109.

21. Ibid., 110.

22. Ibid., 114.

23. Examples are Nick Galifianakis in North Carolina in 1972, Albert Gore in Tennessee in 1970, LeRoy Collins in Florida in 1968, Henry Howell in Virginia in 1973, Robert King High in Florida in 1966, and Ralph Yarborough in Texas in 1970 (Yarborough lost to a conservative Democrat in the primary).

24. The quotation comes from remarks by Senator Goldwater to newsmen in Atlanta in 1961. The full sentence was as follows: "We're not going to get the Negro vote as a bloc in 1964 and 1968, so we ought to go hunting where the ducks are." Tindall, *Disruption of the Solid South*, 60.

25. Bernard Cosman, *Five States for Goldwater: Continuity and Change in Southern Presidential Voting Patterns* (University: Univ. of Alabama Press, 1966), 59–118. Also, see Bartley and Graham, *Southern Elections: Precinct Data*, 345–407.

26. Table 3-2 also shows that starting in 1964, black voters in Southern cities voted almost unanimously for Democratic presidential nominees.

27. CBS News Election Day survey, as cited in Theodore H. White, *The Making of the President 1972* (New York: Atheneum, 1973), 343–44.

28. Reg Murphy and Hal Gulliver, *Southern Strategy* (New York: Charles Scribner's Sons, 1971), 249. George McGovern's view of Nixon's Southern strategy, which apparently carried little weight with the Southern electorate, deserves quoting at length. "What is this southern strategy?" McGovern rhetorically asked during a 1972 address to the South Carolina General Assembly. "It is this. It says to the South: Let the poor stay poor, let your economy trail the nation, forget about decent homes and medical care for all your people, choose officials who will oppose every effort to benefit the many at the expense of the few—and in return, we will try to overlook the rights of the black man, appoint a few southerners to high office, and lift your spirits by attacking the 'eastern establishment' . . . It is a clever strategy. But it's not for the benefit of the people of the South. And it's not for the benefit of the American nation." Quoted in Jack Bass and Walter DeVries, *The Transformation of Southern Politics* (New York: Basic Books, 1976), 31.

29. Murphy and Gulliver, *Southern Strategy*, 2 (italics in the original).

30. One participant in the Atlanta meeting, Harry Dent, former chairman of the South Carolina Republican party and a Thurmond associate, claims there was no deal. He described the meeting thus: "Nixon's position on the Supreme Court got the most enthusiastic response. Thurmond was particularly pleased to hear him declare that as president he would only appoint strict constructionists. . . .

   "Nixon made clear his support of the Supreme Court's ruling overturning the old separate, but equal, system of education for blacks and whites. He neither committed himself to retreat from that decision nor to suggest that he would support repealing the 1954 High Court decision, as has sometimes been speculated by some writers. Nixon did, however, express his opposition to busing as a means of achieving racial balance in schools.

   "After the session, Nixon asked Thurmond to accompany him in his car to the airport. Thurmond accepted. The press played up this ride to the airport as if some sinister deals were made between Nixon and Thurmond. This was not the case." Harry S. Dent, *The Prodigal South Returns to Power* (New York: John Wiley & Sons, 1978), 82.

31. The gains were steady in a regional sense; the state-by-state situations varied enormously and were anything but steady.

32. The brief mention of various elections in the next few paragraphs previews their more detailed treatment in the state chapters.

33. Interview with Robert Vance, chairman of the Alabama Democratic party at the time, conducted by Jack Bass and Walter DeVries, July 16, 1974.

34. The term is Donald S. Strong's and appears in his "Alabama: Transition and Alienation," in William C. Havard, ed., *The Changing Politics of the South* (Baton Rouge: Louisiana State Univ. Press, 1972), 457.

35. Bartley and Graham, *Southern Politics*, 103.

36. Interview with Robert Shaw, Georgia Republican party chairman, conducted by Jack Bass and Walter DeVries, April 27, 1974.

37. Raleigh *News and Observer*, Nov. 8, 1968. The observation was made by James C. Gardner, the defeated 1968 GOP candidate for governor of North Carolina.

38. The Republican Thad Cochran won the three-way contest with 45.0 percent of the votes cast. Evers, the black activist, received 22.9 percent. The Democratic nominee, Maurice Dantin, polled 31.8 percent.

39. Interview with Pat Moran, former Arkansas Public Service Commission chairman and an assistant to Sen. Dale Bumpers, conducted by the author, July 19, 1978.

40. Key, *Southern Politics*, 285.

41. Interview with Governor Carter, conducted by Jack Bass and Walter DeVries, Nov. 20, 1973. Carter went on to say, "And I think that although we still have a very easily identifiable Republican party mechanism in Georgia, the trend is toward the Democrats. I would predict that . . . in 1974 you'll see a trend begin in a similar fashion at least in Tennessee. The same thing has already happened in Florida, and I think that South Carolina might be moving away from the impact of Strom Thurmond's defection to the Republican party primarily on the basis of the racial question."

42. The question used in the surveys done by the University of Michigan's Center for Political Studies is "Generally speaking, do you usually think of yourself as a Republican, a Democrat, an independent, or what?"

43. The fascinating generational differences among these party identifiers and the implications of these differences for the future are explored in Chapter 15 along with a host of other survey information.

44. Chiles was quoted by Jack Pridgen, his press secretary, in an interview with Pridgen, conducted by the author, July 13, 1978.

45. Raleigh *News and Observer*, Nov. 1, 1976.

46. Carter carried all the Southern states except Virginia. His percentages were the following: Georgia, 66.7; Arkansas, 65.0; South Carolina, 56.2; Tennessee, 55.9; Alabama, 55.7; North Carolina, 55.2; Florida, 51.9; Louisiana, 51.7; Texas, 51.1; Mississippi, 49.6; and Virginia, 48.0.

47. Paul R. Abramson, "Class Voting in the 1976 Presidential Election," *Journal of Politics* 40 (Nov. 1978), 1070.

48. Ibid.

49. University of Michigan, 1976 National Election Study. The computations were done by the author using the computer facilities of the Brookings Institution. In the rest of the nation Carter did not carry a majority of white voters either: Ford had 52 percent to Carter's 47 percent. When the rest of the country is broken into three regions, the 1976 survey shows that whites in the Northeast favored Carter 53 percent to 47 percent, but Ford carried the whites in the Midwest and West by about the same margin as in the South—54 percent to 45 percent.

50. New Orleans *Times-Picayune*, Nov. 4, 1976.

51. The Republican David Treen's capture of the Louisiana governorship in 1979 appears in both figures under 1980; the peculiar circumstances of his election are considered in Chapter 8.

52. The following are the county-level correlations between the GOP victors and the Reagan pattern in their states:

	Reagan 1980
Denton (Alabama)	.94
East (North Carolina)	.93
White (Arkansas)	.89
Hawkins (Florida)	.84
Mattingly (Georgia)	.73

See the Appendix for an explanation of the correlation technique.

53. One qualification is necessary: John Anderson's independent candidacy was received differently in the South, where the Illinois congressman was far weaker than in the rest of the nation (see Table 15-2).

54. University of Michigan, 1980 National Election Study. These calculations were made by the author using the computer facilities of the Brookings Institution.

55. Jackson (Miss.) *Clarion-Ledger*, Oct. 28, 1980.

56. In 1980 Vice-President Walter F. Mondale, the former Minnesota senator and close associate of Hubert Humphrey, was again Carter's running mate.

57. The 1981 Democratic gubernatorial victory of Charles S. Robb in Virginia appears for the first time in the 1982 figures, offsetting the Trible gain in the regional net figures.

58. At the state legislative level, the 1982 balloting was a standoff, the GOP controlling 16.7 percent of the seats after the elections, compared with 16.6 percent in 1980.

59. This is Paul T. David's Composite B Index, which David presented in his *Party Strength in the United States 1872–1970* (Charlottesville: Univ. Press of Virginia, 1972). To construct the index every two years requires the occasional use of interpolation. Since the entire House is elected biennially, it is a simple matter to average a party's vote in all of a state's congressional districts to obtain the first of the three index components. Governorships, which usually run for four years, require the creation of an artificial figure for the election that comes at midterm, which is the average of the preceding and following elections. With Senate seats David faced a slightly more complicated situation. Because each state has two senators serving staggered six-year terms, there is a Senate election in every state in two election years out of three. David adopted this formula: "Use the actual popular vote figures in computing the percentages for any biennial year in which a senator is elected. . . . If neither seat is up, average the percentages for the previous and following senatorial election." David, *Party Strength*, 10. See generally his chap. 2 and his elaboration on odd problems in the introductory note to the data tables, pp. 85–87.

   David updated his party-strength figures for the 1972, 1974, and 1976 elections in three research notes published in the *Journal of Politics* (vol. 36, 785–96; vol. 38, 416–25; and vol. 40, 770–80). For the 1978 and 1980 elections (and for the necessary revision of the 1976 figures), the calculations were done by Eric V. Armen and the author at the Brookings Institution for James L. Sundquist's revised edition of *Dynamics of the Party System*. The 1982 calculations were made by the author at the University of Mississippi. For special rules governing Louisiana after its adoption of the open-primary system, see note 14 in Chapter 8.

60. In the construction of the regional illustration, each state's index figure was weighted for population using the number of members the state was entitled to send to the U.S. House of Representatives.

61. Earl Black describes in detail the Deep South–Rim South distinction on the race issue from 1950 to 1973 in his *Southern Governors and Civil Rights: Racial Segregation as a Campaign Issue in the Second Reconstruction* (Cambridge, Mass.: Harvard Univ. Press, 1976), 48–141.

Chapter 4: Mississippi

1. Charles N. Fortenberry and F. Glenn Abney, "Mississippi: Unreconstructed and Unredeemed," in William C. Havard, ed., *The Changing Politics of the South* (Baton Rouge: Louisiana State Univ. Press, 1972), 493.

2. In 1960 the Kennedy-Johnson Democratic ticket was second with 36.3 percent; the Republicans, led by Richard Nixon, finished third with 24.7 percent. The victorious unpledged slate cast Mississippi's electoral votes for Sen. Harry F. Byrd of Virginia.

3. Strom Thurmond and the Dixiecrats had carried Mississippi in 1948 with nearly the exact figure—87.2 percent!

4. Humphrey's race and McGovern's correlate at a nearly perfect .96. See the Appendix for an explanation of the correlation technique.

5. For an excellent account of the formation of this coalition, see William Simpson, "The Birth of the Mississippi 'Loyalist Democrats' (1965–1968)" *Journal of Mississippi History* 4 (Feb. 1982), 27–45. The article is especially revealing on the bitter factional struggles among black leaders.

6. The slogan was found on various 1963 GOP campaign advertisements in the Republican party file at the Mississippi Department of Archives and History, Jackson.

7. The statement is from a Rubel Phillips campaign brochure found in the Republican party file at the Mississippi Department of Archives and History, Jackson.

8. Neal R. Peirce, *The Deep South States of America* (New York: W. W. Norton, 1974), 196. At least one prominent Mississippi Republican, W. D. (Billy) Mounger, held to Walker's reasoning nearly a decade later. "Eastland is a national Democrat," Mounger told reporters in 1975. "I think he has been playing house with Ted Kennedy and George McGovern behind the scenes in Washington." Jackson *Clarion-Ledger*, May 16, 1975.

9. Jackson *Clarion-Ledger*, Nov. 1, 1967.

10. Ibid.

11. Ibid.

12. Ibid.

13. Numan V. Bartley and Hugh D. Graham, *Southern Elections: County and Precinct Data, 1950–1972* (Baton Rouge: Louisiana State Univ. Press, 1978), 375.

14. While the South Carolina Democratic establishment in 1968 was sending an integrated and unchallenged delegation to the Chicago convention and while its leaders were nominally supporting Humphrey's candidacy in the state, Governor Williams of Mississippi and state officeholders were backing Wallace openly, *Clarion-Ledger*, Nov. 3, 1968.

15. See Fortenberry and Abney, "Mississippi," 493–95, for a discussion of Democratic party factional struggles through 1971.

16. A sample of Evers's 1971 campaign statements follows: "For too long poor blacks and whites have been ignored. What we have now is a society filled with hate and very little opportunity for a man to help himself improve his own life. Welfare does little to help and mean white folks in control of the state government don't let local people use federal programs to work out their own problems. . . . What we've got to do is change Mississippi . . . from a divided state to a place of brotherhood where blacks and whites can work and live together in peace with opportunities for all. . . . I'm going to change the tax system so that the rich folks pay a fair share. Right now a fellow earning $6,000 pays at the same rate as a plantation owner earning $250,000. We're also going to change that sales tax so that things like

medicine and food aren't taxed." The quotation is from a 1971 Evers campaign letter on file at the Mississippi Department of Archives and History, Jackson.

17. Evers's county-level vote correlates at .95 with McGovern's, and at .94 with the county-level percentage of blacks.

18. Numan V. Bartley and Hugh D. Graham, *Southern Politics and the Second Reconstruction* (Baltimore: Johns Hopkins Univ. Press, 1975), 154.

19. Jack Bass and Walter DeVries, *The Transformation of Southern Politics* (New York: Basic Books, 1976), 215.

20. The quotation is from a talk Carmichael gave to a class of political science students at the University of Mississippi, March 31, 1982.

21. *Clarion-Ledger*, Nov. 8, 1972.

22. *New York Times*, May 15, 1978.

23. *New York Times*, Jan. 21, 1976.

24. Finch gained considerable publicity by working at various jobs during the campaign, a gimmick that had been used successfully in other parts of the country and was partly responsible for the success of a Florida Democratic gubernatorial candidate in 1978.

25. *New York Times*, Oct. 20, 1975.

26. Ibid.

27. Ibid.

28. Ibid., Aug. 18, 1975.

29. Interview with Carmichael, conducted by the author, March 31, 1982, in Oxford, Miss.

30. *Clarion-Ledger*, Nov. 8, 1975; *New York Times*, Oct. 20, 1975.

31. Interview with Carmichael.

In 1983 Carmichael tried to remedy the situation by shedding the Republican label and making a strong appeal to black voters in a bid to win the lieutenant governor's office as an independent. "If I can get 50 percent of the black vote, there is no question I will be elected," Carmichael told a reporter. *Clarion-Ledger*, Sept. 20, 1983.

If logic mattered in politics, Carmichael would have had a fair shot at his goal since his Democratic opponent, Lt. Gov. Brad Dye, had once been closely associated with the segregationist John Bell Williams, serving as Williams's 1967 campaign manager. Carmichael centered his surface campaign on the need to replace the state's 1890 constitution, which he called "anti-black and anti-business." Dye, the epitome of the old-style courthouse politician, conducted a vigorous person-to-person campaign throughout the state, stressing his experience in state government and arguing that changes in the constitution should be made through the amendment process rather than by a special convention, as Carmichael urged. *Clarion-Ledger*, Oct. 28, 1983.

When the votes came in, Carmichael once more found out how hard it is to break the state's biracial Democratic coalition. Black voters apparently remained with the Democratic nominee, and Dye won with 63.5 percent to Carmichael's 36.5 percent.

32. *New York Times*, Jan. 21, 1976.

33. Evers's vote correlates with the county-level percentage of blacks at .86.

34. Both Cochran, from the congressional district that includes the capital of Jackson, and the Republican Trent Lott, from the Gulf Coast congressional district, had first been elected to the U.S. House in the Nixon landslide of 1972.

35. *Washington Post*, Oct. 10, 1978.
36. *Clarion-Ledger*, Nov. 5, 1978.
37. Ibid.
38. Interview with Mike Retzer, chairman of the Mississippi Republican party, conducted by the author, Jan. 24, 1979.
39. *New York Times*, Nov. 25, 1978.
40. *Clarion-Ledger*, Nov. 5, 1978.
41. On the Sunday before the election, a get-out-the-vote parade went from Vicksburg to Clarksdale and back through Greenwood to Indianola, featuring Evers with the boxing champion Muhammad Ali and the singer Kris Kristofferson, who were filming a movie in Natchez. A large crowd viewed the procession. Ibid.
42. *Washington Post*, Oct. 10, 1978.
43. *Clarion-Ledger*, Nov. 9, 1978.
44. The officeholder sought anonymity for these remarks, made in an interview conducted by the author in 1979.
45. Montgomery's rating by the conservative Americans for Constitutional Action in 1972 was 100 percent; his rating by the liberal Americans for Democratic Action that year was zero. Michael Barone, Grant Ujifusa, and Douglas Matthews, *The Almanac of American Politics 1976* (New York: E. P. Dutton, 1975), 461.
46. Interview with Montgomery, conducted by the author, Jan. 26, 1979.
47. Interview with Lott, conducted by the author, Jan. 23, 1979.
48. *New York Times*, Jan. 29, 1979.
49. To win the Democratic nomination, Winter defeated Lt. Gov. Evelyn Gandy, a former assistant to Sen. Theodore G. Bilbo and a veteran of state politics who was allied with the Eastland faction of the party. In the first primary many black voters supported a candidate favored by Charles Evers, but blacks apparently swung to Winter over Gandy in the runoff. *Congressional Quarterly Weekly Report*, July 28, 1979; Aug. 11, 1979; Oct. 27, 1979; and Nov. 10, 1979.
50. Conservative Republicans, such as Wirt Yerger and W. D. (Billy) Mounger, backed a Delta planter, Leon Bramlett, in the 1979 GOP gubernatorial primary. Bramlett, a former Democrat, entered the race late and with weak name recognition. His well-financed effort, however, came very close to denying the nomination to Carmichael. Bramlett received 15,148 votes to Carmichael's 17,161. (The low GOP totals reflect the relative insignificance of the Republican primary in a state where most state-legislative and local offices are determined in the Democratic primary.) The figures from the 1979 primary appeared in the *Jackson* (Miss.) *Daily News*, July 17, 1980.
51. Over the objections of blacks, Governor Winter ended the dual party chairmanship arrangement during the spring of 1980, when he installed his choice, Danny Cupit, as state chairman. The *Clarion-Ledger* wrote that Cupit, who is white, "has walked the fine line of diplomacy between blacks and whites and moderates and conservatives in the party." State Rep. Fred Banks, a leading black politician, said that blacks would not be comfortable with a single party chairman. "Even though I recognize it's time to have one head . . . there is not enough trust there yet," Banks asserted. *Clarion-Ledger*, March 23, 1980.
52. Carter's two presidential races in Mississippi correlate at .82.
53. *Minneapolis Tribune*, Oct. 23, 1980.
54. A Mississippi State University survey conducted Sept. 18, 1982, found that 80 percent of the state's blacks favored Stennis and 20 percent preferred Barbour.

These results were reported in the *Clarion-Ledger*, which sponsored the poll, on Sept. 27, 1982. There is no reason to suspect that this ratio changed during the remaining weeks of the campaign.

55. *New York Times*, June 10, 1982.

56. For a good account of this court struggle, see Art Harris's June 1, 1982, *Washington Post* article on the subject.

57. *New York Times*, Oct. 14, 1982. This informative article was written by Adam Clymer.

58. Ibid.

59. Ibid.

60. Memphis *Commercial Appeal*, Nov. 5, 1982.

61. *Clarion-Ledger*, Feb. 8, 1981.

62. *New York Times*, July 9, 1981.

63. Interview with Wright, conducted by the author, July 27, 1982.

In Washington, Congressman Dowdy declined to join the Conservative Democratic Forum, the group of predominantly conservative Southern Democrats popularly known as the boll weevils. Asked if this decision was in deference to blacks and organized labor in his district, Dowdy said, "I think it would be misunderstood if I did. I vote with them. If you got the records out, . . . [they would show that] on many, many occasions I vote with the position of many of them who are known as boll weevils." When asked if such votes upset labor and blacks, Dowdy responded, "I don't vote with them [the boll weevils] all the time. And on some major issues . . . I felt I should vote against their position—the tax cut, different budget resolutions that have come up. Those have been the noticeable differences."

On the Mississippi Republican party, Dowdy minced no words: "Republicans in Mississippi are—a large number of them in my opinion—are [in the GOP] because they like what they think the Republican party now stands for in a racial sense. And that's a strong part of the Republican party in Mississippi. In my district, a lot of the people who are in the Republican party are racists. And they feel more comfortable—and naturally they should—with the Republican party." Interview with Dowdy, conducted by the author, July 15, 1982.

64. To win the nomination, Allain defeated Evelyn Gandy in the Democratic runoff primary. *Clarion-Ledger*, Aug. 24, 1983. A third candidate, the conservative Delta businessman Mike Sturdivant, was eliminated in the first primary despite having spent $1.6 million, over twice Allain's primary-campaign outlay. The spending figures were reported in the Memphis *Commercial Appeal*, Sept. 25, 1983.

65. Alvin Chambliss, a black civil rights lawyer from Oxford and a leading Evers supporter, added: "Access is not enough . . . we want blacks on agencies, boards and commissions . . . we want black people running agencies, boards and commissions.

"It's time for us to start supporting our own. . . . We have no permanent friends." *Clarion-Ledger*, Sept. 12, 1983.

66. *Jackson Daily News*, Sept. 12, 1983.

67. Of course, over the years Evers made his share of enemies among his fellow black leaders. Bill Minor, a journalist who has covered Mississippi politics for over thirty-five years, called Evers "the unsinkable exponent of Machiavellian politics in the Magnolia State" and added: "Once more, *le grand* Charles comes forth and offers himself on behalf of the entire black race in Mississippi at the head of a gubernatorial crusade. He did that in 1971, but then it was something special because blacks had just attained the vote in substantial numbers.

"Now the blush of enthusiasm for an Evers gubernatorial candidacy no longer exists in the black community." *Clarion-Ledger*, Aug. 28, 1983.

68. *Commercial Appeal*, Oct. 21, 1983.
69. Tupelo (Miss.) *Daily Journal*, Sept. 28, 1983.
70. *Clarion-Ledger*, Oct. 2, 1983.
71. Minor's column drew a sharp response from Ebbie Spivey of Canton, the Republican party chairwoman: "Bill Minor's assertion that the Republican Party has abandoned the Bramlett campaign is completely untrue. Leon Bramlett has been and continues to be the best hope we have ever had to win the governor's race." *Clarion-Ledger*, Oct. 4, 1983.
72. *Jackson Daily News*, Oct. 12, 1983.
73. *Clarion-Ledger*, Oct. 13, 1983.
74. Ibid., Oct. 18, 1983.
75. Ibid., Oct. 13, 1983.
76. Ibid., Oct. 24, 1983. This article was headlined, "Candidate Allain Lashes Back at Bramlett on 'Family Issue.' "
77. *Clarion-Ledger*, Oct. 26, 1983.
78. In describing Spell's efforts to get journalists to break the story, the *Clarion-Ledger* wrote, "News-gathering organizations across the state were plied with documents, offered interviews with alleged male prostitutes and threatened with losing the year's top political scoop to another news outlet." This Oct. 26, 1983, article was headlined, "Political Story of Season Built from Rumor to Roar."
79. Ibid.
80. Ibid.
81. Ibid.
82. Bill Minor wrote, "A loose cannon has been unleashed in Mississippi politics . . . . Almost universally, the reaction has been one of disgust about the entire episode, a feeling that Mississippi politics has become mired deeper in the mud than ever before." *Clarion-Ledger*, Oct. 30, 1983. Norma Fields, the veteran capital reporter for the Tupelo *Daily Journal*, began her weekly column, "It is a tragedy for Mississippi no matter which way the governor's race goes this year, for Mississippi politics has been forever tainted with tactics heretofore deemed untouchable. It is a nightmare for those of us covering this Faulknerian tragedy and trying to make some kind of sense out of it in the public print." *Daily Journal*, Nov. 1, 1983.
83. *Clarion-Ledger*, Oct. 26, 1983.
84. *Clarion-Ledger*, Nov. 3, 1983.
85. Tupelo *Daily Journal*, Nov. 4, 1983.
86. Incidentally, Bill Minor, the veteran political analyst, accurately predicted, in a column written ten days before the election, what would happen: "Allain, no matter the intensity of his denial that the allegations are untrue, has already suffered some loss of public esteem . . . My initial impression is that the deviant sex charges hurled at him have not cost him the election, but have caused his once-comfortable lead to drop several percentage points." *Clarion-Ledger*, Oct. 30, 1983.
87. Ibid., Nov. 11, 1983.

Chapter 5: South Carolina

1. After all, it was Mississippi that teamed up with South Carolina to provide the Dixiecrat ticket of Thurmond and Wright in 1948. It was also in Mississippi and

South Carolina that the proportion of blacks was the highest in the region—49.2 percent and 42.9 percent, respectively, in the 1940 census—and as a result white fears and resistance in these two states reached the highest level in the region.

2. Senator Johnston carried his party loyalty to the extent of seconding the nomination of Sen. Hubert Humphrey for the vice-presidency during the Atlantic City convention. At the same time, the South Carolina Democratic party chairman, Yancey McLeod, put the argument for supporting the Johnson-Humphrey ticket in bread-and-butter terms: "I hope that every office-holder, office seeker and the state, city and county employees will realize that South Carolina in this matter is a two-party state and that a Republican victory in November will almost undoubtedly precipitate Republican opposition two years from now in the whole political spectrum. . . . " *The State*, Aug. 28, 1964.

3. Humphrey's county-level support negatively correlates with Johnson's four years earlier; the coefficient is −.27. The correlation coefficient comparing Kennedy's race with Johnson's is .82. See the Appendix for an explanation of the correlation technique.

4. Alexander P. Lamis, "The Disruption of a Solidly Democratic State: Civil Rights and South Carolina Electoral Change, 1948–1972," *Journal of Political Science* 5 (Fall 1977), 69–72. In 1972 McGovern ran a pattern similar to Humphrey's; the two national nominees' races correlate at .95.

   The Piedmont turnabout in 1968 is illustrated in a scatter diagram of the Johnson-Humphrey correlation in my dissertation, "Southern Two-Party Politics: Dynamics of Electoral Competition in the South since the Early 1960s" (Vanderbilt University, 1982), 68 (fig. 6).

5. The dip in Democratic strength visible in Figure 5-1 in 1954 did not involve an early GOP gain; rather it reflected a peculiar U.S. Senate race that witnessed the Democrat Strom Thurmond's general-election victory as a write-in candidate. See note 28 in Chapter 2. Since Thurmond did not win in 1954 as the Democratic nominee, the party's strength "dropped" that year. For an account of this bizarre 1954 election, see Alberta Lachicotte, *Rebel Senator: Strom Thurmond of South Carolina* (New York: Devin-Adair, 1966), 77–105.

6. William D. Workman, Jr., *The Case for the South* (New York: Devin-Adair, 1960).

7. Bartley and Graham, *Southern Politics and the Second Reconstruction* (Baltimore: Johns Hopkins Univ. Press, 1975), 97.

8. Interview with Lee Bandy, Washington correspondent for *The State*, conducted by the author, Jan. 16, 1979. Thurmond expressed his motive differently: "Well, I had known that the Republican party was more conservative before I came to the Senate, but I didn't realize there was as much difference up here in the parties. . . . After I got up here I soon found that the Republican party was more in line with my thinking and the philosophy of the people of South Carolina than the Democratic party . . . at the national level and so that is the reason that I changed parties. I felt more at home in the Republican party." Interview with Thurmond, conducted by Jack Bass and Walter DeVries, Feb. 1, 1974.

9. Thurmond has run all of his re-election campaigns since the switch with little or no reference to the Republican party and, as much as possible, without reference to other Republicans on the ballot. Asked about this, Thurmond replied, "The Republican party hasn't been in existence long enough to run as a ticket; it isn't strong enough. I'm an independent at heart. You'll find good ones on both tickets." Interview with Thurmond, conducted by the author, July 18, 1978.

10. The emphasis placed here on the race issue and the spurt it gave Republicans in South Carolina—and elsewhere—does not imply that race was the only or the chief motivation of all Republican leaders. Many of them were committed ideological conservatives on economic issues and viewed the building of the Republican party as a means of exerting influence for their philosophical position in the politics of their state. J. Drake Edens, a former GOP state chairman in South Carolina, articulated this view when describing his reasons for getting involved in party affairs: "I was convinced that the Democrats were going to break the country financially, that they were completely irresponsible in fiscal matters, and I guess as much as anything else that is what got me involved in politics. I was one Southern Republican . . . [for whom] race has never been an issue with me. It wasn't in the beginning, it's not now, it never has been." Interview with Edens, conducted by Jack Bass, Feb. 13, 1974.

11. Interview with Joan McKinney, Washington correspondent for the Charleston (S.C.) *News and Courier*, conducted by the author, July 17, 1978.

12. Jack Bass and Walter DeVries, *The Transformation of Southern Politics* (New York: Basic Books, 1976), 261–63.

13. James Clyburn, a leading black politician in South Carolina who served in the West administration, told an interviewer in 1974 of the irony in Governor West's position favoring exemption of the state from the provisions of the Voting Rights Act: "It's real funny. I said to the governor one time when he was raising hell about the Voting Rights Act, and one of the commitments he wanted from McGovern [in 1972] and got from him was that he would get South Carolina out from under the Voting Rights Act . . . . I said, 'That's a . . . shame. How the hell do you think you got in?'. . . He [West] knows darn well that without the black vote he wouldn't have gotten here. . . . It is just that simple. I don't know why people play this down." Interview with Clyburn, conducted by Jack Bass.

    Clyburn, who was instrumental in a short-lived black third-party movement, the United Citizens party, had praise for Governor West's personal attitude toward the problems faced by blacks. But the trouble comes, Clyburn said, "with the people he surrounded himself with. The most conservative elements around the governor had the most influence on him." *The State*, Jan. 12, 1975, as cited in Bass and DeVries, *Transformation of Southern Politics*, 264. Clyburn added, in the interview with Bass, "I think that the John West administration has done a good job in articulating the problems . . . but you are going to have to have somebody outside who is not a [product] of that legislature up there who will make anything happen in this state, and that is the only way I see it really happening for black people."

14. Numan V. Bartley and Hugh D. Graham, *Southern Elections: County and Precinct Data, 1950–1972* (Baton Rouge: Louisiana State Univ. Press, 1978), 388.

15. Peirce, *The Deep South States of America* (New York: W. W. Norton, 1974), 402.

16. The Zeigler-McGovern correlation coefficient is .91.

17. Peirce, *Deep South States*, 404–6.

18. Interview with McKinney.

19. Peirce, *Deep South States*, 400.

20. *The State*, Oct. 28, 1974. Edwards showed no sign of exploiting racial issues.

21. Prior to the fall campaign Thurmond was asked why he did so much better at the polls than other Republican candidates in the state. He responded, "People know where I stand. I'm not shifty. I try to be stable, consistent." Interview with Thurmond, conducted by the author.

22. The correlation figures are .81 and .91, respectively.
23. Interview with Thurmond, conducted by the author. The senator went on to say, "For state politics, it would suit me to run as an individual."
24. Peirce, *Deep South States*, 400.
25. Interview with Bandy.
26. Interview with McKinney.
27. *New York Times*, March 21, 1978. This informative article was written by Wayne King.
28. *Atlanta Constitution-Journal*, Sunday, May 13, 1978; the editorial writer was William E. Rone, Jr. Turnipseed remained active on the South Carolina political scene. In 1980 he won the Democratic nomination for Congress from the Columbia-centered district, but was defeated by U.S. Rep. Floyd Spence, the conservative Republican incumbent. In 1982 Turnipseed ran for lieutenant governor, leading the first primary with 45 percent to State Rep. Mike Daniel's 31 percent. The following account of the Democratic runoff campaign appeared in *The State*, June 20, 1982: "Turnipseed is obviously aware that Daniel is trying to jolt the state's voters, especially through the business and corporate community, into helping spread the word to be afraid of Turnipseed.

"But during a Columbia news conference late last week, Turnipseed kept saying, 'They don't need to fear me.'

"Turnipseed conceded that 'maybe I have gone a little overboard in representing the under-represented. I've been a lightening rod, and I know that.'

"He says if elected, he will be a representative of everybody, including business and industry.

" 'But I'll never be a part of trying to protect a cheap labor force,' Turnipseed said."

Daniel won the Democratic nomination, 51.9 percent to Turnipseed's 48.1 percent. *New York Times*, June 24, 1982. Daniel was a two-to-one winner in November over Norma Russell, a Republican state senator. *The State*, Nov. 4, 1982.
29. Interview with U.S. Rep. Carroll Campbell, conducted by the author, Jan. 17, 1979.
30. Ibid.
31. Interview with Edward L. (Ed) Young, conducted by the author, July 17, 1978.
32. Interview with Campbell. He added, "I think the Republican party is going to pick up black voters in the same manner in which it is attracting white voters. And I think that is going to be a philosophy . . . based on concern for human needs and at the same time for the integrity of the free enterprise system. . . . The hope for the Republican party in the South is the growing black middle class, because the Republican party has middle-class values. . . . We ought to recognize that color of skin has nothing to do with values."

Continuing his critical analysis of the Republican position in South Carolina, Campbell said his party has spent too much time trying to put together an ideologically purist party: "We try to out-conservative one another. We have let our umbrella come down halfway and not been broad enough to bring in enough people to make the coalition the size that you need to win. And that umbrella has to be raised to the extent to cover enough people."

Although the two Democratic congressmen from South Carolina who were interviewed for this book offered less enlightening assessments of the electoral situation, one of them, U.S. Rep. Butler Derrick, did agree with Campbell on the umbrella opening: "They [South Carolina Republicans] are probably going to be perceptive enough to broaden their base and that will give the Democrats some real problems on the local and state level." Interview with Derrick, conducted by the author, Jan. 18, 1979.

33. The percentage was calculated from figures released before the November election by the South Carolina State Election Commission, as reported in *The State*, Oct. 21, 1982. James B. Ellisor, the commission's director, said blacks made up 27.6 percent of the state's voting-age population. In the 1980 census blacks were 30.5 percent of South Carolina's population. *The State*, Oct. 10, 1982.

34. The South Carolina Constitution had been changed to allow a governor to serve two consecutive terms.

35. *The State*, Nov. 4, 1982.

36. Ibid.

37. *Congressional Quarterly Weekly Report*, Oct. 9, 1982, p. 2589.

38. Interview with Napier, conducted by the author, July 28, 1982.

39. Ninety-seven percent of the district's blacks voted for Tallon, according to an exit poll conducted by WPDE-TV of Florence, S.C. The poll is reported in Thomas E. Cavanagh, "Black Gains Offset Losses in '82 Elections," *Focus* (Nov.–Dec. 1982). Hartnett, the other Republican congressman elected in 1980, won re-election with 54.9 percent of the vote over the Democrat W. Mullins McLeod. After the election Hartnett observed, "I said 53.7 percent would be a landslide in a district that's 33 percent black. . . . We did exactly what we hoped we would do." *The State*, Nov. 4, 1982. The partisan makeup of the other four seats did not change in 1982, leaving the state's six-member U.S. House delegation evenly split between Republicans and Democrats as a result of Napier's loss.

Chapter 6: Alabama

1. Bartley and Graham, *Southern Politics and the Second Reconstruction* (Baltimore: Johns Hopkins Univ. Press, 1975), 98–99.

2. The Hill-Johnson correlation is .82. For an explanation of the correlation technique, see the Appendix.

3. Whereas Stevenson's race in 1956 and Kennedy's in 1960 correlate at a high .88, the Kennedy-Johnson correlation is a nearly random .12.

4. V. O. Key, Jr., *Southern Politics in State and Nation* (New York: Alfred A. Knopf, 1949), 41–46. Before the early 1960s, South Alabama voted overwhelmingly for Democratic presidential candidates. Walter Dean Burnham wrote that South Alabama was "such a citadel of Democracy that it chose to accept Al Smith's wetness and Catholicism in 1928 rather than run the dangers of jeopardizing the local system of social control through a party bolt." Burnham, "The Alabama Senatorial Election of 1962: Return of Inter-Party Competition," *Journal of Politics* 26 (Nov. 1964), 803. In North Alabama are found the strongest New Deal counties, areas that benefited from the Tennessee Valley Authority projects and that consistently supported New Deal Democrats. Ibid., 805–10. Also, in North Alabama, part of which encompasses an extension of the Appalachian Mountains, there was a residue of Civil War pro-Union sentiment similar in origin to the Mountain Republicanism found in Tennessee, North Carolina, and Virginia. These traditionally

Republican counties in Alabama included Cullman and Winston, the latter known as the "Free State of Winston" because it seceded from the Confederacy when Alabama left the Union. (For a tongue-in-cheek account of Winston County's "defiance" of the South, see Key, *Southern Politics*, 282–83.)

5. The full sentence was "In the name of the greatest people that have ever trod this earth, I draw the line in the dust and toss the gauntlet before the feet of tyranny, and I say: Segregation now—segregation tomorrow—segregation forever." Jack Bass and Walter DeVries, *The Transformation of Southern Politics* (New York: Basic Books, 1976), 62.

6. Martin's races in 1962 and 1966 are negatively related; the correlation coefficient is −.12. The GOP candidate in 1966 received 31.0 percent of the vote to Mrs. Wallace's 63.4 percent.

7. Strong, "Alabama: Transition and Alienation," in William C. Havard, ed., *The Changing Politics of the South* (Baton Rouge: Louisiana State Univ. Press, 1972), 457.

8. Sparkman's race correlates with Mrs. Wallace's at only .33.

9. *Montgomery Advertiser*, Nov. 6, 1968.

10. Ibid.

11. The Allen-Wallace correlation is .85. Another interesting correlation coefficient emphasizes the gulf between the Alabama Democracy and the national party at this juncture: With the electoral pattern of the 1968 Democratic presidential nominee, Humphrey, the Democrat Allen's 1968 race correlates at −.70; in other words, where Humphrey was strong, Allen was weak, and vice versa. This disparity reached an even more extreme position in the early 1970s. The county-level voting pattern of the 1970 Alabama Democratic gubernatorial nominee (again Wallace) was completely opposite to that of the 1972 Democratic presidential standard-bearer (McGovern). The correlation coefficient is −.87, nearly a perfect negative score!

12. Neal R. Peirce, *The Deep South States of America* (New York: W. W. Norton, 1974), 256. It is amusing how forgetful politicians become when reviewing their past. In an interview with the *New York Times* as he left office, Wallace said his deepest regret was allowing what he described as his philosophical opposition to federal intervention to be taken as an indication that he personally hated blacks. "I was not an enemy of blacks in those days," maintained Wallace. "I was the enemy of the federal government, big government. It's very unfortunate that it involved race when we raised those issues." *New York Times*, Jan. 7, 1979.

13. For a detailed analysis of the National Democratic Party of Alabama, see Hardy T. Frye, *Black Parties and Political Power: A Case Study* (Boston: G. K. Hall, 1980).

14. *Montgomery Advertiser*, Nov. 1, 1970.

15. Cashin's vote correlates with the county-level percentage of blacks at .90 and with McGovern's pattern at .87.

16. Frye quotes a *Birmingham News* analysis shortly after the 1972 voting that concluded, "Is the National Democratic Party of Alabama a political force that carries weight at the state level in elections? Tuesday's election results would say no." *Black Parties*, 150.

17. Peirce, *Deep South States*, 300. On Vance's role, also see Frye, *Black Parties*, 76–80, 126–49.

18. Interview with Robert Vance, then chairman of the Alabama Democratic party, conducted by Jack Bass and Walter DeVries, July 16, 1974. Vance was later named to the U.S. Court of Appeals for the Fifth Circuit by President Carter.

19. *Montgomery Advertiser,* Nov. 8, 1972.
20. Interview with Ray Jenkins, conducted by Jack Bass and Walter DeVries, Feb. 5, 1974.
21. To lend support to Jenkins's deprecation of the wisdom of the Blount strategy, Sparkman's race correlates with McGovern's at −.42.
22. In an article headlined, "Elvin McCary: The Man Few People Wanted in Governor's Race," the *Huntsville* (Ala.) *Times* on Nov. 3, 1974, reported, "He ran the campaign from his vest pocket, without staff or party support, and often without outside contributions. No one bets he will defeat Wallace—or, for that matter, even come close. McCary is doing what he says is essential if the Alabama Republican Party ever hopes to put the state government in a 'real two-party system.' "
23. Interview with Jenkins.
24. Regarding James E. (Big Jim) Folsom, the former governor, Jenkins said, "Basically, Jim was as solid a populist as ever came down the road. I mean he really was. He was good; he really fully appreciated the needs of the poor people of Alabama. He fully appreciated the . . . powerful influence exerted by agencies like the Farm Bureau, and he was determined to break it. He . . . had as fine a program as any governor ever could hope to have. But now he had a malapportioned legislature that made it impossible for him to achieve anything. . . . Plus the fact that he was such a wretched administrator. He was a heavy drinker always. In his last administration, he was an out-and-out alcoholic. You would go for six weeks without the Governor doing anything and that sort of thing. The two things combined plus Jim's gentle personality and gentle nature and unwillingness to hurt anybody. He simply lacked the ruthlessness that you have to have in politics to accomplish anything. Those things pretty much made him a failure. . . . But on the race question, he was way ahead on that. His Christmas message in 1949 is really one of the nicest, just simple statements about justice towards the black man that anybody could possibly ever write." Interview with Jenkins. For an account of Alabama politics during Folsom's first term as governor, see William D. Barnard, *Dixiecrats and Democrats: Alabama Politics, 1942–1950* (University: Univ. of Alabama Press, 1974).
25. Interview with Jenkins.
26. Ibid.
27. Interview with George Wallace, conducted by Jack Bass and Walter DeVries, July 15, 1974.
28. Interview with Bill Harris, chairman of the Alabama Republican party, conducted by the author, Jan. 24, 1979.
29. Ibid.
30. Interview with U.S. Rep. Jack Edwards, conducted by the author, Jan. 26, 1979.
31. Interview with Jenkins.
32. Interview with Harris.
33. Interview with Edwards, conducted by the author, July 27, 1982. In an earlier interview, conducted Jan. 26, 1979, Congressman Edwards emphasized the importance of the Alabama GOP broadening its range to "take in some of that middle ground that is fertile and ripe for the picking if somebody will just appeal to them. Maybe I'm wrong, but maybe one day, if I am right, we will prevail." Steven K. Smith elaborates on what he calls "the problem of the purists" in his "Southern Congressional Politics since the Great Society" (Ph.D. diss., Univ. of South Carolina, 1983).

34. There were no statewide elections in Alabama in 1976. Carter's victory in the state that year, with 55.7 percent of the vote, followed regional trends, to the consternation of GOP officials. Edgar Weldon, Republican party chairman, noted after the 1976 election, "It's very discouraging as a Republican to offer candidates and go out and have a majority maybe [among white voters], and get beat because the black community doesn't care who you are or what you stand for. They're going to straight-ticket vote." *Montgomery Advertiser*, Nov. 4, 1976.

35. For a survey of the Alabama partisan scene during the 1978 elections, see Margaret K. Latimer, " 'No Party' Politics at the End of the Wallace Era," *Publius* (Winter 1979), 215–27.

36. *Washington Post*, Sept. 25, 1978.

37. Sunday *Atlanta Constitution-Journal*, Feb. 26, 1978.

38. Interview with B. J. Richey, news editor of the Washington bureau of a newspaper group that included the *Birmingham News, Huntsville Times, Mobile Press,* and *Mobile Register,* conducted by the author, Jan. 24, 1979.

39. *Washington Post*, Sept. 27, 1978.

40. Ibid., Sept. 25, 1978.

41. Ibid.

42. Ibid. Graddick ran on one issue—capital punishment. According to the *Washington Post*, "Graddick calls himself a 'man of convictions' who will lock up criminals and see to it that murderers and rapists get the electric chair. 'I'll fry them until their eyeballs pop out and smoke comes out of their ears,' he told one reporter—a statement he now denies making." Ibid.

43. Interview with Edwards (1979).

44. *Birmingham News*, Oct. 22, 1978. The article was headlined, "Battling Odds Nothing New for Governor-hopeful Hunt."

45. *Washington Post*, Oct. 3, 1978.

46. Interview with Edwards (1979).

47. Peggy Roberson, Washington correspondent of the *Montgomery Advertiser*, wrote that Martin had "suddenly changed his perception of Heflin since he switched races," and she quoted Heflin on the matter: "One week I was the damnedest radical ever to come down the pike and now I hear that we will be 'two voices for conservatism' " in the Senate. *Montgomery Advertiser*, Oct. 11, 1978.

48. *Washington Post*, Nov. 5, 1978. Stewart had faced similar charges in the primary: "When Mrs. Allen charged Stewart was a 'flaming liberal' and a tool of organized labor, he responded by citing his efforts to save consumers $200 million a year in lower utility payments. 'Is that liberal?' he asked." *Congressional Quarterly Weekly Report*, Oct. 14, 1978. To establish his own conservative credentials, Martin had Sen. Barry Goldwater of Arizona speak for him in Mobile, where the former GOP presidential standard-bearer called Martin a conservative in the same mold as the late Senator Allen. *Mobile Press*, Nov. 4, 1978.

49. *Birmingham News*, Nov. 8, 1978. When he announced his candidacy, Martin was quoted in the *Alabama Journal* of June 30, 1978, as saying that the nation "is in the same mood it was [in] when the Republican party made its sweep in 1964." If he had any justification for that assertion, it was not readily apparent even in late June but certainly not in November.

50. The Reagan-Denton correlation coefficient is .94, a nearly perfect positive relationship.

51. *Congressional Quarterly Weekly Report*, Oct. 11, 1980.

52. The *Mobile Press* reported, "Stewart is an arrogant and abrasive man. He'll tell you that himself . . . he takes pride in it." Sept. 14, 1980. In an article headlined "Did Stewart Cook His Own Goose?" Tom Scarritt, Washington correspondent of the *Birmingham News*, discussed the "charm" issue: "The moral of Sen. Donald Stewart's defeat, an aide in another Alabama congressional office said last week, is that it doesn't hurt to be nice to people, even if you're a senator. . . .

   "Stewart's approach was different. His office tried to impress the voters with his accomplishments, rather than courting them. Stewart visited the state religiously, but he sometimes seemed too busy to listen to the people, or even to be polite. . . .

   " 'Donald was just rude sometimes,' an aide said." *Birmingham News*, Sept. 26, 1980.

53. *New York Times*, Nov. 1, 1980.

54. Ibid.

55. A survey conducted at the University of Alabama, Tuscaloosa, Oct. 26 to Nov. 2, 1980, revealed that black Alabamians favored Folsom 81 percent to 19 percent. Information on the income of respondents in the survey was not available, but another class-related variable that was available, level of education, suggested the presence of a moderate class cleavage among whites in this election. Whites with at least some college education favored Denton by 64 percent to 36 percent. Among whites with a high school education or less, Folsom held a slight lead over Denton, 54 percent to 46 percent. The survey, identified as Capstone Poll No. 3, was conducted by Patrick R. Cotter, who kindly made these cross-tabulations available to me.

56. *Birmingham News*, Nov. 5, 1980.

57. Peirce, *Deep South States*, 256.

58. When Wallace's bid for black support was developing in the summer of 1982, Peggy Roberson of the *Montgomery Advertiser* articulated this amused surprise during an interview while explaining Wallace's general appeal: "So almost everybody you talk to has some little reason for remembering Wallace with great affection, except the blacks. And I'll be damned, some of them—it just freaks me out—will go for Wallace on the grounds that they are all racists anyway and at least we know what old Wallace is and what he is up to. And he is better than Folmar." Interview with Roberson, conducted by the author, July 15, 1982.

59. Governor James declined to run for re-election.

60. *Birmingham News*, Sept. 30, 1982.

61. *New York Times*, Sept. 26, 1982.

62. One of McMillan's brochures carried this message: "Alabama is at a crossroads. We can move forward, stand still or fall backward. We can elect a leader who fits the times and has a common sense approach to government; or we can continue to be distracted by shallow, simplistic political rhetoric. The time has come to elect a leader who can make things better for you as an Alabamian. Things *can* be better with George McMillan as Governor!" The heading on the brochure read, "Because We Don't Have 4 Years To Waste."

63. *New York Times*, Sept. 26, 1982.

64. *Montgomery Advertiser*, Aug. 8, 1982.

65. *New York Times*, Sept. 12, 1982.

66. *Birmingham News*, Sept. 12, 1982. This first-rate profile article about Pickett was written by the *News* staff writer Frank Sikora.

67. Ibid. Pickett further noted, "He made us more determined to fight for our rights. If

he had been a fence-straddler, an appeaser, we might not have won some civil rights as quickly as we did."

68. *Birmingham News*, Sept. 26, 1982.
69. *Montgomery Advertiser*, Sept. 24, 1982.
70. Natalie Davis of Birmingham Southern College, who conducted numerous surveys during the 1982 election season, said her last poll, taken Sept. 27, the day before the runoff, showed Wallace was supported by 33 percent of those blacks likely to vote. Telephone conversation with Davis, Dec. 16, 1982. To discover why black voters would support such a symbol of racial hatred, Frank Sikora, a *Birmingham News* reporter, visited one Black Belt county where Wallace outpolled McMillan by over two to one. The first part of his artcle, filed from Hayneville, Ala., went as follows:

"Back in 1965, Robert Strickland was out on U.S. 80 with the Selma-to-Montgomery march, singing a song that said:

" 'Ain't gonna let George Wallace turn us around.'

"Wednesday, Strickland, 57, stood by his pickup truck in front of the Lowndes County Courthouse and pointed at the 'Wallace' stickers on it.

" 'George Wallace changed,' he said. 'We've changed, too. I think black folks just decided that this man is worth giving our support to.

" 'George Wallace made some mistakes, sure. Why, I remember thinking once that the worst thing in the world would be a vote for George Wallace. But he's like Saul, who was struck down and then got up to do good.

" 'I think Wallace knows he has a chance to help people. He's said he regretted the past. And down here, the folks believe him. That's all.'

"Strickland's attitude is typical of those of many black voters here in Lowndes County . . . . " *Birmingham News*, Sept. 30, 1982.
71. *Birmingham News*, Sept. 29, 1982.
72. *New York Times*, Oct. 16, 1982. The material in quotation marks was attributed to Folmar's campaign manager.
73. *Birmingham News*, Sept. 3, 1982.
74. Interview with Roberson. Tom Scarritt, Washington correspondent of the *Birmingham News*, agreed with this view of the GOP nominee, saying, "Folmar has made no effort to appeal to blacks." Interview with Scarritt, conducted by the author, July 15, 1982.
75. An exit poll of voters on Election Day taken by ABC News and the *Washington Post* found that 89 percent of Alabama's blacks voted for Wallace. This figure was provided by Thomas E. Cavanagh, research associate at the Joint Center for Political Studies in Washington. Davis's last Birmingham Southern general-election poll, conducted Oct. 31, gave Wallace the support of 90 percent of the blacks.
76. For two useful treatments of this election, see Bradley Moody, "Realignment or Persistence: Patterns of Voting in the 1982 Alabama Gubernatorial Election" (Paper presented at the Annual Meeting of the American Political Science Association, Chicago, Sept. 1–4, 1983), and Patrick R. Cotter, "George Wallace and the Changing Party Politics of Alabama" (Paper presented at the Annual Meeting of the Southern Political Science Association, Birmingham, Nov. 3–5, 1983). In his table 3 Moody reports that the correlation between Wallace's 1982 general election and Carter's 1980 pattern in Alabama is .72, which is a fair measure of how far the Wallace-led Democracy in Alabama has traveled since the early 1970s, when the Wallace-McGovern correlation was −.87, as discussed in note 11 above.

Chapter 7: Georgia

1. The correlations between Stevenson's two races and Kennedy's 1960 result were not nearly as strong as those found elsewhere in the South, but compared with what followed they do offer some sense of voter stability. The correlation coefficient for Stevenson in 1956 and Kennedy in 1960 is .75, but Kennedy in 1960 and Johnson in 1964 yield a correlation of −.01.
2. Numan V. Bartley and Hugh D. Graham, *Southern Politics and the Second Reconstruction* (Baltimore: Johns Hopkins Univ. Press, 1975), 68. On North Georgia, Bartley wrote, "The predominately white residents of the hill country were less immediately concerned with racial issues, and the North Georgia towns only occasionally demonstrated the same dedication to the social and ideological status quo that dominated the voting tendencies of the South Georgia towns." Numan V. Bartley, *From Thurmond to Wallace: Political Tendencies in Georgia 1948–1968* (Baltimore: Johns Hopkins Univ. Press, 1970), 58.
3. Bartley and Graham, *Southern Politics*, 68.
4. Bernd, "Georgia: Static and Dynamic," in William C. Havard, ed., *The Changing Politics of the South* (Baton Rouge: Louisiana State Univ. Press, 1972), 353.
5. *Atlanta Constitution*, Sept. 1, 1970.
6. Interview with Harris, conducted by Jack Bass and Walter DeVries, April 22, 1974. Harris was a key backer of Goldwater in 1964 but had been associated with the Talmadge family throughout his career.
7. Neal R. Peirce, *The Deep South States of America* (New York: W. W. Norton, 1974), 313.
8. *Atlanta Constitution*, Sept. 1, 1970.
9. Interview with Jimmy L. Bentley, Jr., conducted by Jack Bass and Walter DeVries, April 29, 1974.
10. Interview with Bentley.
11. *Atlanta Constitution*, Sept. 1, 1970. Prior to his defeat Bentley foresaw the possibility of major switchovers to the GOP. He has, of course, a personal vendetta against those who scuttled his political career, and his remarks must be read in light of that bitterness: "This thing [the possibility of major switchovers] had substance there for about twenty-four months. But when Republicans in this state just slashed it to the ground, all of my old friends in the state, in courthouses, in city halls, who had taken it seriously, you know, that maybe the kid knows what he's talking about, they were waiting to see. And I never did even get to first base, and a television announcer [Suit] was given a job. It became somewhat of a joke, I mean, in the eyes of a lot of people. They quit taking the Republicans seriously after '70." Interview with Bentley.
12. *Atlanta Constitution*, Sept. 24, 1970.
13. Bartley and Graham, *Southern Politics*, 149–50.
14. *Atlanta Constitution*, Sept. 25, 1970.
15. Bartley and Graham report the Wallace-Carter correlation coefficient as .95. *Southern Politics*, 150.
16. Interview with Charles Kirbo, conducted by Jack Bass and Walter DeVries, May 1, 1974.
17. Bartley and Graham, *Southern Politics*, 149.
18. Interview with Carl Sanders, conducted by Jack Bass and Walter DeVries, April 24, 1974.

19. Numan V. Bartley and Hugh D. Graham, *Southern Elections: County and Precinct Data, 1950–1972* (Baton Rouge: Louisiana State Univ. Press, 1978), 363–65.
20. Jack Bass and Walter DeVries, *The Transformation of Southern Politics* (New York: Basic Books, 1976), 144.
21. Interview with Robert Shaw, conducted by Jack Bass and Walter DeVries, April 27, 1974.
22. Bartley and Graham, *Southern Politics*, 180.
23. David S. Broder, *The Changing of the Guard: Power and Leadership in America* (New York: Penguin Books, 1981), 368.
24. For those who wonder how black Democratic politicians deal with these racist appeals by white leaders in their party, the following excerpt from a 1974 interview with State Rep. Bobby Hill, a black leader from Savannah, may serve to cast light on this question:

    Hill: It's obvious what kind of image [Nunn is] trying to portray. He's trying . . . not to part company too far from the kind of campaign he ran, which was extremely racist. But I have a different kind of insight. I served with him for four years on the Judiciary Committee up in the House. . . . When the chips are down on an issue, I think we can count on him.

    Bass: How do you feel about . . . a candidate like Nunn? I assume on the basis of what you've said that he uses race as a political issue because he feels it's necessary. Is that correct?

    Hill: Well, that makes for a hypocrite and it also makes for a hypocritical kind of analysis, which you have to give. And if you know the guy personally, you know that you've had unstrained relationships with him. And I know that, when we close the door and get in a smoke-filled room, we can count on him. I know that for a fact. And I also know that he's got to win. . . . And so I understand that.

    Interview with Hill, conducted by Jack Bass and Walter DeVries, May 3, 1974.
25. Bartley and Graham, *Southern Elections: Precinct Data*, 363–65.
26. *Atlanta Constitution*, Aug. 15, 1974.
27. Interview with Dave Nordan, conducted by the author, Jan. 23, 1979.
28. Rex Granum, in a 1974 *Atlanta Constitution* news analysis, summed up the partisan situation: "Even the most cursory review of the state's political scene readily shows that in the short span of eight years the Republican party, which once threatened to be Georgia's victorious political institution, first stumbled and now has fallen miserably." *Constitution*, Nov. 4, 1974.
29. In 1976, Carter swept his home state as the Democratic presidential nominee with 66.7 percent of the vote, his highest percentage in the South.
30. Cook centered his campaign on taxes, promising to cut them by 10 percent. He told the *Atlanta Journal*, "I think that if there is any issue that will get people in the state to forsake that straight [Democratic] ticket voting, just because their granddaddies did, I think it's the tax issue." *Journal*, Nov. 5, 1978.
31. *Congressional Quarterly Weekly Report*, July 26, 1980.
32. *Atlanta Journal*, Aug. 10, 1980.
33. Ibid., Aug. 20, 1980.
34. *Washington Post*, Nov. 18, 1980. This informative article was written by Art Harris.
35. Ibid.
36. At the outset of the runoff, Miller predicted Talmadge would conduct a racist campaign: "That's what happens to old politicians when they get in trouble. They resort to what they know best." *Atlanta Journal*, Aug. 6, 1980.

37. *Atlanta Journal*, Aug. 27, 1980.
38. Ibid.
39. *Congressional Quarterly Weekly Report*, Oct. 11, 1980.
40. *Atlanta Journal*, May 12, 1980.
41. Ibid., Oct. 29, 1980.
42. The Reagan-Mattingly correlation coefficient is .73.
43. Two other urban examples were Muscogee County (Columbus), Mattingly 58 percent, Reagan 38 percent; and Richmond County (Augusta), Mattingly 53 percent, Reagan 44 percent.
44. Eugene Talmadge, Herman's father, "often bragged that he did not want to carry a county that had a streetcar." V. O. Key, Jr., *Southern Politics in State and Nation* (New York: Alfred A. Knopf, 1949), 116.
45. Wright-McNeill and Associates, a Washington firm that conducted polls in 1980 for the Republican party, reported that 39 percent of Georgia's blacks voted for Mattingly. A Wright-McNeill document prepared for the Republican National Committee, which contained this figure, was cited in Pearl T. Robinson, "Whither the Future of Blacks in the Republican Party?" *Political Science Quarterly* 97 (Summer 1982), 226.
46. *Washington Post*, Nov. 18, 1980.
47. *Atlanta Constitution*, Sept. 1, 1982. One *Constitution* article, headlined, "Joe Frank Harris Is White Knight of Religious Right," contended that the publicity surrounding Harris's no-tax-rise pledge obscured his strong support among fundamentalist Christian groups. The July 20, 1982, article noted, "Harris is a staunch Methodist layman, a non-smoker and teetotaler, a devout family man . . . and his campaign is salted with subtle religious appeals."
48. *New York Times*, Sept. 2, 1982.
49. *Atlanta Constitution*, Sept. 2, 1982.
50. Ibid. On Election Day, Speaker Murphy responded to Bell's campaign attacks: "He [Bell] has seen fit to run all over Georgia calling Democrats crooks. Most of us think he is an idiot." *Atlanta Constitution*, Nov. 3, 1982.
51. *Atlanta Constitution*, Sept. 2, 1982.
52. Ibid., Nov. 3, 1982.
53. Ibid.
54. Ibid.
55. Ibid. Mike Christensen wrote this article.
56. Ibid. A look at the 1982 congressional results supports Ginn's conclusion: nine of Georgia's ten U.S. House seats were won by Democrats, making it the most Democratic delegation in the South. The lone Republican, the two-term incumbent Newt Gingrich, who was expected to win handily, was held to 55.2 percent by Jim Wood, a Forest Park newspaper publisher. Gingrich represented a suburban Atlanta district.
57. *Atlanta Constitution*, Nov. 3, 1982. The *Constitution* endorsed Harris in the campaign.

Chapter 8: Louisiana

1. T. Harry Williams, *Huey Long* (New York: Alfred A. Knopf, 1970), 414.
2. Quoted in Neal R. Peirce, *The Deep South States of America* (New York: W. W. Norton, 1974), 59–60.
3. V. O. Key, Jr., *Southern Politics in State and Nation* (New York: Alfred A. Knopf,

1949), 3. Controversy over the career of this remarkable politician still rages. In two delightful sentences in *Southern Politics*, Professor Key illuminated the spirit of the debate: "Long dramatized himself as the champion of the people against the sinister interests and his production was by no means pure melodrama. For there are sinister interests and there are champions of the people, even though there may always be some good about the sinister and at least a trace of fraud in self-styled champions" (157).

4. Ibid., 301.

5. David M. Landry and Joseph B. Parker, "The Louisiana Political Culture," in James Bolner, ed., *Louisiana Politics: Festival in a Labyrinth* (Baton Rouge: Louisiana State Univ. Press, 1982), 11.

6. Perry H. Howard, *Political Tendencies in Louisiana*, rev. ed. (Baton Rouge: Louisiana State Univ. Press, 1971), 251–397.

7. Bolner, *Louisiana Politics*, xvii.

8. On this election, see William C. Havard, Rudolf Heberle, and Perry H. Howard, *The Louisiana Elections of 1960* (Baton Rouge: Louisiana State Univ. Press, 1963).

9. The Kennedy-Johnson correlation coefficient is .89.

10. Landry and Parker wrote, "Largely because of the Latin tradition of tolerance, racism was rarely as intense or, one might argue, was never as institutionalized in South Louisiana as it was in other parts of the South. In the French parishes, for example, a higher percentage of blacks were registered to vote prior to the 1965 Voting Rights Act than in any other area of the South. Nor did the Ku Klux Klan find much support in South Louisiana primarily because the Klan is anti-Catholic as well as antiblack." "The Louisiana Political Culture," in Bolner, *Louisiana Politics*, 2.

11. Concerning this sectional division, Adrian Laborde, a veteran Alexandria newspaper editor, noted, "North Louisiana is Waspish, always has been. South Louisiana is pretty heavily Latin flavored, as you know, especially southwest Louisiana. A lot of French people, a lot of Catholic people, a lot of liberals . . . people who like the good life, not as straitlaced as the people of North Louisiana. The point to make there, I think, and very few would admit it, is that North Louisiana is more conservative on the old race issue. There's a lot more racism. There has been, let's put it that way. From [Alexandria] on north . . . at least, it has been more overt." Interview with Laborde, conducted by Jack Bass and Walter DeVries, Jan. 12, 1974.

12. The Johnson-Humphrey correlation is a weak .30.

13. Humphrey and McGovern produce a correlation coefficient of .90.

14. The construction of David's party-strength index for Louisiana after the mid-1970s required special rules. If there is a "runoff" general election between candidates of the two major parties, disregard the open-primary results and treat the runoff like a general election in a more traditional electoral system. If the runoff is between candidates of the same party, however, treat it like a purely one-party affair; thus, the winner gets the 100 percent he or she would get in an uncontested general election. If there is no runoff, use the open-primary results only if candidates of both major parties finish first and second. If the top two in the open primary are of the same party, treat the results like a party primary. See note 59 in Chapter 3 for the general rules governing the calculation of David's index.

15. Howard, *Political Tendencies in Louisiana*, 375–90.

16. Ibid., 391–92.

17. Ibid., 391.
18. Ibid.
19. Perry H. Howard, "Louisiana: Resistance and Change," in William C. Havard, ed., *The Changing Politics of the South* (Baton Rouge: Louisiana State Univ. Press, 1972), 564.
20. The Kennedy-McKeithen and Johnson-McKeithen correlations are .22 and .18.
21. Bartley and Graham, *Southern Politics*, 157.
22. New Orleans *Times-Picayune*, Nov. 8, 1971.
23. Grenier and Howard, "The Edwards Victory," in Mark T. Carleton, Perry H. Howard, and Joseph B. Parker, eds., *Readings in Louisiana Politics* (Baton Rouge: Claitor's, 1975), 497.
24. Interview with Governor Edwards, conducted by Jack Bass, Sept. 25, 1973. Treen described Edwards as follows: "Well, he's just a fun-loving Cajun Catholic. And, sure, that hurt him and helped me . . . in North Louisiana. And those characteristics helped in South Louisiana against me. They wanted a . . . Cajun governor." Interview with Treen, conducted by Jack Bass and Walter DeVries, Jan. 31, 1974.
25. Interview with Edwards. Because of his close ties with blacks, Edwards's views concerning the changing role of race in Louisiana politics are instructive: "I think there's less resentment of blacks by the white and much less fear of whites by blacks. That's number one. Number two is that the Voting Rights Act of 1965, in my opinion, probably was the only effective civil rights legislation that has ever passed. I think the rest is so much garbage and rhetoric. The Voting Rights Act . . . provided the catalyst for . . . black power at the polls, not only in electing huge numbers of black legislators, local officials and even now some congressmen, but more important in making white politicians sensitive to their needs and desires . . . ." Interview with Edwards.
26. Governor McKeithen was re-elected in 1967 without GOP opposition. On the ups and downs of McKeithen's career, see Howard, *Political Tendencies in Louisiana*, 375–97.
27. Baton Rouge *State Times*, Jan. 27, 1972.
28. Bass and DeVries, *The Transformation of Southern Politics* (New York: Basic Books, 1976), 181. For an analysis of the effects of Louisiana's unique voting arrangement, see Thomas A. Kazee, "The Impact of Electoral Reform: 'Open Elections' and the Louisiana Party System," *Publius* 13 (Winter 1983), 131–39.
29. Interview with Victor Bussie, Louisiana AFL-CIO president, conducted by Jack Bass and Walter DeVries, Jan. 15, 1974.
30. For an account of that election, see Michael Barone, Grant Ujifusa, and Douglas Matthews, *The Almanac of American Politics 1976* (New York: E. P. Dutton, 1975), 338.
31. The alleged fraud occurred in the 1976 Democratic primary. (The open-primary system was not extended to federal elections until 1978.) The Democrat, Richard Tonry, was convicted in 1978 of misuse of campaign money.
32. Interview with U.S. Rep. Robert L. Livingston, Jr., conducted by the author, July 17, 1978.
33. Ibid.
34. Louisiana is the only Deep South state with registration by party. Two Rim South states—North Carolina and Florida—require party registration.
35. Interview with Treen. Registered Republicans by law could not vote in the Democratic primary.

36. Interview with Jay Stone, administrative assistant to U.S. Rep. W. Henson Moore, Republican of Louisiana, conducted by the author, July 18, 1978.
37. Ibid.
38. Interview with Livingston. He added that the GOP must use up-to-date campaign techniques such as phone banks and extensive polling: "The more technically oriented candidates will dominate. If an old-time Southern politician goes at it without the new techniques, he will lose, Republican or Democrat."
39. Through an informal process, the state's Republicans decided that Treen would be their candidate in the 1979 open primary. Congressman Moore had considered running and was a "candidate" in the informal process but did not become an actual candidate after Treen received the nod of the party. Treen and Moore had announced earlier that they would not both run. Interviews with Kenneth R. (Bucky) Allen, Washington correspondent of the *Alexandria Daily Town Talk*, conducted by the author, July 17, 1978, and Jan. 23, 1979.
40. The first two Democrats to back Treen, Mouton and Henry, were censured almost immediately at a meeting of the Democratic State Central Committee. Mouton responded, "It's like telling me I have to endorse Lucifer over God because Lucifer is a Democrat. I bet many of those who voted against me were supporters of the States Rights Party or have voted for Republicans like Eisenhower or Nixon." Baton Rouge *Morning Advocate*, Nov. 18, 1979. Several months after the election, at the state Democratic convention in Shreveport, all four of the Democratic candidates who supported Treen were condemned by a vote of 343 to 166. The condemnation resolution called the endorsements "reprehensible and . . . a betrayal of the trust placed in them by the Democratic voters of this state." *Times-Picayune*, March 23, 1980.
41. *Congressional Quarterly Weekly Report*, Oct. 20, 1979.
42. *Morning Advocate*, Nov. 21, 1979. At the New Orleans announcement of his endorsement, Fitzmorris declared, "I will cover every nook and corner of Louisiana. I'm going to be preaching the gospel of honesty and integrity and the gospel of Dave Treen and I'm going to be out there every single hour that God gives me breath." In 1983 Fitzmorris was defeated in his effort to win back his old job; Lt. Gov. Bobby Freeman, a Democrat, was re-elected with 58 percent of the vote to Fitzmorris's 42 percent in the "runoff" general election.
43. *Morning Advocate*, March 23, 1980.
44. *Congressional Quarterly Weekly Report*, Oct. 20, 1979.
45. *Times-Picayune*, Dec. 9, 1979.
46. Ibid.
47. *Morning Advocate*, Dec. 1, 1979. Governor Edwards, who was barred by law from seeking a third consecutive term, added that "it makes no difference who wins, I can beat him in four years."
48. *Morning Advocate*, Dec. 4, 1979.
49. Ibid.
50. It is hard to study this election without agreeing that Louisiana is *sui generis*.
51. *Morning Advocate*, Dec. 9, 1979.
52. *Times-Picayune*, Dec. 10, 1979.
53. For a discussion of friends-and-neighbors voting, see Key, *Southern Politics*, 37–41.
54. Jenkins received 38.8 percent against Long's 57.6 percent in the open primary. Jenkins attacked Long for supporting the Panama Canal treaties and charged, "Americans are overtaxed and our senator is the chairman of the tax-writing com-

mittee. As chairman of that committee he's helped guide us into the worst infla-
tionary recession in this century." *Morning Advocate*, July 11, 1980. After his
victory, Long lashed out at Jenkins for Jenkins's statement announcing that he had
received 55 percent of the votes of whites in his losing effort. Long said, "The
inference there is a matter of injecting racism into the campaign, to suggest that
unless one gets a majority of the white vote, he should not be permitted to be
elected to office. . . . I hope that this is the last time that a candidate who is beaten
by as much as 20 percent of the votes calls upon his opponent to apologize for the
fact that black Americans voted for the winner." *Morning Advocate*, Sept. 15,
1980. For those with a keen eye for hypocrisy, Long's "indignation" in 1980 over
Jenkins's remark is likely to recall the senator's participation in filibusters in the
1950s and 1960s opposing civil rights for blacks.

55. Several minor candidates polled a total of 1.3 percent in the October 22 open
primary.

56. For an account of one lively debate, see Jack Wardlaw's "Louisiana Politics" column in the *Times-Picayune*, Sept. 4, 1983.

57. *Morning Advocate*, Sept. 15, 1983. At every opportunity Treen, whose campaign
slogan was "Keep It Treen," attacked Edwards's veracity. "Want to tell when Edwin
Edwards is telling a falsehood?" Treen shouted at a South Louisiana audience.
"Watch his mouth. When his lips aren't moving, he's telling you the truth."
Times-Picayune, Sept. 11, 1983.

The personal attacks seemed to slide easily off the nimble Edwards. Reporting on
the former governor's energetic motorcade tour of the state, Iris Kelso, a *Times-Picayune* columnist, wrote:

"Edwards . . . makes fun of himself and refers to his racy image.

"He frequently says that if the Treen people don't stop spreading false rumors
about him, he's going to start some 'true rumors' that are worse.

"At one stop, he said, 'Man, people know how bad I am. They also know how
good I am.' " *Times-Picayune*, Oct. 6, 1983.

58. See a fine report by John LaPlante in the *Morning Advocate*, Oct. 2, 1983,
headlined, "Treen Trying Hard to Erode Edwards' Black Support."

59. *Morning Advocate*, Oct. 2, 1983.

60. Edwards campaign brochure entitled, "25 Years of Friendship." The brochure also
pointed out that as a congressman Treen had voted against the 1975 extension of
the Voting Rights Act.

61. *Morning Advocate*, Oct. 25, 1983. Edward C. Renwick, a Loyola University political analyst, told Alan Katz of the *Times-Picayune*, "Although it's still too early to
say until we've studied hundreds of precinct returns, I suspect that Treen got no
more than 5 percent of the black vote." *Times-Picayune*, Oct. 24, 1983.

62. *Morning Advocate*, Oct. 25, 1983.

63. Bankston, Moore, and Despot were quoted ibid.

64. Ibid.

Chapter 9: Arkansas

1. Arkansas's governor is elected for a two-year term.

2. In his 1964 race Rockefeller received 43.0 percent of the vote, the high-water mark
for post-Reconstruction Republicans in the state up to that election.

3. Looking back at the Rockefeller years, several observers in 1978 offered comments
like this one by Kenneth Danforth, press secretary to Sen. Dale Bumpers, Demo-

crat of Arkansas: "The Arkansas Republican party was built on the resources of one man. If it hadn't been for Winthrop, the Republicans would not have had a party." Interview with Danforth, conducted by the author, July 17, 1978.

4. Rockefeller's losing 1964 campaign is unrelated to Goldwater's Arkansas vote that year, an early indication of Rockefeller's different appeal. The correlation coefficient is .05.

5. For an account of Rockefeller's political career, see John L. Ward, *The Arkansas Rockefeller* (Baton Rouge: Louisiana State Univ. Press, 1978).

6. The earlier presidential elections followed regional patterns. Consistently high relationships in voter support for national Democratic nominees ended with the 1964 election. While Arkansas did not join the Goldwater sweep, that campaign disrupted county-level trends. Kennedy's candidacy in 1960 and Johnson's in 1964 produce a correlation coefficient of .21, compared with a coefficient of .85 for Stevenson's in 1956 and Kennedy's in 1960. This disrupted national pattern persisted through the 1968 and 1972 elections.

7. Jim Ranchino, *Faubus to Bumpers: Arkansas Votes, 1960–1970* (Arkadelphia: Action Research, 1972), 55–56.

8. *Arkansas Gazette* (Little Rock), Nov. 3, 1968.

9. Ibid., Nov. 1, 1968.

10. Ibid., Nov. 3, 1968.

11. Rockefeller's 1966 and 1968 races correlate at .88.

12. *Arkansas Gazette*, Nov. 3, 1968.

13. Bernard and Rockefeller's races in 1968 were only moderately related, correlating at .46.

14. Ranchino, *Faubus to Bumpers*, 53–54. Ranchino called this finding "one of the political mysteries of 1968."

15. Richard E. Yates explained what makes this hilly northwestern part of the state in the Ozarks different: "The hill country was antisecessionist and Unionist and blamed the plantation east—and, indeed, the whole plantation South—for the calamities of the Civil War. The considerable Republican strength in the mountain counties is an enduring monument to this hostility." Yates, "Arkansas: Independent and Unpredictable," in William C. Havard, ed., *The Changing Politics of the South* (Baton Rouge: Louisiana State Univ. Press, 1972), 235. The strongest counties for Ford in 1976 are located in this part of the state, as Map 9-1 shows.

16. Numan V. Bartley and Hugh D. Graham, *Southern Elections: County and Precinct Data, 1950–1972* (Baton Rouge: Louisiana State Univ. Press, 1978), 353.

17. Ranchino, *Faubus to Bumpers*, 65–67.

18. *Arkansas Gazette*, Sept. 5, 1970.

19. Ibid., Nov. 1, 1970.

20. Ibid.

21. Bartley and Graham, *Southern Elections: Precinct Data*, 353.

22. Ranchino, *Faubus to Bumpers*, 71.

23. The correlation coefficient between Bumpers's races in 1970 and 1972 is .24.

24. A senior aide to Bumpers suggested in 1978 that the Republican party in Arkansas in the late 1960s "maybe never really did exist. It was just Rockefeller's personal organization under the Republican masthead. Rockefeller realized that liberal Democrats and blacks were most dissatisfied, and he did his picking." Interview with Pat Moran, administrative assistant to Senator Bumpers, conducted by the author, July 19, 1978.

25. *Arkansas Gazette*, Nov. 5, 1970.
26. Interview with Bethune, conducted by the author, July 29, 1982.
27. Jack Bass and Walter DeVries, *The Transformation of Southern Politics* (New York: Basic Books, 1976), 94.
28. *Arkansas Gazette*, May 31, 1972.
29. Ibid. This successful tactic of McClellan's was not forgotten by Pryor six years later when, after McClellan's death, he won a hotly contested Democratic runoff for McClellan's Senate seat by criticizing his opponent, U.S. Rep. Jim Guy Tucker, for supporting the labor law reform bill in 1977 and by "accusing him of siding with Northern liberals in Congress." *New York Times*, June 15, 1978. Danforth, Bumpers's press assistant, said of Pryor, "David is like an old shoe to folks there; he comes across like he is from Arkansas. It is a matter of salesmanship. He's just as liberal as Tucker. He 'sugar coats it' to make it acceptable to Arkansas. Pryor is really for the common man." Interview with Danforth.
30. The *Arkansas Gazette* noted that "bad blood from the primary may have helped" Babbitt (Nov. 8, 1972).
31. Ibid., Nov. 6, 1974.
32. Ibid., Nov. 2, 1976.
33. Ibid., Nov. 3, 1976.
34. Ibid. Also in 1976 Arkansas gave Jimmy Carter his second-highest percentage in the South, 65.0 percent, slightly behind Georgia.
35. Pryor defeated Congressman Tucker in the Democratic primary runoff. See note 29 for a description of Pryor's 1978 primary-election tactics.
36. Senator McClellan died the preceding year.
37. Interview with Danforth.
38. Clinton, who received highly favorable publicity as a consumer advocate while attorney general (he was elected to that position in 1976), was characterized as being in the Bumpers-Pryor mold, all moderate-to-liberal Democrats with a good sense of what sells in Arkansas. Interview with Silvia Spencer, a former UPI reporter in Little Rock, conducted by the author, July 12, 1978. Clinton served as McGovern's field coordinator in Texas in 1972, a fact that was omitted from his official gubernatorial biography. Bass and DeVries, *Transformation of Southern Politics*, 104.
39. Interview with Moran.
40. Interview with U.S. Rep. Bill Alexander, Democrat of Arkansas, conducted by the author, July 21, 1978.
41. Ibid. He said that the wrong (meaning a liberal) Democrat could lose the Senate seat in 1978, and he strongly implied, in his preprimary remarks, that Tucker was the wrong Democrat.
42. Brief interview with Sen. Dale Bumpers, conducted by the author, July 19, 1978.
43. Ibid.
44. Rockefeller's influence was important to Bethune's earlier involvement in state politics. In a 1982 interview Bethune said, "I got into the Republican party because of Rockefeller. I was very much interested in the types of things he was trying to do in Arkansas—stop the gambling in Hot Springs, improve the prison system, have a more progressive legislative agenda for the state, involve blacks in government. These were the themes of the Rockefeller administration. It was moderate Republican politics. . . When I was encouraged to be a candidate for office, I had to choose whether to take the easier course and run as a Democrat or was I going to

stay with the Republican effort. So I stayed with the Republicans, and I got my brains beat out in 1972 for attorney general. I did well in central Arkansas [around Little Rock] but got killed in the small towns out in the state." Interview with Bethune.

45. Prior to the November election, a Bumpers assistant noted that a victory by Bethune "would give a great surge to the Republican hopes in the state." Interview with Danforth.

46. *Arkansas Gazette*, Nov. 8, 1978. Bethune was not the first Republican to win a U.S. House seat. Aided by Rockefeller's sweep in 1966, John Paul Hammerschmidt won in the district that includes the Republican northwestern part of the state. (Hammerschmidt's closest challenge came in 1974 when Bill Clinton, then a law professor at the University of Arkansas at Fayette, held him to 51.5 percent.) Hammerschmidt, unlike Bethune, is not a statewide figure. Bethune himself characterized his colleague as "a rather low-keyed congressman—a good congressman— but a low-key guy who tends to his own business." Interview with Bethune.

47. For example, Tom Hamburger, Washington correspondent of the *Arkansas Gazette*, said, "I see it [the GOP win] more as a problem of Bill Clinton's political style than the strength of the Republican party in the state." Interview with Hamburger, conducted by the author, July 27, 1982.

48. *Arkansas Gazette*, Nov. 6, 1980.

49. *Congressional Quarterly Weekly Report*, Oct. 11, 1980. Robert Johnston wrote, "The defeat of the 'wunderkid' of Arkansas politics was certainly the headline story in Arkansas of the 1980 election. It may well be [that] this startling event owed much to the quixotic intervention of a septuagenarian turkey farmer [Montrose Schwartzlose] from Kingsland, Arkansas, who doesn't have a telephone and spent less than $5,000 . . . against one of the most successful politicians in Arkansas." Johnston, "The 1980 Election in Arkansas" (Paper presented at the Feb. 1981 meeting of the Arkansas Political Science Association).

50. *Arkansas Gazette*, Nov. 6, 1980. The article was headlined, "Anatomy of a Smashing Victory."

51. Quoted in a column by Jeffrey Katz, Memphis *Commercial Appeal*, Feb. 15, 1982.

52. *Arkansas Gazette*, Nov. 2, 1980.

53. As a result, the state's AFL-CIO took a neutral stance in Bumpers's re-election campaign. *Arkansas Gazette*, Sept. 14, 1980.

54. *Arkansas Gazette*, Nov. 2, 1980.

55. Clark's run was not given much credence until near the end. One reporter wrongly predicted, "Clark's lightly-funded effort is not expected to provide Bumpers with much more of a challenge than he received from John H. Jones, the 1974 GOP contender who won 15.1 percent of the vote." *Congressional Quarterly Weekly Report*, Oct. 11, 1980.

56. *New York Times*, May 27, 1982.

57. Ibid., Oct. 28, 1982.

58. Jeffrey Katz of the Memphis *Commercial Appeal* wrote, "His new, more personalized style of campaigning reassured the voters that he had shed his arrogance. While he kept saying he had relearned the importance of listening to his constituents, his audience had decided that it might be worthwhile listening again to Clinton." Nov. 4, 1982.

59. Ibid.

60. Memphis *Commercial Appeal*, Nov. 6, 1982.

61. "He said he had tried to help blacks by supporting rural medical clinics, resurrecting the Mississippi County Midwife Program when federal funds were cut, and by taking other actions, but had little success gaining their [blacks'] support." Ibid.

62. Ibid.

63. Ibid.

Arkansas's four U.S. House districts saw a bevy of competitors in 1982. Bethune had a close race, defeating the Democrat Charles L. George with only 54 percent of the votes. Congressman Alexander, an important House Democratic leader, was forced by the Democrat-turned Republican Chuck Banks of Osceola to conduct a vigorous general-election campaign, a rarity for him. Banks attacked Alexander for opposing Reagan's 1981 tax cut, and he accused the Democrat of voting with the Eastern liberals 60 percent of the time. Former President Ford campaigned for Banks, asserting that an Arkansas congressman should not have close ties with Eastern liberals. "That kind of ideology and thinking has gotten us into the kind of trouble we're just coming out of at the present time," Ford said. Alexander met the assault head on. According to a newspaper account, "Alexander says the Reagan tax cut was unfair because it helped the rich far more than the poor." He charged that Reaganomics "was suggested by the ruthless Republican politicians on Wall Street to take advantage of the American taxpayers," adding that the Republican party had recruited Banks "on the hope that Reaganomics would work, rather than fail as it has." Memphis *Commercial Appeal*, Oct. 25, 1982. Alexander won with 65 percent of the vote. Hammerschmidt withstood, at 66 percent of the votes, a spirited run by the Democrat Jim McDougal of Kingston, who asserted on the stump, "Arkansas can't afford Reaganomics, and we need a congressman with the courage to vote for the people of this district rather than blindly voting for Reagan and the rich." Ibid. Congressman Beryl Anthony, Jr., a Democrat, defeated a Republican opponent, Bob Leslie, 66 percent to 34 percent, in a campaign that generally featured the same issues raised in the other three contests.

Chapter 10: North Carolina

1. The highlands of North Carolina, Virginia, and Tennessee have harbored substantial Republican sentiment since the Civil War era, a Mountain Republican legacy that had its origin in the debate over secession. V. O. Key, Jr., explained, "The yeoman of the hills was reluctant to abandon the Union for the cause of the [lowland] planter and his slaves. When the people voted on secession or related issues, the upland farmers showed hostility toward secession. . . . The highland yeomanry did not want to fight a rich man's war; the Democratic party was, or at least became, the planters' party and the war party. The Democratic party forced the hills into The War, and for this it has never been forgiven." *Southern Politics in State and Nation* (New York: Alfred A. Knopf, 1949), 282–83. This Mountain Republican strength has persisted into the current period. The GOP strongholds in the uplands, however, were too weak to sustain state-level majorities until they were joined with the new wave of Republicanism that flowed from the disruption of the Southern Democracy during the civil rights upheaval of the 1960s.

2. This division of the state was adopted from Preston W. Edsall and J. Oliver Williams, "North Carolina: Bipartisan Paradox," in William C. Havard, ed., *The Changing Politics of the South* (Baton Rouge: Louisiana State Univ. Press, 1972), 400.

3. See note 1 above for the origins of Mountain Republicanism.

4. The Piedmont Crescent counties contained 36.6 percent of the state's population in the 1970 census. Edsall and Williams, "North Carolina," 397.

5. Bernard Cosman, *Five States for Goldwater: Continuity and Change in Southern Presidential Voting Patterns* (University: Univ. of Alabama Press, 1966), 93–118.

6. A Raleigh *News and Observer* reporter pointed this out shortly after the election: "The victory over the emotionalism of the racial issue was most striking in Eastern North Carolina, traditional home of massive Democratic majorities and strong racial attitudes. While 'black belt' counties from Virginia's Southside to Louisiana's Delta counties were reversing historic habits and going for Goldwater, Eastern North Carolina stuck fast to old habits." Nov. 5, 1964.

7. Raleigh *News and Observer*, Sept. 3, 1964.

8. Ibid., Oct. 7, 1964.

9. Ibid.

10. The Kennedy-Johnson correlation coefficient is .88.

11. The break in Democratic presidential-support patterns that occurred in 1968 and persisted in 1972 was milder than similar disruptions exhibited in the Deep South states. Johnson's 1964 county-level vote correlates with Humphrey's at .68; the Johnson-McGovern correlation is .53. Humphrey and McGovern ran similarly; the coefficient is .85.

12. Edsall and Williams, "North Carolina," 391.

13. Numan V. Bartley and Hugh D. Graham, *Southern Politics and the Second Reconstruction* (Baltimore: Johns Hopkins Univ. Press, 1975), 132.

14. Raleigh *News and Observer*, May 8, 1968.

15. Ibid., Oct. 19, 1968. Ervin, whose Republican opponent in 1968 was Robert V. Somers, went on to concede "that there is dissatisfaction within the Democratic Party of North Carolina." He said, however, that "the Democratic Party has been a great instrument of service to the people, to all the nation. No organization is perfect. The only perfect person that I know is my wife and she made a foolish mistake when she married me."

16. Jane Pettis Wiseman, "The 'New Politics' in North Carolina: James Gardner and the 1968 Governor's Race" (M.A. thesis, History Department, Univ. of North Carolina, Chapel Hill, 1971), 30 (table 4). Wiseman wrote, "Perhaps the campaign's greatest paradox lay in Gardner's 'eastern strategy.' . . . Gardner's intense concentration on the east may have affected his judgment of the electorate's temper in the rest of the state. He expected the non-Wallace voters to remain steady in their party loyalties. . . . The Republican base in the west and Piedmont needed reassurance from Gardner, but his pandering to Wallace and his vacillating endorsement of presidential hopefuls caused them to abandon him" (94–95). A 1968 survey of the Comparative State Elections Project found that Gardner attracted the votes of 45 percent of Wallace's North Carolina supporters to Scott's 55 percent. But among Nixon supporters 29 percent defected to the Democrat Scott; 97 percent of Humphrey's supporters voted for Scott. This cross-tabulation appears in table 3-4 of Arlon Keith Kemple, "Changes in Party Competitiveness and the Evolution of Interparty Processes: The North Carolina Republican Party" (Ph.D. diss., Univ. of North Carolina, Chapel Hill, 1979), 139.

17. The Moore-Scott correlation coefficient is .86.

18. Numan V. Bartley and Hugh D. Graham, *Southern Elections: County and Pre-*

cinct *Data,* 1950–1972 (Baton Rouge: Louisiana State Univ. Press, 1978), 379, 381–82.

19. Raleigh *News and Observer,* Nov. 8, 1968. Gardner's observations apply with equal force to the 1964 gubernatorial election. The Democratic nominee, Dan K. Moore, used the race issue to defeat Richardson Preyer in the primary. For example, Moore was quoted in the *News and Observer,* June 2, 1964, as saying, "My opponent in the second primary owes his lead and owes a major part of his entire vote to the bloc Negro vote in North Carolina. This is his 'Go Forward' vote; this is his 'mainstream' vote, and it hangs like a millstone around his neck today." For his part, Preyer vowed "to maintain 'the North Carolina way' in race relations if he is elected Governor. He opposed the civil rights bill." Ibid., May 29, 1964. But Preyer was also quoted as saying, "In North Carolina we want to light the torch of knowledge, not the torch of hate that divides our people. We cannot let North Carolina slip into another Alabama or Mississippi." Ibid., May 30, 1964. Preyer struck a left-of-center stance on economic issues: "One of my opponents says that raising the minimum wage from 85 cents to $1.00 an hour will drive away new industries. I am not interested in sweatshop industries looking for cheap labor." Ibid., May 29, 1964. It is ironic that Moore, after using the race issue to defeat Preyer, received roughly 90 percent of the votes in black precincts in Greensboro, Raleigh, and Charlotte in his successful general election campaign against the Republican Robert L. Gavin. Bartley and Graham, *Southern Elections: Precinct Data,* 379, 381–82.

20. Helms, a former Raleigh newspaper editor, campaigned for Willis Smith, the segregationist Democrat elected to the U.S. Senate in 1950 after the race-baiting primary runoff described in Chapter 3, and later worked on Smith's staff. During the 1960s Helms was a broadcasting executive in Raleigh and served on the Raleigh City Council. For more on Helms's background, see W. Lee Johnston, "The New Right in North Carolina: From a Minority Faction in the State's Democratic Party to the Dominant Faction in the State's Republican Party," *Journal of the North Carolina Political Science Association* 3 (1983), 9–23.

21. Raleigh *News and Observer,* Nov. 2, 1972.

22. Interview with Phil Kirk, conducted by the author, July 19, 1978.

23. For example, in Greensboro Galifianakis won 86 percent of the votes of blacks in the first primary. Bartley and Graham, *Southern Elections: Precinct Data,* 381. It was partly to avoid a fate such as Jordan's in the Democratic primary that led Sen. Strom Thurmond of South Carolina to switch to the Republican party in 1964.

24. *News and Observer,* Nov. 8, 1972.

25. Galifianakis responded by calling himself a fiscal conservative and likening himself to Senator Ervin in this regard. The Helms quotations are from the Raleigh *News and Observer,* Nov. 3, 1972.

26. The McGovern-Bowles correlation is only .59, but the McGovern-Galifianakis correlation is .81.

27. Helms received 48 percent of the vote in the East. Richard J. Trilling and Daniel F. Harkins, "The Growth of Party Competition in North Carolina," in Thad Beyle and Merle Black, eds., *Politics and Policy in North Carolina* (New York: MSS Information Corp., 1975), 90. See their chapter generally (pp. 81–94) for another view of North Carolina party competition.

28. The answer might have come in Helms's 1978 re-election effort had his Demo-

cratic opponent been more in the Scott-Bowles Democratic tradition, but he was not.

Claude Sitton, managing editor of the Raleigh *News and Observer*, had this to say about Helms's future in a 1974 interview when asked if Helms would be a one-termer: "Not necessarily, because Helms has quite a bit of support, personal support that he's built up. You know, people vote for reasons of personality as well as party policy. Probably more for reasons of personality, in many cases. Many of them like Helms; I'm not sure that many of them have that good an understanding of what Helms stands for. Not only that, Helms is a very intelligent politician. Helms is already beginning to moderate his views somewhat to fit those of the public generally. . . . But I wouldn't say that Helms would necessarily be a one-term senator. I hope so, but I wouldn't predict it, no." Interview with Sitton, conducted by Jack Bass and Walter DeVries.

29. *News and Observer*, May 8, 1978.
30. Neal R. Peirce, *The Border South States* (New York: W. W. Norton, 1975), 145–46.
31. *News and Observer*, Nov. 3, 1974.
32. *News and Observer* article by Ferrel Guillory, Nov. 3, 1974, as cited in Jack Bass and Walter DeVries, *The Transformation of Southern Politics* (New York: Basic Books, 1976), 233. After observing Morgan's political maneuvers, Rowland Evans and Robert Novak called him "a throwback to shrewd courthouse Democratic politicians of the old one-party South—canny, non-ideological, and supremely flexible." Quoted in Peirce, *Border South States*, 145.
33. Interview with Martin Donsky, a former Raleigh *News and Observer* reporter who was writing for *Congressional Quarterly* at the time of the interview, conducted by the author, July 14, 1978. A similar observation was made by Robert M. Auman, a research assistant to U.S. Rep. Ike F. Andrews, Democrat of North Carolina, in an interview conducted by the author, July 21, 1978.
34. *News and Observer*, Nov. 3, 1974.
35. North Carolina voter records reveal that Republican party registration did not pass the 25.0 percent mark from 1966 through 1982, indicating the persistence of strong Democratic party allegiance. Of course, party-registration figures are not the same as party-identification estimates derived from public opinion surveys, but the former do roughly gauge relative party strength over time.

In 1966, the first year for which registration figures in North Carolina were centrally compiled and published, 17.8 percent of the state's voters (344,700 of a total of 1,933,763) registered as Republicans. Two years later the figure increased to 21.6 percent (448,637 of 2,077,538). It remained stable in 1970 and rose to 23.0 percent in 1972. GOP registration reached 23.6 percent in 1974 and 1976, and in 1980 it climbed to 24.4 percent (677,077 of 2,774,844). In 1982 Republican registration fell slightly to 23.9 percent (640,675 of 2,674,787). These figures were provided by the State Board of Elections in Raleigh.

Only two other Southern states—Louisiana and Florida—required voter registration by party.

36. The Morgan-Hunt correlation coefficient is .96.
37. *News and Observer*, Nov. 2, 1976.
38. Ibid. The article also reported that Hunt collected $409,000 for the general election and that his GOP opponent raised only $51,000.
39. Interview with Rob Christensen, conducted by the author, July 26, 1982.

40. *News and Observer*, Nov. 1, 1976.
41. The Carter-Hunt correlation is .91. In 1976 many of the eastern counties that had abandoned Humphrey and McGovern produced high percentages for Carter.
42. *News and Observer*, Nov. 3, 1976.
43. *New York Times*, May 31, 1978.
44. Ibid.
45. Ibid.
46. Ibid.
47. *Washington Post*, Oct. 31, 1978.
48. Ibid.
49. *Congressional Quarterly Weekly Report*, Oct. 14, 1978.
50. Ibid.
51. *News and Observer*, Nov. 8, 1978.
52. The Hunt-Ingram county-level correlation is .67; the Morgan-Ingram correlation is .57. The *Charlotte Observer* in a Nov. 12, 1978, article described Governor Hunt's positioning during this election:
    "Hunt, who was on something of a political hot seat in the Ingram-Helms race because many of Hunt's loyalists were unhappy with Ingram, was careful not to criticize Ingram at a recent press conference. But he made it clear he felt Ingram had been outgunned all the way by Helms and was lucky to come as close as he did.
    " 'We did all we were asked to do and made every effort we could,' Hunt said. 'But when you realize how limited (financially) he was, he actually did very well with what he had.'
    "The governor added, 'Obviously Helms had a lot of people who agree with him and who personally admire him, and he was able to get his message out.' The article was headlined, "The $7-Million Question: Why Didn't He Win Big?"
53. Also in 1976 Helms prevented Governor Holshouser's selection as a delegate to the national convention. *Charlotte Observer*, Sept. 18, 1980.
54. W. Lee Johnston, "Special Interest Politics: The North Carolina Congressional Club" (Paper presented at the Annual Meeting of the Southern Political Science Association, Memphis, Nov. 5–7, 1981), 3.
55. Ibid., 10.
56. Ibid., 14. Johnston attributed the quotation to a March 20, 1981, telephone interview with Ellis.
57. *Charlotte Observer*, Nov. 5, 1980.
58. Ibid., Oct. 28, 1980.
59. East spent $500,000 alone on his television campaign, which was described in newspaper reports as a blitz or a barrage. Raleigh *News and Observer*, Nov. 5, 1980.
60. Ibid.
61. *Charlotte Observer*, Sept. 24, 1980.
62. Ibid.
63. Ibid., Oct. 28, 1980.
64. Raleigh *News and Observer*, Nov. 5, 1980.
65. Interview with Christensen.
66. The county-level electoral patterns of East and Reagan correlate at .93.
67. *Charlotte Observer*, Sept. 18, 1980.
68. There was no statewide race in 1982.

69. *New York Times*, Sept. 24, 1982. Saying that Hunt has "the aspect of an over-worked country doctor" as he "dashes from one ailing campaign to the next," the *Times* wrote, "At other times Mr. Hunt uses a dose of Democratic populism. Noting that several Congressional Club candidates went to Houston seeking contributions, Mr. Hunt crowed, 'But we're not willing to go to Texas and get down on our knees before the big oil millionaires and ask for that kind of money.' "
70. The headline of a postelection newspaper article proclaimed, "Hunt Emerges as a Big Winner from GOP Congressional Losses." *News and Observer*, Nov. 4, 1982.
71. Ibid.
72. Ibid.
73. Ibid.

Chapter 11: Virginia

1. V. O. Key, Jr., wrote, "Virginia Republicans, although they are strong in a number of counties, make less of a show in state politics than either the North Carolina or Tennessee Republican organizations. . . . [I]n the mountain counties of southwestern Virginia the Republicans are fighters, but . . . in most of the remainder of the state they are a faction of the Byrd organization." *Southern Politics in State and Nation* (New York: Alfred A. Knopf, 1949), 284–85.
2. Ralph Eisenberg, "Virginia: The Emergence of Two-Party Politics," in William C. Havard, ed., *The Changing Politics of the South* (Baton Rouge: Louisiana State Univ. Press, 1972), 41.
3. J. Harvie Wilkinson III, *Harry Byrd and the Changing Face·of Virginia Politics, 1945–1966* (Charlottesville: Univ. Press of Virginia, 1968); Eisenberg, "Virginia," 39–91; and Key, *Southern Politics*, 19–35.
4. Francis Pickens Miller, a national Democrat, made a spirited race against John S. Battle, the organization's candidate, in the 1949 gubernatorial primary. The organization made a strong effort to defeat Miller, whom Byrd labeled the labor candidate. Eisenberg, "Virginia," 47. Miller lost to Battle by seven percentage points.
    In 1953 State Sen. Ted Dalton of Roanoke "threw another scare into the organization. Dalton campaigned with a progressive platform (for Virginia). He stressed programs to raise minimum teachers' salaries, appropriate more money to state mental institutions, and launch vigorous industrial development activities. Dalton also attacked the organization, the appointive powers of judges, and election laws, and he called for repeal of the poll tax." Eisenberg, "Virginia," 49. The organization's candidate in 1953 defeated Dalton 54.8 percent to 44.3 percent. These contests are noted at length here not only for what they show about the nonmonolithic nature of Byrd Virginia politics but also because the sons of Miller, Dalton, and Battle played important roles as candidates in later elections.
5. Eisenberg, "Virginia," 51.
6. Ibid., 55. For example, Godwin asserted, "The Governor of our state and our state leaders will exhaust every effort and avail themselves of every method legally open to them to keep our schools racially separate. . . . We are convinced our system of public free schools in Virginia cannot survive on an integrated basis." *Richmond News Leader*, July 1, 1958, as quoted in Wilkinson, *Harry Byrd*, 265.
7. Wilkinson, *Harry Byrd*, 250–51.

8. Eisenhower carried Virginia with 56.3 percent and 55.4 percent in 1952 and 1956, respectively, as did Nixon in 1960 with 52.4 percent.

9. Eisenberg, "Virginia," 64.

10. *Richmond Times-Dispatch*, Oct. 13, 1965, as quoted in Wilkinson, *Harry Byrd*, 274.

11. Wilkinson, *Harry Byrd*, 270–71.

12. Numan V. Bartley and Hugh D. Graham, *Southern Elections: County and Precinct Data, 1950–1972* (Baton Rouge: Louisiana State Univ. Press, 1978), 405–6.

13. On Godwin's move away from the pay-as-you-go doctrine, Charles McDowell, a veteran writer for the *Richmond Times-Dispatch*, noted, "Oh, there is a feeling on the part of Godwin and a lot of the old Byrd characters that progress ain't so bad really, and even spending some state money isn't so bad if it is done by the right people, and the right people were the Byrd people, the country club people, bankers and big merchants, the power structure." Interview with McDowell, conducted by Jack Bass, Oct. 30, 1973.

14. Wilkinson, *Harry Byrd*, 303.

15. *Richmond News Leader*, Nov. 3, 1965, as quoted in Wilkinson, *Harry Byrd*, 284.

16. Wilkinson, *Harry Byrd*, 312.

17. Ibid., 313.

18. Ibid., 333. Rawlings himself was defeated in the general election by William L. Scott, a conservative Republican who was elected to the U.S. Senate six years later.

19. Bartley and Graham, *Southern Elections: Precinct Data*, 405–6.

20. The Republican James P. Ould, Jr., and the Conservative F. Lee Hawthorne received 33.5 percent and 7.9 percent, respectively, against Spong. The Republican Lawrence M. Traylor and the Conservative John W. Carter won 37.4 percent and 7.9 percent, respectively, against Byrd.

21. Eisenberg, "Virginia," 72.

22. Ibid.

23. Ibid.

24. Ibid.

25. Ibid., 75–76.

26. Ibid., 76.

27. Of this action Howell later said it made his supporters "so mad they could spit." Interview with Howell, conducted by Jack Bass, March 13, 1974.

28. Eisenberg, "Virginia," 77.

29. Interview with McDowell. Later in the interview McDowell described Howell's good qualities that he said Battle never appreciated: "His feel for the plain people. His obvious regard for the plain people . . . working people, black people, ordinary people, what their problems are; he wants to help them. He had a demagogic way of advocating their cause very often. He has a marvelous gentle streak in him, too. He is not an easy guy at all."

30. Interview with McDowell.

31. The correlation between Holton's 1965 race and his 1969 victory is .62, which strongly suggests that Holton's increased strength in 1969 came from areas other than those he had carried four years earlier. The correlation coefficient is from Louis Seagull, *Southern Republicanism* (New York: John Wiley & Sons, 1975), 170.

32. Larry Sabato, *Virginia Votes, 1969–1974* (Charlottesville: Institute of Government, Univ. of Virginia, 1976), 19. The portion of Table 11.1 dealing with the general election lends support to Sabato's conclusion.

33. Miller defeated Richard Obenshain, a conservative Republican. Eisenberg wrote that Obenshain "on the ticket was the conservative to balance Holton's moderate image." Eisenberg, "Virginia," 78.

34. Jack Bass and Walter DeVries, *The Transformation of Southern Politics* (New York: Basic Books, 1976), 354.

35. Rawlings won the Democratic nomination narrowly over a more conservative opponent in a primary that attracted a very low turnout. Sabato, *Virginia Votes 1969–1974*, 24.

36. Bass and DeVries, *Transformation of Southern Politics*, 355.

37. Sabato, *Virginia Votes 1969–1974*, 24. This position by Holton, in retrospect, appeared to be an important one for two-party development in Virginia. In an interview in 1974, Richard Obenshain, chairman of the Virginia GOP during the middle 1970s and a leading conservative Republican figure, was asked if the decision to run a Republican candidate in 1970 had not been a major factor encouraging former Governor Godwin to run for the governorship in 1973 as a Republican rather than as an independent. Obenshain responded, "I am inclined to believe that [because] the party did run a candidate in 1970 [that] was one of many contributing causes that added a strong element of credibility to the premise which was simply there all the time that the Republican party would run a candidate for governor in 1973 come hell or high water." Interview with Obenshain, conducted by Jack Bass, March 7, 1974.

38. Sabato, *Virginia Votes 1969–1974*, 25–26.

39. Ibid., 28.

40. Ibid.

41. Bass and DeVries, *Transformation of Southern Politics*, 355.

42. Norfolk *Virginian-Pilot*, July 28, 1971, as cited in Sabato, *Virginia Votes 1969–1974*, 39.

43. Throughout this period the Republican party made all its nominations for statewide office by convention.

44. Asked in a 1974 interview why he ran as an independent, Howell replied, "I can't broker a convention. . . . It is very difficult to go out and get people. See, I don't have any organizations. I've just got concerned citizens, some of whom have been with me for a long time. They come and go. I am not capable in a month's time . . . of getting delegates elected to a convention. People who go to the polls and vote for you aren't interested in going to a school to elect delegates." Interview with Howell, conducted by Jack Bass, March 13, 1974.

45. Sabato, *Virginia Votes 1969–1974*, 39.

46. Ibid., 39–42.

47. This special election is described ibid., 39–58.

48. Interview with McDowell.

49. Bartley and Graham, *Southern Politics*, 178.

50. Interview with McDowell.

51. Interview with William Spong, conducted by Jack Bass, March 8, 1974.

52. *Washington Post*, Nov. 5, 1973.

53. Ibid., Nov. 6, 1973. Howell's proposed taxes, known as the ABC plan, would have placed higher taxes on alcohol, banks, and corporations. "Godwin bitterly denounced the plan, charging it would impede industrial growth and actually result in higher taxes for most people," according to an article in the *Washington Post*, Nov. 7, 1973.

54. *Washington Post*, Nov. 7, 1973. Bass and DeVries describe in depth a controversy

involving a network television report on the morning of the election that called Howell a proponent of busing. *Transformation of Southern Politics*, 362–63. Howell appeared to attribute his narrow loss to Godwin's use of the busing issue: "And then, of course, Godwin's main thing was all of those pretty little white children, his saturation TV, you may have seen them, walking together. So he, for the first time, went back to an easy way to win an election, and that is to try to set . . . the whites against blacks." Interview with Howell.

55. Neal R. Peirce, *The Border South States* (New York: W. W. Norton, 1975), 86–87.

56. Sabato, *Virginia Votes 1969–1974*, 89.

57. Larry Sabato, *Virginia Votes 1975–1978* (Charlottesville: Institute of Government, Univ. of Virginia, 1979), 15.

58. Howell's correlation in 1977 with Carter in 1976 is .87. Also, Howell's race in 1973 correlates with his 1977 race at .89. These coefficients are from Robert S. Montjoy and James O. Glanville, "The 1977 Election: A New Equilibrium?" *University of Virginia News Letter* 54 (Feb. 1978).

59. Sabato, *Virginia Votes 1975–1978*, 20.

60. Sabato contends that, with the rise of two-party competition in Virginia, the Democratic party primary is now dominated by liberals, organized labor, blacks, and urban voters, all part of Howell's long-time constituency. *Virginia Votes 1975–1978*, 36. The 1977 Miller-Howell contest was the first statewide Democratic primary since 1970 and the last through the early 1980s; the Democrats nominated their candidates for U.S. senator in 1978 and 1982 and for governor in 1981 by convention. For a first-rate analysis of the 1977 race, see Alan Abramowitz, John McGlennon, and Ronald Rapoport, "Voting in the Democratic Primary: The 1977 Virginia Gubernatorial Race," in Robert P. Steed, Laurence W. Moreland, and Tod A. Baker, eds., *Party Politics in the South* (New York: Praeger, 1980), 81–95.

61. *New York Times*, Nov. 9, 1977. Another thorough account of this election is found in the *Washington Post*, Nov. 9 and 10, 1977.

62. Sabato, *Virginia Votes 1975–1978*, 71. Any number of other reasons have been offered to explain Howell's defeat, including the divisiveness of the Howell-Miller primary. Sabato, who worked in Howell's 1977 campaign, also offered these observations: "[Howell's] economic and social policies genuinely threatened the continued dominance of Virginia's elite, a threat that fully mobilized the elite. Howell's background, manners, and comportment were decidedly 'plebeian'; Howell did not look or act like Virginians' conception of a Governor. (This perception of Howell appeared repeatedly in polls during the campaign.)" Ibid., 75.

63. *Washington Post*, June 5, 1978.

64. The *Washington Post* reported, "The most puzzling aspect of the Republican convention to Democrats was its failure to nominate former Governor Linwood Holton. All the Democratic candidates have said in interviews that Holton would have been the toughest Republican foe and many of their campaign staffers have been frank to say he could not be beaten." June 5, 1978. In searching for reasons in an article headlined, "Promising Future Dimmed for Holton," a *Post* reporter mentioned Holton's insistence that the GOP oppose Byrd in 1970 and pointed out that this decision was "unpopular with the party right wing." The reporter also wrote, "[Holton's] repeated conciliatory gestures to Virginia's blacks—including personally escorting his children to class at an all-black city school during anti-busing protests in Richmond—drew the wrath of GOP conservatives both in and outside of the state." June 4, 1978.

65. During the campaign Warner received considerable publicity because of his marriage to the actress Elizabeth Taylor. The marriage, however, ended in divorce several years after the election, a not inconsiderable development for Warner's 1984 re-election prospects.

66. *Washington Post*, June 11, 1978. The candidate who finished a distant second to Miller in the multicandidate field had the backing of Howell. Ibid.

67. *Baltimore Sun*, Nov. 6, 1978.

68. Ibid.

69. Miller's campaign manager said, "There are those who think Henry Howell is the greatest person in Virginia and others who don't. To have him involved in the campaign would take away from the central issue of who is best qualified to serve in the U.S. Senate." *Washington Post*, Sept. 28, 1978. In its editions the following day, the *Post* reported the angry reaction of Howell supporters to this decision, especially in the Tidewater.

70. *Washington Post*, Oct. 15, 1980. Byrd's endorsement was heralded as breaking a two-generation Byrd family tradition of "golden silence" on presidential preference. Ibid.

71. Sabato reports that in his losing effort Carter received over 95 percent of the vote in forty-three selected urban black precincts. See Sabato's chapter "The 1980 Presidential Election: Virginia Leads the 'Solid' South" in his *Virginia Votes 1979–1982* (Charlottesville: Institute of Government, Univ. of Virginia, 1983). Also on this election see David B. Magleby, "The 1980 Election: Understanding the Reagan Victory in Virginia," *University of Virginia News Letter* 57 (March 1981).

72. Throughout the period under study, Republicans scored notable successes in races for the U.S. House. After the 1974 elections Virginia's ten-member delegation was evenly divided between Democrats and Republicans. Two of the five Democrats, W. C. (Dan) Daniel of the Southside Fifth District and David E. Satterfield III of the Third District, encompassing the Richmond area, were solid conservatives, at least as conservative as their Republican colleagues, judging from their voting records (Michael Barone, Grant Ujifusa, and Douglas Matthews, *The Almanac of American Politics 1976* [New York: E. P. Dutton, 1975], 878, 881); both were re-elected in 1976. In Northern Virginia's two congressional districts, the Eighth and the Tenth, two liberal Democrats—Herbert E. Harris II and Joseph L. Fisher—defeated conservative Republican incumbents in 1974 and were re-elected in 1976. The fifth Democrat in the delegation after the 1974 election was the veteran Thomas N. Downing of the Tidewater First District, another conservative.

When Downing decided to retire in 1976, the then twenty-nine-year-old Republican Essex County prosecutor, Paul S. Trible, Jr., defeated the winner of a divisive Democratic primary, 48.6 percent to 47.4 percent, to give the GOP a majority of the House delegation. Along with his five Republican colleagues—G. William Whitehurst (Second District), Robert W. Daniel, Jr. (Fourth), M. Caldwell Butler (Sixth), J. Kenneth Robinson (Seventh), and William C. Wampler (Ninth)—Trible was re-elected in 1978. The four Democrats were also re-elected in 1978.

But in 1980 the Republican Thomas J. Bliley, Jr., a former mayor of Richmond, replaced the conservative Democrat Satterfield, who retired. And the two liberal Democratic congressmen from Northern Virginia were defeated narrowly by the Republicans Stan Parris in the Eighth and Frank Wolf in the Tenth. The other Republican incumbents coasted to re-election victories, several without Democratic opponents. After the 1980 elections the conservative Democrat Dan Daniel in the Fifth became the lone member of his party in Virginia's ten-member delegation.

73. *Washington Post*, March 20, 1981.
74. Ibid.
75. *Washington Post*, May 30, 1981. The Norfolk *Virginian-Pilot* reported Howell's characterization of Robb's approach as baseball politics: "Chuck Robb has been told not to rock the boat, to stick with generalities. . . . Me, I play football.

"Yes, both parties want to look like each other. But someday some young people will come along who will be willing to 'play football.'

"We came close, but we didn't win against the 'Big Boys.' " May 30, 1981.
76. *Virginian-Pilot*, May 30, 1981.
77. *Washington Post*, March 23, 1981.
78. Three James Madison University researchers report that Robb's electoral pattern was closely related to Howell's 1977 gubernatorial loss; the correlation coefficient is .81. This similarity at the voter level emphasizes the partisan continuity developing in Virginia despite the apparent ideological distance between Howell and Robb. Kay M. Knickrehm, B. Douglas Skelley, and Devin C. Bent, "Decomposition and Realignment in Virginia" (Paper presented at The Citadel Symposium on Southern Politics, Charleston, S.C., March 25–27, 1982), 21.
79. *Washington Post*, Nov. 5, 1981.
80. Ibid., Oct. 28, 1981.
81. *New York Times*, Nov. 2, 1981.
82. The three 1982 Democratic U.S. House victories came in the Ninth, Fourth, and Sixth districts. State Sen. Frederick Boucher, a Democrat, defeated Rep. William C. Wampler, a nine-term Republican veteran, in Southwest Virginia's Ninth. State Delegate Norman Sisisky, a Democrat, defeated Rep. Robert W. Daniel, Jr., a Republican, in the Fourth, centered in Southside Virginia. And the Democrat James Olin, a retired businessman, won an open seat in the Sixth, which includes Roanoke and Lynchburg. The Democrat John McClennon, a William and Mary political science professor whose works are cited at several points in this chapter, won a respectable 43.7 percent of the votes in the Tidewater district while losing to the Republican Herbert H. Bateman. McGlennon labored under the handicap of having received his party's nomination secondhand; the first Democratic nominee, also a professor, grew tired of the campaign trail and quit after a few months.
83. For example, Robb told reporters after the election, "There is what is sometimes referred to as fire in the belly. It is clear that Paul wanted very much for a long, long period to be a United States senator . . . . Dick Davis didn't have that fire in the belly . . . ." *Washington Post*, Nov. 4, 1982.
84. Alan I. Abramowitz, John McGlennon, and Ronald Rapoport, "The Transformation of the Virginia Electorate" (Paper presented at the Annual Meeting of the Southern Political Science Association, Atlanta, Oct. 28–30, 1982), 6 (table 3).
85. Ibid., 7 (table 4).
86. Ibid., 10.

Chapter 12: Tennessee

1. V. O. Key, Jr., *Southern Politics in State and Nation* (New York: Alfred A. Knopf, 1949), 75–78.

2. Ibid., 76.

3. Correlations between these three elections are nearly perfect, averaging .97.

4. Numan V. Bartley and Hugh D. Graham, *Southern Elections: County and Precinct Data, 1950–1972* (Baton Rouge: Louisiana State Univ. Press, 1978), 391.

5. Numan V. Bartley and Hugh D. Graham, *Southern Politics and the Second Reconstruction* (Baltimore: Johns Hopkins Univ. Press, 1975), 105–6.

6. Bartley and Graham, *Southern Elections: Precinct Data,* 392.

7. This modus vivendi between conservative Democrats and Republicans is described by Norman L. Parks in his "Tennessee Politics since Kefauver and Reece: A 'Generalist' View," *Journal of Politics* 28 (Feb. 1966), 149–51.

8. Parks, "Tennessee Politics," 151. Parks's analysis of the West Tennessee potential for the Republican party proved to be on target: "Conceivably Memphis could be converted into the Republican and political capital of the state, for this city combines all the segregationist passions of the old South with the conservatism, wealth, and drive of modern business. . . . Though their [the Republicans'] literature screamed about 'stinking socialism,' the chief concern was obviously fear and hostility toward the Negroes and a scarcely concealed contempt for the white tenant and lower income workers." Ibid., 161–62.

9. The Baker-Kuykendall correlation coefficient is .98. The Kuykendall-Goldwater and Baker-Goldwater correlations are .99 and .98.

10. For an account of Governor Clement's career, see Lee Seifert Greene, *Lead Me On: Frank Goad Clement and Tennessee Politics* (Knoxville: Univ. of Tennessee Press, 1982).

11. J. Leiper Freeman, *Political Change in Tennessee, 1948–1978: Party Politics Trickles Down* (Knoxville: Bureau of Public Administration, Univ. of Tennessee, 1980), 20.

12. Bartley and Graham, *Southern Elections: Precinct Data,* 392. This does not imply that Baker ran a racist campaign, an implication the record does not support; rather as the Republican nominee he was benefiting from a Memphis pattern similar to Goldwater's in 1964. In his 1972 re-election campaign against a Democrat linked to Wallace, Baker attracted 40 percent of the votes of blacks in Memphis, while holding a percentage similar to his 1966 showing in lower-income white precincts. See Table 12-1.

13. Freeman, *Political Change in Tennessee,* 20. Also in 1966 the Republican Kuykendall won a congressional seat in Memphis.

14. Ibid.

15. The correlation coefficient for Kennedy in 1960 with Johnson in 1964 is .94. The Johnson-Humphrey correlation, however, is .69.

16. In addition to the data presented in the two tables, this assertion is supported by precinct correlations reported in William M. Berenson, Robert D. Bond, and J. Leiper Freeman, "The Wallace Vote and Political Change in Tennessee," *Journal of Politics* 33 (May 1971), 516–18. See also the survey data in Yung Wie and H. R. Mahood, "Racial Attitudes and the Wallace Vote: A Study of the 1968 Election in Memphis," *Polity* 3 (Aug. 1971), 532–49.

17. Freeman, *Political Change in Tennessee,* 13.

18. David Halberstam, "The End of a Populist," *Harper's,* (Jan. 1971), p. 38, as cited in Jack Bass and Walter DeVries, *The Transformation of Southern Politics* (New York: Basic Books, 1976), 297.

19. Bartley and Graham, *Southern Politics,* 158.

20. Ibid., 159.
21. Freeman supports this point concerning Nashville by using precinct correlation data adapted from an unpublished paper by Mike Bennett, "An Analysis of the Gore-Brock Senate Race" (Vanderbilt Univ., 1971), prepared under his supervision. The Bennett analysis shows that Knoxville and Chattanooga followed the Memphis pattern. Freeman wrote, "In all the cities except Nashville race seemed a stronger factor than economics in differentiating between votes for Brock and votes for Gore." *Political Change in Tennessee*, 22.
22. "Hooker was plagued throughout the campaign by a speculative collapse in the Minnie Pearl fried chicken franchise business that had added to his wealth and to the wealth of his close friends but had enmeshed a larger number of later participants and smacked less of scandal than poor business judgement." Bartley and Graham, *Southern Politics*, 153.
23. *Nashville Tennessean*, Oct. 22, 1970.
24. The correlation coefficient is .92. John Means of the Tennessee News Bureau, a one-man Washington news-gathering operation, contended that "Brock rode Dunn's coattails more than the other way." Means stressed the importance of Dunn's Memphis base. Interview with Means, conducted by the author, Jan. 25, 1979.
25. Freeman, *Political Change in Tennessee*, 14.
26. Bass and DeVries, *Transformation of Southern Politics*, 298.
27. Tennessee is the only Southern state without a runoff primary.
28. Bass and DeVries, *Transformation of Southern Politics*, 302.
29. The Blanton-Gore correlation is .90.
30. Of course, Blanton represented many of these West Tennessee counties in Congress. But this same pattern persisted in 1976 for the Democratic senatorial nominee, as Map 12-1 shows.
31. These two races were highly correlated with Blanton's victory two years earlier; the coefficients averaged .96.
32. *Washington Post*, Oct. 17, 1976.
33. Ibid. Sasser no doubt was helped by the October revelation by Brock, under intense press questioning, that he had paid only $2,026 in federal income taxes in 1975 on an income of $51,670. Buttons and bumper stickers soon appeared with the slogan "I Paid More Taxes Than Bill Brock." *New York Times*, Oct. 28, 1976.
34. *New York Times*, Oct. 28, 1976.
35. A scatter diagram of the .89 correlation of Gore in 1970 with Sasser in 1976 isolated eleven counties as "far-outliers." These are presented in Map 12-1, which also delineates the three grand divisions of Tennessee. See the Appendix for a discussion of the use of scatter diagrams.
36. The Memphis classified precinct breakdown for Sasser was not available, but the similarity of the Carter-Sasser pattern statewide (coefficient of .98) strongly suggests a showing by Sasser similar to Carter's in Memphis. For Carter's Memphis precinct results in 1976, see Table 3-5.
37. The Johnson-Carter correlation is .92.
38. Gore's district, which had a black population of only 6 percent in 1970, gave McGovern slightly over 35 percent of its votes, which means that a significantly higher percentage of whites in the district supported the South Dakota liberal than was the Southern norm that year.
39. Interview with Gore, conducted by the author, Jan. 25, 1979. Gore added, "At the same time there is a realization that the role of government is changing, that the

government has become too heavy-handed, has become too large . . . and it has become stale. The spirit of the New Deal, once it became institutionalized, lost much of its imagination. . . . People are apprehensive about a bureaucracy that feeds on itself, gets more and more top-heavy." Congressman Gore was the leading Democratic candidate to succeed Senator Baker, who announced that he would not seek re-election in 1984.

40. Shirley Chapman, *Democrats Challenge Traditional Republicanism in Upper East Tennessee* (Johnson City: East Tennessee State Univ., 1977), 15.
41. Ibid., 26.
42. Ibid., 27–28.
43. Ibid., 37.
44. *Congressional Quarterly Weekly Report*, Oct. 14, 1978. Baker downplayed his ambition for higher office, saying, "I am running for the Senate, not the presidency." *Nashville Tennessean*, June 4, 1978.
45. Freeman, *Political Change in Tennessee*, 26.
46. In 1981 Blanton was convicted on charges growing out of a scheme to sell state liquor licenses; he was sentenced to three years in prison. *New York Times*, June 10, 1981.
47. *Nashville Tennessean*, Nov. 9, 1978. Butcher's wife, Sonya, appeared to agree with this assessment. The *Tennessean* writer Charles L. Fontenay noted, "And Mrs. Butcher, commenting somewhat bitterly on her belief that the voters mistrusted her husband's wealth, said she was disappointed that 'a man can be crucified for his success.' " Ibid. In 1983 Butcher's successful financial wizardry went awry, and he was forced into bankruptcy as his banking empire collapsed. Ibid., June 30, 1983.
48. Interview with Ken Jost, administrative assistant to Congressman Gore, conducted by the author, Jan. 16, 1979.
49. *Congressional Quarterly Weekly Report*, Oct. 14, 1978. Chiles's walk across the Sunshine State is described in the Florida chapter.
50. Freeman, *Political Change in Tennessee*, 31.
51. Memphis *Commercial Appeal*, Nov. 8, 1978. A reporter found irony in this result: "In his rough clothing, his blond hair whipped in snow, rain and high wind, he [Alexander] was a contrast to the fashionably dressed Butcher . . . who, ironically, came from much more humble beginnings, including a rural Union County home without electricity." Ibid.
52. Freeman, *Political Change in Tennessee*, 32.
53. The only contest in 1980 was for Tennessee's presidential electors, which fell narrowly to Reagan. A scatter diagram of this election, made available by Leiper Freeman, shows a strong relationship between Carter's county-level patterns in 1976 and 1980, suggesting no disruption of the state's Democratic coalition because the movement away from the Democratic nominee in 1980 was uniform throughout the state.
54. *New York Times*, Feb. 1, 1981.
55. Memphis *Press-Scimitar*, Sept. 24, 1982. The article was headlined, "Beard Shows Sharp Teeth But Sasser Bites Him Back."
56. *Nashville Banner*, Sept. 24, 1982. The editorial added, "Nor can we embrace the publicity and advertising approach Rep. Beard's campaign has taken in the past few days. His latest television commercial, showing Fidel Castro lighting his cigar with a dollar bill and thanking 'Senor Sasser' for foreign aid, is sadly lacking in taste and substance. It appalls the senses . . . ."

57. *New York Times*, Oct. 6, 1982.
58. Ibid.
59. Ibid. Doug Hall, Sasser's press assistant, added, "They went too far. If they had been more subtle about it, they could have caused us more damage."
60. Ibid. Before the campaign heated up, Morris Cunningham, Washington correspondent of the Memphis *Commercial Appeal*, said, "I think that Beard is having a problem trying to identify himself with the mainstream of political thinking in Tennessee and to get away from a lot of real right-wing votes that he has cast in the past." Interview with Cunningham, conducted by the author, July 30, 1982.
61. *Nashville Tennessean*, Sept. 8, 1982.
62. *Congressional Quarterly Weekly Report*, Oct. 9, 1982.
63. *Nashville Tennessean*, Sept. 8, 1982.
64. Ibid. Alexander even managed to turn attention back to the Democrats' nadir during the last part of Blanton's term in office. A *Tennessean* reporter, Joel Kaplan, tells the story:

    "I would like you to ask yourselves, 'Are you better off today than you were four years ago?' " Tyree asked [during the September debate], mimicking the question Ronald Reagan asked as he toured the country during his 1980 presidential campaign against Jimmy Carter.

    While Tyree's question was an attempt to focus attention on Tennessee's dismal economic situation, for which he blames Alexander and his fellow Republicans, it also enabled the governor to bring up the scandal-ridden administration of former Gov. Ray Blanton.

    "Four years ago, our state government was a laughing stock," Alexander said. "We were embarrassed all over the country. It wasn't so long ago we heard stories of whiskey licenses being sold and money passing through the governor's office."
65. William F. Buckley's "Firing Line," taped in Nashville, Nov. 11, 1982. There were two open congressional seats in Tennessee in 1982, and the parties split them. Beard's seat went to the Republican Don Sundquist of Memphis, who focused his attention on the well-to-do Memphis suburbs of Shelby County. And in a newly created, sprawling district north of Knoxville (Tennessee in 1982 picked up the U.S. House seat it had lost after the 1970 census), the son of a former governor, the Democrat Jim Cooper, defeated the daughter of Senator Baker, the Republican Cissy Baker, 65.8 percent to 34.2 percent. The two Republican incumbents from East Tennessee districts were returned in 1982, as were the five Democratic incumbents, giving Tennessee a six-to-three House delegation favoring the Democrats.

Chapter 13: Florida

1. Actually in 1940 the Palmetto State outnumbered the Sunshine State by 2,389 people: South Carolina, 1,899,803; Florida, 1,897,414. The exact 1980 figures were Florida, 9,746,421; South Carolina, 3,122,814.
2. V. O. Key, Jr., *Southern Politics in State and Nation* (New York: Alfred A. Knopf, 1949), 83.
3. Manning J. Dauer, "Florida: The Different State," in William C. Havard, ed., *The Changing Politics of the South* (Baton Rouge: Louisiana State Univ. Press, 1972), 92–113. A similar outline was offered by Charles Stafford, Washington correspondent of the *St. Petersburg Times*, in an interview conducted by the author, July 11, 1978.

4. Eisenhower carried Florida in 1952 with 55.0 percent and in 1956 with 57.2 percent. In 1960 Nixon won the state with 51.5 percent.
5. Voting consistency was quite high in presidential elections prior to 1964. Stevenson's losing races in 1952 and 1956 correlate at .97; Stevenson's 1956 race correlates at .93 with Kennedy's losing Florida effort in 1960. But this consistency ended in 1964. There is only a random relationship between Kennedy's county-level pattern in 1960 and Johnson's in 1964; the coefficient is −.04.
6. Among the Southern states Florida has the lowest percentage of blacks after Texas: 15.3 percent in the 1970 census and 13.8 percent in the 1980 census. See Table 3-3.
7. For example, Holmes, Walton, and Washington counties in the North Florida Panhandle gave Kennedy 65.7, 71.0, and 63.0 percent of their votes, respectively. Johnson received only 27.0, 39.5, and 35.5 percent, respectively, in these counties four years later.
8. Interview with Stafford.
9. The correlation coefficient between Eisenhower in 1956 and Nixon in 1968 is .93.
10. The Kennedy-Humphrey correlation is −.30.
11. Humphrey's county-level pattern correlates with McGovern's at .90.
12. For Collins's approach to the race issue, see David R. Colburn and Richard K. Scher, *Florida's Gubernatorial Politics in the Twentieth Century* (Tallahassee: Univ. Presses of Florida, 1980), 77.
13. Numan V. Bartley and Hugh D. Graham, *Southern Politics and the Second Reconstruction* (Baltimore: Johns Hopkins Univ. Press, 1975), 63. The 1964 gubernatorial election was for a special two-year term because the Florida legislature decided to separate gubernatorial and presidential elections.
14. Ibid., 125.
15. Colburn and Scher, *Florida's Gubernatorial Politics*, 83.
16. Jack Bass and Walter DeVries, *The Transformation of Southern Politics* (New York: Basic Books, 1976), 122.
17. *Tallahassee Democrat*, Nov. 6, 1968.
18. The coefficient is .82.
19. Kirk's eccentric behavior as governor is viewed in retrospect by a number of observers as having made him a "guaranteed one-termer." Interview with Walter Wurfel, a deputy White House press secretary in the Carter administration and a former newsman in Florida, conducted by the author, July 13, 1978. In terms of two-party development, Wurfel said, "Kirk's election was the worst thing that could have happened to the Republicans. He wasn't interested in the Republican party— party was a matter of convenience for him." U.S. Rep. L. A. (Skip) Bafalis, a Florida Republican, in discussing Kirk's 1970 defeat observed that the state's first Republican governor since Reconstruction lost "because of a lot of stupid things he did." Interview with Bafalis, conducted by the author, July 21, 1978.
20. *St. Petersburg Times*, Sept. 4, 1970.
21. Ibid., Nov. 1, 1970.
22. Ibid., Sept. 5, 1970. Florida's NAACP field secretary, Marvin Davies, asserted that "racism is the dominant theme of the current political campaigns." He said that implicit in all the antibusing statements is this message to white parents: "I will keep your white child out of the black community." Ibid., Aug. 22, 1970.
23. Ibid., Nov. 1, 1970.
24. Ibid.

25. Interview with Jack Pridgen, press secretary to Sen. Lawton Chiles, conducted by the author, July 13, 1978.
26. *St. Petersburg Times*, Nov. 1, 1970.
27. Ibid. Pridgen asserted that it was impossible for Chiles's GOP opponent to get to the right of him: "Chiles was down-home, a country populist . . . ." Interview with Pridgen.
28. Bass and DeVries, *Transformation of Southern Politics*, 124.
29. Quoted during the interview with Pridgen.
30. Interview with Askew, conducted by Jack Bass and Walter DeVries, July 8, 1974.
31. Senator Gurney did not run for re-election. Bass and DeVries wrote, "The incumbent . . . had fallen on hard times. He retired in the face of Federal and state grand jury investigations involving $300,000 in unreported campaign funds and alleged kickbacks for federal housing contracts in connection with fundraising in his behalf." *Transformation of Southern Politics*, 125. Gurney was later tried on five felony charges and was acquitted of three; a mistrial was declared on the other two.
32. Interview with Eli M. Feinberg, administrative assistant to Senator Stone, conducted by the author, July 20, 1978.
33. Interview with Representative Bafalis.
34. Interview with Stafford.
35. Mark Stern reached a similar conclusion: "A Miami-based Jewish candidate with strong Miami backing had brought together the old Democrats of the Panhandle with the big-city Democrats of the south to win the Senate seat." "Florida's Elections," in Manning J. Dauer, ed., *Florida's Politics and Government* (Gainesville: Univ. Presses of Florida, 1980), 80.
36. The *St. Petersburg Times* reported, "Thurmond hit consistently on the theme that the Republicans reflect the South's political philosophy much better than the Democrats." Nov. 3, 1974.
37. Askew's first election correlates with his 1974 re-election pattern at −.28.
38. *St. Petersburg Times*, Nov. 4, 1974. Dyckman went on to emphasize Askew's low-key style: "But even his critics mute what they say about him because of his unusual style—outwardly disarming and inwardly stubborn—that makes it possible for him to win graciously and lose calmly." Ibid.
39. Askew provided an example of his position on the race issue in a 1972 speech: "If the people remain divided against themselves on the race issue, they'll have no time to demand a fair-shake on taxes, on utility bills, on consumer protection, on government services, on environmental preservation, and other problems." Quoted in Neal R. Peirce, *The Deep South States of America* (New York: W. W. Norton, 1974), 453. In a 1974 interview Askew assessed the role of race in the South and the rest of the country: "I think that the South right now is poised . . . to become very much a part of the Democratic national party. Some of the problems that have characteristically been thought of as Southern problems in terms of race are not just Southern problems anymore. I think that some of the other parts of the country are now facing up to a lot of self-questioning that the South has gone through and I think come out pretty well. I think that the South is going to solve its racial problems before other parts of the country will." (He added, "When I say 'other parts of the country,' I'm talking about parts that are urban where you have a large black population.") Interview with Askew.
40. *St. Petersburg Times*, Nov. 4, 1974.
41. These were Alachua (Gainesville), Dade (Miami), Duval (Jacksonville), Volusia

(Daytona Beach), Leon (Tallahassee), and Hillsborough (Tampa). The nine of the fifteen largest urban counties that Carter lost to Ford were Sarasota, Lee, Palm Beach, Broward, Brevard, Pinellas, (St. Petersburg), Polk, Orange (Orlando), and Escambia (Pensacola).

42. About 95 percent of the blacks in four Florida cities voted for Carter. *The Black Vote: Election '76* (Washington: Joint Center for Political Studies, Aug. 1977), 52.

43. A *Miami Herald* reporter said Carter put together "a Democratic 'lunch bucket' coalition of blue collar whites, blacks and relatively liberal Jewish voters." *Miami Herald*, Nov. 3, 1976.

44. *St. Petersburg Times*, Nov. 3, 1976.

45. Interview with Pridgen.

46. *St. Petersburg Times*, Oct. 24, 1976.

47. *Florida Times-Union*, Sept. 14, 1978. Shevin's campaign manager, Steve Wilkerson, added, "Bob Graham is a liberal from Miami. That's all there is to it." *Tallahassee Democrat*, Sept. 14, 1978.

48. *Miami Herald*, Nov. 5, 1978. The article continued: "To those who recall his reputation as one of the Legislature's most liberal members, a man at the forefront of so many battles for more money for urban programs, Graham's platform has an unmistakable rightward bent . . . something that must seem a bit curious to members of the Florida Conservative Union, which ranked his 1974 Senate voting record zero on a scale that made 100 the most conservative score.

"Graham, however, rejects attempts to pin him down on philosophical labels, insisting that most state government issues don't lend themselves to simplistic labels such as liberal and conservative."

49. *Miami Herald*, Oct. 29, 1978. In fact, the Democratic combination was dubbed the Graham-Cracker ticket.

50. *St. Petersburg Times*, Nov. 9, 1978.

51. Graham received a gracious endorsement from Shevin: "I want to say that I lost and I lost to a qualified man, and he is a qualified candidate. We will unite and we will beat the Republican candidate." *Tallahassee Democrat*, Oct. 6, 1978.

52. Graham's race correlates with Carter's 1976 victory in Florida at .76 and with Chiles's 1976 re-election pattern at .71.

53. *St. Petersburg Times*, Oct. 24, 1980.

54. *Miami Herald*, Sept. 23, 1980.

55. Ibid., Sept. 10, 1980. Regarding Stone's renomination defeat, Charles Stafford of the *St. Petersburg Times*, commented, "He was perceived as what he was, which was an opportunist. He would jump on whatever bandwagon happened to be popular. And the one time he made a statesmanlike vote [by supporting the Panama Canal treaties], it hurt him. The unions, labor, got on him about common situs picketing, too." Patrick McMahon, Stafford's colleague in the *St. Petersburg Times* Washington bureau, expressed it this way: "The key to the Democrats' success in Florida is that they can kind of mush back and forth from moderate liberal to moderate conservative, and they all kind of stand each other fairly well. And when they can't, as in Dick Stone, they lose. When the right doesn't like him, because of the Panama Canal, and the left with the labor unions starts to pull him apart, then they don't win." Joint interview with Stafford and McMahon, conducted by the author, July 27, 1982.

56. Stone did send Gunter a telegram saying he supported Democrats "from the courthouse to the White House." *St. Petersburg Times*, Oct. 28, 1980.

57. Hawkins also had statewide exposure from two losing races: for the GOP senatorial nomination won by Eckerd in 1974 and as the GOP nominee for lieutenant governor in 1978 on Eckerd's losing ticket. *Miami Herald,* July 14, 1980.
58. A *New York Times* reporter added that Hawkins "espouses Ronald Reagan's plea for 'getting the Government off our backs and out of our pocket book.' She supports the Kemp-Roth proposal to cut Federal taxes, which she says will generate enough revenue through increased economic activity to enable the Government to increase military spending." Oct. 13, 1980.
59. *Miami Herald,* Oct. 31, 1980.
60. Ibid., Nov. 9, 1980.
61. Interview with McMahon, conducted by the author, July 27, 1982.
62. The *St. Petersburg Times* reported: "Bafalis' problems began before he qualified. His search for a running mate was frustrated by embarrassing rejections from several big names. Only at the 11th hour did he line up little-known Leo F. Callahan, the Fort Lauderdale police chief. . . .

    "No sooner had Callahan signed on than he developed health problems that kept him on the sidelines until October.

    "Then Bafalis was left red-faced by disclosures that [Nick] Longworth [Bafalis's campaign manager] had been indicted but never tried for campaign dirty tricks in a 1970 Indiana campaign and by his own involvement in an insolvent West Virginia coal-mining company.

    "Those setbacks were reflected in fund-raising problems that prevented Bafalis from launching the kind of media campaign so critical for success in Florida." Nov. 3, 1982.
63. Ibid.
64. In an article headlined, "GOP Had Golden Chance in Florida; Dogged by Problems, 'They Blew It,' " Robert D. Shaw, Jr., Washington correspondent of the *Miami Herald,* wrote that in February 1982 Chiles's re-election prospects looked "grim." Nov. 7, 1982.
65. *St. Petersburg Times,* Nov. 3, 1982.
66. Ibid.
67. Ibid. Also in the 1982 elections the Democrats won thirteen U.S. House seats to six for the Republicans.
68. On the basis of statewide telephone surveys conducted by the Policy Sciences Program at Florida State University, Beck reported that Republican party identifiers increased from 23 percent in Nov. 1978 to 31 percent in Jan. 1982. During that same period Democratic party identifiers declined from 45 percent to 39 percent. The Florida State surveys also charted ideological differences among these party identifiers. Beck wrote in conclusion, "Traditional Florida politics have been characterized by mass partisan loyalties to the Democratic party that defy the liberal-conservative ideological cleavage, however mild, outside the South. More ideologically based party coalitions seem to have been long overdue in the South. The recent partisan changes in Florida have increased significantly the ideological distinctiveness of the state's party coalitions, bringing them more into line with national patterns. . . . Barring a complete reversal in the climate of the times, there is good reason to believe that a major and lasting transformation of Florida politics has taken place." "Realignment Begins? The Republican Surge in Florida" (Rev. version of Paper presented at the Annual Meeting of the American Political Science Association, New York, Sept. 1981), 15.

Chapter 14: Texas

1. The 1980 census reported that Hispanics made up 21.0 percent of Texas's population (2,985,824 people out of a total population of 14,227,574). In the 1970 census the Hispanic percentage was 18.4.
2. Key, *Southern Politics in State and Nation* (New York: Alfred A. Knopf, 1949), 254.
3. Ibid.
4. Three analysts wrote in 1964 that the "opportunities seem so favorable for overthrow of the one-party system in Texas that its continuation seems incredible." James R. Soukup, Clifton McCleskey, and Harry Holloway, *Party and Factional Division in Texas* (Austin: Univ. of Texas Press, 1964), 65.
5. Key, *Southern Politics*, 259.
6. For a detailed view of party factional alignments in Texas, see Clifton McCleskey, Allan K. Butcher, Daniel E. Farlow, and J. Pat Stephens, *The Government and Politics of Texas*, 7th ed. (Boston: Little, Brown, 1982), 75–121.
7. Interview with Yarborough, conducted by Jack Bass and Walter DeVries, Dec. 10, 1974. Yarborough added that the forces of "predatory wealth [have] gotten smarter. They no longer denounce labor. They used to denounce the Negroes when I was running. . . . Now they put a few on their side."
8. The correlation between the presidential and senatorial races in 1960 is a nearly perfect .96.
9. Interview with Arthur E. Wiese, chief of the *Houston Post*'s Washington bureau, conducted by the author, Jan. 11, 1979.
10. Interview with Cragg Hines, Washington correspondent of the *Houston Chronicle*, conducted by the author, Jan. 10, 1979.
11. Rowland Evans and Robert Novak, *Lyndon B. Johnson: The Exercise of Power* (New York: New American Library, 1966), 352–53. As to where Johnson fits in the Texas political landscape, O. Douglas Weeks wrote, "The sudden elevation of Johnson to the presidency made him remote from the Texas scene and pushed him into closer identification with Kennedy liberalism. To Texans, this liberal role was unconvincing. Johnson to them had always been the temporizer and the compromiser, never moving too far from the center." Weeks, "Texas: Land of Conservative Expansiveness," in William C. Havard, ed., *The Changing Politics of the South* (Baton Rouge: Louisiana State Univ. Press, 1972), 223.
12. Yarborough's county-level pattern correlates with Johnson's winning 1964 pattern in Texas at .96.
13. The Johnson-Connally correlation coefficient is .94. Connally, who was seriously wounded during the Kennedy assassination in Dallas, was opposed in 1964 by the Republican Jack Crichton.
14. The term of office for governor was changed from two years to four years starting with the 1974 election.
15. The Tower races offer exceptional circumstances that are discussed below.
16. Bartley and Graham, *Southern Politics and the Second Reconstruction* (Baltimore: Johns Hopkins Univ. Press, 1975), 83. Jack Bass and Walter DeVries, *The Transformation of Southern Politics* (New York: Basic Books, 1976), 318, cite a precinct analysis by Richard Murray of the University of Houston that makes this same point.
17. Interview with Wiese.

18. *Houston Post,* Nov. 2, 1968.
19. Bartley and Graham, *Southern Politics,* 159–60.
20. *Houston Chronicle,* Nov. 4, 1970.
21. Ibid.
22. Bartley and Graham, *Southern Politics,* 169.
23. Ibid.
24. *Houston Chronicle,* June 4, 1972.
25. Ibid. The *Chronicle* reporter Bo Byers labeled Briscoe a conservative and Grover an ultraconservative.
26. Bartley and Graham, *Southern Politics,* 179–80.
27. Interview with Hines.
28. Bartley and Graham, *Southern Politics,* 170.
29. Sanders called himself a Lyndon Johnson Democrat. *Houston Post,* Nov. 6, 1972.
30. *Houston Post,* Nov. 6, 1972.
31. The McGovern-Sanders correlation coefficient is .81. In the 1972 campaign, "much of the conservative Democratic establishment followed the lead of former Governor Connally in directing its efforts toward the Democrats for Nixon campaign, and the liberals, while supporting Sanders, were unwilling to make any great sacrifices for the man who had beaten Ralph Yarborough." Bartley and Graham, *Southern Politics,* 179.
32. A look ahead at Map 14-1 indicates that Ford's strength in 1976 was urban based. The class-based nature of this urban support was described in note 12 of Chapter 3 and is addressed again below.
33. Also, precinct returns from Fort Worth, more working class than its sister city Dallas, show that a major decline in support for Sanders in 1972 relative to that for Bentsen in 1970 occurred in the white lower-income areas; Sanders received 51 percent to Bentsen's 66 percent. Overall, Bentsen carried Fort Worth (Tarrant County) with 50.1 percent, but Sanders lost it with 40.9 percent. Numan V. Bartley and Hugh D. Graham, *Southern Elections: County and Precinct Data, 1950–1972* (Baton Rouge: Louisiana State Univ. Press, 1978), 397.
34. *Houston Chronicle,* Nov. 3, 1974.
35. Ibid., Nov. 6, 1974.
36. A *Houston Chronicle* reporter, in keeping with the general interpretation of this election, wrote, "If a combination of Connally and Allan Shivers, another extremely popular former Democratic Governor, cannot woo Texas into the Republican column for an incumbent President, it is doubtful that the GOP can build much strength in the state in the near future." Nov. 3, 1976. Connally formally switched to the Republican party in 1973.
37. Background on the state's political geography was provided in an interview with Dolly McClary, administrative assistant to U.S. Rep. Martin Frost, conducted by the author, Jan. 11, 1979, and in an interview with Pam Turner, chief legislative assistant to Senator Tower, conducted by the author, Jan. 10, 1979.
38. See Table 3-5 in Chapter 3.
39. Interview with Wiese. Also contributing to the assessment of Bentsen were interviews with two of his assistants: Mike Naeve, chief legislative assistant, and Jack Devore, press secretary; both interviews were conducted by the author, Jan. 10, 1979.
40. Gramm won the U.S. House seat in 1978 and gained some notice during the first years of the Reagan administration for his labors on behalf of the Republican

President's budget and tax policies. When in January 1983, at the beginning of the Ninety-eighth Congress, House Democrats stripped him of his seat on the Budget Committee as punishment for having defied the Democratic leadership by openly collaborating with the Republicans, Gramm switched to the GOP, resigned his seat, and won it back a month later in a special election as a Republican. *New York Times*, Feb. 14, 1983.

41. *Houston Post*, Nov. 3, 1976. Jon Ford, political editor of the Austin *American-Statesman*, wrote, "Steelman's reputation as a moderate or liberal on environmental matters (for example, his opposition to the Trinity River barge canal, which cost him key support in his home county) cooled some members of his own party. Voting records indicate he is a fiscal conservative in the GOP mold."

42. Austin *American-Statesman*, Nov. 12, 1978; *Houston Chronicle*, Nov. 5, 1978.

43. Dan Dutko, former administrative assistant to U.S. Rep. Robert Krueger, the 1978 Democratic senatorial nominee, said that Clements's "money fed conservative Democrats what they wanted to hear." Interview with Dutko, who handled finances for the Krueger campaign and in early 1979 became administrative assistant to Sen. Donald Stewart of Alabama, conducted by the author, Jan. 11, 1979. Others interviewed who stressed Clements's personal financing of his campaign were Wiese, Hines, Devore, and Turner.

44. *Dallas Morning News*, Nov. 12, 1978, as reprinted in Eugene W. Jones, Joe E. Ericson, Lyle C. Brown, and Robert S. Trotter, Jr., *Practicing Texas Politics*, 4th ed. (Boston: Houghton Mifflin, 1980), 158.

45. Ibid., 157.

46. Ibid., 158.

47. "As did Briscoe in the primary, Clements attempted to label Hill a 'liberal claims lawyer who has made a career out of government service' and who surrounds himself with liberals.

   "Hill brushed off the attack, emphasizing his basically conservative fiscal philosophy, echoing [his] no new-taxes line and observing:

   " 'I have been around just long enough to know the score and not long enough to be a professional officeholder.' " Austin *American-Statesman*, Nov. 8, 1978.

48. *New York Times*, May 8, 1978.

49. Interview with Wiese.

50. Ibid.

51. Precinct data from Houston reveal that Hill also did poorly in white middle- and upper-income precincts, getting 37.0 percent and 23.0 percent respectively; in lower-income white areas he polled 60.9 percent. Among Houston blacks, Hill received 95 percent of the votes. These precinct results were reported by Richard Murray and appeared in the *Houston Chronicle*, Nov. 8, 1978.

52. Tower himself told the *Houston Post*, "I think Bill Clements helped a great deal in the win. He got out there and generated the votes." Nov. 9, 1978.

53. *Baltimore Sun*, May 2, 1978.

54. Ibid., Oct. 27, 1978. This article was written by Carl P. Leubsdorf.

55. Interview with Wilson, conducted by the author, Jan. 17, 1979. Perhaps concluding he had better not push his luck one more time, Tower announced in August 1983 that he would not seek re-election in 1984, setting off a scramble for the job among a host of politicians. They included Congressman Kent Hance, former Congressman Robert Krueger, the Democrat-turned-Republican Phil Gramm, and State Sen. Lloyd Doggett. *Dallas Morning News*, Aug. 24, 1983.

56. One Mexican-American leader, Rick Hernandez, a Carter White House official, looked at the bright side of Hill's defeat, telling a Mexican-American gathering that the Clements victory could purify the party. He reasoned that, if many conservative Democrats left the party, the influence of Hispanics could increase. "Texas, whether we like it or not, is going to become a two-party state, and we must control the Democratic party." *Houston Chronicle*, Dec. 3, 1978. The political importance of Texas's Hispanics has no parallel in the other ten Southern states. In the 1978 gubernatorial race, 75.3 percent of the state's Mexican-Americans voted for Hill, according to an analysis done by the Southwest Voter Registration Education Project in San Antonio.

57. Anne Greene, the Harris County Democratic chairman, was one who expressed delight at this prospect. Austin *American-Statesman*, Dec. 2, 1978.

58. Ibid.

59. Ibid.

60. The district was represented by John Nance Garner from 1903 to 1933 and by O. C. Fisher, another conservative Democrat, from 1943 to 1975; it was Krueger's district for two terms before he made his Senate bid in 1978.

61. Joint interview with Loeffler and Adkins, conducted by the author, Jan. 18, 1979. Loeffler said that in the 1978 campaign he opposed President Carter's policies and pointed out to voters that there were "constraints that [Speaker Thomas P.] Tip O'Neill would place on a Democrat representing a conservative area, constraints I would not have to labor under."

62. The conservative Democrat George H. Mahon represented the Nineteenth from 1935 until Kent Hance's election.

63. Interview with Hance, conducted by the author, Jan. 12, 1979.

64. Ibid.

65. Interview with Wilson. For a recent study of the development of the GOP in Texas through the 1978 gubernatorial victory, see Roger M. Olien, *From Token to Triumph: The Texas Republicans since 1920* (Dallas: Southern Methodist Univ. Press, 1982).

66. Interview with Wilson.

67. Ibid. Rep. Ron Paul, an arch-conservative Republican elected from a Houston district in 1978, contended, "We have established a two-party system for the first time. . . . The fact that we have a Republican governor indicates that a lot of conservative Democrats will now become Republicans." Interview with Paul, conducted by the author, Jan. 12, 1979.

68. All the quotations are from an article by Sam Attlesey, a *Dallas Morning News* writer, that appeared in the *Texas Observer*, Dec. 14, 1979.

69. *Texas Observer*, May 15, 1981.

70. While Hightower was the prize of the liberals, Ann Richards, the Democratic nominee for state treasurer, and U.S. Rep. Jim Mattox, the party's candidate for attorney general, were also viewed somewhat favorably by the left-of-center forces.

71. *Texas Observer*, Nov. 26, 1982.

72. *Houston Post*, Sept. 11, 1982.

73. Ibid.

74. *New York Times*, Sept. 13, 1982.

75. Reporting on White's campaign, the *New York Times* wrote that he "has found a good horse in the utility issue, the cornerstone of his quasi-populist campaign. He charges that Mr. Clements has done little to halt the rapid rise in electric rates.

This has become the symbol of Mr. White's effort to exploit class consciousness amid widespread unemployment and to link Mr. Clements to the weak economy.

"His television commercials are filled with sarcasm. One shows a group in elegant attire dining on caviar while the voice-over intones: 'From up here, the view of the economy is rosy.' Then Mr. White appears, dressed in jeans, and says, 'Texans don't need a Governor who will listen only to the big shots on Wall Street.' " *New York Times*, Oct. 31, 1982. The article was written by Robert Reinhold.

76. Ibid., Oct. 14, 1982.

77. Ibid.

78. Ibid.

79. Interview with Leubsdorf, conducted by the author, July 28, 1982. Leubsdorf added that "Clements is apparently losing some of those conservative Democrats he got last time because his opponent is a genuine conservative Democrat."

80. An article with comments from both sides on the effect of the utility issue appeared in the *Dallas Morning News*, Nov. 7, 1982, under the headline "White's Stand on Utility Bills Aided in Win."

81. Ibid., Nov. 7, 1982. The reporter Jackie Calmes added, "This fall, when Clements told a Galveston interviewer that it would not be appropriate to have a housewife on the Public Utilities Commission because 'I don't know of any that are qualified in the sense that I am talking about,' White turned the utility issue into a women's issue, too."

82. *Houston Post*, Jan. 3, 1982. This article, written by Arthur Wiese, continued, "The Texas Democrat, a millionaire former business executive . . . and a politician with deep ties to the state's powerful business community, regards himself as not quite a total centrist. 'I've always said I was somewhat to the right of center,' he said. . . .

" 'Lloyd Bentsen is the most active liberal senator from the South today,' insisted Collins. Bentsen at first declined to 'answer any charge that's that off-base' but he later ventured that 'it's baloney.' "

83. These classified precinct breakdowns were published in the *Houston Post*, Nov. 4, 1982.

84. The 1982 percentage appeared in a San Antonio *Express-News* article, Nov. 7, 1982, and was attributed to Willie Velasquez, executive director of the Southwest Voter Registration and Education Project. The 1978 Hispanic figure, cited in note 56 above, was 75.3 percent. For a study of recent Hispanic electoral behavior, see *Mexican American Voting in the 1982 Texas General Election* (San Antonio: Southwest Voter Registration Education Project, Dec. 1982).

85. *Houston Post*, Nov. 14, 1982.

86. *Amarillo Daily News*, Nov. 4, 1982.

Chapter 15: Southern Politics in the 1980s

1. A network of political scientists in various states interested in promoting the growth of state polls was established in January 1981 at a conference on comparative state polling at the University of Kentucky, which was attended by representatives of nineteen different academic polling units in eighteen states. An account of the organizing conference appeared in Malcolm E. Jewell's informative newsletter, *Comparative State Politics*, March 1981, pp. 21–22.

The potential of extensive, coordinated state polling for understanding American electoral behavior was demonstrated in the 1968 surveys of the Comparative State Elections Project of the Institute for Research in Social Science, University of North Carolina at Chapel Hill, which featured separate samples in thirteen selected states along with a national sample. See the resulting data book produced by Merle Black, David M. Kovenock, and William C. Reynolds, *Political Attitudes in the Nation and the States* (Chapel Hill: Institute for Research in Social Science, 1974), and the analytical study by David M. Kovenock, James W. Prothro, et al., *Explaining the Vote: Presidential Choices in the Nation and the States, 1968* (Chapel Hill: Institute for Research in Social Science, pts. 1 and 2, 1973; pt. 3, 1974).

2. The samples for the surveys of the Center for Political Studies (CPS) are drawn to reflect a random selection of persons within several regional groupings. For the South two such groupings are available. The first consists of the states of the former Confederacy minus Tennessee, which the CPS calls the Solid South. The other is the Border South, defined by CPS as Tennessee, Oklahoma, Kentucky, Maryland, West Virginia, and the District of Columbia. Researchers take different positions on the choice; see Charles D. Hadley, "Survey Research and Southern Politics: The Implications of Data Management," *Public Opinion Quarterly* 45 (Fall 1981), 393–401. To avoid excluding Tennessee and to get the largest number of respondents, I have combined the CPS's Solid South and Border South. This choice for the 1980 CPS National Election Study, which I use exclusively in this chapter, is made easier by the small number of respondents from outside the eleven-state South. Of the subsample's 539 respondents, only 93 were not from the states of the former Confederacy: 23 from Kentucky, 26 from Maryland, 31 from Oklahoma, 13 from West Virginia, and none from the District of Columbia. Furthermore, all calculations were also done using the Solid South definition, and the differences with the Solid South–Border South combination were minuscule.

3. For a discussion of the advantages of party identification as a measure of partisan change, see Raymond Wolfinger and Robert B. Arseneau, "Partisan Change in the South, 1952–1976," in Louis Maisel and Joseph Cooper, eds., *Political Parties: Development and Decay* (Beverly Hills, Calif.: Sage Publications, 1978), 181–87.

4. This Alabama poll, conducted Oct. 26–Nov. 2, 1980, gave the lead in the state among likely voters to Reagan, 48 percent to Carter's 46 percent; the poll's undecided voters were distributed in the direction they said they were leaning. On Election Day, Reagan carried Alabama with 48.8 percent to Carter's 47.4 percent.

5. This black partisan unity is shored up by a stark economic fact of life well known to anyone who lives in the region: Southern blacks tend to be very poor. For example, the 1970 U.S. census found that in South Carolina 49.7 percent of the state's blacks lived below the poverty line. The figure for South Carolina's whites was 12.3 percent. Nationally in 1970 the poverty breakdown was 35.0 percent for blacks and 10.9 percent for whites. The U.S. census found that the general situation had not changed by 1982. *New York Times*, Aug. 3, 1983.

6. Similar findings were revealed in a survey of Columbus, Ga., conducted in Jan., Feb., and March 1981, using income level, educational level, and occupational stratum as measures of economic class. The results were reported by William Chappell, G. James Foster, and Raymond G. Gonzalez, all of Columbus College, in their "Presidential Voting Patterns in the 1980 Election: A Case Study of an Urban Southern Community" (Paper presented at the Annual Meeting of the Southern Political Science Association, Memphis, Nov. 5–7, 1981).

7. For fine introductions to this research, see Paul R. Abramson, *Generational Change in American Politics* (Lexington, Mass.: Lexington Books, 1975), and Philip E. Converse, *The Dynamics of Party Support: Cohort-Analyzing Party Identification* (Beverly Hills, Calif.: Sage Publications, 1976).

8. Wolfinger and Arseneau, "Partisan Change in the South," 207. There is a vast political science literature tracing Southern partisan change using the American National Election Studies of the University of Michigan's Center for Political Studies (formerly known as the Survey Research Center). The Wolfinger and Arseneau chapter is perhaps the best introduction to this material. Other good survey analyses along these lines are Bruce A. Campbell, "Patterns of Change in the Partisan Loyalties of Native Southerners, 1952–1972," *Journal of Politics* 39 (Aug. 1977), 730–61; Bruce A. Campbell, "Change in the Southern Electorate," *American Journal of Political Science* 21 (Feb. 1977), 37–64; Paul Allen Beck, "Partisan Dealignment in the Postwar South," *American Political Science Review* 71 (June 1977), 477–96; Charles D. Hadley and Susan E. Howell, "The Southern Split Ticket Voter, 1952–76: Republican Conversion or Democratic Decline?" in Robert P. Steed, Laurence W. Moreland, and Tod A. Baker, eds., *Party Politics in the South* (New York: Praeger, 1980), 127–51; Charles L. Prysby, "Electoral Behavior in the U.S. South: Recent and Emerging Trends," in Steed, Moreland, and Baker, eds., *Party Politics in the South,* 101–26; and Paul Allen Beck and Paul Lopatto, "The End of Southern Distinctiveness," in Laurence W. Moreland, Tod A. Baker, and Robert P. Steed, eds., *Contemporary Southern Political Attitudes and Behavior* (New York: Praeger, 1982), 160–82.

9. The behavior of Northern blacks voting for Carter is excluded for lack of relevancy, not for lack of interest, since fruitful comparisons could be made with this category of voters to explore important topics beyond the scope of this work. Two other classifications—blacks for Reagan, North and South—were excluded because their numbers were minuscule.

10. The wording for all the CPS questions was taken from the 1980 American National Election Study's codebook.

11. The question was worded as follows: "Some people believe that we should spend much less money for defense. Others feel that defense spending should be greatly increased. Where would you place yourself on [a seven-point scale]?" The reported percentages of those favoring an increase in defense spending were derived by combining points 5, 6, or 7 on the scale.

12. Survey data cited in Chapter 3 showed that the 1976 class breakdown of Democratic party support was nearly identical in the South and the North. A comparison of the North and South in the 1980 election suggests that class voting was more prevalent in Dixie in that election than four years earlier, a fascinating shift in regional direction (see Table 15-4).

13. For an early analysis of this trend, see Philip E. Converse, "On the Possibility of Major Political Realignment in the South," in Allan P. Sindler, ed., *Change in the Contemporary South* (Durham, N.C.: Duke Univ. Press, 1963), 195–222. Converse, of course, could not have anticipated the fury with which the race issue became enmeshed in the convergence tendency he so accurately described.

14. V. O. Key, Jr., *Southern Politics in State and Nation* (New York: Alfred A. Knopf, 1949), 311.

15. Arkansas appeared to follow Deep South patterns in this regard.

16. For a discussion of the importance of race to Southern distinctiveness, see I. A.

Newby's *The South: A History* (New York: Holt, Rinehart & Winston, 1978), esp. chap. 1.

17. Parts of both states—namely, North Florida and East Texas—still exhibited Southern trends, however.

18. If these observations are accurate, the Rim South–Deep South division should become less meaningful in the future. In fact, Figure 2-2, which displays differences in Democratic presidential support between the two subregional categories, indicates that this once-substantial behavioral gap had already narrowed considerably by the 1970s and early 1980s.

19. James L. Sundquist, *Dynamics of the Party System: Alignment and Realignment of Political Parties in the United States* (Washington: Brookings Institution, 1973), 218–44. For Sundquist's views on party-system change since his excellent book first appeared, see his new, thoroughly revised edition, published in 1983 by the Brookings Institution.

20. See, for example, these works by Samuel Lubell: *The Future of American Politics*, 3d ed., rev. (New York: Harper & Row, 1965); *White and Black: Test of a Nation* (New York: Harper & Row, 1964); *The Hidden Crisis in American Politics* (New York: W. W. Norton, 1970); and *The Future While It Happened* (New York: W. W. Norton, 1973).

21. David H. Everson summarized this debate in his *American Political Parties* (New York: Franklin Watts, 1980), 125–55. Useful recent works include John R. Petrocik, *Party Coalitions: Realignment and the Decline of the New Deal Party System* (Chicago: Univ. of Chicago Press, 1981); Bruce A. Campbell and Richard J. Trilling, eds., *Realignment in American Politics: Toward a Theory* (Austin: Univ. of Texas Press, 1980); and Jerome M. Clubb, William H. Flanigan, and Nancy H. Zingale, *Partisan Realignment: Voters, Parties, and Government in American History* (Beverly Hills, Calif.: Sage Publications, 1980).

22. Three of the current national trends are the increased importance of television to the electoral process, the ubiquitous appearance of professional campaign managers, and the general weakening of voter attachment to political parties as reflected in the growing number of persons who claim independence when asked their party affiliation. These trends have contributed to a view that political parties are declining nationwide, and there is much to justify that belief. See, for example, David S. Broder, *The Party's Over: The Failure of Politics in America* (New York: Harper & Row, 1972); Jeff Fishel, ed., *Parties and Elections in an Anti-Party Age: American Politics and the Crisis of Confidence* (Bloomington: Indiana Univ. Press, 1978); Thomas E. Patterson, *The Mass Media Election: How Americans Choose Their President* (New York: Praeger, 1980); and Larry J. Sabato, *The Rise of Political Consultants: New Ways of Winning Elections* (New York: Basic Books, 1981). But, interestingly, the South is providing a partial countermovement as a result of its unprecedented growth in two-party activity. Of course, the national trends—the increased use of the electronic media, the proliferation of campaign consultants, the growth of independents—have taken place in the South simultaneously with the rise of two-party competition, presenting a mixed regional picture.

23. See the Mississippi chapter for a discussion of the 1982 contest to succeed Bowen in the Second District.

24. Michael Barone and Grant Ujifusa, *The Almanac of American Politics 1982* (Washington: Barone, 1981), 500. Bowen's congressional voting record received the following approval rating from the liberal Americans for Democratic Action: 15 per-

cent in 1978, 11 percent in 1979, and 28 percent in 1980. The conservative Americans for Constitutional Action rated him as follows: 88 percent in 1978, 70 percent in 1979, and 43 percent in 1980. Ibid., 600.

25. Interview with Bowen, conducted by the author, July 28, 1982.

26. The shift to a purely philosophical concern in these last few paragraphs is more a shift in degree than in kind. All political analysis—no matter what the author's claim—reflects philosophical preferences to some extent.

27. Key, *Southern Politics*, 307 (emphasis added).

Chapter 16: The 1984 Elections

1. Many volumes have appeared examining the 1984 elections, including: Paul R. Abramson, John H. Aldrich, and David W. Rohde, *Change and Continuity in the 1984 Elections*, rev. ed. (Washington: CQ Press, 1987); Gerald M. Pomper et al., *The Election of 1984: Reports and Interpretations* (Chatham, N.J.: Chatham House, 1985); Ellis Sandoz and Cecil V. Crabb, Jr., eds., *Election 84: Landslide without a Mandate?* (New York: New American Library, 1985); Michael Nelson, ed., *The Elections of 1984* (Washington: CQ Press, 1985); and Austin Ranney, ed., *The American Elections of 1984* (Durham, N.C.: Duke University Press for the American Enterprise Institute for Public Policy Research, 1985). Professor Donald M. Freeman of the University of Evansville has written an invaluable history of the vast literature on presidential elections. His study, which includes a 40-page bibliography, was presented at the Annual Meeting of the American Political Science Association, September 3–6, 1987, in Chicago.

2. *Mississippi Press* (Pascagoula), Oct. 2, 1984.

3. Ibid.

4. *The State* (Columbia, S.C.), Oct. 16, 1984.

5. *New York Times*, Aug. 2, 1984.

6. Ibid.

7. Memphis *Commercial Appeal*, Sept. 14, 1984.

8. Ibid.

9. Ibid.

10. Ibid., Sept. 13, 1984.

11. One problem in getting accurate regional estimates arises because those who conduct surveys define the South differently. The 28-percent figure for the Southern white vote relied on here is taken from the CBS News/*New York Times* 1984 Election Day exit poll, as reported in *Public Opinion* (Dec. 1984–Jan. 1985), 34. This poll adds Kentucky and Oklahoma to the eleven former Confederate states to form its definition of the South. This same survey is also used for the summary estimates displayed in Table 16-3; there the national white vote for Mondale is put at 35 percent. Lacking a separate non-Southern white percentage, I have estimated it at 36 percent to 38 percent, thus arriving at the eight-to-ten percentage-point North-South difference mentioned in the text.

12. In my use in Tables 16-1, 16-4, and 16-5 of the 1984 National Election Study of the University of Michigan's Center for Political Studies (CPS) and in Table 18-1 of the CPS's 1986 National Election Study, I continue to define the South as a combination of the CPS's Solid South and Border South groupings for the reasons explained in note 2 of Chapter 15. The CPS's Solid South is made up of the states

of the former Confederacy minus Tennessee, and its Border South category consists of Tennessee, Oklahoma, Kentucky, Maryland, West Virginia, and the District of Columbia. It is my understanding that the CPS draws a representative stratified random sample within each of its regional categories. Thus, if one combines respondents selectively from states across groupings, such as adding Tennessee to the Solid South's ten states, a strategy not infrequently found in recent years, the resulting totals are not necessarily representative of the population of the newly created combination.

For the sake of completeness, it should be noted that, in drawing the respondents within each regional grouping, not all states are selected for sampling each election year. In 1984 the sampled states and the number of respondents interviewed in each were as follows: *Solid South:* Virginia, 48; Alabama, 53; Arkansas, 60; Florida, 78; Georgia, 92; North Carolina, 65; Texas, 153. *Border South:* Maryland, 47, Tennessee, 102; West Virginia, 52.

13. Harold W. Stanley, "The 1984 Presidential Election in the South: Race and Realignment," in Robert P. Steed, Laurence W. Moreland, and Tod A. Baker, eds., *The 1984 Presidential Election in the South: Patterns of Southern Party Politics* (New York: Praeger, 1986), p. 316.

14. *New York Times*, June 16, 1985.

15. Ibid.

16. Ibid., Sept. 1, 1985.

17. Laurence W. Moreland, Robert P. Steed, and Tod A. Baker wrote: "White support for Reagan was probably higher in South Carolina than in any other state in the South or, indeed, any other state in the nation with the possible exception of Mississippi." Moreland, Steed, and Baker, "South Carolina," in Steed, Moreland, and Baker, eds., *The 1984 Presidential Election in the South*, 145.

18. We do not often like to admit that even in electoral research—one of the most "scientific" subfields of political science—the art or instinct in our craft remains very important.

19. For a useful discussion of these dimensions, see James L. Sundquist's *Dynamics of the Party System: Alignment and Realignment of Political Parties in the United States*, rev. ed. (Washington: Brookings Institution, 1983), 430–32.

20. V. O. Key, Jr., with the assistance of Milton C. Cummings, Jr., *The Responsible Electorate: Rationality in Presidential Voting, 1936–1960* (Cambridge, Mass.: The Belknap Press of Harvard University Press, 1966).

21. To quote Professor Key completely on the point: "The perverse and unorthodox argument of this little book is that voters are not fools. To be sure, many individual voters act in odd ways indeed; yet in the large the electorate behaves about as rationally and responsibly as we should expect, given the clarity of the alternatives presented to it and the character of the information available to it." Ibid., 7.

22. Ibid., 58–59.

23. For a contrasting view of Southern attitudes, see Chapter 10, "The Conservative Advantage in Public Opinion," in Earl and Merle Black, *Politics and Society in the South* (Cambridge, Mass.: Harvard University Press, 1987), which begins on page 213 with this paragraph:

"Conservatism occupies an exalted ideological position in the South. Although the region has sometimes been portrayed as ripe for the construction of successful biracial coalitions of have-littles and have-nots, the growth of the urban middle class and the popularity of middle-class beliefs among southern white workers have worked against explicit class politics and in favor of conservative politics generally. When southerners are queried about their ideological preferences, their beliefs concerning individual versus governmental responsibility for securing jobs and a good standard of living, and their satisfaction with life in their states and localities, the collective thrust of their responses reveals a region in which conservatism flourishes and liberalism withers."

24. William D. Snider, *Helms and Hunt: The North Carolina Senate Race, 1984* (Chapel Hill: University of North Carolina Press, 1985).
25. *Washington Post*, Oct. 28, 1984. The article, written by Helen Dewar, was headlined "$21 Million Dead Heat: N.C. Senate Race Expensive and Mean."
26. Ibid.
27. *The State*, Oct. 7, 1984. This excellent summary article by Lavona Page was headlined "Helms-Hunt Mudfight May Be Nation's Messiest."
28. Ibid.
29. Raleigh *News and Observer*, Nov. 2, 1984.
30. Ibid.
31. Ibid., Nov. 8, 1984.
32. Ibid., Dec. 16, 1984.
33. *News and Observer*, Oct. 6, 1984.
34. *Birmingham News*, Sept. 5, 1984.
35. Ibid., Oct. 23, 1984. This article, written by William Bunch, was headlined: "Both Senate Candidates Rated as Conservatives, Supporters of Reagan."
36. Ibid., Oct. 23, 1984.
37. Ibid.
38. Ibid., Oct. 25, 1984.
39. Ibid., Oct. 30, 1984.
40. *The Political Report*, Jan. 11, 1985. *The Political Report*, a nonpartisan weekly newsletter that closely follows congressional elections, is published by the conservative Free Congress Research and Education Foundation and its Washington-based Institute on Government and Politics.
41. *Birmingham News*, Oct. 29, 1984.
42. Ibid., Nov. 3, 1984.
43. Jackson (Miss.) *Clarion-Ledger*, April 4, 1984.
44. Tupelo (Miss.) *Daily Journal*, Oct. 31, 1984.
45. *Clarion-Ledger*, Aug. 26, 1984.
46. Ibid.
47. Ibid., April 15, 1984.
48. Ibid., June 17, 1984.
49. In low-income white precincts in Jackson, Mondale received 14.7 percent of the vote; in moderate-to-high income white areas he won 9.6 percent. For Winter the comparable figures were 15.8 percent and 11.1 percent. See Table 3-2 in Alexander P. Lamis, "Mississippi," in Steed, Moreland, and Baker, eds., *The 1984 Presidential Election in the South*, 64.
50. Ibid., 63 and 66.
51. *Commercial Appeal*, Jan. 7. 1984.
52. *Clarion-Ledger*, Oct. 21, 1984.
53. *Commercial Appeal*, Oct. 7, 1984.
54. *Clarion-Ledger*, Oct. 31, 1984.
55. Ibid., Oct. 21, 1984.

56. Ibid.
57. *The State*, Aug. 14, 1983.
58. *Congressional Quarterly Weekly Report*, Oct. 13, 1984, p. 1447.
59. *Arkansas Gazette* (Little Rock), Nov. 4, 1984. This article, written by George Wells, was headlined, "Senate Race Has Been Most Memorable Yet."
60. *Arkansas Gazette*, Sept. 23, 1984.
61. Diane K. Blair, "Arkansas," in Steed, Moreland, and Baker, *The 1984 Presidential Election in the South*, 202.
62. *Arkansas Gazette*, Oct. 21, 1984.
63. Ibid.
64. Ibid., Nov. 4, 1984.
65. Ibid.
66. Ibid., Nov. 7, 1984.
67. In 1986 Williams won the point, if not the seat; Fowler did not seek re-election in 1986 in order to run for the Senate, and he was succeeded by a black Democrat, as is related in Chapter 17.
68. *Atlanta Constitution*, Oct. 22, 1984.
69. Ibid., Nov. 8, 1984.
70. New Orleans *Times-Picayune*, Aug. 14, 1984.
71. Ibid., Sept. 9 and 23, 1984; *New York Times*, Sept. 28, 1984.
72. *Nashville Tennessean*, June 17, 1984.
73. Ibid., May 30, 1984.
74. Ibid., Nov. 7, 1984. The article, written by Larry Daughtrey, was headlined: "No Conventional Label Easily Fits Albert Gore, Jr."
75. *Nashville Tennessean*, Sept. 22, 1984.
76. Larry Sabato, "Virginia" in Steed, Moreland, and Baker, *The 1984 Presidential Election in the South*, 298, and Norfolk *Virginian-Pilot*, Oct. 17, 1984.
77. Sabato, "Virginia," 298.
78. *Washington Post*, May 29, 1984. The aide noted that Warner voted for the Martin Luther King, Jr., federal holiday.
79. Harrison released a campaign flyer in October claiming that Warner supported Senator Helms 92 percent of the time and questioning the Republican's civil rights record. She told the Richmond *Times-Dispatch*: "I would not call John Warner a racist. I would call him totally insensitive to how people live in the real world. This man is a real elitist." *Times-Dispatch*, Oct. 24, 1984.
80. *Virginian-Pilot*, Oct. 30, 1984.
81. Sabato, "Virginia," 288.
82. On the homosexual-contribution matter, Doggett said he returned the money when he learned of its source. He added that, although he did not endorse the homosexual way of life, "I'm not going to see them made an object of fear or hate." *New York Times*, Sept. 30, 1984.
83. Ibid.
84. *Congressional Quarterly Weekly Report*, June 9, 1984.
85. Ibid.
86. The accent, incidentally, is from Gramm's native state of Georgia, not the Lone Star State.
87. *Dallas Morning News*, Sept. 3, 1984.
88. The Reagan-Gramm county-level correlation coefficient of .99 is witness to Gramm's success on this point.

89. The Republican victors correlate with Reagan in the top half of the .90s with the exception of Martin in North Carolina. The GOP losers were less close to Reagan's pattern. The correlation coefficients of Reagan with the Southern Republicans follow with the appropriate Democratic opponents in parenthesis: Gramm (Doggett) .99; Cochran (Winter) .97; Thurmond (Purvis) .97; Helms (Hunt) .96; Warner (Harrison) .95; Martin (Edmisten) .92; Bethune (Pryor) .90; Smith (Heflin) .85; Ashe (Gore) .83; Freeman (Clinton) .83.

    For an explanation of the correlation technique, see the Appendix. The coefficients are from Tari Renner, "Southern Electoral Change and the 1984 Republican Vote: A Correlation Analysis" (Paper prepared for delivery at the Citadel Symposium on Southern Politics, Charleston, South Carolina, March 6–7, 1986).

90. These estimates are based on a CBS News/*New York Times* exit poll conducted in Alabama on November 6, 1984, as reported in *Public Opinion* (Dec. 1984–Jan. 1985), 40.

91. These tendencies are shown in cross-tabulations provided by Patrick R. Cotter, to whom the author is grateful for this courtesy. See Patrick R. Cotter, "Split Ticket Voting in the 1984 Election: Presidential and Senate Voting in Alabama" (Paper prepared for delivery at the Southern Political Science Association's Annual Meeting, Nashville, November 1985).

92. These similar tendencies are shown in cross-tabulations provided by David M. Brodsky and Robert H. Swansbrough, both of the University of Tennessee at Chattanooga, to whom the author expresses his appreciation for their kind assistance. Findings from their Tennessee Poll were presented in their "Ticket Splitting in Tennessee" (Paper prepared for delivery at the Citadel Symposium on Southern Politics, March 6–7, 1986, in Charleston, S.C.). Their overall study of recent Tennessee politics makes up one chapter in their forthcoming edited book on recent Southern electoral change to be published by the University of South Carolina Press.

Chapter 17: The 1986 Elections

1. The 1986 victory gave the Democrats a 55-to-45 edge in the Senate, although the next year they lost a seat as the result of the death of Senator Edward Zorinsky, a Nebraska Democrat, and the subsequent appointment of a Republican replacement by a Republican governor.

2. This gave the Democrats 258 seats in the 100th Congress compared with 177 for the Republican party. The Democrats have controlled the U.S. House since the 1954 elections.

3. Thus, of the region's 116 seats, the GOP claimed 39 seats in 1986, or 33.6 percent, as compared with its 37.1 percent in 1984.

4. Nationwide the party gained four more governorships.

5. The Republican party's slow-but-steady progress in state legislative races continued in two of the three states that held elections in 1987. The GOP picked up five seats in Mississippi and three in Virginia; in Louisiana the Democrats gained three seats. These figures are from the Nov. 24, 1987, issue of the *Southern Political Report*, an excellent biweekly newsletter published in Washington by Hastings Wyman, Jr.

6. A Capstone Poll taken in late January showed 61 percent of the respondents believed Wallace's health affected his performance as governor "a great deal," up from 45 percent in a mid-October 1985, poll. *Birmingham News*, Feb. 2, 1986.

7. *New York Times*, April 3, 1986.
8. *Montgomery Advertiser*, May 11, 1986.
9. *Birmingham News*, April 20, 1986.
10. *Birmingham News*, May 4, 1986. The article, written by Michele MacDonald, was headlined "Bill Baxley Running for Dream of Lifetime."
11. *Anniston (Ala.) Star*, March 16, 1986.
12. The percentages for the Democrats in the first primary are from David L. Martin, "The 1986 Alabama Democratic Primaries: A Contest Without a Winner," *Comparative State Politics Newsletter* (Aug. 1986), 2.
13. *Birmingham News*, April 20, 1986.
14. Ibid.
15. *New York Times*, June 23, 1986.
16. Ibid.
17. *Birmingham News*, April 27 and May 4, 1986.
18. Martin, "The 1986 Alabama Democratic Primaries," 2.
19. *Washington Post*, Aug. 2, 1986, and *New York Times*, Aug. 2, 1986.
20. *Washington Post*, Aug. 2, 1986.
21. *New York Times*, Aug. 6, 1986.
22. Patrick R. Cotter and James Glen Stovall, "The 1986 Election in Alabama: The Beginning of the Post-Wallace Era," *PS* (Summer 1987), 661.
23. Martin, "The 1986 Alabama Democratic Primaries," 3.
24. *Birmingham News*, Aug. 22, 1986.
25. *Birmingham Post Herald*, Oct. 2, 1986.
26. Ibid.
27. *New York Times*, June 23, 1986.
28. *New York Times*, Nov. 1, 1986, quoting Gerald Johnson of Auburn University.
29. *Birmingham News*, Oct. 14, 1986.
30. *Birmingham News*, Oct. 14, 1986. This article, written by Rick Bragg, was headlined, "Hunt Hoping To Ride Wave of Democrats' Resentment."
31. The percentage is from an October 1986 Capstone Poll and was provided to the author by Patrick R. Cotter of the University of Alabama at Tuscaloosa.
32. The correlation coefficient between Graddick's runoff pattern and Reagan's 1984 vote in Alabama is .85; the calculation was done by Jeff Whitson, an undergraduate political science major at the University of North Florida.

    Two political scientists at Birmingham-Southern College wrote that Graddick was perceived "as the conservative, law and order, anti-black, pro-business, 'pseudo-Republican.' " They said Baxley was viewed "as the liberal, championing the rights and needs of blacks, poor whites, and a rather small white liberal constituency." H. Irvin Penfield and Natalie M. Davis, "Changing Patterns in Partisanship: Republicans in Alabama" (Paper presented at the Annual Meeting of the Southern Political Science Association, Charlotte, November 5–7, 1987), 1.
33. *New York Times*, July 15, 1986. The article was written by Phil Gailey.
34. *Birmingham Post Herald*, Nov. 5, 1986.
35. This article by Sidney Blumenthal of the *Washington Post* was carried in *The State*, Nov. 2, 1986.
36. *Birmingham Post Herald*, Sept. 19, 1986. This article, written by Ted Bryant, was headlined "Reagan Leads GOP Love Feast."
37. Ibid.
38. *Mobile Press Register*, Sept. 19, 1986.

39. *Birmingham News*, Nov. 5, 1986.
40. In addition, Don Siegelman, the former secretary of state and an up-and-coming Democratic politician often mentioned for higher office, became attorney general. The office of secretary of state was won by Glen Browder, a former political science professor at Jacksonville State University.
41. *Atlanta Journal*, Nov. 9, 1986.
42. In midsummer, for example, I wrote: "If Georgia Democrats choose a senatorial nominee in 1986 who can hold together all elements of the party's diverse 'night-and-day' alliance, Mattingly is a guaranteed one-termer." "The Future of the Two-Party South: Implications from an Analysis of Recent Elections" (Paper presented at the Annual Meeting of the American Political Science Association in Washington, August 28–31, 1986), 56.
43. *Atlanta Journal*, Oct. 7, 1986.
44. *Congressional Quarterly Weekly Report*, Oct. 11, 1986, p. 2417.
45. *Atlanta Journal*, Nov. 10, 1985. This article, written by Hal Straus, was headlined "Fowler Plays to Audiences Down South."
46. Ibid.
47. *Atlanta Journal*, Aug. 7, 1986.
48. Nunn praised Fowler in a 30-second television commercial: "I've known Wyche for 10 years. I've worked with him. He's an outstanding congressman. He will be an outstanding senator." *Atlanta Journal*, Sept. 15, 1986.
49. *Chattanooga* (Tenn.) *News-Free Press*, Sept. 7, 1986.
50. On the absenteeism charge, the *Atlanta Journal* noted that Mattingly's ads "don't mention that until this year, when he has been campaigning for the Senate, Fowler's attendance was at or near the average level for Georgia House members." *Atlanta Journal*, Oct. 7, 1986.
51. *The Political Report*, Feb. 20, 1987.
52. *New York Times*, Oct. 9, 1986.
53. *Atlanta Journal*, Oct. 6, 1986. This profile article was headlined "Mattingly Has Yet To Make Mark: Freshman Senator Is Still Learning Ropes of Lawmaking Process."
54. *Atlanta Journal*, Oct. 21, 1986.
55. Ibid.
56. Ibid., Oct. 24, 1986, and *The Political Report*, Feb. 20, 1987.
57. *Atlanta Journal*, Oct. 1986.
58. Ibid., Nov. 9, 1986.
59. "If they [party officials] had just given me two days' worth of what they spent on Mattingly, I could have whipped Joe Frank," Davis said as he watched the returns come in with 200 supporters at a Cobb County hotel. *Atlanta Journal*, Nov. 5, 1986.
60. Ibid.
61. Ibid., Sept. 4, 1986. A *New York Times* article on Aug. 10, 1986, was headlined "Atlanta Campaign Tests a Friendship of 25 Years."
62. *Atlanta Journal*, Nov. 5, 1986.
63. *Congressional Quarterly Weekly Report*, Oct. 11, 1986, p. 2418.
64. Moore received the party's "endorsement" at a GOP state convention on March 22, 1986. "It's time to bring the Reagan Revolution to Louisiana, and we will," Moore told the 1,000 delegates in his acceptance speech. Baton Rouge *Morning Advocate*, March 23, 1986.

65. See "Moore Not Shocked by Vote But Other Observers Were" in the *Morning Advocate*, Oct. 5, 1986, for a discussion of how GOP spokesmen raised expectations. For example, Senator John Heinz, the Pennsylvania Republican who headed his party's Senate campaign committee, was quoted as saying on September 11 that an outright Moore victory was "a very good possibility."
66. *Morning Advocate*, Oct. 24, 1986.
67. Ibid.
68. Ibid., Oct. 23, 1986.
69. Ibid.
70. *Washington Post*, Oct. 2, 1986. The article, written by Thomas B. Edsall, was headlined "Republicans Target Precincts for Possible Voter Challenges."
71. Ibid.
72. Ibid.
73. Ibid., Oct. 31, 1986. This article was written by David Maraniss.
74. Ibid.
75. New Orleans *Times-Picayune*, Oct. 20, 1986. Breaux remarked during the debate: "Only if you believe in the tooth fairy do you believe he knew nothing about it."
76. *New York Times*, Oct. 31, 1986. This article was written by Dudley Clendinen.
77. Ibid.
78. *Times-Picayune*, Oct. 11, 1987.
79. Ibid., Oct. 8, 1987.
80. Ibid., Oct. 21, 1987. Two independent polls in mid-October confirmed that Roemer had broken out of the pack. Ibid.
81. *New York Times*, Feb. 28, 1987.
82. Tauzin, a Cajun like Edwards, won 9.8 percent, and Brown finished with 8.9 percent.
83. "I have determined," Edwards said in his withdrawal statement, "being the politician that I am . . . that under the circumstances since I did not run first it would be inappropriate for me to continue in this election." *Times-Picayune*, Oct. 25, 1987.
84. In an interview a few days later, Edwards added: "I wish my successor good luck and have no criticism of him, but if Buddy Roemer isn't successful, maybe I'll be back." *Times-Picayune*, Oct. 27, 1987. This article was written by Allan Katz.
85. *Times-Picayune*, Oct. 26, 1987.
86. Ibid. Pointing to Roemer's conservatism, George Despot, a former GOP state chairman, added: "He [Roemer] made what we would classify as a Republican sale. He probably made a better Republican sale than Bob Livingston." *Morning Advocate*, Oct. 26, 1987. The article was headlined: " 'Electability' Issue Hurt GOP."

Paul Hardy, a Republican and a former secretary of state who had abandoned the Democratic party after the 1979 governor's election, defeated Lt. Governor Bobby Freeman in the November 21 runoff. Hardy likened himself to Roemer and asked the voters to make a clean sweep at the top. Freeman led a six-candidate field in the open primary with 40 percent of the vote followed by Hardy at 29 percent. Apparently riding the Roemer wave, Hardy won the second spot for the GOP with 53 percent in the two-candidate general election. *New York Times*, Nov. 23, 1987.

In addition to Hardy's victory, the Republicans can point to steady gains in voter registration. Table 8-2 in the Louisiana chapter recorded GOP registration at 9.1 percent in 1983, up from a mere 2.0 percent in 1970. By 1988 the Republican share had climbed to 15.1 percent. The recent figures are as follows:

	Total Registered	Republicans Registered	GOP Percentage
1984	2,244,469	255,709	11.4%
1986	2,177,381	295,349	13.6
1988	2,183,796	330,829	15.1

SOURCE: Parish Report of Registered Voters, Louisiana Commissioner of Elections, Baton Rouge. The figures are for the quarter ending Dec. 31, except for the 1988 figures, which were tabulated on February 12, 1988, after the registration books closed for Super Tuesday.

87. Harnett lost narrowly to state Senator Nick A. Theodore, a Greenville Democrat. Incidentally, Theodore became the first Greek-American to win a statewide election in the South. Charleston (S.C.) *News and Courier*, Nov. 6, 1986.

88. *The State*, June 15, 1986. Daniel received 47 percent of the votes to Lader's 27 percent.

89. To critics of his role in the 1970 antibusing protest, Campbell had this response: "There are a bunch of hypocrites out there who want to condemn me, but then you ask them the same question: Do you support forced busing? And if they tell you, 'No, I do not,' then they don't have the credibility to question anything." *Charlotte Observer*, Oct. 12, 1986.

90. The article was written by Jerry Adams and appeared in *The State*, Oct. 19, 1986. John Monk's profile article in the *Charlotte Observer* had more such phrases: "dull as dirt" and "the puppet of clever aides" along with this sentence: "Despite the allegations of softness, Daniel has shown ambition and hard work." Oct. 12, 1986. Adams of *The State* also noted that Daniel had "had uncanny luck—he calls it destiny—by running against people who scare the daylights out of the establishment, such as state Sen. Tom Turnipseed in the 1982 Democratic party runoff . . . ."

91. *Charlotte Observer*, Oct. 12, 1986.

92. *Miami Herald*, Oct. 21, 1986. The article, written by Fred Grimm, was headlined "Gubernatorial Campaign Is Taking Some Mean Twists."

93. Ibid.

94. See Broach's fine four-page analysis of the election in the November 1986 issue of his public affairs newsletter *The Carolina Report*. Broach also wrote: "Republican feints at the black vote were just that, designed to counter efforts by some Democrats to stimulate black turnout by portraying Campbell as unfriendly to blacks." Campbell previewed his astute comprehension of the "proper" GOP electoral approach to blacks in his 1979 comments quoted on page 72 of the South Carolina chapter.

95. Like father, like daughter, one could say, since Patterson's father defeated Workman's father, the veteran newspaper editor, in the 1962 Senate election that ushered in the new era of two-party competition in the state.

96. Bill Minor, "Congressman Espy from Mississippi," *Southern Changes* (Dec. 1986), 1.

97. Ibid., 2. A study conducted by the Voter Education Project in Atlanta calculated that Espy received 12 percent of the white vote and put Clark's 1984 white vote at 7 percent. The same organization said Espy received 95 percent of the black vote compared with Clark's 94 percent. The figures are from a Joint Center for Political Studies report in *Southern Exposure* (Summer 1987), 2.

98. *Clarion-Ledger*, Nov. 6, 1986. Minor also noted that Espy "held his own with

Franklin in a televised debate . . . (by comparison, Clark, a less-polished speaker, might have been outmatched)." Minor, "Congressman Espy," 2.

99. *Clarion-Ledger*, Nov. 8, 1987. None of the other Republican candidates for lesser state offices received more than a third of the votes cast, pointing to the party's persistent "down-ticket" weakness. David E. Sturrock, a graduate student at the University of California, Riverside, is investigating the "down-ticket" arena. See his "Toward a Theory of 'Down-Ticket' Realignment in the American South" (Paper presented at the Annual Meeting of the Western Political Science Association, Anaheim, Calif., March 26–28, 1987).

100. New Orleans *Times-Picayune*, Aug. 19, 1987. In these pre-runoff comments, Minor included Sturdivant with Mabus and Reed.

101. *Clarion-Ledger*, Nov. 5, 1987. Adding to the air of change sweeping the state, Mike Moore, a 35-year old Gulf Coast district attorney and a Democrat, won the post of attorney general, and C. B. (Buddie) Newman, the mossback speaker of the Mississippi House of Representatives, decided to retire in 1987 after being stripped of part of his power in a successful 1986 House revolt against him.

102. *New York Times*, May 25, 1986.

103. Ibid., May 29, 1986.

104. White also had to win his party's nomination in a primary, which he accomplished easily with 61 percent of the votes. But, as Diane K. Blair of the University of Arkansas reported, "for Clinton that meant 315,397 of 520,628 votes cast; for White it meant getting 13,831 of 22,346 votes cast. Clearly, the Democratic primary is still the primary of choice because it is still the contest where most state and local races are in fact decided." Blair, "Arkansas State Elections, 1986," *Comparative State Politics Newsletter* (Dec. 1986), 8.

105. *The Political Report*, Oct. 10, 1986.

106. *Arkansas Gazette* (Little Rock), March 4, 1986.

107. Ibid.

108. Ibid., Feb. 16, 1986.

109. Alexander is quoted by Robin Toner in "It's a Long Way, Little Rock to Rio," *New York Times*, Aug. 13, 1986. Toner characterized Alexander's withdrawal from the leadership contest as "a hard tumble from Washington's fast track" and reported the congressman's philosophical acceptance of the blow to his career: "My mother used to say that those things that don't kill you make you strong."

110. Ibid.

111. Raleigh *News and Observer*, May 4, 1986.

112. Ibid., March 23, 1986.

113. Ibid., April 13, 1986.

114. Ibid. This article, written by Rob Christensen, was headlined "Funderburk Says Republicans Need Senate Candidate Like Helms."

115. *Greensboro News and Record*, April 20, 1986.

116. *Asheville Citizen*, Aug. 31, 1986.

117. Ibid.

118. *Charlotte Observer*, Oct. 13, 1986.

119. Paul Luebke, "Newspaper Coverage of the 1986 Senate Race: Reporting the Issues or the Horse Race?" *Comparative State Politics Newsletter* (April 1987), 20. Luebke's article was reprinted from *North Carolina Insight*.

120. *Charlotte Observer*, Oct. 13, 1986. The article was headlined "Tax on Food Is Top Topic in Broyhill-Sanford Debate."

121. Ibid.
122. Ibid., Nov. 5, 1986.
123. *New York Times*, March 1, 1987.
124. *Charlotte Observer*, Nov. 9, 1986. Still others pointed to the contrasts in the candidates' personalities and styles, giving Sanford the edge. See "Key Voters Saw Sanford as Better Leader, Analysts Say," *Charlotte Observer*, Nov. 21, 1986.
125. GOP voter registration in North Carolina continued its slow rise. In 1982 Republicans made up 23.9 percent of the state's registered voters, as reported in note 35 of Chapter 10. In 1984 the percentage increased to 25.6 (838,631 of 3,270,933) in a year that witnessed a substantial growth in total registration. The GOP share reached 27.2 percent in 1986 (836,726 of 3,080,990), and it rose again in 1987, but only slighly, to 27.5 percent (848,817 of 3,086,740). The figures, which are for October of the reported year, were provided by the State Board of Elections in Raleigh.
126. Virginia was the only Southern state to make its nominations by convention.
127. A third candidate, Richard Viguerie, the conservative direct-mail specialist, retained over 15 percent of the delegates to the end.
128. Larry Sabato, *Virginia Votes 1983–1986* (Charlottesville: Institute of Government, University of Virginia, 1987), 61.
129. Ibid., 84.
130. After examining voter turnout in 1985 compared with 1984, Sabato concluded that the decline in Democratic turnout was less than the Republican drop-off and could have made the difference for Wilder. See ibid., 89–93.
131. At this point Sabato has the following footnote: "The 'firebrand' image did not extend to the state Senate, where Wilder had long been considered a member of the 'club' and one of the body's most effective members." Ibid., 105 (note 29).
132. Ibid., 104–5.
133. Ibid., 105.
134. Ibid., 106. Sabato's criticism of Chichester's performance began: "For all of the strengths of Wilder's campaign, he still arguably would not have won, considering his liabilities, if he had faced an able, mainstream opponent who could have run a strong campaign." Ibid., 105.
135. See Sabato's gubernatorial analysis, ibid., 102–4.
136. Ibid., 106.
137. Pickett, a Virginia Beach delegate, defeated state Senator A. Joe Canada, a Virginia Beach Republican, with 49.5 percent of the vote to Canada's 41.9 percent. An independent, Stephen P. Shao, an economics and business professor at Old Dominion University and a native of Shanghai, China, won 8.6 percent as an independent. In the neighboring First District, state Senator Robert C. Scott, a black Democrat, received 44.0 percent against U.S. Representative Herbert H. Bateman, the Republican first elected in 1982. The district is 29 percent black.
138. *New York Times*, Sept. 21 and Nov. 12, 1987.
139. Philip Ashford of the Memphis *Commercial Appeal* quoted a media consultant working for McWherter as follows: "He's stronger on television than a lot of people think. It's a misconception that the media belongs to the 'blow-dries.' Television magnifies everything—including character." Ashford's September 6, 1986, article was headlined "Fine-Tuning of Image Sought."
140. Knoxville *News Sentinel*, Aug. 6, 1986.

141. *Washington Post*, Oct. 12, 1986. The article, written by Thomas B. Edsall, contained this subheading, "In Tennessee, It's the Grand Old Party Vs. Good Old Boy."

142. On this point and generally, see Steven D. Williams, "Democrats Regain Tennessee's Governorship," *Comparative State Politics Newsletter* (Dec. 1986), 6–7.

143. *Commercial Appeal*, Oct. 8, 1986.

144. *Chattanooga News-Free Press*, Nov. 5, 1986.

145. *Dallas Times Herald*, Oct. 7, 1986.

146. *Dallas Morning News*, Oct. 7, 1986.

147. *Dallas Times Herald*, Nov. 5, 1986.

148. *Dallas Morning News*, Dec. 5, 1986. James Dyer of Texas A & M University concluded: "There was not a feeling that Clements could do that much more, but that White deserved being punished because the economy had gone bad. . . . There was just a negative feeling about White." Ibid.

149. V. O. Key, Jr., *Southern Politics in State and Nation* (New York: Alfred A. Knopf, 1949), 82.

150. *Palm Beach Post*, Nov. 5, 1986.

151. *Miami Herald*, Oct. 21, 1986.

152. Ibid.

153. Ibid.

154. Ibid.

155. On Smith's personal spending, a newspaper reported: "He's written checks for $1.2 million—plus $144,000 from relatives and his company—to get a new job. . . . 'I did grow up poor,' says Smith. 'For me to spend that much money hurts. I didn't like writing that check. Personally, I'm pretty tight.'" *St. Petersburg Times*, Sept. 21, 1986. The article had this subheading, "Smith Strikes Gold in His Own Wallet."

156. *Miami Herald*, Oct. 1, 1986; *St. Petersburg Times*, Oct. 3, 1986.

157. *New York Times*, Oct. 2, 1986. The article, written by Jon Nordheimer, was headlined "Florida Democrats in Disarray; G.O.P. Confident."

158. *Miami Herald*, Nov. 5, 1986.

159. Interviewing voters in the North Florida town of Mayo, Jon Nordheimer of the *New York Times* elicited these comments:

   "Martinez is sharp, I kid you not," Alton Buchanan said from behind the counter of his hardware store in Mayo. "He's a descendant of Spanish people, and heck, the Spanish were in Florida even before us.

   "Now if Martinez was from Miami, that'd be different," Mr. Buchanan, who is 38 year old, said. "Being as he's from Tampa, and sounds jes' like us, a good ol' boy I guess you can call it, then no one minds what his name is." *New York Times*, Nov. 2, 1986.

160. *Pensacola Journal Gazette*, Oct. 3, 1986.

161. Mark Stern, "The 1986 Election in Florida: The More Things Change, the More They Remain the Same" (Paper delivered at the Annual Meeting of the Florida Political Science Association, Winter Park, Fla., April 3, 1987), 7.

162. Ibid., 9.

163. The registration figures as of February 6, 1988, were: 2,026,018 Republicans out of a total registration of 5,358,667, or 37.8 percent. The figures for 1986 were: 2,038,831 Republicans out of a total registration of 5,631,188, or 36.2 percent. In

1984 the figures were: 1,895,937 Republicans out of a total of 5,574,472, or 34.0 percent. The information was provided by the Division of Elections, Florida Department of State, Tallahassee; for 1984 and 1986 the figures were calculated in October.

164. The following are part of Suzanne Parker's findings based on polls conducted by the Survey Research Center of the Policy Sciences Program at Florida State University in Tallahassee:

	All Floridians			
	1984	1985	1986	1987
Democrat	39%	35%	31%	32%
Republican	29	35	38	37
Independent	32	30	31	30
N	892	1002	914	850
	Whites			
Democrat	35%	31%	28%	27%
Republican	32	37	40	40
Independent	33	32	31	34

Question: "Generally speaking, do you usually think of yourself as a Republican, a Democrat, an Independent, or what?"

165. The senatorial race may also lead to changes in the state's U.S. House delegation, which remained divided between twelve Democrats and seven Republicans after the 1986 elections (all incumbents were easily re-elected in 1986 and an open seat was held by the Democratic party). At least two congressmen in 1988 were planning to seek Chiles's seat.

166. For example, Paul R. Abramson, John H. Aldrich, and David W. Rohde wrote: "It is clear that candidate quality was at least one of the major causes of the Democratic victories in the South, but candidate quality also was important in Senate races outside the South, and in House races as well." Noting that they were not alone in their assertion on this point, the authors quoted Richard Nixon: "We must face up to the blunt truth that the Republicans lost because the Democrats fielded better candidates." Abramson, Aldrich, and Rohde, *Change and Continuity in the 1984 Elections*, rev. ed. (Washington: CQ Press, 1987), 323–24. For a national perspective on recent elections, see this book generally and Chapter 12, "The 1986 Congressional Election," in particular.

167. Natalie Davis of Birmingham-Southern made this observation in a phone conversation with the author, October 1987.

168. All five of the first-time Democratic victors were outspent by their GOP opponents. For Fowler, Shelby, and Breaux, the deficit ranged from $1.9 million to $3 million; Sanford lagged behind Broyhill by $1 million in campaign expenditures; Graham came closest to his Republican opponent but was still outspent by a quarter of a million dollars in an election that cost nearly $13 million, the second most expensive in the nation in 1986. *New York Times*, Feb. 8, 1987. This article, which reprinted the Federal Election Commission's final totals, was headlined "107 G.O.P. Millions Didn't Save Senate."

Chapter 18: Toward the Future

1. *Montgomery Advertiser*, Nov. 5, 1983. The article was headlined "Run, Jesse, Run."
2. *Atlanta Journal*, April 25, 1984. The article was written by Ann Woolner.
3. Ibid. A black city councilman from Montezuma, Georgia, added: "The net result of the Jesse Jackson campaign [is that] black people will see the power of the black vote, probably more so than ever before." Ibid. On blacks and the ballot, see Steven F. Lawson, *In Pursuit of Power: Southern Blacks and Electoral Politics, 1965–1982* (New York: Columbia University Press, 1985).
4. *Montgomery Advertiser*, Nov. 5, 1983.
5. *New York Times*, Sept. 17, 1984.
6. One white Southern Democratic politician asserted that elimination of the runoff "would build the Republican party overnight." *New York Times*, May 3, 1984. For further treatment of the issue, see Alexander P. Lamis, "The Runoff Primary Controversy: Implications for Southern Politics," *PS* (Fall 1984), 782–87.
7. Ronald Smothers's excellent article on black-white Democratic relations (*New York Times*, Dec. 2, 1984) begins as follows: "In the last days of his successful race in South Carolina's First Congressional District, the incumbent Republican Thomas Harnett ran an advertisement picturing his Democratic opponent Edward Pendarvis with one of his supporters, a black state legislator named McKinley Washington. 'You can judge a candidate by the company he keeps,' said the caption. While many Democrats condemned the ad, which was widely viewed as an ugly appeal to racism, party leaders are considering ways to make themselves and their party less susceptible to such tactics. . . ."
8. *New York Times*, Dec. 2, 1984.
9. In 1984 Hollings characterized Jackson's appeal this way: "Instead of 'I am somebody,' it's 'I am some color.' It's not Rainbow. It's Blackbow." *The State*, Oct. 21, 1984.
10. *The State*, May 31, 1987. The article, written by Lee Bandy and headlined, "Jackson Blamed for Republican Growth," went on to report more of Hollings's opinion of Jackson: "It's always been Hollings' contention that Jackson is interested in promoting Jackson, not trying to broaden the base of the Democratic Party. He tends to view Jackson as a divisive and disruptive figure, one who will go out of his way to create havoc if he doesn't get his way."
11. Brooks is quoted in a column written by Jeff Greenfield and carried in *The State*, Oct. 16, 1987. Brooks added: "Whenever the day comes that a black is elected to national office, it will be someone who is holding public office or someone who is more mainstream and not a radical or militant. And that, unfortunately, is how Jesse Jackson and others who are in the movement are perceived."
12. White independents rose two percentage points in the South by 1986 but declined three points in the North. Income and age differences reveal patterns only slightly altered from those seen in the 1980 figures in Chapter 15.
13. *Congressional Quarterly Weekly Report*, Aug. 1, 1987, p. 1699. The seven-page article, written by Alan Ehrenhalt and titled, "Changing South Perils Conservative Coalition," quotes U.S. Representative Trent Lott, the Mississippi Republican, on the development as follows: "The Boll Weevils are under the ground, but they are waiting, and sooner or later, we will sing our mating song, and they will come out

again." A study of Southern House members from 1947 to 1984 showed that, starting in 1978, there occurred a pronounced rise in liberal votes (as measured by the Americans for Democratic Action scale) among Southern Democrats. William R. Shaffer, "Southern Democratic Congressional Ideology: A Cohort Analysis" (Paper delivered at the Citadel Symposium on Southern Politics, Charleston, S.C., March 6–7, 1986).

14. The discussion in this section draws from my "Realignment as a Synonym for Change: A Conceptual Assessment with Reference to Recent Southern and National Electoral Politics" (Paper delivered at the Annual Meeting of the American Political Science Association in Chicago, Sept. 3–6, 1987).

In addition to the works cited below, the realignment literature includes: Joel H. Silbey, Allan G. Bogue, and William H. Flanigan, eds., *The History of American Electoral Behavior* (Princeton: Princeton University Press, 1978); Jerome M. Clubb, William H. Flanigan, and Nancy H. Zingale, *Partisan Realignment: Voters, Parties, and Government in American History* (Beverly Hills, Calif.: Sage Publications, 1980); and Bruce A. Campbell and Richard J. Trilling, eds., *Realignment in American Politics: Toward a Theory* (Austin: University of Texas Press, 1980).

15. V. O. Key, Jr., "A Theory of Critical Elections," *Journal of Politics* Vol. 17 (Feb. 1955), 3–18.

16. Ibid., 3–4.

17. Key wrote in a footnote at this point: "For example, the 1928 election in the South, in contrast with New England, involved large but short-lived accretions to the Republican ranks." Ibid., 17.

18. Ibid., 16–17.

19. "Secular Realignment and the Party System," *Journal of Politics* Vol. 21 (May 1959), 198–210. This is one of Professor Key's least successful writings, lacking his usual clarity and crisp insight. Essentially, he was grappling with the "aftershocks" theme that James L. Sundquist later effectively elucidated; see reference to Sundquist's elaboration of this theme on page 23 above.

20. *Politics, Parties, and Pressure Groups*, 5th ed. (New York: Thomas Y. Crowell Co., 1964), 253.

21. Ibid., 229.

22. The views of E. E. Schattschneider are found in his book *The Semi-Sovereign People: A Realist's View of Democracy in America* (New York: Holt, Rinehart and Winston, 1960). Key expressed interest in this dimension as well, noting that stable party groupings "may be seriously disturbed by the impact of great new issues that cut across the old party lines, issues that are not made by party leaders but are imposed by internal conditions or external circumstances." *Politics, Parties, and Pressure Groups*, 253.

23. James L. Sundquist, *Dynamics of the Party System: Alignment and Realignment of Political Parties in the United States*, rev. ed. (Washington: Brookings Institution, 1983), 14.

24. Ibid., 3–14.

25. Ibid., 17.

26. V. O. Key, Jr., *Southern Politics in State and Nation* (New York: Alfred A. Knopf, 1949), 76. For a recently published account of how Key's book came to be written, see Alexander P. Lamis and Nathan Goldman, "V. O. Key's *Southern Politics*: The Writing of a Classic," *Georgia Historical Quarterly* Vol. 71 (Summer 1987), 261–85.

27. Often these works rely solely on survey data, especially the party identification of

respondents traced over a series of polls. For example, see John R. Petrocik, "Realignment: New Party Coalitions and the Nationalization of the South," *Journal of Politics*, 49 (May 1987), 347–75. Petrocik "conceives of realignments as transformations of the social group profile of party supporters" (p. 352), which stripped of the jargon appears to mean that, when groups of voters change their partisan attachments, there is realignment. In this "more limited conception," to use Petrocik's characterization, "realignment" can certainly be measured easily enough with survey data on partisan identification, but how this conception of realignment amounts to anything more than a synonym for change is unexplained.

This conceptual flaw aside, Petrocik does a good job of analyzing recent changes in partisan identification in the South, demonstrating, among other things, that the 1984 elections represented a continuation of changes "underway for at least two decades" (p. 357). He also shows that migration from the North was not a significant element in the South's partisan transformation (p. 359) and that the partisan shifts were "not confined to new cohorts" (p. 362).

28. The dealignment interest derives from the revelation through the examination of survey data that there has been a substantial growth in recent years of persons who decline to identify themselves with either the Democratic party or the Republican party but opt for the choice of independent. This is, of course, an important development in the party system that must be examined, but no more so than many other changes. For a useful discussion of the realignment-dealignment debate, see Harold W. Stanley, "Southern Partisan Changes: Dealignment, Realignment or Both?" *Journal of Politics*, 50 (Feb. 1988), 64–88. Stanley concluded: "In sum, *both* realignment and dealignment were the unequivocal conclusion to draw from recent southern partisan changes. . . ." (p. 85).

19 Postscript: The 1988 Elections and Beyond

1. Associated Press dispatch carried in the Charleston (S.C.) *News and Courier*, June 20, 1988.
2. *New York Times*, June 20, 1988.
3. Ibid.
4. Ibid., June 18, 1988.
5. Ibid., October 23, 1988.
6. Ibid.
7. Typical of Senator Bentsen's pitch to Dixie is the following quote from his remarks on a visit to Panama City, Florida. After declaring his pride in being a life-long "Southern Democrat," Bentsen told his audience: "This year, Michael Dukakis reached out to the South. He chose one of you. He took the extra step to bring us home again. He came here and listened to us. He campaigned among us. He asked a Southerner to join him on the ticket, and one reason I accepted was because I want to help bring Texas and Tennessee and Arkansas and Mississippi back into the Democratic Party." *New York Times*, September 18, 1988. This article, written by Warren Weaver, Jr., was headlined: "Bentsen Plays Up Roots in His Tour of the South."
8. Associated Press dispatch carried in *The State* (Columbia, S.C.), July 24, 1988.
9. *Charlotte Observer*, October 22, 1988.
10. Ibid.

11. The 1988 figure is from the *New York Times*/CBS News survey of voters as they left polling places and was reported in the *New York Times's* "Portrait of the Electorate," published November 10, 1988. The ABC News exit polls, which are used to construct Table 19-3, also report 32 percent as Dukakis's share of the white vote in the South as a whole.

12. Wicker's column was carried in *The State*, November 20, 1988. After the 1984 election, similar comments were made by Bill Moyers and are quoted above on page 239.

13. When asked on a network television program if the use of the Horton case represented "an element of Republican racist appeal," Senator Bentsen responded: "When you add it up, I think there is, and that's unfortunate, and I just don't want to see this election won on that kind of packaging and that kind of distortions." *St. Petersburg Times*, October 24, 1988. The article, written by John Harwood, was headlined: "Democrats Charge Bush's Campaign Using Racist Pitch."

14. See pages 24–26 and 241–42.

15. North Carolina Republicans won 10 additional seats in the 120-member House, giving them an unprecedented 46 seats. In the 50-seat Senate they added 3 seats for a total of 13. With these results in mind, the *Charlotte Observer* ran a post-election story on November 14, 1988, appropriately headlined, "N.C. GOP Demanding R-E-S-P-E-C-T." When the legislature assembled in January, House Republicans wasted no time in exercising their increased power. They joined with 20 dissident Democrats to replace Speaker Liston B. Ramsey, whose 8-year autocratic rule had generated considerable bitterness, with another Democrat. In partial return the House Republicans were given a larger role in the committee structure. For more on this development, see a January 17, 1989, *New York Times* article, headlined "G.O.P. Role Grows in North Carolina," and a recently published book on North Carolina politics: Paul Luebke, *Tar Heel Politics: Myths and Realities* (Chapel Hill, N.C.: University of North Carolina Press, 1990), which concludes with a chapter on the 1988 election and its aftermath.

16. Georgia Republicans captured seven more seats in the 180-member House to boost their total to 36. They added one seat in the 56-seat Senate, increasing their presence to 11. All of this prompted two *Atlanta Journal* reporters to open a post-election story as follows: "Jumping to a record number in the Legislature, Georgia Republicans on Wednesday proclaimed 1988 a banner party-building year, laying the foundation for a serious run for the governor's mansion in 1990." The article, written by A. L. May and David K. Secrest, was headlined "Ga. GOP Hails Vote as Big Step to 2-Party State" and appeared on November 10, 1988.

17. The Florida GOP gains in the U.S. House came in the Fourth District, which stretches from the southern part of Duval County (Jacksonville) past Daytona Beach, and in the Ocala-centered Sixth District in north-central Florida. The Republican victors, Craig T. James and Cliff Stearns, respectively, had held no previous public office. In Texas, Democrats won back 2 seats lost in 1984. U.S. Representative Mac Sweeney lost his central Gulf Coast district to the Democrat Greg Laughlin. State Senator Bill Sarpalius, a Democrat, was victorious in a district in the Panhandle; the seat was open because the Republican incumbent ran unsuccessfully for the U.S. Senate. U.S. Representative Pat Swindall, a Georgia Republican under federal indictment for perjury in a money-laundering case, lost decisively to the former actor Ben Jones, a Democrat who was making his second try for the seat. The GOP gained a seat in Louisiana when the Republican Jim

McCrery won a full term in the open primary. Earlier in 1988 he had narrowly won a special election to fill the seat left vacant by Buddy Roemer's inauguration as governor. McCrery was a former Roemer aide and had switched to the GOP only a few months before the special election. Incidentally, a relatively new book on Pelican State politics is Stella Z. Theodoulou, *The Louisiana Republican Party, 1948–1984: The Building of a State Political Party* (New Orleans: Tulane University Studies in Political Science, Vol. 18, 1985).

18. Bill Grant, who was elected in 1986 as a Democrat from Florida's sprawling Second District, which consists of a score of rural and small-town counties east and west of Tallahassee, announced that he could "better represent the values and priorities" of his constituents as a Republican. *New York Times*, February 22, 1989. Four months later Tommy Robinson, of Arkansas's Little Rock-centered district, followed suit, declaring that "there is and will be no room for conservative Southern Democrats in today's national Democratic Party." *New York Times*, July 29, 1989.

19. Raleigh *News and Observer*, November 9, 1988. The article was written by Rob Christensen.

20. Ibid.

21. Ibid. Another *News and Observer* article, headlined "Election Winds All Blew Martin's Way," asserted that the "now-famous 'redneck' remark . . . managed to alienate blacks and white conservatives" (November 13, 1988). ABC News exit poll estimates showed Martin with 65 percent of the white vote and 15 percent of the black vote. Carolyn Smith, ed., *The '88 Vote* (New York: Capital Cities/ABC, Inc., 1989), p. 526; this source is a 874-page data book containing findings from ABC News's 1988 national and state exit polls.

22. Sasser's Republican opponent, Bill Andersen, a Kingsport attorney not well known even in GOP circles, received a little over a third of the vote.

23. U.S. Representative Beau Boulter, the GOP senatorial nominee in 1988, garnered 40.3 percent of the vote to Bentsen's 59.7 percent.

24. Robb won slightly over 70 percent of the votes against the Republican Maurice Dawkins, a 67-year-old black businessman.

25. *St. Petersburg Times*, November 9, 1988.

26. Ibid., November 8, 1988.

27. *Congressional Quarterly Weekly Report*, October 15, 1988, p. 2912.

28. Ibid., 2913.

29. Also in Florida, the Republican Tom Gallagher, a former state senator, was elected insurance commissioner-treasurer. Both Smith and Gallagher were elected in 1988 to unexpired two-year terms.

30. Information on all of these "out-of-the-limelight" GOP gains came from Hastings Wyman, Jr., *Southern Political Report*, November 15, 1988; and David E. Sturrock, "The Quiet Frontier: Recent Developments in Southern Down-Ticket Politics" (Paper delivered at the Citadel Symposium on Southern Politics, Charleston, S.C., March 8-9, 1990).

31. Although Wilder was nominated by convention and without an opponent, Coleman faced two experienced Virginia Republicans in a primary: Paul S. Trible, Jr., a former one-term U.S. senator who declined to run for re-election in 1988, and U.S. Representative Stan Parris, a five-term veteran from Alexandria. Coleman's primary victory with 37 percent of the vote—Virginia does not require a runoff— was described as a come-from-behind feat. *New York Times*, June 15, 1989.

32. *New York Times*, October 15, 1989. The article, written by B. Drummond Ayres,

Jr., was headlined "New Issues and Changing Electorate Reshape Virginia Governor's Race."

33. The *New York Times* headlined its September 25, 1989, report on the campaign this way: "Though Racial Politics Lurks, It Is Muted in Virginia Contest."

34. Larry J. Sabato, "Virginia's National Election for Governor—1989, Part 2, The General Election," 44–46. The quotation is from the typescript of Sabato's work, which is to be published soon as a volume in the series *Virginia Votes* (Charlottesville: Institute of Government, University of Virginia). Sabato also wrote: "Wilder was aided in one other way by his race: it secured for him an enormous amount of free and overwhelmingly favorable publicity in regional and national publications and broadcasts." Ibid., 46.

35. Ibid., 15.

36. Ibid., 29.

37. Ibid., 2. In fact, as Sabato pointed out, "Coleman captured the lion's share of territory, though not the vote-rich population centers. He gained majorities in seventy-three of the ninety-five counties and nineteen of the forty-one cities—the most localities won by a losing general election candidate in this century. Remarkably, Wilder's plurality was built from just twenty-two cities and twenty-two counties. No statistic does more to illustrate the changing center of population gravity in Virginia." Ibid., 4.

38. *New York Times*, April 16, 1989. The article carried the headline "Black Virginia Politician Rests at Brink of History."

39. *New York Times*, November 26, 1989; New Orleans *Times-Picayune*, February 11, 1990. Atlanta *Constitution*, August 9, 1990.

40. *New York Times*, June 14, 1990.

41. *New York Times*, June 6, 1990. A North Carolina candidate can avoid a runoff by winning over 40 percent of the vote, which Gantt narrowly failed to do, necessitating the need for his victorious runoff. The other Southern states with runoffs, including Georgia, require 50 percent, plus one vote, in the first primary for a candidate to avoid a runoff. The controversy over the runoff, which Jesse Jackson raised vociferously in the mid-1980s, re-entered the political limelight in the spring of 1990 when a suit was filed in U.S. District Court challenging the Georgia runoff system as discriminatory to black candidates. See Note 6 in Chapter 18 and its textual reference on Page 299 for earlier mention of this issue. Georgia's Andrew Young has not joined the current legal challenge to the runoff. He explained his position to a *New York Times* reporter as follows: "I'm interested in winning the general election—that's the only thing that counts for me, and I think the best chance of winning the general election is to go into it with a majority in the Democratic Party." *New York Times*, May 22, 1990. The article, written by Robin Toner, was headlined "Young as Candidate: Hard Road, Light Touch."

42. *New York Times*, April 25, 1990. The article was headlined "Chiles Transforms Florida Campaign."

43. Cleveland *Plain Dealer*, April 11, 1990.

44. Ibid., March 14, 1990.

45. *New York Times*, March 1, 1990. The article, written by Roberto Suro, was headlined "Homespun Texan Goes for Republicans' Heart." Williams, known by the nickname "Claytie," is making his first run for public office. He promised, among other things, to teach young criminal offenders "the joy of busting rocks" and says he knows how to get "more bang for the buck" in state government. Ibid.

46. Seven of the eleven Southern states now choose their governors during the elections held in the middle of a presidential term. Two states—Mississippi and Louisiana—conduct their election in the year before a presidential election, and Virginia's is in the year after the quadrennial national contest. North Carolina, as pointed out earlier in this chapter, is the only one to keep its major state elections in the presidential year.

47. *New York Times*, May 31, 1990.

48. Of the remaining 12 U.S. Senate seats, 7 are to be filled in 1992 and 5 in 1994. Thus, by the luck of the electoral calendar, 1990 offers the largest number of regularly scheduled statewide elections for the top 33 statewide offices—7 gubernatorial and 10 senatorial elections. This does not happen again until 2002!

49. A wild card in the Louisiana race against Senator Johnston is David Duke, a former grand wizard of the Ku Klux Klan and founder of the National Association for the Advancement of White People. Duke won a seat in the state House of Representative as a Republican. A master publicity seeker, Duke argues: "I'm the only Republican who can attract a sizable number of the blue-collar, Ronald Reagan, George Wallace voters you need to win." *New York Times*, December 8, 1989. Duke showed his parliamentary skill recently when he secured overwhelming Louisiana House passage of a bill to weaken affirmative action in the state. *New York Times*, May 31, 1990. A recent *New York Times* article on Duke, headlined "Ex-Klansman Puts New Racial Politics to Test," began as follows:

    "It's racial politics for the 90's—not Old South race baiting, but post-civil-rights-era harangue against welfare abuse and programs like affirmative action that his audience sees as helping blacks while hurting whites.

    " 'I'm not a racist like Jesse Jackson,' David Duke said recently, peering into the Cajun country blue-collar crowd of perhaps 200 people at the American Legion hall [in Franklin, Louisiana]. "I'm proud of my heritage like Jesse Jackson is proud of his. But I believe the time has come for equal rights for everyone in this country, even for white people."

    The June 18, 1990, article was written by Peter Applebome. The Louisiana open primary is October 6.

50. The most recent party registration figures in the three Southern states that require such registration reveal slow, steady GOP growth. In Florida, as of February 1, 1990, there were 2,312,735 Republicans out of a total registration of 5,751,154, or 40.2 percent. Prior to the 1988 general election, the GOP percentage was 39.0. (This information was provided by the Division of Election, Florida Department of State, Tallahassee, and updates note 163 in Chapter 17.) In Louisiana, as of April 7, 1990, there were 368,331 registered Republicans out of 2,123,156 registered voters, or 17.3 percent. At the end of 1988, the GOP percentage was 16.5. (The Louisiana Commissioner of Elections provided these figures, which update note 86 in Chapter 17.) In North Carolina, as of April 9, 1990, 30.8 percent of the registered voters were Republicans—969,349 out of 3,147,867. When the registration books closed prior to the November 1988 election, the Republican percentage was 29.6. (These figures, provided by the State Board of Elections in Raleigh, update note 125 in Chapter 17.)

51. I cannot claim credit (or blame) for the idea. The initiative to engage in "future gazing" came from the organizers of a "Future South" symposium, held October 20, 1988, to mark the centennial of Converse College, a quality women's liberal arts institution in Spartanburg, S.C. The occasion brought me into association with

a delightful group of scholars of my generation: David R. Goldfield (urbanization), Robert C. McMath (technology, modernization, and social change), Howard N. Rabinowitz (black-white relations), Margaret R. Wolfe (role of women), and James C. Cobb (overview and moderator). Joe P. Dunn and Howard L. Preston, of Converse, have edited the symposium papers and the University of Illinois Press is to publish them in 1991 as a book under the title *The Future South: An Historical Perspective for the Twenty-First Century*. The rest of this section draws from my chapter in the Converse volume, "The Future of Southern Politics: New Directions for Dixie."

52. Alan I. Abramowitz, "Party Leadership, Realignment, and the Nationalization of Southern Politics" (Paper presented at the Annual Meeting of the Southern Political Science Association, Memphis, November 5–7, 1981). Abramowitz also surveyed local party officials, but I omitted those findings in my use of his fine paper.

53. For example, Clark Surratt, of *The State*, interviewed dozens of Palmetto State Democratic officials concerning their attitude toward the national standard-bearer. The conclusion of his September 25, 1988, article is summed up in the headline: "S.C. Democrats Found Giving Lukewarm Support to Dukakis."

54. David E. Sturrock, "Legislative Elections and the Two-Party South" (Paper delivered at the 1988 Citadel Symposium on Southern Politics, Charleston, S.C., March 3–4, 1988), p. 6. Sturrock's paper draws from his soon-to-be-completed doctoral dissertation on the Southern "down-ticket" arena.

55. See Robert P. Steed, Laurence W. Moreland, and Tod A. Baker, eds., *The Disappearing South?: Studies in Regional Change and Continuity* (Tuscaloosa: University of Alabama Press, 1990).

56. John Egerton, *The Americanization of Dixie: The Southernization of America* (New York: Harper's Magazine Press, 1974). Similarly, twenty years ago Samuel Lubell wrote of "the effort to southernize the North." Lubell, *The Hidden Crisis in American Politics* (New York: W. W. Norton, 1970), 88.

57. Thomas E. Watson, "The Negro Question in the South," *Arena* 6 (1892), p. 548. For an excellent panoramic overview of more than a century of Southern political history, ranging from the Redeemers and the Populists to the Reaganites, see Dewey W. Grantham, *The Life and Death of the Solid South: A Political History* (Lexington: University Press of Kentucky, 1988).

58. To place the burden on leadership is to follow a conception of democracy that views elites as having significant leeway in determining the direction of a political system. For this formulation, I am indebted once more to V. O. Key, Jr., who, in his other great masterpiece, *Public Opinion and American Democracy* (New York: Alfred A. Knopf, 1961), concludes that public opinion rarely controls political action. Instead, Professor Key wrote, it operates "as a system of dikes which . . . fix a range of discretion within which debate at official levels may proceed" (p. 552). And, the responsibility for exercising that discretion rests with political leaders (p. 558). The Southern dikes of opinion, if one views them correctly, that is, comparatively and through their logical dimensions (see Tables 16-5 and 19-4), are plenty broad enough to offer the promise of the Southern political future I have sketched.

59. I would like to express my appreciation to my fine new colleagues in the Political Science Department at Case Western Reserve University—Vince McHale, Ken Grundy, Dixon Long, and Rosanna Perotti. They have contributed mightily to making my permanent academic home at C.W.R.U. a most congenial place to work.

Index

Abbitt, Watkins, 157, 159
Abney, F. Glenn, 332, 347
Abortion, attitudes on, 221, 223; Virginia guber-
natorial election of 1989, effect on, 317
Abramowitz, Alan I., 161, 213, 301, 322, 323,
379, 381, 418
Abramson, Paul R., 37–38, 345, 396, 398, 410
Abscam scandal, 73
Adams, Al, 287–88
Adams, Jerry, 406
Adkins, Howard, 205, 393
Agnew, Spiro, 49, 100, 116, 199
Ailes, Roger, 310
Alabama: Black Belt, turnabout of voting in,
77–79; Democrats, estrangement of from national party, 356, 360; Dixiecrat-Loyalist
split, 82; gubernatorial election of 1986,
266–71, 297; Mississippi and South Carolina, comparison to, 91; New Deal legacy,
355; regional cleavages, 82, 355–6; Republicans, ideological-purity disputes among, 84,
357; Senate election of 1984, 252–53; Senate
election of 1986, 271–72, 295 Wallace's impact on Republicans, 76–77, 83, 84; summary and conclusion, 91–92. See also Wallace, George C.
Alabama Democratic Conference (ADC), 89,
90, 91, 266
Alabama New South Coalition, 266
Albin, Rick, 285
Aldrich, John H., 398, 410
Alexander, Bill, 126, 285, 369, 371, 407

Alexander, Lamar, 31, 169, 174, 175–77, 178,
290, 384, 385
Allain, Bill, 59–61, 62, 351
Allen, James B., 79–80, 83, 84, 86, 91, 235,
327–8, 329
Allen, Kenneth R. (Bucky), 366
Allen, Maryon, 86, 358
Andersen, Bill, 415
Anderson, John: and the South, 346, support in
1980 measured, 214, 216, 217
Anderson, Thomas J., 173
Andrews, Ike F., 143, 251–52
Antilynching bill of 1938, 8
Anthony, Beryl, Jr., 371
Applebome, Peter, 417
Arkansas: busing issue in 1970 gubernatorial
election, 122–23; Democrats break with seg-
regationist past, 122; gubernatorial election of
1986, 284, 297; Republicans and blacks,
121, 122, 124, 129, 371; Republicans'
strength in Ozarks, 122, 368; two-party poli-
tics, phases of, 120; Senate election of 1984,
256–57; Senate election of 1986, 284–85,
295; summary and conclusion, 129–30. See
also Bumpers, Dale; Clinton, Bill; Rockefeller, Winthrop
Armen, Eric V., 346
Armey, Dick, 262
Armstrong, David, 255
Arnall, Ellis, 96
Arrington, Richard, 266
Arseneau, Robert B., 217, 395, 396

419